Law and Practice of International Arbitration in the CIS Region

Law and Practice of International Arbitration in the CIS Region

Edited by

Kaj Hober

Yarik Kryvoi

Published by:
Kluwer Law International B.V.
PO Box 316
2400 AH Alphen aan den Rijn
The Netherlands
Website: www.wolterskluwerlr.com

Sold and distributed in North, Central and South America by:
Wolters Kluwer Legal & Regulatory U.S.
7201 McKinney Circle
Frederick, MD 21704
United States of America
Email: customer.service@wolterskluwer.com

Sold and distributed in all other countries by:
Quadrant
Rockwood House
Haywards Heath
West Sussex
RH16 3DH
United Kingdom
Email: international-customerservice@wolterskluwer.com

Printed on acid-free paper.

ISBN 978-90-411-6701-9

e-Book: ISBN 978-90-411-6703-3
web-PDF: ISBN 978-90-411-8954-7

© 2017 Kluwer Law International BV, The Netherlands

All rights reserved. No part of this publication may be reproduced, stored in a retrieval system, or transmitted in any form or by any means, electronic, mechanical, photocopying, recording, or otherwise, without written permission from the publisher.

Permission to use this content must be obtained from the copyright owner. Please apply to: Permissions Department, Wolters Kluwer Legal & Regulatory U.S., 76 Ninth Avenue, 7th Floor, New York, NY 10011-5201, USA. Website: www.wolterskluwerlr.com

Printed in the United Kingdom.

MIX
FSC® C103993

Editors

Prof Dr Kaj Hober is Professor of International Investment and Trade law at Uppsala University. Prior to that he was Professor of East European Law at Uppsala University (1997-2009) and Professor of International Law at the Centre for Petroleum & Mineral Law & Policy, University of Dundee (2010). He has more than thirty years of experience – as legal advisor, counsel and arbitrator – of international arbitration, including East-West disputes and investment treaty disputes. He has written several books and numerous articles on Soviet and Russian law, international arbitration and international investment and trade law. He is also an associate member of 3 Verulam Buildings, Gray's Inn, London and Chair of the Board of the Arbitration Institute of the Stockholm Chamber of Commerce.

Prof Dr Yarik Kryvoi is the Senior Research Fellow in International Economic Law and Director of the Investment Treaty Forum at the British Institute of International and Comparative Law. He is also a Professor of Law at the University of West London and teaches arbitration at the Chartered Institute of Arbitrators. He has several years of experience practicing international dispute resolution with leading international law firms in London, Washington, D.C. and Saint Petersburg. Professor Kryvoi has advised governments, international organisations and major international corporations on issues of international law and dispute resolution under ICSID, UNCITRAL, ICC, LCIA and SCC rules. He is the founder of the CIS Arbitration Forum and has also served as a counsel for the Economic Court of the Commonwealth of Independent States advising on issues of international administrative law. He holds law degrees from Harvard, Moscow, Nottingham, Utrecht and St Petersburg and is admitted to practice in New York.

Contributors

Zhanyl Abdrakhmanova is a partner at Centil Law Firm based in Dushanbe, Tajikistan. She has been focusing on contract law, corporate law, international private law, M&A, and arbitration and mediation issues in both Kyrgyzstan and Tajikistan for the last six years. She has taken the lead and has been heavily involved in numerous project finance, M&A and other various large-scale cross-border transactions in Kyrgyzstan and Tajikistan. Zhanyl has also protected interests of major foreign investors in their disputes with the Kyrgyz authorities. Zhanyl has previously held key positions in the public authorities and has also been an independent national expert for international organizations such as UNDP, World Bank, DFID on the issues related with the foreign investments and protection of creditor rights.

Aliaksandr Danilevich is an attorney at law and partner at Danilevich & Volozhinets law office in Minsk, Belarus, where he is responsible for international commercial arbitration, international litigation and sports law. Dr Danilevich is a member of the Court of Arbitration for Sport in Lausanne, included in the list of ICSID arbitrators and an arbitrator in International Arbitration Court by Belarusian Chamber of Commerce. He is also a member of Rugby Europe Legal Committee. Currently, Dr Danilevich is an associate professor at the International Private and European Law Department of the Belarusian State University in Minsk; he is lecturing on International Commercial Arbitration and International Civil Proceedings. Dr Danilevich was a member of a working group elaborating the new Belarusian law on domestic arbitration.

Dmitry Davydenko is an international legal practitioner and legal scholar with a focus on resolution of disputes involving Russian and CIS-related parties. Dr Davydenko is Chief expert of the Center for Arbitration and Mediation at the Russian Chamber of Commerce and Industry, Executive Secretary of the Maritime Arbitration Commission at the Russian Chamber of Commerce and Industry, Director of the CIS Arbitration Forum. He is listed as an arbitrator at International Commercial Arbitration Court and Maritime Arbitration Commission at the Russian Chamber of Commerce and Industry and other institutions. He is the author of numerous articles on arbitration and

Contributors

alternative dispute resolution as well as on related legal matters such as private international law and procedure.

Asel Duissenova is a Deputy Chairperson of Kazakhstan International Arbitration (KIA) and practicing arbitrator. She is a leading researcher at the Research Institute of Private Law at the Caspian University and associate professor at the Adilet Higher School of Law, Caspian University, Ph.D. She has participated in more than sixty international research and practice conferences, workshops and round tables related to pressing issues of civil law and alternative dispute resolutions law (Almaty, Astana, Atyrau, Aktobe, Ust-Kamenogorsk, Shymkent, Pavlodar, Karaganda, Tashkent, Bremen, Hague, Rotterdam, etc.).

Sargis Grigoryan is the head of the arbitration practice of GPartners Law Firm in Armenia and the head of the firm's worldwide CIS/Armenia Dispute Resolution Group. During his thirteen years of practice, Mr Grigoryan has advised clients in more than eighty arbitration and litigation proceedings across a host of various jurisdictions. He holds Master's Degrees (LL.M.) from Uppsala (2003) and Stockholm (2006) Universities and a Graduate Diploma in Law (GDL) from the College of Law, London, UK (2013).

Maksud Karaketov is an associate at CENTIL Law Firm. He is majoring in corporate law, arbitration and mediation. Maksud received his law degree from Tashkent State University of Law (Uzbekistan), LL.M. and Ph.D. from Nagoya University (Japan) with specialization in Alternative Dispute Resolution. His Ph.D. dissertation was entitled 'Creating an appropriate model of court-connected mediation for Uzbek Judicial system'. His works on legislation in Uzbekistan, Kazakhstan and Japan have been published in CIS Arbitration, Getting the deal through, Jurisprudence Journal of Tashkent State University of Law and Nagoya Journal of Law and Politics.

Gunduz Karimov is the managing partner of the Baku office of Baker & McKenzie and the Head of the Maritime and Energy Law Center of Baku State University. He practices in the areas of dispute resolution, intellectual property, compliance and pharmaceuticals and healthcare. Dr Karimov has been teaching private international law, intellectual property, commercial law courses at Baku State University since 2000. He also served as Associate Dean for Student Affairs in the Faculty of Law of Baku State University. Mr Karimov has an international law degree from the faculty of international law and international relations of Baku State University, an LL.M. degree from Indiana University in Bloomington and Ph.D. in Intellectual Property Law from Institute of Philosophy and Law in Azerbaijan. UK. He has also successfully completed a two-year course at the ICC Advanced Arbitration Academy jointly developed by ICC and CIArb. Gunduz Karimov is also a member of the Azerbaijan Bar Association and has been registered trademark attorney of Azerbaijan. Gunduz Karimov is recognized as a leading attorney in Azerbaijan by various ranking publications such as Chambers Global, Legal 500 and IFLR.

Contributors

Rolf Knieper has been Professor of Law at the University of Bremen (Germany) from 1973 until his retirement in 2006. He holds the title of doctor iuris from the University of Frankfurt am Main/Germany and doctor honoris causa from the State University of Tbilisi/Georgia as well as Chisinau/Moldova. He has been visiting scholar at Harvard Law School (USA) and visiting researcher at the IMF and the World Bank. In 2010, he has taught comparative contract law as 'distinguished chair professor' at National Taiwan University. Rolf has gained his practical experience of legal, economic and social problems and developments by contributing to legal and judicial reform of countries in different parts of the world. He continues to advise governments of the region until today and has assisted Turkmenistan to draft its Civil Code, its Civil Procedure Code and its Law on Arbitration. Rolf has been nominated as arbitrator for the first time in 1990. Thereafter he has served as arbitrator/chairperson/committee-member in commercial and investment disputes under Rules of ICSID, ICC, LCIA, UNCITRAL, SCC and at the PCA. He is listed on the Panel of Arbitrators of ICSID and of the Kazakhstan International Arbitrage (KIA).

Alexey Kostin is presently Chairman of International Commercial Arbitration Court and Maritime Arbitration Commission at the Russian Chamber of Commerce and Industry – oldest arbitral institutions in this country. Prof. Dr Kostin has been involved in numerous arbitral proceedings in different capacities for almost forty years, mainly as arbitrator under different rules (SCC, LCIA, UNCITRAL, etc.). He is also Head of Department of Private International and Comparative Law at the Moscow State Institute (University) at the Russian Ministry of Foreign Affairs, member of various academic and professional bodies (LCIA and CIArb, councilor of IFCAI and VIAC, listed arbitrator in plural institutions). As academic and practitioner, he writes and speaks extensively on topics related to international arbitration.

Shirinbek Milikbekov is an associate at Centil Law Firm. In recent years, he has focused on corporate law, subsoil and energy, aviation, telecommunication law and dispute settlement in Tajikistan. Shirinbek holds a Master's Degree in Law and Business from Bucerius Law School/WHU School of Management, Germany and a Bachelor's Degree in International and Business Law from the American University of Central Asia, Kyrgyzstan.

Foziljon H. Otakhonov is Chairman of International Commercial Arbitration Court at the Chamber of Commerce and Industry of Uzbekistan. He served as Chairman of Tashkent City Economic Court between 1997–2004 and was the Minister of Justice of Uzbekistan between 2006–2007. He has also been serving as a chairman of board of commercial bank Kapitalbank since 2012. As a leading figure in the arbitration field in Central Asia, Mr Otakhonov has an extensive experience in commercial arbitration, corporate governance and banking law. He has been a speaker, moderator or chairman in national and international symposiums and seminars. He teaches and extensively writes on, *inter alia*, commercial law, arbitration and corporate law in both Uzbek and Russian languages. Mr Otakhonov holds a law degree from Tashkent State University

Contributors

School of Law and a doctoral degree from Tashkent State University of Law. In 2002, he was awarded the Dostlik Medal by the President of Uzbekistan.

Olena Perepelynska (FCIArb) is a Partner and Head of CIS Arbitration Practice at Integrites Law Firm. Olena is a President of the Ukrainian Arbitration Association (UAA), where she has coordinated the Working Group for elaboration of proposals to improve arbitration legislation in Ukraine as well as a number of educational activities of the UAA, including the annual Arbitration School and a series of Master Classes in arbitration. Olena has a law degree from the Institute of International Relations, Kyiv Taras Shevchenko National University, and diploma in International Arbitration from the Chartered Institute of Arbitrators, UK. She also has successfully completed two-year course in the ICC Advanced Arbitration Academy for Central & Eastern Europe. Olena Perepelynska is a Fellow of the Chartered Institute of Arbitrators and is included in the lists of arbitrators of various arbitration institutions in Austria, Belarus, Czech Republic, Georgia, Hong Kong, Kazakhstan, Kyrgyzstan, Lithuania, Malaysia, Poland, Romania, Russian Federation, Ukraine and Vietnam.

Alexandr Svetlicinii is assistant professor at the University of Macau, Faculty of Law, where he also served as Acting Programme Coordinator for the Master of International Business Law. Prior to joining the University of Macau, Dr Svetlicinii was Senior Research Fellow at the Jean Monnet Chair of European Law of the Tallinn Law School, Tallinn University of Technology. Dr Svetlicinii received his law degree from the Free International University of Moldova (Chisinau), LL.M. International Business Law (Cum Laude) with specialization in EU Law from the Central European University (Budapest), Master of Research (Law) from the European University Institute (Florence) and Ph.D. in Law from the European University Institute (Florence). His works on commercial arbitration in Moldova have been published in the European Business Law Review, Journal of International Arbitration and Vindobona Journal of International Commercial Law and Arbitration. The author acknowledges the support from the University of Macau Multi-Year Research Grant MYRG2016-00131-FLL.

Alisher Umirdinov is an Associate Professor at the Nagoya University of Economics, Faculty of Business Law. He completed his LL.D. at Nagoya University, Graduate School of Law in 2012. He did his post-doctoral research, at School of Law, SOAS, University of London (SOAS University, School of Law) from January 2013 till January 2014 under the supervision of Professor Peter Muchlinski. During his stay in the United Kingdom, Dr Umirdinov also got an opportunity of being a visiting junior researcher at the Centre for Energy, Petroleum and Mineral Law and Policy (CEPMLP), Dundee University. He also participated in the legal assistance programs of JICA for Central Asian Countries for several years in Osaka, Japan. Dr Umirdinov's interest areas include international investment law, commercial arbitration, competition law and policy in post-soviet transition countries, as well as oil and gas law. He has also authored articles in the field of State contracts, investment protection, natural resource and competition law and policy in Uzbek, Japanese and English languages.

Contributors

Diora Ziyaeva is a Senior Associate at Dentons LLP in New York, specializing in the fields of International Arbitration and US Litigation. Diora focuses her practice on investor-state arbitration, on commercial arbitration and on issues and disputes relating to public international law, as well as corporate law with an emphasis on the oil and gas sector. She has experience litigating complex cases and has been involved in several important proceedings under the rules of ICSID, ICC, LCIA, UNCITRAL, SCC, and the PCA, including proceedings relating to the energy sector and involving states and state-owned entities. Diora is qualified to practice law in New York and regularly advises on investment law, enforcement and contract law in the legal systems of the Russian Federation and the Central Asian states. Diora is a noted speaker and lecturer having given numerous presentations throughout the world. She has authored many articles and books on international arbitration. She holds an LL.M. from Harvard University, an LL.B. from the University of World Economy and Diplomacy (UWED) and is fluent in several languages.

Summary of Contents

Editors	v
Contributors	vii
CHAPTER 1 Characteristics and Trends of Law and Practice of International Arbitration in the CIS Region *Yarik Kryvoi & Kaj Hober*	1
CHAPTER 2 Armenia *Sargis Grigoryan*	51
CHAPTER 3 Azerbaijan *Gunduz Karimov*	89
CHAPTER 4 Belarus *Aliaksandr Danilevich*	125
CHAPTER 5 Kazakhstan *Asel Duissenova & Maksud Karaketov*	169
CHAPTER 6 Moldova *Alexandr Svetlicinii*	211

Summary of Contents

CHAPTER 7
Russia
Alexey Kostin & Dmitry Davydenko   255

CHAPTER 8
Tajikistan
Shirinbek Milikbekov & Zhanyl Abdrakhmanova   311

CHAPTER 9
Turkmenistan
Rolf Knieper & Diora Ziyaeva   345

CHAPTER 10
Ukraine
Olena Perepelynska   383

CHAPTER 11
Uzbekistan
Foziljon Otakhonov & Alisher Umirdinov   439

Appendices   485

Appendix 1
Map of the Commonwealth of Independent States   487

Appendix 2
Satistics of Cases Involving States of the CIS Region with Leading Arbitration Institutions   489

Appendix 3
The Most Important Domestic Enactments on International Arbitration in the CIS Region   493

Appendix 4
Ratification of Selected Arbitration Related Conventions by CIS States   495

Appendix 5
Agreement on the Settlement of Disputes Relating to the Exercising of Economic Activity 1992 (the Kiev Agreement)   499

Appendix 6
Convention on Legal Assistance in Civil, Family Relations and Criminal Matters 1993 (the Minsk Convention)   505

Appendix 7
Convention on Legal Assistance in Civil, Family Relations and Criminal
Matters 2002 (the Kishinev Convention) 537

Appendix 8
Annex 16 to the 2014 Treaty on the Eurasian Economic Union Protocol on
Trade in Services, Incorporation, Activities and Investments 583

Index 603

Table of Contents

Editors	v
Contributors	vii

CHAPTER 1
Characteristics and Trends of Law and Practice of International Arbitration in the CIS Region
Yarik Kryvoi & Kaj Hober   1

List of Abbreviations				1
§1.01	Introduction			2
§1.02	International Commercial Arbitration			4
	[A]	Development of Commercial Arbitration in the Region		4
		[1]	Historical Background of Arbitration in CIS Region	4
		[2]	Development of Arbitration in Post-Soviet Era	6
	[B]	Sources of Arbitration Law in the CIS States		8
		[1]	Overview of International Treaties	8
			[a] New York Convention 1958	8
			[b] Agreement on the Settlement of Disputes Relating to the Exercising of Economic Activity 1992 (the Kiev Agreement)	9
			[c] Convention on Legal Assistance in Civil, Family Relations and Criminal Matters 1993 (the Minsk Convention)	9
			[d] Convention on Legal Assistance in Civil, Family Relations and Criminal Matters 2002 (the Kishinev Convention)	10
		[2]	National Legislation	11
	[C]	CIS States Practice in Commercial Arbitration		13
		[1]	Disputes in Domestic Arbitration Institutions	13

Table of Contents

		[2]	Disputes in Foreign Arbitration Institutions		15
			[a] Corruption Considerations		16
			[b] Impact of Sanctions Against Russia		18
	[D]	Trends in Law and Practice of Arbitration in CIS Region			19
		[1]	Common Features		19
		[2]	Distinctive Features		22
			[a] Arbitrators' Qualifications		23
			[b] Arbitrability		23
			[c] Public Policy		25
			[d] Enforcement of Arbitral Awards		27
§1.03	Investor-State Arbitration				28
	[A]	Development of Investor-State Arbitration			28
		[1]	Historical Background		28
		[2]	Overview of Investment Climate in the Region		29
	[B]	Legal Framework			30
		[1]	International Agreements		30
			[a] Washington Convention 1965		31
			[b] Energy Charter Treaty (ECT) 1994		31
			[c] CIS Convention for the Protection of Investor's Rights 1997 (the Moscow Convention)		33
			[d] EAEU Convention for the Promotion and Mutual Protection of Investments 2008		34
			[e] Treaty on the EAEU 2014		35
		[2]	Model BITs		36
	[C]	CIS States Practice in Investment Treaty Arbitration			38
		[1]	General Overview		38
		[2]	Notable Cases		39
	[D]	Enforcement of International Investment Arbitral Awards			42
		[1]	Peculiarities of Enforcing International Investment Arbitral Awards in the CIS Region		43
		[2]	Issues of State Immunity		44
§1.04	Concluding Remarks				46
Appendix I Ratification of Selected Arbitration Related Conventions by CIS States					48
Appendix II The Most Important Domestic Enactments on International Arbitration in the Region					50

CHAPTER 2
Armenia
Sargis Grigoryan   51

List of Abbreviations			51
§2.01	General Introduction		52
	[A]	Historical Development of the Legal System	52
	[B]	The Legal Profession	53

xviii

	[C]	Sources of Arbitration Law	53
	[D]	International Legal Framework	54
	[E]	Available Dispute Resolution Mechanisms	55
	[F]	Judicial System	55
	[G]	Arbitration Institutions	56
	[H]	Sovereign Immunity and International Arbitration	56
§2.02	The Arbitration Agreement		57
	[A]	Introduction	57
	[B]	Validity of the Arbitration Agreement	58
		[1] General Provisions	58
		[2] Requisites of a Valid Arbitration Agreement	58
	[C]	Concluding the Arbitration Agreement	58
	[D]	The Doctrine of Separability	59
	[E]	Invalidity of the Arbitration Agreement	59
	[F]	Arbitrability	60
	[G]	Effect of Arbitration Agreement on Third Parties	61
	[H]	Termination of Arbitration Agreement	61
	[I]	Drafting an Arbitration Clause	61
§2.03	Applicable Law		62
	[A]	Introduction	62
	[B]	The Law Governing the Arbitration Agreement	62
	[C]	The Law Governing the Arbitration (*Lex Arbitri*)	63
	[D]	Restrictions on Party Autonomy	63
§2.04	The Arbitrators		64
	[A]	Appointment of Arbitrators	64
	[B]	Qualifications of Arbitrators	64
	[C]	Powers and Duties of Arbitrators	65
	[D]	Challenges and Replacement of Arbitrators	66
	[E]	Compensation of Arbitrators	67
§2.05	Jurisdiction of the Arbitral Tribunal		67
	[A]	Introduction	67
	[B]	The Arbitrator's Determination of Their Jurisdiction	67
	[C]	Court Review of Arbitrators' Jurisdiction	68
§2.06	The Procedure Before the Arbitral Tribunal		68
	[A]	Introduction	68
	[B]	General Principles	69
	[C]	Commencing the Arbitral Proceedings	69
	[D]	Conduction of Arbitration	70
		[1] Written Submissions	70
		[2] Post-hearing Briefs	70
		[3] Evidence	71
		[4] Witness and Experts Testimony	71
	[E]	Hearings	72
§2.07	The Arbitral Award		72
	[A]	Introduction	72

Table of Contents

		[B]	Deliberation and Voting	73
		[C]	Different Kinds of Awards	73
		[D]	Interim Measures	73
		[E]	Emergency Arbitration	74
		[F]	Interest and Costs	74
		[G]	Effects of the Award	75
			[1] Execution	75
			[2] Res Judicata and Lis Pendens	75
		[H]	Correction and Interpretation of the Award	76
§2.08	Setting Aside the Award			76
		[A]	Introduction	76
		[B]	Invalid Awards	76
		[C]	Challengeable Awards	76
			[1] Grounds for Challenging the Award	76
			[2] Waiver of Right to Challenge	77
§2.09	Recognition and Enforcement of the Arbitral Award			78
		[A]	Enforcement of Domestic Awards	78
		[B]	Enforcement of Foreign Arbitral Awards	79
			[1] Introduction to Recognition and Enforcement	79
			[2] Interim Awards	80
			[3] Grounds for Refusing Recognition and Enforcement	80
			[4] Procedures for Recognition	81
§2.10	Investor-State Arbitration			82
		[A]	General Overview	82
Appendix 1 List of Bilateral Investment Treaties the Country Has Ratified				86
Bibliography				87

CHAPTER 3
Azerbaijan
Gunduz Karimov   89

List of Abbreviations				89
§3.01	General Introduction			90
		[A]	Historical Development of the Legal System	90
		[B]	The Legal Profession	91
		[C]	Sources of Arbitration Law	92
		[D]	International Legal Framework, Supremacy of International Law	95
		[E]	Available Dispute Resolution Mechanisms	96
		[F]	Judicial System	97
		[G]	Arbitration Institutions	99
		[H]	Sovereign Immunity and International Arbitration	99
§3.02	The Arbitration Agreement			101
		[A]	Introduction	101
		[B]	Validity of the Arbitration Agreement	101
		[C]	Capacity of the Parties to Conclude an Arbitration Agreement	103

	[D]	Intention of the Parties in Arbitration	104
	[E]	The Doctrine of Separability	104
	[F]	Arbitrability	105
		[1] Disputes Capable of Settlement by Arbitration	105
		[2] Disputes Not Capable of Settlement by Arbitration	106
		[3] Special Provisions on Consumer and Labour Disputes	107
	[G]	Effect of Arbitration Agreement on Third Parties	108
	[H]	Termination of Arbitration Agreement	108
	[I]	Drafting Arbitration Clauses	109
§3.03	Applicable Law		109
	[A]	The Law Governing the Arbitration Agreement	109
	[B]	The Law Governing the Arbitration (*Lex Arbitri*)	110
	[C]	Party Autonomy on Choice of Law Issues	110
	[D]	Restrictions on Party Autonomy	111
	[E]	National Public Policy	112
§3.04	The Procedure Before the Arbitration Tribunal		112
	[A]	General Principles of Arbitration Procedure (Party Autonomy, Speed, Impartiality, Etc.)	112
	[B]	Commencing and Conduct of the Arbitral Proceedings	113
§3.05	Recognition and Enforcement of the Arbitral Award		114
	[A]	Enforcement of Foreign Arbitral Awards	114
§3.06	Investor-State Arbitration		115
	[A]	General Overview of Law and Practice Related to Investor-State Arbitration	115
	[B]	List of Investor-State Disputes (Concluded and Pending)	117
	[C]	Reform Proposals	118
Appendix I List of Bilateral Investment Treaties of Azerbaijan			120
Bibliography			121

CHAPTER 4
Belarus
Aliaksandr Danilevich 125

List of Abbreviations			125
§4.01	General Introduction		126
	[A]	Historical Development of the Legal System	126
	[B]	The Legal Profession	126
	[C]	Sources of Arbitration Law	127
	[D]	International Legal Framework, Supremacy of International Law	128
	[E]	Available Dispute Resolution Mechanisms	129
	[F]	Judicial System	129
	[G]	Arbitration Institutions	129
	[H]	Sovereign Immunity and International Arbitration	130
§4.02	The Arbitration Agreement		131
	[A]	Introduction	131

Table of Contents

	[B]	Validity of the Arbitration Agreement	131
		[1] General Provisions	131
		[2] Requisites of a Valid Arbitration Agreement	132
	[C]	Concluding the Arbitration Agreement (Written, Oral, by Conduct)	132
	[D]	The Doctrine of Separability	133
	[E]	Invalidity of the Arbitration Agreement	133
	[F]	Arbitrability	133
		[1] Disputes Capable of Settlement by Arbitration	133
		[2] Disputes Not Capable of Settlement by Arbitration	134
		[3] Special Provisions on Consumer and Labor Disputes	135
	[G]	Effect of Arbitration Agreement on Third Parties (Parties Substitution, Guarantee Agreements, Group of Companies Doctrine)	135
	[H]	Termination of Arbitration Agreement	136
		[1] Termination with Respect to Existing Dispute	136
		[2] Complete Termination	136
	[I]	Drafting Arbitration Clauses	136
§4.03		Applicable Law	137
	[A]	Introduction	137
	[B]	The Law Governing the Arbitration (*Lex Arbitri*)	137
	[C]	Party Autonomy on Choice of Law Issues	137
	[D]	Restrictions on Party Autonomy	138
		[1] General Observations	138
		[2] Reasonable Connection Test	138
		[3] National Public Policy	138
		[4] Mandatory Rules of Municipal Law	139
		[5] International Public Policy	139
	[E]	No Explicit Choice of Law	139
		[1] Introduction	139
		[2] Relevant Conflict of Law Rules	139
	[F]	The Law Governing the Arbitration Agreement	140
§4.04		The Arbitrators	140
	[A]	Appointment of Arbitrators	140
		[1] Appointment of Arbitrators under Municipal Law	140
		[2] Appointment under Institutional Rules	141
	[B]	Qualifications of Arbitrators	141
	[C]	Powers and Duties of Arbitrators	142
	[D]	Challenges and Replacement of Arbitrators	142
		[1] Challenges under Municipal Law	142
		[2] Challenges under Institutional Rules	142
	[E]	Compensation of Arbitrators	143
§4.05		Jurisdiction of the Arbitration Tribunal	143
	[A]	Introduction	143

	[B]	The Arbitrators' Determination of Their Jurisdiction	144
	[C]	Court Review of Arbitrators' Jurisdiction	144
	[D]	Institutional Rules	144
§4.06	The Procedure Before the Arbitration Tribunal		145
	[A]	Introduction	145
	[B]	General Principles of Municipal Judicial Procedure	145
	[C]	General Principles of Arbitration Procedure (Party Autonomy, Speed, Impartiality, Etc.)	145
	[D]	Commencing the Arbitral Proceedings	146
		[1] Municipal Law	146
		[2] Institutional Rules	146
	[E]	Conduct of Arbitration	146
		[1] Written Submissions	146
		[2] Post-hearing Briefs	146
		[3] Evidence (Admissibility, Documentary Evidence)	147
		[4] Witness and Experts Testimony	147
	[F]	Hearings	147
§4.07	The Arbitral Award		148
	[A]	Introduction	148
	[B]	Deliberation and Voting	148
	[C]	Different Kinds of Awards (Separate, Interim, Consent, Default, Etc.)	148
	[D]	Interest and Costs	148
	[E]	Effects of the Award	148
		[1] Execution	148
		[2] Res Judicata and Lis Pendens	149
	[F]	Correction and Interpretation of the Award	149
		[1] Municipal Law	149
		[2] Institutional Rules	150
§4.08	Setting Aside the Award		150
	[A]	Introduction	150
	[B]	Invalid Awards	150
	[C]	Challengeable Awards	150
		[1] Grounds for Challenging the Award	150
		[2] Waiver of Right to Challenge	151
	[D]	Review of Jurisdictional Awards	151
§4.09	Recognition and Enforcement of the Arbitral Award		151
	[A]	Enforcement of Domestic Awards	151
		[1] Enforcement Domestically	151
		[2] Enforcement Abroad	153
	[B]	Enforcement of Foreign Arbitral Awards	153
		[1] Introduction to Recognition and Enforcement	153
		[2] Separate, Partial and Interim Awards	154
		[3] Grounds for Refusing Recognition and Enforcement	154

Table of Contents

		[a]	Lack of Capacity and Invalidity of Arbitration Agreement	154
		[b]	Procedural Violations	154
		[c]	Excess of Mandate	154
		[d]	Arbitral Award Not Binding	155
		[e]	Non-arbitrability	155
		[f]	Public Policy	155
	[4]		Procedures for Recognition	156
§4.10	Investor-State Arbitration			156
	[A]		General Overview of Law and Practice Related to Investor-State Arbitration	156
	[B]		List of Investment Treaties the Country Has Ratified	158
	[C]		List of Investor-State Disputes (Concluded and Pending)	159
	[D]		Reform Proposals	160
Appendix I Belarus' BITs				161
Bibliography				163

CHAPTER 5
Kazakhstan
Asel Duissenova & Maksud Karaketov 169

List of Abbreviations			169
§5.01	General Introduction		170
	[A]	Historical Development of the Legal System	170
	[B]	The Legal Profession	170
	[C]	Sources of Law on Arbitration	171
	[D]	International Legal Framework, Supremacy of International Law	172
	[E]	Available Dispute Resolution Mechanisms	173
	[F]	Judicial System	173
	[G]	Arbitration Institutions	174
	[H]	Sovereign Immunity and International Arbitration	174
§5.02	The Arbitration Agreement		175
	[A]	Introduction	175
	[B]	Validity of the Arbitration Agreement	176
		[1] General Provisions	176
		[2] Requisites of a Valid Arbitration Agreement	176
	[C]	Concluding the Arbitration Agreement (Written, Oral, by Conduct)	176
	[D]	The Doctrine of Separability	177
	[E]	Invalidity of the Arbitration Agreement	177
	[F]	Arbitrability	178
		[1] Disputes Capable of Settlement by Arbitration	178
		[2] Disputes Not Capable of Settlement by Arbitration	178
		[3] Special Provisions on Consumer and Labor Disputes	179

	[G]	Effect of Arbitration Agreement on Third Parties (Substitution of Parties, Guarantee Agreements, Group of Companies Doctrine)	179
	[H]	Termination of Arbitration Agreement	180
		[1] Termination with Respect to Existing Dispute	180
		[2] Complete Termination	180
	[I]	Drafting Arbitration Clauses	181
§5.03		Applicable Law	181
	[A]	Introduction	181
	[B]	The Law Governing the Arbitration (*Lex Arbitri*)	181
	[C]	Party Autonomy on Choice of Law Issues	182
	[D]	Restrictions on Party Autonomy	182
		[1] General Observations	182
		[2] Reasonable Connection Test	182
		[3] National Public Policy	182
		[4] Mandatory Rules of Municipal Law	183
		[5] International Public Policy	183
	[E]	No Explicit Choice of Law	183
		[1] Introduction	183
		[2] Relevant Conflict of Laws Rules	184
	[F]	The Law Governing the Arbitration Agreement	184
§5.04		The Arbitrators	184
	[A]	Appointment of Arbitrators	184
		[1] Appointment of Arbitrators under Municipal Law	184
		[2] Appointment under Institutional Rules	185
	[B]	Qualifications of Arbitrators	185
	[C]	Powers and Duties of Arbitrators	186
	[D]	Challenges and Replacement of Arbitrators	186
		[1] Challenges under Municipal Law	186
		[2] Challenges under Institutional Rules	187
	[E]	Compensation of Arbitrators	187
§5.05		Jurisdiction of the Arbitration Tribunal	188
	[A]	Introduction	188
	[B]	The Arbitrators' Determination of Their Jurisdiction	188
	[C]	Court Review of Arbitrators' Jurisdiction	188
	[D]	Institutional Rules	189
§5.06		The Procedure Before the Arbitration Tribunal	189
	[A]	Introduction	189
	[B]	General Principles of Municipal Judicial Procedure	189
	[C]	General Principles of Arbitration Procedure (Party Autonomy, Speed, Impartiality, Etc.)	189
	[D]	Commencing the Arbitral Proceedings	190
		[1] Municipal Law	190
		[2] Institutional Rules	190
	[E]	Conduct of Arbitration	191

Table of Contents

		[1]	Written Submissions	191
		[2]	Post-hearing Briefs	191
		[3]	Evidence (Admissibility, Documentary Evidence)	192
		[4]	Witness and Expert Testimony	192
	[F]	Hearings		192
§5.07	The Arbitral Award			193
	[A]	Introduction		193
	[B]	Deliberation and Voting		193
	[C]	Different Kinds of Awards (Separate, Interim, Consent, Default, Etc.)		193
	[D]	Interest and Costs		194
	[E]	Effects of the Award		194
		[1]	Execution	194
		[2]	Res Judicata and Lis Pendens	194
	[F]	Correction and Interpretation of the Award		195
		[1]	Municipal Law	195
		[2]	Institutional Rules	195
§5.08	Setting Aside the Award			195
	[A]	Introduction		195
	[B]	Invalid Awards		196
	[C]	Challengeable Awards		196
		[1]	Grounds for Challenging the Award	196
		[2]	Waiver of Right to Challenge	197
	[D]	Review of Jurisdictional Awards		197
§5.09	Recognition and Enforcement of the Arbitral Award			198
	[A]	Enforcement of Domestic Awards		198
		[1]	Enforcement Domestically	198
		[2]	Enforcement Abroad	198
	[B]	Enforcement of Foreign Arbitral Awards		198
		[1]	Introduction to Recognition and Enforcement	198
		[2]	Separate, Partial and Interim Awards	199
		[3]	Grounds for Refusing Recognition and Enforcement	199
			[a] Lack of Capacity and Invalidity of Arbitration Agreement	199
			[b] Procedural Violations	199
			[c] Excess of Mandate	199
			[d] Arbitral Award Not Binding	200
			[e] Non-arbitrability	200
			[f] Public Policy	200
		[4]	Procedures for Recognition	200
§5.10	Investor-State Arbitration			201
	[A]	General Overview of Law and Practice Related to Investor-State Arbitration		201
	[B]	List of Investments the Country Has Ratified		201

		[C]	List of Investor-State Disputes (Concluded and Pending)	202
		[D]	Reform Proposals	202

Appendix 1 Kazakhstan's BITs 204
Appendix 2 Investor-State Disputes Against Kazakhstan 206
Bibliography 207

CHAPTER 6
Moldova
Alexandr Svetlicinii 211

List of Abbreviations 211
§6.01 General Introduction 212
    [A] Historical Development of the Legal System 212
    [B] The Legal Profession 213
    [C] Sources of Arbitration Law 214
    [D] International Legal Framework, Supremacy of International Law 215
    [E] Available Dispute Resolution Mechanisms 217
    [F] Judicial System 218
    [G] Arbitration Institutions 218
    [H] Sovereign Immunity and International Arbitration 220
§6.02 The Arbitration Agreement 220
    [A] Introduction 220
    [B] Validity of the Arbitration Agreement 221
        [1] General Provisions 221
        [2] Requisites of a Valid Arbitration Agreement 221
    [C] Concluding the Arbitration Agreement (Written, Oral, by Conduct) 221
    [D] The Doctrine of Separability 222
    [E] Invalidity of the Arbitration Agreement 222
    [F] Arbitrability 222
        [1] Disputes Capable of Settlement by Arbitration 222
        [2] Disputes Not Capable of Settlement by Arbitration 223
        [3] Special Provisions on Consumer and Labor Disputes 223
    [G] Effect of Arbitration Agreement on Third Parties 224
    [H] Drafting Arbitration Clauses 224
§6.03 The Arbitrators 225
    [A] Appointment of Arbitrators 225
        [1] Appointment of Arbitrators under Municipal Law 225
        [2] Appointment under Institutional Rules 226
    [B] Qualifications of Arbitrators 226
    [C] Powers and Duties of Arbitrators 226
    [D] Challenges and Replacement of Arbitrators 226
        [1] Challenges under Municipal Law 226
        [2] Challenges under Institutional Rules 227

Table of Contents

	[E]	Compensation of Arbitrators	227
§6.04		Jurisdiction of the Arbitration Tribunal	227
	[A]	Introduction	227
	[B]	The Arbitrators' Determination of Their Own Jurisdiction	228
	[C]	Court Review of Arbitrators' Jurisdiction	228
	[D]	Institutional Rules	228
§6.05		The Procedure Before the Arbitration Tribunal	228
	[A]	Introduction	228
	[B]	General Principles of Municipal Judicial Procedure	229
	[C]	General Principles of Arbitration Procedure (Party Autonomy, Speed, Impartiality, Etc.)	229
	[D]	Commencing the Arbitral Proceedings	229
		[1] Municipal Law	229
		[2] Institutional Rules	230
	[E]	Conduct of Arbitration	230
		[1] Written Submissions	230
		[2] Post-hearing Briefs	230
		[3] Evidence (Admissibility, Documentary Evidence)	231
		[4] Witness and Experts' Testimony	231
	[F]	Hearings	231
§6.06		The Arbitral Award	232
	[A]	Introduction	232
	[B]	Deliberation and Voting	232
	[C]	Different Kinds of Awards (Separate, Interim, Consent, Default, Etc.)	232
	[D]	Interest and Costs	233
	[E]	Effects of the Award	233
		[1] Execution	233
		[2] Res Judicata and Lis Pendens	233
	[F]	Correction and Interpretation of the Award	234
		[1] Municipal Law	234
		[2] Institutional Rules	234
§6.07		Setting Aside the Award	234
	[A]	Introduction	234
	[B]	Invalid Awards	235
	[C]	Challengeable Awards	235
		[1] Grounds for Challenging the Award	235
		[2] Waiver of Right to Challenge	236
	[D]	Review of Jurisdictional Awards	236
§6.08		Recognition and Enforcement of the Arbitral Award	236
	[A]	Enforcement of Domestic Awards	236
		[1] Enforcement Domestically	236
		[2] Enforcement Abroad	237

	[B]	Enforcement of Foreign Arbitral Awards				237
		[1]	Introduction to Recognition and Enforcement			237
		[2]	Separate, Partial and Interim Awards			238
		[3]	Grounds for Refusing Recognition and Enforcement			238
			[a]	Lack of Capacity and Invalidity of Arbitration Agreement		238
			[b]	Procedural Violations		239
			[c]	Excess of Mandate		240
			[d]	Arbitral Award Not Binding		240
			[e]	Non-arbitrability		240
			[f]	Public Policy		241
		[4]	Procedures for Recognition			241
§6.09	Investor-State Arbitration					242
	[A]	General Overview of Law and Practice Related to Investor-State Arbitration				242
	[B]	List of BITs of the Republic of Moldova				244
	[C]	List of Investor-State Disputes (Concluded and Pending)				246
§6.10	Reform Proposals					248
Bibliography						249

CHAPTER 7
Russia
Alexey Kostin & Dmitry Davydenko — 255

List of Abbreviations			255
§7.01	General Introduction		256
	[A]	Historical Development of the Legal System	256
	[B]	The Legal Profession	257
	[C]	Sources of Arbitration Law	257
	[D]	International Legal Framework, Supremacy of International Law	258
	[E]	Available Dispute Resolution Mechanisms	259
	[F]	Judicial System	259
	[G]	Arbitration Institutions	260
	[H]	Sovereign Immunity and International Arbitration	261
§7.02	The Arbitration Agreement		262
	[A]	Introduction	262
	[B]	Validity of the Arbitration Agreement	262
		[1] General Provisions	262
		[2] Requisites of the Valid Arbitration Agreement	262
	[C]	Concluding the Arbitration Agreement	263
	[D]	The Doctrine of Separability	263
	[E]	Invalidity of the Arbitration Agreement	264
	[F]	Arbitrability	264

Table of Contents

		[1]	Disputes Capable of Settlement by Arbitration	264
		[2]	Special Provisions on Consumer and Labour Disputes	265
	[G]	Effect of the Arbitration Agreement on Third Parties		265
	[H]	Termination of the Arbitration Agreement		265
	[I]	Drafting Arbitration Clauses		266
§7.03	Applicable Law			266
	[A]	Introduction		266
	[B]	The Law Governing the Arbitration (*Lex Arbitri*)		267
	[C]	Party Autonomy on Choice of Law Issues		267
	[D]	Restrictions on Party Autonomy		268
		[1]	General Observations	268
		[2]	Close Connection Test	268
		[3]	National Public Policy	268
		[4]	Mandatory Rules of Municipal Law	268
		[5]	International Public Policy	269
	[E]	No Explicit Choice of Law		270
		[1]	Introduction	270
		[2]	Relevant Conflict of Law Rules	270
	[F]	The Law Governing the Arbitration Agreement		270
§7.04	The Arbitrators			271
	[A]	Appointment of Arbitrators		271
		[1]	Appointment of Arbitrators under Municipal Law	271
		[2]	Appointment under Institutional Rules	272
	[B]	Qualifications of Arbitrators		273
	[C]	Powers and Duties of Arbitrators		274
	[D]	Challenges and Replacement of Arbitrators		275
		[1]	Challenges under Municipal Law	275
		[2]	Challenges under Institutional Rules	275
	[E]	Compensation of Arbitrators		276
§7.05	Jurisdiction of the Arbitral Tribunal			276
	[A]	Introduction		276
	[B]	The Arbitrators' Determination of Their Jurisdiction		276
	[C]	Court Review of Arbitrators' Jurisdiction		277
	[D]	Institutional Rules		277
§7.06	The Procedure Before the Arbitral Tribunal			277
	[A]	Introduction		277
	[B]	General Principles of Municipal Judicial Procedure		277
	[C]	General Principles of Arbitration Procedure		279
	[D]	Commencing the Arbitral Proceedings		280
		[1]	Municipal Law	280
		[2]	Institutional Rules	280
	[E]	Conduct of Arbitration		281

			[1]	Written Submissions	281
			[2]	Evidence (Admissibility, Documentary Evidence)	281
			[3]	Witness and Experts Testimony	281
		[F]	Hearings		281
§7.07	The Arbitral Award				282
		[A]	Introduction		282
		[B]	Deliberation and Voting		282
		[C]	Different Kinds of Awards		283
		[D]	Interest and Costs		284
		[E]	Effects of the Award		285
			[1]	Execution	285
			[2]	Res Judicata and Lis Pendens	286
		[F]	Correction and Interpretation of the Award		286
			[1]	Municipal Law	286
			[2]	Institutional Rules	286
§7.08	Setting Aside the Award				287
		[A]	Introduction		287
		[B]	Invalid Awards		287
		[C]	Challengeable Awards		288
			[1]	Grounds for Challenging the Award	288
			[2]	Waiver of Right to Challenge	288
		[D]	Review of Jurisdictional Awards		289
§7.09	Recognition and Enforcement of the Arbitral Award				289
		[A]	Enforcement of Domestic Awards		289
			[1]	Enforcement Domestically	289
			[2]	Enforcement Abroad	289
		[B]	Enforcement of Foreign Arbitral Awards		290
			[1]	Introduction to Recognition and Enforcement	290
			[2]	Separate, Partial and Interim Awards	291
			[3]	Grounds for Refusing Recognition and Enforcement	291
				[a] Lack of Capacity and Invalidity of Arbitration Agreement	292
				[b] Procedural Violations	292
				[c] Arbitral Award Not Binding	292
				[d] Non arbitrability	293
				[e] Public Policy	293
			[4]	Procedures for Recognition and Enforcement	294
§7.10	Investor-State Arbitration				295
		[A]	General Overview of Law and Practice Related to Investor-State Arbitration		295
Appendix 1. List of Investment Treaties Russia Has Ratified					297
Appendix 2. List of Investor-State Disputes (Concluded and Pending)					299
Bibliography					302

Table of Contents

CHAPTER 8
Tajikistan
Shirinbek Milikbekov & Zhanyl Abdrakhmanova   311

List of Abbreviations			311
§8.01	General Introduction		312
	[A]	Historical Development of the Legal System	312
	[B]	The Legal Profession	313
	[C]	Sources of Arbitration Law	313
	[D]	International Legal Framework, Supremacy of International Law	314
	[E]	Available Dispute Resolution Mechanisms	314
	[F]	Judicial System	315
	[G]	Arbitration Institutions	315
	[H]	Sovereign Immunity and International Arbitration	315
§8.02	Arbitration Agreement		315
	[A]	Introduction	315
	[B]	Validity of the Arbitration Agreement	316
		[1] Requirements of a Valid Arbitration Agreement	316
	[C]	Concluding the Arbitration Agreement	316
	[D]	The Doctrine of Separability	316
	[E]	Invalidity of the Arbitration Agreement	317
	[F]	Arbitrability	317
		[1] Disputes Capable of Settlement by Arbitration	317
		[2] Disputes Not Capable of Settlement by Arbitration	318
	[G]	Effect of Arbitration Agreement on Third Parties (Party Substitution, Guarantee Agreements, Group of Companies Doctrine)	318
	[H]	Termination of Arbitration Agreements	319
	[I]	Drafting Arbitration Clauses	319
§8.03	Applicable Law		319
	[A]	Introduction	319
	[B]	The Law Governing the Arbitration	320
	[C]	Party Autonomy on Choice of Law Issues	320
	[D]	Restrictions on Party Autonomy	320
	[E]	No Explicit Choice of Law	320
		[1] Introduction	320
		[2] Relevant Conflict of Law Rules	321
	[F]	The Law Governing the Arbitration Agreement	321
§8.04	The Arbitrators		321
	[A]	Appointment of Arbitrators	321
	[B]	Qualification of Arbitrators	322
	[C]	Powers and Duties of Arbitrators	322
	[D]	Challenges and Replacement of Arbitrators	323
	[E]	Compensation of Arbitrators	323

§8.05	Jurisdiction of the Arbitration Tribunal		324
	[A] Introduction		324
	[B] The Arbitrators' Determination of Their Jurisdiction		324
§8.06	The Procedure Before the Arbitration Tribunal		325
	[A] Introduction		325
	[B] General Principle of Non-interference		325
	[C] General Principles of Arbitration Procedure		325
	[D] Commencing the Arbitration Proceedings		325
	[E] Conduct of Arbitration		326
		[1] Written Submissions	326
		[2] Post-hearing Briefs	326
		[3] Evidence (Admissibility, Documentary Evidence)	326
		[4] Witness and Expert Testimony	326
	[F] Hearings		326
§8.07	The Arbitral Award		327
	[A] Introduction		327
	[B] Deliberation and Voting		327
	[C] Different Kinds of Awards (Separate, Interim, Consent, Default, Etc.)		327
	[D] Interest and Costs		328
	[E] Effects of the Award		328
		[1] Execution	328
		[2] Res Judicata and Lis Pendens	328
	[F] Correction and Interpretation of the Award		328
§8.08	Setting Aside the Award		329
	[A] Introduction		329
	[B] Invalid Awards		329
	[C] Challengeable Awards		330
		[1] Grounds for Challenging an Award	330
		[2] Waiver of Right to Challenge	330
	[D] Review of Jurisdictional Awards		331
§8.09	Recognition and Enforcement of the Arbitral Award		331
	[A] Enforcement of Domestic Awards		331
		[1] Domestic Enforcement	331
		[2] Enforcement Abroad	331
	[B] Enforcement of Foreign Arbitral Awards		332
		[1] Introduction to Recognition and Enforcement	332
		[2] Separate, Partial and Interim Awards	333
		[3] Grounds for Refusing Recognition and Enforcement	333
		[4] Procedures for Recognition	335
§8.10	Investor-State Arbitration		336
	[A] General Overview of Law and Practice Related to Investor-State Arbitration		336
	[B] List of Investment Promotion Treaties Signed by Tajikistan		337

Table of Contents

| | | [C] | List of Investor-State Disputes (Concluded and Pending) | 337 |
| | | [D] | Reform Proposals | 337 |

Appendix I List of BITs Signed by Tajikistan 339
Bibliography 342

CHAPTER 9
Turkmenistan
Rolf Knieper & Diora Ziyaeva 345

List of Abbreviations 345
§9.01 General Introduction 346
    [A] Historical Development of the Legal System 346
    [B] The Legal Profession 347
    [C] Sources of Arbitration Law 348
    [D] International Legal Framework, Supremacy of International Law 349
    [E] Available Dispute Resolution Mechanisms 351
    [F] Judicial System 351
    [G] Arbitration Institutions 352
    [H] Sovereign Immunity and International Arbitration 353
§9.02 The Arbitration Agreement 353
    [A] Introduction 353
    [B] Validity of the Arbitration Agreement 353
        [1] General Provisions 353
        [2] Requisites of a Valid Arbitration Agreement 354
    [C] Concluding the Arbitration Agreement (Written, Oral, by Conduct) 355
    [D] The Doctrine of Separability 355
    [E] Invalidity of the Arbitration Agreement 356
    [F] Arbitrability 356
        [1] Disputes Capable of Settlement by Arbitration 356
        [2] Disputes Not Capable of Settlement by Arbitration 357
    [G] Termination of the Arbitration Agreement 357
        [1] Termination with Respect to an Existing Dispute 357
§9.03 Applicable Law 357
    [A] Introduction 357
    [B] The Law Governing the Arbitration (*Lex Arbitri*) 357
    [C] Party Autonomy on Choice of Law Issues 358
    [D] Restrictions on Party Autonomy 358
        [1] General Observations 358
        [2] Reasonable Connection Test 359
        [3] National Public Policy 359
        [4] Mandatory Rules of Municipal Law 359
    [E] No Explicit Choice of Law 359
        [1] Introduction 359

		[2]	Relevant Conflict of Law Rules	360
§9.04	The Arbitrators			360
	[A]	Appointment of Arbitrators		360
		[1]	Appointment of Arbitrators under Municipal Law	360
	[B]	Qualifications of Arbitrators		360
	[C]	Powers and Duties of Arbitrators		361
	[D]	Challenges and Replacement of Arbitrators		361
		[1]	Challenges under Municipal Law	361
			[a] International Arbitration	361
			[b] Domestic Arbitration	361
	[E]	Compensation of Arbitrators		362
§9.05	Jurisdiction of the Arbitration Tribunal			362
	[A]	Introduction		362
	[B]	The Arbitrators' Determination of Their Jurisdiction		362
	[C]	Court Review of Arbitrators' Jurisdiction		363
	[D]	Institutional Rules		364
§9.06	The Procedure Before the Arbitration Tribunal			364
	[A]	General Principles of Arbitration Procedure		364
	[B]	Commencing the Arbitral Proceedings		364
		[1]	Municipal Law	364
	[C]	Conduct of Arbitration		364
	[D]	Hearings		365
§9.07	The Arbitral Award			365
	[A]	Introduction		365
		[1]	International Arbitration	365
		[2]	Domestic Arbitration	365
	[B]	Deliberation and Voting		366
	[C]	Different Kinds of Awards (Separate, Interim, Consent, Default, Etc.)		366
		[1]	Interim Awards	366
		[2]	Consent Awards	366
		[3]	Default Awards	367
	[D]	Interest and Costs		367
	[E]	Effects of the Award		368
		[1]	Res Judicata and Lis Pendens	368
	[F]	Correction and Interpretation of the Award		368
		[1]	Municipal Law	368
§9.08	Setting Aside the Award			369
	[A]	Introduction		369
	[B]	Challengeable Awards		369
		[1]	Grounds for Challenging the Award	369
		[2]	Waiver of Right to Challenge	370
	[C]	Review of Jurisdictional Awards		370
§9.09	Recognition and Enforcement of the Arbitral Award			370

	[A]	Enforcement of Domestic Awards	370
		[1] Enforcement Domestically	370
		[2] Enforcement Abroad	371
	[B]	Enforcement of Foreign Arbitral Awards	371
		[1] Introduction to Recognition and Enforcement	371
		[2] Separate, Partial and Interim Awards	372
		[3] Grounds for Refusing Recognition and Enforcement	372
		[a] Lack of Capacity and Invalidity of Arbitration Agreement	372
		[b] Procedural Violations	373
		[c] Excess of Mandate	373
		[d] Arbitral Award Not Binding	373
		[e] Non-arbitrability	374
		[f] Public Policy	374
		[g] Sovereign Immunity	374
		[4] Procedures for Recognition	374
§9.10	Investor-State Arbitration		375
	[A]	General Overview of Law and Practice Related to Investor-State Arbitration	375
	[B]	List of Investment Treaties the Country Has Ratified	375
	[C]	List of Investor-State Disputes (Concluded and Pending)	376
§9.11	Reform Proposals		377
	[A]	Ratify the NY Convention	377
	[B]	Review the BITs as to the Consistency of Dispute Resolution Provision	377
	[C]	Set up an Independent Association for Lawyers to Regulate Admission to the Bar	378
	[D]	Finalize and Open the New International Commercial Arbitration Court at the Turkmen Chamber of Commerce	378
	[E]	Abolish the Arbitration Court of Ashgabat	378
	[F]	Ratify the U.N. Convention on the Immunity of Property of States	379
	[G]	Align the National Arbitration of Annex 1 of the CPC to the UNCITRAL Model Law	379
	[H]	Introduce a System of Tenure for Judges	379
Appendix I Turkmenistan BITs			380
Appendix II Investor-State Disputes Against Turkmenistan			381
Bibliography			381

CHAPTER 10
Ukraine
Olena Perepelynska 383

List of Abbreviations 383
§10.01 General Introduction 384

	[A]	Historical Development of the Legal System	384
	[B]	The Legal Profession	386
	[C]	Sources of Arbitration Law	387
	[D]	International Legal Framework, Supremacy of International Law	388
	[E]	Available Dispute Resolution Mechanisms	389
	[F]	Judicial System	390
	[G]	Arbitration Institutions	390
	[H]	Sovereign Immunity and International Arbitration	391
§10.02	The Arbitration Agreement		391
	[A]	Introduction	391
	[B]	Validity of the Arbitration Agreement	392
		[1] General Provisions	392
		[2] Requisites of a Valid Arbitration Agreement	392
	[C]	Concluding the Arbitration Agreement (Written, Oral, by Conduct)	394
	[D]	The Doctrine of Separability	394
	[E]	Invalidity of the Arbitration Agreement	394
	[F]	Arbitrability	395
		[1] Disputes Capable of Settlement by Arbitration	395
		[2] Disputes Not Capable of Settlement by Arbitration	397
		[3] Special Provisions on Consumer and Labour Disputes	399
	[G]	Effect of Arbitration Agreement on Third Parties (Parties Substitution, Guarantee Agreements, Group of Companies Doctrine)	400
	[H]	Termination of Arbitration Agreement	401
		[1] Termination with Respect to Existing Dispute	401
		[2] Complete Termination	401
	[I]	Drafting Arbitration Clauses	402
§10.03	Applicable Law		402
	[A]	Introduction	402
	[B]	The Law Governing the Arbitration (*Lex Arbitri*)	402
	[C]	Party Autonomy on Choice of Law Issues	403
	[D]	Restrictions on Party Autonomy	403
		[1] General Observations	403
		[2] Reasonable Connection Test	403
		[3] National Public Policy	404
		[4] Mandatory Rules of Municipal Law	404
		[5] International Public Policy	404
	[E]	No Explicit Choice of Law	405
		[1] Introduction	405
		[2] Relevant Conflict of Law Rules	405
	[F]	The Law Governing the Arbitration Agreement	405
§10.04	The Arbitrators		406

Table of Contents

	[A]	Appointment of Arbitrators		406
		[1]	Appointment of Arbitrators under Municipal Law	406
		[2]	Appointment under Institutional Rules	406
	[B]	Qualifications of Arbitrators		407
	[C]	Powers and Duties of Arbitrators		407
	[D]	Challenges and Replacement of Arbitrators		408
		[1]	Challenges under Municipal Law	408
		[2]	Challenges under Institutional Rules	408
	[E]	Compensation of Arbitrators		409
§10.05	Jurisdiction of the Arbitration Tribunal			410
	[A]	Introduction		410
	[B]	The Arbitrators' Determination of Their Jurisdiction		410
	[C]	Court Review of Arbitrators' Jurisdiction		410
	[D]	Institutional Rules		410
§10.06	The Procedure Before the Arbitration Tribunal			411
	[A]	Introduction		411
	[B]	General Principles of Municipal Judicial Procedure		411
	[C]	General Principles of Arbitration Procedure (Party Autonomy, Speed, Impartiality, Etc.)		411
	[D]	Commencing the Arbitral Proceedings		412
		[1]	Municipal Law	412
		[2]	Institutional Rules	412
	[E]	Conduct of Arbitration		412
		[1]	Written Submissions	412
		[2]	Post-hearing Briefs	412
		[3]	Evidence (Admissibility, Documentary Evidence)	413
		[4]	Witness and Experts Testimony	413
	[F]	Hearings		413
§10.07	The Arbitral Award			414
	[A]	Introduction		414
	[B]	Deliberation and Voting		414
	[C]	Different Kinds of Awards (Separate, Interim, Consent, Default, Etc.)		414
	[D]	Interest and Costs		414
	[E]	Effects of the Award		415
		[1]	Execution	415
		[2]	Res Judicata and Lis Pendens	415
	[F]	Correction and Interpretation of the Award		416
		[1]	Municipal Law	416
		[2]	Institutional Rules	416
§10.08	Setting Aside the Award			416
	[A]	Introduction		416
	[B]	Invalid Awards		417
	[C]	Challengeable Awards		417

		[1]	Grounds for Challenging the Award	417
		[2]	Waiver of Right to Challenge	418
	[D]	Review of Jurisdictional Awards		418
§10.09	Recognition and Enforcement of the Arbitral Award			418
	[A]	Enforcement of Domestic Awards		418
		[1]	Enforcement Domestically	418
		[2]	Enforcement Abroad	419
	[B]	Enforcement of Foreign Arbitral Awards		419
		[1]	Introduction to Recognition and Enforcement	419
		[2]	Separate, Partial and Interim Awards	420
		[3]	Grounds for Refusing Recognition and Enforcement	421
			[a] Lack of Capacity and Invalidity of Arbitration Agreement	421
			[b] Procedural Violations	421
			[c] Excess of Mandate	422
			[d] Arbitral Award Not Binding	422
			[e] Non-arbitrability	422
			[f] Public Policy	423
		[4]	Procedures for Recognition	424
§10.10	Investor-State Arbitration			424
	[A]	General Overview of Law and Practice Related to Investor-State Arbitration		424
	[B]	List of Investment Treaties the Country Has Ratified		425
	[C]	List of Investor-State Disputes (Concluded and Pending)		425
	[D]	Reform Proposals		426
Appendix I Ukraine's BITs				428
Appendix II Investor-State Disputes Against Ukraine				430
Bibliography				432

CHAPTER 11
Uzbekistan
Foziljon Otakhonov & Alisher Umirdinov   439

List of Abbreviations			439
§11.01	General Introduction		441
	[A]	Historical Development of the Legal System	441
	[B]	The Legal Profession	443
	[C]	Sources of Arbitration Law	444
	[D]	International Legal Framework, Supremacy of International Law	445
	[E]	Available Dispute Resolution Mechanisms	446
	[F]	Judicial System	447
	[G]	Arbitral Institutions	448
	[H]	Sovereign Immunity and International Arbitration	449
§11.02	The Arbitration Agreement		450

Table of Contents

	[A]	Introduction	450
	[B]	Validity of the Arbitration Agreement	450
		[1] General Provisions	450
		[2] Requirements for a Valid Arbitration Agreement	451
	[C]	The Doctrine of Separability	451
	[D]	Invalidity of the Arbitration Agreement	452
	[E]	Arbitrability	452
	[F]	Effect of Arbitration Agreement on Third Parties	453
	[G]	Termination of Arbitration Agreement	454
	[H]	Drafting Arbitration Clauses	454
§11.03	Applicable Law		455
	[A]	The Law Governing the Arbitration (*Lex Arbitri*)	455
	[B]	Party Autonomy on Choice of Law Issues	455
	[C]	No Explicit Choice of Law	456
		[1] Introduction	456
		[2] Relevant Conflict of Law Rules	456
	[D]	The Law Governing the Arbitration Agreement	457
§11.04	The Arbitrators		458
	[A]	Appointment of Arbitrators	458
		[1] Appointment of Arbitrators under Municipal Law	458
		[2] Appointment under Institutional Rules	458
	[B]	Qualifications of Arbitrators	458
	[C]	Challenges and Replacement of Arbitrators	459
		[1] Challenges under Municipal Law and Institutional Rules	459
	[D]	Compensation of Arbitrators	460
§11.05	Jurisdiction of the Arbitral Tribunal		460
	[A]	Arbitrators' Determination of Their Jurisdiction	460
	[B]	Court Review of Arbitrators' Jurisdiction	461
	[C]	Institutional Rules	461
§11.06	The Procedure Before the Arbitral Tribunal		461
	[A]	Introduction	461
	[B]	General Principles of Municipal Judicial Procedure	462
	[C]	General Principles of Arbitral Procedure	462
	[D]	Commencing the Arbitral Proceedings	462
	[E]	Conduct of Arbitration	463
		[1] Written Submissions	463
		[2] Evidence	463
		[3] Witness and Experts Testimony	464
	[F]	Hearings	464
§11.07	The Arbitral Award		464
	[A]	Introduction	464
	[B]	Deliberation and Voting	465
	[C]	Different Kinds of Awards	465
	[D]	Interest and Costs	466

				Table of Contents

	[E]	Effects of the Award		466
		[1]	Execution	466
		[2]	Res Judicata and Lis Pendens	467
	[F]	Correction and Interpretation of the Award		467
§11.08	Setting Aside the Award			468
	[A]	Introduction		468
	[B]	Challengeable Awards		468
		[1]	Grounds for Challenging the Award	468
§11.09	Recognition and Enforcement of the Arbitral Award			470
	[A]	Enforcement of Domestic Awards		470
		[1]	Enforcement Domestically	470
		[2]	Enforcement Abroad	470
	[B]	Enforcement of Foreign Arbitral Awards		470
		[1]	Introduction to Recognition and Enforcement	471
		[2]	Grounds for Refusing Recognition and Enforcement	472
			[a] Public Policy	473
		[3]	Procedures for Recognition	474
§11.10	Investor-State Arbitration			474
	[A]	General Overview of the Law and Practice Related to Investor-State Arbitration.		474
	[B]	List of Investment Treaties the Country Has Ratified		480
	[C]	List of Investor-State Disputes (Concluded and Pending)		481
§11.11	Reform Proposals			482

Appendices	485

Appendix 1
Map of the Commonwealth of Independent States   487

Appendix 2
Satistics of Cases Involving States of the CIS Region with Leading
Arbitration Institutions   489

Appendix 3
The Most Important Domestic Enactments on International Arbitration in
the CIS Region   493

Appendix 4
Ratification of Selected Arbitration Related Conventions by CIS States   495

Appendix 5
Agreement on the Settlement of Disputes Relating to the Exercising of
Economic Activity 1992 (the Kiev Agreement)   499

Table of Contents

Appendix 6
Convention on Legal Assistance in Civil, Family Relations and Criminal
Matters 1993 (the Minsk Convention)   505

Appendix 7
Convention on Legal Assistance in Civil, Family Relations and Criminal
Matters 2002 (the Kishinev Convention)   537

Appendix 8
Annex 16 to the 2014 Treaty on the Eurasian Economic Union Protocol on
Trade in Services, Incorporation, Activities and Investments   583

Index   603

CHAPTER 1
Characteristics and Trends of Law and Practice of International Arbitration in the CIS Region

*Yarik Kryvoi & Kaj Hober**

LIST OF ABBREVIATIONS

BIT	Bilateral Investment Treaty
CCI	Chamber of Commerce and Industry
CIS	Commonwealth of Independent States
CIETAC	China International Economic and Trade Arbitration Commission
CPC	Commercial Procedure Code
DIAC	Dubai International Arbitration Centre
ECHR	European Court of Human Rights
ECT	Energy Charter Treaty
EAEU	Eurasian Economic Union
EU	European Union
FDI	Foreign Direct Investment
FTAC	Foreign Trade Arbitration Commission at the USSR Chamber of Commerce
HKIAC	Hong Kong International Arbitration Center
ICAC	International Commercial Arbitration Court
ICC	International Chamber of Commerce

---

* The authors wish to thank Dmitry Davydenko and Olena Perepelynska for their comments on earlier drafts of the paper and Anna Lanshakova and Yelena Burova for their excellent research assistance.

ICSID	International Centre for Settlement of Investment Disputes
JSC Act	Joint Stock Company Act
LCIA	London Court of International Arbitration
MAC	Maritime Arbitration Commission
MFN	Most Favoured Nations Provision
MIGA	Multilateral Investment Guarantee Agency
OECD	Organisation for Economic Co-operation and Development
PCA	Permanent Court of Arbitration
SCC	Stockholm Chamber of Commerce
SIAC	Singapore International Arbitration Centre
UNCITRAL	United Nations Commission on International Trade Law
UNCITRAL Model Law	UNCITRAL Model Law on International Commercial Arbitration 1985
UNCTAD	United Nations Conference on Trade and Development
USSR	Union of Soviet Socialist Republics

§1.01 INTRODUCTION

1.1. Until 1990s businesses from the Commonwealth of Independent States (CIS) were relatively unfamiliar with the practice of international arbitration. During the Soviet period, all foreign trade was conducted by so-called foreign trade organisations, forming part of the State monopoly of foreign trade and thus owned and controlled by the Soviet State. After the dissolution of the Soviet Union at the beginning of the 1990s only a handful of local enterprises engaged in international trade, and therefore in international arbitration.

1.2. The situation has dramatically changed since then. With the growth of the wealth of these countries, their engagement in world trade,[1] growth of foreign investments in the region,[2] the businesses in the region started to include arbitration clauses in their commercial contracts. Currently, parties from CIS countries represent a significant number of users of international arbitration administered by the London Court of International Arbitration (LCIA), the Arbitration Institute of the Stockholm Chamber of

---

1. The Commonwealth of Independent States (CIS) has become a significant trading partner of the European Union (EU) in recent years, with imports and exports growing from EUR 129.9 billion in 2002 to EUR 433.5 billion in 2013 (+ 234%). Russia's weight among the eleven countries comprising the CIS is considerable, accounting for 78.3% of EU-28 imports from the CIS and 70.6% of EU-28 exports to the CIS. See EU-Commonwealth of Independent States (CIS) – statistical overview, http://ec.europa.eu/eurostat/statistics-explained/index.php/EU-Common wealth_of_Independent_States_(CIS)_-_statistical_overview (accessed 23 March 2017).
2. FDI inflows to the whole CIS region averaged in 2000–2006 about USD 19 billion a year. Over half of it (USD 11 billion a year on average) was coming to the Russian Federation. See Alina Kudina & Malgorzata Jakubiak, *EU Eastern Neighbourhood: Economic Potential and Future Development*, Working paper on FDI and investment climate (2008), http://www.case-research.eu/sites/default/files/FDI%20and%20investment%20climate.pdf (accessed 23 March 2017).

Commerce (SCC), and the International Chamber of Commerce (ICC).[3] The world's largest arbitration award is also related to the region.[4] In addition, various international arbitration centres have been established in the CIS countries.

1.3. CIS states are not generally perceived as arbitration-friendly due primarily to the weak rule of law and corruption. However, as other chapters of this book demonstrate, many countries in the region are undertaking legislative efforts to make their legal systems supportive of international arbitration to encourage continued international trade.[5] Arbitration institutions based in the CIS region consider significantly more cases compared to institutions based abroad.

1.4. This chapter will give an overview of common features of law and practice of international arbitration in the CIS region. The similarities between jurisdictions stem from the shared common Soviet roots and the civil law tradition. In some respects, the law and practice is similar, which is reflected in approaches to the qualification of lawyers, proclamation of supremacy of international law, ratification of several regional conventions relevant to arbitration. After the collapse of the Soviet Union legal systems have been slowly drifting away from the Soviet legacy and not only similarities but also significant differences emerged, which may be illustrated by approaches to optional arbitration clauses, arbitrability of corporate and other categories of disputes as well as state immunity and enforcement of arbitration awards.

1.5. The chapter will also touch upon regional conventions relatively unknown in the West. For example, the 2008 Eurasian Economic Union (EAEU) Convention for the Promotion and Mutual Protection of Investments and the 2014 Treaty on the Eurasian Economic Union contain consent of parties to these conventions, including Russia, to arbitration of disputes between investors and states, including using the International Centre for Settlement of Investment Disputes (ICSID) Rules or ICSID Additional Facility Rules for States which have not ratified the ICSID Convention.

1.6. Despite the proliferation of disputes involving CIS-based parties, studies of arbitration law and practice in the region have not yet resulted in a comprehensive monograph. Although much has been written about arbitration in some of the larger

---

3. SCC Statistics 2015, Stockholm Chamber of Commerce, http://www.sccinstitute.com/media/18 1705/scc-statistics-2015.pdf (accessed 20 March 2017); LCIA Registrar's Report 2015, http://www.lcia.org/LCIA/reports.aspx (accessed 23 March 2017); *See also* Jacomijn van Haersolte-van Hof, Every Third LCIA Case Involves a CIS-related Party, CIS Arbitration Forum, 3 November 2015 http://www.cisarbitration.com/2015/11/03/each-third-lcia-case-involves-a-cis-related-party/ (accessed 23 February 2017).
4. *Hulley Enterprises Limited (Cyprus) v. The Russian Federation*, PCA Arbitration (No. AA 226), Award dated 18 July 2014; *Yukos Universal Limited (Isle of Man) v. The Russian Federation, Yukos Universal Limited (Isle of Man) v. The Russian Federation*, UNCITRAL, PCA Case No. AA 227, Final Award dated 18 July 2014; *Veteran Petroleum Limited (Cyprus) v. The Russian Federation*, PCA Case No. AA 228 – Final Award dated 18 July 2014.
5. On 8 April 2016, Kazakhstan adopted the Law No. 488-V On Arbitration which replaced two previous laws – the Law No. 23-III On International Arbitration dated 28 December 2004 and the Law No. 22-III On Arbitration (treteiskii sud) dated 28 December 2004; New Law on Arbitration of Russian Federation entered into force on 1 September 2016.

countries such as Russia and Ukraine, other countries have been studied significantly less. This book fills this gap.

1.7. The first part of this chapter will address various features of international commercial arbitration, including the historical background, legislative framework, common and distinctive features of arbitration in CIS states, such as arbitrability, public policy, and enforcement of arbitral awards. The second part of this chapter will deal with the investor-state arbitration involving CIS countries.

§1.02 INTERNATIONAL COMMERCIAL ARBITRATION

[A] Development of Commercial Arbitration in the Region

[1] Historical Background of Arbitration in CIS Region

1.8. States of the CIS region share a number of similarities, including history, close economic ties and Russian as the commonly spoken language. They also share the common heritage of Soviet law, which was a starting point for development of national legal systems in the 1990s.[6] As a result, the laws and practices of commercial arbitration have common roots, although with time the legal systems are drifting further apart, influenced by differences in political systems, attitudes towards the rule of law and openness to foreign investment and trade.

1.9. Alternative dispute resolution in the former Soviet Union has undergone dramatic changes with transition to the market economy and greater openness which followed the collapse of the Soviet Union.[7] To better understand the law and practice of international arbitration in the region it is important to take a historic journey into the Soviet past.

1.10. Domestic arbitration was almost unknown to the Soviet legal system: disputes between the state-owned companies were resolved by the state arbitrazh system – a quasi-judicial authority – and disputes involving individuals were resolved by state courts.[8] By contrast, disputes involving foreign counterparts were submitted to the Foreign Trade Arbitration Commission (FTAC) and Maritime Arbitration Commission (MAC) at the All-Union Chamber of Commerce and Industry (CCI). As regards Soviet foreign trade organisations, they preferred arbitration either in the SCC or pursuant to so-called US-USSR Optional Clause Agreement [9], unless the parties agreed to arbitration in Moscow before FTAC or MAC.

---

6. Ivan Zykin, *Commercial Arbitration in the CIS*, Int. A.L.R. 1(1), G1 (1997).
7. Roman Khodykin, *Arbitration in Russia: Hot Topic in a Cold Winter*, in Contemporary Issues in International Arbitration and Mediation: The Fordham Papers 2011, edited by Arthur W. Rovine, 274 (Martinus Nijhoff Publishers 2012).
8. Vladimir Khvalei, *supra* 11, p. 22.
9. Kaj Hobér, Transforming East European Law. Selected Essays on Russian, Soviet and East European Law (Juridiska Föreningen i Uppsala 1997), pp. 376–377.

1.11. Although the USSR, Belarus and Ukraine where among the first states to ratify the New York Convention,[10] the real practice of implementation was virtually non-existent in the Soviet Union. The USSR adhered to the principle of state foreign trade monopoly and organisations meticulously followed their obligations because they cared about their reputation.[11] It was not until almost thirty years after the signing of the New York Convention that the Soviet Union adopted an Act implementing the New York Convention into domestic law.[12] This implementation was followed by the liberalisation of the state foreign trade monopoly and the establishment of joint ventures with foreign partners became allowed.[13]

1.12. Until the 1980s no foreign arbitral award had been enforced in the Soviet Union, and no Soviet foreign trade organisation had ever refused to abide by an award rendered against it.[14] This changed in 1990s when, compared to Western countries, the share of awards voluntarily implemented declined in the region, meaning that the parties had to resort to courts more often. The absence of domestic Soviet legislation on enforcement of awards had created many practical problems for creditors. Since all foreign trade organisations were state-owned companies, basic assets such as buildings and large equipment were immune from the execution under Soviet law.[15]

1.13. Many Western commentators have criticised FTAC and MAC for their alleged lack of impartiality.[16] These concerns were related to the organisational structure of FTAC and MAC: only Soviet citizens had been appointed as arbitrators; the rules of procedure and method of determining the applicable law were unfair. It was also argued that FTAC and MAC were in fact national courts and not arbitral tribunals, and a risk of rendering pro-Soviet awards existed.[17] Nevertheless, despite all these fears

---

10. UNCITRAL, Status. Convention on the Recognition and Enforcement of Foreign Arbitral Awards (New York 1958) http://www.uncitral.org/uncitral/en/uncitral_texts/arbitration/NYConvention_status.html (accessed 27 February 2017).
11. Boris Korabelnikov, Mezhdunarodny Kommercheski Arbitrazh, 26 (2nd ed., Moscow 2013).
12. Vladimir Khvalei, *Arbitration in CIS Countries: the Same as Everywhere?*, in Arbitration in CIS Countries: Current Issues, edited by Association for International Arbitration, 21 (Maklu 2012).
13. On 13 January 1987, the Presidium of the USSR Supreme Soviet adopted Decree on 'Questions concerning the Establishment and Operation of Joint Ventures in the Territory of the USSR'. For a comprehensive analysis of joint ventures, *see* Kaj Hober, Joint Ventures in the Soviet Union. A Legal Treatise, (Transnational Juris Publications 1989).
14. Kaj Hobér, Transforming East European Law. Selected Essays on Russian, Soviet and East European Law (Juridiska Föreningen i Uppsala 1997), p. 414; Kaj Hober, Enforcing Arbitral Awards Against Russian Entities, (Transnational Juris Publications 1994), pp. 13–59; Alexander S. Komarov, *Arbitration in Russia: Features of the International Commercial Arbitration Court at the Chamber of Commerce and Industry of the Russian Federation*, in International Commercial Arbitration: Different Forms and their Features, edited by Giuditta Cordero-Moss, 301 (Cambridge University Press 2013).
15. Fundamental Principles of Civil Legislation of the USSR and the Union Republics, Art. 22.
16. *See*, e.g., Samuel Pisar, *The Communist System of Foreign Trade Adjudication*, 72 Harv. L. Rev. 1409 (1959); Eugene Leff, *The Foreign Trade Arbitration Commission of the USSR and the West*, 24 Arb. J. (1969); Robert Jarvis, *The Soviet Arbitration Commission: A Practitioner's Perspective*, 21 Tex. Int'l L. J. 341 (1986).
17. *See*, e.g., King-Smith, *Communist Foreign Trade Arbitration*, 10 Harv. Int'l. L. J. 34, 40 (1969).

FTAC and MAC had a reputation of a high-degree professional competence and fairness during all the period of their existence.[18]

1.14. Following the dissolution of the Soviet Union, all CIS countries have introduced domestic commercial arbitration institutions and adopted corresponding arbitration laws.

[2] Development of Arbitration in Post-Soviet Era

1.15. The CIS is a regional international organisation formed during the break-up of the Soviet Union. Out of fifteen former Soviet Union republics, nine are Member States, two are associate members (Ukraine and Turkmenistan) and Georgia withdrew in 2008 after the Georgia-Russia war. Three Baltic States (Estonia, Lithuania and Latvia) refused to join the CIS and are currently European Union (EU) Member States.

1.16. The CIS was meant to preserve the links which existed between Soviet republics. Currently it plays more of a symbolic role helping to coordinate in the areas of trade, legal cooperation, security and some other areas. In addition to the CIS, a number of other intergovernmental organisation emerged in the post-Soviet space. Eight of CIS Member States are members of the CIS Free Trade Area. A greater degree of integration is achieved within the EAEU, which unites Armenia, Belarus, Kazakhstan, Kyrgyzstan, and Russia.

1.17. The CIS and the EAEU have their own dispute resolution bodies. The Economic Court of the CIS deals primarily with disputes between states and interprets international conventions concluded within the framework of the CIS, as well as other CIS enactments. In addition, CIS institutions can also apply to this court. The Court of the EAEU also considers disputes arising out of implementation of the Treaty on the Eurasian Economic Union, international treaties concluded within the Eurasian Union and institutions of the Union. Unlike the Economic Court of the CIS, not only states but also commercial entities can submit their applications to the Court of the EAEU.

1.18. Following the collapse of the Soviet Union, the number of arbitrations involving the former Soviet Union republics has significantly increased for several reasons. First, as the economy became more open to the rest of the world, the inflow of foreign investments has increased dramatically.[19] For example, in Russia, foreign direct investment (FDI) inflows grew from USD 700 million in 1992 to USD 6,241 million in 1997, in Kazakhstan from USD 100 million to USD 1,321, in Belarus from USD 7 million to USD 200 million during the same years.[20]

---

18. Kaj Hobér, Transforming East European Law. Selected Essays on Russian, Soviet and East European Law (Juridiska Föreningen i Uppsala 1997), p. 426; Kaj Hobér, *Arbitration in Moscow*, 3(2) Arb. Int'l 119–163 (1987).
19. Towards Human Resilience: Sustaining MDG Progress in an Age of Economic Uncertainty (United Nations 2011), p. 89.
20. Klaus Meyer & Christina Pind, *The Slow Growth of Foreign Direct Investment in the Soviet Union Successor States*, 7(1) Econ. Transition, 201, 203 (1999) (citing IMF Balance of Payments Statistics Yearbook and International Statistics).

1.19. Since the collapse of the Soviet Union in 1991, Russia and other former Soviet republics were struggling to establish functioning institutions and the rule of law. Some countries (such as the Baltic States) did it relatively well and joined the EU. Other republics, particularly in Central Asia, plunged into civil wars and regional conflicts, which devastated their economies and societies. Countries of the region significantly differ on their level of economic development, ranging from Kazakhstan with USD 10,510 GDP per capita to Tajikistan with USD 925.9 per capita in 2015.[21] However, many aspects of international arbitration remain unregulated regardless of their level of economic development. In countries which have no significant experience with domestic and international arbitration much is left to the discretion of courts, which leads to a greater legal uncertainty for international arbitration users.

1.20. With the growth of foreign trade with the CIS countries,[22] the use of international arbitration as a mechanism for resolving the disputes with the CIS counterparts has also increased.[23] As discussed in more detail below, arbitration institutions in the CIS region consider significantly more disputes compared to arbitration institutions based abroad. However, foreign counterparts are still reluctant to arbitrate in the region due to the lack of experience of domestic courts with arbitration, a perceived risk of bias in favour of local parties, and worries about corruption.[24] The lack of information about regional institutions discourages non-CIS parties from referring their disputes to arbitration in the region. One of the goals of this book is to shed more light on international arbitration inside these countries. In the recent years most of the CIS countries have modernised their arbitration laws, and have become more arbitration-friendly. For instance, Russia and Kazakhstan in 2016 introduced changes to their arbitration laws. Nevertheless, many CIS countries still have limited practical experience with international arbitration.

1.21. In Russia, the system of commercial courts (arbitrazh courts), in many respects, lead the reform efforts in the area of judiciary. But the task is a difficult one because of lack of experience and due to the vast territory of the Russian Federation. While the Constitutional Court, the Supreme Court and the Supreme Commercial Court are relatively well regarded, the lower level courts have less experience in arbitration and are under increased risk of corruption.[25]

---

21. The World Bank, *GNI per capita, Atlas method (current US$)*, http://data.worldbank.org/ (accessed 12 December 2016).
22. Eurostat Statistics Explained, EU-Commonwealth of Independent States (CIS) – statistics on international trade by EU Member State and CIS countries, http://ec.europa.eu/eurostat/statistics-explained/index.php/EU-Commonwealth_of_Independent_States_(CIS)_-_statistical_overview (accessed 23 February 2017).
23. *See* Statistical Information of Arbitral Institutions: the Stockholm Chamber of Commerce, http://www.sccinstitute.com/statistics/statistics-2008-2014/, the London Court of International Arbitration, http://www.lcia.org/LCIA/reports.aspx (accessed 23 February 2017).
24. Steven Finizio & Kenneth Beale, *Expert View: CIS Arbitration Overview*, 5(5) Com. Dis. Res. (September–October 2014) http://cdr-news.com (accessed 23 February 2017).
25. Ethan Burger, *Corruption in Russia's Arbitrazh Courts*, BNA's Eastern Europe Report, Vol. 14, No. 12, December 2004.

1.22. Western lawyers dealing with Russia complain that 'many foreign investors have found it difficult, if not impossible, to have their rights recognised, particularly when they find themselves in conflict with a politically powerful or well-connected Russian party.'[26] Practitioners also note the trend of 'criminalisation of business law', i.e., when commercial transactions are interpreted by law enforcement bodies as criminal activities.[27] This is why, they suggest, demand for dispute resolution abroad will not dry out. Businesses will continue to seek justice, even if it comes with a significant cost associated with arbitration abroad.

[B]   Sources of Arbitration Law in the CIS States

[1]   Overview of International Treaties

1.23. Soviet law followed a dualist approach, separating domestic and international law. Following the collapse of the Soviet Union, constitutions of nearly all countries explicitly provide either for supremacy of international law or that international law constitutes a part of domestic law and, in one form or another, prevails over domestic law.[28] This section gives an overview of the most important international agreements relevant to international dispute resolution.

[a]   New York Convention 1958

1.24. All states except for Turkmenistan are parties to the 1958 New York Convention on the Recognition and Enforcement of Foreign Arbitral Awards.[29] The CIS laws on the recognition and enforcement of international arbitral awards are in line with the New York Convention.

1.25. Few CIS countries made declarations and reservations to the New York Convention.[30] For instance, Belarus, Moldova and Russia declared that the provision of the Convention would apply in respect of arbitral awards made in the territories of non-contracting States only to the extent to which they grant reciprocal treatment.[31] Armenia declared that it '[would] apply the Convention only to differences arising out of legal relationships, whether contractual or not, which are considered as commercial

---

26. Jeffrey Hertzfeld, Corporate Governance in Russia: The Foreign Direct Investor's Perspective, 31 May – 2 June 1999 at 6, OECD, https://www.oecd.org/daf/ca/corporategovernanceprinciples/1921803.pdf (accessed 27 February 2017).
27. *See* Ethan S. Burger, *Corruption in the Russian Arbitrazh Courts: Will There Be Significant Progress in the Near Term?*, 38 The Int'l Law. 15, 26 (2004).
28. *See,* e.g., Art. 151 of the Constitution of the Republic of Azerbaijan (12 November 1995); Art. 15(4) of the Constitution of the Russian Federation (12 December 1993); Art. 9(2) of the Constitution of Turkmenistan (18 May 1992); Art. 9 of the Constitution of Ukraine (28 June 1996); Preamble to the Constitution of the Republic of Uzbekistan (8 December 1992).
29. Status, Convention on the Recognition and Enforcement of Foreign Arbitral Awards (New York, 1958), UNCITRAL, http://www.uncitral.org/uncitral/en/uncitral_texts/arbitration/NYConvention_status.html (accessed 23 February 2017).
30. *See* New York Arbitration Convention, http://www.newyorkconvention.org/countries (accessed 3 April 2017).
31. *Id.*

under the laws of the Republic of Armenia'.[32] Tajikistan made a reservation that it would not apply the Convention with regard to differences related to immovable property.[33]

[b]   *Agreement on the Settlement of Disputes Relating to the Exercising of Economic Activity 1992 (the Kiev Agreement)*

1.26. All CIS Member States are parties to the 1992 Agreement on the Settlement of Disputes Relating to the Exercising of Economic Activity (the Kiev Agreement),[34] which aims at creating equal opportunities for commercial entities from CIS states to protect their rights and lawful interests. The Agreement established a general principle that commercial entities from CIS Member States have the same rights and obligations as commercial entities of the host state.[35]

1.27. Under the Kiev Agreement, Member States mutually recognise and enforce court judgments rendered in other Member States.[36] Official documents issued by competent bodies of one State party to the Convention do not require any additional procedures to be recognised in another state.[37] Courts and other state bodies of CIS Member States are obliged to render mutual legal assistance such as notifying the parties to disputes, delivery of documents, conducting expertise, taking evidence from witnesses and experts, and other procedural actions.[38]

[c]   *Convention on Legal Assistance in Civil, Family Relations and Criminal Matters 1993 (the Minsk Convention)*

1.28. All CIS states are parties to the CIS Convention on Legal Assistance in Civil, Family Relations and Criminal Matters (the Minsk Convention),[39] which plays a significant role in legal practice. According to the Russian Ministry of Justice, they have processed around 60,000 documents annually within the framework of the Convention. The Convention covers service of court documents, recognition of civil and criminal judgments, and cooperation between national authorities in the areas covered by the Convention. It provides that requests for legal assistance should be processed through the countries' central authority (ministries of justice). Assistance requests, for example, may include taking evidence from experts, witnesses and litigants, service of

---

32. *Id.*
33. *Id.*
34. Agreement of CIS countries of 20 March 1992 'On the Settlement of Disputes Relating to the Implementation of Economic Activity' (the Kiev Agreement), to 52.minjust.ru/sites/default/files/page/2012/06/status_1.doc (accessed 27 February 2017).
35. *Ibid.*, Art. 3.
36. *Ibid.*, Art. 7.
37. *Ibid.*, Art. 6.
38. *Ibid.*, Art. 4.
39. The Convention on Legal Assistance and Legal Relations in Civil, Family and Criminal Matters of 22 January 1993, as amended on 28 March 1997, http://www.cis.minsk.by/page.php?id =614 (accessed 15 March 2017).

documents, recognition and enforcement of judgments. Among other provisions, the Minsk Convention guarantees immunity of experts and witnesses who appear in a court of a contracting state on behalf of someone.

1.29. Similar to the Kiev Agreement, the Minsk Convention provides that documents made in the territory of one contracting state by an official body or a specially authorised person in accordance with the established procedure for and with an official seal are accepted in other contracting states without any additional authorisation. Judgments rendered by contracting parties on civil and family matters, including those confirming amicable settlements are enforced in other Contracting States in absence of grounds listed in Article 55 of the Convention (e.g., when the judgment does not have the effect of res judicata, the defendant was not duly notified about the process).

1.30. The most important effect of the Kiev Agreement and the Minsk Convention is that they simplify the procedure for recognition and enforcement of foreign court judgments, as well as ensure cooperation between courts and ministries of justice. However, they do not cover recognition and enforcement of foreign arbitral awards, which is regulated by the New York Convention or the European Convention on International Arbitration 1961.[40]

1.31. Both Kiev and Minsk Conventions are applied by domestic courts in the region quite extensively, most frequently in the context of the enforcement of foreign court judgments. However, there is still some level of inconsistency in the application of these Conventions.[41]

[d] *Convention on Legal Assistance in Civil, Family Relations and Criminal Matters 2002 (the Kishinev Convention)*

1.32 In 2002, CIS countries signed another multilateral treaty with a subject matter identical to the Minsk Convention, namely, the Convention on Legal Assistance in Civil, Family Relations and Criminal Matters (the Kishinev Convention).[42] The Convention represents amended and modified version of the Minsk Convention. The major changes are related to the issues of legal assistance in criminal matters.[43]

---

40. Yelena Burova, CIS Regional Conventions on Cross-Border Litigation and Its Application by Russian Courts, CIS Arbitration Forum, 9 December 2016, http://www.cisarbitration.com/2016/12/09/cis-regional-conventions-on-cross-border-litigation-and-its-application-by-russian-courts (accessed 27 February 2017).
41. *Id.* (e.g., courts mistakenly apply Kiev and Minsk Conventions in proceedings on the recognition and enforcement of foreign arbitral awards).
42. The Convention on Legal Assistance and Legal Relations in Civil, Family and Criminal Matters of 7 October 2002, https://online.zakon.kz/Document/?doc_id=1034672 (assessed 4 July 2017).
43. For comparative analysis of the provisions of the Minsk and Kishinev Conventions *See* Sergey V. Bakhin, Pravovaya Pomosch i Pravovye Otnosheniya po Grazhdanskim i Semejnym Delam. Korrektirovka Reglamentacii v Ramkax SNG (Kishinevskaya Konvenciya 2002), Zhurnal Mezhdunarodnogo Chastnogo Prava. 2005, No. 4, p. 3-12.

1.33 The Kishinev Convention replaces the Minsk Convention of 1993 and the Protocol thereto of 28 March 1997.[44] However, the Minsk Convention continues to apply in relations with state parties to the Kishinev Convention and states which have not yet ratified the Kishinev Convention.[45]

1.34 For more information regarding ratification of the most important regional conventions please *see* Appendix 4.

[2]   National Legislation

1.35. National arbitration laws have been adopted by all the CIS countries.[46] According to United Nations Conference on Trade and Development (UNCTAD), all CIS States except for Kazakhstan, Kyrgyzstan, Tajikistan and Moldova have adopted the UNCITRAL Model Law on Arbitration.[47] Even those which have not, generally follow most of the Model law provisions. Nowadays, many countries in the region are undertaking legislative efforts to make their legal systems supportive of international arbitration and to bring the arbitration law in line with the UNCITRAL Model Law.

1.36. For example, in 2016, Russia revised its arbitration law, introducing a number of essential changes.[48] The new law sought to provide clearer and more detailed regulation of the arbitration process in order to encourage businesses to use arbitration more actively, decreasing the workload of the state courts, and to eliminate 'pocket' (established by commercial companies to hear disputes with their counterparties) and sham arbitrations.[49]

1.37. The key changes to Russian arbitration law include the widening of the scope of arbitrable disputes (corporate disputes are considered to be arbitrable with certain important exceptions) and the introduction of the term 'permanent arbitration institution' (an institution which administers the disputes on a permanent basis as opposed to ad hoc arbitration). In addition, parties and/or arbitral tribunals in Russian-seated arbitrations are allowed to request the assistance/supervision of Russian courts in the taking of evidence; obtaining material (physical) evidence and documents; appointing the arbitrators; and considering challenges to arbitrators and to the jurisdiction of the

---

44. Article 120(3) of the Kishinev Convention.
45. Article 120(4) of the Kishinev Convention.
46. *See*, e.g., the Law of Republic of Armenia on Commercial Arbitration of 22 January 2007 No. ZR-55; the Law of the Republic of Belarus 'On international commercial arbitration' of 9 July 1999; the Law on Arbitration of Kazakhstan of 8 April 2016, No. 488-V ZRK; the International Commercial Arbitration Law of Ukraine of 24 February 1994 No. 4002-XII.
47. Status, UNCITRAL Model Law on International Commercial Arbitration (1985), with amendments as adopted in 2006, UNCITRAL http://www.uncitral.org/uncitral/en/uncitral_texts/arbitration/1985Model_arbitration_status.html (accessed 23 February 2017).
48. The Federal law of Russian Federation on Arbitration of 29 December 2015 No. 382-FZ, the Federal law on amending the associated laws due to adoption of the Arbitration Law of 29 December No. 409-FZ (in force from the 1 September 2016).
49. *See* more Marianna Rybynok, New Russian Law on Arbitration and International Standards, CIS Arbitration Forum, 7 September 2016 http://www.cisarbitration.com/2016/09/07/new-russian-law-on-arbitration-and-international-standards/ (accessed 15 March 2017).

tribunal). The new law enables the parties to waive the right to set aside the award and simplifies recognition of foreign declaratory judgments and awards, which now do not require the initiation of separate enforcement proceedings.[50]

1.38. On the one hand, some provisions of the new Russian Arbitration Law can be considered arbitration-friendly. On the other hand, state control over arbitration has substantially increased, as demonstrated by the complicated procedure for establishment of permanent arbitration institutions.[51] The requirement for foreign arbitral institutions to obtain a licence to perform arbitration activity in Russia may negatively influence the choice of Russia as a seat for international arbitration. In light of this, Russian ICAC will benefit from the new law, which grants it a privileged position compared to foreign and other domestic arbitrations.[52] Moreover, though the new law proclaims arbitrability of corporate disputes, it is subject to a number of conditions usually not found in countries with arbitration-friendly regulations as discussed on more detail later in this chapter.

1.39. It will only be possible to give a more definitive assessment of the Russian arbitration law once its provisions are tested in practice. As of now, parties envisaging arbitration in Russia should carefully select a licensed arbitral institution and ensure that the dispute is neither excluded from arbitration or may be considered to involve a public interest.[53]

1.40. Until recently, domestic and international arbitration in Kazakhstan was regulated by two different laws. In 2016, Kazakhstan enacted one single law for all arbitrations.[54] The key changes include the possibility for the parties to withdraw unilaterally from the arbitration agreement before the dispute arises, the establishment of new qualification requirements for arbitrators, the widening of the scope of confidentiality principle in arbitration, and the identification of non-arbitrable disputes.[55]

1.41. Ukraine, as one of the major arbitration users in the CIS region, has prepared a draft act introducing changes to the arbitration law, which was registered with the

---

50. Federal Law 'On Arbitration (Arbitral Proceedings) in the Russian Federation' dated 31 December 2015.
51. Maxim Kulkov & Sergey Lysov, *Russian Arbitration Law 2016: Key Issues*, http://kkplaw.ru/files/PLC-RussianArbitrationLaw2016_%20key%20issues.pdf (accessed 3 April 2017).
52. *Id.*
53. *See*, e.g., Reform of the Russian Arbitration Law, http://www.luther-lawfirm.com/en/blog/complex-disputes/das-neue-russische-schiedsverfahrensgesetz-en.html (accessed 3 April 2017).
54. Law of the Republic of Kazakhstan on Arbitration of 8 April 2016 No. 488-V, http://online.zakon.kz/Document/?doc_id=35110250 (accessed 22 March 2017).
55. *See* more, O novellakh zakona 'Ob arbitrazhe', prinyatogo v aprele 2016 goda, https://www.zakon.kz/4788935-o-novellakh-zakona-ob-arbitrazhe.html (accessed 15 March 2017); Pravovoj vestnik – novyj zakon RK 'Ob arbitrazhe', https://www.szp.kz/ru/press_center/news/2016/april/1083/ (accessed 15 March 2017).

Parliament of Ukraine pending adoption.[56] The draft law introduces a pro-arbitration approach to arbitration agreements, fills existing gaps in the matters of judicial assistance to international arbitration (support in obtaining court-ordered interim measures in support of arbitration and assistance in taking evidence), limits the number of court instances that may exercise judicial control and provides support to international arbitration.[57]

1.42. Overall, the changes mark progression towards a more pro-arbitration regime. Further reforms of national arbitration laws will hopefully make arbitration more transparent and reliable, in turn improving trust among arbitration users and judges.

[C] CIS States Practice in Commercial Arbitration

[1] Disputes in Domestic Arbitration Institutions

1.43. Each CIS country has a CCI with affiliated arbitration courts, which are usually the busiest in the country. For example, the International Commercial Arbitration Court (ICAC) at the Russian Federation Chamber of Commerce and Industry ('the Russian ICAC') resolves over 300 cases annually, the ICAC at the Ukrainian Chamber of Commerce and Industry ('the Ukrainian ICAC'), considered over 900 cases in 2015 and between 300 and 600 on average in the previous ten years.[58] In addition, in some countries arbitration active arbitration institutions are affiliated with regional chambers of commerce.

1.44. Although a significant number of disputes involving CIS parties end up in Western arbitration institutions, the bulk of arbitration cases are resolved within the region. For example, the busiest Western arbitration institution, the ICC, in 2015 had only 39 cases involving CIS countries, while the Moscow-based ICAC had 314 cases.

---

56. The Draft Act on Introduction of Amendments to Certain Legislative Acts of Ukraine on the Matters of Judicial Control and Support of International Commercial Arbitration of 31 March 2016, No. 4351.
57. *Ibid.*; *See also* Olena S. Perepelynska, Expert Opinion, Ukraine Reforms its Arbitration-Related Procedural Legislation, http://www.integrites.com/web/uploads/Ukraine%20Reforms.pdf (accessed 15 March 2017).
58. 2015 Report of the Ukrainian Chamber of Commerce and Industry, http://www.ucci.org.ua/media/report2015en/index.html#8 (accessed 15 March 2017).

Figure 1.1   Cases Involving CIS Related Parties in Major Arbitration Institutions for the Period from 2010 to 2015

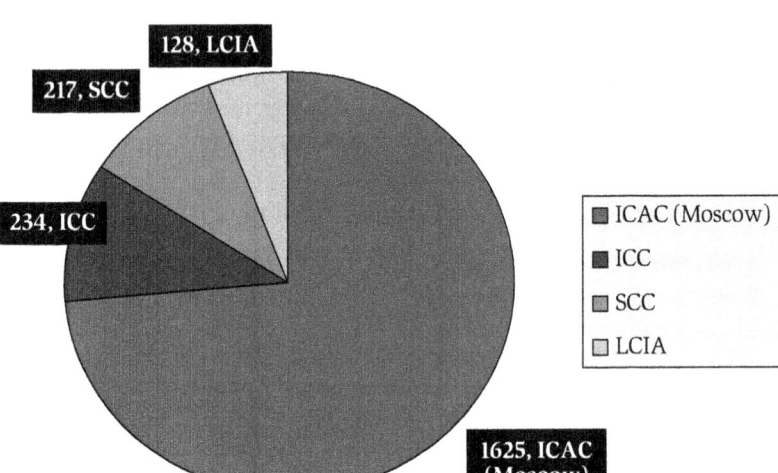

Sources: ICAC, ICC, SCC, LCIA.

1.45. The busiest CIS-headquartered institutions include the Russian ICAC and the Ukrainian ICAC. When it comes to global arbitration institutions the most popular are the ICC followed by the LCIA and the Arbitration Institute at SCC.[59] The A recent study concluded that the most commonly selected applicable law was English law followed by Russian, Swiss and Swedish law.[60] As venues for arbitration, the parties most often preferred the United Kingdom, Russia, Sweden, Switzerland and France.[61]

1.46. When it comes to appointing arbitrators in arbitration institutions headquartered in the CIS, nationals of those states dominate, while at global arbitral institutions almost exclusively lawyers from outside the region are getting appointments.[62] In cases involving the CIS countries, legal scholars, and less often practitioners, serve as arbitrators.

---

59. Maksim Kulkov & Nikolay Pokryshkin, *Obshhaya kharakteristika arbitrazhnykh razbiratelstv s uchastiem kompanij iz SNG*, Legal Insight, No. 1 (27) p. 11 (2014).
60. Dmitry Davydenko, Vybor arbitrazhnyx reglamentov i primenimogo materialnogo prava, Legal Insight No. 1 (27), p. 37 (2014).
61. *Id.*, p. 40.
62. *Rynok uslug arbitrov v. SNG*, Legal Insight No. 1 (27), p. 54 (2014).

Figure 1.2 Nationals CIS Countries Appointed as Arbitrators at the ICC for the Period from 2006–2015

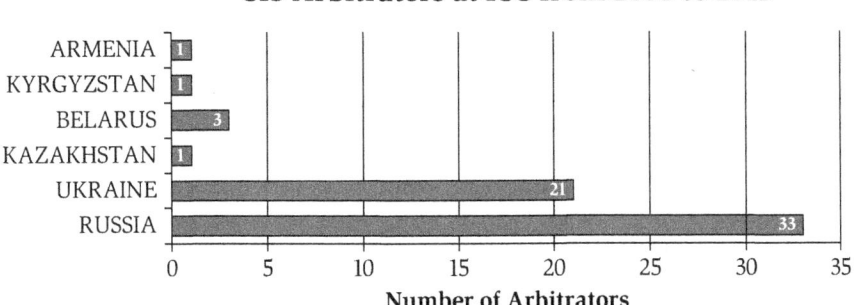

Source: ICC.

[2] Disputes in Foreign Arbitration Institutions

1.47. Statistics from various European arbitration institutions also demonstrate the increasing number of arbitration cases involving Russian companies. For example, Russian parties were second only to local Swedish companies appearing before the SCC.[63] In addition, the majority of investor-state disputes at the SCC concerned CIS countries.[64] Approximately a third of the LCIA's cases involve either a Russian/CIS party or a party ultimately controlled by Russian/CIS entity.[65] The majority of these cases are governed not by Russian law, but by English law with the choice of London as the seat of arbitration and appointment of English arbitrators.[66] Moreover, CIS businesses often operate via foreign registered companies, which make the real number of Russia-related disputes even higher.

1.48. A recent study conducted by the Legal Insight Journal and the CIS Arbitration Forum suggests that the number of disputes involving CIS countries has been constantly rising.[67] Most disputes in the region concern supply, share purchase and loan agreements.[68] The largest disputes from the region most often concern oil and gas sectors.[69]

---

63. SCC Statistics 2015, Stockholm Chamber of Commerce, http://www.sccinstitute.com/media/1 81705/scc-statistics-2015.pdf (accessed 20 March 2017).
64. *Id.*
65. Jacomijn van Haersolte-van Hof, *Every Third LCIA Case Involves a CIS-related Party*, CIS Arbitration Forum, 3 November 2015, http://www.cisarbitration.com/2015/11/03/each-third-lcia-case-involves-a-cis-related-party/ (accessed 23 February 2017).
66. *Ibid.*
67. Maksim Kulkov & Nikolai Pokryshkin, *Obshaya kharakteristika arbitrazhnykh razbiratelstv s uchastiem kompanii iz SNG*, Legal Insight, No. 1(127), pp. 9–12 (2014).
68. *Ibid.*, p. 16.
69. *Ibid.*, p. 15.

1.49. The reason why some parties prefer not to choose Russian law is the unpredictability of the outcome of disputes, since Russian commercial law has yet to recognise a number of western legal concepts.[70] It should be noted, however, that after this study was published a large-scale modernisation of Russian civil law has occurred, and now many western legal concepts have been adopted in Russia and expressly specified in the Civil Code (such as indemnities, escrow account, security deposit, optional agreement, etc.)[71] One of the reasons why Russian parties prefer to refer their disputes to arbitration and foreign courts rather than to Russian courts is a lack of trust in domestic courts.[72]

[a]   *Corruption Considerations*

1.50. Corruption drives many large disputes from the region to litigation or arbitration abroad. Resolving a dispute outside of the region helps avoid the administrative pressure by local officials and allows for the appointment of the most suitable arbitrators for a particular case. The enforcement of arbitration awards abroad may also be easier than enforcing decisions of domestic courts.

1.51. For example, according to commentators, corruption exists in Russian courts, but pressure on judges can also be exercised in other ways.[73] For instance, it is not unheard of that administrative pressure by the local authorities may influence the judge's decision. The situation is even more difficult for foreign investors who rarely have serious political support in Russia, unlike some of their powerful and well-connected Russian colleagues.[74] Despite the increase in popularity of Russian arbitration institutions and the formation of new domestic tribunals, many foreign investors prefer to insert dispute resolution clauses in their commercial contracts which provide for international arbitration outside Russia. Russian oligarchs also take their disputes to foreign courts and tribunals. These cases, as well as significant arbitral proceedings, sometimes arise out of very questionable contracts and allegations of bribery and corruption.[75]

---

70. Mikhail A. Rozenberg, Commercial Dispute Resolution in Russia, https://www.chadbourne.com/sites/default/files/publications/commercialdisputeresolutioninrussia_rozenberg.pdf (accessed 22 March 2017).
71. *See* Faegre Baker Daniels. English Law Concepts Introduced Into Russian Legislation 6 February 2015, http://www.jdsupra.com/legalnews/english-law-concepts-introduced-into-76782/ (accessed 27 March 2017).
72. *See* discussion of corruption in Russian courts in *Michael Cherney v. Oleg Vladimirovich Deripaska* [2008] EWHC 1530 (Comm).
73. Dolad 'Rossiya: Korrupcijya v sudakh' – Rossiiskaya associaciya advokatov za prava cheloveka (Report 'Russia: Corruption in Courts' – Russian Association of Advocates) rusadvocat.com/doklad.rtf.
74. Yaraslau Kryvoi, Bribery and Russia-Related Arbitration in Arbitration in CIS Countries. Current Issues. pp. 113–126 (Association for International Arbitration ed., 2012).
75. For instance, arbitral proceedings in IPOC case involved allegations of corruption of high-level Russian officials, including a former Minister of Communications and Information Technologies of the Russian Federation. *See* discussion of this case in IPOC International Growth Fund Limited v LV Finance Group Limited, Court of Appeal, 18 June 2008, Civil Appeal No. 30 of 2006, British Virgin Islands, reprinted in Yearbook Commercial Arbitration Vol. XXXIII, p. 408 (2008).

1.52. Practitioners note that arbitration users often prefer to avoid their home jurisdiction, which is particularly typical for Russia and Ukraine. The arbitration users prefer to avoid national substantive law, which imposes various restrictive norms, and to exclude courts of CIS countries from resolving disputes because of the perceived low quality of their work.[76]

1.53. Another example demonstrating the willingness of parties to 'move offshore' is the *Yukos* cases. In several awards, related to alleged unlawful expropriation of assets of the once largest Russian oil company, totalling over USD 50 billion, none of the arbitrators were from the CIS region or spoke Russian and none of the lawyers recorded as representing the parties were from the CIS region.[77]

1.54. Western parties are even less willing to accept Russian law or dispute resolution in Russia or other countries of the region. CIS-related parties use not only arbitration abroad, but also English courts to resolve large scale disputes.[78] According to some London legal practitioners, in 2012 'at least 60% of the work of the [high courts] commercial and the Chancery Division is Russian and Eastern European based, and that figure is unlikely to go down'.[79] The Brussels Regulation allows judgments rendered in London to be enforced in all EU countries, which makes it attractive to litigants. However, the situation with the Brussels Regulation in the UK will probably change when the UK leaves the EU.

1.55. English courts often take a broad view of their jurisdiction. For example, in *Cherney v. Deripaska*, the court ruled that jurisdiction will be asserted where the claimant will not receive substantial justice in the natural forum due to bias or a failure of natural justice.[80] In *BTA v. Ablyazov* the court, for similar reasons, extended its jurisdiction noting that the dispute could not be decided in Kazakhstan because of possible state interference. In some cases, however, the courts have taken the view that a CIS court would be more appropriate, for example, if the transaction took place there, the events and witnesses were based there and if the dispute was based on Russian law, then Russian courts were more appropriate.

---

76. Dmitry Gololobov, *Businessmen v. Investigators: who is Responsible for the Poor Russian Investment Climate?*, II(2) Russian L.J., 114, 117 (2014).
77. *Hulley Enterprises Limited (Cyprus) v. The Russian Federation*, PCA Arbitration (No. AA 226), Award dated 18 July 2014; *Yukos Universal Limited (Isle of Man) v. The Russian Federation*, Yukos Universal Limited (Isle of Man) v. The Russian Federation, UNCITRAL, PCA Case No. AA 227, Final Award dated 18 July 2014; *Veteran Petroleum Limited (Cyprus) v. The Russian Federation*, PCA Case No. AA 228 – Final Award dated 18 July 2014.
78. Rupert D'Cruz, Tatiana Menshenina, Patrick Heneghan, *International Dispute Resolution Involving Russian and CIS Companies*, Corporate Disputes Magazine, April-June 2014 Issue, https://www.corporatedisputesmagazine.com/ (accessed 23 February 2017).
79. Jane Croft & Neil Buckley, *Oligarchs pick London to do battle*, 17 February 2012, Financial Times, https://www.ft.com/content/75e4e812-5978-11e1-abf1-00144feabdc0 (accessed 16 December 2016).
80. *Deripaska v. Cherney* [2009] EWCA Civ 849.

[b] Impact of Sanctions Against Russia

1.56. The United Nations General Assembly by Resolution in 2014 called upon states not to recognize changes in status of Crimea region of Ukraine as well as "desist and refrain" from actions aimed at disrupting Ukraine's territorial integrity and national unity.[81] In light of this, the European Union and the United States have imposed a wide spectrum of economic sanctions against Russia in oil and gas, financial, and military sectors.[82] The EU sanctions programme also prohibits the satisfaction of any claim out of any contract or transaction brought by the sanctioned party.[83]

1.57. With fears of the negative impact of the sanctions on arbitration, Russian oil giant, Rosneft, proposed a ban on Russian companies entering into arbitration in the EU countries, instead moving the venue for disputes to its successful Asian competitors, such as Singapore International Arbitration Centre (SIAC), China International Economic and Trade Arbitration Commission (CIETAC), Hong Kong International Arbitration Center (HKIAC), and Dubai International Arbitration Centre (DIAC).[84] The supporters of these measures argue that the potential risks in arbitration brought under existing contracts and future arbitration clauses are related to: (a) the mere possibility to arbitrate; (b) the independence and impartiality of arbitrators from the EU; (c) the enforceability of arbitral awards.[85]

1.58. In response to these concerns, several EU-based arbitration institutions in a joint report stated that the sanctions do not impose general prohibition for Russian parties to seek arbitration before EU-based arbitration institutions.[86] First of all, sanctions apply to a limited number of Russian and Ukrainian persons and entities, whereas the overwhelming majority of businesses are not affected. If the subject of dispute itself is affected by sanctions, it will not matter where the arbitration will be seated, which EU arbitral institution will administer it, which law governs the dispute, and where the award is sought to be enforced. Thus, if the dispute itself is subject to sanctions moving the seat of arbitration outside of the EU will not make any difference.

---

81. UN GA Resolution of 27 March 2014, (A/RES/68/262).
82. Council Decision (EU) of 23 June 2014 No. 629/2014, Council Regulation (EU) of 23 July 2014 No. 629/2014. The US Sectoral Sanctions Identifications List includes persons determined by OFAC to be operating in sectors of the Russian economy identified by the Secretary of the Treasury pursuant to Executive Order 13662, https://www.treasury.gov/resource-center/sanctions/Programs/Pages/ukraine.aspx (accessed 15 February 2017).
83. Council Regulation (EU) from 23 June 2014 No. 692/2014, Art. 6, Council Regulation (EU) from 31 July 2014 No. 833/2014, Art. 11.
84. *See* Anna Zanina, *Sudebnye reform*, Gazeta Kommersant, http://kommersant.ru/doc/2600275 (accessed 17 February 2017).
85. Dmitry Kurochkin & Francesca Albert, *The Future of Commercial Arbitration with Russian Parties in the World of Sanctions*, http://whoswholegal.com/news/features/article/32061/the-future-commercial-arbitration-russian-parties-world-sanctions (accessed 15 February 2017).
86. International Chamber of Commerce Report, *The Potential Impact of the EU Sanctions against Russia on International Arbitration Administered by EU-based Institutions*, 17 June 2015, http://sccinstitute.com/media/80988/legal-insight-icc_lcia_scc-on-sanctions_17-june-2015.pdf (accessed 15 February 2017).

1.59. A person or entity subject to EU sanctions is not per se prevented from seeking arbitration with the ICC, LCIA or SCC. In practice, the EU sanctions legislation have only added a limited number of administrative steps in the case management process. For instance, after failing the request for arbitration institutions would check the parties against a list of sanctioned individuals and entities.[87] Arbitral institutions recommend informing the institution in advance in order to define if any additional administrative requirements need to be fulfilled, for example 'filing an application with the relevant national authorities for an exemption under the sanction regulation'. This, of course, may cause delay of the proceedings.

1.60. Regarding the risk of non-enforcement of awards, it cannot be stated with full confidence that the EU courts would automatically refuse the enforcement of awards which are not in compliance with the sanctions. Such refusal will depend on the interpretation of the public policy concept by each particular country.[88]

1.61. In 2016, the Russian Arbitration Association conducted a survey on the impact of sanctions on arbitration.[89] According to the results of the survey, 75% of respondents expressed preference to refer their dispute to a reputable arbitration institution regardless of the location of the institution in the state that imposed sanctions; 85% of respondents noted that the seat of arbitration in the sanctioned country does not affect the independence and impartiality of arbitrators. The survey also demonstrates that, despite the sanctions, the ICC, LCIA and SCC remained preferable institutions for arbitration of Russia-related disputes in 2014–2015.

1.62. Therefore, as long as the favourite arbitration venues for Russian business disputes continue to maintain their reputation as fair and independent, it is unlikely that sanctions may affect the choice of arbitration venues and arbitration seats in the countries which imposed sanctions against Russia.

[D]   **Trends in Law and Practice of Arbitration in CIS Region**

[1]   Common Features

1.63. All CIS countries are civil law jurisdictions with roots in the Soviet legal system. As this book demonstrates, when it comes to supremacy of international law, most states proclaim that international law prevails over domestic law with a few exceptions, the most common being contradiction to the Constitution.[90] Most countries also

---

87. *Ibid.*
88. Irina Moutaye & Elena Billebro, *Choice of Arbitration Venue in Light of Sanctions against Russia*, http://www.sccinstitute.com/media/76670/choice-of-arbitration-venue-in-light-of-the-sanctions-against-russia.pdf (accessed 15 February 2017).
89. 2016 Russian Arbitration Association survey on the impact of sanctions on arbitration, http://arbitrations.ru/upload/medialibrary/e1e/2016-raa-survey-on-sanctions-and-arbitration.pdf (accessed 17 February 2017).
90. *See*, e.g., Art. 6 of the Constitution of Armenia of 5 July 1995 ('If a ratified international treaty stipulates norms other than those stipulated in the laws, the norms of the treaty shall prevail.').

provide for direct applicability of international law, unless there is a requirement to adopt an implementing act in the international law instrument in question.[91] As in most civil law jurisdictions, in addition to courts of general jurisdiction which consider civil and criminal cases, all countries have specialised commercial courts, which usually deal with issues related to arbitration.[92]

1.64. CIS states typically have a less strict approach to the qualifications required to practice law, and in particular arbitration. Most legal systems distinguish between advocates and licensed (or qualified) lawyers. Advocates usually have the broadest scope of powers, including the right to represent clients in all courts.[93] Licensed lawyers, depending on the jurisdiction in question can render more limited services, without the possibility to represent clients in some courts,[94] or without representation in courts at all.[95]

1.65. Just as all CIS countries share the common heritage of Soviet law, all of them, except Turkmenistan, are parties to the 1958 United Nations Convention on the Recognition and Enforcement of Foreign Arbitral Awards (the New York Convention).[96] Most countries follow the UNCITRAL Model Law on Arbitration[97] and closely watch arbitration laws in Russia and other CIS countries and therefore share many similarities.

1.66. For example, all states recognise the principle of separability of the arbitration clause, meaning that the validity of the arbitration clause does not depend on the validity of the rest of the contract.[98] All jurisdictions require that the arbitration agreement should be made in writing, although writing does not necessarily mean a single document signed by both parties, but can also be the exchange of documents (letters, faxes, electronic messages) signed by respective parties.[99] In addition, the legislation of all CIS countries being in line with the New York Convention provides for

---

91. *See*, e.g., Art. 4(3) of the Constitution of Kazakhstan of 30 August 1995 ('International treaties ratified by the Republic shall have priority over its laws and be directly implemented except in cases when the application of an international treaty shall require the promulgation of a law.').
92. *See*, e.g., Law of Ukraine on the Judicial System and Status of Judges No. 1402-VIII of 2 June 2016.
93. *See*, e.g., Law of Kazakhstan on Advocates's Activity No. 195-I of 5 December 1997.
94. *See*, e.g., Art. 12(1) of Code of Civil Procedure Code of Ukraine of 18 March 2004 and Art. 16(2) of the Code of Administrative Court Procedure of Ukraine of 6 July 2005.
95. *See*, e.g., Regulation of the Ministry of Justice of the Republic of Belarus dated 7 March 2014 'On Some Issues Concerning Licensing of the Legal Services' Provision dated 3 April 2014.
96. The list of contracting states is available at http://www.newyorkconvention.org/countries (accessed 17 February 2017).
97. UNCITRAL Model Law on International Commercial Arbitration (1985), with amendments as adopted in 2006, http://www.uncitral.org/uncitral/en/uncitral_texts/arbitration/1985Model_arbitration_status.html (accessed 17 February 2017).
98. *See*, e.g., Art. 5 and Art. 20 of the Law of the Republic of Kazakhstan on Arbitration of 8 April 2016, No. 488-V ZRK.
99. *See*, e.g., Art. 210 of the Civil Code of the Republic of Moldova of 6 June 2002 and Art. 7(4) of the Law on International Commercial Arbitration of the Republic of Moldova of 22 February 2008, No. 24-XVI.

Chapter 1: International Arbitration in the CIS Region   §1.02[D]

the same grounds for setting aside arbitral awards and refusing the recognition and enforcement of arbitral awards.[100]

1.67. Unusual aspects of international arbitration in the region include the cautious approach of courts' to optional arbitration clauses (which give more procedural options to one party compared to the other).[101] Another such aspect is the possibility under Russian civil law, in some cases for a shareholder or a public prosecutor, to apply to a court to invalidate the entire contract containing an arbitration clause, even though they are not parties to the contract. Law of several other CIS countries contain similar provisions.

1.68. A distinct characteristic of the CIS arbitration market is that international law firms, rather than domestic firms, often represent parties in international arbitration, usually in close cooperation with local firms.[102] However, this is not usually the case for disputes considered in institutions located in the CIS region. A number of domestic CIS firms also successfully represent parties in large cases in the region and elsewhere. Other common procedural features of the CIS arbitration include such measures as reducing the number of the parties' submissions, full payment of arbitration costs by the claimant, squeezing proceedings into one hearing limited by time, and resolving disputes mainly on the basis of documentary evidence.[103]

1.69. CIS-related disputes are also known for the use of the so-called guerrilla tactics, meaning that the parities 'will try to exploit the procedural rules for their own advantage, seeing to delay the hearing and (if they get any opportunity) ultimately to derail the arbitration so that it becomes abortive or ineffective'.[104] Some authors divide guerrilla tactics into hard measures (physical attempts to influence the parties, the parties' counsels or the arbitrators) and soft measures (aimed to delay the anticipated negative arbitral award, or to create grounds to set aside or not enforce the anticipated negative award).[105]

1.70. The hard measures aimed against a party's counsel are generally uncommon. Nevertheless, in one of the Russian cases an enforcement agency took away the computers from an office of a law firm representing a party in a high-profile arbitration

---

100. *See*, e.g., Arts 34(2), 35, 36 of the Law of Republic of Armenia on Commercial Arbitration of 22 January 2007 No. ZR-55; Art 43 of the Law of the Republic of Belarus 'On international commercial arbitration' of 9 July 1999; cl. 3, Art. 50 of the Law on Arbitration of Kazakhstan, *supra* 66; Art. 223 of the Economic Procedure Code of Tajikistan of 5 January 2008; Art. 34 of the International Commercial Arbitration Law of Ukraine of 24 February 1994 No. 4002-XII.
101. Judgment of Russian Supreme Commercial Court No. BAC-1831/12 of 28 March 2012.
102. Rynki juridicheskikh uslug v sfere mezhdunarodnogo arbitrazha v stranakh SNG, Legal Insight, No. 1 (27) p. 42 (2014). p. 42.
103. Vladimir Khvalei, *supra* 11, p. 28.
104. Michael Hwang, *Why Is There Still Resistance to Arbitration in Asia?*, in Global Reflections on International Law, Commerce and Dispute Resolution – Liber Amicorum in Honour of Robert Briner 401, edited by Gerald Asken et al. 2005.
105. Vladimir Khvalei, Guerrilla Tactics in International Arbitration, Russian View – Chapter IV Alternative Dispute Resolution (Guerrilla Tactics), Austrian Yearbook on International Arbitration, Wien: Manz, Beck, Stampfi, 2011, pp. 336, 346–347.

proceeding against a Russian state company.[106] These actions were explained by the necessity of investigating a related criminal case.[107] In other cases, putting pressure on arbitrators through issuing anti-suit injunctions in order to prohibit not only the parties from continuing an arbitration proceeding, but also the arbitrators can be an effective from the standpoint of the final result.[108] With respect to the soft type of guerrilla tactics, these measures often include bringing parallel claims before different tribunals and courts, filing for insolvency, intentional destruction of evidence or challenging witnesses, counsel and arbitrators, etc.[109]

1.71. Sometimes debtors owing substantial amounts may file for insolvency or even for dissolution of the company in order to avoid payment to creditors.[110] For example, in one of the Ukrainian ICAC cases, Malaysian company obtained a favourable arbitral award.[111] When it tried to enforce it in the Netherlands, it found out that the respondent was dissolved by its shareholders shortly before the awards were rendered. Parties may also try to avoid enforcement by means of transferring all of the debtor's assets to some affiliates or third parties.[112] Such situation occurred with the same debtor as in the previously described case.[113] These kinds of debtors' actions are possible because under current Ukrainian legislation is practically impossible for claimants to obtain interim or provisional measures to ensure enforcement of an award.[114] Other examples of using guerrilla tactics in international arbitration by CIS-related parties include contract annulment by courts while arbitration is pending,[115] filing for prohibiting the other party to participate in arbitral proceedings, initiating parallel court/arbitral proceedings.[116] When the risk of using the guerrilla tactics is significant, it is often suggested that the parties apply for interim measures.[117]

[2] Distinctive Features

1.72. Despite the common arbitration tradition, there are some distinctive features in the arbitration legislation of the CIS countries, particularly when it comes to arbitrability of disputes, public policy, and qualification of arbitrators.

---

106. *Id.*, pp. 339–340.
107. *Id.*
108. *Id.*
109. Olena Perepelynska, *Guerrilla Tactics in Arbitration: Ukrainian Style*, http://www.sk.ua/sites/default/files/guerrilla_tactics_in_arbitration.pdf (accessed 27 April 2017).
110. *Id.*
111. Ukrainian ICAC Case No. 319n/2007.
112. *Id.*
113. Ukrainian ICAC Cases No. 322u/2006 and No. 179u/2007.
114. Olena Perepelynska, *supra.*
115. *CJSC TEKOM Corporation v. OJSC Zaporozhye Aluminium Smelter*, Ukrainian ICAC case No. 216u/2003.
116. MAC at UCCI Case No. 12r/2005; Ukrainian ICAC Cases No. 199p/2008 and 200p/2008; Russian ICAC Cases No. 127/2008 and No. 130/2008.
117. Markian Malskyy, *Resolving disputes involving Russian and CIS companies*, Financier Worldwide, https://www.financierworldwide.com/resolving-disputes-involving-russian-and-cis-companies#.WQNg4tLyvcs (accessed 28 April 2017).

[a] Arbitrators' Qualifications

1.73. Every country has its own requirements for the arbitrator's qualifications. What is common for all CIS countries is that all of them recognise that the arbitrator shall be independent and impartial. Higher education, professional qualifications of the arbitrator (such as compulsory legal background if the case is heard by a sole arbitrator),[118] and expertise in particular fields[119] are essential when it comes to the appointment of arbitrators. Some countries have adopted age requirements.[120] For example, in Russia, Uzbekistan and Tajikistan arbitrators must be twenty-five years or older, and at least thirty years in Kazakhstan. Good reputation (people that had previous criminal conviction cannot serve as arbitrators) is also an important consideration when appointing arbitrators in most of the CIS countries.[121] Interestingly, the law in Turkmenistan broadly defines the qualification requirements which an individual must fulfil to serve as an arbitrator, only requiring that an individual must be 'capable'.[122]

1.74. It is important to note that although arbitration institutions in the CIS region maintain lists of recommended arbitrators, the parties may usually also appoint arbitrators who are not on those lists. This is different to the situation which existed in the Soviet times when the parties' choice was limited to those who were listed.[123]

[b] Arbitrability

1.75. In general, most civil law cases are regarded as arbitrable with a few exceptions, which differ from one jurisdiction to another. Depending on the jurisdiction, the disputes not capable of arbitration may include disputes related to immovable property,[124] insolvency disputes,[125] and tax and labour disputes.[126]

1.76. The laws of most countries are silent on the arbitrability of corporate disputes, and this uncertainty gives courts the opportunity to form the practice regarding the issue. For example, although Armenian legislation does not clearly specify whether corporate disputes are arbitrable or not, in practice, arbitration clauses are often used in corporate agreements involving a foreign party. In Belarus, corporate disputes are

---

118. *See*, e.g., Art. 13 of Arbitration Law of Belarus, *supra* 68, Art. 14 of the Arbitration law of Uzbekistan of 16 October 2006 No. 3PY-64.
119. *See*, e.g., the Rules of Arbitration of the Arbitration Court of the Banks Association of Armenia.
120. *See* cl. 2 Art. 13 of the Law on Arbitration of Kazakhstan, *supra* 66.
121. *See*, e.g., Arts 80(1), 86 of Russian Criminal Code; Art. 11(9–11) of Russian Arbitration Law, *supra* 75; cl. 3 Art. 13 of the Law on Arbitration of Kazakhstan, *supra* 66; Art. 15 of the Law of the Republic Tajikistan on International Commercial Arbitration of 18 March 2015 No. 1183.
122. Article 2(1)(2) of the Law of the Republic of Turkmenistan on International Commercial Arbitration of 16 August 2014 No. 101-V.
123. Katherine Ward, *Arbitration with the Soviets: The Importance of Forum Selection in Dispute Resolution Clauses in Non-Maritime Joint Enterprise Agreements*, University of Chicago Legal Forum, No. 1, p. 699 (1990).
124. *See*, e.g., Art. 444 of the Civil Procedure Code of the Republic of Azerbaijan (1 September 2000).
125. Article 2(4) Law of the Republic of Armenia 'On Arbitration Courts and Arbitration Procedures' of 5 May 1998.
126. Law of the Republic of Kazakhstan on Arbitration, *supra* 66.

also arbitrable, for example, when the charter of incorporation contains an arbitration clause.[127]

1.77. In most common law jurisdictions, corporate disputes (particularly those arising out of shareholders' agreements) may be referred to arbitration and be adjudicated according to a foreign law as chosen by the parties.[128] Only in a few cases will the jurisdiction of arbitral tribunals be denied and the dispute resolution clauses and the provision of the chosen applicable law be ignored. This may be the case, for example, if it is deemed to violate public policy or the mandatory rules of corporate law, or if it violates the rights of third parties.[129]

1.78. For example, in the *Megafon* case, the claim was brought by several Russian shareholders of the Russian Joint Stock Company (JSC) OAO Megafon, and in essence, was directed against foreign shareholders of the company. In addition, the shareholders' agreement was subject to Swedish law providing for arbitration in Stockholm. The Federal Arbitrazh Court of Western Siberia found that the shareholders' agreement was invalid under Russian law. The reasoning of the court was based on the idea that since some provisions of the agreement were contradicting certain statutory provisions, which according to the court were mandatory under Russian law, the shareholders' agreement violated Russian public policy and was therefore invalid.[130]

1.79. Until 2016 corporate disputes in Russia were considered non-arbitrable. In many cases, the Russian state commercial courts took the position that corporate disputes are not 'arbitrable' since the state commercial courts have exclusive jurisdiction over such disputes.[131] In the famous case of *Novolipetsk Steel Mill (NLMK) v. Nikolay Maksimov*, the arbitrazh courts annulled awards, and found corporate disputes to be non-arbitrable in accordance with sections 33(1) 2 and 225-1 of the Russian Arbitrazh Procedural Code, which provide for the exclusive jurisdiction of commercial courts to hear corporate disputes.[132] Russia has recently addressed the issue of arbitrability of corporate disputes in its legislation, essentially making these disputes arbitrable with a few important exceptions, such as certain categories of shareholder disputes.[133]

---

127. *See* IAC by BelCCI, award of 16 December 2002, case No. 333/28-02.
128. *Russel v. Northern Bank Development Corp. Ltd.* [1992] 1 W.L.R. 588; *See Re Greater Beijing Region Expressways Ltd.* [1999] 3 H.K.L.R.D. 862 CA; *Muir v. Lampl* [2005] 1 H.K.L.R.D. 338; *Kwok Ping Sheung Walter v. Sun Hung Kai Properties Ltd.* [2008] 3 H.K.C. 465; [2009]2 H.K.L.R.D. 11 CA.
129. Strembelev, Sergey & Kryvoi, Yaraslau., *Arbitrability of Corporate Disputes in Russia: To Be or Not to Be* (23 January 2014). CIS Arbitration Forum Working Paper 1/2014; Journal 'Zakon', April 2013, No. 4, pp. 108–118. Available at SSRN: https://ssrn.com/abstract=2383736 or http://dx.doi.org/10.2139/ssrn.2383736.
130. Ruling of the Arbitrazh Court of Khanty-Mansiyskiy Autonomous District of 29 December 2004, No. А75-3725-Г/04-860/2005; Ruling of the Eight Appeal Arbitrazh Court of 8 June 2005, No. А75-3725-Г/04-860/2005; Ruling of the Federal Arbitrazh Court of West-Siberian District of 31 March 2006, No. Ф04-2109/2005.
131. *Id.*
132. *See* Decrees of the RF Supreme Court of 9.4.2015 No. 305 ES15 1789 and of the Commercial Court of Moscow District of 17.12.2014 No. А40-26424/11-83-201.
133. Article 45 of the Federal Law 'On Arbitration (Arbitral Proceedings) in the Russian Federation' of 31 December 2015.

1.80. The issue of arbitrability of corporate disputes also remains one of the most controversial issues in the arbitration law of Ukraine. The Commercial Procedural Code of Ukraine (the CPC) provides an exclusive domain for the State over corporate disputes.[134] Prohibition to bring corporate disputes to arbitration established in the Ukrainian CPC appears to contradict the provisions of the Ukrainian Arbitration Act, which explicitly allows arbitration with respect to disputes between an enterprise and its shareholders, as well as disputes between shareholders of an enterprise.

1.81. This contradiction has always been construed in favour of the CPC, as the Arbitration Act stipulates that if any other law establishes restrictions of arbitrability of certain disputes this other law should apply.[135] The position of the Supreme Court of Ukraine is that shareholders shall not submit their corporate disputes related to activities of companies registered in Ukraine, including those arising from corporate governance, to international commercial arbitration.[136]

1.82. It is still unclear how the meaning of 'corporate disputes' is to be understood under Ukrainian law. In *Bonduelle v. Cherkasagroproekt*, the High Commercial Court of Ukraine confirmed that a dispute related to the sale of shares was arbitrable because it did not fall within the definition of corporate disputes under the Ukrainian CCP, since one of the parties to the dispute was not a participant in the company whose shares were sold.[137] In 2016, the Presidium of the High Commercial Court of Ukraine issued a resolution concerning disputes arising from corporate relations. It replaced the previous guidance which recommended commercial courts to consider corporate disputes non-arbitrable in international arbitration.[138] The resolution, however, failed to clarify whether corporate disputes could be subjected to international arbitration, nor mentioned that they were non-arbitrable.

[c]   *Public Policy*

1.83. The concept of public policy is known to the legislation of all countries. However, the issue is treated differently from country to country, and the concept found rather more unusual interpretation in practice of CIS courts. While the concepts of international, and especially transnational public policy, are unknown to legislation of CIS countries, issues of national public policy are treated differently among the CIS

---

134. The Commercial Procedure Code of Ukraine of 6.11.1991 № 1798-XII, Art. 12(2).
135. Article 1(4) of the International Arbitration Act states that: 'This Law shall not affect any other law of Ukraine by virtue of which certain disputes may not be submitted to arbitration or may be submitted to arbitration only according to provisions other than those of this Law'.
136. Ruling of the Supreme Court of Ukraine of 24 October 2008 No. 13 'On the courts' practice related to corporate disputes', para. 9, http://zakon5.rada.gov.ua/laws/show/v0013700-08 (accessed 3 April 2017).
137. Judgment of the High Commercial Court of Ukraine of 15 April 2013, Case No. 7/5026/1561/2012.
138. Resolution of the Presidium of the High Commercial Court of Ukraine issued the Resolution 'On Certain Aspects of Jurisprudence in Disputes arising from Corporate Relations' No. 4 dated 25 February 2016.

countries. There is no uniform position between scholars and practitioners who tend to divide public policy into domestic, international, and transnational.

1.84. The legislation of the CIS countries does not give a clear definition of public policy, in most cases referring just to foundations of law and order of the state, or the basis of the rule of law.[139] This uncertainty gives the courts discretional powers to interpret this concept, and sometimes public policy is interpreted in a very broad manner in order not to enforce awards rendered against state-controlled entities.

1.85. For example, in one of the cases the Supreme Court of Russia found that awarding damages to a person for making unauthorised modifications with equipment owned by another person was contrary to Russian public policy.[140] In an early case in 2003, the Federal Arbitrazh court for the Volgo-Viatskiy Region refused enforcement of an ICC award, reasoning that the enforcement of this award may lead to the insolvency of the defendant, which in turn could negatively impact on the social and economic situation in that region of Russia.[141] Similarly, in *Konditerskaya Fabrika A.V. K v. AVK.Jug*, the commercial court refused to enforce the award, reasoning that recovering an amount in United States dollars from the debtor would be contrary to Russian foreign exchange law, and therefore, would contradict Russian public policy.[142]

1.86. Although foreign arbitration users might expect that public policy can be broadly interpreted in the region, in practice most CIS countries rarely set aside or refuse to enforce awards on the basis of expansive interpretation of public policy.[143] In a recent decision, the High Specialised Court of Ukraine explicitly stated that courts should avoid relying on public policy as a ground to refuse recognition and enforcement of arbitration awards, which should be limited to those stipulated in international treaties ratified by Ukraine.[144]

---

139. *See* paras 98–102 of the Methodical recommendations on certain issues considering the economic courts of the Republic of Belarus of cases involving foreign individuals and legal assistance, approved by the Decree of the Presidium of the Supreme Economic Court of the Republic of Belarus of 26 June 2013 No. 25; decision of the Supreme Court of Kazakhstan of 23 October 2005 No. 10; Information Letter of Presidium of High Commercial Court of Russian Federation of 22 December 2005 No. 96.
140. Ruling of the Supreme Court of Russian Federation No. 305- Э c14-2600 in case No. A40-87194/13-68-844 of 12 January 2015.
141. *United World v. Krasny Yakor*, judgment of 17 February 2003, case No. A43-10716.
142. *Konditerskaya Fabrika A.V. K v. AVK. Jug*, Presidium of Russian Federation Supreme Commercial Court, Case No. 9722/01 (2002). The judgment was later annulled by the Presidium of Russian Supreme Commercial Court, which ruled that enforcement of a foreign arbitral award in foreign currency did not run counter to Russian foreign exchange legislation. *See also*, Vladimir Khvalei & Jonas Benedictson, *Recognition and Enforcement of Foreign Arbitral Award in the Russian Federation*, 1 Stockholm Int'l Arb. Rev. 23, 39 (2005).
143. *See* Dmitry Davydenko & Eugenia Kurzynsky-Singer. *Substantive Ordre? Public in Russian Case Law on the Recognition, Enforcement and Setting Aside of International Arbitral Awards* 20(2) Am. Rev. Int'l Arb. (2010) p. 233. *See also* Information Letter of Presidium of High Commercial Court of Russian Federation of 26 February 2013 No. 56, para. 4.
144. The Highest Specialised Court of Civil and Criminal Cases of Ukraine, Overview of case law related to the recognition and setting aside of international arbitration awards by Ukrainian courts dated 11 December 2015; *see also* Taras Tertychnyi, Ukrainian High Court Summarizes Case Law on the Enforcement and Setting Aside of International Arbitration Awards, CIS

[d] Enforcement of Arbitral Awards

1.87. Foreign arbitral awards are recognised and enforced in CIS states either by virtue of international treaties or according to the principle of reciprocity. All the CIS states, except for Turkmenistan, are parties to the 1958 New York Convention.

1.88. The procedure of enforcement of foreign arbitral awards is regulated by national legislation, notably by the codes of civil or commercial procedure.[145] Even if a party obtains a favourable award it may face difficulties with its enforcement in the region because of complicated procedures. First of all, the procedure can be time consuming – the court's ruling on the enforcement may be subject to appeal in the court of cassation or in exceptional situations in the highest courts of the state, which may uphold the ruling, render another ruling, or remand the case for reconsideration to the lower court.[146]

1.89. After a claimant successfully obtains a judgment of recognition and enforcement of his award and a writ of execution, he will face another challenge at the execution stage. Basically, the execution should be done through the bailiff service (*sudebnye pristavy* in the Russian legal system) according to the Law on Execution Procedure.[147] The execution writs are not automatically forwarded to the bailiffs; creditors must take the initiative. If the debtor has no easily accessible assets, then the efforts of the bailiffs may come to naught. It is questionable whether the bailiffs, particularly in Russia, do their best to recover the amounts owed; some commentators contend that the bailiffs, due to their work overload, are prone to quickly declare defeat and are unwilling to put effort to auction off equipment or ferret out hidden assets of a debtor.[148] Overall, it might take up to twenty months from submission of the request for enforcement to the time a creditor in Russia actually receives the money, depending on the number of court instances the claimant must engage with and on the accessibility of the debtor's assets.[149]

1.90. With respect to the grounds for refusal of recognition and enforcement of foreign arbitral awards the national legislation in the CIS countries repeats the provisions of the 1958 New York Convention, including Turkmenistan which has not joined the New

---

Arbitration Forum, 4 April 2016, http://www.cisarbitration.com/2016/04/04/ukrainian-high-court-summarises-case-law-on-the-enforcement-and-setting-aside-of-international-arbitration-awards/ (accessed 27 February 2017).

145. *See*, e.g., Russian Code of Commercial Procedure of 24.7.2002, Chapter 241; the Code of Commercial Procedure of Belarus of 15.12.1999, Chapter 28; the Code of Commercial Procedure of Ukraine of 6.11.1991, Chapter XIV-1.
146. *See*, e.g., Art. 245(3) of the Russian Code of Commercial Procedure; Art. 249 of the Code of Commercial Procedure of Belarus.
147. *See*, e.g., Federal Law of Russian 'On Execution Procedure' of 2.10.2007 No. 229-FZ; Law of the Republic of Kazakhstan 'On Execution Procedure and Status of Judicial Bailiffs' of 28.10.2015 No. 369-V; Law of the Republic of Ukraine 'On Execution Procedure' of 2.6.2016 No. 1404-VIII.
148. Kathryn Hendley, Enforcing Judgments in Russian Arbitrazh Courts, http://www.ucis.pitt.edu/nceeer/2003-816-04g-Hendley.pdf (accessed 4 April 2017).
149. Maxim Kulkov, Enforcement of International Arbitral Awards in Russia, ABA Teleconference Handout, 18 November 2009.

York Convention.[150] The most frequent ground for refusal of recognition and enforcement of awards in some states in the region is the alleged breach of public policy. Other grounds for refusing enforcement of arbitral awards than public policy include non-arbitrability, procedural violations, and invalidation of contracts containing an arbitration clause invalidation of contracts containing an arbitration clause.

§1.03 INVESTOR-STATE ARBITRATION

[A] Development of Investor-State Arbitration

[1] Historical Background

1.91. In order to access the Soviet market, Western countries began concluding bilateral investment treaties (BITs) with the Soviet Union in order to settle outstanding issues and regulate the future ones. The first Soviet BIT was concluded with its northern neighbour, Finland, in 1989. It was followed by signing BITs with Organisation for Economic Co-operation and Development (OECD) countries, including France, Germany and Canada.[151] Most of the Soviet BITs include arbitration clauses allegedly of limited scope, providing for arbitration only with respect to matters concerning compensation for expropriation.[152] Therefore, under such clauses it has been argued that it would not be possible to arbitrate claims arising out of discrimination, unfair treatment or other measures.

1.92. After the Soviet Union disintegrated in 1991, its successor republics urgently sought to attract foreign investors to support the recovery of their economies.[153] Former Soviet states started to conclude bilateral treaties to facilitate cooperation on legal matters within the post-Soviet space. The peak of concluding international treaties concluded by CIS states was in early 1990s. The largest number was concluded by Russia, followed by Ukraine and Belarus. Kazakhstan, Uzbekistan and Moldova each concluded over forty BITs. Tajikistan and Turkmenistan tended to conclude less treaties.[154] In addition most CIS States are contracting parties to the Energy Charter Treaty (ECT).

1.93. Overall, the countries in the region have concluded more than 550 investment treaties, including BITs, free trade agreements, and other treaties containing

---

150. The Law of the Republic of Turkmenistan 'On International Commercial Arbitration' of 16.8.2014, Art. 47.
151. USSR-Finland BIT of 8 February 1989, USSR-Germany BIT of 13 June 1989, USSR-France BIT of 4 July 1989, USSR-Canada BIT of 20 November 1989, http://investmentpolicyhub.unctad.org/IIA/CountryBits/175 (accessed 21 March 2017).
152. *See*, e.g., Art. 7 of the USSR-Finland BIT of 8 February 1989, http://investmentpolicyhub.unctad.org/Download/TreatyFile/3449 (accessed 21 March 2017).
153. Noah Rubins & Azizjon Nazarov, *Investment Treaties and the Russian Federation: Baiting the Bear?*, 9(2) Bus. L. Int'l, p. 103 (May 2008).
154. Data is available at International Investment Agreements Navigator, UNCTAD, http://investmentpolicyhub.unctad.org/IIA (accessed 28 March 2017).

investment-related provisions.[155] Typically these treaties provide more than one option for arbitration, including resort not only to ICSID itself, but also to ICSID Additional Facility Rules when the dispute falls outside the scope of the ICSID Convention, the SCC Rules, as well as ad hoc proceedings under the UNCITRAL Rules.[156]

Figure 1.3 Total Number of BITs Signed by the CIS Countries

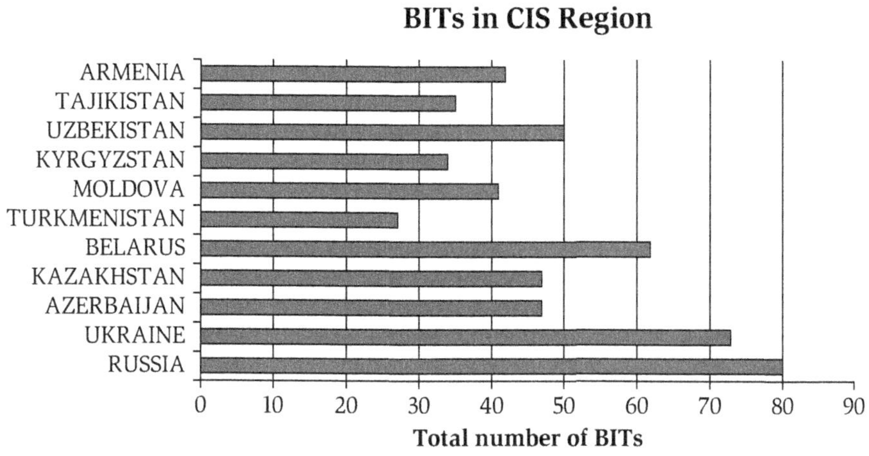

BITs in CIS Region

Country	Total number of BITs
ARMENIA	~42
TAJIKISTAN	~35
UZBEKISTAN	~50
KYRGYZSTAN	~33
MOLDOVA	~40
TURKMENISTAN	~27
BELARUS	~62
KAZAKHSTAN	~47
AZERBAIJAN	~47
UKRAINE	~73
RUSSIA	~80

Source: UNCTAD (2017).

[2] Overview of Investment Climate in the Region

1.94. The dissolution of the Soviet Union led to the growth of foreign investment in the region. For example, in Russia FDI inflows from USD 1.2 billion in 1992 to USD 74.8 billion in 2008, in Kazakhstan from USD 0.1 billion to USD 16.9 billion, to Ukraine from USD 0.2 billion to USD 10.7 billion during the same period.[157] BITs have, since the 1990s, been a core element of the CIS states' policy to encourage investor confidence and certainty as to the business environment, providing for arbitration as a dispute resolution mechanism with respect to the disputes between the investor and the host State.[158]

---

155. Information on the number of BITs signed by each country is available at Mapping BITs, http://mappinginvestmenttreaties.com/country (accessed 10 March 2017); *see also* Independent Study of Bryan Cave LLP, *supra* 118.
156. United Nations Commission on International Trade Law (UNCITRAL), UNCITRAL Arbitration Rules, U.N. G.A. Res. 31/98, adopted 15 December 1976.
157. Klaus Meyer & Christina Pind, *The Slow Growth of Foreign Direct Investment in the Soviet Union Successor States*, 7(1) Economics of Transition, (1999), 201, 203.
158. According to the independent study of Bryan Cave LLP 'International Investment Arbitration in the Commonwealth of Independent States: Year in Review 2015', countries in the region have concluded at least 554 investment treaties, including bilateral investment treaties, free trade

1.95. Economic growth in the CIS region slowed sharply in 2014 due to economic recession in the region and, arguably, in part due to the Russian-Ukrainian crisis, the annexation of Crimea by Russia, followed by the imposition of economic sanctions against Russia by the US and EU.[159] On the whole, in 2008–2015 mutual FDI in the five EAEU countries (Armenia, Belarus, Kazakhstan, Kyrgyzstan and Russia) was more sustainable than in other post-Soviet countries.[160] The top nationalities of the investors in the region include the USA, Netherlands, Turkey, Kazakhstan, Ukraine, United Kingdom, Russia, France, Germany, Ireland, Greece, Italy, Lithuania, Austria, Cyprus.[161] The growth of investments in the region, in turn, led to the growth of claims against the states in investment arbitration.[162] Out of all of the CIS state, Russia has faced the most high-profile cases since 1993.[163]

[B] Legal Framework

1.96. The legal framework for investment arbitration is provided by public international law treaties which comprise of BITs and MITs, such as the ICSID Convention and ECT, as well as regional instruments. Trying to create a favourable investment climate, all CIS states have adopted investment protection laws which provide certain privileges to foreign investors.[164] Consent to arbitrate disputes between states and foreign investors can typically be expressed in treaties, domestic laws or investment agreements.

[1] International Agreements

1.97. All CIS countries are parties to the basic international treaties in the area of foreign investments, such as the Convention Establishing the Multilateral Investment Guarantee Agency (MIGA), which gives investors the opportunities to insure against non-commercial risks in the state with a developing economy, and the Washington

---

agreements and other treaties containing investment-related provisions. Available at https://d11m3yrngt251b.cloudfront.net/images/content/8/4/v2/84187/2015-CISYIR-FINAL.pdf (accessed 2 March 2017).
159. Viljar Veebel & Raul Markus, *Lessons from the EU-Russia Sanctions 2014-2015*, 8(1) Baltic J. L. & Pol., 165, 176 (2015).
160. *Ibid.*
161. Bryan Cave LLP study, *supra* 118.
162. Kaj Hober, Leading Arbitrator's Guide, p. 140.
163. *See*, e.g., *Compagnie Noga d'Importation et d'Exportation v. the Russian Federation*, *Berschader v. the Russian Federation*, *Cesare Galdabini SpA v. the Russian Federation*, *Sedelmayer v. the Russian Federation*, *RosinvestCo UK Ltd. v. the Russian Federation*, *Veteran Petroleum Limited (Cyprus) v. the Russian Federation*, *Yukos Universal Limited (Isle of Man) v. the Russian Federation*, *Renta 4 S.V.S.A. v. the Russian Federation*, *Yucos capital S.A.R.L. v. the Russian Federation*.
164. *See*, e.g., Law of the Republic of Azerbaijan on Protection of Foreign Investments, the Law of Republic of Belarus on Investments of 12 July 2013, Federal Law of Russian Federation of 9 July 1999 No. 160-FZ 'On foreign investments in Russian Federation', Laws of the Republic of Uzbekistan of 30 April 1998 No. 609-I 'On foreign investments', of 29 December 1998 No. 719-I 'On investment activities', of 30 April 1998 No. 611-I 'On guarantees and means of protection of foreign investors' rights'.

Convention on the Settlement of Investment Disputes (ICSID) (except Russia, Kyrgyzstan, and Tajikistan). The ECT is also signed and ratified by the majority of the CIS countries, except Belarus and Russia. Belarus has signed but not ratified the ECT which means that it applies provisionally. As explained in some detail below, Russia signed the ECT in 1994 which provisionally applies pending ratification, which never took place. In 2009, Russia claims that it formally withdrew from the ECT.

[a]   Washington Convention 1965

1.98. All CIS states except for Russia, Tajikistan and Kyrgyzstan have also ratified the Convention on the Settlement of Investment Disputes between States and Nationals of Other States (the ICSID Convention).[165] The ICSID Convention is a self-contained arbitration system that prohibits the review of arbitral awards by the national courts of any Member State. Awards are subject only to review by an international ad hoc committee and thereafter become automatically enforceable. ICSID arbitral awards are final and binding, and all contacting states are required to recognise them.[166]

1.99. Foreign investors may nevertheless have access to ICSID arbitration involving the countries that have not ratified the Convention via Additional Facility Rules where it is allowed by investment treaties. Unlike the ICSID awards, awards rendered under the ICSID Additional Facility Rules are subject to the supervision of a national court, and their enforcement is covered by the New York Convention Regime.

1.100. It is interesting to note that although Russia, Tajikistan and Kyrgyzstan are not parties to the ICSID Convention, ICSID Additional Facility rules can still be used by them by virtue of regional conventions discussed in more detail below.

[b]   Energy Charter Treaty (ECT) 1994

1.101. The ECT[167] has been signed and ratified by the majority of the CIS countries, except Belarus and Russia.[168] Belarus has signed but not ratified the ECT which means that it applies it provisionally. Russia signed the ECT in 1994 but never ratified it. In 2009, during arbitrations involving former shareholders of Yukos oil company, Russia declared that it would no longer seek to ratify the Treaty and formally withdrew from the ECT.

---

165. Database of ICSID Member States, https://icsid.worldbank.org/en/Pages/about/Database-of-Member-States.aspx (accessed 27 February 2017).
166. For a more detailed analysis of the ICSID arbitration regime *see* Yaraslau Kryvoi, International Centre for Settlement of Investment Disputes, (Kluwer Law International 2016).
167. The 1994 Energy Charter Treaty, The treaty and related documents are available at http://www.energycharter.org/process/energy-charter-treaty-1994/energy-charter-treaty/ (accessed 20 March 2017).
168. Constituency of the Energy Charter Conference, http://www.energycharter.org/who-we-are/members-observers/ (accessed 27 February 2017).

1.102. The Treaty aims at providing investment protection in the energy sector and also provides for a specific regime for transit disputes. The ECT operates as an investment protection tool to reduce commercial risks in the energy sector by granting investors non-discriminatory treatment (national treatment and most-favoured national treatment) and granting compensation in the case of expropriation and other losses, as well as enabling free transfer of capital.[169]

1.103. The ECT also offers freedom of energy transit, improvement of energy efficiency, and international dispute settlement, including investor-state arbitration and inter-state arbitration. Under Article 26(4) of the ECT, parties may choose ICSID Arbitration, arbitration under the ICSID Additional Facility Rules, ad hoc arbitration under the UNCITRAL Rules, or arbitration under the SCC Rules. The ECT arbitral awards are also final and binding, and each contracting party is obliged to provide for the effective enforcement of such awards.

1.104. With respect to Russia's withdrawal from the ECT, some commentators believe it is linked to the arbitrations between Russia and the former shareholders of the Yukos oil company. Another perspective is set out in the Russian Oil and Gas Report:

> The main point in the ECT is the 'obligation on member countries to facilitate energy materials and products transit across their territory, in line with the principle of freedom of transit.' In effect, this means that once Russia ratified the treaty, it would have had to permit free transit of Central Asian gas to Europe across Russian territory. The Russian authorities regard this prospect as completely unacceptable: Russia would only receive transit fees for Central Asian gas, and wouldn't be able to control gas flows. At present Russia buys gas from Kazakhstan, Uzbekistan, and Turkmenistan before selling it to Europe – as Russian gas. Moreover, the ECT would require Gazprom to sell Russian gas to consumer countries at the border, so that subsequent sales would be handled by the gas companies of those countries. This would be extremely disadvantageous for Gazprom, which is striving for access to end consumers: that is, it seeks access to the domestic markets of its partner states.[170]

1.105. Russia has officially demonstrated its discontent with the existing frameworks of bilateral and multilateral cooperation in the energy sector. It argued that the existing legal mechanisms have failed to prevent and resolve conflict situations, which makes it necessary to efficiently improve the legal framework of the world trade in energy resources, and with that stresses the interest of Russia in an agreement regulating global energy cooperation.[171] In 2009, Russia proposed a new energy charter called the

---

169. Johan Billiet, International Investment Arbitration. A Practical Handbook (Maklu Publishers 2016), p. 46.
170. *Russia officially refuses to ratify the Energy Charter Treaty*, Russian Oil and Gaz Report (10 August 2009).
171. Conceptual Approach to the New Legal Framework for Energy Cooperation of 21.4.2009. http://www.kremlin.ru/ref_notes/258 (accessed 5 April 2017).

integral approach to new legal base of international energy cooperation'. This approach implies that either a new energy charter should be elaborated or serious amendments to the current charter should be made.[172]

1.106. The applicability of the ECT was the central legal issue in the world's largest investor-state arbitration to date in which former shareholders of Yukos oil company alleged violations of the ECT. In 2009, The Permanent Court of Arbitration (PCA) tribunal seated in the Netherlands upheld its jurisdiction under the ECT, explaining that Russia had agreed to apply provisionally as a whole pending its entry into force, including its dispute resolution provisions when it signed the treaty.[173] In 2014 the tribunal held that Russia breached Article 13(1) of the ECT by unlawfully expropriating the Yukos shareholders' assets and awarded them compensation amounting to USD 50 billion.[174] Russia challenged the award at the Hague District Court, which in 2016 set aside the award concluding that Russia 'was only bound by the treaty provisions reconcilable with Russian law'.[175] The court concluded that because the ECT had never been ratified by the Russian Parliament, 'the arbitration clause of Article 26 ECT does not have a legal basis in Russian law and is incompatible with the starting points laid down in that law'. Russia has appealed this judgment.

[c] *CIS Convention for the Protection of Investor's Rights 1997 (the Moscow Convention)*

1.107. The Convention on the Protection of Investor's Rights 1997 remains in force for Armenia, Belarus, Kazakhstan, Kyrgyzstan, Moldova, Tajikistan.[176] The convention contains guarantees to investors similar to those found in many BITs, but applies irrespective of the nationality of the investor. For example, the convention gives

---

172. *Id.*; *See also* Irina Pominova, Risks and Benefits for the Russian Federation from Participating in the Energy Charter Treaty: Comprehensive Analysis, Occasional Paper, Energy Charter Secretariat, Knowledge Centre 2014; Russia's withdrawal from the Energy Charter Treaty (August 2009), http://www.nortonrosefulbright.com/knowledge/publications/22691/russias-withdrawal-from-the-energy-charter-treaty (accessed 5 April 2017); Andrei Belyi, Rossiya I Dogovor Energeticheskoy Khartii, 4 EKO No. 6, 2010, pp. 97–114.
173. *Yukos Universal Ltd. v. Russian Federation*, Interim Award on Jurisdiction and Admissibility, PCA Case No. AA 227 (30 November 2009), available at http://ita.law.uvic.ca/documents/YULvRussianFederation-InterimAward-30Nov2009.pdf; *Hulley Enterprises Ltd. v. Russian Federation*, Interim Award on Jurisdiction and Admissibility, PCA Case No. AA 226 (30 November 2009), available at http://ita.law.uvic.ca/documents/HELvRussianFederation-InterimAward-30Nov2009.pdf; *Veteran Petroleum Trust v. Russian Federation*, Interim Award on Jurisdiction and Admissibility, PCA Case No. AA 228 (30 November 2009), available at http://ita.law.uvic.ca/documents/VPLvRussianFederation-InterimAward-30Nov2009.pdf. (accessed 5 April 2017).
174. *Yukos Universal Limited (Isle of Man) v. The Russian Federation*, UNCITRAL, PCA Case No. AA 227; *Hulley Enterprises Limited (Cyprus) v. The Russian Federation*, UNCITRAL, PCA Case No. AA 226; *Veteran Petroleum Limited (Cyprus) v. The Russian Federation*, UNCITRAL, PCA Case No. AA 228.
175. The Hague District Court Judgment C/09/477160, dated 20 April 2016, unofficial English translation available at http://deeplink.rechtspraak.nl/uitspraak?id = ECLI:NL:RBDHA:2016:4230 (accessed 5 April 2017).
176. UNCTAD Investment Policy Hub, Convention on Protection of Investor Rights (CIS Investor Rights Convention (1997)), http://investmentpolicyhub.unctad.org/IIA/mostRecent/treaty/3408 (accessed 27 February 2017).

protection to investors in case of adverse changes in legislation (Article 5), nationalisation (Article 9), compensation of damages caused to the investor (Article 10) and guarantees on the use of profits (Article 12). It contains an article which confirms the right of the parties to have recourse to arbitration and international courts, but as the CIS Economic Court explained, this does not establish jurisdiction of any specific court or tribunal.[177] The convention does not contain any provision on the recognition and enforcement of arbitral awards. For the purposes of issuing authoritative interpretations of regional international treaties such as the 1997 Moscow Convention, members of CIS in 1992 established the CIS Economic Court.

1.108. Several claims were filed against the Republic of Kyrgyzstan in the Moscow ICAC under the Moscow Convention.[178] The claimants argued that a broadly drafted dispute resolution provision of the Convention entitles potential claimants to bring arbitration proceedings against the states-parties to the Convention in any arbitration court of the investor's choice.[179] The Kyrgyz Republic initiated annulment proceedings before in Russian courts, and in the meantime applied to the CIS Economic Court seeking clarification of Article 11. In 2014, the CIS Economic Court agreed with Kyrgyzstan that the provisions of the Convention cannot be treated as the consent of the state to refer disputes to international arbitration.

[d]   *EAEU Convention for the Promotion and Mutual Protection of Investments 2008*

1.109. In 2008, several CIS States signed the Agreement on Promotion and Reciprocal Protection of Investments in the Member States of the Eurasian Economic Community.[180] In addition to similar guarantees provided by the Moscow Convention, it also contains investor-state dispute resolution provisions. In particular, Article 9 provides that investors can resort to arbitration institutions affiliated with national chambers of commerce, UNCITRAL arbitration, ICSID or ICSID additional facility arbitration. Belarus, Kazakhstan, Kyrgyzstan, Russia and Tajikistan are parties to this Agreement. Interestingly, Russia, which is not a party to ICSID Convention, agreed to use ICSID Additional Facility Rules to resolve disputes between investors and contracting states.

---

177. Decision of the Economic Court of the Commonwealth of Independent States dated 23 September 2014 № 01-1/1-14.
178. *Lee John Beck and Central Asian Development Corporation v. Kyrgyz Republic*, Award of 13 November 2013; *OKVV et al. v. Kyrgyz Republic*, Award of 23 November 2013; *Stans Energy Corp. and Kutisay Mining LLC v. - The Kyrgyz Republic*, PCA Case No. 2015-32.
179. According to Art. 11, 'disputes on implementation of investments in the framework of this convention should be considered by courts or arbitration courts of States of the parties to the disputes. The Economic Court of the Commonwealth of Independent States or international arbitration courts.'
180. Agreement on Promotion and Reciprocal Protection of Investments in the Member States of the Eurasian Economic Community dated 12 December 2008 http://investmentpolicyhub.unctad.org/IIA/country/18/treaty/3252 (accessed 27 February 2017).

[e]   Treaty on the EAEU 2014

1.110. In 2014, Russia, Belarus and Kazakhstan signed and ratified the Treaty on the EAEU.[181] Armenia has acceded to the Treaty,[182] and the relevant accession agreement was ratified by the Parliaments of Armenia and Russia.[183] In 2015, Kyrgyzstan also joined the treaty.[184] The Treaty, which entered in force in 2015 and replaced 2008 EAEU Convention, provides a full suite of investment protections, along with a binding investor-state arbitration mechanism.

1.111. The EAEU aims to create an environment for a stable development of the Member States' economies in order to raise the living standards of their population, as well as to increase the competitiveness of and cooperation between the national economies in the conditions of the global economy. The Treaty confirms the creation of an economic union that provides for free movement of goods, services, capital and labour and pursues coordinated, harmonised and single policy in the sectors determined by the document and international agreements within the Union.[185]

1.112. The Treaty also secured the Member States' agreement to pursue a coordinated energy policy and form common energy markets (electric energy, gas, oil and oil products) based on common principles; determines regulatory treatment of the turnover of pharmaceuticals and medical devices; establishes new long-term priorities of transport policy in the territory of the EAEU.[186] Another important novelty of the EAEU Treaty is a possibility to apply national treatment to the citizens of all the four countries in regards to social security, including health care.[187]

1.113. The Treaty contains a protocol similar to those found in many BITs:

6. Procedure for Settlement of Investment Disputes
84. All disputes between a recipient state and an investor of another Member State arising from or in connection with an investment of that investor on the territory of the recipient state, including disputes regarding the size, terms or order of payment of the amounts received as compensation of damages pursuant to paragraph 77 of this Protocol and the compensation provided for in paragraphs 79-81 of this Protocol, or the order of payment and transfer of funds provided for in paragraph 8 of this Protocol, shall be, where possible, resolved through negotiations.

---

181. Treaty on the Eurasian Economic Union 2014, http://www.un.org/en/ga/sixth/70/docs/treaty_on_eeu.pdf (accessed 20 March 2017).
182. Press release of the President of Armenia of 10 October 2014, www.president.am/ru/pressrelease/item014/10/10/Prezident-Serzh-Sargsyan-Minsk-Supreme-Eurasian-Economic-Council/#!officialPhotos (accessed 20 March 2017).
183. The Parliament of Armenia ratified the accession treaty with the EAEU on 4 December 2014, https://ria.ru/economy/20141010/1027795213.html (accessed 20 March 2017). The State Duma ratified Armenia's Accession treaty with the EAEU on 10 December 2014.
184. The President of Kyrgyzstan signed the Treaty on 21 May 2015, http://thediplomat.com/2015/05/kyrgyzstan-finally-joins-the-eurasian-economic-union/ (accessed 20 March 2017).
185. The Treaty on the Eurasian Economic Union is effective (1 January 2015), http://www.eurasiancommission.org/en/nae/news/Pages/01-01-2015-1.aspx (accessed 5 April 2017).
186. *Id.*
187. *Id.*

85. If a dispute may not be resolved through negotiations within 6 months from the date of a written notification of any of the parties to the dispute on negotiations, it may be referred to the following, at investor's option:
   1) a court of the recipient state duly competent to consider relevant disputes;
   2) international commercial arbitration court at the Chamber of Commerce of any state as may be agreed by the parties to the dispute;
   3) ad hoc arbitration court, which, unless the parties to the dispute agree otherwise, shall be established and act in accordance with the Rules of Arbitration of the United Nations Commission on International Trade Law (UNCITRAL);
   4) the International Centre for Settlement of Investment Disputes established pursuant to the Convention on the Settlement of Investment Disputes between States and Nationals of Other States of March 18, 1965, in order to resolve the dispute under the provisions of the Convention (provided that it has entered into force for both Member States that are parties to the dispute) or under the Additional Facility Rules of the International Centre for Settlement of Investment Disputes (if the Convention has not entered into force for one or both the Member States that are parties to the dispute).
86. An investor having referred a dispute for settlement to a national court or one of the arbitration courts specified in sub-paragraphs 1 and 2 of paragraph 85 of this Protocol shall not have the right to redirect the dispute to any other court or arbitration. The choice made by an investor with respect to a court or arbitration referred to in paragraph 85 of this Protocol shall be final.
87. Any arbitration decision on a dispute considered pursuant to paragraph 85 of this Protocol shall be final and binding on the parties to the dispute. Each Member State shall ensure enforcement of such decisions in accordance with its legislation.[188]

1.114. In other words, this treaty extends common dispute resolution provisions (including ICSID and UNCITRAL options) to investors coming from the Member States of the EAEU.

[2]   Model BITs

1.115. Generally speaking, model BITs represent an expression of a state's investment policy, and present the starting position of a state in his negotiations with a potential contracting party.[189] With the emergence of a market economy in the Soviet Union in the late 1980s, it started concluding BITs, and adopted a model BIT in 1987.[190] After the dissolution of the USSR, Russia remains the only Soviet Union successor that has a model BIT. The first model BIT was adopted in 1992.[191] The current Russian BIT model

---

188. Annex 16 to the Treaty on the Eurasian Economic Union of 29 May 2014, Protocol on Trade in Services, Incorporation, Activities and Investments http://www.un.org/en/ga/sixth/70/docs/treaty_on_eeu.pdf (accessed 5 April 2017).
189. Chester Brown, Commentaries on Selected Model Investment Treaties (Oxford University Press 2013), p. 2.
190. Approved by the Resolution of the Council of Ministers of the USSR of 27 November 1987 No. 1353.
191. Model BIT, approved by Resolution of the government of the Russian Federation of 11 June 1992 No. 395, as amended on 26 June 1995.

was approved by the government in 2001 and was later revised.[192] Though the new model BIT is more developed than the first one, it is still described as minimalist due to the inclusion of only the basic provisions and lack of details.[193] It consists of twelve articles, which significantly differs from the sophisticated and detailed model BITs of the United States (thirty-seven articles)[194] and Canada (fifty-two articles).[195]

1.116. Unlike the 1992 BIT, the revised model initially did not even contain provisions on fair and equitable treatment, national treatment, or most favoured nation. These provisions were included again after revision of the Model BIT in 2002.[196] However, these standards are relatively weak: fair and national treatment, most favoured nation are limited to 'management' and 'disposal' of investments.[197] The 1992 and 2001 model BITs, like the majority of Russian BITs, do not include umbrella clauses, and the 2016 Guidelines on the negotiation of BITs[198] do not envisage the inclusion of such clauses in future Russian BITs.

1.117. Also, the revised model BIT lacks several protections found in other countries' BITs, such as rules on entry and sojourn of foreign nationals, prohibition to impose restrictions on the nationality of top managerial personnel, and obligations on transparency.[199] Both model BITs impose six-month cooling-off periods, and the 2016 Guidelines similarly recommend the inclusion of such a period in Russia's BITs. Both the 1992 and the 2001 model BITs, as well as the 2016 Guidelines on the negotiation of BITs, provide that investments may only be nationalised when such a measure is accompanied by prompt, adequate and effective compensation.

1.118. As for dispute resolution, while the 1992 BIT provided for the resolution of investor-state disputes in the SCC, the new model BIT has replaced this provision stipulating that investment disputes may be referred to a state court or an arbitration tribunal of the contracting party hosting the investment; ad hoc arbitration under the UNCITRAL Rules; or arbitration under the ICSID Convention or ICSID Additional

---

192. Model BIT, approved by Resolution of the government of the Russian Federation of 9 June 2001 No. 465, as amended on 11 April 2002 and 17 December 2010.
193. Sergey Ripinsky, Chapter 14. Russia, in Chester Brown (ed.), Commentaries on Selected Model Investment Treaties (Oxford 20013), p. 597.
194. 2012 U.S. Model Bilateral Investment Treaty, U.S. Department of State, https://www.state.gov/documents/organization/188371.pdf (accessed 13 March 2017).
195. 2004 Canada Model Bilateral Investment Treaty, http://www.italaw.com/documents/Canadian2004-FIPA-model-en.pdf (accessed 13 March 2017).
196. 2001 Russia Model BIT, *supra* 16, Art. 3.
197. Sergey Ripinsky, *supra* 17, p. 620.
198. Guidelines on the negotiation of BITs, adopted by the government of the Russian Federation on 30 September 2016. These Guidelines supersede the 1992 and 2001 model BITs and lay out recommendations as to the contents of future BITs.
199. Even though the current model BIT is missing these relevant provisions, some BITs concluded by Russia do include them. For example, 'umbrella clauses' can be found in the Russia-China BIT (2009), Russia-Denmark BIT (1996); obligations regarding entry and sojourn of foreign nationals in connection with an investment can be found in Russia-China BIT (2006), Russia-Kazakhstan BIT (1998); prohibition of certain performance requirements can be found in Russia-Japan BIT (1998); obligation on transparency of domestic legislation can be found in Russia-Kazakhstan BIT (1998).

Facility Rules.[200] Though unlike the 1992 Russian model BIT, the current version provides that an arbitral award shall be final and binding upon both parties to the dispute. The enforcement of arbitral awards against Russia, however, can be problematic.[201]

[C] CIS States Practice in Investment Treaty Arbitration

[1] General Overview

1.119. Depending on the treaty in question, claims against the CIS states may be filed with ICSID, ad hoc arbitration under the UNCITRAL Rules, or ICSID Additional Facility Rules[202] (for those countries that failed to ratify the ICSID Convention), and the SCC either under the SCC Arbitration Rules or UNCITRAL Rules. Russia and Ukraine remain top respondent states and claimants' home states among all CIS countries in investment arbitrations. According to the UNCTAD statistics,[203] the CIS countries were involved as respondents in the following number of cases.

---

200. 2001 Russia Model BIT, *supra* 16, Art. 8(2).
201. 2001 Russia Model BIT, *supra* 16, Art. 8(3); *See also* Noah Rubins & Azizjon Nazarov, *Investment Treaties and the Russian Federation: Baiting the Bear*, 9(2) Bus. L. Int'l 100, 112 (2008).
202. ICSID Additional Facility Rules (2006), https://icsid.worldbank.org/en/Documents/resources/AFR_2006%20English-final.pdf (accessed 6 March 2017).
203. *See* UNCTAD statistical information on Investment Dispute Settlement, http://investmentpolicyhub.unctad.org/ISDS/FilterByCountry (accessed 7 March 2017).

Figure 1.4   Total Number of Investment Disputes Involving CIS Countries as Respondents in Various Tribunals

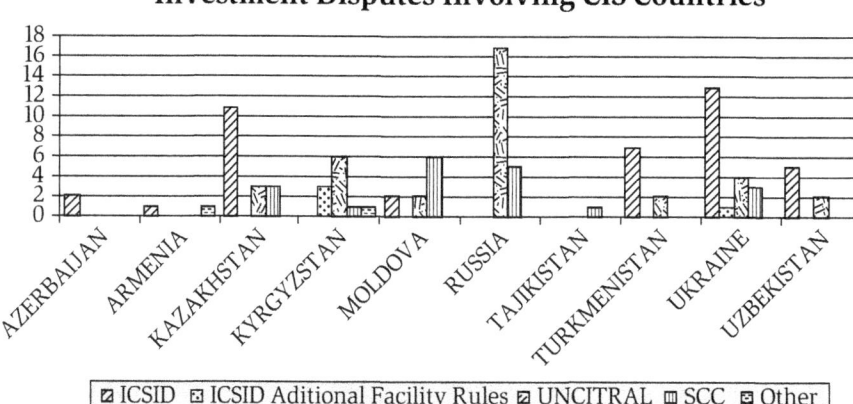

Source: UNCTAD (2017).

1.120. The ICSID annual reports demonstrate that in 2014, under the ICSID Convention and Additional Facility Rules, Eastern Europe and Central Asia accounted for 25% of newly ICSID registered cases, in 2015 it was up to 33%, and 22% in 2016.[204] Claims against CIS countries to ICSID have been brought most frequently by investors from the United States, the Netherlands, Turkey and CIS.[205] The oil, gas and mining industry represent the industries where the investment disputes against the CIS states most frequently arise, followed by the construction and communication industries.[206] Most of the claimants invoke breaches of fair and equitable treatment and (indirect) expropriation claims under various BITs.[207]

[2]   Notable Cases

1.121. In most of the cases Russia was the respondent in the proceedings held in institutional arbitration, namely under the Rules of SCC. One of the earliest SCC cases, *Compagnie Noga D'importation et D'exportation S.a. v. Russia* (1993), concerned the termination of a food-for-oil contract between a Swiss company and the Russian

---

204. ICSID Annual Reports, available at https://icsid.worldbank.org/en/Pages/resources/ICSID-Annual-Report.aspx (accessed 3 March 2017).
205. Bryan Cave LLP Independent study, *supra* 118.
206. *Ibid.*
207. *See also* Dmitry Davydenko & Saba Seculovic, Russia losing battles but winning wars with foreign investors: cases overview, CIS Arbitration Forum, 22 June 2016, http://www.cisarbitration.com/2016/06/22/russia-losing-battles-but-winning-wars-with-foreign-investors-cases-overview/ (accessed 10 March 2017); for a discussion of early cases against Russia, Ukraine, Moldova and the Kyrgyz Republic, please *see* Kaj Hober, Investment Arbitration in Eastern Europe: In Search of a Definition of Expropriation (Juris Publications 2007).

Government. The contract provided for binding arbitration of any disputes at the Chamber of Commerce of Stockholm, Sweden, under Swiss law. This dispute also gave rise to a landmark case on the enforcement of arbitral awards and state immunity, with the Paris Court of Appeal stating that a 'general waiver of immunity from enforcement doesn't amount to a waiver from diplomatic immunity'.[208]

1.122. Another notable SCC case against Russia was initiated in 1998 by Mr Sedelmayer under the Germany-Russia BIT, claiming expropriation of the investor's property as a result of certain directives ordering transfer of the claimant's assets in a JSC to a state agency.[209] In 1998, Mr Sedelmayer obtained a favourable award ordering Russia to pay damages in the amount of USD 2.35 million plus interest.[210] Despite obtaining a favourable award, it took more than twelve years to enforce it in the different jurisdictions.

1.123. When it comes to investment arbitrations, the *Yukos* case attracts the most attention. In this case the ECT-based claims arising out of indirect expropriation were brought by former Yukos shareholders against Russia under the UNCITRAL Rules. In 2014, the tribunal found that the measures undertaken by Russia amounted to indirect expropriation and issued an arbitral award requiring Russia to pay over USD 50 billion in compensation.[211] In 2016, the Hague District Court annulled all three awards, reasoning the tribunal did not have jurisdiction, since Russia never ratified the ECT, and that Russia had no duty to provisionally apply the ECT dispute resolution provisions as it is contrary to Russian domestic law.[212] The decision on the appeal against the judgment setting aside the awards is still pending at the Court of Appeal in the Hague.

1.124. One of the issues facing foreign investors filing claims against Russia is the extension of arbitration through most favoured nation (MFN) clauses. The majority of modern BITs include provisions that guarantee qualified investors MFN status. In *Berschader v. Russian Federation*, two Belgian investors signed a contract for the construction of a new Supreme Court in Moscow.[213] When the company had almost completed its obligations under the contract, Russia annulled the contract with

---

208. *Gouvernement de la Fédération de Russie v. Compagnie Noga d'importation et d'exportation*, Cour d'appel de Paris, Case No. 615/2000, judgment of 27 July 2000.
209. *Mr. Franz Sedelmayer v. Russian Federation*, Case No. T 6-583-98SCC award of 7 July 1998, http://arbitration.org/sites/default/files/awards/arb156.pdf (accessed 10 March 2017).
210. *Ibid. See also* Kaj Hober, Investment Arbitration in Eastern Europe: In Search of a Definition of Expropriation (Juris Publications 2007) pp. 45–58 and Appendix 1 which contains the award.
211. *Yukos Universal Limited (Isle of Man) v. The Russian Federation*, UNCITRAL, PCA Case No. AA 227; *Hulley Enterprises Limited (Cyprus) v. The Russian Federation*, UNCITRAL, PCA Case No. AA 226; *Veteran Petroleum Limited (Cyprus) v. The Russian Federation*, UNCITRAL, PCA Case No. AA 228.
212. Judgment of the Hague District Court of 20 April 2016 in the joined Cases No. C/09/477160 / HA ZA 15-1; C/09/477162 / HA ZA 15-2, C/09/481619 / HA ZA 15-112, http://www.italaw.com/sites/default/files/case-documents/italaw7258.pdf (accessed 13 March 2017).
213. *Berschader v. Russian Federation*, SCC case No. V, award of 21 April 2006, available at http://www.italaw.com/sites/default/files/case-documents/ita0079_0.pdf (accessed 27 March 2017).

millions remaining unpaid.[214] In 2004, the Berschader filed in its claim against Russia before the SCC under the 1989 Belgium-USSR BIT, arguing that the expansive dispute resolution clause of the Norway-Russian BIT should apply by operation of the MFN clause.[215] However, the tribunal rejected the jurisdictional objection stating that the terms of the Belgian treaty were inadequately clear to permit the use of the Norwegian arbitration clause.[216]

1.125. In *RosInvestCo v. Russian Federation* the tribunal constituted under the rules of the Arbitration Institute of the SCC also dealt with the issue of extending procedural clauses through MFN clauses. It agreed to extend application of procedural provisions of the Denmark-Russia BIT on the basis of the MFN clause in UK-Soviet BIT noting in relation to procedural clauses such as arbitration clauses that it

> [was] a normal result of the application of MFN clauses, the very character and intention of which is that protection not accepted in one treaty is widened by transferring the protection accorded in another treaty.[217]

1.126. Recently, in light of events in Crimea, multiple investment arbitration claims have been brought against Russia for the recovery of alleged losses occurring as result of shutting down or nationalising Ukrainian businesses without any compensation.[218] Despite Russia's position that an international arbitral tribunal does not have jurisdiction, the tribunals in two of the cases nonetheless already issued interim awards holding that it has jurisdiction to hear claims of Ukrainian investors.[219]

1.127. In a number of cases involving CIS States, parties have agreed to settle before the arbitral tribunal rendered the award.[220] For instance, the proceedings were

---

214. *Id.*
215. *Id.*
216. *Id.*
217. *RosInvest v. Russian Federation*, Award on Jurisdiction dated 5 October 2007, http://www.italaw.com/sites/default/files/case-documents/ita0719.pdf, paras 131–133. (accessed 6 April 2017).
218. *Stabil LLC and others v. The Russian Federation*, PCA Case No. 2015-35; *LLC Lugzor and others v. Russian Federation*, PCA case No. 2015-29; *Privatbank and Finance Company Finilon LLC v. Russian Federation*, PCA Case No. AAA568; *Everest Estate LLC and others v. The Russian Federation*, PCA Case No. AA577; *Aeroport Belbek LLC and Mr Kolomoisky v. The Russian Federation*, PCA Case No. 2015-07; *PJSC Ukrnafta v. The Russian Federation*, PCA Case No. 2015-34; *JSC Oschadbank v. The Russian Federation*; *see also* Yuriy Sidorenko, 14 Iskov protiv Rossii: Perspektivy, Paradoksy i Riski, https://legal.report/author/ataka-na-rossiyu-v-investicionnom-arbitrazhe.-otkroetsya-li-tureckij-front (accessed 6 March 2017).
219. *See* PCA Press Release of 9 March 2017, Arbitration Between Pjsc Privatbank And Finance Company Finilon LLC As Claimants And The Russian Federation, https://pcacases.com/web/sendAttach/2093 (accessed 10 March 2017); PCA Press Release of 9 March 2017, Arbitration Between Aeroport Belbek LLC and Mr. Igor Valerievich Kolomoisky as claimants and the Russian Federation, https://pcacases.com/web/sendAttach/2090 (accessed 10 March 2017).
220. *See*, generally, Yaraslau Kryvoi & Dmitry Davydenko, *Consent Awards in International Arbitration: From Settlement to Enforcement* (7 November 2015) 40 Brooklyn J. of Int'l L. (2015) pp. 827–868, Available at SSRN: https://ssrn.com/abstract=2580572 (accessed 10 March 2017).

concluded with a settlement in *Fondel B.V. v. Republic of Azerbaijan*,[221] *Barmek Holding A.S. v. Republic of Azerbaijan* under Turkey-Azerbaijan BIT,[222] and in the case related to mining industry *Global Gold Mining LLC v. Republic of Armenia* under the US-Armenia BIT.[223]

[D] Enforcement of International Investment Arbitral Awards

1.128. After receiving the award, parties may either comply voluntarily, enforce it in national courts, sell the award, or challenge it (non-ICSID awards) or apply for annulment (ICSID awards). When arbitral tribunals render awards against states in many cases CIS states such as Kazakhstan, Tajikistan comply voluntarily with international investment arbitral awards.[224] However, in some cases countries resist the enforcement of the awards either by challenging them, or by raising various defences during the enforcement proceedings.[225]

1.129. The regime of challenging and enforcing ICSID and non-ICSID awards is different. While the issues of annulment and enforcement of ICSID awards are regulated by the ICSID Convention, the regime for setting aside, recognising and enforcing non-ICSID awards is the same as that for awards issued by international commercial arbitration tribunals under the New York Convention.

1.130. When enforcing international investment awards in CIS countries, parties may face several obstacles. The following part discusses the reasons and common defences that several CIS countries use to resist the enforcement of international investment arbitral awards.

---

221. Information on the outcome of the case *Fondel Metal Participations B.V. v. Republic of Azerbaijan*, ICSID Case No. ARB/07/1, is available at http://www.italaw.com/cases/3632 (accessed 10 March 2017).
222. Information on the outcome of the case *Barmek Holding A.S. v. Republic of Azerbaijan*, ICSID Case No. ARB/06/16, is available at http://www.italaw.com/cases/3453 (accessed 10 March 2017).
223. Information on the outcome of the case *Global Gold Mining LLC v. Republic of Armenia*, ICSID Case No. ARB/07/7, is available at http://www.italaw.com/cases/3641 (accessed 10 March 2017).
224. Information on voluntary compliance with awards in cases *Joseph C Lemire v. Ukraine*, ICSID Case No. ARB/06/18; *Biedermann International, Inc. v. The Republic of Kazakhstan and The Association for Social and Economic Development of Western Kazakhstan 'Intercaspian'*, SCC Case No. 97/1996; *Mohammad Ammar Al-Bahloul v. The Republic of Tajikistan*, SCC Case No. V (064/2008) available at Global Arbitration Review, Investment Arbitration Review 2016, Country Reports, http://globalarbitrationreview.com/know-how/topics/2000010/investment-treaty-arbitration-2016 (accessed 10 March 2017).
225. *See*, e.g., Luke Peterson, Kazakhstan fails in bid to set aside half billion dollar Energy Charter Treaty award, Investment Arbitration Reporter, 9 December 2016, http://www.iareporter.com/articles/kazakhstan-fails-in-bid-to-set-aside-half-billion-dollar-energy-charter-treaty-award (accessed 2 April 2017); Luke Peterson, How many states are not paying awards under investment treaties? Investment Arbitration Reporter, 7 May 2019, http://www.iareporter.com/articles/how-many-states-are-not-paying-awards-under-investment-treaties (accessed 2 April 2017).

[1] Peculiarities of Enforcing International Investment Arbitral Awards in the CIS Region

1.131. Non-enforcement of awards by states may have a negative impact on the investment climate in the CIS region, and may result in a decrease in foreign investments. Nevertheless, a few states for various reasons resist the enforcement using annulment proceedings under the ICSID Convention, or judicial review before national courts.[226] The main reason for resisting the enforcement of an arbitral award by the state is usually the amount of the compensation which, along with other costs (arbitrators', arbitral institutions', experts', counsels' fees), constitute significant amounts of money.[227] Russia is one of the CIS states which has so far not honoured the awards which have been rendered against it.[228]

1.132. In the previously mentioned case of *Mr. Sedelmeyer v. Russia*, Russia failed to pay voluntarily the damages in the amount of USD 2,350,000 issued by the SCC Tribunal. Mr Sedelmayer sought enforcement of the award against Russia's various assets abroad, in Sweden and Germany. While German courts ruled that certain assets of the Russian Federation were immune, Mr Sedelmeyer succeeded in Germany and also in the Swedish courts which declared that a building owned by the Russian trade mission was not immune.[229] Russia refused to recognise the judgment of the Swedish court, arguing that the Swedish court violated the Vienna Convention on Diplomatic Relations because the property was immune and that Swedish authorities failed to explain to the court the extent of Sweden's international obligations.[230] The Sedelmayer enforcement saga lasted over twelve years and demonstrated how difficult the enforcement process can be.[231]

1.133. In some cases, the state refusing the enforcement of arbitral awards fails to provide any legal reasoning, in other cases, states implement changes to national legislation to justify the non-enforcement of the award.[232] For example, in the three parallel *Yukos* arbitrations against Russia the Tribunal rendered the largest ever awards in the history of international arbitration.[233] To avoid complying with these awards,

---

226. Alan S. Alexandroff & Ian A. Laird, Compliance and Enforcement, in The Oxford Handbook of International Investment Law, edited by Peter Muchlinski, Federico Ortino & Christoph Schreuer pp. 1174–1175.
227. Aleksandra Anufrieva, Ispolnenie Reshenij Mezhdunarodnykh Investicionnykh Arbitrazhej: Rabotaet li Sistema?, Zakonodatelstvo, No. 3, p. 73–80 (March 2016).
228. Elliot Glusker, *Arbitration Hurdles Facing Foreign Investors in Russia: Analysis of Present Issues and Implications*, 10(3) Repperdine Disp. Res. J. (2010) 595, 607.
229. *Sedelmayer v. Russian Federation*, Decision of the Supreme Court of Sweden, 1 July 2011; *Sedelmayer v. Russian Federation*, Decision of the Supreme Court of Germany, 4 October 2005; All the judgment on the case are available at http://arbitration.org/award/37 (accessed 10 March 2017).
230. Yaraslau Kryvoi, Chasing the Russian Federation, CIS Arbitration Forum, CIS Arbitration Forum, 13 July 2011 http://www.cisarbitration.com/2011/07/13/chasing-the-russian-federation/ (accessed 10 March 2017).
231. *Ibid.*
232. Anufrieva A.A., *supra* 58.
233. *Yukos Universal Ltd v. Russian Federation*, PCA Case No. AA 227, UNCITRAL ad hoc arbitration, Final Award, 18 July 2014; *Veteran Petroleum Ltd v. Russian Federation*, PCA Case

Russia challenged the three arbitral awards in the Dutch courts since the Hague was the seat of those arbitrations, and subsequently a Dutch court set them aside, holding that the Tribunal could not have established jurisdiction based on the provisional application of the ECT.[234]

1.134. In addition to the dispute under the ECT former Yukos shareholders also filed claims under the European Convention of Human Rights (ECHR) claiming the violation of their rights under several articles of Convention, including Article 6 (right to a fair trial), Article 1 of Protocol No. 1 (protection of property), Articles 1 (obligation to respect human rights), 7 (no punishment without law), 13 (right to an effective remedy), 14 (prohibition of discrimination), and 18 (limitation on use of restrictions on rights). The ECHR issued a decision partly in favour of the claimant.[235] In this case the Constitutional Court of Russia found that the decision of the ECHR violated the Russian Constitution, and Russia may not enforce decisions under European Convention on Human Rights if they contradict the country's Constitution.[236]

1.135. The case of *JKX Oil plc v. Ukraine* represents the Ukrainian 'saga' on the enforcement of emergency arbitrator's award.[237] The Kiev Court of Appeal, after numerous circulations of the case on several instances, refused to enforce and recognise the SCC emergency arbitration award rendered against Ukraine, stating that the enforcement of the emergency award would violate the public order of the Ukraine, since it would reduce the applicable tax rate for the claimant which could be implemented only under the Tax Code of Ukraine. The Supreme Court of Ukraine overruled the decision not finding any violation of the Ukrainian public order[238]

1.136. As these examples illustrate, even after obtaining a favourable award, investors risk facing several challenges at the enforcement stage in some CIS countries.

[2]   Issues of State Immunity

1.137. Although States must recognise and enforce the award either under the ICSID Convention or the New York Convention, each State's laws relating to sovereign immunity from execution continue to apply. The doctrine of state immunity means that

---

No. AA 228, UNCITRAL ad hoc arbitration, Final Award, 18 July 2014; *Hulley Enterprises Ltd v. Russian Federation*, PCA Case No. AA 226, UNCITRAL ad hoc arbitration, Final Award, 18 July 2014.

234. Judgment of the Hague District Court of 20 April 2016 in the joined Cases No. C/09/477160 / HA ZA 15-1, C/09/477162 / HA ZA 15-2, C/09/481619 / HA ZA 15-112.
235. Judgment of the European Court of Human Rights of 31 July 2014, Case of OAO Neftyanaya Kompaniya Yukos v. Russia, http://www.italaw.com/sites/default/files/case-documents/italaw7752.pdf (accessed 21 March 2017).
236. Judgment of the Constitutional Court of Russia of 19 January 2017, http://doc.ksrf.ru/decision/KSRFDecision258613.pdf (accessed 21 March 2017).
237. *See* the progress of the case at http://www.italaw.com/cases/3153 (accessed 21 March 2017).
238. Judgment of the Supreme Court of Ukraine of 24 February 2016, available at http://www.italaw.com/sites/default/files/case-documents/italaw7392.pdf (accessed 5 April 2017).

a state is generally immune from lawsuits in another state's courts[239] or arbitration tribunals. International law has developed two approaches to the state immunity doctrine: absolute immunity, which means that the sovereign state is completely immune from foreign jurisdiction in all cases; and restrictive immunity, which provides immunity to foreign states for their 'public' acts, but not for their 'private' acts, including commercial activities.[240]

1.138. Despite the adoption of general international law approaches to immunity,[241] approaches to the doctrine of state immunity vary from state to state: depending on the will of the state to comply with the awards, the state may adopt a particular strategy of protection of its property.[242] The Soviet Union traditionally adhered to the theory of absolute immunity, which is explained by the then existing system of foreign trade, i.e., the monopoly of foreign trade; and unity between economic and political power of the State.[243] Despite the development of the theory of restrictive immunity in the 1970s and its adoption by several developed countries, the Soviet Union remained loyal to the theory of absolute immunity.[244] Since all CIS states are former Soviet Union republics, they all closely follow the development of Russian law in many aspects.[245]

1.139. Following the dissolution of the Soviet Union, the CIS countries had initially adopted the principle of absolute immunity in national legislation. CIS countries such as Armenia, Belarus, Ukraine still follow the doctrine of absolute immunity, allowing the execution of foreign judgments and arbitral awards against a state only with the consent of that state.[246] In 1999, Kazakhstan made the first step towards recognition of the restrictive immunity doctrine by incorporating this theory into its new Civil Procedure Code.[247]

---

239. United Nations Convention on Jurisdictional Immunities of States and Their Property Art. 5, G.A. Res. 59/38, U.N. Doc. A/RES/59/38, at 3 (16 December 2004) ('A State enjoys immunity, in respect of itself and its property, from the jurisdiction of the courts of another State subject to the provisions of the present Convention.'). 'State immunity' is sometimes called 'sovereign immunity.' See, e.g., Sean D. Murphy, Principles of International Law 302 (2d ed. 2012).
240. Malkolm N. Shaw, International Law (Cambridge University Press 2008) 6th ed. pp. 701–704.
241. See, e.g., 1972 European Convention on State Immunity, http://www.wipo.int/edocs/trtdocs/en/ce-csi1/trt_ce_csi1.pdf (accessed 6 March 2017); 2004 United Nations Convention on Jurisdictional Immunities of States and Their Property, http://legal.un.org/ilc/texts/instruments/english/conventions/4_1_2004.pdf (accessed 6 March 2017).
242. Anastasia Bessonova, Doktrina gosudarstvennogo immuniteta kak sposob zaschity gosudarstvennogo imushchestva ot ispolneniya po reshenniyam mezhdunarodnykh investitsionnykh arbitrazhej, Arbitrazhnyj I grazhdanskyj process, № 12, 12–17 (2015).
243. Ibid.
244. Maydan Sulejmanov., Razvitiye zakonodatelsva Respubliki Kazakhstan o Mezhdunarodnom Kommercheskom Arbitrazhe, Doklad na 11-om Mnogostoronnem arbitrazhnom kongresse, http://zangerlf.com/ru/publications/156 (accessed 7 March 2017).
245. Kaj Hober, Selected Writings of Investment Treaty Arbitration, (Studentlitteratur 2013) p. 520.
246. See, e.g., Art. 239 of the Economic Procedural Code of the Republic of Belarus, Art. 553 of the Civil Procedure Code of the Republic of Belarus; Art. 245 of the Civil Procedure Code of the Republic of Armenia of 17 June 1998.
247. According to the Art. 427 of the Civil Procedure Code of the Republic of Kazakhstan, '[a] foreign state enjoys jurisdictional immunity in Kazakhstan, including immunity from legal process, immunity from claim and immunity from enforcement of a judicial act, except for the cases, provided for in this Code'.

1.140. Until 2016, Russian procedural laws contained contradictory provisions on the immunity issues: while the Civil Procedure Code followed the doctrine of absolute immunity, the Commercial Procedure Code contained provisions on restrictive immunity of a state.[248] This uncertainty was overcome with the adoption in 2015 of the Law on Jurisdictional Immunities of Foreign States which finally endorsed a restrictive theory of sovereign immunity and introduced the principle of reciprocity in issues regarding the application of jurisdictional immunities.[249] Basically, the law resembles the provisions of the UN Convention on Jurisdictional Immunities of States and Their Property recognising the doctrine of restrictive immunity.

1.141. The general rule under the law is that foreign states have immunity from lawsuits in Russian courts, including immunity from interim measures and the execution of judgments. According to this law, foreign states cannot invoke immunity in disputes arising out of civil transactions or involvement in commercial or other economic activity, claims to property, for compensation of harm or labour disputes (with the foreign state acting as an employer). The law distinguishes between consent of a foreign state to adjudication and waiver from immunity from enforcement. A state can consent in an international treaty, a written agreement or a notification to court. In addition, immunity is waived when the state has itself instituted the proceeding, intervened in the proceeding, taken any other step relating to the merits or concluded an arbitration agreement. It is important to note that this law established the principle of reciprocity, meaning that immunity can be restricted in relation to States, which restrict immunity of the Russian Federation and its property on its territory.

1.142. Legislators in other CIS jurisdictions may use this law as a model in the future.

§1.04 CONCLUDING REMARKS

1.143. The CIS states and businesses from the region have made significant progress in many areas since the collapse of the Soviet Union.[250] However, as this chapter shows, arbitration users still face various challenges while arbitrating against CIS states and CIS-related parties, as well as in CIS jurisdictions. Investors and lawyers advising them need to understand the law and practice of arbitration in the CIS countries to minimise their risks and to do so before agreeing to arbitrate disputes.

---

248. According to previous version of Art. 401 of Civil Procedure Code of Russian Federation, immunity of the state may be restricted only with the consent of the state. Under Art. 251 of Commercial Procedure Code of Russian Federation, foreign state has judicial immunity and interim relief immunity only if the foreign state is acting with the capacity of the carrier of power.
249. Federal Law of 3 November 2015 No. 297-FZ 'On Jurisdictional Immunity of Foreign State and Foreign Property in Russian Federation'; See also, Anastasia Rogozina, New Rules on Jurisdictional Immunities of States in Russian Courts, CIS Arbitration Forum, 13 November 2013 http://www.cisarbitration.com/2015/11/13/new-rules-on-jurisdictional-immunities-of-states-in-russian-courts/ (accessed 8 March 2017).
250. Elliot Glusker, *Arbitration Hurdles Foreign Investors in Russia: Analysis of Present Issues and Implications*, 10 Pepp. Disp. Resol. L. J. 595, 620 (2010).

1.144. The legal framework of many CIS states has significantly improved in recent years as a result of reform of several CIS states' legislation on arbitration. Apart from certain controversial proposals regarding the increased regulation of arbitration, the new legislation can be seen as a significant step forward in the development of a more arbitration-friendly climate in the region.

APPENDIX I RATIFICATION OF SELECTED ARBITRATION RELATED CONVENTIONS BY CIS STATES

Country	New York Convention*	Washington Convention**	Minsk Convention***	Energy Charter Treaty****	Eurasian Economic Union	Kishinev Convention
Armenia	29 December 1997	16 September 1992	22 November 1994	18 December 1997	4 December 2014	21 January 2005
Azerbaijan	29 February 2000	18 September 1992	1996	2 December 1997	-	-
Belarus	15 November 1960	10 July 1992	10 June 1993	not ratified	9 October 2014	1 August 2003
Russia	24 August 1960	not ratified	11 November 1994	not ratified	26 September 2014	-
Ukraine	10 October 1960	7 June 2000	16 March 1995	6 February 1998	-	-
Kazakhstan	20 November 1995	21 September 2000	20 April 1994	18 October 1995	1 October 2014	29 March 2004
Kyrgyzstan	18 December 1996	Signed, not ratified	19 January 1996	08 April 1997	20 May 2015	2 September 2004
Moldova	18 September 1998	5 May 2011	26 February 1996	10 June 1996	-	-
Tajikistan	14 August 2012	Tajikistan "not ratified" the Washington Convention	21 November 1994	17 June 1997	-	18 April 2005
Turkmenistan	Turkmenistan "not ratified" the New York Convention	26 September 1992	21 January 1998	10 July 1997	-	-

Country	New York Convention*	Washington Convention**	Minsk Convention***	Energy Charter Treaty****	Eurasian Economic Union	Kishinev Convention
Uzbekistan	7 February 1996	26 July 1995	21 February 1994	22 December 1995	-	-

* Convention on the Recognition and Enforcement of Foreign Arbitral Awards, 1958, http://www.uncitral.org/uncitral/en/uncitral_texts/arbitration/NYConvention_status.html (accessed 27 February 2017).

** Convention on the Settlement of Investment Disputes between States and Nationals of Other States, 1966, https://icsid.worldbank.org/en/Documents/icsiddocs/ICSID%20Convention%20English.pdf (accessed 27 February 2017).

*** The Convention on Legal Assistance and Legal Relations in Civil, Family and Criminal Matters, 1993, http://www.cis.minsk.by/page.php?id =614 (accessed 15 March 2017).

**** The 1994 Energy Charter Treaty, The treaty and related documents are available at http://www.energycharter.org/process/energy-charter-treaty-1994/energy-charter-treaty/ (accessed 20 March 2017).

***** Treaty on the Eurasian Economic Union 2014, http://www.un.org/en/ga/sixth/70/docs/treaty_on_eeu.pdf (accessed 20 March 2017).

****** The Convention on Legal Assistance and Legal Relations in Civil, Family and Criminal Matters, 2002, https://online.zakon.kz/Document/?doc_id = 1034672 (assessed 4 July 2017).

APPENDIX II THE MOST IMPORTANT DOMESTIC ENACTMENTS ON INTERNATIONAL ARBITRATION IN THE REGION

Country	Law
Armenia	The Law of the Republic of Armenia 'On Commercial Arbitration', of January 22, 2007 No. ZR-55
Azerbaijan	The Law of the Republic of Azerbaijan 'On International Commercial Arbitration', of 18 November 1999
Belarus	The Law of the Republic of Belarus 'On International Arbitration Court', of 29 May 2009 No. 698
Russia	Federal Law of the Russian Federation 'On Arbitration in the Russian Federation' of December 29, 2015 No. 382-FZ
Ukraine	The Law of the Republic of Ukraine 'On International Commercial Arbitration' of February 24, 1994 No. 4002-XII
Kazakhstan	The Law of the Republic of Kazakhstan 'On Arbitration', of April 8, 2016 No. 488-V ZRK
Kyrgyzstan	The law 'On arbitration courts in the Kyrgyz Republic', of 30 July 2002
Moldova	The Law of the Republic Of Moldova 'On International Commercial Arbitration', of February 22, 2008 No. 24-XVI
Tajikistan	The Law of the Republic of Tajikistan 'On international commercial arbitration', of March 18, 2015 No. 1183
Turkmenistan	The Law of Turkmenistan 'On International Commercial Arbitration', of August 16, 2014 No. 101-V
Uzbekistan	The Law of the Republic of Uzbekistan 'On Arbitration Courts', of 16 October 2006, No. 3PY-64

CHAPTER 2
Armenia

Sargis Grigoryan

LIST OF ABBREVIATIONS

ACBAA	Arbitration Court of the Banks Association of Armenia
ACCCIA	Arbitration Court of the Chamber of Commerce and Industry of Armenia
Advocacy Act	Advocacy Act of Armenia No. 29 dated 13 January 2005
Armenian Arbitration Act	Commercial Arbitration Act of Armenia No. 55 dated 22 January 2007
CIS	Commonwealth of Independent States
Civil Code	Civil Code of Armenia No. 239 dated 28 July 1998
Code of Civil Procedure	Code of Civil Procedure of Armenia No. 247 dated 7 August 1998
Constitution of Armenia	Constitution of Armenia (amended) dated on 6 December 2015
EBRD	European Bank for Reconstruction and Development
EAEU	Eurasian Economic Union
Geneva Convention	European Convention on International Commercial Arbitration, 1961, Geneva
ICSID	Convention on the Settlement of Investment Disputes between States and Nationals of other Sates, 1965, Washington
Judicial Code	Judicial Code of Armenia No. 135 dated 7 April 2007

Enforcement Act	Law on Compulsory Enforcement of Judicial Acts No. 221 dated 5 May 1998
New York Convention	United Nations Convention on the Recognition and Enforcement of Foreign Arbitral Awards, 1958, New York
SJC	Supreme Judicial Council of Armenia
UNCITRAL	United Nations Commission on International Trade Law
UNCITRAL Model Law	UNCITRAL Model Law on International Commercial Arbitration 1985
WTO	World Trade Organization

§2.01 GENERAL INTRODUCTION

[A] Historical Development of the Legal System

1.1. Armenia declared its independence from the Soviet Union on 21 September 1991, which led to the formation of a national judicial system in what is regarded as the first phase of judicial reform. Armenia adopted its Constitution in 1995 which was revised in 2005 and 2015. The Constitution declares a division of power among the executive, legislative and judicial branches, providing also for an independent judiciary and personal freedoms.

1.2. On 6 December 2015, a referendum was held for constitutional amendments – under the Constitution, the National Assembly is elected by proportional electoral contest. It also introduces the concept of 'constitutional laws' as a special segment of legislation e.g., judicial code, electoral code, etc ... Constitutional laws will have to be adopted by a favourable vote of three-fifths of all Members of Parliament.

1.3. In October 2014 Armenia's President signed the accession treaty to the Eurasian Economic Union (EAEU) with the presidents of Belarus, Kazakhstan and Russia at the Commonwealth of Independent States (CIS) summit in Minsk, Belarus. The treaty came into force in January 2015 and is undoubtedly the most comprehensive form of economic integration of the post-Soviet countries since the break-up of the Soviet Union. With the EAEU membership, there is a strong likelihood that Armenia will adopt more protectionist trade and investment policies pursued by other EAEU Member States.

1.4. However, over the last decade, the Government of Armenia have made considerable efforts to upgrade the commercial, tax and financial legislation in order to improve the business and investment environment. Nevertheless, significant gaps in the legal and regulatory framework remain. In addition, as is often the case in early transition countries, implementation of the law by courts and officials remains an issue.[1]

---

1. *See Armenia Country Report on Human Rights Practices*, the US Department of State, 2015.

1.5. Experience in transition countries suggests that advances in law reform and economic development progress or regress hand in hand. Given the positive correlations throughout the countries' operations between legal transition, on the one hand, and overall economic progress, on the other hand, it is reasonable to expect that the future success of the transition process in Armenia will depend in part on the country's ability to strengthen the rule of law and improve the quality of courts.[2]

[B] The Legal Profession

1.6. The Advocacy Act of 2004 by which a professional association of advocates was established, known as the Chamber of Advocates, requires bar admission as a prerequisite for practicing the law in Armenia including the representation in civil and criminal proceedings.

1.7. Article 17 of the Advocacy Act requires that a foreign advocate is entitled to practice in Armenia on the basis of his or her home country license but must register with the Chamber of Advocates. A foreign advocate cannot provide legal assistance on issues related to state or official secrets of the Republic of Armenia or be elected in the bodies of the Chamber of Advocates.

1.8. There is no requirement for foreign law firms to obtain special permissions to practice law beyond the usual company registration procedures. In March 2011, the Business Entry One-stop Shop was launched within the Ministry of Justice.[3] Companies and individual entrepreneurs can now obtain the name reservation, business registration and tax identification number at a single location and at the same time. An application for a taxpayer identification number is filed to tax authority at the one-stop shop and the State Registrar of the Ministry of Justice of Armenia the tax identification number is issued by.

[C] Sources of Arbitration Law

1.9. On 25 December 2006 Armenia adopted a new law on commercial arbitration (the Armenian Arbitration Act). It provides a coherent and modern framework for the conduct of both domestic and international commercial arbitration in Armenia and for the enforcement in Armenian courts of arbitral awards made in other countries.

1.10. Armenia's new law is based on the Model Law on International Commercial Arbitration, which was promulgated over twenty years ago by the United Nations Commission on International Trade Law (UNCITRAL). At least fifty countries, in

---

2. The Government of Armenia adopted 2012–2016 Strategic Programme for legal and judicial reforms in Armenia, which, among other things, aims to strengthen the independence, professionalism and accountability of the justice system. For a general discussion, see also *Commercial Law of Armenia: Assessment by the EBRD*, June 2012, EBRD Report.
3. https://www.e-register.am, operated by the Ministry of Justice of Armenia.

addition to Armenia, have adopted national arbitration laws based on the UNCITRAL Model Law.

1.11. The new law is designed to eliminate certain difficulties and uncertainties that arose under the previous law, for example, party autonomy[4] is recognized and court intervention is expressly excluded except as specified in the Act.[5] If wisely used and implemented, the new legislative instrument can provide the basis for a busy, effective and efficient system for the resolution of commercial disputes in Armenia.

1.12. On 19 June 2015, a package of laws related to arbitration was adopted aiming to bring the Armenian Arbitration Act in compliance with the latest version of the UNCITRAL Model Law and to improve the arbitral practice established by the Court of Cassation of Armenia.[6]

1.13. There are also other legislative instruments such the Code of Civil Procedure, the Judicial Code, the Law on Compulsory Enforcement of Judicial Acts, the Consumer Credit Act which make passing reference to the ability to arbitrate disputes in these subject matter areas.

1.14. Case law continues to play a lesser role in the development of arbitral law in Armenia. Further, much of the practice of arbitration is contained in awards of arbitral tribunals, which are generally not published. The legal framework for arbitration in Armenia is not likely to change in the next decade. However, the developing case law can shed light into different aspects of the framework and varying factual scenarios under it.

[D]   International Legal Framework

1.15. International conventions are an important source of law in Armenia. Article 1 of the Constitution of Armenia provides that such conventions prevail over the national legislation once they have been ratified by the Armenian Parliament and published in the Official Gazette.[7] The supremacy of international law is extremely important for both international arbitration proceedings with seat in Armenia and the enforcement of foreign arbitral awards.

1.16 Armenia is a party is the New York Convention on the Recognition and Enforcement of Foreign Arbitral Awards of 1958 (ratified on 29 December 2007). Armenia made two declarations: (1) it will apply the Convention only to recognition and

---

4. Article 19(1) state as general principle that 'the parties are free to agree on the procedure to be followed by the arbitral tribunal in conducting the proceedings.'
5. Article 5 states as another general principle that the court should not intervene except as provided by the Act.
6. On 18 July 2014 the Cassation Court, the highest court in Armenia, in the case EKD/1910/02/13 delivered a decision which jeopardize the arbitration system. In this case the Cassation Court needed to answer a question whether an arbitral tribunal was entitled to decide the matter of invalidity of the contract. The Court held that only state courts had jurisdiction over the invalidity issue.
7. The legislative database of the Republic of Armenia is available on www.arlis.am.

enforcement of awards made in the territory of another contracting state; and (2) apply the Convention only to differences arising out of legal relationships, whether contractual or not, which are considered as commercial under the laws of Armenia.

1.17 Armenia also ratified the Convention on the Settlement of Investment Disputes between States and Nationals of Other States (ratified on 16 September 1992) and is a signatory to the Treaty on Settling of Disputes Related to Commercial Activity (1994). Armenia also has ratified the Energy Charter Treaty (ratified on 18 December 1997) and the Treaty's Trade Amendment which incorporates rules and practices of the World Trade Organization (WTO) – e.g., regarding non-discrimination and transparency – into the Treaty's trade provisions.

1.18 Armenia is also a party to the Convention on the Protection of the Rights of the Investor signed in Moscow on 28 March 1997. The Convention provides certain guarantees for the protection of rights of the investors and has a number of features e.g., it applies to investors both of the state signatories to the Convention and to the investor of non-Member States as well.[8]

[E] Available Dispute Resolution Mechanisms

1.19. In 2015 Armenia introduced conciliation is an alternative out-of-court dispute resolution instrument which is in compliance with UNCITRAL Model Law on International Commercial Conciliation of 2002. The Code of Civil Procedure provides the framework for the conduct of conciliation proceedings. The Ministry of Justice of Armenia maintains a list of certified mediators.

1.20. Article 103 of the Civil Procedural Code, which came into force in 2015, establishes that the court shall leave the case unheard if one of the parties refers to the agreement on resolving the dispute through mediation, unless the court finds that the agreement is null and void, lost its force, or evidently incapable of being performed. Even though an agreement to resolve a dispute in mediation is binding and enforceable, and courts cannot hear the case until the parties exhaust the possibility to try to resolve such dispute via mediation, the process itself is not binding and it can be terminated at any time by either party or the mediator.

[F] Judicial System

1.21. Article 167 of the Constitution provides that the constitutional justice shall be administered by the Constitutional Court by ensuring the supremacy of the Constitution. Article 163 of Constitution provides that the judicial system in Armenia consists of the Constitutional Court, the Cassation Court, appellate courts, general jurisdiction first instance courts, and the administrative court.

---

8. Article 3 of the Convention.

1.22. The National Assembly elects the judges of the Constitutional Court by at least three fifths of the votes of the total number of the members of parliament, for a twelve-year term. The Constitutional Court shall consist of nine judges. The judges of the Cassation Court are appointed by the President of the Republic of Armenia upon nomination by the National Assembly. First instance and appellate court judges are appointed by the President of the Republic upon nomination by the Supreme Judicial Council (SJC).

1.23. According to Article 174 of the Constitution the SJC shall consist of ten members. Five of the members of the SJC shall be elected by the General Assembly of Judges from among judges having at least ten years of experience. Five of the members of the SJC shall be elected by the National Assembly by at least a three-fifths majority vote of the total number of parliamentarians, from among legal scholars and other reputed lawyers that are citizens of only the Republic of Armenia, and have voting rights, strong professional qualities, and at least fifteen years of professional work experience. The members elected by the National Assembly may not be judges.

1.24. Article 5 of the Armenian Arbitration Act says that the functions referred to in the Act shall be performed by the Court of General Jurisdiction of Kentron and Nork-Marash Administrative District.

[G]   Arbitration Institutions

1.25. As one of the leading arbitral institutions in Armenia the Arbitration Court of the Banks Association of Armenia (ACBAA) is a recognized forum to hear financial disputes among their members, commercial banks.[9] This is an independent arbitral institution with a short tradition and its own set of rules.[10] Other arbitral institutions include the Arbitration Court of the Chamber of Commerce and Industry of Armenia (ACCCIA).[11] It has a set of published arbitration rules. Under the Rules, the arbitrator must inform the secretariat of any circumstances which may raise justified doubts as to their own impartiality or independence in connection with the dispute. The parties have the right to apply to the President of the Chamber of Commerce and Industry for the removal of an arbitrator.

[H]   Sovereign Immunity and International Arbitration

1.26. Armenian doctrine favours an extensive notion of foreign state's immunity from the jurisdiction of domestic courts.[12] The rules of state immunity are enshrined in

---

9. The official website of the Banks Association of Armenia is http://www.uba.am.
10. During 2015, the Court administered about 2,500 financial disputes - most frequently parties brought disputes arising out of consumer credit agreements, commercial loan agreements and credit card service agreements.
11. The official website of the Arbitration Court of the Chamber of Commerce and Industry of Armenia is http://www.arbitrage.am.
12. For a general discussion, see М. М. Богуславский. Международное частное право, 2-е издание, переработанное и дополненное. М.: Международные отношения, 1994.

Article 245(1) of the Code of Civil Procedure which provides that state immunity is absolute. However, the Code establishes that foreign states and their instrumentalities are not immune from the jurisdiction of domestic courts if the state or state instrumentalities consent to suit.

1.27. There is no reported court practice on the immunity of foreign states and their instrumentalities from proceedings in Armenia. There are cases involving embassies but they pertain more to diplomatic immunity.

1.28. The doctrine of immunity does not preclude participation of the state and its instrumentalities in arbitral proceedings if there is a valid arbitration agreement.[13] Enforcement of arbitral awards rendered in such arbitrations can be successfully sought in Armenia against public entities subject to the usual defences.

Hence, having considered that the Armenian courts generally adopted an arbitration-friendly approach, an agreement to arbitrate may be sufficient to constitute a waiver of immunity before the Armenian courts.

§2.02 THE ARBITRATION AGREEMENT

[A] Introduction

1.29. In Armenia, the agreement to arbitrate is the foundation stone of arbitration and it serves to evidence the consent of the parties to submit to arbitration.[14] Article 7(1) of the Armenian Arbitration Act distinguishes two types of arbitration agreement:

(1) an agreement to submit the future disputes to arbitration; it usually takes the form of arbitration clause in the main contract;
(2) an agreement to existing disputes to arbitration which is usually called as a submission agreement.

1.30. Further, under the Armenian law, there should be a defined legal relationship between the parties whether contractual or not, since there must be an arbitration agreement to form the basis of arbitral proceedings.

1.31. Concluding, to be valid and enforceable, the terms of an arbitration agreement must be clear and certain, in particular, there must be a clear reference to arbitration by the parties to make arbitration the means for final and binding resolution of disputes between them.[15]

---

13. H. Fox and P. Webb, The Law of State Immunity, Oxford International Law Library, 3rd edition, 2015.
14. See 'How to Arbitrate in Armenia', the Commercial Law and Economic Regulation project conducted by Bearing Point and the International Law Institute.
15. For a general discussion see 'Improving the Efficiency of Arbitration Agreements and Awards: 40 Years of Application of the New York Convention', ICCA Congress Series No. 9, Paris 1998.

[B] Validity of the Arbitration Agreement

[1] General Provisions

1.32. The Armenian Arbitration Act requires that an agreement to arbitrate shall be in writing and incorporated into a document signed by the parties or in an exchange of letters, telex, telegrams or other means of telecommunication which provides a record of the agreement.

1.33. Here, the Act is entirely influenced by the UNCITRAL Model Law and New York Convention which sets out what is required for a formally valid arbitration agreement: 'agreement in writing' and 'signed by the parties or contained in an exchange of letter or telegrams'. It aims to help prove the parties' agreement to refer their disputes to arbitration.

[2] Requisites of a Valid Arbitration Agreement

1.34. To recognize and give effect to an arbitration agreement under the Act the following requirements must be met:

- the agreement is in writing;
- the parties to the arbitration agreement have legal capacity;[16]
- the dispute arises in respect of defined legal relationship whether contractual or not; and
- the dispute concerns a subject-matter of capable of settlement by arbitration.

11.35. It is to be noted that in Armenia that an arbitration agreement should be a formal agreement, and that all the terms should be contained in one document. Signature of a written agreement by the parties is required for an arbitration agreement to be valid under the Armenian Armenia Act[17] and the same goes to the New York Convention.[18]

[C] Concluding the Arbitration Agreement

1.36. Thus, for the purposes of the Armenian Arbitration Act, the requirement for writing may be satisfied by any means of telecommunication that provides 'a record of the agreement'. Furthermore, signature of a written agreement by the parties is required for an arbitration agreement to be valid under the Act. The court will usually seek to give effect to the parties' intention to refer disputes to arbitration and to allow the arbitral tribunal full jurisdiction except in cases of hopeless confusion.

---

16. The prevailing criteria is that legal capacity should be governed by the personal law of each party, *see Yukos International UK B.V. v. the Ministry of Justice of Armenia*, Rosneft ojsc, EAKD/1494/02/10.
17. Article 7(2).
18. Article II(2).

1.37. It is to be note that an oral agreement to arbitrate, sometimes known as a 'parol submission', is not valid as a matter of Armenian law.

[D] The Doctrine of Separability

1.38. Armenia recognizes the principle of the separability of the arbitration agreement which is enshrined in Article 16 of the Armenian Arbitration Act. It means that the arbitration clause in a contract is considered to be separate from the main contract of which it forms part and, as such, survives the termination of that contract. Article 16(1) of the Armenian Arbitration Act provides that:

> The arbitral tribunal may rule on its own jurisdiction, including any objections with respect to the existence or validity of the arbitration agreement. For that purpose, an arbitration clause which forms part of a contract shall be treated as an agreement independent of the other terms of the contract. A decision by the arbitral tribunal that the contract is null and void shall not entail ipso jure the invalidity of the arbitration clause.

1.39. It means that by the arbitration clause the arbitral tribunal has a ground to decide on its own jurisdiction, even if it is alleged that the main contract has been terminated or proven to be null and void.

[E] Invalidity of the Arbitration Agreement

1.40. Article 8(1) of the Armenian Arbitration Act places the court under an obligation to refer the parties to arbitration if the court is seized with a claim on the same subject-matter unless it finds that the arbitration agreement is null and void, inoperative or incapable of being performed.

1.41. In 2014, the Court of Cassation asked a question whether an arbitral tribunal was entitled to decide the matter of invalidity of the contract.[19] The Court eventually held that only state courts had jurisdiction over the invalidity issue. The Court relied on the proper mechanisms of the civil rights protection. It referred to Article 13(1) of the Civil Code which stated that the protection of civil rights [...] is conducted by court. The Court reasoned that according to the Constitution[20] and the European Convention for the Protection of Human Rights and Fundamental Freedoms[21] every person whose rights and freedoms are violated shall have an effective remedy before a national authority, and thus it is the state's duty to create effective mechanisms to protect such rights. The Court went further saying that that the protection of civil rights could be done through judicial, administrative and public (arbitration) means, from which the most guaranteed option was the judicial option because in such case the protection was conducted in accordance with the judicial procedure strictly envisaged by the law,

---

19. *Mantashanner v. Prometey Bank* (EAKD1910/02/13).
20. Article 18.
21. Article 13.

which included firm guarantees to find out the circumstances which were important for the case and to ensure the execution of the judicial rights of the parties.[22]

[F] Arbitrability

1.42. Article 2(4) of the Armenian Arbitration Act determines which types of dispute may be resolved by arbitration. The Act determines the term 'commercial' which should be given a wide interpretation so as to cover matters arising from all relationships of a commercial nature,[23] whether contractual or not. Certain disputes involving sensitive matters of public policy such as antitrust, validity of acts of state, bankruptcy, patents and trademarks may not, in principle, be submitted to arbitration.

In addition, the Act does not specify whether corporate disputes (including disputes concerning title to shares and participation interests in companies incorporated in Armenia) are arbitrable, although no explicit prohibition in the applicable legislation exists. In commercial practice, arbitration clauses are often used in corporate agreements involving a foreign party, e.g., share purchase agreements or joint venture agreements.[24] Concluding, a wide range of corporate disputes (including corporate management, share ownership, derivative claims against directors and even challenges of the corporation's transactions with third parties) is clearly arbitrable under the Armenian Arbitration Act

In addition, arbitration of employment disputes is provided by Article 264(3) of the Labor Code of 2004, including for matters concerning collective issues. However, in practice, it is extremely rare for employment disputes resolved through arbitration in Armenia.

1.43. All civil law disputes capable of being referred to court will be deemed arbitrable, subject to the exceptions stated in the legislation. For example, the Insolvency Act of 2006 expressly provides for the non-arbitrability of insolvency disputes and the same goes to a number of other types of disputes that are predominantly public or administrative in nature, such as those connected to privatization. Public procurement is also designated as a non-arbitrable subject as provided by the Public Procurement Act of 2010.

1.44. Article 34(2)(b) of the Armenian Arbitration Act reproduces the essence of Article V of the New York Convention and describes the grounds on which an award may be set aside. One of the grounds that a court may consider of its own initiative

---

22. *See also* M. Manukyan, 'Eleven Months without Jurisdiction to Decide on the Invalidity of a Contract', Kluwer Arbitration Blog, 27 October 2015.
23. However, in *Mantashanner v. Prometey Bank* (EAKD1910/02/13) the Court defined that the nullity and voidability of the main contract is barred from arbitration referring to 'public policy' as the basis of the bar.
24. Those corporate disputes may only be referred to arbitration provided that all the shareholders, the company, and other parties who are acting as claimants or defendants have signed the respective arbitration agreement. The consent is required since the award must be binding on all the shareholders (res judicata).

includes non-arbitrability of the subject-matter of the dispute or violation of public policy.[25]

[G] Effect of Arbitration Agreement on Third Parties

1.45. The 'group of companies doctrine' was not recognized under the applicable Armenian law. It is highly disputed among scholars, and both arbitral tribunals and the have taken differing views.[26] Armenian courts will base their decision whether a third party must submit to, or can be included in, arbitration proceedings on the applicable national law instead of general principles of international law. To determine the applicable law, the courts will make a thorough conflict of laws analysis and either opt for the law applicable to the arbitration agreement or, if the third party requires protection, the law that is possibly applicable to the legal relationship between the third party and one of the parties to the arbitration agreement. Consequently, the courts will assess the agreement under the applicable law, both regarding its content and formal validity.

1.46. Armenian courts will carefully examine whether the result is in line with domestic public policy. There is no set answer to this question. The decision rather shows that the court will decide on a case-by-case basis whether the outcome is contrary to fundamental principles of Armenia law.

[H] Termination of Arbitration Agreement

1.47. Armenian law does not contain any specific rules regarding the termination of the arbitration agreement, thus in practice the courts, based on *lex fori*, apply general rules on the termination of obligations. Thus, Articles 466–469 of the Civil Code of Armenia allow the parties by agreement to bring the arbitration agreement to arbitrate to an end. Arbitration is consensual and there is no reason why the parties cannot agree to vary their arbitration agreement so as to bring about its termination.[27] The parties may jointly agree that the existing dispute shall be resolved by the court rather than pursuant to the arbitration agreement contained in their contract.

There is a statutory requirement for the termination of the arbitration agreement to be in writing.

[I] Drafting an Arbitration Clause

1.48. In Armenia, it is important to ensure that the wording adopted in an arbitration agreement is certain and adequate to fulfil the intentions of the parties and to

---

25. *Pacific China Holdings Ltd (In Liquidation) v. Grand Pacific Holdings Ltd*, CACV 136 of 2011 and FAM 18 of 2012.
26. Fouchard Gaillard Goldman on International Commercial Arbitration, Savage and Gaillard (ed), 1999.
27. D. Sutton and J. Gill, Russel on Arbitration, 22nd edition, pp. 79–80, 2003.

encompass a broad scope of arbitration issues. A well-drafted arbitration clause must cover the following matters: (1) what arbitral rules will apply; (2) how many arbitrators there will be; (3) how the arbitrators will be appointed; and (4) where the arbitration will be held. It may also be advisable to state (5) the language in which the arbitration will be held.

§2.03 APPLICABLE LAW

[A] Introduction

1.49. In domestic arbitrations between parties in Armenia the issue of the choice of law to be applied does not usually arise – the arbitration will be subject in all respects to Armenian law. And it recognizes the doctrine of the autonomy of the parties. However the issue does arise in international arbitration and can be of fundamental importance. It is possible for at least three different laws to apply to a dispute referred to arbitration: (1) the law governing the performance obligations under the contract, (2) the law of the arbitration agreement (*'lex arbitri'*) and, (3) the procedural law (*'lex fori'*).

1.50. Article 1284 of the Civil Code of Armenia provides that the parties are free to choose the applicable laws, whether they make an express choice or provide how the laws are to be chosen. Article goes further stating that the different laws can operate simultaneously on different aspects of the main agreement.[28]

1.51. If the parties have not made an express choice, the governing law of the main contract is determined by Chapter 80 of the Civil Code of Armenia. For example, Article 1285(1) provides that:

> In the absence of agreement of the parties to a contract on the applicable law, the law of the state shall be applied of where the party was founded, has its residence or basic place of activity who is:
>
> - the pledgor–in a contract of pledge;
> - the seller–in a contract of purchase and sale;
> - the lessor–in a contract of lease…

[B] The Law Governing the Arbitration Agreement

1.52. The law of an arbitration agreement usually follows the governing law of the main contract. In theory, as arbitration agreement is separable from the main contract between the parties; the agreement to arbitrate may have a different law from the main contract.

1.53. Where there is no express choice of a governing law of the arbitration agreement, the court will apply Armenian law to regulate substantive matters relating to that

---

28. *See* A. Haikyantc, 'Civil Code of Armenia', Yerevan, Armenia, 2011, pp. 489–492.

agreement, including in particular the interpretation, validity, voidability and discharge of the agreement to arbitration. It is to be noted that similar matters relating to the reference and enforcement of the award. The court will also apply the proper law of the arbitration agreement to determine whether a particular dispute falls within the wording of the arbitration clause.

[C] The Law Governing the Arbitration (*Lex Arbitri*)

1.54. According to the Armenian Arbitration Act and treaties lex arbitri shall govern the following issues for the purposes of arbitration proceedings and further enforcement of the arbitral award: (1) validity of arbitration agreement (for both form and substance), (2) arbitrability of the subject matter of the dispute, and (3) rules of the arbitral procedure.

[D] Restrictions on Party Autonomy

1.55. In Armenia, there are restrictions on the principle of the party autonomy which are enshrined in Article 1258 of the Civil Code of Armenia:

1. A norm of foreign law subject to application in accordance with Paragraph 1 of Article 1253 of this Code shall not be applied when the consequences of its application would clearly contradict the bases legal order (public policy) of the Republic of Armenia. In such a case if necessary the respective norm of the law of the Republic of Armenia shall be applied.
2. A refusal to apply a norm of foreign law may not be based merely on the difference of the legal, political, or economic system of the respective foreign state from the legal, political, or economic system of the Republic of Armenia.

It means that the court that applies a foreign law as the law chosen by the parties is not obliged to apply provisions of that law which are incompatible with the national public policy.

1.56. The court has the powers in respect of matters that affect public policy or the public interest.[29] Article 1258 of the Civil Code of Armenia qualifies the autonomy of the parties by such safeguards as are necessary in the public interest. Moreover, enforcement of an arbitral award may be opposed on the ground that it is contrary to public policy,[30] and an application may be made to set aside an award because it is in conflict with the public policy of Armenia. It means there was a serious irregularity causing substantial injustice to the applicant where the award was obtained by fraud or the award or the way in which it was procured was contrary to public policy.[31]

---

29. In Armenia, the Civil Code uses 'public interest', however, it is not the same thing with public policy but they may overlap. *See also* footnote 29, *supra*, pp. 458–469.
30. Article 36(1)(b)(ii) of the Armenian Arbitration Act.
31. Article 34(2)(b)(ii) of the Armenian Arbitration Act.

§2.04 THE ARBITRATORS

[A] Appointment of Arbitrators

1.57. As a principle, the parties are free to determine the procedure to appoint arbitrators as provide by Article 11(1) of the Armenian Arbitration Act.[32] Usually each party nominates one arbitrator and the party-appointed arbitrators designate the third arbitrator, who will generally be the chairman of the arbitral tribunal. The parties may also entrust a third person or institution to make the appointment.

1.58. Any natural person may be chosen to act as an arbitrator, the only general rule being that the person chosen must have legal capacity and be 25 or older.

1.59. Article 11(3) provides that where the parties are unable to reach the agreement upon the appointment of an arbitrator:

a) in an arbitration with three arbitrators, each party shall appoint one arbitrator, and the two arbitrators thus appointed shall appoint the third arbitrator; if a party fails to appoint the arbitrator within thirty days of receipt of a request to do so from the other party, or if the two arbitrators fail to agree on the third arbitrator within thirty days of their appointment, the appointment shall be made, upon request of a party, by the court;
b) in an arbitration with a sole arbitrator, if the parties are unable to agree on the arbitrator, he shall be appointed, upon request of a party, by the court.

1.60. It is to be noted that a decision of the court shall be subject to no appeal. Moreover, the court or other authority, in appointing an arbitrator, shall have due regard to any qualifications required of the arbitrator by the agreement of the parties and to such considerations as are likely to secure the appointment of an independent and impartial arbitrator.[33]

1.61. In addition, there are no formal requirements for the appointment of arbitral tribunals. Appointment is often effected on the parties' behalf by their lawyers. Where the tribunal is to consist of single arbitrator, and the parties agree on the name, a letter from each of the parties or representatives to the proposed arbitrator, and his acceptance, should be sufficient to achieve his appointment.

[B] Qualifications of Arbitrators

1.62. In Armenia, the most important qualification for an arbitrator is that he/she should be experienced in the law and practice of arbitration.

1.63. It is also becoming increasingly important for arbitrators to show their awareness on the particular area of business and on the different traditions, aims and expectations

---

32. *See*, R. Petrosyan, 'Civil Procedural Code of Armenia', Yerevan, Armenia, 2012, pp. 684–675.
33. When considering a potential nominee, it is crucial to check whether the nominee has any financial interest in the dispute, a party, its counsel or a major witness or beneficiary or whether there are any past business relationships with a party or counsel.

of the people of that world. The Rules of Arbitration of the ACBAA provide that the member(s) of the tribunal must have special qualification in the financial industry.[34]

1.64. It is to be noted that there is no practice to interview a potential candidate, even if, the individual is not known to the counsel or the party appointing them.

[C] Powers and Duties of Arbitrators

1.65. The first source of an arbitral tribunal's powers is the arbitration agreement between the parties under which the tribunal has been appointed, of course, within the limits allowed by the applicable law i.e., the governing law of the arbitration agreement and the law of the place of arbitration.

1.66. The Armenian Arbitration Act[35] gives the arbitral tribunal a wide discretion in procedural matters (e.g., to rule on jurisdiction, to decide all procedural and evidential matters, to make provisional orders), subject to the parties' agreement in many cases. Importantly, the exercise of that discretion is subject to the arbitral tribunal discharging its duty to act impartially as between the parties, giving each party a reasonable opportunity of putting its case and dealing with that of its opponents.

1.67. As stated above, the arbitral tribunal is expressly given the power to rule on its own substantive jurisdiction, as to:

(a) whether there is a valid arbitration agreement;
(b) whether the tribunal is properly constituted; and
(c) what matters have been submitted to arbitration in accordance with the arbitration agreement.[36]

1.68. The arbitral tribunal also has the duty to apply procedures designed to the circumstances of the particular case, avoiding unnecessary delay or expense, so as to provide a fair means of the resolution of the matters falling to be determined. The specific duties of the arbitral tribunal imposed by the Act are:

(a) to act fairly and impartially between the parties;
(b) to possess the qualifications required by the arbitration agreement;
(c) to be physically and mentally capable of conducting the proceedings;
(d) to adopt suitable procedure and to avoid unnecessary delay or expense;
(e) importantly, not to exceed its substantive jurisdiction and powers.

---

34. It is also common practice that arbitration clauses specify that tribunal are to be composed of 'financial lawyers'.
35. Chapter 4 of the Armenian Arbitration Act.
36. Article 16 of the Armenian Arbitration Act.

1.69. Thus, it is the tribunal's general duty to act fairly by giving each party should be given a reasonable opportunity of putting his case and dealing with that of his opponent. An obligation to act impartially as between the parties is also required as part of the general duty imposed on the tribunal by the Act[37] – failure to observe this fundamental requirement may lead to the removal of biased arbitrator in accordance with Article 12 of the Act.

1.70. Finally, the arbitral tribunal has also duty not to exceed its jurisdiction or powers in conducting arbitration; otherwise, any resulting award may be challenged for serious irregularity.

[D] Challenges and Replacement of Arbitrators

1.71. Article 12 of the Armenian Arbitration Act says that before accepting an appointment, an arbitrator should consider whether he is suited to the particular case:

> he/she shall disclose any circumstances likely to give rise to justifiable doubts as to his/her impartiality or independence. An arbitrator, from the time of his/her appointment and throughout the arbitral proceedings, shall without delay disclose any such circumstances to the parties unless they have already been informed of them by him/her.

1.72. Article 13(2) provides machinery for challenge a party who intends to challenge an arbitrator shall, within fifteen days after becoming aware of the constitution of the arbitral tribunal or after becoming aware of any circumstance mentioned above, send a written statement of the reasons for the challenge to the arbitral tribunal. Unless the challenged arbitrator withdraws from his office or the other party agrees to the challenge, the arbitral tribunal shall decide on the challenge.

1.73. If the challenge is not successful, the party may request, within thirty days after having received notice of the decision rejecting the challenge, the court to decide on the challenge. This decision shall be subject to no appeal. The challenged arbitrator or the arbitral tribunal are entitled to continue the arbitral proceedings and make an award.

1.74. In addition, it is to be noted that once a tribunal has been appointed, it continues in place with full authority until that authority is terminated by operation of law, by act of the parties or a court order. Article 14(1) of the Armenian Arbitration Act says that parties acting together can remove the arbitral tribunal in whole or in part, or agree to revoke the reference itself. Another example, the authority of an arbitrator ceases on his death because it is personal. However, it is uncertain whether the insolvency of an arbitrator is likely to affect his formal capacity to continue to act.

---

37. Article 11(5) of the Armenian Arbitration Act.

[E] Compensation of Arbitrators

1.75. In most cases the arbitral tribunal enters into an express agreement with the parties about the level of fees and the right to be paid certain expenses. The level of fees may be agreed directly with each arbitrator as normally occurs in an ad hoc arbitration or be fixed by the institution managing the arbitration in accordance with the terms of appointment specified in the relevant arbitration rules.

1.76. For instance, the ACBAA charges arbitrators' fees based in part on a percentage scale of the amount in dispute. The arbitrators' fees are managed by the Court and fixed on the basis of the relevant scale found in the relevant appendix, taking into consideration the diligence of the arbitrators, the time spent, the rapidity of the proceedings and the complexity of the dispute. Based on the amount in dispute, the scale provides a minimum and a maximum for one arbitrator.

§2.05 JURISDICTION OF THE ARBITRAL TRIBUNAL

[A] Introduction

1.77. Separability and competence-competence are two of the best-known concepts in arbitration which are also enshrined in the Armenian Arbitration Act. They are different, but often linked, because they share a common goal: *to prevent early judicial intervention from obstructing the arbitration process.*[38]

[B] The Arbitrator's Determination of Their Jurisdiction

1.78. Article 16(1) of the Armenian Arbitration Act, as identified earlier, defines the power of an arbitral tribunal to rule on its jurisdiction (competence-competence) including any objections with respect to the existence or validity of the arbitration agreement, without having to resort to a court. As regards the separability, an arbitration clause shall be treated as an agreement independent of the other terms of the contract. As a consequence, a decision by the arbitral tribunal that the contract is null and void shall not entail ipso jure the invalidity of the arbitration clause. Article 16(2) of the Act requires that any objections relating to the arbitrators' jurisdiction be made at the earliest possible time.

1.79. Thus, the arbitral tribunal to continue with the proceedings even where the existence or validity of the arbitration agreement has been challenged by one of the parties for reasons directly affecting the arbitration agreement, and not simply on the basis of allegations that the main contract is void or otherwise ineffective. The party challenging the competence of arbitral tribunal need not delay its objection until the

---

38. For a general discussion, *see* Alan S. Rau, *Everything You Really Need to Know About 'Separability' in Seventeen Simple Propositions*, 14 March 2003, American Review of International Arbitration.

recognition and enforcement stages, but rather may raise the objection during the arbitral proceedings.

1.80. The Act provides in Article 16(3) that *'if the arbitral tribunal rules as a preliminary question that it has jurisdiction, any party may [appeal to the court], within thirty days after having received notice of the ruling ... '* While the matter is pending in the court, the arbitral tribunal may continue the arbitral proceedings. The decision of the court is subject to no appeal.

[C] Court Review of Arbitrators' Jurisdiction

1.81. The courses of action open to a party who disputes the arbitral tribunal's jurisdiction are various and Article 16(3) of the Armenian Arbitration Act allows any party to apply to the court for a determination of the tribunal's jurisdiction under the Act. The Act goes further, stating *'...while such a request is pending, the arbitral tribunal may continue the arbitral proceedings and make an award.'*

1.82. In Armenia, not only must the applicant specify ground why the court should decide the matter but he must also satisfy the court that there is a good reason for making an order in the course of the reference. The court must decide the matter during a hearing and the process will usually take two months.

1.83. The applicant must also satisfy the court that the application is made without delay i.e., as soon as he becomes aware of any issue as to the substantive jurisdiction of the tribunal. Article 16(2) of the Armenian Arbitration Act provides that a plea that the arbitral tribunal does not have jurisdiction shall be raised not later than the submission of the statement of defence. Moreover, the Act also says that a party is not precluded from raising such a plea by the fact that he has appointed, or participated in the appointment of, an arbitrator

§2.06 THE PROCEDURE BEFORE THE ARBITRAL TRIBUNAL

[A] Introduction

1.84. The general principle of the role of the Armenian court in arbitration is provided in Article 5 of the Act which states that in matters governed by the Act the court should not intervene except as provided by the Act. This statement of principle in the very first section of the Armenian Arbitration Act is clear recognition of the policy of party autonomy underlying the Act and the desire to limit and define the court's role in arbitration so as to give effect to that policy.

1.85. Thus, parties have great latitude in setting procedural ground rules and often do so to varying degrees in arbitration clauses that they write into their contracts. An arbitral tribunal's authority to establish procedures for the conduct of the arbitration, and to deal with the taking evidence, is quite broad and comprehensive, limited only by the constraints of administrating authorities arbitration rules on the subject or the laws of Armenia. Article 18 of the Act assures that the process will be fair and that basic notions of due process are preserved.

1.86. Before discussing the conduct of the arbitral proceedings, it is to be noted that Article 332 of the Civil Code of Armenia imposes a time limit for bringing a claim – it also applies to arbitrations as it does to legal proceedings. The effect of a statutory time limit is to provide a procedural bar to the remedy which has to be raised by way of defence to the claim. However, it does not go to the jurisdiction of the arbitral tribunal, but it does provide a defence to the claim.

1.87. It rarely happens that the parties agree to impose a time limit for commencing arbitral proceedings or to provide that a claim shall be barred or extinguished if arbitration is not commenced within the time limit.

[B] General Principles

1.88. Article 19(1) of the Armenian Arbitration Act provides that the parties are free to agree on the procedure to be followed by the arbitral tribunal in conducting the proceedings. However, the guiding principle is partially restricted; the procedure to be followed by the parties must be in compliance with certain mandatory rules and public policy requirements. If this principle is not applied, the arbitral award may be set aside[39] or refused recognition and enforcement.[40]

1.89. The second concept to be applied in relation to arbitral procedure is an equality of the parties which is adopted in Article 18 of the Armenian Arbitration Act. It states that the parties shall be treated with equality and each party shall be given a full opportunity of presenting his case.

1.90. Finally, the Act imposes a mandatory duty on the arbitral tribunal in Article 12 to act fairly and impartially as between the parties and adopt procedures suitable to the circumstances of the particular case, avoiding unnecessary delay or expense.

[C] Commencing the Arbitral Proceedings

1.91. Arbitration is commenced as prescribed by the provisions of the arbitration agreement and the law governing the arbitration proceedings. Thus, Article 21 of the Armenian Arbitration Act regulate when the proceedings are deemed to have commenced:

> the arbitral proceedings in respect of a particular dispute commence on the date on which a request for that dispute to be referred to arbitration is received by the respondent.

---

39. Article 34(2)(2)(b) of the Armenian Arbitration Act.
40. Article 36(1)(2)(b) of the Armenian Arbitration Act.

1.92. The Act does not regulate issues associated with the form of the notice commencing the proceedings. However, the party must ensure that sufficient information is provided in the notice commencing the arbitration to enable not only the respondent, but also the institution to gauge the nature of the dispute and the level of the party agreement of the proposed arbitrators, seat and language of the proceedings to enable an appropriate tribunal to be appointed. In addition, the notice must contain the description of the claims, the facts supporting it and the relief sought.

1.93. The notice of arbitration is usually validly served by ordered post. It means that the notice is treated as effectively served, if it is addressed, pre-paid and delivered by post to the addressee's last known principal business address.

[D] Conduction of Arbitration

[1] Written Submissions

1.94. In Armenia, there is an increasing trend toward standardization of the conduct of arbitration ranging from the nature and scope of the arbitral proceeding to the professional conduct of the lawyers and arbitrators.

1.95. An arbitral tribunal's authority to establish procedures for the conduct of the arbitration, and to deal with the taking of evidence, is quite broad and comprehensive, limited only by the constraints of the law of the place of arbitration. Thus, Article 18 of the Armenian Arbitration Act assures that the process will be fair and that basic notions of due process are preserved.[41]

1.96. Article 23 of the Act contains a mandatory provision to the effect that each party shall state the facts supporting his claim or defence, as the case may be, and may submit documents or references to the evidence that will rely upon. And, most domestic proceedings now involve a compulsory document exchange, although the extent of such an exchange is left to the arbitrators' discretion.[42]

[2] Post-hearing Briefs

1.97. The Armenian lawyer is not accustomed to a post-hearing procedure in which presentation of his case is concluded with oral summations. However, the parties may obtain final versions of the full record (which may include memoranda, transcribed testimony, evidence and other materials) at or before the end of the hearings.[43]

---

41. In domestic arbitrations, a party is entitled to be represented by counsel who must be qualified.
42. In Armenia, the process of exchanging pleadings and written evidence prior to a hearing usually consumes two months.
43. Article 55(1) of the Code of Civil Procedure usually serves as a guiding principle.

[3] Evidence

1.98. Armenia is the civil law country and the arbitrator takes a more active part in the conduct of the arbitral proceedings and in the presentation of evidence, including the examination of witnesses. However, there is a trend in domestic arbitral procedures that the initiative as regards evidence is almost wholly in the hands of the parties.

1.99. Under the Armenian Arbitration Act, the extent to which production of documents will be ordered is left to the arbitrators to decide as they consider appropriate, in the absence of any agreement of the parties to the contrary. For example, the arbitral tribunal has the power to determine the admissibility, relevance, materiality and weight of any evidence (Article 19(2)). The arbitral tribunal may also meet at any place it considers appropriate for consultation among its members, for hearing witnesses, experts or the parties, or for inspection of goods, other property or documents (Article 20(2)).

1.100. The methods of presenting evidence to an arbitral tribunal are the following:[44]

(a) production of documents;
(b) testimony of witnesses of fact (*mainly written*);
(c) opinions of expert witnesses (*mainly written*).

[4] Witness and Experts Testimony

1.101. It is not common practice in Armenia to submit written statements of the witnesses on whose evidence the parties intend to rely. Those statements are simply signed by the witnesses. An arbitral tribunal has discretion to determine the evidentiary weight to be given to witness evidence. The content of the testimony of witnesses are usually made known to the arbitrators and to the other side in advance of the oral testimony of those witnesses.

1.102. The third method of presenting evidence to an arbitral tribunal is by the use of expert witnesses. Expert evidence is normally furnished in the form of written report at the same time as any written statements of witnesses of fact. Where expert evidence is submitted by the parties, the rules regarding the admissibility of expert evidence applied by arbitral tribunals are in general the same as those applied in other forms of evidence in the same arbitration. In addition, the requirement of independence and impartiality is also embodied in the Act which enables parties to challenge the appointment of a tribunal appointed expert on grounds of justifiable doubts as to his impartiality or independence in the same way that such a challenge would be made to the appointment of the arbitrator.

---

44. The arbitral tribunals usually apply relevant provisions of the Code of Civil Procedure.

1.103. Article 26 of the Armenian Arbitration Act endorses the authority of a tribunal to appoint its own expert and the role of the expert is to provide non-binding advice to the tribunal, which is then responsible for reaching its own conclusions.

[E] Hearings

1.104. Article 24(1) of the Armenian Arbitration Act provides that the arbitral tribunal has the power decide whether to hold oral hearings for the presentation of evidence or for oral argument, or whether the proceedings shall be conducted on the basis of documents and other materials.

1.105. Further, Article 24(2) implies that the parties shall be given sufficient advance notice of any hearing (usually fifteen days) and of any meeting of the arbitral tribunal for the purposes of inspection of goods, other property or documents.

1.106. In practice, if there is to be an oral hearing the arbitral tribunal decides when and where the hearing or indeed any part of the proceedings shall be held. There is no a requirement that the parties must be represented by a qualified lawyer.[45]

1.107. It is to be noted that the tribunal has the power to proceed in the absence of a party, and a hearing may take place even if one of the parties is not present.[46] Where an arbitration hearing proceeds in the absence of one of the parties, the tribunal should consider the evidence and submissions before it in order to determine whether they are sufficient to establish the claim. It is to be noted that the tribunal is not bound to accept the evidence of the party attending and may find, even if it is uncontroverted, that it falls short of establishing the case to be proved.

§2.07 THE ARBITRAL AWARD

[A] Introduction

1.108. There is no statutory definition of an award in Armenian arbitration law. In principle, an arbitral award is a final determination of a particular issue or claim in the arbitration. The distinction must be drawn between an award and procedural orders which address the procedural mechanisms to be adopted in the arbitration.

1.109. Article 31(1) of the Armenian Arbitration provides that the award shall be made in writing and shall be signed by the arbitrators. The award shall state the reasons upon which it is based as well as its date and the place of arbitration.

---

45. However, it is required that the parties must be represented by a qualified lawyer in the arbitration-related court proceedings.
46. In practice where one party does not participate the tribunal records in details in its award the opportunities to participate that the absent party was given.

[B] Deliberation and Voting

1.110. Article 29 of the Armenian Arbitration Act provides that when there are three arbitrators, any award or other decision of the arbitral tribunal shall be made by a majority of the arbitrators. However, this article makes exception to this rule, in relation to the questions of procedure and allows the presiding arbitrator to decide such questions on his own, '...*if so authorized by the parties or all members of the arbitral tribunal.*'

1.111. It is common practice that if an arbitral tribunal is composed of more than one arbitrator, there should be discussion between the arbitrators before the award is drawn up.

1.112. It is to be emphasized that the Armenian Arbitration Act neither requires nor prohibits 'dissenting opinions'. However, in practice, arbitrators taking a minority position do occasionally dissent, and when do, they write an opinion that often forms part of the award.

[C] Different Kinds of Awards

1.113. Article 32(1) of the Armenian Arbitration Act uses the expression '*final award*', '*... the arbitral proceedings are terminated by the final award...*'. However, there are various different kinds of award that may be made during the course of arbitration, for example, interim, interlocutory, or partial awards.

1.114. It is noteworthy to mention that the Act does not impose any restrictions to the effect that the parties cannot terminate the arbitral proceedings by agreement.[47] Current practice provides a six months limit for the arbitrators to render the final award from the signing of some sort of terms of reference. However, extensions are common, particularly in large arbitrations.

[D] Interim Measures

1.115. Broadly speaking, the Armenian Arbitration Act adopts the amendments to the Model Law involving interim measures as adopted by UNCITRAL in 2006. Article 17 of the Act provides that unless otherwise agreed by the parties, the arbitral tribunal may, at the request of a party, grant interim measures.

An interim measure granted by a tribunal may be in the form of an interim decision which must be recognized as binding and can be enforced upon application to the competent court. The grounds for refusing recognition or enforcement of an interim measure include several of the grounds for refusing recognition or enforcement of an arbitration award as stipulated by Articles 34, 35 and 36 of the Armenian Arbitration Act.

---

47. Article 32(2)(b) of the Armenian Arbitration Act.

Further, Article 17(2) of the Act an arbitral tribunal has the right to issue a 'preliminary order': an order 'directing a party not to frustrate the purpose of an interim measure'. The application for an interim measure is 'with notice'; the application for a preliminary order is 'without notice'. If granted, the preliminary order preserves the status quo until the on-notice hearing of the interim measure. The tribunal can then discharge the preliminary order or adopt it as an interim measure, with variations to its terms if the tribunal considers this to be appropriate. According to Article 17(3)(5), a preliminary order is binding on the parties but is not enforceable by a court. Interim measures are to be enforced by courts.

In addition, Article 17(6) of the Act also provides that an applicant for an interim measure or a preliminary order is liable for any subsequent costs or damages caused to the other party if the tribunal later determines that the measure or order should not have been granted.

Finally, a party is entitled to request, before or during arbitral proceedings, interim measures from the competent court in accordance with Articles 97–102 of the Code of Civil Procedure and it will have the same powers to grant an interim measure as an arbitral tribunal has (Article 17(7) of the Armenian Arbitration Act).

[E] Emergency Arbitration

1.116. In Armenia, the arbitration institutions have not introduced yet provisions that provide for some form of emergency relief, either through the appointment of an emergency arbitrator or through the expedited formation of the tribunal.

[F] Interest and Costs

1.117. In Armenia, arbitral tribunals generally award simple interest; the tribunal must award interest according to as a set of rules to be found in Article 411 of the Civil Code of Armenia. These rules determine the liability to pay interest, the period it must cover and rate to be applied.

1.118. On costs, the arbitral tribunal may fix and apportion between the parties the costs of arbitration in the final award and they include: the fees and expenses of the arbitrators; any administrative expenses of the applicable arbitration institution; fees and expenses of experts; and reasonable legal costs incurred by the parties.

1.119. In making costs awards, there are generally three ways in which costs can be allocated:

- the losing party bears all the costs;
- costs divided equally; and
- parties bear their own costs.

[G] Effects of the Award

[1] Execution

1.120. As discussed above,[48] an award made by the tribunal in accordance with an arbitration agreement is final and binding both the parties. It means that, subject to any contrary agreement by the parties and to the right of challenge, once made the award is immediately enforceable. If a party refuses to comply with the award, execution proceedings will be necessary.

1.121. There is one principal method of execution of an award available in Armenia. It is to obtain permission of the court to enforce the award in the same manner as a judgment. A party wishing to enforce an award must apply to the court for permission within one year when the award is rendered in accordance with the Law on Compulsory Enforcement of Judicial Acts.

[2] Res Judicata and Lis Pendens

1.122. Armenia has a well-established doctrine of res judicata which is codified in Article 91(1) of the Code Civil Procedure. Judgments are binding upon the parties when rendered (subject to any appeal) and constitute a bar to re-litigating the same dispute. Thus, Code has a broader notion of res judicata, which expresses both the binding nature of a judgment or award on the parties (positive res judicata) and the mirror image of the prohibition upon re-litigating claims which have been decided (negative res judicata).

1.123. Armenia recognizes the principle of res judicata in arbitration as well in Article 91(4) of the Code Civil Procedure: (1) the effect of an award on existing disputes between the parties; (2) its effect on subsequent disputes between the parties; and (3) its effect on third parties.

1.124. Res judicata questions appear much more frequently between the court and the tribunal than between different arbitral tribunals. The party can initiate parallel proceedings before the court if he considers that:

 (a) there is no agreement to arbitrate;
 (b) the arbitration agreement is invalid or unenforceable;
 (c) the arbitration agreement has expired or otherwise has terminated;
 (d) the dispute is not arbitrable; or
 (e) the dispute does not fall within the scope of the agreement to arbitrate.

1.125. The court may also have jurisdiction if the respondent does not raise lack of jurisdiction based on an agreement to arbitrate or does raise any such defence too late in the state proceedings.

---

48. *See* section 1.108, *supra*.

[H] Correction and Interpretation of the Award

1.126. The Armenian Arbitration Act in Article 33(1) separates two different matters: the interpretation and clarification. The Act provides for interpretation of a specific point or a part of the arbitral award only when the parties agree that such a request should be to the arbitral tribunal.

1.127. Further, the Act enables the party to request the arbitral tribunal to correct in the award any errors in computation, any clerical or typographical errors or any errors of similar nature. The arbitral tribunal may correct any error of the type on its own initiative within thirty days of the date of the award.

§2.08 SETTING ASIDE THE AWARD

[A] Introduction

1.128. In Armenia, a party to the arbitral proceedings may apply to the court to challenge an award on the grounds specified in Article 34(2) of the Armenian Arbitration Act i.e., serious irregularity affecting the tribunal, the proceedings or the award or that the arbitral tribunal had no substantive jurisdiction over the dispute in question.

1.129. Under the Act, an application for setting aside an award must be made within three months of receiving the award or, if a request for an interpretation, correction or additional award has been made, within three months of that request being disposed of by the arbitral tribunal.

[B] Invalid Awards

1.130. The Armenian Arbitration Act does not distinguish types of the awards for purposes of setting aside procedure. Thus, all the awards rendered in Armenia can be equally challenged on the grounds provided by the Act. However, it is to be mentioned that the threshold for invalidity is high; an award is invalid only if it is clearly incompatible with basic principles of Armenian law or public policy, such as when an award orders a party to carry out illegal actions, or when an award is contrary to Armenian law.

[C] Challengeable Awards

[1] Grounds for Challenging the Award

1.131. Armenian courts declare to be enforcement- and arbitration-friendly as the challenge of an award is limited to clearly exceptional cases. The Court of General Jurisdiction will refuse the challenge of an arbitral award only on the basis of a violation of public policy where it leads to a result which is 'manifestly' incompatible with the essential principles of Armenian law.

Thus, Article 34(1) makes it clear that an application to have an award set aside is intended to be the only method of challenging an award and the only grounds on which an award may be set aside are those provided by Article 34(2) of the Act which reproduces the essence of Article V of the New York Convention.

The expression 'challenge of an arbitral award' (վճռի վիճարկումը) covers any form of judicial recourse for the setting aside (i.e., the annulment), in whole or in part, of an arbitral award.

1.132. Before looking at the grounds on which an award can be set aside, the Court of General Jurisdiction must first verify whether the award can no longer be contested before the arbitrators. The four grounds on which the party making the application entitled to rely are concerned with largely procedural regularities either in the course of the arbitration or in the award itself. The applicant must prove that

(a) a party to the arbitration was under some incapacity or the arbitration agreement was not valid;
(b) he was not given proper notice of the appointment of an arbitrator or of the arbitral proceedings or was otherwise unable to present his case;
(c) the tribunal exceeded its powers or failed to deal with all issues that were put to it;
(d) the composition of the arbitral tribunal or the arbitral procedure was not in accordance with the agreement of the parties or was not in accordance with the Act.

The grounds mentioned above can no longer be invoked to request the setting aside of the award if the party was aware of them during the arbitration proceedings, but failed to raise them at that point.

1.133. However, there are two further grounds specified in Article 34(2)(b), however, which may be raised by the court's own initiative:

(a) where the subject-matter of the dispute is not capable of settlement by arbitration under Armenian law; or
(b) where the arbitral award is in conflict with the public policy of Armenia.

1.134. Finally, if a challenge is successful the court making the decision may refer the arbitral award back to the arbitral tribunal for re-consideration or it may vary the award or set the award aside in whole or in part.

[2] Waiver of Right to Challenge

1.135. A party who wishes to challenge an award for a serious irregularity should not only act promptly in making his application to the court but should also take care not to lose his right to object. Article 4(1) of the Act provides that a party who knows that any provision of the Act from which the parties may derogate or any requirement under the arbitration agreement has not been complied with and yet proceeds with the arbitration without stating his objection to such non-compliance without undue delay or, if a time-limit is provided therefor, within such period of time, shall be deemed to have waived his right to object.

1.136. It means, in practice, that the objection, which should be recorded in writing and sent to the tribunal and the other parties, should not only identify the irregularity, but also make clear that any further participation in the arbitration will be without prejudice to the objection.

In addition, if all parties are non-Armenian, they can waive their right to initiate proceedings to set aside the award, before or after the dispute arose. This waiver must expressly refer to setting aside proceedings; a general waiver to invoke 'any legal recourse' will not be sufficient in that respect.

Finally, parties cannot validly expand the scope of the judicial review beyond the grounds for annulment which are provided under the Armenian Arbitration Act.

§2.09 RECOGNITION AND ENFORCEMENT OF THE ARBITRAL AWARD

[A] Enforcement of Domestic Awards

1.137. Under the Armenian Arbitration Act, the court will grant judgment on an award made in Armenia unless:

- the appeal period to set the award aside has not yet elapsed;
- there is a pending appeal, application to set aside the order, or declaration of invalidity;[49]
- the award has been set aside.

1.138. The Act contains in Articles 35 and 36 a system that is almost identical to Articles IV – VI of the New York Convention for the enforcement of an arbitral award 'irrespective of the country in which it was made'.

1.139. The court cannot refuse recognition of the domestic award unless:

(a) one of the parties was not qualified to enter into the arbitration agreement;
(b) the arbitration agreement is invalid under the law elected by the parties or, failing any indication in that regard, under the laws of Armenia;
(c) the party against whom the award is invoked was not given proper notice of the appointment of an arbitrator or of the arbitration proceedings or was otherwise unable to present his case;
(d) the award deals with a dispute not contemplated by or not falling within the terms of the arbitration agreement, or it contains decisions on matters beyond the scope of the agreement;

---

49. However, the Act does not clearly prohibit the party to appeal the order.

(e) the mode of appointment of arbitrators or the applicable arbitration procedure was not observed.

1.140. Additionally, the court can set aside an award if:

(a) the subject-matter of the dispute is not capable of settlement by arbitration under the laws of Armenia;
(b) the recognition or enforcement of the award would be contrary to the public policy of Armenia.

[B] Enforcement of Foreign Arbitral Awards

[1] Introduction to Recognition and Enforcement

1.141. Today court practice in enforcing foreign arbitral awards in Armenia is greatly influenced by both objective and subjective factors. The inexperience of the court in these matters is only due to unfamiliarity with the application of international legal instruments, but also to the fact that the Armenian judiciary is still not used to applying adversarial procedure, which seems more essential in dealing with matters connected to international arbitration as opposed to usual domestic litigation.[50]

Cases connected with the enforcement of foreign arbitral awards in judicial practice in Armenia are not numerous. At the same time, due to established traditions, the form and contents of these court decisions are substantially different as compared with judicial practice in the majority of western legal systems. One of the main differences is that the section concerning the decision's reasoning is usually very short.

Armenia as a signatory to the New York Convention applies its provisions for recognition and enforcement of arbitral awards irrespective of the country in which it was made subject to the limited grounds[51] for refusing recognition and enforcement which are identical to those found in Article V of the Convention.

1.142. Thus, Armenia recognizes arbitral awards as binding and enforce them in accordance with domestic procedures, subject to the conditions laid down in the New York Convention. Armenia does not impose discriminatory conditions, higher fees or charges for recognition and enforcement of the Convention awards compared to domestic awards. The practical result will be that the award may be enforced in the same manner as a judgment of the court to the same effect.

1.143. To obtain recognition and enforcement of a New York Convention award the party applying for recognition and enforcement is required to attach a duly authenticated original award or a duly certified copy and the original arbitration agreement or

---

50. Unfortunately, the great majority of judges who have to deal with cases of enforcement of foreign arbitral awards are not knowledgeable in foreign languages, which excludes them from foreign sources of information about the practice of international arbitration.
51. Article 36 of the Armenian Arbitration Act.

a duly certified copy. Where the arbitral award or arbitration agreement is not in Armenian, the applicant is required to produce a certified official translation.

1.144. In the case of enforcement of a foreign arbitral award, Armenian law has no statutory limitation periods applicable to actions for enforcement, however, the case law provides a one-year time limit for certain actions for enforcement of the awards.[52]

Finally, consideration must also be given to whether the agreement between the parties contains or gives rise to any agreed contractual limitation on the period for enforcement.

[2]   Interim Awards

1.145. Articles 35 and 36 do not specify the types of award the Act covers and whether it applies to interim awards or other forms of provisional relief. However, there is no strict statutory requirement of 'finality'.[53] There may be circumstances in which an interim award will be treated as binding and enforceable pursuant to the Act and the New York Convention, notwithstanding that it is not the final award in the arbitration.[54]

[3]   Grounds for Refusing Recognition and Enforcement

1.146. The provisions of the Armenian Arbitration Act (Articles 35 and 36) governing recognition and enforcement of awards are almost identical to those set out in the New York Convention. It is to be noted that the Act does not permit any review on the merits of an award and the grounds provided by Article 36 are the only on which recognition and enforcement may be refused.

1.147. It is important that under the Armenian Arbitration Act (which follows the New York Convention) shifts the burden of proof from the party seeking enforcement of the arbitral award to the party against whom enforcement is sought. Thus, once the party seeking enforcement has provided evidence of a binding award and the arbitration agreement, the onus is then on the resisting party to provide the existence of one or more of the limited grounds set out in Article 36 of the Act.

1.148. However, Article 36(1)(b) further provides that the court may refuse enforcement of its own motion if the subject matter of the dispute cannot be settled by arbitration under the law, or if the award is contrary to the public policy of Armenia.

1.149. Thus, the court has no discretion but to recognize and enforce a New York Convention award unless the party opposing the enforcement proves one or more of the grounds specified in the Armenian Arbitration Act. These grounds of refusal are exhaustive, and if no one of the grounds is present the award will be enforced.

---

52. EKD/0024/16/12 2015 (Interpipe Ukraine case).
53. Most domestic arbitration rules permit the issuance interim awards in this sense of the term.
54. It is to be noted that that an interim award, if final, is subject to a set aside action upon issuance.

Recognition and enforcement of an arbitral award may be refused if the opposing party proves that:

(a) the parties to the arbitration agreement were under some incapacity or the said agreement is not valid;
(b) the party against whom the award was invoked was not given proper notice of the appointment of the arbitrator or of the arbitral proceedings or was otherwise unable to present his case;
(c) the arbitral award exceeds the scope of the terms of submission to arbitration (ultra petita), i.e., where the tribunal has gone beyond the terms of the arbitration agreement upon which its jurisdiction is based;
(d) the arbitral procedure or the composition of the arbitral tribunal did not comply with the agreement between the parties, or failing such agreement, was not in accordance with the lex arbitri;
(e) the award has not yet become binding on the parties or has been set aside or suspended by in the place of the award.

1.150. 36(1)(b) of the Armenian Arbitration Act contains two further grounds for refusal of recognition and enforcement, which may be raised either by the party resisting recognition and enforcement or by the court of its own motion. Those two grounds are that:

(a) the subject-matter of the dispute is not capable of settlement by arbitration under the laws of Armenia (e.g., divorce, bankruptcy etc.);
(b) the recognition or enforcement of the award would be contrary to the public policy of Armenia.

The recourse to public policy is justified that the non-conformity with basic principles of morality, religious and justice is evident.[55]

1.151. The court in Armenia has taken the position that these grounds for refusal of recognition and enforcement of arbitral awards must be interpreted and applied in the same way as by courts everywhere.

[4] Procedures for Recognition

1.152. Article 35(1) of the Armenian Arbitration Act provides that the party relying on an award or applying for its enforcement shall supply the original award or a copy thereof to the court. If the award is not made in Armenia, the court requests the party to supply a notarized translation.

1.153. The application to recognize an award must be supported by written evidence (usually in the form of a witness statement) which exhibits the arbitration agreement

---

55. *See* A. Haikyantc, 'Civil Code of Armenia', Yerevan, 2011, pp. 458–469.

and the award. The court, the Court of General Jurisdiction of Kentron and Nork-Marash Administrative District, will decide the recognition application by holding a hearing.

The application for the enforcement of an award including the execution statement to be submitted to the Compulsory Enforcement Office of Armenia costs 8,000 Armenian Drams (USD 17).

§2.10 INVESTOR-STATE ARBITRATION

[A] General Overview

1.154. Armenia officially welcomes and promotes foreign investment and the country has received respectable rankings on some global indexes measuring business climate (e.g., the World Bank's Doing Business). In January 2015, the enactments on the EAEU trading bloc went into effect, creating a single economic market of 176 million people covering Armenia, Belarus, Kazakhstan, Kyrgyzstan, and Russia. Armenia's investment and trade policy is relatively open; foreign companies are entitled by law to the same treatment as Armenian companies. However, Armenia's investment climate poses several challenges: corruption remains a significant obstacle and access to justice is limited.

1.155. Five sectors of the economy – telecommunication, utilities, transport, warehousing and banking – have been the major drivers for foreign investment. Armenia also attracts foreign investment in the mining industry as a key contributor to the national economy. Ore concentrates and metals accounted for just over half of Armenia's exports in last years, solidifying their status as the country's most important export products.

1.156. There are only inflows of foreign direct investment. The Central Bank of Armenia recently reported that FDI in Armenia increased by USD 50.55 Million in the third quarter of 2016. FDI averaged USD 78.87 Million from 1993 until 2016, reaching an all time high of USD 425.89 Million in the fourth quarter of 2008 and a record low of – USD 67.53 Million in the fourth quarter of 2014.

1.157. The Government of Armenia, particularly, the Prime Minister's office, is solely responsible for negotiating investment agreements. Other ministries or state sector agencies must also approve the investment agreements. Major asset-privatization agreements with foreign investors must be submitted to the Armenian parliament for approval. The Civil Code of Armenia of 1998 is the main legal framework for governing the investment agreements. The Foreign Investments Act of 1996 is also applicable with other secondary legislative instruments.

1.158. Since 1992, Armenia has signed forty-two bilateral investment treaties, most of which are in force. Armenia's first BIT was signed with China in 1992. The BIT regime provides the most fundamental substantive protections including national treatment, MFN treatment and fair and equitable treatment.

1.159. EU relations with Armenia are based on the EU-Armenia Partnership and Cooperation Agreement, which provides for wide-ranging cooperation in the areas of political dialogue, trade, investment, economy, law-making and culture. The PCA with Armenia was signed in April 1996 and entered into force at the beginning of July 1999.

1.160. Armenia is also a party to the Convention on the Protection of the Rights of the Investor signed in the City of Moscow on 28 March 1997. The Convention provides certain guarantees for the protection of rights of the investors and has a number of features e.g., it applies to investors both of the state signatories to the Convention and to the investor of non-Member States as well.

1.161. Although Armenia does recognize the importance of foreign investments in the domestic economy, there is no an investment treaty programme in place. However, Armenia continues to expand its network of bilateral and regional investment treaties.

1.162. In 2014, Armenia adopted the 2104–2025 Long Term Development Strategy, which, among other things, aims to promote foreign investment in Armenia. In 2013, the Government of Armenia also endorsed a sophisticated business environment improvement programme. The Development Foundation of Armenia (DFA) is a national authority for investment, export and tourism promotion. The DFA facilitates the establishment and the development of foreign companies in Armenia by promoting business and supporting investors throughout the investment life cycle.

1.163. The Foreign Investments Act of 1996 provides guarantees for foreign investors to invest and operate in Armenia as well as certain standards of protection. The Act provides that the foreign investor and its investment are to be treated no less favourably than a national of Armenia. Foreign investments are not subject to any specific admission or registration requirements. However, there are certain sectors, which require a licence to operate; if the investor intends to operate in the mining sector, he is required by the Licences Act of 2001 to obtain an operation license.

1.164. It is to be noted that the Land Code also prohibits foreign investors to acquire real estate in Armenia. However, the investor can establish a subsidiary company to purchase real estate. Non-resident individuals are taxed only on their Armenian-source income. Non-resident entities are subject to Armenian tax only on income that has a source in Armenia. Non-resident entities are those whose existence is established under foreign law.

1.165. The Ministry of Economic Development and Investments of Armenia is responsible for development of investment policy, which aims to develop a good and modern investment climate, which provides opportunities for all investors: public and private, large and small, and foreign and domestic.

1.166. A foreign investor wishing to file a request for arbitration would name the Government of Armenia, the Prime Minister's Office as the respondent. There is no pre-determined ministry or state agency responsible for disputes arising out investment treaties. In case of an actual investment dispute, the Government of Armenia will establish a team, which would be authorized by a relevant governmental decree to represent Armenia. It is likely that the Ministry of Justice would be mandated to act on behalf of the Government of Armenia.

1.167. There is no Armenian model BIT in the sense of an official, published model BIT. However, most of Armenia's treaties have been drafted in accordance with a new Russian model. The model contains some of the most fundamental substantive protections, including national treatment, MFN treatment and fair and equitable treatment.

1.168. All international agreements signed by Armenia are deposited with the Ministry of Foreign Affairs, which is also responsible for archiving all international documents including diplomatic correspondence. Parliamentary ratification records are published in the Official Gazette, which is also available online.

1.169. Armenian BITs usually contain a very broad definition of 'investment', recognizing that current investments take a wide variety of forms. The examples cover investments that are owned or controlled by nationals or companies of one of the BIT partners made in the territory of the other. Investments can be made either directly or indirectly through one or more subsidiaries, including those of third countries. Control is not specifically defined in BITs. Ownership of over 50% of the voting stock of a company would normally convey control but in many cases the requirement could be satisfied by less than that proportion. The samples also provide a non-exclusive list of assets, claims and rights that constitute investment. These include both tangible and intangible property, interests in a company or its assets, a claim to money or performance having economic value, and associated with an investment, intellectual property rights, and any right conferred by law or contract (such as government-issued licenses and permits).

1.170. Armenian BITs typically do not use the term 'investor', instead, referring to 'nationals' and 'companies'. The definition of 'company' is broad in order to cover virtually any type of legal entity, including any corporation, company, association, or other entity that is organized under the laws and regulations of a party. The term 'national' means a natural person who is a national of a party under its own laws.

1.171. Armenia's BITs set forth the substantive rights and protections that contracting parties are obligated to accord to foreign investors and their investments. The general obligations undertaken by Armenia in many BITs often require providing investments with:

(1) fair and equitable treatment;
(2) full protection and security; and
(3) national treatment and most favoured nation treatment.

1.172. In addition, Armenia agrees in many BITs not to engage in conduct that restricts by arbitrary or discriminatory measures the operation, maintenance, expansion, or disposition of investments, and to provide effective means of asserting claims and enforcing rights so as to resolve any disputes arising out of the investments. Importantly, very few BITs also require Armenia to observe all obligations undertaken toward investor.

1.173. Armenian BITs also typically define the conditions under which property may be expropriated. For example, one BIT formulation provides that property may only be expropriated for a public purpose, in a non-discriminatory manner, according to due process of law, and upon payment of prompt, adequate and effective compensation. Compensation is usually defined as equivalent to the fair market value of the expropriated investment immediately before the action was taken or became known.

1.174. All BITs provide dispute settlement procedures. Some BITs require that a case be submitted in the first instance to the local courts, but if the case has not been resolved within a certain period of time, then, the investor may pursue an international arbitration. Other BITs allow the investor to file an international arbitration after a specified consultation period has elapsed, generally, three and six months. The investor is afforded a wide choice of submitting the dispute to international arbitration:

- the International Centre for Settlement of Investment Disputes (ICSID);
- an ad hoc tribunal established under the Arbitration Rules of the UNCITRAL;
- an arbitral proceeding under the Arbitration Institute of the Stockholm Chamber of Commerce (SCC).

1.175. There is no established practice regarding confidentiality issues that may arise during the course of investment arbitration proceedings. However, the Government of Armenia certainly would require confidentiality in investment arbitration.

1.176. Armenia has been a party to one known investment treaty arbitration: *Global Gold Mining LLC v. Armenia* ICSID Case No. ARB/07/7, under the US-Armenia BIT, where on 9 May 2008, settlement agreed by the parties and proceeding discontinued at their request. The case was related to the mining industry.

APPENDIX 1 LIST OF BILATERAL INVESTMENT TREATIES THE COUNTRY HAS RATIFIED

Country	Date of Signature	Date of Entry into Force
United Kingdom of Great Britain and Northern Ireland	27.05.1993	11.07.1996
Kirghizstan	04.07.1994	27.10.1995
Romania	20.09.1994	24.12.1995
Cyprus	18.01.1995	01.07.1996
Bulgaria	10.04.1995	27.03.1996
Islamic Republic of Iran	06.05.1995	26.02.1997
Iraq	07.11.1992	
France	04.11.1995	21.06.1997
Georgia	04.06.1996	18.02.1997
Egypt	09.01.1996	01.03.2006
Canada	08.05.1997	29.03.1999
Israel	19.01.2000	25.06.2003
Belarus	26.05.2001	02.10.2002
Russian Federation	15.09.2001	08.02.2006
Austria	17.10.2001	01.02.2003
Tajikistan	02.04.2002	18.11.2002
Qatar	22.04.2002	08.10.2007
Oriental Republic of Uruguay	06.05.2002	15.12.2013
India	23.05.2003	30.05.2006
Finland	05.10.2004	20.03.2007
Kingdom of the Netherlands	10.06.2005	01.08.2006
Lithuania	25.04.2006	16.03.2007
Argentina	16.04.1993	20.12.1994
Belgium	07.06.2001	19.12.2003
China	04.07.1992	18.03.1995
Germany	21.12.1995	04.08.2000
Italy	23.07.1998	13.01.2003
Kazakhstan	06.11.2006	01.08.2010
Kuwait	25.06.2010	04.09.2013
Latvia	07.10.2005	21.04.2007
Lebanon	01.05.1995	01.10.1998
Spain	26.10.1990	28.11.1991
Sweden	08.02.2006	01.05.2008
Switzerland	19.11.1998	04.11.2002

Chapter 2: Armenia

Country	Date of Signature	Date of Entry into Force
Turkmenistan	19.03.1996	
Ukraine	07.10.1994	07.03.1996
United Arab Emirates	20.04.2002	
United States of America	23.09.1992	29.03.1996
Vietnam	01.02.1993	28.04.1993

Bibliography

Books and Journals

D. Sutton and J. Gill, *Russel on Arbitration*, 22nd edition, 2003.

P. Fouchard, E. Gaillard, B. Goldman, *International Commercial Arbitration*, Savage and Gaillard (ed), 1999.

H. Fox and P. Webb, *The Law of State Immunity*, Oxford International Law Library, 3rd edition, 2015.

A. Haikyantc, *Civil Code of the Republic of Armenia*, Yerevan, 2011.

R. Petrosyan, *Civil Procedural Code of the Republic of Armenia*, Yerevan, 2012.

М. Богуславский, *Международное частное право. 2-е издание, переработанное и дополненное: Международные отношения*, 1994.

Commercial Law of Armenia: Assessment by the EBRD, June 2012, the EBRD Report.

Improving the Efficiency of Arbitration Agreements and Awards: 40 Years of Application of the New York Convention, ICCA Congress Series No. 9, Paris 1998.

How to Arbitrate in Armenia, the Commercial Law and Economic Regulation project conducted by Bearing Point and the International Law Institute, 2012.

Alan S. Rau, *Everything You Really Need to Know About 'Separability' in Seventeen Simple Propositions*, March, 2003, American Review of International Arbitration.

Legislation

Constitution of Armenia (amended) dated on 6 December 2015.

Judicial Code of Armenia No. 135 dated 7 April 2007.

Code of Civil Procedure of Armenia No. 247 dated 7 August 1998.

Civil Code of Armenia No. 239 dated 28 July 1998.

Land Code of Armenia No. 185 dated on 15 June 2001.

Advocacy Act of Armenia No. 29 dated 13 January 2005.

Commercial Arbitration Act of Armenia No. 55 dated 22 January 2007.

Law on Compulsory Enforcement of Judicial Acts of Armenia No. 221 dated 5 May 1998.

Licences Act of Armenia No. 193 dated on 8 August 2001.

Cases

Yukos International UK B.V. v. the Ministry of Justice of Armenia, Rosneft ojsc, EAKD/1494/02/10.
Mantashanner v. Prometey Bank, EAKD1910/02/13.
Pacific China Holdings Ltd (In Liquidation) v. Grand Pacific Holdings Ltd, CACV 136 of 2011 and FAM 18 of 2012.
Interpipe Ukraine (EKD/0024/16/12 2015).
Global Gold Mining LLC v. Armenia, ICSID Case No. ARB/07/7.

CHAPTER 3
Azerbaijan

Gunduz Karimov

LIST OF ABBREVIATIONS

Arbitration Law	Law on International Commercial Arbitration of the Republic of Azerbaijan dated 18 November 1999
AZN	National currency – Azerbaijan manat
CIS	Commonwealth of Independent States
Civil Code	Civil Code of the Republic of Azerbaijan dated 1 September 2000
Civil Procedure Code	Civil Procedure Code of the Republic of Azerbaijan dated 1 September 2000
Constitution of Azerbaijan	Constitution of the Republic of Azerbaijan dated 12 November 1995
Geneva Convention	European Convention on International Commercial Arbitration, 1961, Geneva
ICAC	International Commercial Arbitration Court under Baku Arbitration Mediation Centre
ICSID Convention	Convention on the Settlement of Investment Disputes between States and Nationals of other States, 1965, Washington
New York Convention	United Nations Convention on the Recognition and Enforcement of Foreign Arbitral Awards, 1958, New York
PIL Law	Law on Private International Law of the Azerbaijan Republic dated 6 June 2000
PSA	Production Sharing Agreement
Regulations of ICAC	Regulations of the Azerbaijan International Commercial Arbitration dated 11 November 2003
UNCITRAL	United Nations Commission on International Trade Law

UNCITRAL Model Law	UNCITRAL Model Law on International Commercial Arbitration 1985
USD	United State Dollar
USSR	Union of Soviet Socialist Republics

§3.01 GENERAL INTRODUCTION

[A] Historical Development of the Legal System

1.1. Since ancient times, the country of Azerbaijan has gone through some major historic events which have had an enormous influence not only on its religious and political systems but, to some extent, on the legal system as well. Initially Christian in some parts when Azerbaijan was part of the Caucasus Albania, and Zoroastrian in other parts, Azerbaijan was invaded by the Arabian Khalifa in a mid-seventh century and forced to adopt Islam as its main religion. This had a significant influence on the cultural, political and legal system during that period. Basically, starting from mid-seventh century, the court adjudication system of the country was based on sharia law.[1]

From the fifteenth to seventeenth centuries, sharia law played an important role in the legal thinking of Azerbaijani leaders. It was further developed in the sixteenth century, when Shah Ismayil Khatai united Azerbaijan under the Safavid dynasty. The 'Qanun-name' (code of laws) of Uzun Hasan, his predecessor, was the first legislative act intended to regulate tax, culture, crime and trade issues. The 'Qanun-name' applied to the same relations during the ruling of the Safavid dynasty. Later, Shah Tahmasib I adopted the Decree 'On providing customs privileges to certain merchants'.

Between 1813 and 1828, after numerous wars, Russia and Iran divided the disintegrated Azerbaijan between them. As a part of the Russian empire and then the Soviet Union for around 200 years, Azerbaijan adopted a different alphabet and absorbed European culture, but kept Islam. As a consequence of the Russian invasion, Azerbaijan's legal system was adapted to the legal system of Russia, which, in turn, was based on the German legal system. The Azerbaijani legal system is therefore based on the pandect system.

1.2. In 1918, Azerbaijan gained independence by becoming the first democratic republic among the Muslim countries. Though its status as a republic remained for only twenty-three months until Communist Russia regained its position in Azerbaijan in 1920, it contributed very positive changes to the legal system. At the beginning of 1919, the Ministry of Justice, which acted as Trial Chamber of Azerbaijan, created a special commission for the preparation of draft laws relating to the judicial system.[2]

---

1. Masuma Melikova & Xayyam Ismayilov, State and Law of Azerbaijan in Ancient and Middle-Age Times (in Azeri), p. 7 (Baku, Hugug Adabiyyati, 2001). Xayyam Ismayilov, History of State and Law of Azerbaijan (in Azeri), p. 121 (Baki, Nurlar, 2006).
2. Supreme Court of Azerbaijan, overview of Azerbaijan judicial history, http://www.supremecourt.gov.az/ru/static/view/27 (accessed 26 June 2017).

1.3. The period from 1921 through to 1991 resulted in massive changes in the legislation, as several Soviet-type laws, decrees and regulations were enacted. With regard to arbitration called 'arbitrazh', the Council of Ministers of the Soviet Union approved the Decree 'On further improvement of the organization and activity of bodies of state arbitrazh', establishing arbitrazh under the Council of Ministers of the USSR, state arbitration at the Council of Ministers of the Union and autonomous republics, and state arbitration at territorial, regional and city executive committees. It further declared that this system would be the single system governing arbitration in the USSR.[3]

1.4. Later, following the Perestroika movement, on 16 April 1988, Decree No. 490 'On Regulations on the State Arbitrazh of the USSR' and the rules for consideration of economic disputes state arbitration were adopted. In May of the same year, the Regulations of Azerbaijan State Arbitrazh bodies extended the jurisdiction of arbitrazh courts to cooperatives (first commercial firms) and enterprises.[4]

1.5. The country gained its next stage of independence in 1991 by adopting the Act of State Sovereignty of the Republic of Azerbaijan on 18 October 1991. In 1995, Azerbaijan adopted the Constitution of Republic of Azerbaijan on the referendum. The Constitution established the system of division of power: presidential, legislative and judicial branches of government.[5]

1.6. In 2001, Azerbaijani joined the Council of Europe. Since then it has improved and modified its judicial and legal system by adopting new laws following trends in the legal systems of various European countries. However, the law still remains statutory. Court precedents are not considered sources of law, with the exception of the judgments of the European Court of Human Rights.

[B] The Legal Profession

1.7. The legal profession has been popular among Azerbaijani youth for a number of political and social reasons. While in Soviet time, young graduates of the law school wished to become prosecutors, this trend changed in the mid-2000s, with more and more candidates sitting the bar exam in Azerbaijan and abroad. Commercial law has become popular due to the growth of the economy.

1.8. The Azerbaijani system has its own particular institution for lawyers. The Bar Association in Azerbaijan is an independent legal institution which professionally operates in the area of legal protection. External legal services in Azerbaijan are provided by advocates, who are registered members of the Azerbaijani bar, and unregistered lawyers employed in local and international law firms. The protection that advocates enjoy under the Azerbaijani Law on Advocates and Legal Services (the 'Advocates Law') does not extend to unregistered lawyers. There is no law that

---

3. Masuma Melikova, *supra* n. 1, pp. 213 and 573.
4. *Ibid.*, p. 626.
5. Constitution of the Republic of Azerbaijan, Arts 82 and 83 (I) (12 November 1995).

explicitly governs the activities of unregistered lawyers. The Advocates Law regulates advocates and their legal services.

In order to be licensed as an advocate, a lawyer has to meet the following requirements:

(a) have a higher legal education;
(b) have three years' legal experience, such as legal training, advocate assistant or adjunct professor in the university;
(c) successfully pass the 'Qualification Commission's exam' consisting of an oral interview and a written test; and
(d) successfully pass the mandatory training in the educational and scientific institution of the relevant executive authority.

There are around 800 practising advocates in Azerbaijan.

[C] Sources of Arbitration Law

1.9. According to Vidadi Mirkamal, 'fundamentally, sources of arbitration law regulate the scope of relations on the international level through conventions, to which Azerbaijan is a party, and on a national level by enacting relevant laws.'[6] The arbitration practice in Azerbaijan is relatively new and is constantly undergoing development. Unlike the other countries of the former Soviet Union, such as Russia or Ukraine, Azerbaijan did not have an arbitration practice during Soviet time. However, after the flow of foreign investments into the country, and due to the fact that the legal system of the country was still in flux, foreign investors chose arbitration as a dispute resolution mechanism in privatization and investment agreements between them and the State/state entities in Azerbaijan. This later resulted in the arbitration proceedings, and all of them were conducted outside Azerbaijan. Further, as a country which declared its adherence to international business law standards, in the late 1990s, Azerbaijan acceded to major international instruments and adopted internal laws.

1.10. The adoption of many laws, as well as declaring the Constitution of the Republic of Azerbaijan a fundamental act, has lead to a strictly systematized law system. Sources and types of law are listed in the Constitution of the Republic of Azerbaijan. The Constitution itemizes the following:

(a) the Constitution itself;
(b) acts adopted by referendum;
(c) laws;
(d) orders;
(e) decrees of Cabinet of Ministers of the Republic of Azerbaijan; and
(f) normative acts of central executive power bodies.[7]

---

6. Vidadi Mirkamal, International Arbitration Process (in Azeri), p. 29 (2011).
7. Constitution of the Republic of Azerbaijan, Art. 148 (12 November 1995).

Moreover, Article 149 of the Constitution sets the hierarchy of legal acts. First of all, the Constitution and acts adopted by referendum have priority. Further, laws should not contradict the Constitution. Below these, decrees of the President of the Republic of Azerbaijan should not contradict the Constitution and laws of the Republic of Azerbaijan. Decrees of the Cabinet of Ministers of the Republic of Azerbaijan should not contradict the Constitution, the laws of the Republic of Azerbaijan and decrees of the President of the Republic of Azerbaijan. Finally, at the bottom of the hierarchy, are acts of central bodies of executive power. Such acts should not contradict the Constitution, the laws of the Republic of Azerbaijan, decrees of the President of the Republic of Azerbaijan and decrees of Cabinet of Ministers of the Republic of Azerbaijan.

1.11. In addition, the Law on Normative Legal Acts, adopted on 21 December 2010, provides a solution for collisions in law. The Law ensures the priority of the Constitution over acts adopted by referendum; in turn, acts passed via referendum prevail over laws in case of any conflict between them. The most important point is that if any provisions of civil relations contradict the Civil Code of Azerbaijan, the latter prevails in all cases.[8]

1.12. The first experience and real commitment to arbitration in Azerbaijan arose on 20 September 1994 with the signing of an Agreement on the development and production sharing of the 'Azeri', 'Chirag' and 'Guneshli' (deep-water) fields in the Azerbaijan sector of the Caspian Sea ('Contract of the Century').[9] The dispute resolution venue of the Contract of the Century is the London Court of International Arbitration.

1.13. The governing arbitration statute in Azerbaijan is the Law of the Republic of Azerbaijan On International Commercial Arbitration (the 'Arbitration Law'), dated 18 November 1999. Azerbaijan is a party to the New York Convention on Recognition and Enforcement of Foreign Arbitral Awards (New York Convention), dated 10 June 1958. The Republic of Azerbaijan ratified the New York Convention on 29 February 2000. Moreover, Azerbaijan did not make any reservations against this Convention. One could argue that the arbitration clause in the Contract of the Century was not enforceable for Azerbaijan until 29 February 2000 when Azerbaijan ratified the New York Convention. It actually appears that this argument has some merit.

1.14. Azerbaijani authors view the UNCITRAL Model Law on International Commercial Arbitration of 1985 (the 'Model Law') as an incentive to ensure uniformity of different pieces of the legislation in the arbitration process.[10] This conclusion could be derived from the mere fact that the Arbitration Law of 18 November 1999 is purely based on the UNCITRAL Model Law.

---

8. Law on Normative Legal Acts, Art. 2.5 (21 December 2010).
9. Azerbaijan, http://www.azerbaijans.com/content_772_en.html (accessed 2 February 2016).
10. Vidadi Mirkamal, *supra* n. 6, p. 39.

This major law, i.e., the Arbitration Law, consists of thirty-six articles. Thus, the Arbitration Law provides that the parties to a contractual dispute are entitled to international arbitration of their dispute only if: (a) the parties to a contractual dispute are located in different jurisdictions; and (b) the parties agreed to arbitrate the dispute outside of their respective jurisdictions or the place of the performance of the parties' obligations under the contract is outside their respective jurisdictions. Arbitrations with an international element, for example, if the place of business of one of the parties is abroad or the subject matter of the dispute is related to another country, can be subject to the Arbitration Law.[11]

1.15. It would be fair to say that Azerbaijani law distinguishes international arbitration from domestic arbitration and currently recognizes international arbitration only as a dispute resolution mechanism between foreign and Azerbaijani companies.

In other words, section 1(1)(3) of the Arbitration Law permits 'international commercial arbitration' where:

(a) The parties to an arbitration agreement have, at the time of the conclusion of that agreement, their places of business in different states.
(b) One of the following places is situated outside the state in which parties have their places of business:
   (i) the place of arbitration is specified in the arbitration agreement;
   (ii) any place where a substantial part of the obligations of the commercial relationship is to be performed or the place with which the subject matter of the dispute is most closely connected; or
   (iii) the parties have expressly agreed that the subject matter of the arbitration agreement relates to more than one country.[12]

1.16. Additionally, the Civil Procedure Code of the Republic of Azerbaijani (the 'CPC'), effective 1 September 2000, contains provisions on the enforcement and recognition of foreign arbitral awards. Two chapters of the CPC contain articles on the recognition and enforcement of foreign arbitral awards (Chapters 47 and 50).

1.17. As stated above, the Arbitration Law governs only international arbitration, whereas domestic arbitration between local entities is not defined under Azerbaijani law. The CPC permits parties to settle disputes through ad hoc arbitration with the consent of the parties. It does not, however, provide for any mechanism or procedure for such arbitration. To date, there has been no domestic arbitration between local entities.

---

11. Law on International Commercial Arbitration of the Republic of Azerbaijan, Art. 1 (18 November 1999).
12. Law on International Commercial Arbitration of the Republic of Azerbaijan, Art. 2 (18 November 1999).

[D] International Legal Framework, Supremacy of International Law

1.18. Within the international framework, Azerbaijan has ratified a number of international documents. Accordingly, the State attempts to make relevant amendments to the national law system, taking into account the nature of such documents. By becoming a member of the World Bank, Azerbaijan signed the Washington Convention on the Settlement of the Investment Disputes between States and Nationals of Other States (entered into force on 18 October 1992), which provides for arbitration in the International Centre for Settlement of Investment Disputes ('ICSID'). ICSID aims to provide the balance between the interests of investors and host States. More than 550 such cases have been administered by ICSID as of 2015.[13] Since the ratification of the latter, ICSID has considered three cases where Azerbaijan appeared as a respondent to the host state for the respective investors (discussed below).

1.19. Being part of Europe, Azerbaijan has ratified the European Convention on Foreign Commercial Arbitration (the 'Geneva Convention'), dated 21 April 1961.[14] The Geneva Convention's applicability to international commercial arbitration is announced in the title and preamble. Unlike the New York Convention, it was not the intention of the drafters of the Convention that its scope be universal. The Convention originated from consultations on East-West trade held within the Economic Commission for Europe; hence, the inclusion of 'European' in the title. However, its application does not only relate to arbitration between a Western and an Eastern European party, e.g., Cuba and Burkina Faso are parties to the Convention.[15] The remarkable part of the Geneva Convention is contained in Article II, which extends the conclusion of arbitration agreements to 'legal persons of public law' as well.[16] This, in turn, eliminates the prohibition of state bodies to enter arbitration. However, the European Convention is without prejudice to matters of recognition and enforcement of arbitral awards.

1.20. Another very advanced document is the Energy Charter Treaty, the fundamental aim of which is 'to strengthen the rule of law on energy issues, by creating a level playing field of rules to be observed by all participating governments, thereby mitigating risks associated with energy-related investment and trade'.[17] Azerbaijan ratified the Treaty in 1997.

1.21. As part of the Commonwealth of Independent States (CIS), Azerbaijan has ratified a number of CIS documents, such as the Agreement On Mutual Enforcement of Economic, Commercial and Arbitral Decisions in Commonwealth Independence States, which describes the procedure of recognizing and enforcing decisions issued by

---

13. World Bank, https://icsid.worldbank.org/en/ (accessed 26 June 2017).
14. United Nations Treaty Collection, https://treaties.un.org/pages/ViewDetails.aspx?src=TREATY&mtdsg_no=XXII-2&chapter=22&lang=en (accessed 26 June 2017).
15. United Nations Treaty Collection, https://treaties.un.org/pages/ViewDetails.aspx?src=TREATY&mtdsg_no=XXII-2&chapter=22&lang=en (accessed 26 June 2017).
16. European Convention on International Commercial Arbitration, Art. II (21 April 1961).
17. International Energy Charter, http://www.energycharter.org/process/overview/ (accessed 26 June 2017).

economic and commercial courts, as well as by arbitral awards. Azerbaijan became a party to this Agreement on 4 December 1998.

1.22. The Minsk Convention On Legal Assistance in Civil, Family Relations and Criminal Cases, dated 22 March 1993 (effective for Azerbaijan since 1996); and the Agreement On The Settlement Of Disputes Relating To The Implementation Of Economic Activity, signed in Kiev, 20 March 1992 (effective for Azerbaijan since 2002) are among the CIS acts dealing with international dispute resolution. Dealing with international documents creates a system of the joint cooperation for the unification of acts and standards.

1.23. The Constitution of Azerbaijan adheres to the monism concept[18] by stating that in the event of a contradiction between Azerbaijan's international treaties and Azerbaijani laws (except the Constitution and acts adopted by referendum), provisions of international agreements shall prevail.[19]

1.24. What is more, under the monist model, Azerbaijan ensures the doctrine of incorporation of international law, which means the automatic application of rules to the national legal system. The possibility to apply the provisions of the international treaties is envisaged in Article 148 of the Constitution, which stipulates that the international agreements to which the Republic of Azerbaijan is a party constitute an integral part of the legislation system of the Republic of Azerbaijan.

[E]   Available Dispute Resolution Mechanisms

1.25. Besides arbitration, mediation and conciliation are possible dispute resolution mechanisms in the local judicial system to resolve cases among the parties. Also, judges in the state courts may volunteer to arbitrate the parties' adverse positions. As an interesting factor, a 'mediation bench' appeared recently in the yard of the Baku Court of Appeals which was intended to prompt the parties to solve their disputes amicably.

1.26. After establishing the International Commercial Arbitration Court ('ICAC') in 2003 (discussed in more details below), later, in April 2008, in order to expand alternative dispute resolution mechanisms, the Baku Mediation Centre was created following the successful history of the establishment of the ICAC in Azerbaijan.

Within a year of existence, the Baku Mediation Centre considered sixty-three cases, seven of them with a foreign element.[20] In 2009, Baku hosted two international seminars: one with the Arbitration Institute of the Stockholm Chamber of Commerce and one with the Venice National and International Arbitration Court. The themes of

---

18. Ziyafat Asgarov, Elshad Nasirov, Mubariz Ismayilov, Constitution of the Republic of Azerbaijan and Fundamental Basis of Law, p. 43 (Qapp-Poliqraf, 2005).
19. Constitution of the Republic of Azerbaijan, Art. 151 (12 November 1995).
20. Legal reforms support centre, report by Alida Makhmudova, 'The Development of International Commercial Arbitration in Azerbaijan', available at http://www.legalreform.az/news.php?readmore = 34 (accessed 26 June 2017).

the seminars were devoted to the disadvantages of the legislation and law enforcement practice, including the lack of a system of communication and coordination between the court (which relevant court is the Supreme Court of Azerbaijan) and arbitration, a complication that affects the development of the arbitration procedure in Azerbaijan.[21]

The Azerbaijan Arbitration and Mediation Centre continues to operate successfully in the field of international cooperation. So far, there are signed cooperation agreements with institutions in arbitration and mediation from more than twenty countries.[22]

[F]　**Judicial System**

1.27. As briefly mentioned above, Azerbaijan is a traditional civil law jurisdiction. As a part of the Russian empire for 200 years, the country followed the changes and developments in the whole jurisdiction. The Soviet era was no different. Starting from 1922, the then-Azerbaijan Soviet Social Republic fully integrated into the Soviet judicial system, which was characterized by introducing the so-called basics of the Soviet legislation (called '*основы советского законодательства*' in Russian) at the federal level, leaving the members of the Union limited rights to form their own national legislation and judiciary.[23]

Formation of the national justice system took a long time. Due to limited human resources, the Soviets allowed lawyers to become judges at the age of 25. Until September 2016, the independent Azerbaijan granted this right from the age of 30. After the amendments to the Constitution in September 2016, there are no major requirements for the candidates to judges, other than higher education and five years of legal experience.

In 1959, the Presidium of the USSR liquidated the Ministry of Justice and transferred all management functions to the Supreme Court of Azerbaijan. Later, in 1970, a new Decree established the Ministry of Justice and from then a new stage in national justice history began.[24]

1.28. After the declaration of independency in 1991, the state commenced reforms in different areas, including the judicial system. The laws 'On Constitutional Court', 'Courts and Judges', 'Prosecution', 'Police', 'Operative-search activity' and other laws were radically different from previous ones. Codified laws, such as the Civil and Civil Procedural Code, Criminal Code, Labour Code and others, marked new rules and procedures.[25] The country has also accepted some European concepts, such as the prohibition against prosecutors interfering in the commercial activity of entrepreneurs and legal entities. In contrast, this right still exists with prosecutions in Russia.

---

21. Ibid.
22. Azerbaijan Arbitration and Mediation Centre, http://www.arbitr.az/news.php?readmore=137 (accessed 26 June 2017).
23. Ziyafat Asgarov, *supra* n. 18, p. 48 (Qapp-Poliqraf, 2005).
24. Supreme Court of Azerbaijan, http://www.supremecourt.gov.az/static/view/27 (accessed 26 June 2017).
25. The Court System of Azerbaijan, http://courts.gov.az/judicial_power/ (accessed 26 June 2017).

1.29. In a relatively short period, the relevant changes were executed in the judicial branch accordingly. Today, the Azerbaijani judicial system has a three-tiered scheme:

(a) trial courts;
(b) regional appellate courts; and
(c) the Supreme Court of the Republic of Azerbaijan.

Trial courts are the courts of first instance and include district courts, administrative-economic courts and courts on grave crimes.

Jurisdictional issues between district courts and administrative-economic courts differ depending on the basis of subjects of the dispute, as well as on the nature of a dispute.[26]

Administrative-economic courts have jurisdiction over economic disputes arising from civil, administrative and other legal relationships between legal entities, as well as between legal entities and individuals engaged in entrepreneurial activities without forming a legal entity.[27]

In civil, family, labour and housing disputes where at least one party is a natural person and he/she does not have a status of an individual entrepreneur, these disputes should be considered by district courts.[28]

In accordance with the Law on Courts and Judges, dated 10 June 1997, the courts on grave crimes consider grave criminal actions.[29]

Appellate courts and the Supreme Court have civil, criminal, administrative-economic and military panels.[30]

1.30. Decisions of the first instance court may be appealed to appellate courts; if the party is not satisfied at this stage, he/she can refer to the Supreme Court. Decisions of the civil and administrative-economic panels of the Supreme Court may be revised in an additional appeal to the Plenum of the Supreme Court of the Republic of Azerbaijan. The decisions of the Supreme Court are final and binding.[31]

1.31. The Constitutional Court of Azerbaijan plays a separate and important role in the judicial system. Its authority includes settling disputes between the three branches of power and interpreting the Constitution and other legal acts.[32]

The Supreme Court's administrative-economic panel is the leading institution in Azerbaijan by virtue of the controlling power over arbitration and the level of sophistication of the judges.

---

26. Civil Procedure Code of the Republic of Azerbaijan, Art. 24.2 (1 September 2000).
27. *Ibid.*, Art. 26.1 (1 September 2000).
28. *Ibid.*, Art. 25.1 (1 September 2000).
29. Law on Courts and Judges of Azerbaijan, Art. 25 (10 June 1997).
30. Gunduz Karimov, Doing Business in Azerbaijan, p. 104 (Baker & McKenzie, 2015).
31. Civil Procedure Code of the Republic of Azerbaijan, Art. 422 (1 September 2000).
32. Constitution of the Republic of Azerbaijan, Art. 130 (12 November 1995).

[G] Arbitration Institutions

1.32. Although Azerbaijan adopted Arbitration Law in 1999, no local institution was effective in Azerbaijan until 2003 when as a part of a project on 'The creation and organization of the arbitration courts in Azerbaijan' funded by USAID, a legal entity was established. Shortly after, in November of 2003, this legal entity established the ICAC as an independent legal organization (currently the only authority on international arbitration in the country).[33] The ICAC became the first professional arbitration institution intended to resolve international commercial disputes in Azerbaijan.

1.33. The ICAC has its own official regulations, arbitrators and schedule of fees. Its members are selected on a competitive basis. The ICAC operates its own Presidium and Secretariat. Moreover, for the proper functioning of the institution, the ICAC keeps its building stocked with the necessary technical equipment.[34]

1.34. Pursuant to its Charter, the ICAC considers commercial disputes within 120 days. The Charter provides for three grounds for a dispute to be brought before the arbitral tribunal: independent arbitration agreement, arbitral clause and arbitral note. The registration fee, which is paid at the time of filing of statement of claim, is USD 300 and is not refundable. The arbitration fee shall be paid in advance and in the national currency (AZN (manats)) if the claim amount is expressed in AZN manats. If the claim amount is expressed in any foreign currency, the arbitration fee shall be paid in USD. The ICAC also provides for special rules governing the diminution of the arbitration fee, its apportionment, extra expenses and payment procedure.[35]

1.35. Arbitration proceedings generally take place in Baku – the capital of Azerbaijan. The parties can, however, agree to hold the hearing at any place within the country. In this case, the payment of additional expenses incurred in connection with the arbitration held outside Baku is borne by the disputing parties. The parties also have the opportunity to select any arbitrator, which guarantees a professional and skilled person in dispute resolution. Further, although arbitration proceedings are typically conducted in the Azerbaijani language, the parties may also agree to conduct the hearing in another language.[36]

[H] Sovereign Immunity and International Arbitration

1.36. Commonly used, independence is understood as there being equality among the other members of the international community and superiority within each member's boundaries. Thus, based on this, generally two types of relations are present:

(a) relations of common nature; and

---

33. Azərbaycan Beynəlxalq Kommersiya Arbitraj Məhkəməsi, http://www.arbitr.az/bkam/BKAM_haqqinda.html (26 June 2017).
34. *Ibid.*
35. *Ibid.*
36. Regulations of Azerbaijan International Commercial Arbitration, Art. 12.

(b) special relations.

Special relations purport to the equality of the parties and party autonomy as fundamental conditions contrary to the relations of common nature where the state appears as a leading subject of relations.[37] In civil theory the state gains the status of special (sui generis) subject of civil law.[38]

1.37. Under Article 5.2 of the Civil Code, civil legal relationships of state authorities and self-governing with other persons shall also be regulated by civil legislation, provided that the law does not specify otherwise. It further provides in Article 43.2 that Azerbaijan participates in civil relationships in the same manner as other legal entities. In such cases, Azerbaijan exerts control using bodies which are not legal entities.[39] Therefore, Azerbaijan may submit itself to the jurisdiction of foreign courts or to a foreign law as any other Azerbaijani entity may do in a foreign trade transaction.

1.38. Specifically, Azerbaijani legislation, by enacting the Private International Law (PIL) Law, confirmed the position of the limitation of sovereign immunity. Pursuant to the PIL Law, it is applicable to civil transactions with foreign element to which the state is a party, and the subject matter of transactions is not connected with the performance of state's sovereign functions. The nature of such legal transactions shall be determined in accordance with the reasons they were concluded for.[40]

1.39. Azerbaijan deviated from the Soviet protection methods on the basis of sovereign immunity defence by entering into various production sharing agreements ('PSAs') with the global oil companies. On 20 November 1994, the Republic of Azerbaijan signed a major PSA, the Contract of the Century (as discussed above). Due to its tremendous importance in the development of the 'Azeri', 'Chirag' and 'Guneshli' deep-water oil fields, the Contract of the Century has been drafted on 400 pages and in 4 languages. A total of 13 companies (Amoco, BP, McDermott, Unocal, SOCAR, LukOil, Statoil, Exxon, TPAO, Pennzoil, Itochu, Ramco and Delta) from eight countries (Azerbaijan, USA, Great Britain, Russia, Turkey, Norway, Japan and Saudi Arabia) have participated in signing the Contract of the Century.[41]

In those PSAs, the State Oil Company of the Azerbaijan Republic ('SOCAR') represents the Government. SOCAR is fully owned by the state but is a commercial party to all PSAs concluded in Azerbaijan, in the capacity of a business organization. As an illustration, in accordance with the provisions of the 'Agreement on The Exploration, Development and Production Sharing for the Shah Deniz Prospective Area in the Azerbaijan Sector of The Caspian Sea', disputes arising between the parties (not

---

37. Zavar Gafarov, Ataxan Abilov, Private International Law, pp. 117–118 (Qanun, 2nd ed. 2007).
38. Sabir Allahverdiyev, Civil Law of the Republic of Azerbaijan, p. 630, vol. 1, General Section (1st Book) (Digesta, 2003).
39. Civil Code of the Republic of Azerbaijan, Art. 43.2 (1 September 2000).
40. Law on Private International Law, Art. 16 (6 June 2000).
41. President of Azerbaijan, http://en.president.az/azerbaijan/contract (accessed 26 June 2017).

all) shall be referred to arbitration, the procedure of which is illustrated in the appendix.[42]

SOCAR encountered very few disputes during its commercial activity as a party to the PSAs. In 2003, a dispute between Frontera Resources Corporation and SOCAR was arbitrated by the Swedish Arbitration Institute under the rules of UNCITRAL. Frontera Resources Corporation acted as a claimant. The arbitral panel found that the halting of exports of crude oil from the Kursangi & Karabagli oil fields in the Republic of Azerbaijan was in violation of the Agreement on Rehabilitation, Exploration, Development and Production Sharing between SOCAR, Frontera, Delta/Hess and SOCAR Oil Affiliate.[43] Certainly, the nature of the relations are unique, but this shows the approach of the Republic of Azerbaijan toward limiting its state sovereignty in the commercial contracts.[44] Such limitation means that the state no longer acts as a subject of administrative relations. It would rather act as a legal entity with the 'abandoned immunity'.

§3.02 THE ARBITRATION AGREEMENT

[A] Introduction

1.40. Given that Azerbaijani arbitration legislation follows the language of the UNCITRAL Model Law on International Commercial Arbitration, a general definition of an arbitration agreement in Azerbaijani does not differ from the international conventions and the legislation of the other CIS countries. Basically, the national legislation reflects Article II(2) of the New York Convention with some additions to the possible forms of exchange due to the new technologies.

[B] Validity of the Arbitration Agreement

1.41. An agreement by the parties to refer to arbitration of any disputes arising from contractual obligations or differences between them creates the basis of modern international commercial arbitration.[45]

The validity of an arbitration agreement is an important issue because it can be considered as a substantive issue and procedural.[46] The court or arbitral tribunal rule on the validity of arbitration clauses. However, the substance lies in the elements which define the validity.

---

42. Production Sharing Agreement on The Exploration, Development and Production Sharing for the Shah Deniz Prospective Area in the Azerbaijan Sector of The Caspian Sea at http://www.bp.com/content/dam/bp-country/en_az/pdf/legalagreements/PSAs/SD-PSA.pdf (accessed 26 June 2017).
43. PlainSite, http://www.plainsite.org/dockets/jme2i9rw/new-york-southern-district-court/frontera-resources-azerbaijan-corporation-v-state-oil-company-of-the-azerbaijan-republic/ (accessed 26 June 2017).
44. Zavar Gafarov, *supra* n. 37, p. 119.
45. Alan Redfern, Martin Hunter, Nigel Blackaby & Constantine Partasides, Law and Practice of International Commercial Arbitration, §1-08 (UK, Kluwer Law International 2004).
46. Habil Isgandarli, International Arbitration, p. 38 (Qanunvericilik və şərhlər, 2004).

Provided that the Azerbaijani Arbitration Law does not specify the elements of validity, the current view according to Vidadi Mirkamal is that the essentials of arbitration agreement are as follows:

(a) form of arbitration agreement;
(b) capacity of the parties; and
(c) intention of the parties.[47]

1.42. An arbitration agreement appears first as a contract, and thus the requirements governing validity of contracts should also apply to it. The Civil Code provides that an agreement concluded in violation of the conditions stipulated in the Civil Code shall be invalid. A disputed agreement shall also be deemed an invalid agreement due to its consideration by the court as invalid. In the event there is a dispute in respect of an agreement, the agreement shall be invalid from the moment of its conclusion. The right to dispute belongs to the interested party. An invalid agreement shall not result in any legal consequences, except for consequences relating to its invalidity. Such agreement shall be invalid from the moment of its conclusion.[48] An agreement concluded by a legal entity in contradiction to the purposes of its activity as set forth in its charter or agreement concluded by a legal entity not having a special permit (licence) required for undertaking a certain activity, may, in the event it has been proven that the other party participating in the agreement knew or should have known of its illegality, be considered by court as invalid upon a claim of that legal entity, its founders or body supervising the legal entity's activity.[49]

1.43. The application of the above-cited provisions of the Civil Code is somewhat limited in the Arbitration Law. Thus, Article 354.2 of the Civil Code provides that claims on finding a disputed agreement invalid or on applying the consequences of its invalidity may be brought within one year of the date of the end of such coercion or threat that influenced the conclusion of the agreement or the date when the claimant became aware or should have become aware of the circumstances giving ground to the invalidity of the agreement. The one-year period is generally considered very short for disputing arbitration agreements as it may take several months before the parties actually resort to arbitration after they have entered into commercial relations.

1.44. The second distinctive nature of an arbitration agreement lies in its procedural character. An arbitration agreement does not substantially regulate an issue; instead it serves as a reference for further substantive agreements. At the same time, procedurally, its regulation falls out of compliance with relevant civil procedure codes. It is subject to sui generis source, a national law or international convention.[50]

---

47. Vidadi Mirkamal, Arbitration Agreement, p. 50 (Baki-2005).
48. Civil Code of the Republic of Azerbaijan, Art. 337 (1 September 2000).
49. Civil Code of the Republic of Azerbaijan, Art. 349 (1 September 2000).
50. Vidadi Mirkamal, *supra* n. 47, p. 20 (Baki-2005).

1.45. Further, the Azerbaijani national legislation has adopted the concept of written form and included this into the Arbitration Law, which requires in Article 7 that 'an arbitration agreement is concluded in written form'.

An agreement is considered as concluded in writing if it is reflected in a document signed by the parties, or is signed by a letter, teletype, telegraph or other means of electronic communication to which the other party does not object. An arbitration clause in the contract shall be deemed an arbitration agreement, if the contract is concluded in writing and reference is made to the clause forming part of the contract.[51]

The Regulations of the ICAC set out that an arbitration agreement must be made in written form and contain a more detailed definition of this concept. According to Article 2 of the Regulations, an arbitration agreement is in the written form if:

(a) the agreement 'is contained in a document signed by the parties';
(b) the agreement is 'contained ... in an exchange of letters, telex, telegrams or other means of telecommunication which provide a record of the agreement'; and
(c) the agreement 'refers to a contract concluded in writing and becomes a part of that contract'.[52]

Azerbaijani courts follow the 'current worldwide attitude [that] is toward the enforcement of arbitration agreement in most cases having the evidence of [an] agreement'.[53]

[C] Capacity of the Parties to Conclude an Arbitration Agreement

1.46. According to Article 43.1 of the Azerbaijani Civil Code, a legal entity is a specially established organization which has passed state registration as provided by law, owns its own property, bears liability for its obligations to the extent of its property, has the right to acquire and exercise property and personal non-property rights on its own behalf, is liable for its obligations and acts as a plaintiff or a defendant in court. A legal entity has its own balance sheet. Article 44.1 of the Civil Code concerns the capacity of legal entities. Under that Article, a legal entity has civil rights and bears civil liability from the moment of state registration.[54]

1.47. The capacity of natural persons is linked to their national law or, if they are stateless or a refugee, the law of domicile or residence applies.[55] Under Article 442.1 of the CPC, procedural legal capacity of foreign legal entities is defined by the law of the country, where the legal entity was established, regulating the establishment of that legal entity.

---

51. Law on International Commercial Arbitration of the Republic of Azerbaijan, Art. 7 (18 November 1999).
52. Regulations of Azerbaijan International Commercial Arbitration Art. 2(2).
53. Gary Born, International Commercial Arbitration, p. 14 (Wolters Kluwer, 2nd. ed., 2001).
54. Civil Code of the Republic of Azerbaijan, Art. 44 (eff. 1 September 2000).
55. Zavar Gafarov, *supra* n. 37, pp. 86–87 (Qanun, 2nd ed. 2007).

1.48. The PIL Law also covers the issues of law applicable to legal entities. Article 12 regulates this by defining the status of a legal entity, its civil legal capacity, the establishment and termination of its activities, and its organizational and legal forms. Furthermore, under Article 11 of the PIL Law, the law of the jurisdiction in which an entity is established determines the legal capacity of that entity. Although, under the PIL, a company's legal status is governed by the law of the jurisdiction where such company is incorporated, the rights and obligations of the parties to the agreements involving foreign investors, including agreements on the creation of Azerbaijani joint ventures with foreign participation, however, are not always required to be governed by Azerbaijani law. Under the PIL, the law of any foreign jurisdiction can govern a contract with an Azerbaijani entity if the contract also involves an entity with a 'foreign element'.

[D]   Intention of the Parties in Arbitration

1.49. A more uncertain issue is the intention of the parties. Azerbaijani judges (as well as arbitrators) as continental system lawyers, may consider parties' intentions during interpretation of a disputed arbitration agreements. For example, Article 404 of the Civil Code can be used by analogy. It provides that in the course of the contract terms' interpretation, the court shall take into consideration not only the actual meaning of the words and phrases thereof, but the essence of the parties' will, and shall compare the actual meaning of the contract with its other terms and conditions. Given the above, all relevant circumstances, including the preceding negotiations, the practice of relationship established between the parties, the parties' business traditions and the consequent behaviour of the parties, shall be taken into account.[56]

1.50. Given that Azerbaijani court decisions are not publicly available, drawing practical conclusions about the applicability of these provisions appears difficult. Nevertheless, it can be the key to answer a number of the undefined questions within the arbitration agreement. There are many factors that should be well thought-out while stating the intention, such as the nationality of the parties; the place where the contract is signed, paid and performed; the enforceability of the award; and the availability to challenge the award in the court. As the practice of the national arbitration institution has no experience with regard to enforcement of intention issues, it is difficult to make a conclusion about the ICAC approach to such a matter.

[E]   The Doctrine of Separability

1.51. The validity of the arbitration agreement/clause remains separate from the main contract. A good basis for this point has been transformed into a specific theory called

---

56. Idris Asgarov, Comments to Civil Code of the Republic of Azerbaijan, p. 612 (Qanun, 2011).

the 'doctrine of separability'. This doctrine stresses the severability of the arbitration agreement and provides an independent view on it.[57]

The principle that an arbitration clause is independent from the main contract is widely accepted in theory and practice.[58]

1.52. The doctrine of separability has been reflected in most international documents, such as the UNCITRAL Rules and UNCITRAL Model Law on International Commercial Arbitration, as well as in Arbitration Law.

It can be concluded that there are always two significant issues:

(a) the validity of the main contract; and
(b) the validity of the arbitration clause.

1.53. The Arbitration Law enshrines the separability doctrine in the following manner:

> [An a]rbitration clause which forms part of a contract shall be treated as an agreement independent of the other terms of the contract. A decision by the arbitral tribunal that the contract is null and void shall not entail ipso jure the invalidity of the arbitration clause.[59]

In addition, the Civil Code of Azerbaijan contains Article 352, which states that the invalidity of part of a transaction does not result in the invalidity of the other parts of the contract, provided the contract could be concluded without including the invalid part into the transaction. This article can serve as a strong argument in support of the doctrine of separability.

[F] **Arbitrability**

[1] Disputes Capable of Settlement by Arbitration

1.54. If the parties concluded the arbitration agreement, it means they intend to refer any type of their disputes to the arbitration court. Usually most of the clauses state 'any dispute arisen from the contract shall be referred to arbitration'.[60]

The arbitrability of disputes in Azerbaijan lies within the requirements of the Civil Procedure Code, the Arbitration Law and the New York Convention. Although the laws of Azerbaijan recognize both local and foreign (international) arbitration, Azerbaijan adopted no legislative act regulating domestic arbitration. Azerbaijani state does not generally encourage arbitration, either locally or internationally as a dispute resolution mechanism between Azerbaijani companies. Thus there does not exist an operational domestic arbitration forum in the Republic of Azerbaijan. Therefore, the

---

57. Vidadi Mirkamal, *supra* n. 47, pp. 86–87 (Baki-2005).
58. *Ibid.*, p. 87 (Baki-2005).
59. Law on International Commercial Arbitration of the Republic of Azerbaijan, Art. 16(1) (18 November 1999).
60. Vidadi Mirkamal, *supra* n. 6, p. 118 (2011).

provisions of the Azerbaijani legislation related to the arbitration demand interpretation in light of the above-mentioned circumstances.

1.55. The Civil Procedure Code provides that it shall apply throughout the territory of the Republic of Azerbaijan, irrespective of any circumstances.[61] Under Article 6, justice in respect of civil cases and economic disputes fall under sole jurisdiction of courts, and they carry in the manner provided for by the law. The Civil Procedure Code provides in Article 26.1 that regardless of the organizational or other affiliation or the subordination, economic disputes in the civil proceedings between legal entities, persons carrying out entrepreneurial activities without establishing a legal entity and who obtained entrepreneur status in the manner provided for by the law, fall under the jurisdiction of administrative-economic courts. Article 28 of the Civil Procedure Code provides that except as otherwise provided by the intergovernmental agreements, international agreements or the parties' agreement, cases with the participation of foreigners, stateless persons and foreign legal entities (emphasis added – GK) fall under jurisdiction of the courts.

The persons to whom this provision applies are foreigners, stateless persons and foreign legal entities.[62] It defines those cases with participation of these persons fall under jurisdiction of the courts, unless: (i) intergovernmental agreements; (ii) international agreements; and (iii) the agreement of the parties provide otherwise. Together with Articles 3.2 and 26 of the Civil Procedure Code, this provision prohibits two Azerbaijani legal entities to refer their disputes to foreign arbitration.

Corporate disputes and their arbitrability is a hot topic in contemporary international Arbitration Law. Unfortunately, as the local legislation does not invoke any reference to 'corporate disputes', difficulties arise with the application of national arbitration tools to such type of disputes. Considering the experience of the CIS countries, it appears that some countries have had the same problems, but they have at least started to develop a position as cases are submitted to the courts. The most recent and popular book on Corporate Law in Azerbaijan is also silent about the arbitrability of corporate disputes (See, for example, Emin Karimov, Azerbaijan Law of Corporations, Baki, Qanun Neshriyyati, 2014).

[2] Disputes Not Capable of Settlement by Arbitration

1.56. Arbitrability of international disputes (i.e., where one of the parties is an Azerbaijani person and the counterpart is foreign) has limits to the exclusive jurisdiction issues. The position of the Azerbaijani legislation defines that national courts have exclusive jurisdiction over certain types of disputes. In particular, in accordance with the CPC, the exclusive jurisdiction covers: disputes relating to property rights over immovable property, including claims in respect of lease or pledge of the property, if such property is located in Azerbaijan; disputes relating to the invalidation of

---

61. Civil Procedure Code of the Republic of Azerbaijan, Art. 2 (1 September 2000).
62. Civil Procedure Code of the Republic of Azerbaijan, Art. 28 (1 September 2000).

decisions, recognition of validity or invalidity, or dissolution of a legal entity whose legal address is in the Republic of Azerbaijan; disputes relating to claims in respect of recognition of validity of patents, marks or other rights, if registration or application for registration of these rights has been carried out in the Republic of Azerbaijan and a judgment or order on compulsory enforcement measures was requested and enforced in the Republic of Azerbaijan; disputes relating to claims against carriers arising out of transportation contracts; disputes relating to termination of marriage between the citizens of the Republic of Azerbaijan with foreigners or stateless persons – if both spouses have their place of residence in Azerbaijan.[63]

The list of matters which fall under exclusive jurisdiction is exhaustive, thus any other dispute which does not fall within the above scope seems to be arbitrable, i.e., can be subject to arbitration proceedings.

[3]   Special Provisions on Consumer and Labour Disputes

1.57. In accordance with Article 26 of the Law On Consumers' Rights Protection of the Republic of Azerbaijan dated 15 September 1995, all the rights of consumers should be protected through courts.[64] Given that the arbitration practice in general is developing in Azerbaijan, it seems too early to talk about the arbitration of consumer disputes.

1.58. The Labour Code of the Republic of Azerbaijan dated 1 February 1999, contains useful provisions on the arbitration of labour disputes. The Labour Code stipulates the notion of collective labour disputes, which are disputes based on claims made by employees or agencies of trade unions, employers, their associations or the relevant executive authorities relating to the conclusion, amendment and execution of collective agreements and other labour, social and economic issues.[65] This type of arbitration is ad hoc. In case of the affirmative decision by both parties to initiate labour arbitration, it should be organized not later than five working days after such decision was made in the form of an agreement. Moreover, the regulation, place of the dispute, terms and technical assistance to the arbitration can be determined by the parties subject to mutual consent.[66]

1.59. The decision rendered by arbitral tribunal has a binding effect if the parties previously agreed on this. In this case, the dispute shall be deemed finally settled and continuation of the dispute is not allowed.[67] The Labour Code does not envisage similar mechanism for individual labour disputes. In summary, Azerbaijani law provides arbitration-type adjudication only for collective labour disputes.

---

63. Civil Procedure Code of the Republic of Azerbaijan, Art. 444 (1 September 2000).
64. Law On Consumers' Rights Protection of the Republic of Azerbaijan, Art. 26 (19 September 1995).
65. The Labour Code of the Republic of Azerbaijan, Art. 3(15) (1 February 1999).
66. The Labour Code of the Republic of Azerbaijan, Art. 268(2) (1 February 1999).
67. *Ibid.*, Art. 268(6).

[G] Effect of Arbitration Agreement on Third Parties

1.60. Neither the Arbitration Law nor any other legal source provides guidelines on the effect of an arbitration agreement on third parties. However, in international practice, situations exist when an arbitration agreement extends to non-signatories. Extension of the arbitration agreement to non-signatories is 'the expression most used, [and] covers situations in which a party's standing to sue or to be sued under an arbitration agreement is considered, whenever this party is not named or designated in the arbitration agreement or the contract containing it, or appears to have signed the arbitration agreement or the contract on behalf of a third party'.[68]

1.61. Traditionally there are five doctrines through which a non-signatory can be bound by arbitration agreements entered into by others: (1) assumption; (2) agency; (3) estoppel; (4) veil piercing; and (5) incorporation by reference. And in one separate category is included the 'group of companies doctrine' because of its application in various jurisdictions.[69] The ICAC has adopted none of these theories. Given the conservative approach taken by judges in state courts, one could conclude, by analogy, that the same approach would be taken by the Azerbaijani arbitrators.

[H] Termination of Arbitration Agreement

1.62. The Arbitration Law does not list the grounds for termination, as generally the arbitration clause relates to the main contract and subsequently depends on its performance. The Civil Code proclaims the principle of good faith in the execution of obligations. The principle demands each party to perform its obligations in the proper time and place, in case of the absence of relevant provisions on time and place, in accordance with the customs of business circulation.[70] Moreover, the Code ensures that the termination of the contract is subject to the parties' agreement. Additionally, any agreement on amending or terminating a contract shall be made in the same form as the contract.[71]

Thus, if the parties fulfil their obligations properly, the contract is terminated, and such termination can be a ground for dissolving an arbitration agreement. In case of any amendment to the arbitration agreement the parties must follow the same structure or system used to conclude the main contract. Any breach of the contract may be a ground for termination of the arbitration clause.[72]

---

68. Andrea M. Steingruber, Consent in International Arbitration, p. 298 (UK, Oxford University Press, 2012).
69. Bernard Hanotiau, Complex Arbitrations: Multiparty, Multicontract, Multi-issue and Class Actions, The Hague, p. 4 (Kluwer Law International, 2005).
70. Civil Code of the Republic of Azerbaijan, Art. 425 (1 September 2000).
71. Civil Code of the Republic of Azerbaijan, Arts 421.1 and 423.1 (1 September 2000).
72. Vidadi Mirkamal, *supra* n. 6, p. 121 (2011).

[I] Drafting Arbitration Clauses

1.63. An objective necessity requires an arbitration agreement to be very precise. Generally, when drafting an arbitration clause, parties often have difficulties in defining their objectives.[73] The standard arbitration clauses recommended by various international arbitral organizations may help in this case.

The ICAC also provides its recommendations for drafting an arbitration clause:

> Disputes arising from the contract, or breach, termination or invalidation of thereof and which are referred to the International Commercial Arbitration Court shall be resolved by one or more arbitrators as final in accordance with the Regulations.[74]

§3.03 APPLICABLE LAW

[A] The Law Governing the Arbitration Agreement

1.64. The PIL Law contains the legal principles to be applied to civil legal relations with foreign elements. One of the main requirements is that 'Consent of the parties to determine the applicable law should be clearly stated or directly proceed from the terms of the contract and the circumstances of the case as a whole'.[75] Moreover, application of foreign law cannot be restricted due to its general character.[76] Party autonomy in this case also sets out criteria under which the relevant body determining the applicable law must take into consideration the intention of the parties.[77]

1.65. A 'foreign element' is generally understood to exist where: (i) the parties to the contract belong to different jurisdictions; (ii) the place of performance under the contract is outside Azerbaijan; or (iii) the contract's subject matter is located outside Azerbaijan.[78] Article 4 of the PIL Law restricts the application of any foreign legal provisions to any dispute with a foreign element which contradicts either the Constitution or acts adopted by referendum of the Republic of Azerbaijan. Additionally, Article 5(1) reads as follows: 'regardless of the law applicable to the present law, the mandatory rules of the Republic of Azerbaijan must be applied'.

1.66. Pursuant to the Arbitration Law, the arbitral tribunal shall decide the dispute in accordance with the rules of law chosen by the parties as applicable to the substance of the dispute.[79] The same article provides that in the absence of an explicit choice of

---

73. Habil Isgandarli, *supra* n. 46, p. 52 (Qanunvericilik və şərhlər, 2004).
74. Regulations of Azerbaijan International Commercial Arbitration, Final Provisions.
75. Law on International Private Law, Art. 1.3 (6 June 2000).
76. *Ibid.*, Art. 1.4.
77. Mehman Sultanov, Some Aspects of Development of Conflict of Rules in the Law on International Private Law, Azerbaijan Law Journal, 2 (6) (2003).
78. Zavar Gafarov, *supra* n. 37, pp 9–10 (Qanun, Baku, 2007).
79. Law on International Commercial Arbitration of the Republic of Azerbaijan, Art. 28(1) (18 November 1999).

law, any reference to any State's law or legal system shall be construed as directly referring to the substantive law of that State and not to its conflict of laws rules.[80]

1.67. The Regulations of the ICAC follow the above-described way of determining the governing law. Disputes referred to the ICAC shall be resolved on the basis of the applicable substantive law.[81]

1.68. In the event that, after applying the above two methods, the substantive law still cannot be determined by an arbitral court, both the Arbitration Law and the Regulations of the ICAC suggest a third method – the reference to the conflict of laws rules which the arbitral tribunal considers applicable.[82]

[B] The Law Governing the Arbitration (*Lex Arbitri*)

1.69. The existence of the autonomy of parties with regard to the regulation of the arbitration proceedings are determined by lex arbitri, which should be taken as the starting point. Lex arbitri applies to the law of the place where arbitration takes place and mainly covers the legislation relating to the arbitration proceedings. Thus, the national legislation regulates the issues of validity of arbitration agreements, the rules governing the arbitral proceedings and interim measures, etc. The Arbitration Law deals with some of these issues. The law provides for the procedural requirements to deal with the whole process.[83]

[C] Party Autonomy on Choice of Law Issues

1.70. Article 6 of the Civil Code sets out the principles of civil law regulation in the Republic of Azerbaijan. Equality of the subjects of civil relationships, autonomy of will of the subjects of civil relationships, freedom of property of the participants to civil turnover, the inviolability of property, freedom of contract and protection of civil rights by the courts are among the core principles of the Civil Code. In general, the Azerbaijan economy has been liberalized over the years which, in turn, has affected the harmonization of the legal instruments used to regulate economic relations. As a guiding principle, courts usually respect and strictly support party autonomy issues in civil contracts. Party autonomy on the choice of law issues is not an exception.

1.71. The PIL Law, in its Article 1.1, provides that legal norms should be applied to civil law relationships with a foreign element. Pursuant to Article 1.2 of the PIL Law, the law applicable to civil law relationships with a foreign element is determined, along with this Law, on the basis of other legislative acts, by international agreements to which the Republic of Azerbaijan is a party and commonly accepted international

---

80. Law on International Commercial Arbitration of the Republic of Azerbaijan, Art. 28(1) (18 November 1999).
81. Regulations of International Commercial Arbitration Court of Azerbaijan, Art. 15(1).
82. Law on International Commercial Arbitration of the Republic of Azerbaijan, Art. 28(2), Regulations of International Commercial Arbitration Court of Azerbaijan, Art. 15(1).
83. Vidadi Mirkamal, *supra* n. 6, pp. 136–137 (2011).

customs, as well as by the agreement of the parties (emphasis added – GK). Further, the PIL Law understands the principle of party autonomy as: '[the] consent of the parties to determine the applicable law should be clearly stated or directly proceed from the terms of the contract and the circumstances of the case as a whole'.[84] This wholly covers the law governing the arbitration agreement, which is usually the law agreed between the parties. This results in the application of party autonomy principle in arbitration.[85]

1.72. Article 19(1) of Arbitration Law provides that 'subject to the provisions of this Law, the parties are free to agree on the procedure to be followed by the arbitral tribunal in conducting the proceedings'.[86]

This is basically a reflection of the above-mentioned principle and reiterates the same concept contained in the corresponding article of the UNCITRAL Model Law. The freedom to choose the procedure is one of the advantages provided by the arbitration process. Therefore, it is of the utmost importance that the parties refer to their intention to arbitrate, as they can coordinate the process themselves in the manner they see fit. For example, the parties can decide on the time and place, choice of arbitrators, law applicable to arbitration, and the schedule of meetings and hearings.[87]

1.73. Although the parties are able to choose the law governing the process, the place and many other issues, there are certain limitations. The parties cannot choose provisions that breach the rules of the state the law of which has been selected as governing law.

As referred to earlier, not all claims or disputes are arbitrable. Party autonomy is a sensitive category in these cases.

[D] Restrictions on Party Autonomy

1.74. As mentioned above, the PIL Law follows the widely accepted civil law principles of party autonomy on choice of law issues. Thus, it provides that agreements and other actions of the parties intending to make certain relations subject to another law by disregarding the rules determined by the applicable law shall be considered invalid. In that case, the law of the relevant state whose application is determined in accordance with the law shall apply. Further, irrespective of the law to be applied in accordance with the PIL Law, the mandatory norms of the Republic of Azerbaijan regulating the relevant relationships shall apply and any choice of law which violates such mandatory norms is invalid.[88]

---

84. Law on International Private Law, Art. 1.3 (6 June 2000).
85. Alan Redfern, *supra* n. 45, at § 1-60.
86. Law on International Commercial Arbitration of the Republic of Azerbaijan, Art. 19(1) (18 November 1999).
87. Vidadi Mirkamal, *supra* n. 6, p. 124 (2011).
88. Zavar Gafarov, *supra* n. 37, p. 77.

[E] **National Public Policy**

1.75. Various laws regulating the rules of international private law reflect the concept of public policy in different forms. Thus, the CPC says that the rogatory letters issued by foreign courts shall not be executed if the execution is contrary to the sovereignty of the Republic of Azerbaijan and the general principles of law. The CPC further states that the recognition and enforcement of decisions of foreign courts and arbitral tribunals is possible if they are not contrary to the legislation of the Republic of Azerbaijan and legal order and are mutually guaranteed. The compulsory enforcement of the decisions can be waived on similar grounds.[89]

1.76. Article 4 of the PIL Law states that foreign legal provisions are not applied in the Republic of Azerbaijan if they contradict either the Constitution or acts adopted by referendum. Under Article 34 of the Arbitration Law, the arbitral decision can be annulled by the Supreme Court if it determines that the arbitral decision is contrary to the Constitution of the Republic of Azerbaijan. Finally, under Article 157 of the Family Code of the Republic of Azerbaijan, dated 28 December 1999, the legal provisions of the foreign family law are not applied if such application would contradict the fundamental principles of legal order of the Republic of Azerbaijan. In this event, the Azerbaijani law would be applied. However, although the laws provide for the theoretical basis of public policy arguments, up to date there have not been publicly available cases or disputes considered in Azerbaijan where a party invoked public policy considerations.

§3.04 THE PROCEDURE BEFORE THE ARBITRATION TRIBUNAL

[A] **General Principles of Arbitration Procedure (Party Autonomy, Speed, Impartiality, Etc.)**

1.77. The Constitution of the Republic of Azerbaijan proclaims the principle of equality before the law and courts in its Article 25.[90] In addition, the CPC states that justice in civil and commercial cases shall be provided through the principle of equality before the law and the courts.[91] Thus, this principle has two sides of application: substantive and procedural.[92]

1.78. The Constitutional Court of the Republic in its Decision on Interpretation of Article 373 of the Civil Procedural Code, dated 27 December 2001 noted that 'the principle of equality before the law and courts should be provided by the same rules, procedural forms and warranties to the parties in civil cases. Each person shall have an opportunity to defend himself in the process by the same means'.[93]

---

89. Civil Procedure Code of the Republic of Azerbaijan, Art. 465 (1 September 2000).
90. Constitution of the Republic of Azerbaijan, Art. 25(I) (12 November 1995).
91. Civil Procedural Code of the Republic of Azerbaijan, Art. 8.1 (1 September 2000).
92. Vafaddin Ibayev, The International Civil Process, p. 41 (Baku, Elm, 2005).
93. Decision of the Constitutional Court of Azerbaijan Republic regarding the interpretation of Art. 373 of the Civil Procedural Code, dated 27 December 2001 // Decisions of the Constitutional Court of Azerbaijan Republic, p. 178 (1998–2003).

1.79. It is apparent that the principle has a very distinct basis in procedural issues and thus, the same may be applicable to the execution of the principle in arbitration proceedings. Article 18 of the Law on Arbitration is the best illustration of the principle.

1.80. The second very crucial principle is impartiality of the arbitrators. Impartiality means the disposition to one of the parties (direct or indirect), lack of prejudice toward him and trust of the parties in decision-making processes.[94]

1.81. Notwithstanding that the Law on Arbitration is based on the Model Law, it does not contain provisions on disclosure, which play a huge role in the principle of impartiality. Alternatively, the Law on Arbitration contains articles regarding the process of challenging an arbitrator.

[B] Commencing and Conduct of the Arbitral Proceedings

1.82. The moment of commencement of the process is the date on which a request for that dispute to be referred to arbitration is received by the respondent, unless the parties agreed on other rules. Consideration of relevant documents belongs to the parties, as they can submit or may add a reference to the documents or other evidence.[95]

1.83. The Regulations of the ICAC describe the requisites of a statement of claim:

(a) the parties' names, addresses and other details;
(b) demand of the relief sought;
(c) grounds on which the ICAC's powers are based;
(d) the applicant's explanation of the factual and legal situation with reference to the claim based on evidence;
(e) cost of the claim;
(f) name of the arbitrator and the arbitrator chosen by the applicant, or the name of the arbitrator and the arbitrator to be appointed by the Chairman of the ICAC upon request;
(g) list of documents attached to the application; and
(h) the signature of the applicant.[96]

1.84. In case the applicant's statement of claim does not meet the requirements of Article 22, the Executive Secretary of the ICAC advises him to eliminate these gaps within one month. In other cases, the ICAC will rule on termination of the investigation.[97]

---

94. Vidadi Mirkamal, *supra* n. 6, p. 168.
95. Law on International Commercial Arbitration of the Republic of Azerbaijan, Art. 23(1) (18 November 1999).
96. Regulations of International Commercial Arbitration Court of Azerbaijan, Art. 22.
97. Regulations of International Commercial Arbitration Court of Azerbaijan, Art. 24.

1.85. When the arbitral tribunal is organized and arbitrator(s) are selected due to institutional rules, the arbitration tribunal examines all the documentation and, if needed, may require additional documents or other evidence.[98] Further, the legislation ensures the possibility of taking oral hearings or written proceedings.[99]

1.86. The decision to hold oral hearings must be delivered to parties and, taking into account their time, must provide parties with thirty days to prepare for the proceedings. Additional oral hearing may be conducted with due attention to capabilities of the parties.[100]

1.87. As a primary rule, the parties shall be given advance notice of any hearing or meeting of the arbitral tribunal for the purposes of inspecting goods or other property and documents. The parties' communication on each document or other information supplied must be continuous.[101]

1.88. If a party has been duly notified of the time and place of a hearing and does not attend without any good reason, then the tribunal shall not take this fact into account and shall continue the process. Still the party may ask for consideration of the dispute without its participation.[102]

§3.05 RECOGNITION AND ENFORCEMENT OF THE ARBITRAL AWARD

[A] Enforcement of Foreign Arbitral Awards

1.89. The general rule is that if there is no challenge to the arbitral award, it should be enforced, i.e., to have legal implications for the losing party. We pointed out above that the Arbitration Law does not distinguish between domestic and foreign arbitral awards. The Regulations of the ICAC state that the ICAC's binding awards are enforceable in accordance with the legislation of Azerbaijan.

1.90. Foreign arbitral awards are recognized and enforced based on the New York Convention and Arbitration Law. In addition, the CPC contains provisions related to the decisions of foreign courts and arbitral awards. In line with Article IV of New York Convention, the party that applies to seek the recognition and enforcement of an arbitral award shall submit:

(a) a duly authenticated original award or duly certified copy thereof; and
(b) the original agreement or a duly certified copy thereof.[103]

---

98. Regulations of International Commercial Arbitration Court of Azerbaijan, Art. 29.
99. Law on International Commercial Arbitration of the Republic of Azerbaijan, Art. 24(1) (18 November 1999).
100. Regulations of International Commercial Arbitration Court of Azerbaijan, Art. 30.
101. Law on International Commercial Arbitration of the Republic of Azerbaijan, Art. 24(3) (18 November 1999).
102. Regulations of International Commercial Arbitration Court of Azerbaijan, Art. 35.
103. New York Convention on the Recognition and Enforcement of Foreign Arbitral Awards, Art. IV(1) (1958).

Chapter 3: Azerbaijan §3.06[A]

1.91. Meanwhile, the Convention obliges that an award or agreement be presented in an official language of the state on which the award relies. The translation shall be certified by an official or sworn translator or by a diplomatic or consular agent.[104] The Arbitration Law and the CPC require the same documents. If such documents are in a foreign language, the party shall supply a duly certified translation thereof into the Azerbaijani language.[105]

1.92. Additionally, the Law on the Enforcement of the Republic of Azerbaijan guarantees the execution of the awards rendered by international arbitral tribunals, arbitration courts and the courts of foreign countries.[106] The execution period of such awards is three years.[107]

1.93. The Arbitration Law contains the same grounds to reject recognition and enforcement of the arbitral award as the New York Convention and Model Law. The grounds are exhaustive. The Arbitration Law identifies five separate grounds to refuse recognition and enforcement based on request of the party against whom it is invoked. Two other grounds relate to the public policy of the place of enforcement and arbitrability.[108]

1.94. Notwithstanding that Azerbaijan has a legal basis for the functioning of arbitral institutions, its arbitration practice is limited mostly to obtaining the awards for recognition and execution. In the past seventeen years, around 100 arbitral awards were accepted for recognition by the Supreme Court. Most of them have been successfully recognized.

§3.06 INVESTOR-STATE ARBITRATION

[A] General Overview of Law and Practice Related to Investor-State Arbitration

1.95. As Azerbaijan enjoys an abundance of natural resources, both onshore and offshore, the country has developed as the largest recipient of foreign direct investment in the South Caucasus region. In addition, Azerbaijan has significantly increased its capital investments abroad by involving state-run and private companies of Azerbaijan.[109] Azerbaijan has been a party to the ICSID Convention since 1992. This stipulates the conclusion of multilateral and bilateral investment treaties with foreign states. The national legislation provides additional privileges for foreign investors.[110]

---

104. *Ibid.*, Art. IV(2).
105. Law on International Commercial Arbitration of the Republic of Azerbaijan, Art. 35 (18 November 1999); Civil Procedural Code of the Republic of Azerbaijan, Art. 475 (1 September 2000).
106. Law on the Enforcement of the Republic of Azerbaijan, Art. 6 (27 December 2001).
107. *Ibid.*, Art. 13.1.4.
108. Alan Redfern, *supra* n. 45, at § 10-34.
109. Capital Flows Across Borders in Azerbaijan, http://www.freeeconomy.az/site/assets/files/1391/capital_flows_across_borders_in_azerbaijan.pdf (accessed 26 June 2017).
110. Law on Protection of Foreign Investments, Art. 5 (15 January 1992).

1.96. Under the law, the following entities and individuals may be considered as foreign investors in Azerbaijan: (i) foreign legal persons; (ii) foreign citizens, stateless persons, and citizens of Azerbaijan with a permanent residence abroad, subject to registration in their country of residence for engaging in economic activity; (iii) foreign states; and (iv) international organizations.[111]

1.97. Pursuant to the Foreign Investment Law, foreign investment may take one of the following forms: (i) participation in enterprises and organizations established with legal entities and citizens of the Republic of Azerbaijan on a shared basis; (ii) establishment of enterprises wholly owned by foreign investors; (iii) purchase of enterprises, property, buildings, structures, shares in enterprises, other shares, bonds, securities and certain other property, which, under the law of the Republic of Azerbaijan, may be owned by foreign investors; (iv) acquisition of rights to use land and other natural resources, as well as other proprietary rights; and (v) conclusion of agreements with legal entities and citizens of the Republic of Azerbaijan providing for other forms of foreign investment.[112]

1.98. To ensure that foreign investors consider Azerbaijan as a reputable place to invest, the legislation provides for certain guarantees. For instance:

(a) if the subsequent legislation of the Republic of Azerbaijan deteriorates the conditions of investment, it will apply the foreign investment law in force at the time of the investment within ten years of the law at the time of the investment;
(b) foreign investors are guaranteed immediate, adequate and effective compensation in case of nationalization and requisition;
(c) foreign investors are entitled to recover damages, including lost profits, incurred by them as a result of actions of state bodies or their officials; and
(d) foreign investors are entitled to repatriate profits derived from foreign investments subject to applicable taxes and duties.[113]

1.99. With regard to arbitration, the legislation sets grounds for free access to international arbitration. Two conditions should be met in order to refer to arbitration: the law does not prohibit a specific type of dispute to be arbitrable; and the parties agree to submit their dispute to the international arbitration.[114]

1.100. As a part of the ongoing business law reforms, the President of the Republic of Azerbaijan signed the Decree On Actions for provision of organization of 'one window principle in activities of business subjects' dated 25 October 2007 to simplify the procedures of starting a business in the country. According to the Decree, the registration organ overseeing the 'one window' principle is the Ministry of Taxes of the

---

111. *Ibid*, Art. 2.
112. *Ibid*, Art. 3.
113. Law on Protection of Foreign Investments, Art. 10 (15 January 1992).
114. Gunduz Karimov, Doing Business in Azerbaijan, p. 10 (Baker & McKenzie, 2016).

Republic of Azerbaijan. The 'one window' system has been in operation since 1 January 2008. Under the new system, a simplified one-step procedure has been introduced (compared to the previous fifteen-step procedure) and the timeframe for the procedure has been reduced from thirty days to three days.[115]

1.101. Moreover, Azerbaijan has set a 'not-less-favoured' regime for foreign investors through bilateral treaties.[116] The Republic of Azerbaijan has concluded over thirty-seven bilateral treaties with different counties (most of the CIS countries, USA, Germany, France, Saudi Arabia, etc.) some are currently under negotiation.[117]

1.102. The 'Doing Business 2009' report prepared by the World Bank and the International Finance Corporation illustrates that Azerbaijan is very strong with regard to its reforms in the area of foreign investments. The business environment in Azerbaijan is considered positive. In the 'Global competitiveness report' prepared for 2009–2010, Azerbaijan increased by 18 places from last year's report to place 51st among 133 countries and claimed 1st place among the CIS countries.[118]

[B]   List of Investor-State Disputes (Concluded and Pending)

1.103. Unlike in domestic arbitration, with regard to international arbitration Azerbaijan could be considered as an investor-friendly country. 'Azerbaijan opened [a] very attractive investment climate to many companies operating in different fields with reasonable protection mechanisms'.[119] During the twenty-five years of Azerbaijan's independence and its membership in the World Bank, ICSID considered three cases where Azerbaijan acted as a respondent-host state.

1.104. In Fondel Metal B.V. v. Republic of Azerbaijan, the claimant filed a suit with the Secretary-General. The proceedings were concluded with a settlement, as agreed upon by the parties and discontinued at the parties' request (Order taking note of the discontinuance issued by the Tribunal on 23 January 2009 pursuant to Arbitration Rule 43(1)).[120]

Barmek Holding A.S. referred its claim to ICSID based on the Bilateral Treaty between Turkey and Azerbaijan of 1994. The outcome was a settlement agreed upon

---

115. Minister of Economy of Azerbaijan, http://www.economy.gov.az/index.php?option = com_content&view = article&id = 88:az%C9%99rbaycan-respublikas%C4%B1n%C4%B1n-investisiya-m%C3%BChiti-haqq%C4%B1nda&catid = 17:investisiyalar&lang = en (accessed 26 June 2017).
116. Azerbaijan Business and Investment Opportunities Yearbook, Volume 1 Strategic, Practical Information and Opportunities, p. 114 (International Business Publication, USA, 2016).
117. Ibid., pp. 114–115.
118. Minister of Economy of Azerbaijan, http://www.economy.gov.az/index.php?option = com_content&view = article&id = 88:az%C9%99rbaycan-respublikas%C4%B1n%C4%B1n-investisiya-m%C3%BChiti-haqq%C4%B1nda&catid = 17:investisiyalar&lang = en (accessed 26 June 2017).
119. Hasan Allahverdiyev & Zahid Məmmədov, Investisiya proseslərinin tanzimlənməsi, p. 9 (Baku, 2003).
120. World Bank, https://icsid.worldbank.org/en/Pages/cases/casedetail.aspx?CaseNo = ARB/07/1 (accessed 26 June 2017).

by the parties and recorded at their request in the form of an award (Award embodying the parties' settlement agreement rendered on 28 September 2009, pursuant to ICSID Arbitration Rule 43(2)).[121]

The third case is Azpetrol International Holdings B.V., Azpetrol Group B.V. and Azpetrol Oil Services Group B.V. v. Republic of Azerbaijan.[122] In contrast to previous cases, this was not settled by the parties' agreement and therefore took a substantial time to obtain an award. The award states that the case was dismissed for lack of jurisdiction.[123] Details are unavailable.

[C]   Reform Proposals

1.105. In the author's view, the major impediment for the development of the arbitration institution in Azerbaijan is the lack of domestic arbitration. The practice of the ICAC is very limited as very few foreign legal entities or foreign investors in Azerbaijan choose the ICAC as a dispute resolution mechanism with their Azerbaijani counterparts. Nevertheless, international organizations and some non-governmental organizations continue to cooperate with the Azerbaijani authorities in the field of international and local arbitration with the aim of increasing the visibility and popularity of out-of-state dispute adjudication mechanisms. In 2014, the World Bank launched the Judicial Services and Smart Infrastructures Project in Azerbaijan. In 2016, the World Bank issued a report on the activities and assessment conducted during the project. 'The objective of the project is to improve the access, transparency and efficiency of delivery of selected justice services. A draft report assessing needs and demands for alternative dispute resolution (ADR) mechanisms in Azerbaijan was discussed with the consultant team, the PIU and the World Bank team via video conference in February 2016. An updated assessment reflecting the comments received during and prior to the video conference discussion is expected within the next weeks and will inform the design of the pilot ADR system'.[124]

1.106. The necessity to encourage parties to refer to arbitration will directly affect the development of arbitration. The Azerbaijani Arbitration Law is silent on many aspects, thus difficulties arise in all stages of application of an arbitration agreement. Moreover, the experience of the Supreme Court in the recognition and enforcement of arbitral awards is limited. One of the issues is in the law system, which highly affects arbitration is the absence of a 'public policy' in Azerbaijan. Azerbaijan has not established its public policy, thus the wording of the Model Law, i.e., 'the award is in conflict with the public policy', was replaced with 'the Constitution of the Azerbaijan'.

---

121. World Bank, https://icsid.worldbank.org/en/Pages/cases/casedetail.aspx?CaseNo = ARB/0 6/16 (accessed 26 June 2017).
122. https://icsid.worldbank.org/en/Pages/cases/casedetail.aspx?CaseNo = ARB/06/15 (accessed 26 June 2017).
123. *Ibid.*
124. http://documents.worldbank.org/curated/en/2016/04/26218883/azerbaijan-judicial-services -smart-infrastructure-project-p144700-implementation-status-results-report-sequence-04 (accessed 26 June 2017).

Moreover, this article has been amended by changing 'the legislation of the Republic of Azerbaijan' to 'the Constitution'.

1.107. Among others, the Azerbaijan Arbitration and Mediation Center conducted a Research and Practical Seminar on Mediation and Arbitration in Baku on 2 May 2014. The aim of the seminar was to increase awareness on arbitration and encourage young lawyers to undertake research activities. During the seminar, representatives of the CIS countries shared opinions about the status of arbitrators and mediators, national regulatory issues, ethics, codes of conduct for arbitrators and mediators, arbitration and mediation procedures.[125]

---

125. Azerbaijan Arbitration and Mediation Center, http://www.arbitr.az/news.php?readmore =136 (accessed 26 June 2017).

APPENDIX I LIST OF BILATERAL INVESTMENT TREATIES OF AZERBAIJAN

No.	Short title	Status	Date of signature	Date of entry into force
1	Albania - Azerbaijan BIT (2012)	Signed	09/02/2012	
2	Austria - Azerbaijan BIT (2000)	In force	04/07/2000	28/05/2001
3	Azerbaijan - Belarus BIT (2010)	Signed	03/06/2010	
4	Azerbaijan - BLEU (Belgium-Luxembourg Economic Union) BIT (2004)	In force	18/05/2004	27/05/2009
5	Azerbaijan - Bulgaria BIT (2004)	Signed	07/10/2004	
6	Azerbaijan - China BIT (1994)	In force	08/03/1994	01/04/1995
7	Azerbaijan - Croatia BIT (2007)	In force	02/10/2007	30/05/2008
8	Azerbaijan - Czech Republic BIT (2011)	In force	17/05/2011	09/02/2012
9	Azerbaijan - Egypt BIT (2002)	Signed	24/10/2002	
10	Azerbaijan - Estonia BIT (2010)	Signed	07/04/2010	
11	Azerbaijan - Finland BIT (2003)	In force	26/02/2003	10/12/2004
12	Azerbaijan - France BIT (1998)	In force	01/09/1998	24/08/2000
13	Azerbaijan - Georgia BIT (1996)	In force	08/03/1996	10/07/1996
14	Azerbaijan - Germany BIT (1995)	In force	22/12/1995	29/07/1998
15	Azerbaijan - Greece BIT (2004)	In force	21/06/2004	03/09/2006
16	Azerbaijan - Hungary BIT (2007)	In force	18/05/2007	26/02/2008
17	Azerbaijan - Iran, Islamic Republic of BIT (1996)	In force	28/10/1996	20/06/2002
18	Azerbaijan - Israel BIT (2007)	In force	20/02/2007	16/01/2009
19	Azerbaijan - Italy BIT (1997)	In force	25/09/1997	04/02/2000
20	Azerbaijan - Jordan BIT (2008)	Signed	05/05/2008	
21	Azerbaijan - Kazakhstan BIT (1996)	In force	16/09/1996	30/04/1998
22	Azerbaijan - Korea, Republic of BIT (2007)	In force	23/04/2007	25/01/2008
23	Azerbaijan - Kyrgyzstan BIT (1997)	In force	28/08/1997	28/08/1997
24	Azerbaijan - Latvia BIT (2005)	In force	03/10/2005	10/05/2006
25	Azerbaijan - Lebanon BIT (1998)	Signed	11/02/1998	
26	Azerbaijan - Lithuania BIT (2006)	In force	08/06/2006	01/07/2007
27	Azerbaijan - Macedonia, The former Yugoslav Republic of BIT (2013)	Signed	19/04/2013	
28	Azerbaijan - Moldova, Republic of BIT (1997)	In force	27/11/1997	28/01/1999
29	Azerbaijan - Montenegro BIT (2011)	In force	16/09/2011	02/11/2012

Chapter 3: Azerbaijan

No.	Short title	Status	Date of signature	Date of entry into force
30	Azerbaijan - Norway BIT (1996)	Signed	25/09/1996	
31	Azerbaijan - Pakistan BIT (1995)	Signed	09/10/1995	
32	Azerbaijan - Poland BIT (1997)	In force	26/08/1997	10/02/1999
33	Azerbaijan - Qatar BIT (2007)	Signed	28/08/2007	
34	Azerbaijan - Romania BIT (2002)	In force	29/10/2002	29/01/2004
35	Azerbaijan - Romania BIT (2006)	Signed	11/10/2006	
36	Azerbaijan - Russian Federation BIT (2014)	Signed	29/09/2014	
37	Azerbaijan - San Marino BIT (2015)	Signed	25/09/2015	
38	Azerbaijan - Saudi Arabia BIT (2005)	Signed	09/03/2005	
39	Azerbaijan - Serbia BIT (2011)	In force	08/06/2011	14/12/2011
40	Azerbaijan - Switzerland BIT (2006)	In force	23/02/2006	25/06/2007
41	Azerbaijan - Syrian Arab Republic BIT (2009)	In force	08/07/2009	04/01/2010
42	Azerbaijan - Tajikistan BIT (2007)	In force	17/03/2007	26/02/2008
43	Azerbaijan - Turkey BIT (1994)	Terminated on 02/05/2013, to be replaced by new	09/02/1994	08/09/1997
44	Azerbaijan - Turkey BIT (2011)	In force	25/10/2011	02/05/2013
45	Azerbaijan - Ukraine BIT (1997)	In force	21/03/1997	09/12/1997
46	Azerbaijan - United Arab Emirates BIT (2006)	In force	01/11/2006	24/08/2007
47	Azerbaijan - United Kingdom BIT (1996)	In force	04/01/1996	11/12/1996
48	Azerbaijan - United States of America BIT (1997)	In force	01/08/1997	02/08/2001
49	Azerbaijan - Uzbekistan BIT (1996)	In force	27/05/1996	02/11/1996

Bibliography

Legislation

Constitution of the Republic of Azerbaijan (dated 12 November 1995); http://www.president.az/azerbaijan/constitution.
Civil Procedure Code of the Republic of Azerbaijan (dated 1 September 2000); http://www.e-qanun.az/code/9.
Civil Code of the Republic of Azerbaijan (dated 1 September 2000);

http://www.e-qanun.az/code/8.
The Labour Code of the Republic of Azerbaijan (dated 1 February 1999);
http://www.e-qanun.az/code/7.
Law On Advocates and Legal Services of Azerbaijan (dated 19 December 1999);
http://www.e-qanun.az/framework/257.
Law on Courts and Judges of Azerbaijan (dated 10 June 1997);
http://www.e-qanun.az/framework/3933.
Law on the Enforcement of the Republic of Azerbaijan (dated 27 December, 2001);
http://www.e-qanun.az/framework/1406.
Law on Private International Law of Azerbaijan (dated 6 June 2000);
http://www.e-qanun.az/framework/509.
Law on International Commercial Arbitration of the Republic of Azerbaijan (dated 18 November 1999);
http://www.e-qanun.az/framework/90.
Law On Consumers' Rights Protection of the Republic of Azerbaijan (dated 19 September 1995);
http://www.e-qanun.az/framework/9479.
Law on Protection of Foreign Investments of the Republic of Azerbaijan (dated 15 January 1992);
Regulations of Azerbaijan International Commercial Arbitration (2003);
http://www.arbitr.az/bkam/esasname.html.

Literature

Alan Redfern, Martin Hunter, Nigel Blackaby and Constantine Partasides, Law and Practice of International Commercial Arbitration (UK, Kluwer Law International 2004).
Azerbaijan Business and Investment Opportunities Yearbook, Volume 1 Strategic, Practical Information and Opportunities (International Business Publication, USA, 2016).
Doing Business in Azerbaijan, Baker & McKenzie, 2015.
Gary Born, International Commercial Arbitration (Wolters Kluwer, 2nd. ed., 2001).
Hasan Allahverdiyev, Zahid Məmmədov, Investisiya proseslərinin tanzimlənməsi (Baku, 2003).
Habil İsgəndərli, Beynəlxalq Arbitraj (Qanunvericilik və şərhlər, 2004).
Idris Asgarov, Comments to Civil Code of the Republic of Azerbaijan (Qanun, 2011).
Masuma Melikova and Xayyam Ismayilov, State and Law of Azerbaijan in Ancient and Middle-Age Times (in Azeri) (Baku, Hugug Adabiyyati, 2001).
Mehman Sultanov, Some Aspects of Development of Conflict of Rules in the Law On International Private Law, Azerbaijan Law Journal, 2 (6) (2003).
Sabir Allahverdiyev, Civil law of the Republic of Azerbaijan, General Section (1st Book) (Digesta, 2003).
Vafaddin Ibayev, The International Civil Process (Baku, Elm, 2005).
Vidadi Mirkamal, Arbitration Agreement (Monograph, Baki-2005).

Vidadi Mirkamal, International Arbitration Process, available at http://www.legalreform.az/yukle/Beynelxalq%20Arbitraj%20_SAYTA.pdf (2011).
Xayyam Ismayilov, History of State and Law of Azerbaijan (in Azeri) (Baki, Nurlan, 2006).
Zavar Gafarov, Ataxan Abilov, Private International Law (Qanun, 2nd ed. 2007).
Ziyafat Asgarov, Elshad Nasirov, Mubariz Ismayilov, Constitution of the Republic of Azerbaijan and Fundamental Basis of Law (Qapp-Poliqraf, 2005).

Webliography

Azərbaycan Beynəlxalq Kommersiya Arbitraj Məhkəməsi, http://www.arbitr.az/bkam/BKAM_haqqinda.html.
Capital Flows Across Borders in Azerbaijan, http://www.freeeconomy.az/site/assets/files/1391/capital_flows_across_borders_in_azerbaijan.pdf (accessed 21 July 2016).
International Energy Charter, http://www.energycharter.org/process/overview/.
Minister of Economy of Azerbaijan, http://economy.gov.az/index.php?lang=en.
PlainSite, http://www.plainsite.org/dockets/jme2i9rw/new-york-southern-district-court/frontera-resources-azerbaijan-corporation-v-state-oil-company-of-the-azerbaijan-republic/.
President of Azerbaijan, http://en.president.az/azerbaijan/contract.
Production Sharing Agreement on The Exploration, Development and Production Sharing for the Shah Deniz Prospective Area in the Azerbaijan Sector of The Caspian Sea at http://www.bp.com/content/dam/bp-country/en_az/pdf/legal agreements/PSAs/SD-PSA.pdf.
Supreme Court of Azerbaijan, http://www.supremecourt.gov.az/static/view/27.
The Court System of Azerbaijan, http://courts.gov.az/judicial_power/.
United Nations Treaty Collection, https://treaties.un.org/pages/ViewDetails.aspx?src=TREATY&mtdsg_no=XXII-2&chapter=22&lang=en.
United Nations Treaty Collection, https://treaties.un.org/pages/ViewDetails.aspx?src=TREATY&mtdsg_no=XXII-2&chapter=22&lang=en.
World Bank, https://icsid.worldbank.org/apps/ICSIDWEB/about/Pages/default.aspx.
World Bank, https://icsid.worldbank.org/apps/ICSIDWEB/cases/Pages/casedetail.aspx?CaseNo=ARB/07/1&tab=PRO.

CHAPTER 4
Belarus

Aliaksandr Danilevich

LIST OF ABBREVIATIONS

BelCCI	Belarusian Chamber of Commerce and Industry
BSSR	Belarusian Soviet Socialist Republic
BIT	Bilateral investment treaty
Civil Code CC	Civil Code of Belarus No. 218-Z dated December 7, 1998
Commercial Procedure Code	Commercial Procedure Code of Economic Procedure No. 219-Z dated December 15, 1998.
Domestic Arbitration Law	Law of Belarus "On Arbitration Courts" No. 301-Z dated July 18, 2011
Geneva Convention	European Convention on International Commercial Arbitration, 1961, Geneva
IAC by the BelCCI	International Arbitration Court by the Belarusian Chamber of Commerce and Industry
LIAC Law	Law of Belarus "On International Arbitration Court" No. 698 dated May 29, 2009
ICSID Convention	Convention on the Settlement of Investment Disputes between States and Nationals of other States, 1965, Washington
Law on International TreatiesIT	Law on International Treaties No. 421-3 dated July 23, 2008
New York Convention	United Nations Convention on the Recognition and Enforcement of Foreign Arbitral Awards, 1958, New York
UNCITRAL	United Nation Commission on International Trade Law
UNCITRAL Model Law	UNCITRAL Model Law on International Commercial Arbitration 1985
USSR	Union of Soviet Socialist Republic

§4.01 GENERAL INTRODUCTION

[A] Historical Development of the Legal System

1.1. Development of arbitration law in Belarus began with the independence achievement of the country that was associated with the disintegration of the Soviet Union in 1991. Until that time, the country was under the Russian occupation of *Rzecz Pospolita*, which included the lands of modern Belarus, Poland, Lithuania and Ukraine (1569–1795).[1]

1.2. Notwithstanding the formation of the formally autonomous Belarusian Soviet Socialist Republic (BSSR) in 1919, all powers with regard to foreign trade belonged to the central Soviet government in Moscow. In 1991, Belarus inherited the Soviet civil law legal system and the national norms of private international law based on the typical legislation of the Union of Soviet Socialist Republic (USSR) after the collapse of the Soviet Union.

1.3. The National Law On International Arbitration Court (IAC Law), based on the United Nation Commission on International Trade Law (UNCITRAL) Model Law of 1985, was adopted on July 9, 1999.[2] The law changed insignificantly in 1999[3] and in 2014.[4] The changes were not related to the changes in the UNCITRAL Model Law in 2006.[5] Activities of the "domestic" arbitration courts are governed by the Law of July 18, 2011 No. 301-Z (in version of January 1, 2015) On Arbitration Courts.[6]

[B] The Legal Profession

1.4. In Belarus, there exists special legislation regarding different forms of legal profession, such as advocates,[7] judges,[8] notaries,[9]

---

1. *See*: Юхо, Я.А. Кароткі нарыс гісторыі дзяржавы і права Беларусі /Я.А. Юхо. – Мінск: Універсітэцкае, 1992. – 270 с.
2. Law of the Republic of Belarus No. 279-Z of July 9, 1999 [Amended as of July 1, 2014]. On International Arbitration Court (Tribunal), http://law.by/main.aspx?guid=3871&p0=H19900279e.
3. National Registry of Legal Acts of Republic of Belarus', January 14, 2000, No 4, 2/119.
4. National Legal Web Portal of the Republic of Belarus, July 10, 2014, 2/2172.
5. UNCITRAL Model Law on International Commercial Arbitration 1985 with amendments as adopted in 2006, https://www.uncitral.org/pdf/english/texts/arbitration/ml-arb/07-86998_Ebook.pdf.
6. Law of Republic of Belarus of July 18, 2011 No 301-Z (in version of January 1, 2015) On arbitration courts, http://www.pravo.by/main.aspx?guid=3871&p0=H11100301.
7. Law of Republic of Belarus of December 30, 2011 No 334-Z On Advocacy and Legal Practice in the Republic of Belarus, http://www.rka.by/content/zakon-ob-advokature-i-advokatskoy.
8. Code of Republic of Belarus On Judicial System and Judges Status of June 29, 2006 No 139-Z (in version of January 4, 2014), http://etalonline.by/?type=text&regnum=Hk0600139#load_text_none_1_.
9. Edict of the President of Republic of Belarus of November 27, 2013 No 523 (in version of August 8, 2016) On Organization of Notarial Activity in Republic of Belarus / National Legal Internet Portal of Republic of Belarus, November 29, 2013, 1/14639; Law of Republic of Belarus of July 18, 2004 No 305-Z (in version January 5, 2016) On Notariate and Notarial Activity, http://belnotary.by/zakonodatelstvo/zakon-o-notariate/.

prosecutors,[10] investigators.[11] Providing legal services as well as any other form of legal assistance is subject to a licensing in Belarus.[12] In general, there are two types of licenses – a lawyer's license which gives the broadest scope of powers, including the right to provide "legal aid" in all courts *(the advocates)*;[13] and a lawyer's license, the owner of which is entitled to render legal services, but does not have the right to represent his client before the court.[14] However, the second type of license, which is a limited license, allows representing the client in arbitral courts.

[C]   **Sources of Arbitration Law**

1.5. The legislation of Belarus on international commercial and domestic arbitration is based on the UNCITRAL Model Law 1985. The institutional international and domestic arbitration courts are legal entities and shall be registered by the Ministry of Justice.[15] The model rules are approved by the government for the domestic arbitration court.[16]

1.6. Some clarifications on arbitration are given by the Resolutions of the Supreme Court Plenum of the Republic of Belarus, particularly on consequences of the

---

10. Law of Republic of Belarus of May 8, 2007 No 220-Z (in version of July 18, 2016) On Procuracy of Republic of Belarus, http://www.pravo.by/webnpa/text.asp?&p0 = H10700220.
11. Criminal Procedure Code of Republic of Belarus of July 16, 1999, No 295-3, http://etalonline. by/?type = text&regnum = HK9900295.
12. Presidential Decree of September 1, 2010 No 450 On Licensing of Certain Types of Activities, http://www.pravo.by/webnpa/text.asp?RN = P31000450; The Presidential Decree of June 14, 2012 No 265 On Some Issues of Legal Practice, http://president.gov.by/ru/official_documents _ru/view/ukaz-265-ot-14-ijunja-2012-g-1491/.
13. Edict of the President of Republic of Belarus of June 14, 2012 No 265 On some issues of Advocate Activity, http://minjust.gov.by/ru/about-licensing/a/.
14. Licensing of the provision of legal services by the second type of lawyers is governed by the Regulation of the Ministry of Justice of the Republic of Belarus of March 7, 2014 No 58 On Some Issues Concerning Licensing of the Activity of the Legal Services Provision, National Legal Web Portal of the Republic of Belarus, April 3, 2014, 8/285034; the Regulation of the Ministry of Justice of the Republic of Belarus of November 30, 2010 No 105 On Some Measures Related to Realization of the Attorney's Activities and Legal Services, National registry of Legal Acts of Republic of Belarus, January 1, 2011, No 1, 8/23112.
15. The Resolution of the Council of Ministers of the Republic of Belarus of May 29, 2009 No 698 On State Registration of International Arbitration Courts Operating on a Permanent Basis, National registry of Legal Acts of Republic of Belarus, June 9, 2009, No 136, 5/29855. Registration of domestic arbitration courts is provided additionally by the Regulation of the Ministry of Justice of the Republic of Belarus of December 2, 2011 No 272 On Some Issues Concerning State Registration of Institutional Arbitration Courts' and the Instruction on the Procedure of Maintenance of Register of Arbitrators and Institutional Arbitration Courts, National Registry of Legal Acts of Republic of Belarus, December 29, 2011, No 144, 8/24555.
16. Regulation of the Council of Ministers of the Republic of Belarus of January 12, 2012 No 52 On Approval of the Model Rules of the Arbitration Court operating on a Permanent Basis accepted Model Rules of institutional (domestic) arbitration court. http://news.21.by/other-news/2012/ 01/25/451575.html.

conclusion of an arbitral agreement for the consideration of a dispute by the economic courts,[17] and on the annulment of awards.[18]

[D] International Legal Framework, Supremacy of International Law

1.7. Article 8(1) of Belarusian Constitution[19] is a foundational norm, according to which "Belarus recognizes the priority of universally recognized principles of international law and ensures internal legislation's conformity with them." The Law on the International Treaties of Belarus[20] dealing with the legal force of international treaties was enacted in 2008.

1.8. Article 33(1) of Law on International Treaties states that: "International treaties to which Belarus is a party are subject to diligent execution by Belarus in accordance with international law." According to Article 33(2) of Law on International Treaties, "the legal norms contained in the international treaties in force to which Belarus is a party form part of the legislation applicable in the territory of Belarus and are subject to direct application, except in cases where an international treaty states or implies that the application of specific norms in question requires the enactment of internal normative legal acts; and have the legal force of the normative legal act that expresses the consent of Belarus to be subject to the corresponding international treaty."[21]

1.9. In order of priority, ratified self-executing treaties have the force of law; the inter-state treaties confirmed by Presidential Decrees have the force of a Presidential Decree; intergovernmental treaties confirmed by governmental orders have the force of a Ministerial Council award; while interdepartmental treaties have the force of a departmental statutory act.

1.10. Today it may be asserted that Belarusian legislation recognizes the priority of ratified international treaties.[22] This opinion is based on the provisions of Article 116 of the Belarusian Constitution, according to which the Constitutional Court renders final awards with respect to the conformity of legislative acts of state organs with inter-state

---

17. Chapter 3 of the Resolution of the Plenum of the Highest Economic Court of the Republic of Belarus of October 31, 2011 No 21 On Some Issues of the Resolution by the Economic Courts of Cases with the Participation of Foreign Persons, http://www.pravo.by/main.aspx?guid = 3871 &p0 = X21100021.
18. On Application by the Courts of the Legislation Concerning Recognition and Enforcement of the Awards of the Foreign Courts and Foreign Arbitral Awards of December 23, 2014 No 18, http://www.court.by/jurisprudence/Post_plen/civ_proc/forein/af5a2f40566c0ca8.html.
19. National Registry of Legal Acts of Republic of Belarus', January 5, 1999, No 1, 1/0.
20. National Registry of Legal Acts of Republic of Belarus, August 4, 2008, No 184, 2/1518.
21. Article 20(2) of the Law on Normative Legal Acts of Belarus of January 10, 2000 contains a provision similar to that expressed above / National Registry of Legal Acts of Republic of Belarus, January 21, 2000, No 7, 2/136.
22. *See*: Салеев И. Соотношение международных договоров и внутреннего законодательства Республики Беларусь / Белорусский журнал международного права и международных отношений 2000 – № 3, http://evolutio.info/content/view/364/51/.

formations, such as the Republic of Belarus, international treaties and other ratified international treaties of Belarus.[23]

1.11. With respect to commercial arbitration, Belarus participates in the European Arbitration Convention (European Convention of April 21, 1961 on International Commercial Arbitration[24]), and the New York Convention (New York Convention of June 10, 1958 on the Recognition and Enforcement of Foreign Arbitral Awards[25]); it has also acceded to the 1965 Convention on the Settlement of Investment Disputes between States and Nationals of other States, 1965 (ICSID Convention).[26]

[E]   Available Dispute Resolution Mechanisms

1.12. In Belarus, the following mechanisms for the settlement of dispute are settled by law: state courts – general courts and economic (commercial) courts; international arbitration courts – institutional and ad hoc; domestic arbitration courts – institutional, ad hoc; mediation – voluntary mediation; in-court mediation.[27]

[F]   Judicial System

1.13. The structure of the judicial system is regulated by Chapter 6 of the Constitution, Presidential Decree of November 29, 2013 No. 6 "On the improvement of the judicial system of the Republic of Belarus." In the system of courts of general jurisdiction, specialized courts may be established.[28] According to paragraph 2 of the Decree No. 6, the courts system consists of the Constitutional Court, the Supreme Court, regional (Minsk city) courts, the economic courts of regions (of city of Minsk) and departmental (city) courts.

[G]   Arbitration Institutions

1.14. The Ministry of Justice maintains a register of permanent arbitration courts, which is published on the official website of the Ministry.[29] On February 1, 2016, three permanent "domestic" arbitration courts with the rights of legal entities were registered, as well as twenty-two arbitration courts in the form of separate subdivisions of legal entities.[30] Two international courts of arbitration are registered – the International

---

23. A similar norm is enshrined in Art. 54 Law on the Constitutional Procedure of January 8, 2014 / National Legal Internet Portal of Republic of Belarus, January 16, 2014, 2/2122.
24. 484 UNTS 349.
25. 330 UNTS 3.
26. International Centre for Settlement of Investment Disputes, https://icsid.worldbank.org/apps/ICSIDWEB/icsiddocs/Pages/ICSID-Convention.aspx.
27. On the basis of the Law of Belarus of July 12, 2013 No 58-3 On Mediation, http://www.court.by/brest/extrajudicial-mediation/a34340f977c1411c.html.
28. Article 109 of the Belarusian Constitution.
29. See at: http://minjust.gov.by/ru/arbitration-registry/.
30. Ministry of Justice of Republic of Belarus, Registrar of arbitrators and permanently functioning arbitration institutions, http://minjust.gov.by/ru/arbitration-registry/.

Arbitration Court at the Belarusian Chamber of Commerce and Industry (BelCCI)[31] and the International Arbitration Court "Chamber of Arbitrators" by the Belarusian Lawyers Union.[32]

[H] Sovereign Immunity and International Arbitration

1.15. The possibility of Belarus to be a party in an arbitration clause is defined in legislation.[33] The disputes between an investor and Belarus shall be settled out of court by negotiation, unless otherwise provided by legislative acts of Belarus.[34]

1.16. If disputes which are not under exclusive jurisdiction of Belarusian courts and which have arisen between a foreign investor and Belarus are not settled out of court through negotiations within three months from the date of the receipt of the written proposals for their settlement out of court, then such disputes by the investor's choice may also be resolved: (a) by an arbitral tribunal, which shall be established to address each specific dispute under the Arbitration Rules of the UNCITRAL, unless the parties to the dispute shall otherwise agree; (b) by the International Centre for Settlement of Investment Disputes (ICSID), if a foreign investor is a citizen or legal person of the state – party to the Convention on the Settlement of Investment Disputes between States and Nationals of Other States of March 18, 1965.[35]

1.17. Article 36 of the Law of Belarus on Concessions[36] also considers the issues of immunity and arbitration, saying that the concession agreement may include the waiver of State immunity for the execution of an arbitral award. This means that Belarus does not legally presume the inclusion of the waiver of the State immunity in any investment agreement. Some Belarusian Bilateral investment treaties (BITs) and

---

31. See at: http://www.cci.by/en/content/international-arbitration-court-general-information. This court is the most authoritative, and is a really active international arbitration court in Belarus.
32. International Arbitration Court "Chamber of Arbitrators" by Belarusian Lawyers Union, http://mpa.by/about.aspx, see also: Danilevich A. A New Arbitration Institution Established in Belarus, CIS Arbitration Forum, 2 January 2011 http://www.cisarbitration.com/2011/01/02/a-new-arbitration-institution-established-in-belarus/.
33. Law of Republic of Belarus On Investments of July 12, 2013 No 53-Z, http://www.pravo.by/main.aspx?guid=3871&p0=H11300053.
34. Article 13 of the Law of Belarus of July 12, 2013 No 53-Z "On investments".
35. See also: Комментарий "Проблемы определения условий инвестиционного договора по праву Республики Беларусь (комментарий к Закону Республики Беларусь от 12 июля 2013 No 53-3 'Об инвестициях') (часть 2)" (Я.И.Функ) ConsultantPlus: Belarus. Technology PROF [Electronic resource] / Jurspectre Ltd., National Centre of Legal Information. – Minsk, 2016; Корочкин А.Ю. Закрепление оговорки об отказе государства от юрисдикционного иммунитета в инвестиционном законодательстве Республики Беларусь. ConsultantPlus: Belarus. Technology PROF [Electronic resource] / Jurspectre Ltd., National Centre of Legal Information. – Minsk, 2016.
36. Law of Republic of Belarus On Concessions of July 12, 2013 No 63-Z, http://www.pravo.by/main.aspx?guid=3871&p0=H11300063&p1=1.

particular investment agreements contain the inclusion of a single meaning waiver of any kind of State immunity of Belarus.[37]

§4.02 THE ARBITRATION AGREEMENT

[A] Introduction

1.18. One of the principles of the international arbitration court activities is the principle of consent jurisdiction of all cases.[38] The arbitration agreement may be concluded in the form of an arbitration clause (separate provision of a civil contract) or a separate agreement.[39]

[B] Validity of the Arbitration Agreement

[1] General Provisions

1.19. Article 11 IAC Law "Definition and form of arbitration agreement" includes the following provisions: "Arbitration agreement is an agreement between the parties to submit to an international arbitration court all or certain disputes which have arisen or which may arise from the binding side relationship. An arbitration agreement may be in the form of an arbitration clause (separate provision of a civil contract) or a separate contract."[40]

1.20. The commercial court, in which the action is brought which is the subject of an arbitration agreement, leaves the claim without consideration, if a party so requests no later than when submitting its first statement on the merits. The commercial court refuses to comply with the request if it comes to a conclusion that the arbitration agreement is invalid, inoperative or incapable of being performed.[41] It should be noted that the court may not refuse its jurisdiction ex officio. Belarusian state courts over the past few years have shifted from overly harsh assessment of the shortcomings of arbitration agreements to a more "pro-arbitration" approaches.[42]

---

37. Agreement Between the Government of Republic of Belarus and the Governement of Russian Federation on Conditions of Sale of Shares of Joint-Stock Company "Betransgas" (Moscow, November 25, 2011); Agreement between the Governement of Republic of Belarus and the Governement of People's Republic of Bangladesh on Concerning the Encouragement and Reciprocal Protection of Investment (Dhaka, November 12, 2012) / ConsultantPlus: Belarus. Technology PROF [Electronic resource] / Jurspectre Ltd., National Centre of Legal Information. – Minsk, 2016.
38. Article 3 IAC Law.
39. Paragraph 12 of the Resolution of Plenum of the Supreme Economic Court of Republic of Belarus dated October 31, 2011 No 21 "On Some Issues of the Resolution by Economic Courts of Cases with the Foreign Persons Involvement" / "National Registry of Legal Acts of Republic of Belarus", November 23, 2011, No 130, 6/1092.
40. Relevant to Art. 7 of the UNCITRAL Model Law of 1985.
41. Article 13 IAC Law.
42. Сысуев Т.В. Арбитражное соглашение: форма и содержание, Промышленно-торговое право, 2014, No 01.

[2] Requisites of a Valid Arbitration Agreement

1.21. The norms of the Civil Code on the validity of transactions can be used in an arbitration clause. However, it must be considered that the Belarusian Supreme Court finds that the arbitration clause is a procedural institute.[43]

1.22. According to legislation and court practice, the court shall refuse to apply the legal consequences of an arbitration agreement in the following cases: (a) the form of an arbitration agreement does not correspond to the requirement of the legislation; (b) an arbitration agreement does not determine the kind of an arbitration, particular arbitration institute, or arbitration rules; (c) an arbitration agreement is void, inoperative, incapable of being performed; and (d) the subject matter of the dispute is not arbitrable under Belarusian legislation.[44]

1.23. The legislation specifies that in assessing the validity of the arbitration agreement the following must be taken into account: (a) whether the form of an arbitration agreement is written; (b) whether the parties acted in their authority, capacity, and free will; (c) whether a dispute on the same subject has already been considered by the economic court, and whether it can be executed (if it is clearly enough defined by an arbitration body), as well as (d) whether the subject of the dispute is within the competence of the court of arbitration.[45]

[C] Concluding the Arbitration Agreement (Written, Oral, by Conduct)

1.24. The arbitration agreement shall be made in writing.[46] It is considered to be concluded if it is contained in a document signed by the parties, or concluded by exchanging messages with the use of mail or any other means of communication providing written confirmation of the will of the parties, including the sending of a statement of claim and the response to it, in which, respectively, one party proposes to consider the case in international arbitration, and the other had no objection to this.[47]

1.25. As mentioned above, Article 11(2) IAC Law states that the reference in the contract to a document containing an arbitration clause constitutes an arbitration

---

43. Paragraph 3 of the Resolution of Plenum of the Supreme Economic Court of Republic of Belarus dated December 23, 2005 No 34 (in version of October 31, 2011) On jurisdiction on disputes upon assignment, http://www.pravo.by/main.aspx?guid=3871&p0=X20500034.
44. Belarus. International Arbitration 2015 by T. Sysouev and A. Khrapoutski, http://www.iclg.co.uk/practice-areas/international-arbitration-/international-arbitration-2015/belarus#chapter content1. *See also*: Перерва И.В. Полномочия представителей на заключение арбитражной оговорки/ "Промышленно-торговое право", 2014, N 12.
45. Resolution of Plenum of the Supreme Economic Court of Republic of Belarus dated 31 October 2011 No 21 "On Some Issues of the Resolution by Economic Courts of Cases with the Foreign Persons Involvement," *see* above.
46. Article 11(2) IAC Law.
47. Article 4 of Arbitration Rules of the International Arbitration Court at the BelCCI contains provisions similar to IAC Law. *See also*: Каменков В.С. Недействительность третейского соглашения / ConsultantPlus: Belarus. Technology PROF [Electronic resource] / Jurspectre Ltd., National Centre of Legal Information. – Minsk, 2016.

agreement, provided that the contract is in writing and includes the content of links to make that clause a part of the contract.

[D] The Doctrine of Separability

1.26. According to Article 22(1) IAC Law, an arbitration clause which forms part of the contract shall be considered as an agreement independent of the other terms of the contract. Issuance by the IAC of an award on invalidity of the contract itself does not imply the invalidity of the arbitration clause.

[E] Invalidity of the Arbitration Agreement

1.27. The validity of an arbitration clause depends on the compliance with the conditions for the validity of transactions in accordance with the Civil Code. It should be noted that the validity of an arbitration agreement not only depends on the validity of the consent of the parties, but also on the following factors: (a) the arbitration agreement should apply to the dispute that is likely to be the subject of arbitration (the objective nonarbitrability); (b) parties to an arbitration agreement shall not be entitled to be subjects of legal arbitration (subjective non-arbitrability).

1.28. Viewed in relation to a question settled in Article 4(2) IAC Law, according to Article 43(2) IAC Law, an arbitration agreement is considered invalid by law, which the parties have subjected it to or, in the absence of such an indication – by the law of Belarus, using two principles – *lex voluntatis* and *lex loci arbitri*.[48]

1.29. Belarusian jurisprudence shows that the refusal of recognition and enforcement of arbitral awards, and its annulment may be based not on invalidity only, but also on not concluded arbitration agreement.[49] The Law on Domestic Arbitration courts specifically regulates that in case of the failure to fall within conformity with the requirements of the Articles 9–11 of the Law with regard to the form of the agreement, its parties or the procedure of its alteration, the arbitration agreement is considered to be invalid.[50]

[F] Arbitrability

[1] Disputes Capable of Settlement by Arbitration

1.30. Civil disputes between any legal subjects, arising from the foreign trade and other forms of international economic relations may be resolved by an international arbitration court by the consent of the parties, if the registered office or place of

---

48. Based on the provisions of Art. V(1) of the New York Convention 1958, Art. IX of the European Convention 1961.
49. Перерва И.В. "Незаключенность арбитражного соглашения: обжалование компетенции МАС при БелТПП" // "Промышленно- торговое право", 2015, No 08.
50. Article 12.

residence of at least one of the parties is outside Belarus. Other disputes of economic character may be transmitted to an international arbitration court by the consent of the parties if it is not prohibited by the legislation of the Republic of Belarus.[51] Thus, the law on international commercial arbitration courts allows for the consideration of an "internal" dispute, which is what happens in practice, such as the IAC at the BelCCI. Meanwhile in accordance with domestic court of arbitration "is to resolve any disputes arising between the parties have concluded an arbitration agreement."[52] The corporate disputes are also arbitrable under Belarusian law, usually when the charter of incorporation contains the arbitration clause.[53]

[2] Disputes Not Capable of Settlement by Arbitration

1.31. The dispute cannot be referred to an arbitration court by virtue of an outright ban, established by the legislation. In particular, in accordance with Article 23(2) of the Law of the Republic of Belarus of July 13, 2012 No. 415-Z "On economic insolvency (bankruptcy),"[54] a bankruptcy case cannot be referred to an arbitral tribunal.[55]

1.32. Based on existing court practice, disputes referred to in Articles 47 and 236 of the Commercial Procedure Code (exclusive court jurisdiction) are considered not arbitrable.[56] The cases not subjected to arbitration courts include the disputes relating to violation of the antimonopoly legislation; legislation on patents, trademarks, intellectual and industrial property; disputes related to tax and other administrative relationships (licensing, liquidation of legal entities, etc.); and disputes, the subject of which is associated with the law on securities and rights to real estate, as well as disputes relating to labor legislation. Both of these grounds of public order policy are closely linked.[57]

1.33. The Domestic Arbitration Law[58] expressly provides that an internal arbitration court cannot resolve disputes: (a) a party to which is the founder of the permanent court of arbitration, established as a nonprofit organization, or a legal entity's separate division (unit), which is a court of arbitration; (b) that directly affect the rights and

---

51. According to Art. 4(2) IAC Law.
52. Article 19 of the Domestic Arbitration Law.
53. *See*: IAC by BelCCI Award of December 16, 2002 Case No 333/28-02 / ConsultantPlus: Belarus. Technology PROF [Electronic resource] / Jurspectre Ltd., National Centre of Legal Information. – Minsk, 2016.
54. National Legal Web Portal of the Republic of Belarus, July 24, 2012, 2/1967.
55. *See also*: Гаврилова О.Г. Арбитражное соглашение при банкротстве: можно ли исполнить? // "Промышленно-торговое право", 2015, No 09.
56. Belarus. International Arbitration 2015 by T. Sysouev and A. Khrapoutski, http://www.iclg.co.uk/practice-areas/international-arbitration-/international-arbitration-2015/belarus#chaptercontent1.
57. М.П.Горонков. Комментарий "Производство по делам о признании и приведении в исполнение решений иностранных судов и иностранных арбитражных решений (комментарий к главе 28 Хозяйственного процессуального кодекса Республики Беларусь) (часть 3)" ConsultantPlus: Belarus. Technology PROF [Electronic resource] / Jurspectre Ltd., National Centre of Legal Information. – Minsk, 2016.
58. Article 19.

legitimate interests of third parties who are not parties to the arbitration agreement; (c) that cannot be subject of arbitration proceedings in accordance with the legislation of Belarus, or the law of a foreign state, if the application of the legislation of a foreign state is provided by the arbitration agreement or other agreement between the parties.

[3] Special Provisions on Consumer and Labor Disputes

1.34. Legislation on consumer protection does not limit the possibility of considering a consumer dispute with the seller of goods or services to arbitration. If there is a valid arbitration agreement, the dispute may be resolved by a domestic arbitral tribunal.

1.35. Employers in agreement with the trade unions can create reconciliation bodies, mediation and arbitration for the settlement of individual labor disputes. Operation of these bodies shall be determined by the parties through which they are created. This should not limit the employee's right to judicial protection.[59] Collective labor disputes can be also resolved by labor arbitration.[60] The labor arbitration is a temporarily acting body established by agreement between an employer (employers, associations of employers) and employees through their representative bodies in order to resolve a collective labor dispute.[61]

[G] Effect of Arbitration Agreement on Third Parties (Parties Substitution, Guarantee Agreements, Group of Companies Doctrine)

1.36. Belarusian legislation does not recognize any obligatoriness and validity of an arbitration agreement for the third non-signatory parties. The Supreme Economic Court of the Republic of Belarus clearly stated on the issue that "In case of realization between the creditor and debtor of assignment of right or transfer of debt in full volume, preexisting agreement upon the settlement of dispute in an arbitration court or arbitration clause are not effective with regard to the new creditor or debtor as the procedural legislation does not stipulate similar institute of assignment of right or transfer of debt as civil legislation. Transition of rights and obligations from one party to another does not result in the transition of the procedural rights and obligations; therefore, arbitration agreement cannot be subject of cession."[62]

---

59. Article 251 of Labour Code, http://www.etalonline.by/Default.aspx?type = text&regnum = HK9 900296#load_text_none_1_12.
60. Article 379 of Labour Code.
61. Article 383 of Labour Code.
62. Article 3 of the Resolution of its Plenum of December 23, 2005 No 34 "On subject matter jurisdiction of disputes after assignment of right or transfer of debt". *See also*: Award of IAC by BelCCI of March 16, 2005 (Case No 464/39-04); Корочкин А. Ю. Оговорка о договорной подсудности и арбитражная оговорка при уступке требования, Промышленно-торговое право, 2010, N 12.

[H] Termination of Arbitration Agreement

[1] Termination with Respect to Existing Dispute

1.37. The ICA Law[63] and the Domestic Arbitration Law[64] allow the parties to the arbitral proceedings to terminate the latter by their agreement. In other words, this would terminate the arbitration agreement with respect to the existing dispute. The Domestic Arbitration Law does not designate an appointing authority. In the case of deadlock situations, the arbitration agreement with respect to the existing dispute shall be terminated, and the claimant may refer this dispute to the state court.[65]

[2] Complete Termination

1.38. An arbitration agreement can cease to be effective following the termination of the contract to which it was concluded[66] or in the view of the existence of the grounds for the termination of the arbitration agreement itself. Analysis of the legislation reveals that there are other grounds for the termination of an arbitration agreement: (a) termination of an arbitration agreement by the parties; and (b) invalidation of an arbitration agreement as a result of the arbitration agreement being annulled or void (non-arbitrability of a dispute).

1.39. In accordance with certain grounds an arbitration agreement cannot be enforceable without direct correlation between dispute and arbitration agreement: (a) rendering of final award; (b) disqualification of an arbitrator (if the arbitration agreement stipulates appointment of a certain arbitrator); (c) expiration of the term of making an award without issue of such award; d) annulment of an arbitral award as a result of arbitration agreement being invalid as a civil transaction.[67]

[I] Drafting Arbitration Clauses

1.40. Despite the existence of a significant number of written articles and books about how to conclude a good arbitration agreement, including in Belarus,[68] in practice, we

---

63. Article 41 of the IAC Law.
64. Article 42 of the Domestic Arbitration Law.
65. For arbitrations with sole arbitration lack of parties' agreement to appoint a sole arbitrator, for arbitration with three arbitrators – default of the respondent to appoint his arbitrator or in disagreement of the two party-appointed arbitrators with regard to the presiding arbitrator – Art. 14(4)(5)(6) of the Domestic Arbitration Law.
66. Chapter 26 of the Civil Code (Arts 378–389).
67. Civil Code states in the Chapter 9 the following grounds for the termination of obligations: enforcement, compensation for release from obligation, set-off, confusion of debts, novation, debt forgiveness and impossibility of enforcement, enactment of a government authority, death of an individual or liquidation of a legal entity.
68. Анищенко А.И., Юрьева М.Ю. Арбитражная оговорка – скрытое оружие. / Промышленно-торговое право. – 2008. – No 3. – C. 41-46; Хвалей В. Как "убить" арбитражное соглашение? / Промышленно-торговое право. – 2004. – No2. – C. 117-145.

have to see a lot of arbitration clauses, which lead the plaintiff to a dead end or substantial monetary and/or time wasting.

1.41. The undesirability of alternative or mixed arbitration clauses must be mentioned. Alternative clauses provide the choice for the claimant between the two courts of arbitration, mixed clauses provide the choice between arbitration and state court. The IAC at the BelCCI treat such arbitration clauses in their favor, recognizing the existence of competence.[69] Chairman of the IAC at the BelCCI Prof. Ian Funk holds a generally positive attitude to the idea of alternative qualifications.[70] The Supreme Economic Court has warned parties to avoid such kind of alternative clauses, but does not forbid it.[71]

§4.03 APPLICABLE LAW

[A] Introduction

1.42. It is necessary to distinguish between the law applicable to the arbitration (Procedural Law), and the law applicable to the merits. The present section deals with the procedural issues.

[B] The Law Governing the Arbitration (*Lex Arbitri*)

1.43. The Law applied for consideration of a particular dispute to a permanent international court of arbitration, as well as to the International Arbitration Court, with the seat in the territory of Belarus.[72] Subject to the provisions of the IAC Law, the parties are free to agree on the order of proceedings of the International Arbitration Court.[73]

[C] Party Autonomy on Choice of Law Issues

1.44. If the parties have agreed in the arbitration agreement to submit the dispute to a permanent international tribunal, then in the absence of an agreement to the contrary, they agreed with the procedure for consideration of the dispute in accordance with the arbitration rules. Thus, the legislation provides for the right of the parties to determine

---

69. Award of IAC by BelCCI of May 16, 2011 (Case No 938/44-10), ConsultantPlus: Belarus. Technology PROF [Electronic resource] / Jurspectre Ltd., National Centre of Legal Information. – Minsk, 2016.
70. Функ Я.И. Во имя справедливости и верности интересам дел // Антикризисное управление, 2008, No 2.
71. On Arbitration Agreement: Clarification of Supreme Economic Court of Republic of Belarus, July 24, 2008, No 03-29/1532 / ConsultantPlus: Belarus. Technology PROF [Electronic resource] / Jurspectre Ltd., National Centre of Legal Information. – Minsk, 2016.
72. Article 4 IAC Law.
73. According to Art. 25 IAC Law. This provision is fully in line with Art. 19 UNCITRAL Model Law 1985.

the order of consideration; in the absence of such an agreement, the application of the rights will be adjusted according to the applicable regulations.[74]

[D] Restrictions on Party Autonomy

[1] General Observations

1.45. The party autonomy is restricted by mandatory rules of law[75] and public policy.[76] The choice of foreign law made by an agreement or other actions of the parties is illegal when it contradicts the imperative rules of choice of law of the section VII "Private International Law" of Civil Code.[77]

[2] Reasonable Connection Test

1.46. If it is impossible to determine the applicable law, the law which has the closest connection to legal relations with a foreign element will be applicable.[78] If a person has two or more citizenships, personal law is the law that has the closest connection with the person.[79] If it is impossible to determine the performance as having decisive significance for the content of the contract, the law of the state with which the contract is most closely connected is applied.[80]

[3] National Public Policy

1.47. Foreign law shall not be applied in instances when its application is contrary to the fundamentals of the law and the public order of Belarus as well as in other cases directly provided for by law. In these instances, the law of Belarus shall be applied.[81]

---

74. Article 12 of IAC Law.
75. Article 1100 of Civil Code.
76. Article 1099 of Civil Code. *See also*: Янович З.Н., Шадуро К.В. "Оговорка о публичном порядке как один из основных институтов международного частного права" / ConsultantPlus: Belarus. Technology PROF [Electronic resource] / Jurspectre Ltd., National Centre of Legal Information. – Minsk, 2016; Функ Я. Сверхимперативные нормы и оговорка о публичном порядке как правовые явления, ограничивающие применение иностранного права при разрешении спора международным арбитражем, ConsultantPlus: Belarus. Technology PROF [Electronic resource] / Jurspectre Ltd., National Centre of Legal Information. – Minsk, 2016; Корочкин А.Ю. Обход закона в коллизионном праве Республики Беларусь, Промышленно-торговое право, 2009, N 05.
77. Article 1097 of Civil Code. *See also*: Леанович Е.Б. Обход закона в международном частном праве и злоупотребление правом (шикана) в гражданском праве. ConsultantPlus: Belarus. Technology PROF [Electronic resource] / Jurspectre Ltd., National Centre of Legal Information. – Minsk, 2016.
78. In accordance with Art. 1093 Civil Code.
79. Article 1103 Civil Code.
80. Article 1125(4) Civil Code.
81. Article 1099 Civil Code.

[4] Mandatory Rules of Municipal Law

1.48. The rules of the section "Private International Law" of the Civil Code shall not impact the effect of the mandatory rules of the law of Belarus, which regulate the corresponding relations regardless of the applicable law.[82] The concept of mandatory rules is not fixed normatively, but the norms concerning currency legislation, legislation on foreign trade and antimonopoly legislation are traditionally considered to fall under this rubric.

1.49. Upon the application of the law of a country (other than Belarus), according to the rules of private international law, the court may apply the mandatory rules of that country if, under the law of that country, such rules are intended to regulate the corresponding relations regardless of the applicable law. In such instances, the court shall take into consideration the purpose and nature of such rules as well as the consequences of application thereof.

[5] International Public Policy

1.50. The concept of international public policy is unknown to the Belarusian legislation, and is not in use even with the issues of recognition and enforcement of foreign arbitration awards.

[E] No Explicit Choice of Law

[1] Introduction

1.51. With respect to agreements and contracts not specified in Article 1125(1–3) Civil Code,[83] and in the absence of the parties' agreement concerning the applicable law, the law of the state where the party whose actions are decisive in terms of the content of such a contract shall be applied. Should it be impossible to determine the main location of the business of the party whose actions are decisive in terms of the content of such a contract, the law of the state where this party resides or is located shall be applied. Should it be impossible to determine the actions that would be considered to be decisive under such a contract, the law of the country to which the contract is most closely related shall be applied.[84]

[2] Relevant Conflict of Law Rules

1.52. In accordance with Article 1127 of the Civil Code, "Domain of Applicable Law," the law applicable to a contract by virtue of the provisions of this article shall cover the following topics: (a) contract interpretation; (b) rights and duties of the parties;

---

82. Article 1100 Civil Code.
83. The principle of specific performance is applied in those provisions.
84. Article 1125(4) Civil Code.

(c) contract performance; (d) consequences of failure to perform or improper performance of the contract; (e) contract termination; (f) consequences of nullity or invalidity of the contract; (h) assignment on demand and transfer of debts in connection with the contract.[85]

1.53. The law of the country where the legal person in question is established shall be applied to contracts concerning the creation of such a legal person with a foreign dimension.[86] According to Article 1127(2) Civil Code, which concerns the subject matter of contract performance and the measures that shall be taken in cases of improper performance, in addition to the law applicable under the contract, the law of the country in which the performance takes place shall also be taken into consideration.

[F] The Law Governing the Arbitration Agreement

1.54. Parties have the right to regulate the law applicable to the contract and to the arbitration agreement.[87] In the event that such a right is not defined, the applicable law will be determined on the basis of the lex arbitri hereunder, as it follows from the New York Convention[88] and Geneva Convention.[89]

§4.04 THE ARBITRATORS

[A] Appointment of Arbitrators

[1] Appointment of Arbitrators under Municipal Law

1.55. The Parties may, by mutual agreement, determine the procedure for the appointment of an arbitrator or arbitrators, subject to the provisions of the IAC Law.[90] The quantity of arbitrators in a panel of the IAC for the resolution of the dispute is

---

85. See Award of IAC by BelCCI of September 2, 2009 (case No 765/46-08); Функ Я., Перерва И. "Определение применимого права при разрешении Международным арбитражным судом при риомражспорусь/ возникших из договоров международной купли-продажи товаров" / Промышленно-торговое право, 2009, N 01, 02; договор международной купли-продажи товаров и договоры международного торгового посредничества
(в 3 книгах). Книга 1. Универсальная международно-правовая унификация купли-продажи товаров"/ ConsultantPlus: Belarus. Technology PROF [Electronic resource] / Jurspectre Ltd., National Centre of Legal Information. – Minsk, 2016.
86. Article 1126 Civil Code. See also: Функ Я. Выбор применимого права в силу коллизионных норм Республики Беларусь/ Таможня и ВЭД, 2005, N 1, 2.
87. See also: Ермоленко, Е.В. Право, применимое к арбитражному соглашению / Е.В. Ермоленко / ConsultantPlus: Belarus. Technology PROF [Electronic resource] / Jurspectre Ltd., National Centre of Legal Information. – Minsk, 2016; Функ, Я. И. Международный арбитраж в Республике Беларусь: пособие / Я.И. Функ / ConsultantPlus: Belarus. Technology PROF [Electronic resource] / Jurspectre Ltd., National Centre of Legal Information. – Minsk, 2016.
88. Articles II (2), V(1)(2) of the New York Convention.
89. Article VI of the Geneva Convention.
90. Article 17 IAC Law.

Chapter 4: Belarus §4.04[B]

determined by agreement of the parties or, in the absence of such agreement, includes three arbitrators.[91]

1.56. Article 17(4) IAC Law establishes the competence of the Chairman of the IAC and the Chairman of the BelCCI as appointment authorities if the timely formation of the panel is not possible. Article 17(5) IAC Law sets out the requirements that must be considered in the appointment of arbitrators by the appointment authorities.

[2] Appointment under Institutional Rules

1.57. According to Article 5 of Rules of IAC at BelCCI the quantity of arbitrators is determined by agreement of the parties or, failing such agreement includes three arbitrators. These are: the arbitrator, a reserve arbitrator, as well as a primary or alternate presiding arbitrator, who may be elected (appointed) only with the consent of a competent individual with adequate experience and the necessary personal qualities.

1.58. For the resolution of disputes between the parties from Belarus, an arbitrator appointed to the case must be included in the list of arbitrators. The presiding arbitrator may be elected (appointed) only from the list of arbitrators. Co-plaintiffs and several defendants elect one main and one reserve arbitrator. Third parties do not have the right to choose the arbitrator.

[B] Qualifications of Arbitrators

1.59. Article 17(1) IAC Law stipulates that no one may be deprived of the right to become an arbitrator because of his nationality or citizenship, unless the parties agree otherwise. The Domestic Arbitration Law in Article 13 stipulates much tougher requirements for arbitrators. According to this norm, an arbitrator must: be disinterested in the outcome of the case, be independent of the parties, and have given consent to discharge of duties of the arbitrator. The arbitrator, resolving a dispute alone, must have a law degree and experience in the legal profession for at least three years. In case of a collective dispute resolution, a law degree and experience in the legal profession for at least three years is required for the chairman of the Arbitral Tribunal, and the other arbitrators shall have any higher education and work experience in the relevant specialty for at least three years.

1.60. An arbitrator may not be a neutral person who:[92] (a) is a public servant, including exercising the powers of the judge in the court; (b) is duly recognized as incapable or partially capable; (c) holds a criminal record; (d) whose powers as a judge of the court, prosecutor, police officer, member of Belarus Investigation Committee, State Committee for forensic examinations of Belarus, the state security agencies, border guard, employee of Belarus State Control Committee bodies, tax and customs authorities, an employee of a private notary, or lawyer were discontinued or ceased on

---

91. Article 16 IAC Law.
92. Article 13 of Domestic Arbitration Law.

grounds relating to the commission of offenses that are incompatible with his professional activities for three years from the date of adoption of such decision, unless otherwise provided by legislation.[93]

[C] Powers and Duties of Arbitrators

1.61. An arbitration panel has the right to determine the admissibility, relevance, materiality and weight of any evidence and request the State court for the provisional measures.[94] Arbitrators should be independent and impartial[95] to hear the case;[96] their main duty is to give to the parties equal possibilities to represent their case,[97] follow procedural rules and parties consent,[98] inform parties on presented evidence,[99] and to correct and/or interpret the award.[100]

[D] Challenges and Replacement of Arbitrators

[1] Challenges under Municipal Law

1.62. In accordance with Article 18 IAC Law, an arbitrator may be challenged only if circumstances give rise to justifiable doubts as to his impartiality or independence, or if he does not possess qualifications agreed to by the parties. A party may challenge an arbitrator whom it has appointed only if the circumstances related to lack of impartiality became known to it after his election.

1.63. A person who knows about the possible appointment (election) of himself or herself as an arbitrator must report on the circumstances that might give rise to justifiable doubts as to his or her impartiality, independence or competence. If the arbitrator did not do so prior to the appointment (election), he or she is obliged to inform the parties of any such circumstances as soon as possible in the course of the proceedings. The arbitrator may challenge himself or herself.

[2] Challenges under Institutional Rules

1.64. Similar requirements are established in Article 9 of the Rules of the IAC at the BelCCI. The parties may also, by mutual agreement, determine the procedure for challenging an arbitrator. The interested party submits to the tribunal a written

---

93. No such special law rules for this exist yet.
94. Article 35 IAC Law.
95. Article 18 IAC Law.
96. Article 20 IAC Law.
97. Article 24 IAC Law.
98. Article 25 IAC Law.
99. Article 32 IAC Law.
100. Article 42 IAC Law.

reasoned statement of such withdrawal. The application for disqualification of an arbitrator shall be filed within fifteen days from the day when the party became aware of the appointment of an arbitrator or of the corresponding of the grounds for his removal.

1.65. If the arbitrator being challenged does not report the rejection, the problem is solved by the other two arbitrators before the hearing of the case. If they fail to reach an agreement before the start of proceedings, or if removal is pending against two or more arbitrators or against a sole arbitrator, the Chairman of the IAC addresses the issue of withdrawal of court staff.

1.66. The statement of rejection is submitted within ten days from the date of receipt of the communication on the election (appointment) of the arbitrator or presiding arbitrator. The application for rejection should be considered by the Chairman of the IAC within a week. Determination by the President of the IAC or by the panel of disqualification of an arbitrator (arbitrators) cannot be appealed.

[E] Compensation of Arbitrators

1.67. The Belarus IAC Law does not provide for an "arbitrator fee" concept. Article 15(2) of the IAC Law establishes that the amount of the arbitration fee and costs, as well as the procedure for their collection, is determined – for a permanent international tribunal arbitration rules and for the ad hoc court – by the agreement between the parties to the dispute and the arbitrators. The arbitrators' remuneration in the IAC fixed by BelCCI paid from the amounts of the arbitration fee;[101] however, the scale of fees of the arbitrators is not envisaged.

1.68. Under Article 44(3) of the Law on Domestic Arbitration, in the domestic permanent arbitration court, remuneration of arbitrators shall be determined in accordance with the scale of remuneration of the arbitrators, which must be provided in the rules of the permanent arbitration court.

§4.05 JURISDICTION OF THE ARBITRATION TRIBUNAL

[A] Introduction

1.69. The IAC Law provides for the right of the International Arbitration Court to decide the question of their competence and make an appropriate award on the competence of the arbitral tribunal, including any objections with respect to the existence or validity of the arbitration agreement.

---

101. Article 49 of the Rules of IAC at BelCCI.

[B] The Arbitrators' Determination of Their Jurisdiction

1.70. International Arbitration Court in Belarus has the right to decide the question of their competence and make an appropriate interim award, considering any objections with respect to the existence or validity of the arbitration agreement.[102]

1.71. A party may make the following statements: (a) the international arbitration court has no jurisdiction later than in the statement of defense. Appointment of an arbitrator, or participated in the appointment of an arbitrator is not precluded from raising such a plea; (b) the panel exceeds the limits of its competence, – as soon as the issue will be raised during the proceedings. The panel may admit a later plea if it recognizes a valid reason for the delay.

[C] Court Review of Arbitrators' Jurisdiction

1.72. When the parties have concluded an arbitration agreement, the arbitration agreement is not an obstacle to filing a claim to an appropriate economic court.[103] Economic courts resolve the dispute on the merits regardless of the application by the defendant and request for the transfer of the dispute to an international arbitration court; if it is found that the arbitration agreement is null and void, it cannot be executed.[104]

[D] Institutional Rules

1.73. According to the Article 11 of Rules of the IAC at the BelCCI, when the panel of arbitrators is not appointed, the question on competence is ruled by the court's president. A plea that the IAC at the BelCCI does not have jurisdiction shall be raised not later than the submission of the statement of defense. A party is not precluded from raising such a plea by the fact that it has appointed, or participated in the appointment of, an arbitrator. A plea that the ICAC is exceeding the scope of its jurisdiction shall be raised as soon as the matter alleged to be beyond the scope of its jurisdiction is raised during the arbitral proceedings. If the panel or the IAC president finds the arbitration court competent, the IAC Presidium may be requested by the party within fifteen days to render a final resolution on the issue of competence.

---

102. Article 22 of IAC Law. *See also*: Interim Award of IAC by BelCCI of March 16, 2005 (Case No 464/39-04). ConsultantPlus: Belarus. Technology PROF [Electronic resource] / Jurspectre Ltd., National Centre of Legal Information. – Minsk, 2016.
103. According to the Para 13 of the Resolution of the Plenum of the Supreme Economic Court of Belarus of October 31, 2011 No 21 On Some Issues of Resolving by the Economic Courts of the Republic of Belarus of Cases Involving Foreign Persons.
104. Article II (3) of the Convention on the recognition and enforcement of foreign arbitral awards, done at New York, June 10, 1958.

§4.06 THE PROCEDURE BEFORE THE ARBITRATION TRIBUNAL

[A] Introduction

1.74. The present chapter considers the procedure before the arbitration court by the example of IAC at the BelCCI that follows the UNCITRAL Model Law approach.

[B] General Principles of Municipal Judicial Procedure

1.75. According to Chapter 2 of the Commercial Procedure Code, the general principles of commercial (economic) procedure are: (1) administration of justice only by the courts considering economic affairs; (2) collective and individual consideration of cases; (3) the independence of judges of the court, considering the economic affairs; (4) procedural economy; (5) the legality of the proceedings in the court seized economic affairs; (6) equality before the law and the court considering economic cases; (7) clarification of the procedural rights and procedural obligations; (8) respect for the dignity of the individual; (9) equal rights and integrity of the parties; (10) competitiveness; (11) publicity of the proceedings; (12) the right to legal assistance; (13) optionality; (14) the immediacy of the trial; (15) obligation of judgments and judicial appeals; (16) judicial review and the regulation of language of procedure and using a foreign law.

[C] General Principles of Arbitration Procedure (Party Autonomy, Speed, Impartiality, Etc.)

1.76. The principles that govern the international court of arbitration in the resolution of the dispute are set in Article 3 of the IAC LAW. These are the principles: (a) equality of rights of the parties; (b) the freedom to choose the panel by the parties, the applicable law, procedure and court language; (c) consensual jurisdiction of all cases; (d) priority of the universally recognized principles of international law; (e) the independence of international arbitration and the arbitrators; (f) confidentiality of the cases; (g) court assistance in a settlement agreement by the parties; (h) the finality of awards. The International Court of Arbitration is also guided by the principles of economic procedural legislation of Belarus, which do not contradict the "special" arbitral principles.

1.77. In domestic arbitration, principles are stipulated in Article 5 of the Domestic Arbitration Law, and they are similar to the aforementioned principles. The "extra" principles are legality and the retribution of arbitrators.[105]

---

[105] *See also*: В.С. "Каменков Принципы третейского разбирательства" / Consultant Plus; Ермоленко Е.В. **Принципы деятельности постоянно действующего международного арбитражного суда в Республике Беларусь.** ConsultantPlus: Belarus. Technology PROF [Electronic resource] / Jurspectre Ltd., National Centre of Legal Information. – Minsk, 2016.

[D] Commencing the Arbitral Proceedings

[1] Municipal Law

1.78. The proceedings in the permanent acting International Arbitration Court begins from the date specified in the arbitration rules.[106]

[2] Institutional Rules

1.79. Unless the parties agree otherwise, international arbitration proceedings for the consideration of a particular dispute commence on the date when the claim is received by the respondent. Rules of the IAC at the Belarusian Chamber of Commerce provide that the proceedings are initiated on the day of admission by the International Court of Arbitration of a statement of claim and payment of the arbitration fee.[107]

1.80. Upon receipt of the statement of claim, the response to the claim and documents attached thereto, the panel prepares a case for trial, and then fixes the time and place of the hearing. This may take into account the wishes of the parties. The parties are notified in advance[108] about the time and place of the hearing.

[E] Conduct of Arbitration

[1] Written Submissions

1.81. Unless otherwise agreed by the parties, the International Arbitration Court determines whether to hold oral hearings or consider the case only on the basis of documents and other written materials. However, in the absence of agreement of the parties to waive an oral hearing, the International Arbitral Tribunal shall hold such hearings if requested by either party.[109]

1.82. Requirements to the statement of claim shall be agreed by the parties or determined by the IAC for consideration of a particular dispute, as defined by the rules of arbitration[110] at the institutional IAC. In the absence of an agreement to the contrary, either party may amend or supplement his statements if the panel does not regard this as impractical in view of possible delays.[111]

[2] Post-hearing Briefs

1.83. Such briefs are not envisaged in the IAC Law or BelCCI Rules. There is no prohibition to do this, and there is also no rule that makes the hearing the absolute end

---

106. Article 28 IAC Law.
107. Article 23 of Rules.
108. Article 26 of the Rules of the IAC at the BelCCI.
109. Article 32 IAC Law.
110. Article 29 IAC Law.
111. Article 29 IAC Law.

of the procedure, after which any additional submission is impossible. In practice, the arbitration tribunals and especially the IAC by BelCCI are not strict on timing and are very flexible if they find this post-hearing brief crucial for the dispute resolution. Nevertheless, as was stated above, the tribunal has the full discretion to decide if the new submission may be admissible without making any delay for the case.

[3]   Evidence (Admissibility, Documentary Evidence)

1.84. The allocation of the burden of proof is not resolved literally by IAC Law and BelCCI Rules; rather, however, it is derived from the adversarial principle.[112] Submissions and evidence provided by one of the parties to the panel shall be transferred to another party. The panel or the party with the arbitrator's consent may refer to the state court or the court of a foreign state with the request of the assistance in receipt of evidence in the matter settled at the International Arbitration Court.[113] The parties are obliged to present evidence confirming the content of the rules of the foreign law to which they make a reference.[114]

[4]   Witness and Experts Testimony

1.85. Belarusian arbitral legislation contains no detailed provisions with regard to the witnesses. The feature of Domestic Arbitration Law is that an arbitration award court may be appealed and annulled if the party seeking annulment of the arbitral award presents evidence that a court decision having legal force set false testimony of a witness or knowingly false expert opinion.[115]

[F]   Hearings

1.86. Unless otherwise agreed by the parties, the panel determines whether to hold oral hearings or consider the case only on the basis of documents and other written materials. However, in the absence of an agreement of the parties to waive an oral hearing the international arbitral tribunal shall hold such hearings if requested by either party.[116]

---

112. См. Бончковский Е.А. Доказывание в арбитражном и хозяйственном процессе, Промышленно-торговое право, 2012, No 12.
113. Article 35 of IAC Law.
114. Article 37 (2) IAC Law.
115. Article 47 Domestic Arbitration Law.
116. Article 32 of IAC Law.

§4.07 THE ARBITRAL AWARD

[A] Introduction

1.87. The main task of the international arbitration court is the timely resolution of disputes within its competence.[117] Accordingly, we can say that rendering an award is a duty of the international tribunal.

[B] Deliberation and Voting

1.88. In a case where the dispute is resolved by a panel of arbitrators, the award is taken by the majority of arbitrators.[118] IAC Law, like most national legislation, does not contain specific requirements for award-making procedures, nor do the Rules of the IAC at the BelCCI.

[C] Different Kinds of Awards (Separate, Interim, Consent, Default, Etc.)

1.89. All acts of the arbitral tribunal, depending on the subject matter can be divided into two types: (a) arbitration award, containing the answers to the court at the plaintiff's statement (final award); (b) Interim award containing the answers to the other questions that arise during the process.

[D] Interest and Costs

1.90. In Belarus, interest is a matter of substantive law.[119] Subject to contractual law provisions, interest on the principal debt is usually awarded. In arbitrations under BelCCI Rules, interest can only be awarded in the form of a lump sum as part of the monetary claim covered by the arbitration fee.

1.91. The amount of the arbitration fee and costs, as well as the procedure for their collection, is determined in accordance with arbitration rules for a permanent international tribunal, and in accordance with the agreement between the parties to the dispute and arbitrators for ad hoc arbitration.[120]

[E] Effects of the Award

[1] Execution

1.92. The enforcement of arbitral awards is made according to the rules of the Commercial Procedure Code[121] and international treaties – the New York Convention

---

117. Article 2(1) IAC Law.
118. Article 38 IAC Law.
119. Article 366 of Civil Code.
120. Article 15(2) IAC Law.
121. Chapters 28-29.

of 1958 and the European Convention of 1961. As soon as the enforcement order is made by a competent economic court, an award may be executed in the regular way in Belarus.

1.93. There are two different ways of enforcement: for the arbitral awards made in Belarus (the easiest way),[122] and for foreign arbitral awards (recognition and enforcement based on New York Convention 1958).[123]

[2] Res Judicata *and* Lis Pendens

1.94. Economic courts shall refuse to accept the statement of claim on the grounds that there is an award by the International Court of Arbitration on the dispute between the same parties on the same subject and on the same grounds.[124] This also applies in respect to a foreign arbitral award, except for the cases when the economic court denied recognition and enforcement of such an award. That is, the ban prohibits resuing attempts to circumvent a resolution.

1.95. The facts established by an award of the international arbitration court, have the prejudice in cases before the state court, involving the same persons, or their successors.[125]

[F] Correction and Interpretation of the Award

[1] Municipal Law

1.96. The interpretation, rectification of an award, or an additional award shall be made in writing, signed by all the arbitrators or a majority. It is also necessary to specify the motives, the date of the act and place of the meeting of the International Arbitration Court.[126]

1.97. Within thirty days after receiving the award, if the arbitration rules or agreement between the parties do not provide otherwise, a party, with notice to the other party, may request the international tribunal to correct any award counting errors, clerical, typographical errors or other errors of a similar nature, and also to ask the international arbitral tribunal to give an interpretation of a specific point or part of the solution.[127] If necessary, the named period can be extended by the tribunal.

---

122. Chapter 29 of Commercial Procedure Code.
123. Chapter 28 of Commercial Procedure Code.
124. On the basis of Art. 164 Commercial Procedure Code.
125. Articles 106 and 182 of Commercial Procedure Code. *See also*: Данилевич А.С. Решение международного арбитражного суда, Белорусский журнал международного права и международных отношений – 2001. – No 4. – C. 49-55.
126. Article 40 IAC Law.
127. Article 42 IAC Law.

[2] Institutional Rules

1.98. These are similar to the IAC Law provisions; in fact, they contain Article 41 of the Rules of IAC at the BelCCI.

§4.08 SETTING ASIDE THE AWARD

[A] Introduction

1.99. Control of the competent regional (first instance) economic court on the submitted application is limited to checking the grounds for cancellation of the legislation. Such control may end at the onset of the following consequences: (a) the annulment of the award; (b) failure to satisfy the request for the annulment; (c) deferred examination of the request for annulment for a period established, to provide the international arbitral tribunal an opportunity to hear again the case or take other action, which will eliminate the grounds for setting aside an award.[128]

1.100. IAC Law applies only to the activities of the arbitral tribunal in the territory of Belarus, that is, the use of it abroad is illegal (Article 4). Such regulation in the Belarusian law potentially eliminates international conflict of jurisdiction, possible under the European Convention of 1961.

1.101. A petition of annulment of an award of the International Arbitration Court may be lodged within three months from the date when the party that has lodged this petition has received an arbitration award, and in the case, when the request has been placed in accordance with rules on correction of an award – from the date of making a corrected award.

[B] Invalid Awards

1.102. The IAC Law and the Law on Domestic Arbitration does not distinguish types of the awards for the purposes of setting aside procedure, so all the awards rendered in Belarus could be equally challenged on the grounds provided in each of these laws as applicable.

[C] Challengeable Awards

[1] Grounds for Challenging the Award

1.103. An award of the International Arbitration Court in Belarus may be annulled in cases where the party petitioning it provides evidence of procedural violations – same as the grounds of refusal to enforcement of an arbitral award in the New York Convention 1958.

---

128. Article 43 IAC Law.

1.104. An award of the International Arbitration Court may be cancelled also in cases where the subject of a dispute cannot be a subject of the arbitration agreement under the legislation of Belarus, or where an award of the panel of the IAC contradicts the public order of Belarus.[129]

[2] Waiver of Right to Challenge

1.105. The right to refuse a possible appeal of the award does not provide for Belarusian legislation.

[D] Review of Jurisdictional Awards

1.106. If the panel of the permanent acting IAC accepts jurisdiction, any party within fifteen days after receiving notice of it may ask the Presidium of the Court to make a final ruling on the issue of competence. At the time of settlement of the question of the competence of the IAC trial, the case is suspended.[130]

1.107. A controversial decision was made by the Cassational Collegium of the Supreme Economic Court of Belarus in case No. 01-17/42MX-1/05/884K in 2005.[131] The court wrongly interpreted the provision of Article V(3) of the Geneva Convention 1961 saying that the interim award on competence may be appealed to the state court. In our opinion, this mistake derives from the bad translation of the Geneva Convention 1961 to Russian; the original statement "subject to any subsequent judicial control..." was translated as "possible appeal of an award." In any event, this case is now widely recognized but not followed.

§4.09 RECOGNITION AND ENFORCEMENT OF THE ARBITRAL AWARD

[A] Enforcement of Domestic Awards

[1] Enforcement Domestically

1.108. In accordance with the Belarusian legislation are domestic arbitral awards. These do not require the recognition of Belarus when decisions on their performance do not apply the New York Convention 1958.[132] The Supreme Economic Court in its

---

129. Article 43 IAC Law. *See also*: Данилевич А.С. Обжалование решения международного арбитражного суда (сравнительно-правовой анализ), Вестник Высшего Хозяйственного Суда Республики Беларусь. – 2002. – No 2. – C. 197-221.
130. Article 22 (5) (6) LIAC.
131. Decision of the Cassational Collegium of the Supreme Economic Court of Belarus of September 21, 2005 on case No 01-17/42MX-1/05/884K ConsultantPlus: Belarus. Technology PROF [Electronic resource] / Jurspectre Ltd., National Centre of Legal Information. – Minsk, 2016.
132. *See*: Перерва, И.В. Особенности определения "национальности" арбитражного решения в праве Республики Беларусь, ConsultantPlus: Belarus. Technology PROF [Electronic resource] / Jurspectre Ltd., National Centre of Legal Information. – Minsk, 2016; Перерва, И.В. Особенности исполнения решений внутренних международных арбитражных (третейских) судов

letter dated April 16, 2002 No. 03-25/771 "On the enforcement of foreign awards, as well as international arbitration courts,"[133] pointed out that the IAC at the BelCCI awards, as well as other awards rendered on the territory of Belarus, do not need recognition.

1.109. Thus, for the issuance of an order to enforce "the local" award, the claimant refers to the economic court at the place of residence of the debtor, or at the location of the debtor's property, if its location or place of residence is unknown.[134] Such a declaration may be filed within six months from the date of expiry of the voluntary execution of the award, which is usually specified in the award.[135]

1.110. The Court may refuse to issue the executive document on the grounds of private[136] and public nature.[137] The court may on its own initiative apply for setting aside if the dispute cannot be subject to arbitration under the law of Belarus, or if the arbitrators' nomination violates the fundamental principles of the law of Belarus. It should be noted that the list of grounds for refusal to issue the executive a document is not exhaustive.[138]

1.111. In general, the issuance of an order of execution may be refused in cases of essentially identical grounds as for the cancellation of the award of the International Arbitration Court,[139] except for the following provisions (they differ from the grounds for annulment): (a) the award was not binding on the parties to the arbitration proceedings, or was revoked, or its execution was suspended by the economic court; (b) the award violates the fundamental principles of the law of Belarus.

ConsultantPlus: Belarus. Technology PROF [Electronic resource] / Jurspectre Ltd., National Centre of Legal Information. – Minsk, 2016.

133. On enforcement of decisions of foreign courts and international arbitration courts: a letter of the Supreme Economic Court of the Republic of Belarus of April 16, 2002 No 03-25/771 // Bulletin of the Supreme Economic Court of the Republic of Belarus. – 2002. – No 6. Sey also: Скобелев В. Исполнение внутренних иностранных арбитражных решений (часть 1)" ConsultantPlus: Belarus. Technology PROF [Electronic resource], Jurspectre Ltd., National Centre of Legal Information. – Minsk, 2016.
134. Article 258 Commercial Procedure Code.
135. *See* on the issue: О доказательствах, подтверждающих неисполнение решения арбитражного (третейского) суда: разъяснение Высш. Хоз. Суда Респ. Беларусь, 27 июня 2008 г., No 03-29/1378, ConsultantPlus: Belarus. Technology PROF [Electronic resource] / Jurspectre Ltd., National Centre of Legal Information. – Minsk, 2016; Decision of Cassational Collegium of Supreme Economic Court of Republic of Belarus of November 04, 2008 (Case No 6-12MX/2008/1220K), ConsultantPlus: Belarus. Technology PROF [Electronic resource] / Jurspectre Ltd., National Centre of Legal Information. – Minsk, 2016.
136. Article 260(1) Commercial Procedure Code.
137. Article 260(2) Commercial Procedure Code.
138. Article 260 Commercial Procedure Code.
139. Article 255 Commercial Procedure Code and Art. 43 IAC Law.

[2] Enforcement Abroad

1.112. Belarusian law does not contain specific rules regarding enforcement of its domestic awards abroad. Such enforcement is subject to applicable international treaties and national legislation in the place of enforcement.

[B] Enforcement of Foreign Arbitral Awards

[1] Introduction to Recognition and Enforcement

1.113. The main documents governing the recognition and enforcement of foreign arbitral awards in Belarus are the New York Convention, IAC Law, Chapter 28 of Commercial Procedure Code, Annex 4 to the Civil Procedural Code, and the Resolution of the Plenum of the Supreme Court of the Republic of Belarus of December 12, 2014 No. 18 "On the application of the recognition and enforcement of the law courts of foreign judgments and foreign arbitral awards."[140]

1.114. The awards of international arbitration courts, which do not require enforcement, shall be recognized without any further proceedings, if the party does not file an objection.[141] The request for recognition and enforcement of a foreign arbitral award is fed by the creditor to the economic court at the location or place of residence of the debtor, or the location of the property of the debtor if the location or place of residence is unknown.[142]

1.115. Request for the recognition and enforcement of a foreign arbitral award is considered in the hearing by the sole judge of the economic court in a period not exceeding one month from the date of its filing to the court. The economic court shall not review a foreign arbitral award on the merits.[143] The decision of the economic court on the case of the recognition and enforcement of a foreign arbitral award shall come into force immediately and may be appealed to the court of cassation and to the supervisory authority.[144]

1.116. A foreign arbitral award may be enforced within a period not exceeding three years from the date of its entry into force (not to be confused with the coming into force of the decision of economic court in the case of the recognition and enforcement of a

---

140. *See*: Горонков, М. Об отдельных вопросах деятельности суда при рассмотрении заявлений о признании и приведении в исполнение решений иностранных судов и иностранных арбитражных решений по хозяйственным (торговым) делам / М. Горонков // Вест. Высш. Хоз. Суда Респ. Беларусь. – 2005. – No3. – C. 67– 75; Горонков, М. Основания и порядок признания и исполнения решений иностранных судов по хозяйственным делам в соответствии с международными договорами Республики Беларусь // Вест. Высш. Хоз. Суда Респ. Беларусь.. – 2000. – No4. – C. 150-170;
141. Article 45 IAC Law.
142. Article 246(1) Commercial Procedure Code.
143. Article 4, Art. 247 Commercial Procedure Code.
144. According to Chapters 32 and 33 of Commercial Procedure Code.

[2] Separate, Partial and Interim Awards

1.117. Enforcement of separate, partial and interim arbitral awards is not regulated by Belarusian legislation and relevant case law is absent.

[3] Grounds for Refusing Recognition and Enforcement

[a] Lack of Capacity and Invalidity of Arbitration Agreement

1.118. In accordance with Article V of the New York Convention of 1958, Article IX(2) of the European Convention of 1961, and Article 248(2) Commercial Procedure Code, recognition or enforcement of the award, regardless of the country in which it was made, may be refused only at the request of the party against whom it is invoked, if that party furnishes to the competent court where recognition or enforcement is sought, evidence that: (a) one of the parties to the arbitration agreement was lacking legal capacity; or (b) the agreement is not valid under the law that the parties have applied, and in the absence of indications of such a law, the law of the country where the award was made.[146]

[b] Procedural Violations

1.119. Belarusian legislation fully implements the provisions of the New York Convention on the use of a narrow circle of procedural irregularities as a ground for refusing recognition and enforcement of foreign and "domestic" awards.[147]

[c] Excess of Mandate

1.120. The practice of cancellation of the award of the international tribunal on the basis of such procedural irregularities has not been studied in the Belarusian legal

---

145. by the rules provided by Chapter 12 of Commercial Procedure Code. *See also*: Горонков М.П. Некоторые последствия признания и отказа в признании и приведении в исполнение решения иностранного суда или иностранного арбитражного решения // Вест. Высш. Хоз. Суда Респ. Беларусь. 2005 – No 7 – С. 40-43.
146. Скобелев В. Исполнение внутренних и иностранных арбитражных Решений. / Consultant-Plus: Belarus. Technology PROF [Electronic resource] / Jurspectre Ltd., National Centre of Legal Information. – Minsk, 2016.
147. *See* on the issue: Перерва И.В. Особенности исполнения решений иностранных международных арбитражных судов на территории Республики Беларусь, Промышленно-торговое право, 2004, N 05-06.

literature; thus, relevant failure cases are not described. V. Skobeleu says anyway on a situation, when the arbitration agreement submitted to an arbitration encompasses all disputes concerning the execution of a contract only but a panel issued an award on the termination of the contract.[148]

[d]   Arbitral Award Not Binding

1.121. Considering the immediate final character of arbitration awards in most jurisdictions, Belarusian courts have never faced the problem of recognition and enforcement of awards not having res judicata.

[e]   Non-arbitrability

1.122. Belarusian legislation does not fix a list of disputes that cannot be subject to arbitration. The question of arbitrability of the dispute should be decided by the court (of course, only if the legislation does not impose an outright ban on the transfer of the dispute to arbitration) by analyzing the nature of the dispute – assessing the presence (or absence) in a dispute of significant public interest, such that resolution cannot occur via a private law (arbitration) order.[149]

[f]   Public Policy

1.123. In Article 1 of the IAC Law, public order is briefly defined as the basics of Belarus law; however, this definition does not add clarity about the concept and the content of public policy. Some clarification on the concept of "the foundations of law and order of the Republic of Belarus" made by the Supreme Economic Court,[150] stated that public policy comprises the basic principles of the various branches of law, with the exception of the principles outlined in the Constitution of Belarus. These are to be understood as: in civil law – the principles contained in Article 2 of the Civil Code;[151]

---

148. Скобелев В.П. Исполнение внутренних и иностранных арбитражных решений (часть 2) ConsultantPlus: Belarus. Technology PROF [Electronic resource] / Jurspectre Ltd., National Centre of Legal Information. – Minsk, 2016.
149. *Ibidem.*
150. *See* paras 98–102 of the Methodical recommendations on certain issues considering the economic courts of the Republic of Belarus of cases involving foreign individuals and legal assistance, approved by the Decree of the Presidium of the Supreme Economic Court of the Republic of Belarus of June 26, 2013 No 25, Not published officially.
151. the rule of law; the principle of social orientation regulation of economic activity; the principle of priority of public interests; the principle of equality of participants in civil relations; the principle of the inviolability of property; the principle of freedom of contract; the principle of good faith and reasonableness of participants in civil legal relations; the principle of the inadmissibility of arbitrary interference in private affairs; the principle of free exercise of civil rights, ensuring restoration of violated rights and their judicial protection.

and in procedural areas of the law – the principles embodied in the Code of Belarus on Judicial System and Status of Judges.[152]

1.124. It is contrary to the public policy of Belarus for the recognition and enforcement of foreign arbitral awards made in disputes between Belarusian entities (since such disputes fall within the exclusive competence of the state courts of Belarus).[153] In another case, the Supreme Economic Court of Belarus found a violation of the public order of Belarus in the fact that the claim was made by non-properly authorized representative.[154]

[4] Procedures for Recognition

1.125. The procedure for recognition of the award is fully consistent with the procedure provided for the enforcement of foreign arbitral awards.[155]

§4.10 INVESTOR-STATE ARBITRATION

[A] General Overview of Law and Practice Related to Investor-State Arbitration

1.126. Belarus quite rarely sues and is rarely sued in investment disputes; awards against Belarus in such disputes are not common. Belarus is trying to pursue an active policy to attract investment, but the public sector share in the economy is still high. In the public sector share now accounts for about 70% of GDP.[156] Priority areas and sectors for foreign direct investments in Belarus are the pharmaceutical industry, the biotechnology industry, nanotechnologies and nanomaterials, high technologies in the industry, new materials, the petrochemical and chemical industries, the mechanical engineering industry and production of machines and equipment, transport and transportation infrastructure, civil engineering, production of construction materials, agriculture, food industry, information and communication technologies, and tourism.[157] According to the International Monetary Fund data for the year 2014 the inward

---

152. Principles of the judicial authority to be held only by the courts (Art. 2); independence of the judiciary (Art. 2); recognition of compulsory execution on the entire territory of Belarus of court rulings that have entered into force (Art. 4); the legality of the administration of justice (Art. 7); equality of citizens and organizations before the law (Art. 8); the rights of citizens and organizations to judicial protection (Art. 10); the state language of proceedings and proceedings before the courts (Art. 13); mandatory court rulings and judges the requirements (Art. 14).
153. Paragraph 6 of the Resolution of the Plenum of the Supreme Economic Court of Belarus of December 23, 2005 No 34 On the Jurisdiction on Disputes after the Assignment, *see* above.
154. Функ, Я.И. Международный арбитраж в Республике Беларусь: справочник / – Минск: Дикта, 2005. – C. 128 – 130; *see also*: Бабкина Т., Семчик А. Специфика применения оговорки о публичном порядке в процессе приведения в исполнение иностранных арбитражных решений / Журнал международного права и международных отношений. – 2014 – No 3.
155. Chapter 28 of Commercial Procedure Code.
156. On Belarus, Zubr Capital, http://zubrcapital.by/o_belarusi.
157. Official Website of the Republic of Belarus, Investment in Belarus, http://www.belarus.by/en/business/belarus_investment.

direct investment for Belarus was USD 17,737 million and the outward direct investment was USD 633 million.[158]

1.127. Domestic legislation governing investment agreements with the state or state-owned entities comprises first of all the Decree of the President No. 10 of August 6, 2009 "On Creation of Additional Conditions for the Investment Activity in Republic of Belarus."[159] In order to enhance accountability for the implementation of the Decree, this introduces the obligation of investment of investors in the event of nonfulfillment (improper fulfillment) of the investment agreement to compensate the Republic of Belarus and its administrative territorial units expenses incurred during the implementation of investment incentives and preferences.

1.128. Belarus has yearly approved the investment promotion program.[160] The Foreign Investment Advisory Council under the Council of Ministers of the Republic of Belarus (FIAC) was established in order to enhance the effectiveness of efforts to attract foreign investment in the economy and improve the investment environment of Belarus.[161] The National Agency of Investment and Privatization is a state organization established for attracting foreign direct investments in the Republic of Belarus. The aim of the Agency is to improve the investment image of Belarus abroad, promote foreign investment projects in the territory of the country, and encourage potential investors to invest in the enterprises of a pilot privatization project which is being carried out together with the World Bank.[162]

1.129. The basic Law on Investments[163] contains a provision on protection of foreign investors' rights and rules for the investment dispute resolution. Article 13 of this law governs the dispute resolution procedure. If the dispute is not related to the exclusive competence of the Belarusian courts, have arisen between foreign investors and Belarus, and are not settled out of court through negotiations within three months from the date of receipt of the written proposals for their settlement out of court, then such disputes at the option of the investor can be resolved also by the: arbitral tribunal, established to resolve any dispute according to the arbitration rules on international

---

158. International Monetary Fund, IMF Data Access to Macroeconomic & Financial Data, Coordinated Direct Investment Survey (CDIS) http://www.doingbusiness.org/data/exploreeconomies/belarus/#dealing-with-construction-permits.
159. The Official Website of President of Republic of Belarus, http://president.gov.by/uploads/documents/8dek.pdf.
160. Edict of The President of Republic of Belarus dated January 18, 2016 No 30 "On Approval of the State Investment program for the year 2016" / http://www.pravo.by/main.aspx?guid=3871&p0=P31600030.
161. FIAC acts in accordance with the Decision of the Council of Ministers of the Republic of Belarus No. 1795 of December 12, 2001 "On the Foreign Investment Advisory Council under the Council of Ministers of the Republic of Belarus", http://w1.economy.gov.by/fiac/?page=1.php.
162. The National Investment and Privatisation Agency State Institution was established by Decree of the President of the Republic of Belarus No. 273 of May 25, 2010 – National Agency of Investment and Privatization, http://investinbelarus.by/en/about/History.
163. The Law of Republic of Belarus of July 12, 2013 "On Investments", the Official Legal Web-Portal of Republic of Belarus, http://www.pravo.by/main.aspx?guid=3871&p0=P3160003.

trade law of the United Nations Commission (UNCITRAL), if the parties to the dispute shall otherwise agree; or the International Centre for Settlement of Investment Disputes (ICSID), if the foreign investor is a citizen or legal person of a state that is a member of the Washington Convention of March 18, 1965. If an international treaty of Belarus and (or) the agreement between the investor and Belarus provided otherwise in relation to the settlement of disputes between the investor and Belarus, the provisions of these international agreement and (or) a contract are applying. Many of Belarusian BITs contain the similar provisions.

1.130. Belarusian BITs typically prescribe: protection from expropriation; fair and equitable treatment; full protection and security; an umbrella clause; and a most-favored nation clause. Belarus has no established practice of requiring confidentiality in investment arbitration due to the lack of the special legislation on such confidentiality, same as the jurisprudence.

1.131. According to the Law "On Archive and Records Management in the Republic of Belarus"[164] documents of the Ministry of Foreign Affairs and other ministries are to be kept in the state of the National Archival Fund, but for over fifteen years, they must first be kept in the archive of the Ministry. Archives for documents, which are not state secrets, are available for reference in the reading rooms of the archives in accordance with the Decree of the Ministry of Justice of May 24, 2012 No. 133 (in version of December 4, 2013) "On Approval of Regulations on the procedure for use of archival documents in reading rooms of public archives of the Republic of Belarus."[165]

[B] List of Investment Treaties the Country Has Ratified

1.132. Belarus has ratified the following multilateral treaties: (a) The ICSID Convention on the Settlement of Investment Disputes; (b) The Convention Establishing the Multilateral Investment Guarantee Agency (MIGA) (including amendments made by the Council of Governors of MIGA of November 14, 2010).

1.133. In the framework of MIGA Belarus has also ratified (a) the Amendments to the Convention on MIGA establishment of 2010,[166] (b) The Agreement between the Government of Belarus and MIGA on legal protection of guaranteed foreign investment;[167] (c) The Agreement between the Government of Belarus and MIGA on the use of local currency.[168] Two agreements were signed with countries of former USSR – the Convention on the Protection of the Rights of Investors (signed in the City of Moscow on March 28, 1997)[169] and the Agreement on encouragement and mutual protection of

---

164. National registry of Legal Acts of Republic of Belarus, December 7, 2011, No 136, 2/1875.
165. National registry of Legal Acts of Republic of Belarus, June 9, 2012, N 68, 8/25981.
166. National registry of Legal Acts of Republic of Belarus, July 27, 2011, No 84, 2/1851.
167. National registry of Legal Acts of Republic of Belarus, May 21, 2012, No 56, 2/1921.
168. National registry of Legal Acts of Republic of Belarus, May 16, 2012, No 55, 2/1910.
169. National registry of Legal Acts of Republic of Belarus, October 22, 2003, No 3/930.

investments in the states – members of the Eurasian Economic Community (Moscow, December 12, 2008).[170]

1.134. There is a special legislation in Belarus with regard to the pretrial settlement of state-investors disputes.[171] This legislation provides short instructions to the competent state entities on how to settle an investment dispute at the preliminary stage, but no mandatory procedural provisions are set by it.

1.135. Belarus has ratified bilateral agreements on assistance in and protection of investments with fifty-three countries (*see* Appendix 1). There is no model BIT in Belarus.

[C] List of Investor-State Disputes (Concluded and Pending)

1.136. There was only one case of an investment dispute that potentially might have reached the state level. On June 2, 2013 Mr. Gennady Mykhailenko, a Ukrainian citizen, filed a notice of dispute seeking to bring an ICSID claim for USD 175 million on the basis of direct loss and moral damages.

1.137. As it was reported, Gennady Mykhailenko, the former acting director of the Swiss Belarus-based enterprise Upeco Industries, was sentenced to six years in prison with property confiscation by the Čyhunačny District Court of the city of Homiel in 2006. The court found Mykhailenko guilty because of his actions on the post of director of Private Unitary Foreign Enterprise (PUIP) Upeco Industries in the period from 2003 to 2004. During that period, he took out loans from the Homiel Regional Branch of Belvnesheconombank by false pretences and breach of faith, and misappropriated funds amounting to the difference between the declared and actual value of the equipment that was purchased using the loans, which inflicted losses on the enterprise. The court also found that Mykhailenko forged documents that were of significant importance regarding receiving the loan.

1.138. Mr. Mykhailenko in his turn claimed that the trial was politically motivated and that he never pleaded guilty. A press release posted on the website of the law firm that represented his interests stated that the applicant "suffered severe physical and psychological abuse" during his imprisonment and was subject to inhuman conditions. Mr. Mykhailenko also claimed that "Belarusian officials repeatedly sought to persuade him to relinquish his shareholding in the company."

---

170. National registry of Legal Acts of Republic of Belarus, November 24, 2009, No 277, 2/1609.
171. Resolution of Council of Ministers of the Republic of Belarus of 14.2.2012 N 146 "On approval of the pre-trial settlement of disputes (disagreements), related to the implementation of investment" / National Register of Legal Acts of the Republic of Belarus, 21.2.2012, N 22, 5/35271. *See also*: Комментарий к постановлению Совета Министров Республики Беларусь от 14.2.2012 N 146 "Об утверждении Положения о досудебном урегулировании споров (разногласий), связанных с осуществлением инвестиций". ConsultantPlus: Belarus. Technology PROF [Electronic resource] / Jurspectre Ltd., National Centre of Legal Information. – Minsk, 2016.

1.139. In the notice of intent to submit the dispute to arbitration, the Ukrainian investor stated that the Republic of Belarus violated the bilateral agreements on protection of investments with Ukraine and Switzerland. As the Republic of Belarus is a Member-State of the ICSID Convention, Gennady Mykhailenko intended to bring the dispute before ICSID.

1.140. By September 23, 2013, his request had passed the initial review for compliance with formal requirements. There is not any additional information concerning the results of the review or the dispute as a whole, but according to the database of ICSID cases the case has not been considered before the ICSID.

[D] Reform Proposals

1.141. Despite the fact that Belarusian law on arbitration is rather progressive and is based on the model legislation, in our opinion, it is in need of reform. First of all, it concerns the settlement of the legislative rights of the International Arbitration Court of the adoption of interim measures on their own, without the need of recourse to national courts. The last edition of 2010 UNCITRAL Model Law on International Commercial Arbitration may serve as a model for such legislative change.

1.142. We also believe that the law should enable the authorities administering the International Arbitration Court to determine, in the absence of objections to the parties, that the legal proceedings can be carried out by a sole arbitrator. This will optimize the expenses of the parties.

1.143. With regard to domestic arbitration, we consider it reasonable to provide for a ban on the creation of arbitration courts associated with legal entities because it leads to the creation of so-called pocket courts that may not initially be independent and impartial in disputes involving legal entities, under the auspices of which they were established.

1.144. Establishing the amount of fee earnings of the arbitrators in international arbitration in Belarus requires better specification and clarity so as to establish exact, public and coherent criteria for determining the amount of fees, in particular on the basis of the scale, which forms part of the application, or on the basis of an hourly rate established in the regulations. The law should also contain a provision on the right to remuneration of the arbitrator in accordance with the scale of determining the amount of arbitrators' fee or in accordance with an hourly rate.

1.145. Practice shows that the presence of legislation rules for the composition of the appeal against the award of the arbitral tribunal in relation to their competence is often used by the defendant to prolong the arbitration process. We believe that this provision of the legislation is unnecessary; it does not reflect the modern trends in arbitration legislation worldwide.

Chapter 4: Belarus

APPENDIX I BELARUS' BITs[172]

No.	Country	Signed	Ratified (accessed) by Belarus	Entered into force for Belarus
1.	Azerbaijan	03.06.2010	17.05.2011	01.07.2011
2.	Austria	16.05.2001	04.12.2001	01.06.2002
3.	Armenia	26.05.2001		10.02.2002
4.	Bahrain	26.10.2002	20.05.2003	16.05.2008
5.	Bulgaria	21.02.1996	11.07.1996	11.11.1997
6.	Bosnia and Herzegovina	29.11.2004	06.11.2005	22.01.2006
7.	Cambodia	23.04.2014	15.12.2014	14.04.2016
8.	United Kingdom	01.03.1994	17.10.1994	28.12.1994
9.	Venezuela	08.12.2007	23.06.2008	13.08.2008
10.	Vietnam	08.07.1992	04.10.1994	24.11.1994
11.	Germany	02.04.1993	24.02.1994	23.09.1996
12.	Denmark	31.03.2004	22.11.2004	20.07.2005
13.	Egypt	20.03.1997		18.01.1999
14.	Israel	11.04.2000	10.05.2001	14.08.2003
15.	India	27.11.2002	-	23.11.2003
16.	Iraq	23.08.2014	11.07.2016	11.08.2016
17.	Jordan	16.12.2002	19.06.2003	22.12.2005
18.	Iran	14.07.1995	-	23.06.2000
19.	Italy	25.07.1995	17.10.1996	12.08.1997
20.	Qatar	17.02.2001	26.06.2001	06.08.2004
21.	Cyprus	29.05.1998	-	03.09.1998
22.	China	11.01.1993	04.10.1994	14.01.1995
23.	North Korea	24.08.2006	07.05.2007	31.05.2007
24.	Cuba	08.06.2000		16.08.2001
25.	Kuwait	10.07.2001	26.10.2001	14.06.2003
26.	Kyrgyzstan	30.03.1999	15.07.1999	11.11.2001
27.	Laos	01.07.2013	04.01.2014	20.03.2014
28.	Latvia	03.03.1998	06.11.1998	21.12.1998
29.	Lebanon	19.06.2001	17.09.2001	29.12.2002

---

172. Information provided by various open legal resources.

No.	Country	Signed	Ratified (accessed) by Belarus	Entered into force for Belarus
30.	Libya	01.11.2000		23.02.2002
31.	Lithuania	05.03.1999	05.08.1999	16.05.2002
32.	Macedonia	20.06.2001	26.10.2001	22.11.2002
33.	Mexico	04.09.2008	06.07.2009	27.08.2009
34.	Moldova	28.05.1999	10.08.1999	19.11.1999
35.	Mongolia	28.05.2001	26.10.2001	27.01.2002
36.	Netherlands	11.04.1995	25.04.1996	01.08.1996
37.	The United Arab Emirates	27.03.2000	30.08.2000	16.02.2001
38.	Oman	10.05.2004	10.01.2005	18.01.2005
39.	Poland	16.04.1992	-	21.04.1993
40.	The Republic of Korea	22.04.1997	-	09.08.1997
41.	Romania	31.05.1995	25.04.1996	26.06.1996
42.	Saudi Arabia	20.07.2009	15.06.2010	11.08.2010
43.	Singapore	15.05.2000	08.12.2000	13.01.2001
44.	Syria	11.03.1998		01.10.1998
45.	Slovakia	26.08.2005	16.05.2006	01.09.2006
46.	Tajikistan	03.09.1998	29.07.1999	25.08.1999
47.	Turkey	08.08.1995	17.10.1996	20.02.1997
48.	Ukraine	14.12.1995	25.04.1996	11.06.1997
49.	Finland	08.06.2006	08.11.2006	10.04.2008
50.	Croatia	26.06.2001	26.10.2001	14.07.2005
51.	Czech Republic	14.10.1996	11.11.1997	09.04.1998
52.	Switzerland	28.05.1993	-	13.07.1994
53.	Sweden	20.12.1994	25.04.1996	01.11.1996

Bibliography

Danilevich, Dr. Aliaksandr. "Belarus". *In International Encyclopaedia of Laws: Private International Law*, edited by Bea. Verschraegen. Alphen aan den Rijn, NL: Kluwer Law International, 2012. - 134 p.

Анищенко А.И., Юрьева М.Ю. Арбитражная оговорка - скрытое оружие. // Промышленно-торговое право. - 2008. - № 3. - С. 41–46.

Бабкина, Е.В., Семчик, А.А. Специфика применения оговорки о публичном порядке в процессе приведения в исполнение иностранных арбитражных решений // Журнал международного права и международных отношений. - 2014. - № 3.

Бельская И.А. Правовые формы арбитража в Республике Беларусь: общее и специальное в их законодательном регулировании.

Горонков М.П. Комментарий "Производство по делам об обжаловании решений международных арбитражных (третейских) судов, находящихся на территории Республики Беларусь, и о выдаче исполнительного документа (комментарий к статьям 251 - 261 главы 29 Хозяйственного процессуального кодекса Республики Беларусь)" // ConsultantPlus: Belarus. Technology PROF [Electronic resource] / Jurspectre Ltd., National Centre of Legal Information. - Minsk, 2016.

Данилевич А. Взыскание задолженности в Международном арбитражном суде при БелТПП // "Библиотечка журнала 'Юрист' Право и бизнес". - № 4 (88). - Апр. 2014. - С. 22–30.

Данилевич А.С. Международный коммерческий арбитраж: Учеб. пособие. - Мн.: Академия управления при президенте Республики Беларусь, 2004. - 380 с.

Данилевич А.С. Взыскание дебиторской задолженности в арбитраже // Библиотечка журнала "Юрист". Право и бизнес. - 2011. - №3(51). - С. 57–63.

Данилевич А.С. Взыскание дебиторской задолженности в арбитраже // Библиотечка журнала "Юрист". Право и бизнес. - 2011. - №3(51). - С. 57–63.

Данилевич А.С. Как избрать международного арбитра? // Беларусь в современном мире: материалы IV Междунар. науч. конф., посвящ. 87-летию образования Белорус. гос. ун-та (Минск, 30 октября 2008 г. / Редкол.: В.Г. Шадурский [и др.]. - Минск, Тесей, 2008. - С. 115–116.

Данилевич А.С. Обжалование решения международного арбитражного суда (сравнительно-правовой анализ) // Вестник Высшего Хозяйственного Суда Республики Беларусь. - 2002. - № 2. - С. 197–221.

Данилевич Л.С. Принятие решения внешнеторговыми арбитражными судами. // Торгово-промышленное право. - 2002. - № 6. - СС. 145–172.

Данилевич А.С. Решение международного арбитражного суда // Белорусский журнал международного права и международных отношений. - 2001. - № 4. - С. 49–55.

Данилевич А.С. Срок для вынесения решения внешнеторговым арбитражным судом. - Белорусский журнал международного права и международных отношений. - 2002. - № . - С. 29-32.

Данилевич А.С. Эффективность и законная сила решения международного арбитражного суда. // Торгово-промышленное право. - 2002.- №3. - СС. 103-131.

Данилевич А.С., Зиновина О.И. Реализация права государств на экспроприацию иностранных инвестиций в практике Международного центра по урегулированию инвестиционных споров. // Актуальные проблемы международного публичного и международного частного права: Сб. науч. тр. Вып. 6 / Редкол.: Е. В. Бабкина И Ю. А. Лепешков (отв. ред.) [и др.].: сб. науч. тр. - Выпуск 7. / БГУ, 2015 - с. 110-125.

Данилевич А.С., Рак О.А. Понятие и виды процессуального соучастия в международном коммерческом арбитраже. // Актуальные проблемы международного публичного и международного частного права: Сб. науч. тр. Вып. 7 / Редкол.: Е. В. Бабкина И Ю. А. Лепешков (отв. ред.) [и др.].: сб. науч. тр. - Выпуск 8. / БГУ, 2016 - с. 110-134.

Данилевич, А.С. Арбитражная оговорка в инвестиционном договоре с Республикой Беларусь / А.С. Данилевич / Промышленно-торговое право. - 2010. - № 5. - С. 69-71.

Данилевич, А.С. Как заключить выгодное международное арбитражное соглашение? / А.С. Данилевич // Юридический мир. - 2010. - № 12. - С. 44-48.

Жуковская К.И. Передаем корпоративный спор в арбитраж // Промышленно-торговое право. - 2015. - No 11.

Каменков, В.С. Третейское соглашение: понятие, виды, толкование и содержание / Консультант Плюс: Беларусь. Обзор аналитических материалов и консультационных материалов, введенных в информационный банк "Комментарии Законодательства: Белорусский Выпуск" 2014.

Каменков, В.С. Формирование состава арбитражного (третейского) суда // Журнал "Юстиция Беларуси", 2015, № 1, с. 17-21.

Корочкин А.Ю. Закрепление оговорки об отказе государства от юрисдикционного иммунитета в инвестиционном законодательстве Республики Беларусь. ConsultantPlus: Belarus. Technology PROF [Electronic resource]/Jurspectre Ltd., National Centre of Legal Information. - Minsk, 2016.

Манкевич В.В. О компетенции международных арбитражных и третейских судов.

Панкратов, П.О. Инвестиционные споры с участием государств с переходной экономикой / П.О. Панкратов // Промышленно-торговое право. - 2010. - № 2. - С. 66-71.

Перерва И. Арбитражная оговорка и иные виды арбитражного соглашения во внешнеэкономическом договоре // Юрист. - 2002. - №6. - С. 18-21.

Перерва, И.В. Особенности определения "национальности" арбитражного решения в праве Республики Беларусь / И.В.Перерва // Промышленно-торговое право. – 2006. – No 3. – С. 140-149).

Перерва И.В. Арбитражные соглашения в практике Международного арбитражного суда при БелТПП // Промышленно-торговое право, 2015, No 03.

Перерва И.В. Незаключенность арбитражного соглашения: обжалование компетенции МАС при БелТПП ("Промышленно-торговое право", 2015, No 08).

Перерва И.В. Практика рассмотрения в Международном арбитражном суде при БелТПП споров, вытекающих из договоров строительного подряда/.

Рудинская, Н.Н. "Алгоритм действий при подаче искового заявления в международный арбитражный (третейский) суд при БелТПП".

Сысуев Т., Шалбанова А. Признание и приведение в исполнение иностранных арбитражных решений в Республике Беларусь//Юрист. – 2015. – № 3 (166).

Скобелев, В.П. Источники регулирования международного коммерческого арбитража. Часть 2. Национальные источники [Электронный ресурс] / В.П.Скобелев ConsultantPlus: Belarus. Technology PROF [Electronic resource] / Jurspectre Ltd., National Centre of Legal Information. – Minsk, 2016.

Перерва, И.В. Признание и приведение в исполнение решений международных арбитражных судов: автореф. дис.... канд. юрид. наук: 12.00.15 / И.В.Перерва; Белорус. гос. ун-т. – Минск, 2007.

Сысуев, Т.В. Арбитражное соглашение: форма и содержание / Т.В.Сысуев // Промышленно-торговое право. – 2014. – No 1.

Сысуев, Т.В. Международный коммерческий арбитраж. Общие вопросы признания и исполнения иностранных судебных и арбитражных решений / Т.В.Сысуев // Международное регулирование внешнеэкономической деятельности / Д.П.Александров [и др.]; под ред. В.С.Каменкова. – М.: Изд-во деловой и учеб. лит.; Минск: Дикта, 2005.

Тынель А., Функ Я., Хвалей В. Курс международного торгового права / А.Тынель, Я.Функ, В.Хвалей. – Мн.: Амалфея, 2000. – 704 с.

Функ Я.И. Определение составом международного арбитража применимого права на основании коллизионных норм // Промышленно-торговое право, 2015, No 08.

Хвалей В. Как "убить" арбитражное соглашение? // Промышленно-торговое право. – 2004. – №2. – С. 117-145.

Хвалей В. Как убить арбитражное соглашение // Промышленно-торговое право. – 2004. – №2. – С. 117-145.

ХрапуцкийА., ЛобаньК. Хорошийарбитр-гарантуспеха// Директор.–2015.– № 6.

Якимович, О., Данилевич А. Подготовка и подача иска по международным инвестиционным спорам // "Библиотечка журнала 'Юрист' Право и бизнес". - № 1 (73). - Янв. 2013. - С. 57-61.

Institutional arbitration: tasks and powers of different arbitration institutions / Gola; Götz Straehelin; Graf (eds.). - Zurich; Basel; Geneva: Schulthess; München: Sellier Europ. Law Publ., 2009. - VIII, 310 S.

Web Sources

International Arbitration Court at BelCCI, http://www.iac.by/.

Международный арбитражный (третейский) суд "Палата арбитров при Союзе юристов" - http://union.by/structure/primary/IAC/.

Каменков В.С. Формирование состава арбитражного (третейского) суда (сравнительный анализ-обзор) http://elib.bsu.by/bitstream/123456789/108615/1.

New Belarusian Resolution on the Recognition and Enforcement of Foreign Arbitral Awards: Is There No Rose Without a Thorn? by Timour Sysouev and Karyna Loban on May 2, 2015, http://kluwerarbitrationblog.com/2015/05/02/new-belarusian-resolution-on-the-recognition-and-enforcement-of-foreign-arbitral-awards-is-there-no-rose-without-a-thorn/.

Danilevich A. New Legislation on Arbitration in Belarus, http://www.cisarbitration.com/2012/03/08/new-legislation-on-arbitration-in-belarus/.

Danilevich A. A New Arbitration Institution Established in Belarus, http://www.cisarbitration.com/2011/01/02/a-new-arbitration-institution-established-in-belarus/.

Timour Sysouev, Alexandre Khrapoutski. ICLG Litigation & Dispute Resolution 2015: Belarus //ICLG Litigation & Dispute Resolution 2015. - 2015 http://www.sbh-partners.com/sites/default/files/publication/2015-02-11_sysuev_t._hrapuckiy_a._iclg_litigation_dispute_resolution_2015._belarus.pdf.

Danilevich A. Enforcement of Foreign Arbitration Awards in Belarus / Migalhas on International Arbitration. - Issue No 3. - Spring 2010. [Electronic resource]: http://www.migalhas.com.br/arquivo_artigo/art20100414-02.pdf.

Legislation

Code of Republic of Belarus On Judicial System and Judges Status of 29 June 2006 No 139-Z (in version of January 4, 2014), http://etalonline.by/?type=text&regnum=Hk0600139#load_text_none_1_.

Law of the Republic of Belarus No. 279-Z of 9 July 1999 [Amended as of July 1, 2014] On International Arbitration Court (Tribunal), http://law.by/main.aspx?guid=3871&p0=H19900279e.

Regulation of the Council of Ministers of the Republic of Belarus of 12 January 2012 No 52 On Approval of the Model Rules of the Arbitration Court operating on a permanent basis accepted Model Rules of institutional (domestic) arbitration court. http://news.21.by/other-news/2012/01/25/451575.html.

Resolution of Plenum of Supreme Court of Republic of Belarus of 23 December 2014 No 18 On Application by the Courts of the Legislation Concerning Recognition and Enforcement of the Awards of the Foreign Courts and Foreign Arbitral Awards of 23 December 2014 No 18, http://www.court.by/jurisprudence/Post_plen/civ_proc/forein/af5a2f40566c0ca8.html.

Resolution of Plenum of the Supreme Economic Court of Republic of Belarus dated 23 December 2005 No 34 (in version of October 31, 2011) On jurisdiction on disputes upon assignment, http://www.pravo.by/main.aspx?guid=3871&p0=X20500034.

Resolution of the Plenum of the Highest Economic Court of the Republic of Belarus of 31 October 2011 No 21 On Some Issues of the Resolution by the Economic Courts of Cases with the Participation of Foreign Persons, http://www.pravo.by/main.aspx?guid=3871&p0=X21100021.

Law of the Republic of Belarus No. 279-Z of 9 July 1999 [Amended as of July 1, 2014].

Criminal Procedure Code of Republic of Belarus of 16 July 1999, No 295-3, http://etalonline.by/?type=text&regnum=HK9900295.

Labour Code of Republic of Belarus of 26 July 1999 No 296-Z, http://www.etalonline.by/Default.aspx?type=text&regnum=HK9900296#load_text_none_1_12.

Law of Republic of Belarus of 18 July 2004 No 305-Z (in version January 5, 2016) On Notariate and Notarial Activity, http://belnotary.by/zakonodatelstvo/zakon-o-notariate/.

Law of Republic of Belarus of 8 May 2007 No 220-Z (in version of July 18, 2016) On Procuracy of Republic of Belarus, http://www.pravo.by/webnpa/text.asp?&p0=H10700220.

Presidential Edict of 1 September 2010 No 450 On Licensing of Certain Types of Activities, http://www.pravo.by/webnpa/text.asp?RN=P31000450.

Law of Republic of Belarus of 18 July 2011 No 301-Z (in version of January 1, 2015) On arbitration courts, http://www.pravo.by/main.aspx?guid=3871&p0=H11100301.

Law of Republic of Belarus of 30 December 2011 No 334-3 On Advocacy and Legal Practice in the Republic of Belarus, http://www.rka.by/content/zakon-ob-advokature-i-advokatskoy.

Edict of the President of Republic of Belarus of 14 June 2012 No 265 On some issues of Advocate Activity, http://minjust.gov.by/ru/about-licensing/a/.

Edict of the President of Republic of Belarus of 14 June 2012 No 265 On Some Issues of Legal Practice, http://president.gov.by/ru/official_documents_ru/view/ukaz-265-ot-14-ijunja-2012-g-1491/.

Law of Republic of Belarus On Investments of 12 July 2013 No 53-Z, http://www.pravo.by/main.aspx?guid=3871&p0=H11300053.

CHAPTER 5
Kazakhstan

Asel Duissenova & Maksud Karaketov

LIST OF ABBREVIATIONS

CIS	Commonwealth of Independent States
Constitution of the Republic of Kazakhstan	Constitution of The Republic of Kazakhstan dated August 30, 1995
Civil Code	Civil Code of the Republic of Kazakhstan No. 409 dated July 1, 1999
Civil Procedure Code (CPC)	Civil Procedure Code of the Republic of Kazakhstan No. 377-V dated October 31, 2015
Criminal Code	Criminal Code of the Republic of Kazakhstan No. 226-V dated July 3, 2014
Criminal Procedure Code	Criminal Procedure Code of the Republic of Kazakhstan No. 231-V dated July 4, 2014
Code on administrative offenses	Code of the Republic of Kazakhstan on administrative offenses No. 235-V dated July 5, 2014
Law on Arbitration	Law of The Republic of Kazakhstan on Arbitration No. 488 dated April 8, 2016
Geneva Convention	European Convention on International Commercial Arbitration, 1961, Geneva
ICSID Convention	Convention on the Settlement of Investment Disputes between States and Nationals of other States, 1965, Washington
Law on Advocate Practice	Law of The Republic of Kazakhstan on Advocate Practice No. 195-I dated December 5, 1997
Law on Mediation	Law of The Republic of Kazakhstan on Mediation No. 401-IV dated January 28, 2011

New York Convention	United Nations Convention on the Recognition and Enforcement of Foreign Arbitral Awards, 1958, New York
UNCITRAL	United Nations Commission on International Trade Law
UNCITRAL Model Law	UNCITRAL Model Law on International Commercial Arbitration 1985
KIA	Kazakhstan International Arbitration

§5.01 GENERAL INTRODUCTION

[A] Historical Development of the Legal System

1.1. The legal system of Kazakhstan can be traced back to the Kazakh khanate (Казахское ханство) in the fifteenth century. After becoming a member of the Soviet Union, Kazakh legislation was implemented in accordance with Russian law.

1.2. In 1991, the Republic of Kazakhstan became an independent nation and started to develop its own legislation. Generally speaking, the legal system of the Republic of Kazakhstan is based on the Romano-Germanic legal system. The main source of law is a legal act, which includes the norms of the Constitution, regulatory legal acts, international treaties and other obligations of the Republic, as well as regulatory resolutions of the Constitutional Council and the Supreme Court of the Republic.[1]

[B] The Legal Profession

1.3. Kazakhstan has adopted special laws governing various legal professions such as advocates,[2] notaries,[3] prosecutors,[4] investigators,[5] judges.[6]

1.4. Kazakh legislation does not restrict the power of representation by only granting it to advocates.[7] The Civil Procedure Code provides a list of individuals entitled to be legal representatives by order of any party at civil disputes. The list includes advocates, authorized employees of the legal entity, any individual with a law degree, etc.

---

1. Article 4 of the Constitution of the Republic of Kazakhstan (1995), http://adilet.zan.kz/rus/docs/K950001000_.
2. Law of Kazakhstan On Advocate's Activity No. 195-I of December 5, 1997, http://online.zakon.kz/Document/?doc_id=1008408.
3. Law of Kazakhstan On Notariate No. 155-I of July 14, 1997, http://online.zakon.kz/Document/?doc_id=1008028#pos=1;-299.
4. Law of Kazakhstan On Prosecution No. 2709 of December 21, 1995, http://online.zakon.kz/Document/?doc_id=1004024.
5. Criminal Procedure Code, http://online.zakon.kz/Document/?doc_id=31575852&doc_id2=31575852#pos=76;-8&pos2=1364;-8.
6. Constitutional Law of the Republic of Kazakhstan On Judicial System and Status of Judges in the Republic of Kazakhstan No. 132-II of December 25, 2000, http://online.zakon.kz/Document/?doc_id=1021164&doc_id2=31347293.
7. Article 58, CPC of the Republic of Kazakhstan, http://online.zakon.kz/Document/?doc_id=1006061&doc_id2=1006061#pos=113;-106&pos2=1285;-45.

Employees of a legal entity and any person with a law degree and power of attorney can represent parties during civil[8] and administrative litigation.[9]

1.5. However, in criminal litigation, only advocates can represent the rights and interests of the witness, suspect, defendant, convicted, and acquitted.[10]

1.6. A person wishing to become an advocate should be a citizen of Kazakhstan and possess higher legal education, have an advocate's license, be a member of the bar association, and render qualified legal aid within the framework of advocacy. In order to receive an advocate's license, it is necessary to undergo a six-month to one-year training and pass the bar exam.[11]

1.7. The law sets forth three forms of advocate's activity: legal consultation, independently or jointly established advocate law firms or associations, and individual activity, without registration as a legal entity. In spite of the form, the advocate shall be a member of the bar association, established and operating on the territory of the respective administrative-territorial unit.[12]

[C] Sources of Law on Arbitration

1.8. Arbitration as an alternative method for resolving commercial disputes has been used for little more than twenty years in Kazakhstan. During this relatively short period it managed to pass several very dissimilar stages in its development. Thus, in the history of the development of legislation on arbitration in Kazakhstan, four stages can so far be distinguished:[13]

1.9. *The Initial stage (1993–1999)*. On October 5, 1993, the Arbitration Commission of the Chamber of Commerce of the Republic of Kazakhstan was established. Later, the International Arbitration Court of the IUS Law Centre was created. At that time, the standard rules on arbitration, approved by the Resolution of the Cabinet of Ministers of the Republic of Kazakhstan No. 356 dated May 4, 1993, came into effect in Kazakhstan

1.10. *The second stage. Adoption of the Civil Procedure Code (1999–2004)*. The situation changed dramatically with the adoption of the new Civil Procedure Code on July 1, 1999. Shortly before, state arbitration courts had been liquidated and provisions for the new Civil Procedure Code began to spread into economic disputes between legal entities. With the adoption of the Civil Procedure Code, the Law on settlement of

---

8. The reply of the Supreme Court of January 27, 2016 to the question about the representation of the plaintiff with a law degree, http://online.zakon.kz/Document/?doc_id=35192685#pos=1;-267.
9. Article 748, Code on administrative offenses, http://online.zakon.kz/Document/?doc_id=31577399&doc_id2=31577399#pos=848;-8&pos2=7951;-8.
10. Article 66, Criminal Procedure Code of the Republic of Kazakhstan, http://online.zakon.kz/Document/?doc_id=31575852&doc_id2=31575852#pos=83;-8&pos2=1507;12.
11. Article 7, Law On Advocate's Activity.
12. *Ibid*, Art. 19.
13. Suleimenov M.K. & Duissenova A.E., Advantages and Disadvantages of the New Law of Arbitration // https://www.zakon.kz/4796696-dostoinstva-i-nedostatki-novogo-zakona.html.

economic disputes of 1993 was repealed. Enforcement of arbitration awards by state courts is the cornerstone of effective arbitration proceedings.

1.11. Following the adoption of the Civil Procedure Code, the Supreme Court adopted a Regulatory Resolution[14] obliging courts to make orders on compulsory enforcement of arbitral awards. However, the General Prosecutor's Office and the Ministry of Justice, with open support from the Government of the Republic of Kazakhstan, stood together against this Resolution. After significant pressure, the Supreme Court was forced to suspend the operation of its Regulatory Resolution. The Constitutional Court of the Republic of Kazakhstan also adopted the abovementioned resolution. The only phrase that saved the situation in this resolution was: "in the manner prescribed by the legislation." The Civil Procedure Code retains a provision on the liability of the court to leave the claim without the consideration, if the parties entered into an arbitration agreement.[15]

1.12. *The third stage. Adoption of the Law on International Commercial Arbitration and on Arbitration Courts.* On December 28, 2004 the Law "On Arbitration Courts" (for domestic arbitration) and the Law "On International Commercial Arbitration" (for international arbitration) were adopted. The Law on International Commercial Arbitration in general corresponded to the basic provisions of the UNCITRAL Model Law "On International Commercial Arbitration." The Law on arbitration courts included essential restrictions concerning the competence of arbitration courts. If at least one of the parties was a nonresident of the Republic of Kazakhstan, the dispute would be considered according to the Law on International Commercial Arbitration. In the same year, provisions on appealing awards of the arbitration courts, as well as provisions on enforcement of awards of arbitration courts and international commercial arbitration, were included in the Civil Procedure Code.

1.13. *The fourth stage. Adoption of the Law on Arbitration.* A New Civil Procedure Code was adopted on October 31, 2015. In accordance with the new Civil Procedure Code, the Law of the Republic of Kazakhstan "On Arbitration," which combined two previously existing laws, was adopted on April 8, 2016. According to Article 1 of the Law on Arbitration, disputes arising from civil law relations with participation of individuals and (or) legal entities, regardless of the place of residence or location of the subjects of dispute within the state or beyond its borders are arbitrable. Thus, the division of arbitrations in Kazakhstan between domestic and international arbitration has been removed.

[D] **International Legal Framework, Supremacy of International Law**

1.14. In accordance with the Constitution, international agreements ratified by the Republic shall take priority over its laws and shall be used directly, except for cases

---

14. Regulatory Resolution of the Supreme Court of the Republic of Kazakhstan No. 14 dated October 19, 2001, http://online.zakon.kz/Document/?doc_id = 1025730.
15. Article 249, Civil Procedure Code.

when an international agreement states that its application requires issuance of a law. All legal acts and international agreements shall be published. Acts are deemed mandatory on application only after official publication.

1.15. The Republic of Kazakhstan is a party to all major international conventions in the sphere of international commercial arbitration, including the New York Convention, Geneva Convention, Energy Charter Treaty, and ICSID Convention. On October 21, 2000, the Convention entered into force in Kazakhstan. The ICSID Convention was published in the Bulletin of International Agreements of the Republic of Kazakhstan, 2004, No. 11; this is an official publication annexed to the "Meeting of Acts of the President of the Republic of Kazakhstan and the Government of the Republic of Kazakhstan." Moreover, this edition states that the Convention entered into force in Kazakhstan on July 20, 2004. Thus, we have two dates nearly four years apart, and we do not know which is correct.

[E] Available Dispute Resolution Mechanisms

1.16. The legislation of Kazakhstan provides for the resolution of disputes by state courts and arbitration.

1.17. The parties may also resolve their disputes by using nonjudicial procedures such as negotiations and mediation.[16] The law "On Mediation" was adopted in 2011 and is currently in force.[17] The Law regulates both judicial mediation in criminal and civil proceedings and nonjudicial, independent mediation carried out by professional and nonprofessional mediators.

1.18. Moreover, there are optional consent-based mechanisms for dispute resolution: ***notarial endorsement, participatory procedure.***[18]

[F] Judicial System

1.19. The judicial system is a separate branch of the government in the Republic of Kazakhstan. The judicial system consists of the Supreme Court of the Republic of Kazakhstan, which is the highest Court, and local courts including: (1) regional courts and courts equivalent to them; (2) district courts and courts equivalent to them; (3) Other courts, including specialized courts (martial, commercial, administrative, juvenile, and others), as well as the Court of Astana International Financial Centre, which has a special status.[19]

---

16. Suleimenov M.K., Private Procedural Law (Law of Alternative Dispute Resolution) // Lawyer. 2011. No. 2. P. 12-19.
17. Law of the Republic of Kazakhstan "On Mediation" No. 401-IV, dated January 28, 2008, http://online.zakon.kz/Document/?doc_id = 30927376#pos = 1;-255.
18. Karaketov M.Yu, New ADR Regulations enacted in Kazakhstan, http://www.cisarbitration.com /2016/01/26/new-adr-regulations-enacted-in-kazakhstan/.
19. Page 1 Art. 3 the Law of the Republic of Kazakhstan on Judicial System and Status of Judges, 2000, http://adilet.zan.kz/rus/docs/Z000000132_.

1.20. After the adoption of Civil Procedure Code No. 377-V dated October 31, 2015, the judicial system was reformed. The Civil Procedure Code reduced instances of the judicial system and eliminated the supervisory review procedure. As a result, presently the Court of First Instance is the district or equivalent court. The courts of appeal instance are the appellate judicial board on civil and administrative cases of the regional or equivalent court. The Supreme Court of the Republic of Kazakhstan reviews cases under a cassation procedure.

[G] Arbitration Institutions

1.21. An Arbitration Institution in the Republic of Kazakhstan may be established as a permanent arbitration institution or ad hoc. A permanent arbitration institution may be formed by individuals and (or) legal entities. A permanent arbitration institution should approve its rules and arbitrators' registry.[20]

1.22. However, state bodies, public enterprises, subjects of natural monopolies, second-tier banks, and organizations engaged in certain types of banking operations may not establish arbitration institutions.[21]

1.23. Despite the legal requirements for the establishment of arbitration, there is no exact number of existing and operating arbitrations in Kazakhstan. Nevertheless, the following arbitration institutions are considered the most effective and popular: Kazakhstan International Arbitration (KIA), IUS GENTIUM International Arbitration, the Centre of Arbitration of the National Chamber of Entrepreneurs Atameken,[22] IUS International Arbitration, IAC International Arbitration.[23]

[H] Sovereign Immunity and International Arbitration

1.24. Kazakhstan has ratified the UN Convention on Jurisdictional Immunities of States and their Property by adoption of the Law of the Republic of Kazakhstan dated October 27, 2009 "On Ratification of the United Nations Convention on Jurisdictional Immunities of States and their Property."

1.25. In addition, on February 5, 2010 the Law "On Introducing Amendments and Additions to Some Legislative Acts of the Republic of Kazakhstan on Issues of State Immunity and its Property, Improvement of the Activity of Arbitration Courts and International Commercial Arbitration" was adopted. This law in the Civil Code of the Republic of Kazakhstan (special part) and the Civil Procedure Code of the Republic of

---

20. Article 4 of the Law on Arbitration.
21. *Ibid.*
22. The National Chamber of Entrepreneurs of Kazakhstan "Atameken" was created instead of the Chamber of Commerce and Industry in 2013. The Arbitration center "Atameken" was formed by the National Chamber of Entrepreneurs of Kazakhstan "Atameken". This center is a successor of the International Arbitration Court established at the Chamber of Commerce and Industry.
23. For more information, please *see* http://www.arbitrage.kz/; http://www.atamekenarb.kz/; http://www.iusea.com/; http://arbitrazh.kz/; http://rus.arbitration.kz/; http://aca.kz/ru/.

Kazakhstan formalized the doctrine of functional (limited) immunity to foreign states.[24]

1.26. Foreign states enjoy judicial immunity in the Republic of Kazakhstan, including judicial immunity, immunity from suits, and immunity from enforcement of certain judicial acts, unless the state has waived legal immunity or jurisdictional immunity in Kazakhstan.[25]

1.27. As to the co-relation of the court and the arbitral immunity of the state, a foreign state may solve its dispute in arbitration and participate in it only with written consent. This arbitration would require the state to voluntarily waive its jurisdictional immunity on matters relating to the implementation of arbitration functions by the court of the Republic of Kazakhstan.[26]

1.28. The Courts of Kazakhstan have several functions relating to arbitration, including the issuance of a writ of execution to enforce the arbitral award. The conclusion of an arbitration agreement constitutes the parties' waiver of immunity from enforcement of an arbitral award. Consequently, an arbitration agreement does not entail a waiver of judicial immunity but does constitute the parties' consent to the enforcement of an arbitral award.[27]

§5.02 THE ARBITRATION AGREEMENT

[A] Introduction

1.29. An arbitration agreement is a written agreement between parties to settle a dispute which has arisen or may arise from civil law relations in arbitration. The dispute may be submitted to arbitration if there is an arbitration agreement concluded by the parties. Parties may enter into an arbitration agreement due to disputes which have already arisen or which may arise between the parties of any particular civil law relations.[28]

1.30. An arbitration agreement on a dispute still pending before the court can be concluded before the court has made its decision. In this case, the court can leave the application without consideration.[29] Moreover, the court will not review cases if there is an arbitration agreement by the parties in place.[30]

Despite the fact that most Kazakh arbitral institutions provide a model arbitration clause in their rules and homepages, some parties still conclude improper arbitration clauses.

---

24. Suleimenov M.K., State Immunity: Absolute or Limited? // Lawyer. 2010 No. 3. P. 12-19.
25. Articles 477-478, Civil Procedure Code.
26. Article 482 Civil Procedure Code.
27. Suleimenov M.K. & Osipov E., Immunity of International Organizations, http://online.zakon.kz/Document/?doc_id=31115410#pos=1;-169.
28. Article 2 of the Law on Arbitration.
29. Clause 3 of Art. 8 of the Law on Arbitration.
30. Article 152 of the Civil Procedure Code.

[B] Validity of the Arbitration Agreement

[1] General Provisions

1.31. The Law on Arbitration has groundlessly expanded the list of essential requisites for a valid arbitration agreement, giving rise to justifiable criticism from both scholars and practitioners.[31]

[2] Requisites of a Valid Arbitration Agreement

1.32. An arbitration agreement must contain: (1) intention of the parties to refer the dispute to arbitration; (2) indication of the subject, subject to review by arbitration; (3) indication of the particular arbitration; (4) consent of the authorized body of corresponding industry or local executive body in the cases stipulated by clause 10, Article 8 of this Law.[32]

1.33. Additional requisites of an arbitration agreement may be determined by agreement between the parties.

1.34. Establishing additional requisites provides more grounds for refusing recognition and enforcement for not only domestic but also foreign arbitral awards.[33] The state court is able to refuse to recognize foreign arbitral awards when the party proves that the arbitration agreement is not valid under the law of the State to which the parties have subjected it, or in the absence of such an indication according to the laws of the Republic of Kazakhstan.[34] Unlike in Kazakh legislation, other foreign states do not necessarily require such requisites of arbitration agreements. Consequently, other courts may refuse to recognize foreign arbitral awards in Kazakhstan.[35]

[C] Concluding the Arbitration Agreement (Written, Oral, by Conduct)

1.35. According to Article 9 of the Law on Arbitration, an arbitration agreement shall be in writing, either in the form of an arbitration clause in a contract, or in the form of a separate agreement signed by the parties or signed by an exchange of letters, telegrams, telephone messages, faxes, electronic documents, or other documents defining the subjects and content of their expression.

1.36. An arbitration agreement is in writing if it is concluded by an exchange of statements of claim and response to the claim, in which one party asserts the existence of an agreement, and the other does not object. Reference in a contract to a document

---

31. Suleimenov M.K. & Duissenova A.E., Advantages and Disadvantages of the New Law of Arbitration, https://www.zakon.kz/4796696-dostoinstva-i-nedostatki-novogo-zakona.html.
32. Clause 4, Art. 9 of the Law on Arbitration.
33. Tukulov B.A., New Law of the Republic of Kazakhstan "On Arbitration": Attention to some Problem Issues, https://www.zakon.kz/4795629-novyjj-zakon-respubliki-kazakhstan-ob.html.
34. Article 57 of the Law on Arbitration.
35. Tukulov B.A., New Law of the Republic of Kazakhstan "On Arbitration": Attention to some Problem Issues, https://www.zakon.kz/4795629-novyjj-zakon-respubliki-kazakhstan-ob.html.

containing the terms of the transfer of the dispute to arbitration is an arbitration agreement as long as the contract is in writing and the reference makes the arbitration agreement part of the contract.[36]

[D] The Doctrine of Separability

1.37. Prior to the adoption and entry into force of the Law on Arbitration, the doctrine of separability of an arbitration agreement in Kazakhstan was not legislated. Nevertheless, permanent arbitrations are included it in its rules. Thus, for example, according to clause 3, Article 1 of the Rules of KIA, an arbitration agreement is recognized as having legal force regardless of the validity of the contract to which it is part.[37] In a number of rendered awards of KIA arbitrations, the doctrine of autonomy of an arbitration agreement serves as a basis for the availability of competence to consider a particular dispute in case of invalidity or nonconclusion of the main agreement.[38] Currently, the doctrine of autonomy of an arbitration agreement is specified in Article 5 and Article 20 of the Law on Arbitration.

[E] Invalidity of the Arbitration Agreement

1.38. International agreements on arbitration and national procedural legislation, as well as legislation on arbitration, specify grounds for the invalidity of an arbitration agreement. For instance, the Civil Code provides general grounds for invalidity of transactions. Those grounds are also applicable to an arbitration agreement, which can be recognized as a civil law contract.

1.39. In accordance with Article 157 of the Civil Code, when there is a violation of requirements to the form, content, and participants of a transaction, as well as to the freedom of their expression of will, the transaction may be invalidated under the claim of interested persons,[39] an appropriate public authority, or a public prosecutor.

1.40. The Law on Arbitration provides special grounds in case of invalidity of the arbitration agreement. Thus, according to clause 4, Article 8, an arbitration agreement should be accepted by the other party only by adherence to the proposed contract as a whole (contract of adhesion), if such an agreement is concluded after the grounds for a claim. The idea of this provision is to protect the weaker party in a contract, usually a citizen-consumer.

1.41. Apart from invalidity, nonconclusion of an arbitration agreement must be distinguished. The Civil Code of the Republic of Kazakhstan, in contrast to the Russian Civil Code and the codes of a number of other countries, does not provide rules for

---

36. Article 9 of the Law on Arbitration.
37. Case award No. 05/2010/TP / Reports of Judgments of Kazakhstan International Arbitration (2008 – 2013) / Suleimenov M.K. & Duissenova A.E., Almaty: KIA, 2014. pp. 197–216.
38. *Ibid.*
39. An interested person is a person whose rights and legitimate interests are violated or may be violated because of the transaction.

insignificant transactions, and all invalid transactions in accordance with Article 157 of the Civil Code are to be recognized as voidable. However, this concept of nonconclusion of the contract is widely used in the legislation, legal literature, and case law of Kazakhstan.

1.42. Since the arbitration agreement, by its nature, is a civil contract, relevant rules of the Civil Code on contracts should be applied to it. According to clause 1, Article 393 of the Civil Code, a contract is considered concluded when the parties have reached an agreement concerning all significant conditions.[40]

1.43. Neither contract is considered concluded without definition of the subject. The name of the arbitration institution refers to the essential terms of an arbitration agreement.[41] In the absence of such information, the arbitration agreement should be deemed invalid.

[F] Arbitrability

[1] Disputes Capable of Settlement by Arbitration

1.44. According to the Law on Arbitration, disputes arising from civil law relations between individuals and (or) legal entities may be transferred to arbitration upon the agreement of the parties.[42]

1.45. In general, there are three groups of civil law relations regulated by civil legislation: property relations (including corporate relations); personal non-property relations related to property, and personal non-property relations not related to property.[43] Except for the third group, disputes arising from these types of civil law relations are under the competence of arbitration.

[2] Disputes Not Capable of Settlement by Arbitration

1.46. Arbitral tribunals may not consider disputes arising from personal non-property relations (e.g., tax, labor, bankruptcy disputes). Moreover, the disputes between individuals and (or) legal entities of Kazakhstan on the one hand and government agencies, state enterprises, and legal entities owned by the state[44] on the other hand, are not eligible for settlement by Arbitration, except for with the consent of the authorized body of the corresponding industry (in terms of republican property), or the local executive body (for municipal property).[45]

---

40. Conditions of the subject matter of the contract are significant when their terms are found to be significant by law or necessary for contracts of this type, as well as all the conditions for which at the request of one of the parties an agreement must be reached.
41. Article 393 of the Civil Code.
42. Clause 5, Art. 8. Of the Law on Arbitration.
43. Article 1 of the Civil Code.
44. At least 50% of voting shares (stakes in the authorized capital) are directly or indirectly owned by the state.
45. Clause 9, Art. 8 of the Law on Arbitration.

1.47. In order to receive the consent of an authorized body, the applicant should indicate the predicted cost of a future arbitration hearing in its request. After receiving a request, the authorized body has fifteen calendar days to consider and offer a consent or refusal for conclusion of the arbitration agreement in written form. While considering the request, the authorized body should take into consideration the economic and security interests of Kazakhstan.[46]

1.48. This condition is a novelty for Arbitration law, and one which has not yet been evoked. Furthermore, it is not clear whether issued consent is irrevocable or whether under certain conditions, an authorized body has the right to withdraw it. In addition, practitioners have expressed concerns about the way in which arbitration costs are to be predicted in advance, as well as how requirement clause 10 Article 8 of the new Arbitration Act may subsequently give rise to disputes about the validity of the authorized body's consent.[47]

[3] Special Provisions on Consumer and Labor Disputes

1.49. In accordance with the legislation of Kazakhstan, labor disputes may not be subject to consideration in arbitration and there is hence no labor arbitration in Kazakhstan. Disputes on consumer protection are generally arbitrable if the requirements on the validity of an arbitration agreement have been met.[48]

1.50. The Law on arbitration permits concluding an arbitration agreement to the contract of adhesion[49] after such claim or cause of action has arisen under that contract.[50] The main idea of this provision is to protect the weaker party in the contract, which enters into the merger agreement with the inclusion of an arbitration clause. In practice, one of the parties of the contract of adhesion is usually the consumer – an individual person who joined the agreement developed by the seller (provider).[51]

[G] Effect of Arbitration Agreement on Third Parties (Substitution of Parties, Guarantee Agreements, Group of Companies Doctrine)

1.51. The Law on Arbitration is silent regarding the effect of arbitration agreements on third parties.

---

46. *Ibid.*
47. Tukulov B.A., New Law of the Republic of Kazakhstan "On Arbitration": Attention to some Problem Issues. https://www.zakon.kz/4795629-novyjj-zakon-respubliki-kazakhstan-ob.html.
48. Clause 4, Art. 8 of the Law on Arbitration.
49. A contract of adhesion is a contract consisting of standardized and nonnegotiable terms, especially where one party to the contract is in a weaker bargaining position than the other, https://en.oxforddictionaries.com/definition/contract_of_adhesion.
50. Clause 4, Art. 8 of the Law on Arbitration.
51. Suleimenov M.K. & Duissenova A.E., Advantages and Disadvantages of the New Law of Arbitration, https://www.zakon.kz/4796696-dostoinstva-i-nedostatki-novogo-zakona.html.

1.52. In the absence of a clear position by Kazakh legislators regarding the involvement of third parties in the arbitration, permanent arbitration has attempted to fill this gap with relevant norms on third parties in their regulations.

1.53. In practice, this is possible in three ways:

(1) Third parties can participate in arbitration proceedings when: (a) there is consent from both parties, expressed in writing; (b) there is a consent from the third party;[52] (c) the claimant and/or respondent should notify the arbitral tribunal on involvement of a third party prior to the expiry of the period for reply to the statement of claim. In the case of failure to comply with at least one of the following conditions, a third party may not be a party to the arbitration.
(2) Participation of third parties in arbitration is possible only if such party is a party of the arbitration agreement and application on involvement of a third party was made prior to the first session of the court.
(3) Involvement of the third party in arbitration is not permitted.[53]

[H] Termination of Arbitration Agreement

[1] Termination with Respect to Existing Dispute

1.54. According to clause 7, Article 8 of the Law on Arbitration, an arbitration agreement may be terminated by agreement of parties in the same order in which it was concluded. After the termination of the agreement, the dispute may be resolved at the state court.

[2] Complete Termination

1.55. Moreover, prior to the initiation of the dispute, the parties may unilaterally terminate the arbitration agreement in accordance with Article 404 of the Civil Code by notifying the other party within reasonable time.[54] Scholars and practitioners expressed serious concerns about the practical implications of this provision, since the unilateral termination of the arbitration agreement may result in serious legal consequences for the parties. In addition, it is not clear how to determine the time of dispute initiation: either it is when one party sends the other party a claim, or when one of the parties sends the claim to an arbitration institution.

---

52. According to the authors it should also be expressed in writing.
53. Duissenova A.E., Participation of Third Parties in the Arbitration Proceedings // Coll. Materials of the International scientific and practical conference in the framework of annual civil reads "Civil law and civil law", devoted to the anniversary of the Civil Code of the Republic of Kazakhstan (the 15th anniversary of the General Part and the 10th anniversary of the Special Part). Almaty: Research Institute of Private Law KazSLU, LF Zanger, 2009. pp. 442–455.
54. Clause 5, Art. 9 of the Law on Arbitration.

[I] Drafting Arbitration Clauses

1.56. Since the Law on Arbitration provides strict requirements on the essential terms of the arbitration agreement, it would be more effective to use model arbitration clauses, drafted and recommended by permanent arbitration institutions. Almost all arbitration institutions share arbitration clauses on their homepages.[55]

1.57. As a rule, arbitration institutions encourage the parties to indicate that any (or all) disputes arising from this contract or in connection with it shall be settled finally in accordance with its applicable rules, especially in permanent arbitration.

1.58. Moreover, it is desirable to specify the number of arbitrators who will settle the dispute. This is especially important in cases where the parties want the sole arbitrator to consider the matter. Otherwise, in accordance with cl. 2 of Article 14 of the Law on Arbitration, three arbitrators will consider the dispute. Additionally, it is important to specify the place and language of arbitration.

1.59. To avoid the risk of recognition of the arbitration clause being unenforceable, parties should first specify the exact name of the arbitration institution and indicate exactly which disputes shall be solved by the arbitral decision.[56]

§5.03 APPLICABLE LAW

[A] Introduction

1.60. Pursuant to Article 44 of the Law on Arbitration, the arbitral tribunal shall decide the dispute in accordance with the rules of law chosen by the parties as applicable to the substance of the dispute. In the absence of such rules, the arbitral tribunal determines the applicable law in accordance with the legislation of the Republic of Kazakhstan.[57] Should there be no law governing a specific ratio, the arbitration will make a decision in accordance with the customs of trade applicable to that transaction.

[B] The Law Governing the Arbitration (*Lex Arbitri*)

1.61. According to the Law on Arbitration and treaties, *lex arbitri* shall cover the following issues for the purposes of arbitration proceedings and further enforcement of the arbitral award. (1) validity of the arbitration agreement (for both form and substance); (2) arbitrability of the disputed subject; and (3) rules of the arbitral procedure.

---

55. *See* http://www.arbitrage.kz; http://www.atamekenarb.kz; http://www.iusea.com; http://arbitrazh.kz; http://rus.arbitration.kz.
56. Suleimenov M.K. & Duissenova A.E., Advantages and Disadvantages of the New Law of Arbitration, https://www.zakon.kz/4796696-dostoinstva-i-nedostatki-novogo-zakona.html.
57. For more information, please *see* §5.03[E][2] Relevant Conflict of Law Rules.

[C] Party Autonomy on Choice of Law Issues

1.62. Parties are free to choose the law applicable to the substance of the dispute and the law applicable to the arbitration agreement.[58] However, in practice this happens quite rarely. Generally, parties do not indicate the law applicable to the arbitration agreement.[59]

[D] Restrictions on Party Autonomy
[1] General Observations

1.63. Legislators have restricted the party autonomy principle by prohibiting choosing foreign law when the dispute is between individuals and (or) legal entities of Kazakhstan, as well as when one of the parties is a government agency, state-owned enterprises, or legal entity with at least 50% of voting shares (stakes in the authorized capital) directly or indirectly owned by the State. In such disputes, the applicable law should be the legislation of Kazakhstan, unless otherwise stipulated by international treaties ratified by Kazakhstan.[60]

1.64. This condition is a novelty and was not indicated in the previous laws on domestic and international arbitration. In fact, by adopting this mandatory condition, legislators have made arbitration in Kazakhstan unattractive for foreign investors.[61]

[2] Reasonable Connection Test

1.65. The Civil Code allows judges to apply the law of another State most closely connected with respective legal relations, if under the law of that State such rules should regulate the respective relations regardless of the applicable law.[62]

[3] National Public Policy

1.66. The Civil Code restricts the application of foreign law when it contradicts the basis of rule of law (public policy) of the Republic of Kazakhstan. However, the refusal of the application of foreign law cannot be based only on difference between the political and economic systems of the relevant foreign State and Kazakhstan.[63]

1.67. The Law on Arbitration defines the term national public policy as "fundamental principles of the legal system fixed in the legislation of Kazakhstan."[64] Since there is no

---

58. Article 44 of the Law on Arbitration.
59. Suleimenov M.K., Applicable Law, course of lectures.
60. Clause 1, Art. 44 of the Law on Arbitration.
61. Tukulov B.A., New Law of the Republic of Kazakhstan "On Arbitration": Attention to some Problem Issues, https://www.zakon.kz/4795629-novyjj-zakon-respubliki-kazakhstan-ob.html.
62. Article 1091 of Civil Code.
63. Article 1090 of Civil Code.
64. Article 2 of the Law on Arbitration.

clear definition of public policy, the judges interpret it at their sole discretion.[65] As a result, some judges abuse the use of the condition of public policy in recognition and enforcement of arbitral awards.

1.68. For instance, in a recent case the state court annulled the decision of KIA, deeming it against the public policy of Kazakhstan. Notably, the parties of the arbitration were foreign legal entities and the governing law was Kazakh law. This case caused controversy among scholars and practitioners.[66] As a result, the arbitration institutions of Kazakhstan jointly wrote an open letter to the Supreme Court and Ministry of Justice of Kazakhstan to inform them of the judge's major violation of arbitration law.[67]

[4] Mandatory Rules of Municipal Law

1.69. The legislation of Kazakhstan provides a mandatory condition for application of imperative norms of Kazakh legislation over foreign applicable law when there is special significance for the rights and interests of Kazakh citizens and legal entities in the dispute.[68] For instance, an applicable law of the agreement on establishment of a legal entity with foreign shares in Kazakhstan should be decided by Kazakh legislation.[69] Mandatory rules of Kazakh law are also reflected in foreign currency, tax, and subsoil use laws.

[5] International Public Policy

1.70. There is no notion of "international public policy" in the legislation of the Republic of Kazakhstan.

[E] **No Explicit Choice of Law**

[1] Introduction

1.71. What constitutes a law applicable to civil and legal relations with the participation of foreign citizens, foreign legal entities, or complicated by any other foreign element shall be determined on the basis of the Civil Code, other legislative acts, international treaties ratified by the Republic of Kazakhstan, international customs being recognized.

---

65. Suleimenov M.K. & Duissenova A.E., Advantages and Disadvantages of the New Law of Arbitration, https://www.zakon.kz/4796696-dostoinstva-i-nedostatki-novogo-zakona.html.
66. Suleimenov M.K., How Judge Interpreted the Laws at Its Sole Discretion, http://online.zakon.kz/Document/?doc_id=33710017.
67. Open letter of arbitration institutions to the Supreme court and the Ministry of Justice of the Republic of Kazakhstan, http://online.zakon.kz/Document/?doc_id=34233934#pos=6;-147.
68. Article 1091 of Civil Code.
69. Article 1114 of Civil Code.

1.72. If it is impossible to determine the applicable law, the law most closely linked with civil and legal relations shall apply.[70]

[2] Relevant Conflict of Laws Rules

1.73. In contractual obligations, in absence of the parties' explicit choice of law, the law of the country where a party was established or has place of residence or principal place of business shall apply. For instance, in a purchase and sale contract the law of the seller; in a deed of gift the law of the donator; in the lease contract the law of the lessor and the property owner; for loans or other credit contracts the law of the creditor, etc.[71]

[F] The Law Governing the Arbitration Agreement

1.74. According to the Law on Arbitration,[72] an arbitration clause forming part of a contract shall be treated as an agreement independent of the other terms of the contract. Imposition of arbitration decisions on the invalidity of the contract does not entail the invalidity of the arbitration clause. *Lex arbitri* is applicable to the substantive validity of the arbitration agreement, as well as formal validity of the arbitration agreement if the latter needs to be established by arbitrators.[73]

§5.04 THE ARBITRATORS

[A] Appointment of Arbitrators

[1] Appointment of Arbitrators under Municipal Law

1.75. The parties are free to choose any individual regardless of nationality as an arbitrator if he/she meets the general requirements for arbitrators provided in Article 13 of the Law on Arbitration.[74] The number of arbitrators should be odd. Unless the parties have agreed otherwise, the number of arbitrators should be three.[75]

1.76. In accordance with Article 14(6) of the Law on Arbitration, in the absence of agreement by the parties, the chairman of an arbitration institution or the Arbitration Chamber in ad hoc arbitration may upon the request of one of the parties appoint an arbitrator from the registry of the Arbitration Chamber of Kazakhstan within thirty days.

1.77. The chairman and the Arbitration Chamber are entitled to appoint the arbitrators, when: (1) the party has not appointed an arbitrator within thirty days from the

---

70. Article 1084 of Civil Code.
71. Article 1113 of Civil Code.
72. Article 20 of the Law on Arbitration.
73. Article 49 of the Law on Arbitration.
74. For more information, please *see* §5.04[B] Qualifications of Arbitrators.
75. Article 14 of the Law on Arbitration.

date of receipt of the request from the other party, unless otherwise established by the regulations or by agreement of the parties; (2) two arbitrators could not agree on the choice of the third arbitrator, within thirty days, unless otherwise established by the regulations or by agreement of the parties; (3) parties have not agreed on the choice of the sole arbitrator. The decision on appointment of the arbitrators is irrevocable.

[2] Appointment under Institutional Rules

1.78. Pursuant to clause 2, Article 13 of the Law on Arbitration, additional requirements for candidates to the position of arbitrator can be agreed upon by the parties directly or as determined by rules of a permanent arbitration institution.

1.79. In permanent arbitration, formation of the Arbitral Tribunal is made in the manner prescribed by the rules of the permanent arbitration institution and arbitration agreement. In accordance with the rules of institutional arbitration, in the formation of the Arbitral Tribunal consisting of three arbitrators, each party shall appoint one arbitrator and the two appointed arbitrators shall choose the third, presiding arbitrator.[76]

1.80. Some Arbitration rules authorize the chairman or deputy chairman of the Arbitration Institution to appoint the third arbitrator, who presides over the case (the chairman of the Arbitral Tribunal).[77]

[B] Qualifications of Arbitrators

1.81. According to clause 1, Article 13 of the Law on Arbitration, the arbitrator is an individual who is directly or indirectly disinterested in the outcome of the case, is independent and at least 30 years old, and possesses higher education and at least five years of professional experience.

1.82. The arbitrator resolving a dispute solely must hold a law degree. In cases of collective dispute resolutions, the chairman of the Arbitral Tribunal should hold a law degree. Parties may also impose additional requirements on the arbitrators' qualifications. However, this rarely occurs in practice.

1.83. However, the Law on Arbitration contains a list of persons who cannot be arbitrators:

- elected or appointed judges;
- persons declared incapable or partially capable by the court;
- persons with a criminal record;

---

76. *See*, for example, Art. 24 Rules of Kazakhstani International Arbitrage, http://arbitrage.kz/201 6-09-11-09-51-05/2016-09-11-10-08-22.html.
77. For instance, Art. 3.4 International Arbitration Regulation "IUS" // http://www.iusea.com/ index.php?option = com_content&view = article&id = 2&Itemid = 47.

- public officers, deputies of the Parliament of Kazakhstan, maslikhat deputies;[78]
- military officers.[79]

1.84. Moreover, the Law on Arbitration makes it imperative to introduce an arbitrators' registry by the Arbitration Chamber of Kazakhstan. This is a database containing information about all arbitrators operating in Kazakhstan.[80] A similar requirement is provided in respect to permanent arbitration, where a register of arbitrators is also required.[81]

[C] Powers and Duties of Arbitrators

1.85. The Law on Arbitration does not contain a separate article devoted to the powers and duties of arbitrators. The main duty of arbitrators is to independently and impartially review a dispute and make an award.

[D] Challenges and Replacement of Arbitrators

[1] *Challenges under Municipal Law*

1.86. The authority to make decisions on challenges or terminations of an arbitrator's mandate is granted to the chairman of the arbitration institution.[82]

1.87. After the constitution of the Arbitral Tribunal, parties are entitled to challenge the arbitrator by mutual consent if they doubt his/her impartiality and (or) competence based on the following grounds:[83]

- an individual closely connected with the arbitrator[84] is a party to the dispute, or an arbitrator might otherwise stand to gain or lose depending on the outcome of the dispute;
- the arbitrator or a closely related person is the head of the legal entity whose branch or representative office is party to the dispute, or otherwise represents the direction of a person who can expect significant gains or losses depending on the outcome of the dispute;

---

78. Maslikhat is the local representative agency in Kazakhstan. Maslikhat is the elected body elected by the population of a region (a city of republican status, or the capital) or a district (a city of regional status).
79. Clause 3, Art. 13 of the Law on Arbitration.
80. Article 15 of the Law on Arbitration.
81. Article 16 of the Law on Arbitration.
82. Article 18 of the Law on Arbitration.
83. Article 17 of the Law on Arbitration.
84. A closely connected person is a person who is the spouse of the arbitrator or his close relative, the in-law or employee of permanent arbitration; is in a labor or other contractual relation with the arbitrator, or has other connections showing his or her dependence on an arbitrator.

- the arbitrator has acted as an expert, or otherwise determined its position in the dispute or assisted the party in preparation or presentation of its position beforehand;
- the arbitrator has received or demanded compensation in connection with the consideration of the case;
- the arbitrator unreasonably fails to comply with the terms of the arbitration.

1.88. In the event that the parties fail to reach agreement on a procedure for challenging an arbitrator, or such procedure has not been specified by the arbitration institution rules, the party which intends to challenge an arbitrator shall, within thirty days of becoming aware of any circumstance that gives rise to justifiable doubts, send a written statement of the reasons for the challenge to the arbitral tribunal.[85] The decision on the termination of the powers of an arbitrator is irrevocable.

[2] Challenges under Institutional Rules

1.89. According to cl. 3 Article 17 of the Law on Arbitration, persons approached regarding possible appointment as arbitrators shall disclose any circumstances likely to give rise to justifiable grounds as to their impartiality or independence. If these circumstances occurred during the arbitration, the arbitrator shall immediately notify the parties and withdraw himself or herself from the proceeding.

1.90. If an arbitrator rejects a challenge, or if one of the parties does not agree to an arbitrator being challenged, the matter of the challenge should be considered by the members of the arbitral tribunal within ten calendar days from the receipt of a written request from the party.

1.91. According to clause 1, Article 59 of the Law on Arbitration, international and domestic arbitration institutions shall, within two years from the date of entry into force of the Law on Arbitration, make appropriate changes to their rules.

1.92. Since the Law on Arbitration provides such a large amount of time, permanent arbitration institutions have not yet made changes to their rules. Therefore, we do not have sufficient data to consider in more detail challenges under institutional rules at this moment.

[E] Compensation of Arbitrators

1.93. According the Law on Arbitration, costs associated with the resolution of a dispute in arbitration, in addition to other expenses, include: (1) registration fee; (2) arbitrators' fee; (3) additional costs of the arbitral proceedings.[86]

---

85. Article 17 of the Law on Arbitration.
86. Additional expenses include expenses incurred by arbitrators in connection with the participation in arbitration proceedings; this includes travel costs, accommodation and food expenses,

1.94. In permanent arbitration institutions, the Arbitral Tribunal determines each arbitrators' fee based on the schedule of fees specified in the arbitration rules of that institution. If the arbitration rules do not have such a fee schedule, the Arbitral Tribunal determines each arbitrators' fee based on the claim amount, the complexity of the dispute, time spent by arbitrators for the proceeding, and any other relevant circumstances.

1.95. In ad hoc arbitration, the parties determine the arbitrator's fee by mutual agreement. In the absence of such an agreement, arbitrators use the same methods as an Arbitral Tribunal of permanent arbitration.[87]

§5.05 JURISDICTION OF THE ARBITRATION TRIBUNAL

[A] Introduction

1.96. The Law on Arbitration respects the "principle of competence-competence," under which both institutional arbitration and ad hoc arbitration are entitled to determine the presence or absence of its competence.[88]

[B] The Arbitrators' Determination of Their Jurisdiction

1.97. In accordance with clause 1, Article 20 of the Law on Arbitration, the arbitral tribunal may rule on its own jurisdiction, including any objections of one of the parties about the existence or validity of the arbitration agreement.

1.98. A party has the right to declare the lack of jurisdiction of the arbitral tribunal to hear the arbitration passed before the submission of its first statement on the substance of the dispute. Arbitration shall consider such an application within ten calendar days and issue an order about existence or lack of jurisdiction.

[C] Court Review of Arbitrators' Jurisdiction

1.99. Pursuant to Article 10 of the Law on Arbitration, when the state court receives a lawsuit subject to arbitration, it should refer the parties to arbitration unless it finds that the arbitration agreement is null and void, inoperative, or incapable of being performed. Consequently, in this the arbitral tribunal rather than the court reviews the arbitrators' jurisdiction and the validity of the arbitration agreement.[89]

---

and expenses incurred by arbitrators in connection with the inspection and examination of written and physical evidences at their location, etc.
87. Article 41 of the Law on Arbitration.
88. Article 20 of the Law on Arbitration.
89. Tukulov B.A., New Law of the Republic of Kazakhstan "On Arbitration": Attention to some Problem Issues, http://online.zakon.kz/Document/?doc_id=34537267#pos=107;-150.

[D] Institutional Rules

1.100. Rules of all arbitration institutions follow the provisions of the Law on Arbitration. Accordingly, the Arbitral Tribunal is entitled to determine the presence or absence of its jurisdiction.[90]

§5.06 THE PROCEDURE BEFORE THE ARBITRATION TRIBUNAL

[A] Introduction

1.101. The Law on Arbitration, in contrast to the previous law on international commercial arbitration, contains novelties with respect to the arbitration procedure, significantly distinguishing it from the procedure under the UNCITRAL Model Law "On International Commercial Arbitration."

1.102. For instance, it contains provisions on the form and content of the statement of claim,[91] grounds for a refund claim,[92] rights of parties,[93] date of the arbitral proceedings,[94] protocol, and requirements to its content,[95] etc.

[B] General Principles of Municipal Judicial Procedure

1.103. According to Article 7 of the Law on Arbitration, arbitral institutions and arbitrators are independent in making decisions in the absence of any interference of state bodies and other organizations in their activities, except in cases established by this Law. Thus, state courts shall not interfere in arbitration activities.

[C] General Principles of Arbitration Procedure (Party Autonomy, Speed, Impartiality, Etc.)

1.104. Article 5 of the Law on Arbitration sets out the following principles of the arbitration proceeding: (1) autonomy of the parties' will; (2) lawfulness; (3) independence; (4) equality of the parties; (5) justice; (6) confidentiality; (7) the autonomy of an arbitration agreement.[96]

---

90. For more information, please *see* http://www.arbitrage.kz/; http://www.atamekenarb.kz/; http://www.iusea.com/; http://arbitrazh.kz/; http://rus.arbitration.kz/; http://aca.kz/ru/.
91. Article 23 of the Law on Arbitration.
92. Article 27 of the Law on Arbitration.
93. Article 31 of the Law on Arbitration.
94. Article 35 of the Law on Arbitration.
95. Articles 36–38 of the Law on Arbitration.
96. Suleimenov M.K. & Duissenova A.E., Chapter 11 "Arbitration Protection of Civil Rights" (§ 2. Principles of arbitration proceedings) // Protection of civil rights. Monograph. Responsible editor Suleimenov M.K. Almaty, Research Institute of Private Law, KazSLU, LF Zanger, 2011.

1.105. The principle of autonomy of the parties means that the parties subject to prior agreement among themselves have the right to decide the order of conditions of the arbitration proceedings which have led to or may lead to dispute.

1.106. General principles of the arbitration procedure are also set forth in the rules of arbitration institutions. For instance, Article 32 of the Rules of KIA[97] states that "each party should have equal opportunity to present his/her position and protect his/her rights and interests."

[D] Commencing the Arbitral Proceedings

[1] Municipal Law

1.107. The Law on Arbitration contains two articles regarding the arbitration proceeding (Article 25) and the commencement of the arbitration (Article 26). However, these are not in fact consistent with each other. The presence of the two articles was the result of incompetent legal technique, i.e., a combination of the provisions of the previous Law on Arbitration Courts (Domestic Arbitration) and the Law on International Commercial Arbitration.

1.108. According to clause 1, Article 25 of the Law on Arbitration, after receipt of the statement of claim, the Arbitral Tribunal shall issue an order on commencement of the arbitration proceeding within ten calendar days, in accordance with the rules of arbitration or rules agreed upon by the parties. It should then notify the parties of the place of arbitration.

1.109. Unless the parties have agreed otherwise, the arbitral proceedings in respect to a particular dispute (ad hoc arbitration) begin on the day when a request to transfer that dispute to arbitration is received by the respondent.[98]

[2] Institutional Rules

1.110. Pursuant to Article 14 of the KIA Rules, arbitral proceedings are commenced starting on the date of submission of a claim to the KIA. The date of submission of the claim shall be the date that claim was filed at the KIA. If the claim is submitted via post, the date of submission is the date indicated on the departure stamp at the post office.[99]

---

97. Rules of Kazakh International Arbitration, http://arbitrage.kz/2016-09-11-09-51-05/2016-09-11-10-08-22.html.
98. Article 26 of the Law on Arbitration.
99. Rules of Kazakh International Arbitration, http://arbitrage.kz/2016-09-11-09-51-05/2016-09-11-10-08-22.html.

[E] Conduct of Arbitration

[1] Written Submissions

1.111. Copies of all submitted documents, materials, and information by one of the parties to an arbitration institution shall be transmitted to the other party by arbitration within seven calendar days from the date of their receipt by arbitration. Expert opinions must be transferred by arbitration to the parties before the arbitration proceeding.[100]

[2] Post-hearing Briefs

1.112. Unlike the UNCITRAL Model Law, as well as the Arbitration Laws of other Commonwealth of Independent States (CIS) countries, the Kazakh Law on Arbitration contains provisions on possible revisions to the award under newly discovered circumstances. According to Article 51 of the Law on Arbitration, the arbitration award may be reviewed at the request of one of the parties of an arbitration agreement or another person whose rights are affected by newly discovered facts.

1.113. The grounds for the review of an arbitral award based on newly discovered facts are as follows:

(1) deliberately false testimony of a witness, knowingly false expert opinion, knowingly wrong translation, and forgery of documents or physical evidence leading to the adoption of illegal or unjustified decisions established by a final judgment of the court;
(2) criminal actions of the parties, other persons involved in the case, or their representatives; or criminal acts of an arbitrator committed during consideration of the case established by a final judgment of the court;
(3) recognition of a law or other normative legal act used in making the arbitration award as unconstitutional by the Constitutional Court of Kazakhstan.

1.114. Application for review of an arbitral award on newly discovered facts should be submitted and reviewed in the arbitration institution that issued the award. The term of re-reviewing of the dispute is one month.[101]

1.115. Over the course of the twelve-year existence of KIA, an award has been revised due to newly discovered circumstances only once.

---

100. Clause 4, Art. 26 of the Law on Arbitration.
101. Article 51 of the Law on Arbitration.

[3] Evidence (Admissibility, Documentary Evidence)

1.116. Each party must prove the circumstances which it refers as a basis of its claims and objections. If the arbitrator considers the evidence insufficient, he/she may require the parties to submit additional evidence.[102]

1.117. The arbitrators may refuse to accept the evidence presented by the parties if the evidence is not relevant to the dispute or a refusal is justified in view of the time when such evidence was presented. The arbitrator is obliged to examine all the available evidence in the case directly.[103]

1.118. The arbitral tribunal is entitled to determine the admissibility, relevance, materiality, and value of any evidence.[104]

[4] Witness and Expert Testimony

1.119. In accordance with clause 1, Article 34 of the Law on Arbitration, unless otherwise agreed upon by the parties to the arbitration, the arbitral tribunal may:

(1) appoint one or more experts to report on specific issues to be determined by arbitration;
(2) require a party to give the expert any relevant information or produce relevant documents, goods, or other property for inspection or examination;
(3) solve other issues related to expert participation in the arbitration proceeding, including allocation of expenses for payment of examination and expert participation, if these issues were not agreed upon by the parties.

1.120. The expert opinion shall be submitted in writing[105]

[F] Hearings

1.121. In accordance with clause 1, Article 26 of the Law on Arbitration, unless otherwise provided by agreement of the parties, the arbitration shall decide whether to hold oral hearings for the presentation of evidence or to hold proceedings only based on documents and other materials. However, if the parties have not agreed not to hold an oral hearing, the arbitration shall hold such hearings at an appropriate stage of the proceedings at the request of either party.

1.122. The Arbitral Tribunal is obliged to give sufficient advance notice to the parties of any hearing and of any meeting of the arbitral tribunal for the purposes of inspection

---

102. Article 33 of the Law on Arbitration.
103. *Ibid.*
104. Clause 3, Art. 21 of the Law on Arbitration.
105. Clause 2, Art. 34 of the Law on Arbitration.

of goods, other property, or documents. If any party fails to appear at a hearing or to produce documentary evidence, the arbitral tribunal may continue the proceedings and make the award on the evidence before it.[106] Non-presence of the respondent does not mean its recognition of the claimant's claims.[107]

§5.07 THE ARBITRAL AWARD

[A] Introduction

1.123. Pursuant to Article 47 of the Law on Arbitration, the arbitration award must be in writing and signed by the arbitrators (or a sole arbitrator). If an arbitration proceeding is carried out jointly and the signature of an arbitrator is missing, the reason for such absence shall be specified. An arbitrator may not sign the award if he has a dissenting opinion, which shall be attached to the award in writing.

1.124. The award shall contain information about: (1) the date of the award; (2) the place of arbitration; (3) the arbitral tribunal; (4) justification of arbitration competence; (5) the name of the parties; (6) positions of the claimant and respondent; (7) essence of the dispute; (8) regulatory legal acts which were used as a basis for making the award; (9) amount of expenses, etc.[108]

[B] Deliberation and Voting

1.125. After examining the circumstances of the case, the arbitral tribunal makes an award based on the majority of the arbitrators' votes. An arbitrator who does not agree with the decision of the majority of the members of the tribunal has the right to express a dissenting opinion, which is attached to the decision. Parties have the right to make themselves familiar with the dissenting opinion of the arbitrator. Arbitration may, if it deems necessary, postpone an award and call on the parties for an additional meeting.[109]

[C] Different Kinds of Awards (Separate, Interim, Consent, Default, Etc.)

1.126. The Law on Arbitration provides only one type of arbitration award. All arbitration awards are final. In matters not affecting the merits of the dispute, the arbitral tribunal makes an order.[110] The parties may settle the dispute during arbitration independently or by concluding a settlement or mediation agreement.

---

106. Article 26 of the Law on Arbitration.
107. Article 29 of the Law on Arbitration.
108. Article 47 of the Law on Arbitration.
109. Article 45 of the Law on Arbitration.
110. Article 48 of the Law on Arbitration.

[D] Interest and Costs

1.127. The Law on Arbitration contains a separate article devoted to cost-sharing issues related to the resolution of the dispute in arbitration. Thus, according to Article 46 of the Law on Arbitration, allocation of these costs between the parties is made by the arbitration institution in accordance with the parties' agreement, in the absence thereof – in proportion to satisfied and rejected requirements.

1.128. All costs associated with the arbitration may be attributed to the unsuccessful party if the demand for reimbursement of the costs incurred were claimed during the arbitral proceedings and granted by arbitration[111]

1.129. Arbitration institutions establish the amount of arbitration fees themselves, and, as a rule, in the form of a schedule of arbitration fees depending on the amount of the claim.

[E] Effects of the Award

[1] Execution

1.130. Arbitral awards in Kazakhstan can be executed both voluntarily and forcibly. As a rule, most of the awards in Kazakhstan are executed forcibly.

1.131. According to Article 54 of the Law on Arbitration, an award is recognized as mandatory upon application of a written statement to the court, and enforcement is executed in accordance with the civil procedure of Kazakhstan.

1.132. If the deadline is not set in the award, it shall be subject to immediate execution. Since some difficulties can occur during implementation of this regulation in practice, the awards made by the Arbitral Tribunal of permanent arbitration institutions always indicate the deadline for voluntary execution of the award by the parties. Only after the expiration of that period may the party in whose favor the arbitration award is made and which has not been voluntarily executed apply to a competent court to receive the writ for enforcement.[112]

1.133. Additional costs associated with enforcement of the arbitration award shall be borne by the party that has not complied with the judgment voluntarily.[113]

[2] Res Judicata and Lis Pendens

1.134. This issue is not legally settled in Kazakhstan and remains open.

1.135. In accordance with subclause 3 of Article 277 of the Civil Procedure Code, the court shall terminate the proceedings if there is an arbitral award, rendered within the

---

111. Article 46 of the Law on Arbitration.
112. Article 54 of the Law on Arbitration.
113. Article 56 of the Law on Arbitration.

tribunal's jurisdiction, in a dispute between the same parties, regarding the same subject matter and on the same grounds.

[F] Correction and Interpretation of the Award

[1] Municipal Law

1.136. According to Article 50 of the Law on Arbitration, correction, clarification, or making an additional arbitration award are possible within sixty calendar days after the award is received, unless the parties or rules provide otherwise.

1.137. Either party, having notified the other party, may request that the arbitration correct any errors made in the award with regards to calculation, clerical or typographical errors, or errors of a similar nature; a party may also request clarification on any certain clause or any part of the rendered award.

1.138. If it considers the request to be justified, the arbitral tribunal should within thirty calendar days from the day of receipt make the necessary corrections or clarifications. Clarification of the award made is an integral part of the award.

1.139. Unless otherwise agreed by the parties, any of the parties may request that the tribunal make an additional award as to the claims that were made during the arbitral proceedings which were not reflected in the award within sixty calendar days after receipt of the award, having notified the other party.[114]

[2] Institutional Rules

1.140. Article 47 of KIA Rules repeats the rule of Article 50 of the Law on Arbitration. Accordingly, the Arbitral Tribunal of KIA should make corrections and interpretation of the clauses of rendered award upon the request of any party.

§5.08 SETTING ASIDE THE AWARD

[A] Introduction

1.141. Similar to the Model Law approach, setting aside the award is an exclusive recourse against the award.[115]

1.142. Kazakh courts are not entitled to set aside arbitral awards rendered outside of Kazakhstan by foreign international arbitration institutions. Such awards are to be set aside in the country where they were rendered, i.e., outside of Kazakhstan.

1.143. An application for setting aside an arbitral award may be submitted by the parties or third parties not involved in the case, as long as they concern the rights and

---

114. Clause 3, Art. 50 of the Law on Arbitration.
115. Article 52 of the Law on Arbitration.

obligations about which the arbitration rendered an award on the grounds stipulated by the law, within one month from the date of receipt of the award.[116] An application for setting aside an award is considered by the court within ten business days from the date of initiation of the proceeding.[117]

1.144. Application for setting aside an arbitral award should be submitted to the relevant court of Kazakhstan in accordance with: (1) the place where the arbitral tribunal reviewed the dispute, if the arbitration award was rendered in Kazakhstan; (2) the place where permanent arbitration is located, if the arbitration award was rendered according to the law of the Republic of Kazakhstan in a foreign country; (3) the place in Kazakhstan where arbitration was formed, if the arbitration award was rendered according to the law of the Republic of Kazakhstan in a foreign country.[118]

1.145. After considering an application for setting aside an award, the relevant court shall issue an order either on setting aside an arbitral award or refusal of the application to set aside the reward. This order may be appealed in accordance with the legislation of Kazakhstan.

1.146. Because of the recent adoption of the Law on Arbitration and the combining of the Law on Arbitration (Domestic Arbitration) and International Commercial Arbitration, some judges still misinterpret the provisions of the Law on Arbitration and set aside the arbitration award.[119]

[B] Invalid Awards

1.147. The Law on Arbitration does not specify which awards can be deemed valid or invalid. The Kazakh courts are entitled to challenge any arbitration award in Kazakhstan based on the grounds provided by the Law on Arbitration.

[C] Challengeable Awards

[1] Grounds for Challenging the Award

1.148. In Kazakhstan, an arbitration award could be challenged based on the following grounds:[120]

- the award was made regarding a dispute not contemplated by or not falling within the terms of its submission to arbitration, or contains decisions on matters beyond the scope of the submission to arbitration, and due to *non-jurisdiction of the dispute to the arbitration* court;

---

116. Article 464 of the Civil Procedure Code.
117. Article 465 of the Civil Procedure Code.
118. Article 464 of the Civil Procedure Code.
119. Suleimenov M.K., "Court's Chaos still Continuous," https://www.zakon.kz/4814246-sudejjskijj-bespredel-prodolzhaetsja.html.
120. Article 52 of Arbitration law.

- one of the parties of the arbitration agreement was recognized incapable by the court, or the said agreement is not valid under the law to which the parties have subjected it or, failing any indication thereon, under the law of the Republic of Kazakhstan;
- the party making the application was not given proper notice of the appointment of an arbitrator or of the arbitral proceedings, or was otherwise unable to present its case due to excuses recognized by the court as reasonable;
- the composition of the arbitral tribunal or the arbitral procedure was not in accordance with the agreement of the parties;
- there is an effective court decision or rendered arbitral award in regard to the dispute between the same parties on the same subject and on the same grounds; or there is a court or arbitration order on termination of the proceedings due to abandonment of claim by the plaintiff;
- the award does not comply with the requirement on the written form and the signature provided in Article 47 of the Law on Arbitration.

1.149. The last two grounds have been implemented recently by the adoption of the Law on Arbitration. In fact, it is not clear why the legislator included these grounds. Moreover, it is not clear how it is possible for the arbitration award not to comply with the requirement on the written form and the signature provided in Article 47, since an arbitration award cannot be rendered orally.[121]

1.150. In addition, the arbitration award may be challenged if the court finds that:

- the subject matter of the dispute is not capable of settlement by arbitration under the legislation of Kazakhstan; or
- the award conflicts with the public policy of the Republic of Kazakhstan.[122]

[2] Waiver of Right to Challenge

1.151. The Law on Arbitration and the Civil Procedure Code does not provide any provisions regarding the "Waiver of Right to Challenge."

[D] Review of Jurisdictional Awards

1.152. According to Article 20 of the Law on Arbitration, the Arbitral tribunal may rule on its own jurisdiction, including any objections with respect to the existence or validity of the arbitration agreement. If the tribunal issues a ruling on its lack of jurisdiction, then it may not review the dispute on its merits.

---

121. Suleimenov M.K. & Duissenova A.E., Advantages and Disadvantages of the New Law of Arbitration, https://www.zakon.kz/4796696-dostoinstva-i-nedostatki-novogo-zakona.html.
122. Article 52 of the Law on Arbitration.

§5.09 RECOGNITION AND ENFORCEMENT OF THE ARBITRAL AWARD

[A] Enforcement of Domestic Awards

[1] Enforcement Domestically

1.153. Arbitration awards are enforced based on Article 253 of the Civil Procedure Code. In order to enforce the award, the party should apply to the court located in the place where arbitration took place, the place of residence of the debtor, or at the location of the legal entity, if the place of residence or location is unknown, then at the location of the debtor's property.

1.154. The application to issue the enforcement order should be filed no later than three years upon expiry of the deadline for voluntary enforcement of the arbitral award and should include: (1) the original version or a notarized copy of the arbitral award; (2) the original version or a notarized copy of the arbitration agreement, signed in the manner prescribed by the law.[123]

1.155. The application to issue the enforcement order shall be considered by a judge personally within fifteen days from the date of receipt of the application by the court.[124]

1.156. The court, while considering the application on issuance of the enforcement order for the enforcement of the arbitral award, is not entitled to review the award on the merits.[125] After considering the application, the court renders either a ruling on issuing the enforcement order or a refusal to issue such document.[126]

[2] Enforcement Abroad

1.157. Kazakh legislation does not contain specific rules regarding enforcement of its domestic awards abroad. Such enforcement is subject to the applicable international treaty and national legislation in the place of enforcement.

[B] Enforcement of Foreign Arbitral Awards

[1] Introduction to Recognition and Enforcement

1.158. Similar to the enforcement of domestic awards, the recognition and enforcement of foreign awards are also delegated to the local courts of Kazakhstan. The procedure of recognition and enforcement of foreign arbitral awards complies with the New York Convention. The procedure of enforcement of foreign arbitral awards and domestic awards in Kazakhstan are similar.

---

123. Clause 2, Art. 253 of Civil Procedure Code.
124. Clause 3, Art. 253 of Civil Procedure Code.
125. Clause 8, Art. 253 of Civil Procedure Code.
126. Clause 9, Art. 253 of Civil Procedure Code.

[2] Separate, Partial and Interim Awards

1.159. Although Kazakh legislation does not provide any particular rules on recognition and enforcement of separate, partial and interim awards, in practice Kazakh courts do recognize such awards. For instance, in 2011 Mangystauskaya Oblast Specialized Inter-District Economic Court recognized the partial award rendered by the Istanbul Chamber of Commerce. The subject matter of the partial award was recognition of the share purchase agreement as valid and the claimant's right to keep the advancement payment.[127]

[3] Grounds for Refusing Recognition and Enforcement

[a] Lack of Capacity and Invalidity of Arbitration Agreement

1.160. This ground is usually not been practiced by the State courts. However, it may be widely used when one of the parties is a government body, public enterprise, or legal entity of which at least 50% of voting shares are directly or indirectly owned by the state. Prior to the conclusion of the arbitration agreement, these entities should receive consent from the authoritative bodies.[128]

[b] Procedural Violations

1.161. As shown by judicial practice, procedural violations are used as a basis for refusing recognition and enforcement of arbitral awards in Kazakhstan. For example, this ground has been used by the Judicial Board of the Almaty City Court while reviewing the award of the Arbitration Court of the St. Petersburg and Leningrad region. The Judicial Board did not recognize the award because the respondent had not been duly notified and did not receive the arbitration summons.[129]

[c] Excess of Mandate

1.162. According to p. 8 of Article 253 and Article 503 of the Civil Procedure Code, the judge shall not consider the merits of the arbitral award while reviewing the application for issuance of a writ of execution for enforcement of the arbitral award.[130] Therefore, this ground is not applied by the Kazakh courts.

---

127. Lyailya Tleulina, Recognition and enforcement of foreign judgements and commercial arbitration awards in Kazakhstan.
128. Tukulov B.A., New Law of the Republic of Kazakhstan "On Arbitration": Attention to some Problem Issues, https://www.zakon.kz/4795629-novyjj-zakon-respubliki-kazakhstan-ob.html.
129. Ruling of the Judicial Board of Almaty City Court dated July 27, 2011.
130. Page 8, of the Art. 503 of the Civil Procedure Code.

[d]   Arbitral Award Not Binding

1.163. Foreign arbitral awards are final and binding under the New York Convention, and they shall be recognized and enforced on the territory of the Republic of Kazakhstan in accordance with the Civil Procedure Code of the Republic of Kazakhstan.

[e]   Non-arbitrability

1.164. This ground has sometimes been used by Kazakh courts in order not to enforce awards rendered against the Republic of Kazakhstan.

[f]   Public Policy

1.165. Article 2(1) defines public policy as the basis of the rule of law embodied in the legislation of the Republic of Kazakhstan. Since the definition of public policy is not clear, the judges use this ground at their own discretion when recognizing and enforcing arbitral awards. Therefore, the Supreme Court of the Republic of Kazakhstan rendered decision N10 dated October 23, 2005 and declared that "the application of public policy is possible in exceptional cases, when enforcement of the arbitral award infringes upon the basis of law and order of the Republic of Kazakhstan."

[4]   Procedures for Recognition

1.166. The enforcement of foreign awards is conducted in accordance with Articles 501–504 of the Civil Procedure Code. In accordance with p. 3 of Article 503 of the Civil Procedure Code, the party is entitled to file an application to the court for issuance of a writ of execution within three years from the last day of the term of voluntary enforcement of the arbitral award. The application for issuance of a writ of execution is reviewed by the single judge within fifteen business days from the date of receipt of the application.[131] While reviewing the application, the judge shall not consider the merits of the arbitral award.[132] The court notifies the respondent about the application for issuance of a writ of execution and the date and venue of the court hearing. Upon, review of the application, the judge renders a ruling whether to issue a writ of execution or not. This ruling shall be enforced immediately.

1.167. In contrast to the ruling on issuance a writ of execution on enforcement of domestic arbitral award,[133] the ruling on issuance a writ of execution on enforcement of foreign arbitral award cannot be challenged or appealed.

---

131. Page 6 of the Art. 503 of the Civil Procedure Code.
132. Page 8 of the Art. 503 of the Civil Procedure Code.
133. Page 2 of the Art. 254 of the Civil Procedure Code.

§5.10 INVESTOR-STATE ARBITRATION

[A] General Overview of Law and Practice Related to Investor-State Arbitration

1.168. The ICSID Convention was signed by the Republic of Kazakhstan in 1992, ratified in 2000 and entered into force on October 22, 2000. Additionally, Kazakhstan concluded a number of multilateral and bilateral investment treaties (BITs) with foreign states.

1.169. Most of these treaties refer to arbitration procedures as dispute settlement procedures. Nevertheless, not all of them specify that the arbitral award is final and binding. For instance, treaties concluded with India, Netherlands, France, Iran, etc. do not contain a provision regarding the mandatory enforcement of arbitral awards. In other treaties concluded with Russia, Bulgaria, Turkey, Vietnam, etc., it is stated that the parties of the Convention shall enforce the arbitral award in accordance with their legislation.[134] Thus, there is no standard wording of the provision regarding the recognition and enforcement of arbitral awards in the BIT.

1.170. As of today, Kazakhstan has seven pending and ten concluded investment treaty cases.[135] The subject matters of those disputes are various. For instance, oil transportation (*Aktau Petrol v. Kazakhstan*), corporate (*Hourani v. Kazakhstan*), construction (*WWM v. Kazakhstan*) and so on. Generally, the Ministry of Justice either independently or by recruiting external counsel (domestic or international law firms) represents Kazakhstan in the disputes where Kazakhstan is a respondent.

[B] List of Investments the Country Has Ratified

1.171. Kazakhstan has ratified BITs with forty-nine states.[136]

1.172. In addition to the bilateral agreements, the following were also signed: (1) Framework Agreement between the USA and the Government of the Republic of Kazakhstan, the Kyrgyz Republic, the Government of the Republic of Tajikistan, Turkmenistan and the Republic of Uzbekistan on the development of relations in the field of trade and investment (Decree of the Government of the Republic of Kazakhstan of June 1, 2004 N 609); (2) *Agreement on Trade in Services and Investment in the Member States of the Common Economic Space* (Law of the Republic of Kazakhstan of July 8, 2011 No. 455-IV); and (3) Agreement on encouragement and mutual protection of investments in the Member States of the Eurasian Economic Community (EAEU)

---

134. Suleimenov M.K., Recognition and Enforcement of Foreign Arbitration and State Courts on Investment Disputes: The Experience of Kazakhstan, http://online.zakon.kz/Document/?doc_id=31644606.
135. *See* http://investmentpolicyhub.unctad.org/ISDS/CountryCases/107?partyRole=2.
136. *See* http://investmentpolicyhub.unctad.org/IIA/CountryBits/107.

Member States (the Law of the Republic of Kazakhstan dated July 10, 2009 No. 173-IV).[137] Moreover, Kazakhstan is a party to the Energy Charter Treaty.

[C] List of Investor-State Disputes (Concluded and Pending)

1.173. Kazakhstan has been involved in seventeen investment treaty arbitrations as a respondent. As of today, six of them are pending: (1) *Aktau Petrol Ticaret A.S. and Som Petrol Ticaret A.S. v. Republic of Kazakhstan* (ICSID Case No. ARB/15/8);[138] (2) *Hourani v. Kazakhstan Devincci Salah Hourani and Issam Salah Hourani v. Republic of Kazakhstan* (ICSID Case No. ARB/15/13).[139] (3) *Caratube International Oil Company LLP and Devincci Salah Hourani v. Republic of Kazakhstan* (II) (ICSID Case No. ARB/13/13);[140] (4) *World Wide Minerals v. Republic of Kazakhstan*;[141] (5) *GEM Equity Management AG v. Republic of Kazakhstan*.[142] (6) *Alhambra Resources Ltd. and Alhambra Co-peratief U.A. v. Republic of Kazakhstan* (ICSID Case No. ARB/16/12);[143] (7) *Gold Pool v. Kazakhstan*.[144]

[D] Reform Proposals

1.174. The Law "On arbitration" dated April 8, 2016 should be as close as possible to the UNCITRAL Model Law "On International Commercial Arbitration" (hereinafter – the Model Law). The legislator should delete the various novelties that compromise the legal position of arbitration in Kazakhstan. In particular, the following matters should be taken under consideration:

- Eliminate the provision allowing a party to unilaterally terminate the arbitration agreement should a dispute arise.
- Simplify the procedure for participation of government bodies, public enterprises, and legal entities of which at least 50% of voting shares are directly or indirectly owned by the state in arbitration. By removing the need to obtain the consent of the authorized state body to enter into an arbitration agreement.

---

137. *See* http://trade.gov.kz/ru/Torgovo-ekonomicheskoe_sotrudnichestvo/Soglashenija_ob_inv esticionnom_sotrudnichestve/Soglashenija_Respubliki_Kazahstan_po_investicionnomu_sotr udnichestvu/.
138. *See* https://icsid.worldbank.org/apps/ICSIDWEB/cases/Pages/casedetail.aspx?CaseNo = ARB /15/8.
139. *See* https://icsid.worldbank.org/apps/ICSIDWEB/cases/Pages/casedetail.aspx?CaseNo = ARB /15/13.
140. *See* http://www.iareporter.com/articles/caratube-oil-company-takes-new-tack-in-dispute-wi th-kazakhstan-new-claims-brought-to-icsid-while-earlier-losing-award-remains-under-review/.
141. *World Wide Minerals v. Republic of Kazakhstan*, UNCITRAL (Case 2) – *See* more at: http:// www.italaw.com/cases/2354#sthash.KP2btCoK.dpuf.
142. *See* http://globalarbitrationreview.com/news/article/16032/kazakhstan-faces-two-claims-ba nk-recapitalisation/.
143. *See* https://icsid.worldbank.org/apps/ICSIDWEB/cases/Pages/casedetail.aspx?CaseNo = ARB /16/12&tab = PRD.
144. *See* http://investmentpolicyhub.unctad.org/ISDS/Details/736.

- Permit the choice of a foreign law as an applicable law in disputes involving quasi-public sector companies. This is necessary in light of the fact that foreign entities will refuse to conclude contracts with such companies if the possibility of foreign law being applied is excluded.
- Reduce the mandatory requirements for arbitration agreements. For example, it is necessary to exclude the reference to "indication of the matters which are subject to review by arbitration," since the meaning of this requirement is unclear.
- Eliminate the ground "mismatch arbitration award to requirements of writing and signature" for setting aside the arbitration award.

APPENDIX 1 KAZAKHSTAN'S BITs[145]

No.	Country	Signed[146]	Ratified by Kazakhstan	Entered into force for Kazakhstan
1.	Armenia	06.11.2006	22.05.2010	
2.	Austria	12.01.2010	17.10.2012	21.12.2012
3.	Azerbaijan	16.09.1996	05.12.1997	30.04.1998
4.	BLEU (Belgium-Luxembourg Economic Union)	16.04.1998	30.12.1998	06.02.2001
5.	Bulgaria	15.09.1999	15.05.2001	20.08.2001
6.	China	10.08.1992	08.06.1994	13.08.1994
7.	Czech Republic	08.10.1996	11.06.1997	02.04.1998
8.	Egypt	14.02.1993	15.09.1995	08.08.1996
9.	Estonia	20.04.2011	18.04.2011	26.08.2014
10.	Tajikistan	17.12.1999	07.10.2001	16.12.1999
11.	Finland	09.01.2007	11.01.2008	01.05.2008
12.	France	03.02.1998	05.07.2000	21.08.2000
13.	Georgia	17.09.1996	22.11.1996	24.04.1998
14.	Germany	22.09.1992	29.01.1993	10.05.1995
15.	Greece	26.06.2002	30.04.1997	
16.	Hungary	07.12.1994	12.05.1995	03.03.1996
17.	India	09.12.1996	08.05.1998	26.07.2001
18.	Iran	16.01.1996	02.07.1996	03.04.1999
19.	Israel	27.12.1995	12.06.1996	19.02.1997
20.	Italy	22.09.1994	22.05.1995	12.07.1996
21.	Japan	23.10.2014	22.07.2015	
22.	Jordan	29.11.2006	20.03.2008	01.07.2008
23.	Republic of Korea	20.03.1996	22.11.1996	26.12.1996
24.	Kuwait	31.08.1997	22.02.2000	01.05.2000
25.	Kyrgyzstan	08.04.1999	28.10.1997	01.06.2005
26.	Latvia	08.10.2004	17.03.2006	21.04.2006
27.	Lithuania	15.09.1994	20.02.1995	25.05.1995

---

145. See http://invest.mid.gov.kz/ru/pages/soglasheniya-o-pooshchrenii-i-vzaimnoy-zashchite-investiciy.
146. See http://trade.gov.kz/ru/Torgovo-ekonomicheskoe_sotrudnichestvo/Soglashenija_ob_inv esticionnom_sotrudnichestve/Soglashenija_Respubliki_Kazahstan_po_investicionnomu_sotr udnichestvu/.

Chapter 5: Kazakhstan

No.	Country	Signed	Ratified by Kazakhstan	Entered into force for Kazakhstan
28.	Macedonia	02.07.2012		
29.	Malaysia	27.05.1996	11.06.1997	03.0.1997
30.	Mongolia	02.12.1994	29.04.1995	29.04.1995
31.	Netherlands	27.11.2002	08.05.2007	01.08.2007
32.	Pakistan	08.12.2003	17.03.2006	01.10.2009
33.	Poland	21.09.1994	12.05.1995	25.05.1995
34.	Qatar	04.03.2008	11.11.2008	
35.	Romania	02.03.2010	20.07.2012	17.07.2013
36.	Russian Federation	06.07.1998	11.12.1998	11.02.2000
37.	Serbia	07.10.2010	06.10.2010	07.12.2015
38.	Slovakia	21.11.2007		
39.	Spain	23.03.1994	26.04.1995	22.06.1995
40.	Sweden	25.10.2004	17.03.2006	01.08.2006
41.	Switzerland	12.05.1994	08.05.1998	13.05.1998
42.	Tajikistan	16.12.1999	17.10.2001	20.11.2001
43.	Turkey	01.05.1992	29.01.1993	10.08.1995
44.	Ukraine	17.09.1994	20.04.1995	09.01.1997
45.	United Kingdom	23.11.1995	22.11.1996	23.11.1995
46.	United States of America	19.05.1992	18.12.1992	12.01.1994
47.	Uzbekistan	02.06.1997	29.08.1997	08.09.1997
48.	Viet Nam	15.09.2009	10.12.2010	07.04.2014
49.	Afghanistan	27.09.2012		

APPENDIX 2 INVESTOR-STATE DISPUTES AGAINST KAZAKHSTAN

List of concluded investment treaty arbitrations Against Kazakhstan:

1. Türkiye Petrolleri Anonim Ortaklığı v. Republic of Kazakhstan[147]
2. AES Corporation and Tau Power B.V. v. Republic of Kazakhstan (ICSID Case No. ARB/10/16)[148]
3. Anatolie and Gabriel Stati, Ascom Group S.A., Terra Raf Trans Traiding Ltd v. Republic of Kazakhstan (SCC Case No. Case No. 116 2010)[149]
4. KT Asia Investment Group B.V. v. Republic of Kazakhstan (ICSID Case No. ARB/09/8)[150]
5. Caratube International Oil Company LLP v. Republic of Kazakhstan (I) (ICSID Case No. ARB/08/12)[151]
6. Liman Caspian Oil BV and NCL Dutch Investment BV v. Republic of Kazakhstan (ICSID Case No. ARB/07/14)[152]
7. Rumeli Telekom A.S. and Telsim Mobil Telekomunikasyon Hizmetleri A.S. v. Republic of Kazakhstan (ICSID Case No. ARB/05/16)[153]
8. AIG Capital Partners, Inc. and CJSC Tema Real Estate Company v. Republic of Kazakhstan (ICSID Case No. ARB/01/6)[154]
9. CCL Oil v. Republic of Kazakhstan (SCC Case No. 122/2001)[155]
10. Biedermann International, Inc. v. The Republic of Kazakhstan and The Association for Social and Economic Development of Western Kazakhstan "Intercaspian" (SCC Case No. 97/1996)[156] 1996)

---

147. See https://icsid.worldbank.org/apps/ICSIDWEB/cases/Pages/casedetail.aspx?CaseNo = ARB/11/2.
148. See https://icsid.worldbank.org/apps/ICSIDWEB/cases/Pages/casedetail.aspx?CaseNo = ARB/10/16.
149. See http://globalarbitrationreview.com/news/article/28726/kazakhstan-hit-new-ect-claim/.
150. See https://icsid.worldbank.org/apps/ICSIDWEB/cases/Pages/casedetail.aspx?CaseNo = ARB/09/8.
151. See https://icsid.worldbank.org/apps/ICSIDWEB/cases/Pages/casedetail.aspx?CaseNo = ARB/08/12.
152. See https://icsid.worldbank.org/apps/ICSIDWEB/cases/Pages/casedetail.aspx?CaseNo = ARB/07/14.
153. See https://icsid.worldbank.org/apps/ICSIDWEB/cases/Pages/casedetail.aspx?CaseNo = ARB/05/16.
154. See https://icsid.worldbank.org/apps/ICSIDWEB/cases/Pages/casedetail.aspx?CaseNo = ARB/01/6.
155. See http://www.academia.edu/4039503/An_Overview_of_Kazakhstan_s_Investment_Laws_and_its_Investor-state_Arbitral_Awards.
156. See http://www.iisd.org/itn/wp-content/uploads/2010/10/investment_investsd_oct8_2003.pdf.

Chapter 5: Kazakhstan

List of pending investment treaty arbitrations against Kazakhstan:

1. Aktau Petrol Ticaret A.S. and Som Petrol Ticaret A.S. v. Republic of Kazakhstan (ICSID Case No. ARB/15/8);[157]
2. Hourani v. Kazakhstan Devincci Salah Hourani and Issam Salah Hourani v. Republic of Kazakhstan (ICSID Case No. ARB/15/13).[158]
3. Caratube International Oil Company LLP and Devincci Salah Hourani v. Republic of Kazakhstan (II) (ICSID Case No. ARB/13/13);[159]
4. World Wide Minerals v. Republic of Kazakhstan;[160]
5. GEM Equity Management AG v. Republic of Kazakhstan.[161]
6. Alhambra Resources Ltd. and Alhambra Co-peratief U.A. v. Republic of Kazakhstan (ICSID Case No. ARB/16/12).[162]
7. Gold Pool Limited Partnership v. Republic of Kazakhstan.[163]

Bibliography

Suleimenov M. K., Duissenova A. E. Advantages and disadvantages of the new law of arbitration https://www.zakon.kz/4796696-dostoinstva-i-nedostatki-novogo-zakona.html.

Bassin Y., Suleimenov M. Prosecutor's Office and arbitration court // entrepreneur and law. 2001. No. 8.

Suleimenov M. K. Arbitration courts in Kazakhstan: past, present and future. Almaty: KIA, scientific research institute of private law, 2007. pp. 39–42.

Tukulov B. A. New Law of the Republic of Kazakhstan "On Arbitration": attention to some problem issues. https://www.zakon.kz/4795629-novyjj-zakon-respubliki-kazakhstan-ob.html.

Suleimenov M. K. Recognition and enforcement of foreign arbitration and state court awards on investment disputes: experience of Kazakhstan // Report at the International Conference: "Settlement of investment disputes involving countries with economies in transition" 13–15 November 2009, Moscow, Published at KIA website www.arbitrage.kz.

Karaketov M.Yu, New ADR Regulations enacted in Kazakhstan. http://www.cisarbitration.com/2016/01/26/new-adr-regulations-enacted-in-kazakhstan/.

---

157. See https://icsid.worldbank.org/apps/ICSIDWEB/cases/Pages/casedetail.aspx?CaseNo = ARB/15/8.
158. See https://icsid.worldbank.org/apps/ICSIDWEB/cases/Pages/casedetail.aspx?CaseNo = ARB/15/13.
159. See http://www.iareporter.com/articles/caratube-oil-company-takes-new-tack-in-dispute-with-kazakhstan-new-claims-brought-to-icsid-while-earlier-losing-award-remains-under-review/.
160. *World Wide Minerals v. Republic of Kazakhstan*, UNCITRAL (Case 2) – See more at: http://www.italaw.com/cases/2354#sthash.KP2btCoK.dpuf.
161. See http://globalarbitrationreview.com/news/article/16032/kazakhstan-faces-two-claims-bank-recapitalisation/.
162. See https://icsid.worldbank.org/apps/ICSIDWEB/cases/Pages/casedetail.aspx?CaseNo = ARB/16/12&tab = PRD.
163. See http://investmentpolicyhub.unctad.org/ISDS/Details/736.

Suleimenov M. K. Private Procedural Law (Law of Alternative Dispute Resolution) // Lawyer. 2011. No. 2. pp. 12-19.

Duissenova A. E. Participation of third parties in the arbitration proceedings. Research Institute of Private Law KazSLU, LF Zanger, 2009. pp. 442-455.

Suleimenov M. K. State Immunity: absolute or limited? // Lawyer. 2010 No. 3. pp. 12-19.

Lyailya Tleulina., Recognition and enforcement of foreign judgements and commercial arbitration awards in Kazakhstan.

Suleimenov M. K. "Court's chaos still continuous" https://www.zakon.kz/4814246-sudejjskijj-bespredel-prodolzhaetsja.html.

Skvortsov O. Y., Kurochkin S. A., Morozov M. E. Brief lectures // Reading book of alternative dispute resolution: Training materials and practice recommendations. SPb.: ANO "Editors of 'Arbitration court' magazine"; 2009, p. 189.

Suleimenov M. K. Duissenova A. E. Chapter 11 "Arbitration protection of civil rights" (§ 2. Principles of arbitration proceedings) // Protection of civil rights. Research Institute of Private Law, KazSLU, LF Zanger, 2011.

Suleimenov M. K. Recognition and enforcement of foreign arbitration and state courts on investment disputes: the experience of Kazakhstan.http://online.zakon.kz/Document/?doc_id = 31644606.

Suleimenov M. K. Osipov E. Immunity of international organizations; http://online.zakon.kz/Document/?doc_id = 31115410#pos = 1;-169.

Web Sources

List of investment disputes
http://investmentpolicyhub.unctad.org/ISDS/CountryCases/107?partyRole = 1.
Bilateral Investment Treaties (BITs)
http://investmentpolicyhub.unctad.org/IIA/CountryBits/107.
List of ratified agreements on investment cooperation
http://trade.gov.kz/ru/Torgovo-ekonomicheskoe_sotrudnichestvo/Soglashenija_ob_investicionnom_sotrudnichestve/Soglashenija_Respubliki_Kazahstan_po_investicionnomu_sotrudnichestvu/.
Kazakhstan International Arbitration
http://www.arbitrage.kz/.
International Arbitration "IUS GENTIUM"
http://rus.arbitration.kz/.
Centre of Arbitration of the National Chamber of Entrepreneurs Atameken, http://www.atamekenarb.kz/.
International Arbitration "IUS"
http://www.iusea.com/.
International Arbitration "IAC"
http://aca.kz/ru/.
International Centre for Settlement of Investment Disputes
https://icsid.worldbank.org.

Chapter 5: Kazakhstan

Legislation

Constitution of the Republic of Kazakhstan dated August 30, 1995, http://adilet.zan.kz/rus/docs/K950001000_.

Codes of the Republic of Kazakhstan http://adilet.zan.kz/eng/docs/Z970000195_.

Law of the Republic of Kazakhstan on Advocate Practice No. 195-I dated of December 5, 1997, http://online.zakon.kz/Document/?doc_id = 1008408#pos = 1;-213.

Law on the Judicial System and Status of Judges of the Republic of Kazakhstan No. 132-II dated December 25, 2000, http://online.zakon.kz/Document/?doc_id = 1 021164#pos = 1;-205.

Law on Arbitration No. 488-V dated April 8, 2016, http://online.zakon.kz/Document/?doc_id = 35110250#pos = 1;-213.

Civil Code of the Republic of Kazakhstan No. 409 dated July 1, 1999, http://online.zakon.kz/Document/?doc_id = 1013880&doc_id2 = 1006061#pos = 12;-6&pos2 = 1;-8.

Civil Procedure Code of the Republic of Kazakhstan No. 377-V dated October 31, 2015, http://online.zakon.kz/Document/?doc_id = 34329053#pos = 1;-205.

Law of The Republic of Kazakhstan on Mediation No. 401-IV dated January 28, 2011, http://online.zakon.kz/Document/?doc_id = 30927376#pos = 1;-161.

CHAPTER 6
Moldova

Alexandr Svetlicinii

LIST OF ABBREVIATIONS

ADR	Alternative Dispute Resolution
AITA	International Association of Auto Transporters
BIT	Bilateral Investment Treaty
CCP	Code of Civil Procedure
ICAC	International Commercial Arbitration Court attached to the Chamber of Commerce and Industry of the Republic of Moldova
ICC	International Chamber of Commerce
ICSID	International Centre for Settlement of Investment Disputes
MDL	Moldovan Leu (official currency of the Republic of Moldova)
PPP	Public-Private Partnership
SCC	Stockholm Chamber of Commerce
SCJ	The Supreme Court of Justice of the Republic of Moldova
UNCITRAL	United Nations Commission for International Trade Law
USD	United States dollar
USSR	The Union of Soviet Socialist Republics

§6.01 GENERAL INTRODUCTION

[A] Historical Development of the Legal System

1.1 Traditionally, the Moldovan legal system has been categorized as a civil law system where features resembling German law are predominant.[1] During the period when Moldova was a member of the Union of Soviet Socialist Republics (USSR), its legal system was a peculiar mixture of socialist and continental legal traditions. During the first years of independence (1991-1994), the Moldovan legislators attempted to transform those elements of the national legal system that were instrumental for the establishment of the market economy. At the same time, the legislation adopted during the USSR period was enforced continuously until being replaced by the newly adopted legislation.[2] The importance of arbitration as an alternative dispute resolution (ADR) method was recognized during the early years of post-independence – Moldova passed its first Law on Arbitration prior to the adoption of the nation's Constitution.[3]

1.2 After the adoption of the Constitution in 1994, the legal reform was eventually embraced in all fields of law, including commercial law, when specialized laws regulating particular kinds of business transactions were adopted.[4] The process of adopting new legislation accelerated in post-2000 period, which was marked by several major codifications. In 2002, Moldova adopted its new Civil Code[5] and Criminal Code;[6] in 2003, the national legislature passed the Code of Civil Procedure (CCP)[7] and Code of Criminal Procedure[8] as well as the new Labor Code;[9] in 2005, the Enforcement

---

1. See Mariana Harjevschi & Svetlana Andrițchi, *UPDATE: Performing Legal Research: the Moldovan Experience* (April 2012), http://www.nyulawglobal.org/globalex/Moldova1.htm (accessed 29 November 2016).
2. The Declaration of Independence of the Republic of Moldova, adopted on 27 August 1991, provided that "[n]o other laws shall be respected on the [Moldovan] territory but those, that are in conformity with the Republic's Constitution, laws and other legal acts adopted by the legally constituted authorities of the Republic of Moldova". Law No. 691 of 27 August 1991 *on Declaration of Independence of the Republic of Moldova*, published in the Official Gazette No. 11 on 27 August 1991. According to this provision Soviet laws were not abolished automatically and many of them continued to be implemented. An example of this is the application of the 1964 USSR Civil Code with subsequent amendments until 2003 when a new Civil Code was adopted by the Parliament.
3. Law No. 129 of 31 May 1994 on arbitration (court), published in the Official Gazette No. 2 on 25 August 1994.
4. See e.g., Law No. 731 of 15 February 1996 on leasing, published in the Official Gazette No. 49 on 25 July 1996 (subsequently replaced by Law No. 59 of 28 April 2005 on leasing, published in the Official Gazette No. 92-94, 8 July 2005); Law No. 1335 of 1 October 1997 on franchising, published in the Official Gazette No. 82-83 on 11 December 1997.
5. Code No. 1107 of 6 June 2002, published in the Official Gazette No. 82-86 on 22 June 2002.
6. Code No. 985 of 18 April 2002, published in the Official Gazette No. 128-129 on 13 September 2002.
7. Code No. 225 of 30 May 2003 of civil procedure, re-published in the Official Gazette No. 130-134 on 21 June 2013.
8. Code No. 122 of 14 March 2003 of criminal procedure, re-published in the Official Gazette No. 248-251 on 5 November 2013.
9. Labor Code No. 154 of 28 March 2003, published in the Official Gazette No. 159-162 on 29 July 2003.

Code[10] consolidated the regulation of the state-led enforcement of judgments and arbitral awards.

[B] The Legal Profession

1.3 Attorneys who are licensed by the Ministry of Justice can exercise their legal profession in Moldova.[11] The attorneys have to fulfill the following conditions in order to obtain their license: Moldovan citizenship, full business capacity, law degree, impeccable reputation and admission to the Bar.[12] The admission to the Bar is carried out by the Union of Lawyers[13] after the completion of an eighteen-month professional stage and completion of the qualification examination. The traineeship contract concluded between the trainee and his/her mentor attorney should be registered with the Union of Lawyers.

1.4 The attorneys may engage in solo legal practice (individual office) or team up with other licensed attorneys (associated office). As of 15 November 2016, the Ministry of Justice has issued licenses to 2,045 individual and associated attorney offices.[14] While representation by a licensed attorney is required in criminal cases, in civil litigation the legal representation can be carried out by the licensed attorney, trainee attorney and employees.[15] The state guarantees a certain amount of primary and qualified legal aid,[16] an activity coordinated by the National Legal Aid Council.[17]

1.5 Foreign attorneys are allowed to exercise legal practice in Moldova provided they have confirmed their professional qualifications and have been entered into the Register of Foreign Lawyers maintained by the Union of Lawyers.[18] At the same time, legal services provided by foreign lawyers are essentially limited to representation in international commercial arbitration since the Statute of Legal Profession does not permit foreign lawyers to represent their clients in courts and before the state

---

10. Code No. 443 of 24 December 2004 of enforcement, re-published in the Official Gazette No. 214–220 on 5 November 2010.
11. *Ministerul Justiției al Republicii Moldova*, http://www.justice.gov.md/ (accessed 29 November 2016).
12. Law No. 1260 of 19 July 2002 on legal profession, re-published in the Official Gazette No. 159 on 4 September 2010, Art. 10.
13. *Uniunea Avocaților din Republica Moldova*, http://www.avocatul.md/ (accessed 29 November 2016).
14. The excerpt from the Register of individual offices and associated offices is at http://www.justice.gov.md/public/files/file/persoane_autorizate/avocati/2016/Extras_din_Registrul_Cabinetelor_avocatilor_si_Birourilor_asociate_de_avocati_15112016.pdf (accessed 29 November 2016).
15. CCP, Art. 75.
16. *See* Law No. 198 of 26 July 2007 on legal aid guaranteed by the state, published in the Official Gazette No. 157–160 on 5 October 2007.
17. *Consiliul Național pentru Asistența Juridică Garantată de Stat*, http://www.cnajgs.md/ (accessed 24 November 2016).
18. The registry of foreign attorneys is available at http://uam.md/media/files/files/registrul_avoca_ailor_str__ini_7908115.pdf (accessed 29 November 2016). The list of foreign registered attorneys includes lawyers from Romania, Russia, Italy, Spain and the United Kingdom.

authorities.[19] Foreign lawyers can practice law in Moldova on the basis of a contract held with an individual office or an associated office of licensed Moldovan attorneys. In criminal and administrative cases, foreign lawyers must be assisted by a licensed Moldovan attorney.

[C] Sources of Arbitration Law

1.6 The Republic of Moldova has followed a dualist approach in regulating commercial arbitration as one of the available ADR mechanisms.[20] The Law on Arbitration regulates arbitration proceedings that are considered "domestic."[21] The Law on International Commercial Arbitration regulates arbitration proceedings that are considered "international": (1) the parties have place of business in different countries; (2) the place of arbitration or place of execution of a substantial part of obligations are located in a state, different from the state where the parties have their place of business.[22] The Law on International Commercial Arbitration has been modeled after the United Nations Commission for International Trade Law (UNCITRAL) Model Law on International Commercial Arbitration.[23]

1.7 An important source of arbitration law is the CCP, which regulates the challenges (setting aside) of the arbitral awards, their recognition and enforcement, as well as other issues concerning the involvement of the courts and other state authorities in the arbitration process. The fact that challenges of arbitral awards, as well as their recognition and enforcement, are regulated by the CCP as well as the specialized arbitration laws gave rise to certain repetitions and inconsistencies. This prompted the calls for consolidation of arbitration regulations as explained in §6.10 below.

1.8 The Moldovan legal system belongs to the Romano-Germanic family and the judicial precedent is not recognized as a source of law.[24] Nevertheless, the

---

19. Union of Lawyers, Statute of Legal Profession, published in the Official Gazette No. 54–57 on 8 April 2011, Art. 5. *See also* International Bar Association, *Moldova International Trade in Legal Services*, http://www.ibanet.org/PPID/Constituent/Bar_Issues_Commission/ITILS_Moldova.aspx (accessed 29 November 2016).
20. *See* Alexandr Svetlicinii, *The new rules for commercial arbitration in the Republic of Moldova: A step forward?* 2 Revista moldovenească de drept internațional și relații internaționale, 52–58 (2009); Lilia Gribincea, *Soluționarea de către arbitrajul comercial internațional a litigiilor ce apar din contractele comerciale internaționale*, 7 Revista Națională de Drept 13 (2002); Lilia Gribincea, *Importanța Arbitrajului comercial internațional*, 9 Revista Națională de Drept 20 (2005); Oleg Bontea, *Arbitrajul – mijloc jurisdictional de soluționare pe cale pașnică a diferendelor internaționale*, 2 Revista Națională de Drept 62 (2008).
21. Law No. 23 of 22 February 2008 on arbitration, published in the Official Gazette No. 88–89 on 20 May 2008.
22. Law No. 24 of 22 February 2008 on international commercial arbitration, published in the Official Gazette No. 88–89 on 20 May 2008, Art. 1(2).
23. *1985 UNCITRAL Model Law on International Commercial Arbitration*, http://www.uncitral.org/uncitral/en/uncitral_texts/arbitration/1985Model_arbitration.html (accessed 29 November 2016).
24. *See* generally Mihai Poalelungi, *Precedentul judiciar*, in Mihai Poalelungi, Elena Belei & Diana Sârcu (eds.), Manualul judecătorului pentru cauze civile (Supreme Court of Justice), 98–110 (3rd ed., 2013).

harmonization of the national legislation in line with international and European standards, particularly in the field of human rights, have created the need to learn and to observe the standards and interpretations adopted by the international and European courts, such as the European Court of Human Rights.[25]

1.9 The law entrusts the nation's highest court – the Supreme Court of Justice (SCJ)[26] – to generalize judicial practice and analyze the judicial statistics, as well as to issue ex officio explanatory decisions concerning various issues in judicial practice that are not related to interpretations of laws and that are not mandatory for the judges.[27] Making use of its powers, the SCJ has issued several explanatory decisions on the generalization of judicial practice concerning cases where the parties have concluded an arbitration agreement and cases related to the recognition and enforcement of foreign judgments and foreign arbitral awards in Moldova.[28] Customs and trade usages can be also used as a supplementary source of law by the courts but their practical application is hindered by the lack of the legal doctrine and published case law on this subject.[29]

[D] International Legal Framework, Supremacy of International Law

1.10 The respect for international law and international treaties appears as one of the fundamental principles in the Constitution.[30] In line with the principles of international law, the Moldovan legislation provides for the direct application of international treaties unless the adoption of the implementing legislation is required.[31] For the

---

25. *See* generally Alexandr Svetlicinii, *Republic of Moldova as a Respondent State in the European Court of Human Rights*, 2 Eastern European Human Rights Law Journal, No. 2, 8–15 (2005); Mihai Poalelungi & Diana Sârcu, *Jurisprudența Curții Europene a Drepturilor Omului*, in Mihai Poalelungi, Elena Belei & Diana Sârcu (eds.), Manualul judecătorului pentru cauze civile (Supreme Court of Justice), 69–76 (3rd ed., 2013); Radu Panțîru, *Aspecte deficitare în realizarea justiției identificate de către Curtea Europeană a Drepturilor Omului în hotărârile împotriva Republicii Moldova*, in Mihai Poalelungi, Elena Belei & Diana Sârcu (eds.), Manualul judecătorului pentru cauze civile (Supreme Court of Justice), 77–97 (3rd ed., 2013). *See also* Plenum of the Supreme Court of Justice, Decision No. 3 of 9 June 2014 on application by courts of certain provisions of the European Convention on Human Rights and Fundamental Freedoms.
26. *Curtea Supremă de Justiție a Republicii Moldova*, http://www.csj.md/ (accessed 29 November 2016). *See* Law No. 789 of 26 March 1996 on the Supreme Court of Justice, re-published in the Official Gazette No. 15–17 on 22 January 2013.
27. CCP, Art. 17, Law No. 789, Art. 2.
28. *See* Plenum of the Supreme Court of Justice, Decision No. 2 of 30 March 2015 on application by the courts of the legal provisions related to certain issues in the judicial proceedings where parties have concluded an arbitration agreement; Plenum of the Supreme Court of Justice, Decision No. 9 of 9 December 2013 on judicial practice of applying legislation concerning recognition and enforcement of foreign judgments and foreign arbitral awards (as amended by Plenum of the Supreme Court of Justice, Decision No. 2 of 25 April 2016 on modification and completion of the Decision No. 9 of 9 December 2013).
29. *See* Natalia Osoianu, *Custom as a Source of International Private Law of the Republic of Moldova*, 1–2 Studii Juridice Universitare, 151–158 (2011).
30. Constitution of the Republic of Moldova adopted on 29 July 1994, published in the Official Gazette No. 1 on 12 August 1994, Art. 8.
31. Law No. 595 of 24 September 1999 on international treaties of the Republic of Moldova, published in the Official Gazette No. 24–26 on 2 March 2000, Art. 20.

purpose of the present chapter, it should be noted that the Republic of Moldova has acceded to the following international treaties in the field of commercial arbitration: the New York Convention on Recognition and Enforcement of Foreign Arbitral Awards (New York Convention),[32] the Convention on the Settlement of Investment Disputes between States and Nationals of Other States (International Centre for Settlement of Investment Disputes (ICSID) Convention),[33] the European Convention on International Commercial Arbitration[34] and the Energy Charter Treaty.[35]

1.11 As a member of the Commonwealth of Independent States (CIS), the Republic of Moldova has adhered to the 1993 Convention on Legal Assistance in Civil, Family and Criminal Matters[36] and the 1993 Convention on the Amount of State Fees Payable in Case of Economic Disputes between Companies from Different CIS States.[37] At the same time, the Republic of Moldova has not ratified the CIS 1998 Convention on Mutual Enforcement of Judgments of the Economic Courts of the CIS States.[38] As of 8 December 2015, the Republic of Moldova concluded bilateral agreements on judicial assistance with the following countries: Russian Federation (civil, family and criminal matters), Latvia (civil, family and criminal matters), Lithuania (civil, family and criminal matters), Turkey (civil, commercial and criminal matters), Romania (civil and criminal matters), Ukraine (civil and criminal matters), Azerbaijan (civil, family and criminal matters), Czech Republic (civil, family and criminal matters), Hungary (civil,

---

32. Convention on the Recognition and Enforcement of Foreign Arbitral Awards, New York (1958), 330 UNTS 3. Entry into force for Moldova: December 17, 1998; Decision of the Parliament of the Republic of Moldova No. 87 of 10 July 1998 on accession of the Republic of Moldova to the Convention on the Recognition and Enforcement of Foreign Arbitral Awards, published in the Official Gazette No. 71.
33. Convention on the Settlement of Investment Disputes between States and Nationals of Other States, Washington (1965), 575 UNTS 159. Entry into force for Moldova: June 4, 2011.
34. European Convention on International Commercial Arbitration, Geneva (1961), 484 UNTS 349. Entry into force for Moldova: 5 March 1998; Decision of the Parliament of the Republic of Moldova No. 1331 of 26 September 1997 on accession of the Republic of Moldova to the European Convention on International Commercial Arbitration, published in the Official Gazette No. 67–68.
35. Energy Charter Treaty (1994), 2080 UNTS 95. Entry into force for Moldova: 16 April 1998.
36. Convention on Legal Assistance in Civil, Family, and Criminal Matters, Minsk (22 January 1993), in force for the Republic of Moldova from 26 March 1993. It was amended by the Protocol to the Convention on Legal Assistance in Civil, Family, and Criminal Matters, Moscow (28 March 1997), in force for the Republic of Moldova from 24 June 2003. The current Convention on Legal Assistance in Civil, Family, and Criminal Matters, Chisinau (7 October 2002), was not ratified by the Republic of Moldova.
37. Convention on the Amount of State Fees Payable in Case of Economic Disputes between Companies from Different CIS States, Ashgabat (24 December 1993), in force for the Republic of Moldova from 24 December 1993; Protocol to the Convention on the Amount of State Fees Payable in Case of Economic Disputes between Companies from Different CIS States, Minsk (1 June 2001), in force for the Republic of Moldova from 23 December 2002; Protocol on the Amendment of the Convention on the Amount of State Fees Payable in Case of Economic Disputes between Companies from Different CIS States, Moscow (10 December 2010), not ratified by the Republic of Moldova.
38. Convention on Mutual Enforcement of Judgements Issued by the Arbitration, Economic and Commercial Courts of the CIS States, Moscow (6 March 1998).

family and criminal matters), Slovakia (civil, family and criminal matters), Italy (civil matters), Bosnia and Herzegovina (civil and criminal matters).[39]

[E] **Available Dispute Resolution Mechanisms**

1.12 In its declaration concerning the situation in the justice system adopted by the Parliament in 2009, the legislators noted that "the justice system in the Republic of Moldova is gravely affected by corruption and demonstrates serious symptoms of political influence."[40] As a response to the above-mentioned problems, the Parliament has adopted the Strategy for Reform of the Justice System for 2011–2016 in order to enhance the independence and efficiency of the judicial system, to ensure access to justice, to protect human rights and fundamental freedoms in the field of justice and to contribute to the economic development of the country.[41] The Strategy provided, among other things, for the consolidation of the ADR system.[42] The implementation plan of this strategy provides for the adoption of the guiding principles concerning ADR, development of arbitration and mediation institutions, promotion and professional training in ADR within the business community and judicial system,[43] improvement of the recognition and enforcement of foreign arbitral awards.[44]

1.13 In 2015, the Parliament adopted the Law on Mediation,[45] which replaced the existing law from 2007.[46] A study on the effects of the 2007 Law on Mediation on the popularity of mediation indicated that, despite the substantial number of certified mediators (343 mediators and thirty-four mediator's offices), this method of ADR remains unpopular among the society at large,[47] which required the state to strengthen

---

39. Plenum of the Supreme Court of Justice of the Republic of Moldova, Decision No. 2 of 25 April 2016, Annex No. 3.
40. Parliament Decision No. 53 of 30 October 2009 on adoption of the Declaration of the Parliament of the Republic of Moldova concerning the situation in the justice system of the Republic of Moldova and actions necessary for improving the situation in the field of justice, published in the Official Gazette No. 160-161 on 6 November 2009.
41. Law No. 231 of 25 November 2011 on approval of the Strategy for Reform of Justice Sector for 2011–2016, published in the Official Gazette No. 1-6 on 6 January 2012. *See also* Dumitru Postovan, *Dezvoltarea arbitrajului în Republica Moldova*, 7 Revista Națională de Drept 8-13 (2014).
42. Annex to the Law No. 231 on approval of the Strategy for Reform of Justice Sector for 2011–2016, p. 15.
43. *See* Gheorge Avornic, *Importanța disciplinei Arbitrajul comercial internațional pentru formarca competențelor profesionale ale specialiștilor în drept în condițiile economiei de piaț ă*, 7 Revista Națională de Drept 14-17 (2014).
44. Parliament Decision No. 6 of 16 February 2012 on approval of the Plan of Actions for the Implementation of the Strategy for Reform of Justice Sector for 2011–2016, published in the Official Gazette No. 109-112 on 5 June 2012.
45. Law No. 137 of 3 July 2015 on mediation, published in the Official Gazette No. 224-233 on 21 August 2015.
46. Law No. 134 of 14 June 2007 on meditation, published in the Official Gazette No. 188-191 on 7 December 2007.
47. *See* BDR Associates Strategic Communication, *Situația privind nivelul de informare a grupurilor țintă, atitudinea, față de mediere, serviciile de mediere și mediatori* (July 2014), http://mediere.gov.md/sites/default/files/document/attachments/mediere_analiza_situation ala_final.pdf (accessed 29 November 2016).

its efforts in consolidating and promoting mediation. The new law provided a detailed regulatory framework for the professional training of mediators, their organization into the Mediation Council under the Ministry of Justice,[48] provision of mediation services by the certified mediators in civil, criminal and administrative disputes. The Mediation Council has already certified more than eighty mediator offices and several higher education institutions authorized to organize professional mediator trainings.[49]

[F]   Judicial System

1.14 The system of courts[50] in Moldova has been reorganized several times in the post-1990 period and currently represents a three-level hierarchy, consisting of the first instance courts,[51] the courts of appeal[52] and the SCJ. There is also the specialized District Economic Court for resolving disputes arising from commercial relationships.[53] As a single specialized commercial court, the District Economic Court has a high workload: in 2015 alone, it registered 8,565 new cases.[54] The most recent reorganization of the judicial system has abolished the District Economic Court with effect from April 1, 2017.[55]

[G]   Arbitration Institutions

1.15 Pursuant to the Law on Arbitration, the establishment of the arbitration institutions has to be notified to the SCJ.[56] According to the SCJ's data, there are currently twenty-nine arbitration institutions.[57] The most well-known arbitration institution in Moldova is the International Commercial Arbitration Court (ICAC) of the Chamber of

---

48. *Consiliul de Mediere*, http://mediere.gov.md/ (accessed 29 November 2016).
49. See the list of mediator's offices, http://mediere.gov.md/sites/default/files/lista_birourilor_de_mediatori_la_situatia_de_23_11_15.pdf (accessed 29 November 2016).
50. Law No. 514 of 6 July 1995 on judicial organization, re-published in the Official Gazette No. 15–17 on 22 January 2013.
51. For the complete list of the first instance courts see Annex No. 2 to the Law No. 514.
52. There are four courts of appeal located in Chișinău, Bălți, Cahul, and Comrat. *See* Annex No. 3 to the Law No. 514.
53. *See* Law No. 514, Art. 25. Officially this court is called *Judecătoria Economică de Circumscripție* (District Economic Court) because initially it was intended to create several economic courts with the districts determined by the Parliament. As of today only one economic court was established – it is based in Chișinău, and its district is the whole territory of the Republic of Moldova.
54. *See* the Ministry of Justice, *Report on workload of the first instance courts concerning examination of the economic cases in 2015*, http://www.justice.gov.md/public/files/file/Sistemul%20Judiciar/Studii%20si%20Analize/2016/economice_12_luni_20151_2.pdf (accessed 29 November 2016).
55. Law No. 76 of 21 April 2016 on reorganization of courts, published in the Official Gazette No. 184–192 on 1 July 2016.
56. Law No. 23, Art. 6(2).
57. *See the List of arbitration institutions established pursuant to the Law No 129 of 31 May 1994 and Law No. 23 of 22 February 2008*, http://www.csj.md/index.php/despre-curtea-suprema-de-justitie/arbitraje (accessed 29 November 2016).

Commerce and Industry (CCI) established in 1994.[58] The ICAC's roster of arbitrators includes lawyers and other professionals from Moldova, as well as from Romania, Lithuania, Ukraine, Czech Republic, Germany, Poland, Bulgaria, Spain, Russia, Kyrgyz Republic, Slovenia, Russia, Austria, Belarus, Kazakhstan, etc.[59] Following the legislative dualism in regulation of the arbitration proceedings, the ICAC maintains two sets of rules: for domestic and international commercial arbitration. The ICAC's caseload primarily consists of domestic arbitration cases. For instance, in 2014, out of a total of seventy-one requests for arbitration, sixty-two cases concerned domestic arbitration.[60]

1.16 The Permanent Arbitration Court of the Moldovan Stock Exchange established in 2003 has an objective to resolve disputes among the members/agents and their clients in relation to the alleged infringements of the trading procedures and the resulting damages.[61] The awards issued by the Permanent Arbitration Court of the Moldovan Stock Exchange are subject to challenge before the National Commission for Financial Markets.[62]

1.17 The Arbitration Court of the International Association of Auto Transporters (AITA)[63] established in 2005 provides arbitration, mediation and conciliation services to the members of AITA and other parties.[64] The arbitrators of the AITA Arbitration Court come from the ranks of Moldovan practicing lawyers, academics, AITA officials and other professionals. The range of disputes handled by this arbitration institution includes disputes arising out of the legal relations connected with the conclusion, performance or termination of contracts of transportation and shipping, as well as commercial disputes including sale and purchase, exchange, donation, service provision, lease, brokerage, commission, etc.

1.18 The Air Transport Arbitration Court of the Industry Association of Civil Aviation handles disputes arising out of contractual relationships and other legal civil relationships stemming from the execution of international trade agreements and other international economic relations, when at least one party is established outside of the Republic of Moldova, as well as disputes between enterprises with foreign investments, associations and international organizations based in Moldova.[65]

---

58. *Curtea de Arbitraj Comercial Internațional de pe lîngă Camera de Comerț și Industrie a Republicii Moldova*, http://arbitraj.chamber.md/index.php?id = 22 (accessed 29 November 2016).
59. *See ICAC list of arbitrators*, http://arbitraj.chamber.md/index.php?id = 124 (accessed 29 November 2016).
60. *See* Cristina Martin, *Arbitration in Moldova: per aspera ad astra* (12 June 2015), http://aci.md /arbitration-in-moldova-per-aspera-ad-astra/ (accessed 29 November 2016).
61. *See* National Commission for Financial Markets, Decision No. 62/14 of 26 December 2008 on approval of the Rules of the Moldovan Stock Exchange, published in the Official Gazette No. 37–40 on 20 February 2009.
62. *Comisia Națională a Pieței Financiare*, http://www.cnpf.md/ (accessed 29 November 2016).
63. *Asociația Internațională a Transportatorilor Auto din Moldova*, http://www.aita.md/ (accessed 29 November 2016).
64. Information about this arbitration court is available in Romanian at http://www.aita.md/index .php/ro/principala/20-curtea-de-arbitraj/100-curtea-de-arbitraj-de-pe-linga-aita (accessed 29 November 2016).
65. *See* the Regulation of the Air Transport Arbitration Court of the Industry Association of Civil Aviation, published in the Official Gazette No. 152–155 on 16 February 2011.

[H] Sovereign Immunity and International Arbitration

1.19 As mentioned in Section §6.01[D] above, the Republic of Moldova is party to the European Convention on International Commercial Arbitration, which provides that "legal persons of public law" have the right to conclude valid arbitration agreements.[66] In its instrument of ratification,[67] the Republic Moldova has not made any reservations in this regard. The State and its administrative-territorial units can enter into arbitration agreements in their economic relations with third parties.

1.20 For example, the Law on Public-Private Partnership (PPP) provides that parties may agree on mediation or arbitration as a means of settling PPP-related disputes.[68] At the same time, in its 2011 country report the European Bank for Reconstruction and Development noted that arbitration is an unlikely dispute resolution venue for PPP projects for the following reasons: (1) the high perceived cost of international arbitration; (2) the fact that an arbitral procedure would not give immediate relief to public authorities, e.g., they will not have immediate access to the local law mechanism of application of interim measures (such as "step-in rights") in order to avoid the disruption to a core public service.[69]

§6.02 THE ARBITRATION AGREEMENT

[A] Introduction

1.21 Both in domestic and international commercial arbitration, the arbitration agreement is understood as an agreement of the parties to refer all or some disputes arising out of the contractual or non-contractual relations to arbitration.[70] The arbitration agreement can appear in the form of a contract clause or a separate agreement (*compromis*).[71] The SCJ has made a distinction between the two forms based on the timing of the dispute: the arbitration clause is aimed at the resolution of the future disputes while *compromis* refers to the actual and existing dispute between the parties.[72] The Law on Arbitration expressly requires the arbitration agreement to contain the mode of appointment of arbitrators, the appointing authority, the place of arbitration and the applicable arbitration rules.[73] If the arbitration agreement does not

---

66. European Convention on International Commercial Arbitration, Art. 2(2).
67. Parliament Decision No. 1331 of 26 September 1997 on the accession of the Republic of Moldova to the European Convention on International Commercial Arbitration, published in the Official Gazette No. 67 on 16 October 1997.
68. Law No. 179 of 10 July 2008 on public-private partnerships, published in the Official Gazette No. 165–166 on 2 September 2008, Art. 36. *See also* Robert Krč, *Overview of the PPP System in Moldova*, 10 European Procurement & Public Private Partnership Law Review, 292–297 (2015).
69. European Bank for Reconstruction and Development, *Assessment of the quality of the PPP legislation and of the effectiveness of its implementation* (2011), http://www.ebrd.com/downloads/legal/concessions/moldova.pdf (accessed 29 November 2016).
70. Law No. 23, Art. 8; Law No. 24, Art. 7.
71. Law No. 23, Art. 2; Law No. 24, Art. 7(1).
72. Decision No. 2, para. 6.
73. Law No. 23, Art. 8(3).

specify the arbitration institution, it should be considered as ad hoc arbitration.[74] If the parties agree that their disputes should be resolved in court or by an arbitration tribunal, it is considered that the claimant will have the right to choose between these two alternative venues.[75]

[B] Validity of the Arbitration Agreement

[1] General Provisions

1.22 The validity of the arbitration agreement should be assessed in the context of the general legal capacity of the parties to enter into such agreements and in the context of the form and content of the arbitration agreement itself. The law accepts natural and legal persons (including legal persons in public law as specified in Section §6.01[H] above) as parties to the arbitration agreement. The law does not require the arbitration clause to specify the disputes it covers (it will be presumed that any disputes based on the underlying contract are covered) and allows the parties to modify the arbitration clause in the same way it does with other contract clauses.

[2] Requisites of a Valid Arbitration Agreement

1.23 Both in domestic and international commercial arbitration, the law requires the arbitration agreement to be made in the written form. The Law on Arbitration stipulates that failure to respect the form of the arbitration agreement results in its nullity.[76] In case of international commercial arbitration, this defect can be cured if the other party in its reply to the claim does not raise the objections as to the form of the arbitration agreement.[77]

[C] Concluding the Arbitration Agreement (Written, Oral, by Conduct)

1.24 As specified in Section §6.02[B][2] above, the law mandates the arbitration agreement to be made in writing with possibility to cure this defect in cases of international commercial arbitration. The written form is understood under the provisions of the Civil Code as a single document signed by the parties, as well as the exchange of documents (letters, telegrams, faxes, electronic messages) signed by the respective parties.[78] The Law on International Commercial Arbitration further stipulates that the written form is also respected in cases of electronic messages sent via e-mail.[79]

---

74. Law No. 23, Arts 12–15. See Lilia Gribincea, *Arbitrajul ad-hoc*, 7 Revista Naţională de Drept 72–74 (2014).
75. Decision No. 2, para. 7.
76. Law No. 23, Art. 8(2).
77. Law No. 24, Art. 7(7).
78. Civil Code, Art. 210.
79. Law No. 24, Art. 7(4).

[D] The Doctrine of Separability

1.25 The Doctrine of Separability concerns the autonomous nature of the arbitration agreement vis-a-vis the underlying contract and is also recognized in the judicial practices in Moldova. In its explanatory decision concerning the cases where parties have concluded an arbitration agreement, the SCJ has instructed lower courts to follow the Doctrine of Separability when examining the validity of the arbitration clause and the underlying contract.[80]

[E] Invalidity of the Arbitration Agreement

1.26 When considering the validity of the arbitration agreement in line with the Doctrine of Separability, the courts will consider the requirements of the business capacity of the parties, the form of the arbitration agreement and other factors specified in Section §6.02[B][2] above. In its case law, the SCJ upheld the parties' autonomy to agree on arbitration as well as to forfeit the arbitration agreement and to submit their dispute to the court. For example, in 2003 the SCJ upheld the arbitration agreement in the form of an arbitration clause inserted in the contract for the international sale of goods.[81] In that case, the contract provided for the arbitration under the rules of the International Chamber of Commerce (ICC) International Court of Arbitration and the SCJ emphasized the need to respect the parties' choice of the dispute settlement as well as the autonomy of the contract. In another case decided in 2001, the SCJ upheld the parties' choice to forfeit the arbitration when they failed to raise an objection to the jurisdiction of the court within the time frame provided for by the CCP.[82]

[F] Arbitrability

[1] Disputes Capable of Settlement by Arbitration

1.27 The disputes related to property rights, including those arising out of intellectual property rights such as royalties and other types of compensation related to the patents, are eligible for settlement by arbitration. The Law on International Commercial Arbitration enumerates several types of disputes that are eligible for settlement by arbitration: (a) disputes arising out of civil contractual relationships as well as other legal relationships stemming from the implementation of international commercial contracts and other international commercial transactions; (b) disputes between

---

80. Decision No. 2, para. 6. The SCJ made reference to the ECtHR Judgment of 9 December 1994 in the Case 13427/87 *Stran Greek Refineries and Stratis Andreadis v. Greece*, paras 72–73.
81. SCJ Judgment No. 2re-28/2003 of 24 July 2003: "The court shall dismiss the claim in cases where the parties have stipulated in the contract that the dispute has to be resolved through arbitration, and in the present case claimant has advanced the objections even before the claim was decided on the merits by the arbitral tribunal."
82. SCJ Judgment No. 4–2r/a-17/2001 of 12 March 2001: "Although the contract stipulated that resolution of the dispute will be a competence of the arbitrators of the ICAC, parties through their conduct have changed the jurisdiction of the claim."

enterprises with foreign capital, international associations and organizations established in the Republic of Moldova, disputes between their members, as well as disputes between the former and other persons.[83]

[2] Disputes Not Capable of Settlement by Arbitration

1.28 The Law on Arbitration highlights the following types of disputes that are not arbitrable: (1) claims arising out family law;[84] (2) disputes related to the rental of residential properties; (3) claims and property rights related to residential real estate.[85] In its guidance the SCJ also mentions the following types of disputes that enter into the exclusive competence of the courts: (1) disputes concerning public law relationships where one of the parties is a public authority (administrative, fiscal, customs, etc.); (2) issues related to the insolvency proceedings;[86] (3) disputes related to the disposal of public property; (4) disputes related to the right to life and physical integrity; (5) disputes related to non-material rights over intellectual property; (6) disputes related to the transactions that cannot be entered into by private parties.[87]

1.29 The CCP also stipulates that the following cases with foreign element fall under the exclusive jurisdiction of the Moldovan courts: (a) the claim involves the right of ownership over a real estate located on the territory of Moldova; (b) the property insured or place of the accident leading to the payment of insurance is located in Moldova; (c) the claim is related to a contract of transportation and places of dispatch or delivery of the goods or passengers which are located on the territory of Moldova; (d) the case concerns an accident in the sea or air where the aircraft or the vessel bears the flag of Moldova; (e) the vessel or aircraft has been arrested in Moldova; (f) procedures of insolvency of foreign companies located in Moldova; (g) certain categories of marriage disputes when one of the spouses holds Moldovan citizenship; (h) the last domicile of the deceased or the remaining estate is located in Moldova.[88]

[3] Special Provisions on Consumer and Labor Disputes

1.30 The Moldovan legislation is not entirely clear on the issues of the validity of arbitration clauses included in the consumer contracts. The laws regulating arbitration

---

83. Law No. 24, Art. 1(4).
84. These include: claims concerning civil status, separation of common property, establishing domicile of minor children, enforcement of alimony payments, establishment or challenge of paternity, parental rights, adoption, etc. See Decision No. 2, para. 10.
85. Law No. 23, Art. 3(2).
86. The Law on Insolvency provides for the exclusive competence of the courts to conduct the insolvency proceedings. At the same time, the creditors can provide evidence of their claims against the debtor by submitting to the competent court the copy of the final arbitral award, the decision of the court concerning recognition and enforcement of an arbitral award or an exequatur issued by the court. Law No. 149 of 29 June 2012 on insolvency, published in the Official Gazette No. 193–197 on 14 September 2012. See also Nicolae Clima, *Interacțiunea instanțelor de judecată cu Arbitrajul*, 7 Revista Națională de Drept 18–23 (2014).
87. See Decision No. 2, para. 11.
88. CCP, Art. 461(1).

and consumer protection do not exclude the arbitrability of the consumer disputes.[89] The Civil Code does not regulate arbitration clauses as standard contract clauses.[90] At the same time, the Law on Abusive Contract Clauses in Consumer Contracts modeled after the Directive 93/13/EEC[91] qualifies as abusive the clause that has an object of "excluding or limiting the consumer's right to initiate a court proceeding or to exercise any other right provided by law, particularly by requiring the consumer to resolve any dispute exclusively by arbitration, not covered by legal provisions."[92] The similar lack of clarity persists in the area of labor disputes: while arbitration laws do not exclude arbitrability of labor disputes expressly, the Labor Code does not mention arbitration among the venues for the resolution of labor disputes.[93]

[G]   Effect of Arbitration Agreement on Third Parties

1.31 Based on the principle of the privity of contracts, the arbitration agreement produces effects only for its signatories, as well as their successors.[94] The assignment of receivables covered by the arbitration agreement leads to the assignment of the arbitration agreement.[95] The single instance where an arbitration clause does not require the consent of the parties is the testamentary arbitration clause included in the will concluded by a deceased person in relation to his/her successors.[96] The SCJ has emphasized in its explanatory decision that third parties can take part in the arbitration proceedings only if they have been parties to the arbitration agreement or to a *compromis*.[97] As a result, even in a situation of joint liability, the claimant can direct his/her action in arbitration only against those respondents who have expressly agreed on arbitration.

[H]   Drafting Arbitration Clauses

1.32 The ICAC recommends the following model clause to be included in international commercial contracts: "All disputes arising out of or in connection with this Contract, or regarding its conclusion, execution or termination, shall be settled by the Court of International Commercial Arbitration attached to the Chamber of Commerce and

---

89. For example, the Law on Consumer Protection mentions only court proceedings and mediation as possible venues for resolution of consumer disputes. See Law No. 015 of 13 March 2003 on consumer protection, re-published in the Official Gazette No. 176–181 on 21 October 2011, Art. 31.
90. Civil Code, Arts 712–720.
91. Council Directive 93/13/EEC of 5 April 1993 on unfair terms in consumer contracts, OJ L 95/29.
92. Law No. 256 of 9 December 2011 on abusive clauses in consumer contracts, published in the Official Gazette No. 38–41 on 24 February 2012, Art. 5(5)(q). See also Dorin Cimil, *Criteriile de calificare a clauzelor abusive*, 1 Revista Institutului Național de Justiție, 32–40 (2013).
93. Code No. 154 of 28 March 2003, published in the Official Gazette No. 159–162 on 29 July 2003, Art. 351.
94. Civil Code, Art. 668(2).
95. Decision No. 2, para. 12.
96. Law No. 23, Art. 7.
97. Decision No. 2, para. 13.

Industry of the Republic of Moldova, in accordance with the Rules of Arbitration of this Court. The arbitral award shall be final and binding."[98]

1.33 The ICAC recommends the following model clause to be included in domestic commercial contracts: "All disputes arising out of or in connection with this Contract, or regarding its conclusion, execution or termination, shall be settled by the Court of International Commercial Arbitration attached to the Chamber of Commerce and Industry of the Republic of Moldova, in accordance with the Rules of Arbitration of this Court. The arbitral award shall be final and binding."[99]

1.34 The ICAC recommends the following model clauses for the settlement of disputes through mediation: "All disputes arising out of or in connection with this Contract, or regarding its conclusion, execution or termination, before it settlement through judiciary or arbitral way, shall be passed to be settled by the ICAC attached to the Chamber of Commerce and Industry of the Republic of Moldova." or "If, in case of a dispute, arising out of or in connection with this Contract, parties will try to settle it through mediation procedure organized by the International Commercial Arbitration Court attached to the CCI RM, this procedure will be conducted according to the Rules of the Court on mediation."[100]

§6.03 THE ARBITRATORS

[A] Appointment of Arbitrators

[1] Appointment of Arbitrators under Municipal Law

1.35 The arbitration law respects parties' choice as to the appointment of arbitrators. If the arbitration agreement does not stipulate the number of arbitrators, the dispute shall be resolved by three arbitrators (one arbitrator appointed by each party and presiding arbitrators chosen by the arbitrators).[101] In case of domestic arbitration, the other party has fifteen days to appoint an arbitrator following the notification from the party that has already appointed its arbitrator.[102] In case of international arbitration, this period is thirty days.[103] In case of ad hoc arbitration, the parties can refer to the court for the appointment of an arbitrator (if the properly notified party fails to make the appointment within the prescribed time) or a presiding arbitrator (in case where two arbitrators fail to agree within the prescribed time limit).[104]

---

98. Standard clause recommended by the CCI to be included in international commercial contracts, http://arbitraj.chamber.md/index.php?id=117 (accessed 29 November 2016).
99. Standard clause recommended by the CCI to be included in domestic commercial contracts, http://arbitraj.chamber.md/index.php?id=116 (accessed 29 November 2016).
100. Mediation clause recommended by the CCI to be included in internal and international commercial contracts, http://arbitraj.chamber.md/index.php?id=118 (accessed 29 November 2016).
101. Law No. 23, Art. 11(4); Law No. 24, Art. 11(3).
102. Law No. 23, Art. 12(5).
103. Law No. 24, Art. 11(3).
104. Decision No. 2, para. 23.

[2] Appointment under Institutional Rules

1.36 The ICAC Rules on Domestic Arbitration provide the other party with fifteen days to appoint its arbitrator. If the other party fails to make an appointment, the parties fail to appoint a single arbitrator or the arbitrators fail to agree on the presiding arbitrator, the appointment will be made by the ICAC President.[105] In case of international arbitration, the ICAC President shall appoint the presiding arbitrator within five days if the arbitrators fail to agree on the presiding arbitrator within ten days.[106]

[B] Qualifications of Arbitrators

1.37 The Law on Arbitration provides that the following categories of persons cannot serve as arbitrators: (1) persons under guardianship; (2) persons with criminal record; (3) persons dismissed from the positions of judge, attorney, notary, law enforcement officer for actions incompatible with the respective position; (4) persons who cannot serve as arbitrators due to their status/position in accordance with law.[107] Failure to satisfy the above-mentioned qualification requirements may result in the court's refusal to issue an exequatur for an arbitral award issued by such arbitrator(s).[108]

[C] Powers and Duties of Arbitrators

1.38 Under the Law on Arbitration the arbitrators are responsible for any damages caused in the case of: (1) unjustified resignation after the appointment; (2) unjustified failure to participate in the arbitration proceedings or failure to adopt the arbitration award within the prescribed period; (3) disclosure of confidential information without the consent of the parties; (4) other grave infringement of arbitrator's duties.[109]

[D] Challenges and Replacement of Arbitrators

[1] Challenges under Municipal Law

1.39 The laws governing both domestic and international commercial arbitration stipulate that an arbitrator can be challenged due to his/her lack of impartiality, independence or due to the failure to comply with the qualifications agreed by the parties. The parties have fifteen days from the establishment of the arbitration tribunal to submit the challenge of an arbitrator.[110] If the respective arbitrator does not withdraw voluntarily, the arbitration tribunal shall take a decision in that respect. If the

---

105. ICAC Domestic Rules, Art. 12.
106. ICAC International Rules, Art. 5.
107. Law No. 23, Art. 11(2).
108. Decision No. 2, para. 48. *See also* Tatiana Novac, *Arbitrul și judecătorul. Diferențieri statuare*, 7 Revista Națională de Drept 75–78 (2014).
109. Law No. 23, Art. 15, ICAC Domestic Rules, Art. 16. *See also* Dumitru Postovan, "*Dreptul discreționar*" *în activitatea arbitrajului*, 7 Revista Națională de Drept 54–59 (2014).
110. Law No. 23, Art. 14; Law No. 24, Art. 12.

arbitration tribunal rejects the challenge, the interested party can refer the matter to the court within thirty days from the date of rejection. The court does not review the decision of the arbitral tribunal, but decides on the challenge of arbitrator independently. The decision of the court is final and is not open for appeal.[111]

[2] Challenges under Institutional Rules

1.40 Under the ICAC Rules, the challenge of arbitrators is resolved by the ICAC President, while the challenge should be notified to the ICAC within fifteen days from the establishment of the arbitration tribunal. The appointment of the new arbitrator by the ICAC is made within five days.[112] The ICAC International Rules link the right to challenge an arbitrator from the moment when the respective party learns about the existence of the grounds for a challenge. Such a challenge should be notified to the ICAC within fifteen days.[113]

[E] Compensation of Arbitrators

1.41 The Law on International Commercial Arbitration empowers the arbitrators to request the parties to provide a guarantee for the compensation of arbitrators and costs of the arbitration tribunal.[114] The failure to provide such guarantee can lead to the termination of the arbitration proceedings. The Law on Arbitration provides that compensation of arbitrators should be supported by the losing party.[115]

§6.04 JURISDICTION OF THE ARBITRATION TRIBUNAL

[A] Introduction

1.42 The doctrine of *Kompetenz-Kompetenz* or the arbitration tribunal's competence to decide on its own jurisdiction is recognized in the Moldovan arbitration law.[116] This principle has been respected in the jurisprudence of the highest court. In 2006, the SCJ examined a case where a Slovenian company argued against arbitration claiming that its director, who signed the contract containing an arbitration clause, had been relieved of his duties at the time of signing and therefore could not bind the company.[117] The SCJ rejected the argument that the dispute concerned the validity of the contract itself

---

111. Decision No. 2, para. 24.
112. ICAC Domestic Rules, Art. 15.
113. ICAC International Rules, Art. 8.
114. Law No. 23, Art. 34.
115. Law No. 23, Art. 32.
116. Law No. 23 Art. 27(3): "The arbitral tribunal has a right to determine its own competence to rule on the dispute referred to it as well as on the validity of the arbitration agreement." *See also* Aurel Băieșu, *Rolul arbitrajului comercial internațional în înfăptuirea justiției*, 7 Revista Națională de Drept 2–7 (2014).
117. SCJ Judgment No. 2re-211/2006 of 18 May 2006, published in the SCJ Bulletin No. 10/22 (2006).

and that it did not "arise out of or in connection with" the contract, and confirmed the ability of the arbitral tribunal to decide on its own jurisdiction.[118]

[B] The Arbitrators' Determination of Their Own Jurisdiction

1.43 The domestic and international commercial arbitration laws differ as to the possibility to challenge the arbitration tribunal's determination in court. The lack of clarity concerning the applicable procedure and the competent court make the implementation difficult in practice. The Law on Arbitration empowers the arbitrators to decide about the jurisdiction of the arbitration tribunal. Their decision cannot be challenged in court, except in case for setting aside the arbitral award based on the lack of jurisdiction.[119] In case of international commercial arbitration, the preliminary determination of the arbitration tribunal concerning its jurisdiction can be challenged in court.[120] The court's decision on this issue is final and cannot be appealed.

[C] Court Review of Arbitrators' Jurisdiction

1.44 Although the Law on International Commercial arbitration provides for the possibility to challenge the arbitration tribunal's decision concerning its jurisdiction in court, the CCP does not contain any provisions that would designate the competent court or regulate the procedure for such challenges.

[D] Institutional Rules

1.45 In line with the applicable law, the ICAC Rules provide for the competence of the arbitration tribunal to decide about its own jurisdiction.[121] The decision for jurisdiction can be challenged in court only in the process of setting aside the arbitration award. In cases of international commercial arbitration, the ICAC Rules allow the parties to challenge the jurisdiction decision of the arbitration tribunal within thirty days before the Economic Court of Appeal.[122] Since the Economic Court of Appeal no longer exists in the current judicial system, it is unclear which court would be competent to decide on jurisdiction decisions of the arbitration tribunal.

§6.05 THE PROCEDURE BEFORE THE ARBITRATION TRIBUNAL

[A] Introduction

1.46 The procedure before the arbitration tribunal is regulated by the applicable legislation in general terms, thus providing the arbitrators and the parties with

---

118. *See* Alexandr Svetlicinii, *Enforcement of Foreign Arbitral Awards and Foreign Judgments in the Republic of Moldova*, 10 Wuhan University International Law Review 194, 202 (2009).
119. Law No. 23, Art. 27(3).
120. Law No. 24, Art. 16.
121. ICAC Domestic Rules, Art. 39.
122. ICAC International Rules, Art. 18(3).

sufficient freedom to decide on the format of the proceedings and the procedural actions that should be undertaken prior to the adoption of the arbitral award. Both the domestic and international arbitration procedures include the following phases: citation of the parties and the arbitral tribunal, presentation of evidence, hearings (or written exchange of submissions), deliberation of the arbitrators.

[B] General Principles of Municipal Judicial Procedure

1.47 The CCP proclaims the following general principles of municipal judicial procedure: (1) exercise of justice in courts only (prohibition to establish extraordinary courts); (2) independence of judges (in line with the separation of powers provided in the Constitution the judges are independent and subordinated to law only); (3) equality before the law and justice; (4) public character of judicial hearings (under special circumstances the judicial hearings can be conducted behind closed doors with a public announcement of the decisions taken); (5) direct and verbal character of judicial hearings; (6) adversarial character of the proceedings and equality of the parties in procedural rights.[123]

[C] General Principles of Arbitration Procedure (Party Autonomy, Speed, Impartiality, Etc.)

1.48 The Law on Arbitration proclaims the following general principles of arbitration procedure: (1) protection of fundamental human rights and freedoms; (2) legality; (3) freedom of arbitration agreements; (4) establishment of the arbitral tribunal in accordance with the arbitration agreement; (5) adversarial character of the proceedings; (6) protection of the right to defense; (7) confidentiality.[124] In cases of international commercial arbitration, the respective law does not explicitly declare any general principles as it is substantially based on the wording of the UNCITRAL Model Law on International Commercial Arbitration. The SCJ's guidance contains the following principles that should be respected in the arbitration procedure: adversarial character of the proceedings, equality of the parties before the law and justice, impartiality, right to property, contractual freedom, etc.[125]

[D] Commencing the Arbitral Proceedings

[1] Municipal Law

1.49 Under the applicable municipal law, the claimant submits the request to establish the arbitration tribunal to the respective institution, which effectively commences the arbitral proceedings. The respondent has thirty days to reply to the request for

---

123. CCP, Arts 19–27.
124. Law No. 23, Art. 4; ICAC Domestic Rules, Art. 3.
125. *See* Decision No. 2, para. 41.

arbitration submitted by the claimant.[126] The respondent should raise any exceptions to the arbitration within fifteen days from the date of the request for arbitration in a case when the arbitration is conducted on the basis of written submission without any oral arguments.[127] The Law on International Commercial Arbitration also links the commencement of the arbitral proceedings with the receipt of the request for arbitration by the respondent without establishing time limits for replies and exceptions, which are regulated by the relevant institutional rules or procedural rules agreed by the parties.[128]

[2] Institutional Rules

1.50 The arbitration proceedings at the ICAC are commenced by the application submitted by the claimant, which should include the following information: the name of the arbitration institution, names and addresses of the parties, proof of the existence of the arbitration agreement, object and value of the claim, facts and evidence on which the claim is based, proof of payment of the registration fee (USD 200 for international and MDL 1,000 for domestic arbitration) and arbitration fee (no less than USD 500 for international and no less than MDL 1,000 for domestic arbitration), the name of the arbitrator or the request to the arbitration institution to appoint an arbitrator.[129]

[E] Conduct of Arbitration

[1] Written Submissions

1.51 Unless the parties have agreed otherwise, in domestic arbitration all written submissions including citations, conclusions of the hearings and arbitral awards should be made by a registered letter with confirmation of dispatch and receipt. Other information can be communicated by any means which can produce the proof of contents and the fact of communication.[130] In cases of international commercial arbitration, the rules on written submissions laid down in the UNCITRAL Model Law are reproduced verbatim in the Law on International Commercial Arbitration.[131]

[2] Post-hearing Briefs

1.52 The Law on Arbitration does not regulate the submission of post-hearing briefs. It only mandates the following contents to be included in the minutes of the hearing signed by the arbitrators: (1) any measures ordered by the arbitral tribunal with the

---

126. Law No 23, Art. 18.
127. Law No. 23, Art. 19(2).
128. Law No. 24, Arts. 19, 21.
129. ICAC International Rules, Art. 11; ICAC Domestic Rules, Art. 21.
130. Law No. 23, Art. 21.
131. Law No. 24, Art. 3.

corresponding reasoning; (2) brief description of the hearings; (3) claims and arguments of the parties; (4) any other decisions adopted by the tribunal; (5) names of the arbitrators and the parties, place and date of the hearing.[132] Similar contents of the minutes of the hearing are required by the institutional rules for international commercial arbitration.[133]

[3] Evidence (Admissibility, Documentary Evidence)

1.53 Every party bears the burden of proof in relation to the claims or defenses made in the arbitration. The institutional rules on domestic arbitration require all evidence to be submitted to the arbitral tribunal and communicated to the parties prior to the hearings.[134] Any later submission of evidence is allowed only if the need to submit the respective evidence appears from the hearings and if the submission of evidence does not delay the resolution of the dispute.

[4] Witness and Experts' Testimony

1.54 If a party intends to submit witness testimonies, the institutional rules for domestic and international arbitration require the respective party to notify the tribunal and another party about the identity of the witnesses at least fifteen days prior to the hearings.[135] The Law on International Commercial Arbitration authorizes the tribunal to assign experts for the production of an expert examination and to allow the designated expert to examine any types of evidence in possession of the parties. Upon request of the party or on its own motion, the tribunal may request the expert to participate in the hearing where the parties or their experts can question the expert and provide their own opinions.[136]

[F] Hearings

1.55 The Law on Arbitration requires the hearings to be held no earlier than fifteen days from the date of the citation of the parties.[137] The hearings are normally held in a closed session, unless both parties agree on open hearings. The presiding arbitrator presides over the hearings; the debates of the parties are followed by the decisions taken by the arbitral tribunal. In cases of international arbitration, the Moldovan law in line with the UNCITRAL Model Law allows the arbitral tribunal to decide whether the presentation of evidence will be made in oral hearings or on the basis of a written submission.[138]

---

132. Law No. 23, Art. 26.
133. ICAC International Rules, Art. 30.
134. ICAC Domestic Rules, Art. 34.
135. ICAC Domestic Rules, Art. 35, ICAC International Rules, Art. 27.
136. Law No. 24, Art. 26.
137. Law No. 23, Art. 22(3).
138. Law No. 24, Art. 24.

§6.06 THE ARBITRAL AWARD

[A] Introduction

1.56 The term "arbitral award" in domestic arbitration encompasses the following types of decisions adopted by the arbitral tribunal: (1) resolution of the substance of the dispute; (2) termination of the arbitral proceedings without resolving the substance of the dispute; (3) termination of the arbitral proceedings due to the settlement reached by the parties.[139] The Law on International Commercial Arbitration, in line with the UNCITRAL Model Law, distinguishes the arbitral award and the order for termination which can be issued by the arbitral tribunal if the claimant withdraws his claim, if the parties reach an agreement concerning termination of the proceedings, or if the arbitral tribunal finds the continuation of the proceedings unnecessary or impossible.[140] The Law on Arbitration mandates the arbitral award to contain the following information: the date and place of issue, the composition of the arbitral tribunal, the names and addresses of the parties, the reference to an arbitration agreement, the subject of the dispute, the facts and legal reasoning, the signature(s) of the arbitrator(s).[141]

[B] Deliberation and Voting

1.57 The adoption of the arbitral award is preceded by the secret deliberation with the participation of all arbitrators.[142] The award is adopted by a majority of votes (in a case of split votes, the vote of the presiding arbitrator will be decisive).[143] The dissenting opinion of an arbitrator can be attached to the arbitral award. In domestic arbitration, the award should be delivered to the parties within ten days from the date of its adoption by the tribunal.[144]

[C] Different Kinds of Awards (Separate, Interim, Consent, Default, Etc.)

1.58 In domestic arbitration, as mentioned above in Section §6.01[A], the settlement of the parties can be recorded in the consent award. There are also the following types of additional awards that should be issued by the arbitral tribunal within thirty days from the date of the initial award upon request of the party: decision on interpretation of the issues addressed in the arbitral award, decision on correction of the typographic and calculation errors made in the initial award.[145]

1.59 The Law on International Commercial Arbitration is more detailed in relation to different types of awards and covers the following: (1) award on arbitration costs that

---

139. Law No. 23, Art. 28.
140. Law No. 24, Art. 32.
141. Law No. 23, Art. 29(2).
142. Law No. 23, Art. 28.
143. Law No. 24, Art. 29.
144. Law No. 23, Art. 28.
145. Law No. 23, Art. 29.

cannot be estimated at the time of the adoption of the initial award; (2) additional award on issues raised in the claim but not addressed in the arbitral award (should be adopted within sixty days from the date of request); (3) correction award rectifying typographic and calculation errors made in the initial award; (4) interpretation award explaining the provisions of the initial award.[146]

[D]   Interest and Costs

1.60 In domestic arbitration the following costs should be borne by the losing party (in proportion to the part of the claim that was confirmed in the arbitral award): organization of arbitration proceedings, remuneration of arbitrators, collection and presentation of evidence, remuneration of experts and interpreters, travel costs.[147] In international arbitration, the law provides the arbitral tribunal with more flexibility in determining the portion of the costs to be borne by each party and requires the tribunal to issue an additional award on costs if they have been determined only after the completion of arbitration proceedings.[148]

[E]   Effects of the Award

[1]   Execution

1.61 In domestic arbitration, the arbitral award, that has to be delivered to the parties within ten days from the date of its adoption, has the effect of a definitive court judgment and becomes mandatory for immediate execution unless a different term for execution is provided for in the award.[149] The winning party can apply to the court for an exequatur without waiting for the three-month period allowed for the setting aside of the arbitral award. However, if the setting aside proceedings have already been commenced, the court may decide to stay the examination of the request for exequatur.[150] The court announces the request for exequatur within thirty days from its receipt.[151]

[2]   Res Judicata and Lis Pendens

1.62 Pursuant to the CCP the courts shall refuse the claims concerning the same dispute between the same parties that has already been resolved in arbitration, except for cases where the request for the exequatur has been rejected by the court.[152] If the judicial process has already commenced, the court shall order the termination of

---

146. Law No. 24, Arts 33, 35.
147. Law No. 23, Art. 32.
148. Law No. 24, Art. 33.
149. Law No. 23, Arts 28, 33.
150. Decision No. 2, para. 47.
151. CCP, Art. 484.
152. CCP, Art. 169(1)(d).

judicial proceedings once the arbitral award has been issued in relation to the same dispute between the parties.[153]

[F] Correction and Interpretation of the Award

[1] Municipal Law

1.63 In domestic arbitration, the parties to the dispute or the arbitrators ex officio have a right to request the tribunal to decide on the issues raised in the claim but not resolved in the arbitral award. This right should be exercised within fifteen days from the date of the receipt of the arbitral award.[154] In cases of international arbitration, this period is longer – thirty days from the adoption of the arbitral award.[155] In international arbitration, the errors should be corrected within thirty days from the date of the request; the additional award on the issues not resolved in the original award has to be issued within sixty days from the date of the request.

[2] Institutional Rules

1.64 The ICAC Rules follow the municipal law as far as requests for corrections, interpretations and supplemental awards are concerned. In the case of domestic awards, the period for launching the request is fifteen days, while in international arbitration parties have thirty days to file their request with the tribunal.[156]

§6.07 SETTING ASIDE THE AWARD

[A] Introduction

1.65 Setting aside is the only procedural instrument available under Moldovan law for the annulment of the arbitral award by the court.[157] No other procedural means such as appeal, cassation, revision, etc. are allowed. Until July 1, 2016, the District Economic Court was a single judicial entity entrusted with the exclusive competence to examine the challenges of the arbitral awards.[158] After that date, the requests for setting aside of an arbitral award must be submitted to the court that would be competent to resolve the dispute in the absence of an arbitration agreement.[159] The requests for setting aside the award should be filed with the competent court by the interested party

---

153. CCP, Art. 265 (1)(e).
154. Law No. 23, Art. 30.
155. Law No. 24, Art. 35.
156. ICAC International Rules, Art. 39; ICAC Domestic Rules, Art. 44.
157. See generally Ion Druță & Ana Borș, Contestarea hotărîrilor arbitrale. Încuviințarea executării silite a hotărîrilor arbitrale, in Mihai Poalelungi, Elena Belei & Diana Sârcu (eds.), Manualul judecătorului pentru cauze civile (Supreme Court of Justice), 300–318 (3rd ed., 2013).
158. CCP, Art. 35 (abrogated by Law No. 76 of April 21, 2016).
159. CCP, Art. 477(1).

within thirty days from the date of receipt of the award.[160] The state fee for the setting aside of the arbitral award is the same as for the issuance of the exequatur.[161]

[B] Invalid Awards

1.66 The Moldovan law does not distinguish between the invalid and challengeable awards. The CCP contains the exhaustive list of the grounds for challenge,[162] which have been summarized by the SCJ as follows: grounds related to the competence of the arbitral tribunal, grounds related to the arbitral award, grounds related to the arbitration procedure and grounds related to the arbitration agreement.[163]

[C] Challengeable Awards

[1] Grounds for Challenging the Award

1.67 The CCP contains the exhaustive list of the grounds for challenging the award.[164] These can be generally divided into five groups. The *first* group of grounds is related to the competence of the arbitral tribunal where the subject matter of the dispute is not capable of settlement by arbitration under the law. The arbitrability of various types of disputes was discussed in the Section §6.02[F] above. The *second* group of grounds refers to the arbitral award and includes the following: (a) the arbitral award does not contain the disposition and reasons, the place and date of delivery or is not signed by the arbitrators;[165] (b) the award contains provisions that cannot be executed (e.g., the object of the dispute no longer exists or the arbitral award contains determinations that contradict each other); (c) the arbitral award violates fundamental principles of the Moldovan law or good morals.[166] The SCJ in its explanatory decision emphasized the absence of an exhaustive list of fundamental legal principles and provided references to the principles embedded in the Law on Arbitration and the CCP.[167]

1.68 The *third* group of grounds refers to various procedural irregularities: (a) the constitution of the arbitral tribunal or the arbitration proceedings were not in accordance with the arbitration agreement; (b) the interested party was not informed about

---

160. Law No. 23, Art. 31; Law No. 24, Art. 37.
161. CCP, Art. 477(4).
162. CCP, Art. 480.
163. Decision No. 2, paras 40-43.
164. CCP, Art. 480(2). *See also* Law No. 24, Art. 37(2). *See also* Lilia Gribincea, *Overview of International Commercial Arbitration of the Republic of Moldova*, 8 Revista Științifică a Universității de Stat din Moldova, No. 48, 151-156 (2011).
165. According to Art. 29 Law on Arbitration, the arbitral award should contain the following elements: composition of the arbitral tribunal, the date and the place of issuance, the names and addresses of the parties, the reference to the arbitration agreement, the object of the dispute, the facts and legal issues, the legal reasoning, as well as the signatures of the arbitrators.
166. *See* Andrei Smochină, *Încălcarea principiilor fundamentale ale legislației Republicii Moldova sau a bunelor moravuri – temei de desființare a hotărîrii arbitrale*, 7 Revista Națională de Drept 50-53 (2014).
167. Decision No. 2, para. 41.

the election (appointment) of arbitrators or the arbitration hearings, including the place, date and time of the arbitration hearing and was unable to appear before the arbitral tribunal. The *fourth* ground for setting aside of the arbitral award is the invalidity of the arbitration agreement (e.g., due to the failure to respect the written form). Finally, the *fifth* ground for setting aside the SCJ mentions the situation when the arbitral award addressed the issues not covered by the arbitration agreement or which does not fall under the agreement or when the arbitral award contains determinations on issues that go beyond the arbitration agreement.[168]

[2] Waiver of Right to Challenge

1.69 The parties can waive the right to challenge the arbitral award only after its adoption by the arbitral tribunal. The law does not permit the parties to waive the right to challenge in the agreement to arbitrate (arbitration clause).[169]

[D] Review of Jurisdictional Awards

1.70 In international commercial arbitration, the party can challenge the jurisdictional award issued by the tribunal within thirty days from the date of the receipt of the arbitral tribunal's decision on jurisdiction.[170] The review of the jurisdictional award by the court does not suspend the arbitration proceedings. The court's decision on the jurisdictional award is final and cannot be appealed.

§6.08 RECOGNITION AND ENFORCEMENT OF THE ARBITRAL AWARD

[A] Enforcement of Domestic Awards

[1] Enforcement Domestically

1.71 Domestic arbitral awards are enforced in Moldova in the same way as domestic court judgments – the winning party should apply to the court with the request to issue a judicial execution order, which has to be examined by the court within thirty days.[171] The court's decision concerning enforcement can be appealed within fifteen days from the date of decision.[172] The exequatur issued by the court can be presented to the bailiff or other competent institutions and enforced in conformity with the provisions of the Code of Enforcement.[173]

---

168. Decision No. 2, para. 41.
169. CCP, Art. 477(2).
170. Law No. 24, Art. 16(3).
171. CCP, Art. 484(1); Law No. 23, Art. 33(2).
172. CCP, Art. 425.
173. Code No. 443 of 24 December 2004 on enforcement, re-published in the Official Gazette No. 214–220 on 5 November 2010.

[2] Enforcement Abroad

1.72 Since the Republic of Moldova became a party to the New York Convention in 1998, it enforces its domestic awards abroad pursuant to the terms of the Convention or on the basis of the bilateral agreements on judicial cooperation in civil matters concluded with a number of countries.[174] It should also be noted that the Republic of Moldova has acceded to the 1961 Convention Abolishing the Requirement of Legalization of Foreign Public Documents, which facilitates the recognition of documents issued by the Moldovan authorities in the Contracting States of the Convention.[175]

[B] Enforcement of Foreign Arbitral Awards

[1] Introduction to Recognition and Enforcement

1.73 Being a party to the New York Convention,[176] the Republic of Moldova has harmonized its legislation in line with the provisions of the Convention in order to allow for the recognition and enforcement of foreign arbitral awards on its territory. In 2013, the SCJ issued an explanatory decision guiding the courts in the enforcement of foreign arbitral awards, which was substantially amended in 2016.[177] The arbitral award is considered as "foreign" if: (a) it is issued in a foreign country; (b) it is issued on the territory of the Republic of Moldova but under foreign procedural law.[178]

1.74 As far as the enforcement of ICSID investment arbitration awards is concerned, it should be noted that Moldova has limited experience[179] with ICSID arbitration since the ICSID Convention was ratified in 2011. As a result, the enforcement of ICSID awards is not addressed in the relevant guidelines of the SCJ. Moldovan scholars have

---

174. Moldova has concluded such bilateral agreements with the Community of Independent States, Romania, Ukraine, Russian Federation, Turkey, Latvia, Lithuania, and Azerbaijan. The Plenum of the Supreme Court of Justice of the Republic of Moldova has reproduced the list of the bilateral agreements on judicial cooperation in its Decision No. 3 of 9 December 2013 on judicial practice of applying the legislation concerning the recognition and enforcement of foreign judgments and foreign arbitral awards. *See also* Alexandr Svetlicinii, *Enforcement of Foreign Arbitral Awards and Foreign Judgments in the Republic of Moldov*a, 10 Wuhan University International Law Review, 194–213 (2009).
175. The list of Contracting States is available at https://www.hcch.net/en/instruments/conventions/specialised-sections/apostille (accessed 29 November 2016). It should be noted that Germany has formulated an objection to Moldova's accession so the apostille procedure is not applied between these two countries.
176. Moldova applies the Convention only to the recognition and enforcement of awards made in the territory of another Contracting State. Moldova also formulated a reservation with regards to the retroactive application of the Convention.
177. Decision No. 9. *See also* Alexandr Svetlicinii, *Enforcement of Foreign Arbitral Awards in the Republic of Moldova: Evolution of the Pro-Arbitration Policy in the Case Law of the Supreme Court of Justice*, 24 Journal of International Arbitration, No. 3, 249–264 (2007).
178. CCP, Art. 475(1) (2007).
179. *See* e.g., Sergey Usoskin, *Moldova Gets a Mixed Result in the First ICSID Arbitration against it* (14 April 2013), http://www.cisarbitration.com/2013/04/14/moldova-gets-a-mixed-result-in-the-first-icsid-arbitration-against-it/ (accessed 29 November 2016).

argued that ICSID awards should be treated as domestic court judgments and exempted from the application of the New York Convention.[180]

1.75 In a recent case, the SCJ was seized on a matter concerning the recognition and enforcement of a foreign arbitral award issued against Russian Federation in relation to a contract concluded between the Government of the Russian Federation, European Commission and a Moldovan company.[181] The court rejected the applicant's argument that the respondent (the Russian State) had representation and assets in Moldova and held that Moldovan courts were not competent to examine the cases involving a foreign state.

[2]   Separate, Partial and Interim Awards

1.76 Moldovan legislation does not explicitly address the enforcement of separate, partial and interim awards. The explanatory decision of the SCJ clarifies that the term "foreign arbitral award" covers the following types of decisions issued by the arbitral tribunal: final awards on the merits, partial awards on the merits, consent awards, awards concerning arbitration fees and costs.[182] The following types of decisions are not considered "foreign arbitral award": procedural decisions of the arbitral tribunal related to the organization of the arbitration proceedings, decisions related to the interim relief.[183]

[3]   Grounds for Refusing Recognition and Enforcement

1.77 Grounds for refusing the recognition and enforcement are provided in the CCP[184] and follow the wording of Article V of the New York Convention. The debtor or the court acting ex officio can invoke the grounds for refusing the recognition and enforcement. The following sections contain a more detailed assessment of the various grounds for refusal to recognize and enforce a foreign arbitral award in Moldova.

[a]   Lack of Capacity and Invalidity of Arbitration Agreement

1.78 The lack of capacity of either party and invalidity of the arbitration agreement under the applicable law are two of the grounds for the refusal or the recognition and enforcement of foreign arbitral awards.[185] For example, in a case where one of the

---

180. *See* Zinaida Guțu, *Studiul III Reglementarea și aplicarea mecanismelor de recunoaștere și executare a hotăr ârilor arbitrale străine în Republica Moldova*, 3 (Chișinău 2012), http://www.justice.gov.md/public/files/file/reforma_sectorul_justitiei/pilon5/Studiul_regelementarera_si_aplicarea_mecanismului_de_recunoastere_si_executare_a_hotaririi_arbitrale_straine_in_RM-UNDP_Project-2012.pdf (accessed 29 November 2016).
181. *See* SCJ Judgment No. 2r-778/16 of 21 September 2016.
182. Decision No. 9, para. 18.
183. Decision No. 9, para. 19.
184. CCP, Art. 476; Law No. 24, Art. 39.
185. CCP, Art. 476; Law No. 24, Art. 39; Decision No. 9, paras 36–37.

parties is a legal person, the court will examine whether the natural person who signed the arbitration agreement has been properly authorized to act on behalf of the said legal person.

[b]   Procedural Violations

1.79 Procedural violations leading to the refusal of the recognition and enforcement are: (1) the party against whom the award is invoked was not given proper notice of the appointment of the arbitrator or of the arbitration proceedings, or was otherwise unable to present his case;[186] (2) the composition of the arbitral tribunal or the arbitral procedure was not in accordance with the agreement of the parties, or failing such an agreement was not in accordance with the law of the country where the arbitration took place.

1.80 The SCJ in its explanatory decision stipulated that the following procedural situations cannot justify the refusal to recognize the award: (1) the arbitrator(s) refused to change the date of the hearing as requested by the debtor for the accommodation or his/her witness; (2) the arbitrator(s) refused to postpone or suspend the arbitration procedure due to insolvency proceedings; (3) the absence of the parties at the hearing due to their fear of arrest in the country where the arbitration proceedings take place; (4) the representative of the party does not attend the hearings due to refusal of a visa by the competent immigration authorities.[187]

1.81 In relation to the appointment of arbitrators, the SCJ provided the following example derived from the Italian judicial practice.[188] The court refused the recognition of an award where the arbitration agreement provided for the appointment of three arbitrators. However, the two arbitrators appointed by the parties failed to appoint the third arbitrator because they were in agreement as to the resolution of the merits of the case.[189] The refusal to recognize an award could be also based on the failure to respect the arbitration procedure. For example, in a case where the parties agreed that the

---

186. *See* e.g., SCJ Judgment No. 2re-56.2004 of 26 February 2004. The SCJ refused the enforcement of the arbitral award issued by the Court of International Arbitration of the Ukrainian Chamber of Commerce and Industry against a Moldovan respondent on the grounds of improper notification. An examination of the facts of the case shows that the Ukrainian party sent the notice of arbitration to the domicile of the director of the Moldovan company. However, it was established that prior to arbitration both parties had acknowledged the change of the legal address of the Moldovan company in the subsequent amendment to their contract. The Moldovan party used these facts to successfully challenge the enforcement of the award.
187. Decision No. 9, para. 37.
188. *See also* Donella Antelmi & Francesca Santulli, *Arbitration Awards in Italy: Some Argumentative Features in the Discourse Analytical Perspective*, in Vijay K. Bhatia, Giuliana Garzone & Chiara Degano (eds.), Arbitration Awards: Generic Features and Textual Realisations, 91–108 (Cambridge Scholars Publishing, 2012); Michele Sala, *Linguistic and Textual Features of Italian Commercial Arbitration Awards*, in Vijay K. Bhatia, Giuliana Garzone & Chiara Degano (eds.), Arbitration Awards: Generic Features and Textual Realisations, 152–170 (Cambridge Scholars Publishing, 2012).
189. Decision No. 9, para. 39.

dispute would be decided on the basis of the written submissions, the arbitral tribunal admitted the oral testimony of the creditor's legal representative.[190]

[c] Excess of Mandate

1.82 The excess of mandate is another ground for the refusal of recognition in cases where the award deals with a dispute not contemplated by or not falling within the terms of the arbitration agreement, or it contains determinations on matters that are beyond the scope of the arbitration agreement.[191] In 2011, the SCJ refused the recognition and enforcement of an arbitral award issued by the ad hoc tribunal under UNCITRAL Arbitration Rules due to the fact that the arbitral tribunal ruled on the rights of the debtors who had not signed the arbitration agreement and therefore, could not be compelled to arbitrate.[192] Nevertheless, if the debtor participated in the arbitration proceedings without invoking the excess of mandate, they would lose the right to invoke this ground for the refusal to recognize the arbitral award.[193]

[d] Arbitral Award Not Binding

1.83 An award which has not yet become binding on the parties, or has been set aside or suspended by a competent judicial authority of the country in which or under the law of which that award was made, is not eligible for the recognition and enforcement in the Republic of Moldova. The notion of a binding and complete arbitral award is elaborated on in the Section §6.09[B][2] below. The Law on International Commercial Arbitration also stipulates that if the execution of an award was postponed by the competent court in the country of the issuance, the Moldovan court can also refuse the recognition and enforcement.[194] For example, in 2016 the SCJ refused the recognition and enforcement of an arbitral award issued in Stockholm against a Russian party because of the recognition and enforcement proceedings that had been launched before the Russian court, but had not been completed.[195]

[e] Non-arbitrability

1.84 The non-arbitrability of the underlying dispute, as specified in Section §6.02[F][1] above, serves as a ground for the refusal to recognize and enforce a foreign arbitral award in the Republic of Moldova. In its explanatory decision, the SCJ provides additional examples of the types of disputes that enter into the exclusive competence of

---

190. Decision No. 9, para. 39.
191. CCP, Art. 476(1)(c).
192. *See* SCJ Judgment No. 2r-429/11 of 14 September 2011. The SCJ held that the arbitration agreement was not binding on the third parties and the recognition of an arbitral award issued against them would run contrary to Art. 6 ECHR.
193. Decision No. 9, para. 38.
194. Law No. 24, Art. 39(1)(a).
195. SCJ Judgment No. 2r-778/16 of 21 September 2016.

the courts: public law relationships where one of the parties is a public authority (administrative, fiscal, customs); issues related to the insolvency proceedings; disputes concerning the disposal of public property; disputes that concern right to life and physical integrity; noneconomic rights over intellectual property.[196]

[f]   Public Policy

1.85 Foreign arbitral awards that are contrary to the public order of the Republic of Moldova are not enforceable on its territory. Although the law does not define "public order" explicitly, it has been argued that it refers to the fundamental principles of justice and morality and the imperative norms serving the basic political, economic and social interest of the state.[197] In its explanatory decision, the SCJ makes reference to the International Law Association's definition of the international public policy of a state, which includes: (1) the fundamental principles, pertaining to justice or morality which the State wishes to protect even when it is not directly concerned with; (2) the rules designed to serve the essential political, social or economic interests of the State, these being known as "lois de police" or "public policy rules"; and (3) the duty of the State to respect its obligations towards other States or international organizations.[198] The SCJ further specifies that the refusal to enforce a foreign arbitral award on the grounds of public policy should be rendered only when the violation of public policy norms is "substantial, effective and flagrant."[199]

[4]   Procedures for Recognition

1.86 The recognition and enforcement of the foreign arbitral award shall be sought before the Court of Appeal based on the residence/domicile/headquarters of the debtor or the location of the debtor's assets.[200] The winning party should submit to the court the request for recognition accompanied by the original arbitral award and original arbitration agreement (or their certified copies).[201] All of the above-mentioned documents should be submitted in the state language or accompanied with certified

---

196. Decision No. 2, para. 11.
197. *See* Dumitru Visternicean & Mihai Buruiana, *Procedura de recunoaștere și executare a hotărârilor judiciare și arbitrale străine*, in Mihai Poalelungi, Elena Belei & Diana Sârcu (eds.), Manualul judecătorului pentru cauze civile (Supreme Court of Justice), at 296 (3rd ed., 2013).
198. Decision No. 9, para. 42. International Law Association, Committee on International Commercial Arbitration (2002), Final Report on Public Policy as a Bar to Enforcement of International Arbitral Awards, Recommendation 1(d).
199. Decision No. 9, para. 42.
200. *See* e.g., SCJ Judgment No. 2r-510/16 of 8 June 2016. The SCJ confirmed the competence of the Court of Appeal to examine the request for the recognition and enforcement of a foreign arbitral award and rejected the competence of the first instance court. The respective provision of the CCP concerning the competence of the courts of appeal was introduced in 2015. *See* Law No. 135 of 3 July 2015 published in the Official Gazette No. 213–222 on 14 August 2015.
201. CCP, Art. 475. The jurisprudence of the SCJ indicated that these formalities should be followed strictly and the missing of any documents should result in the refusal to recognize the award. *See* e.g., SCJ Judgment No. 2r-429/11 of 14 September 2011; SCJ Judgment No. 2rc-806/16 of

translations.[202] The request for recognition should be submitted within three years from the date when the arbitral award enters into force according to the law of the country under which it was issued.[203] The court has a duty to notify the Ministry of Justice about the commencement of the recognition and enforcement proceedings. The recent SCJ case law indicates that failure to respect this duty by the court may lead to the annulment of its decision on recognition and enforcement.[204]

1.87 The law does not specify the time limit for the examination of the request for the recognition and enforcement by the competent court. The examination can be postponed or suspended in cases where one of the parties has submitted the request for annulment or suspension of the execution of the arbitral award.[205] If the arbitral award has been issued in a state-party of the New York Convention, the court cannot request the parties to provide any additional evidence not mentioned in the Article IV of the New York Convention.[206] The Moldovan courts are also not authorized to re-examine the merits of the arbitral award, to revise or to modify the award, or to request the parties provide any additional evidence concerning their dispute that has been resolved in arbitration. The decision of the Court of Appeal concerning the recognition or the refusal to recognize a foreign arbitral award can be appealed before the SCJ within fifteen days.[207]

§6.09 INVESTOR-STATE ARBITRATION

[A] General Overview of Law and Practice Related to Investor-State Arbitration

1.88 In the view of attracting foreign investment, the Republic of Moldova has concluded bilateral investment treaties (BITs) with its major trading partners. The list reproduced in Section §6.09[B] below contains forty-one BITs, some of which have not yet entered into force. All of the BITs provide a foreign investor with the possibility to initiate investor-state arbitration against the host state. Most of the BITs provide the foreign investor with the choice of ICSID institutional arbitration or UNCITRAL ad hoc arbitration. Several BITs also mention the options to submit the investor-state disputes

---

21 September 2016. In these cases, the recognition of the foreign arbitral awards was refused due to irregularities in the submitted documents.
202. The official translation of documents is regulated by Law No. 264 of 11 December 2008 on authorization and remuneration of translators and interpreters engaged by the Supreme Council of Magistrates, Ministry of Justice, prosecutor's office, law enforcement authorities, judicial institutions, notaries, attorneys and bailiffs, published in the Official Gazette No. 57–58 on 20 March 2009.
203. CCP, Art. 475(6).
204. See e.g., SCJ Judgment No. 2rc-146/16 of 10 February 2016.
205. Decision No. 9, para. 30.
206. Decision No. 9, para 31. See also SCJ Judgment No. 2r-787/16 of 28 September 2016. See also Diana Lazăr, *Cadrul de reglementări privind procedura recunoașterii și executării sentințelor arbitrale străine în sistemul Convenției de la New York din 1958*, 7 Revista Națională de Drept 79–92 (2014).
207. CCP, Art. 475-3(1).

to the ICC International Court of Arbitration (Paris)[208] or the Arbitration Institute of the Stockholm Chamber of Commerce (SCC).[209]

1.89 The Moldovan BITs often contain a "cooling-off clause," which provides for a certain period of time dedicated to the amicable settlement of investment disputes.[210] Only after the expiration of such a period, a foreign investor has the possibility to resort to arbitration. In 2014, the meaning of the "cooling-off clause" inserted in the Moldova-Russia BIT was tested in an emergency arbitration initiated by a Russian investor before the SCC.[211] In that case, the emergency arbitrator issued an arbitral award ordering interim measures prior to the expiration of the six-month period stipulated in the BIT.[212] Despite being the first reported emergency arbitration under an investment treaty, in the context of the Moldovan legal system the case has a limited practical significance. First, only few of the Moldovan BITs provide for an arbitration by the SCC, which is one of the international arbitration institutions which administers emergency arbitrations.[213] Second, although not tested in this case, it is unlikely that emergency arbitration awards will be enforceable in Moldova given the interpretation of the SCJ that excluded the interim measures and other provisional decisions of the arbitral tribunal from the notion of "final arbitral award" that is subject to recognition and enforcement procedure.[214]

1.90 As reflected in the list of reported investor-state disputes reproduced in Section §6.09[C] below, Moldova has a relatively limited experience with investor-state arbitration.[215] The Republic of Moldova appeared as a respondent in a number of cases initiated by investors from Russia, Ukraine, France and the United States, which were decided by the SCC, ICSID and in ad hoc arbitration under the UNCITRAL rules. Although few in number, the investment arbitration cases involving Moldova attracted substantial attention from the legal practitioners and scholars alike, mostly due to the issues discussed therein, as well as legal reasoning and conclusions reached by the arbitral tribunals.[216]

---

208. http://www.iccwbo.org/about-icc/organization/dispute-resolution-services/icc-international-court-of-arbitration/ (accessed 29 November 2016).
209. http://sccinstitute.com/ (accessed 29 November 2016).
210. See e.g., Moldova-Albania BIT, Art. 8(2) (6 months); Moldova-Bulgaria BIT, Art. 9(2) (6 months); Moldova-Croatia BIT, Art. 10(2) (6 months); Moldova-Germany BIT, Art. 11 (6 months).
211. SCC Emergency Arbitration No EA 2014/053 of 29 April 2014. See also Joel Dahlquist, *The First Known Investment Treaty Emergency Arbitration: TSIKinvest LLC v The Republic of Moldova, SCC Emergency Arbitration No EA 2014/053, 29 April 2014*, 17 Journal of World Investment & Trade, 261–27(2016).
212. Moldova-Russia BIT, Art. 10.
213. Moldova-Belgium-Luxembourg BIT and Moldova-Russia BIT.
214. Decision No. 9, para. 19.
215. See Alexandr Svetlicinii, *Arbitration of Investment Disputes: Experiences of the Republic of Moldova*, 11 Vindobona Journal of International Commercial Law and Arbitration, No. 1, 99–112 (2007).
216. See e.g., Michele Potesta, *Mr. Frank Charles Arif v. Republic of Moldova, ICSID Case No. ARB/11/23, Award, 8 April 2013 (Bernardo M. Cremades, Bernard Hanotiau, Rolf Knieper)*, 15 Journal of World Investment & Trade, 1013–1021 (2014); Joel Dahlquist, *The First Known Investment Treaty Emergency Arbitration: TSIKinvest LLC v The Republic of Moldova, SCC*

1.91 For example, in a 2013 ICSID case initiated by a French investor under the Moldova-France BIT, the arbitral tribunal examined a situation where the decisions of the administrative authorities were subsequently annulled by the courts in a lengthy litigation. The arbitral tribunal concluded that the inconsistency between the conduct of the administrative authorities that encouraged the investment and the conduct of judiciary were in breach of the legitimate expectations of the investor.[217] This conclusion was criticized in the academic literature for the unjustified extension of the state's liability for the lawful conduct of its national judiciary.[218]

1.92 In order to strengthen the legal representation of the State in international arbitration, the Government adopted a decision which introduced the public tender procedure for the procurement of legal representation services.[219] It stipulates that in international arbitration proceedings, the interests of the State should be always represented by an external legal counsel, which should be selected from amongst the domestic or foreign law firms. This procedure has been used for the appointment of legal counsel in several investment arbitration cases pending before the SCC.[220]

[B] List of BITs of the Republic of Moldova[221]

No.	Country	Signature	In Force	Arbitration Option
1	Albania	11.6.2004	23.12.2004	ICSID or UNCITRAL
2	Austria	5.6.2001	1.8.2002	ICSID or UNCITRAL
3	Azerbaijan	27.11.1997	28.1.1999	ICSID or UNCITRAL
4	Belarus	28.5.1999	19.11.1999	ICSID or UNCITRAL

Emergency Arbitration No EA 2014/053, 29 April 2014, 17 Journal of World Investment & Trade, 261–271 (2016); Martin Dietrich Brauch, *Energorynok had no ownership or control over energy-related economic activity; ECT case against Moldova dismissed*, Investment Treaty News (26 November 2015), https://www.iisd.org/itn/2015/11/26/energorynok-had-no-ownership-or-control-over-energy-related-economic-activity-ect-case-against-moldova-dismissed-state-enterprise-energorynok-ukraine-v-republic-of-moldova-scc-arbitration-v-2012-175/ (accessed 29 November 2016).

217. See ICSID Case No. ARB/11/23, award of 8 April 2013.
218. See Martins Paparinskis, *Franck Charles Arif v Republic of Moldova: Courts Behaving Nicely and What to Do About It*, ICSID Review, 1–7 (2016).
219. Government Decision No. 764 of 12 October 2012 on representation of the state in courts and before national and international arbitration tribunals, published in the Official Gazette No. 216–220 on 19 October 2012.
220. See Ministry of Justice, *Advertisement as to beginning of the selection procedure for a lawyer(s) and/or office(s) of lawyers that would be invited to undergo a legal expertise and, following that, to represent the Government of the Republic of Moldova's interests in the arbitral proceedings* (1 February 2012), http://www.justice.gov.md/print.php?l = ro&idc = 6&id = 1208 (accessed 29 November 2016).
221. The list of the bilateral treaties concluded by the Republic of Moldova, http://www.mfa.gov.md/img/docs/Lista-Tratate-Bilaterale_24_11_15.pdf (accessed 29 November 2016).

Chapter 6: Moldova §6.09[B]

No.	Country	Signature	In Force	Arbitration Option
5	Belgium-Luxembourg Economic Union	21.5.1996	20.4.2002	UNCITRAL or ICSID or ICC International Court of Arbitration (Paris) or Arbitration Institute of the SCC
6	Bosnia and Herzegovina	9.4.2003	9.6.2008	UNCITRAL or ICSID
7	Bulgaria	17.4.1996	12.6.1997	UNCITRAL or ICSID
8	China	6.11.1992	1.3.1995	ICSID
9	Croatia	5.12.2001	20.3.2007	ICSID or UNCITRAL or ICC International Court of Arbitration (Paris)
10	Cyprus	13.9.2007	27.3.2008	
11	Czech Republic	12.5.1999	21.6.2000	ICSID or UNCITRAL
12	Estonia	18.6.2010	21.4.2011	UNCITRAL or ICSID
13	Finland	25.8.1995	21.6.1997	UNCITRAL or ICSID
14	France	8.9.1997	3.11.1999	ICSID
15	Georgia	28.11.1998	25.2.1999	ICSID or UNCITRAL
16	Germany	28.2.1994	15.6.2006	ICSID
17	Greece	23.3.1998	27.2.2000	ICSID or UNCITRAL
18	Hungary	19.4.1995	16.8.1996	ICSID or UNCITRAL
19	Iran	30.5.1995	Not in force	
20	Israel	22.6.1997	16.3.1999	ICSID or ad hoc
21	Italy	19.9.1997	26.8.2001	UNCITRAL or ICSID
22	Kuwait	29.3.2002	6.4.2004	ICSID or ad hoc
23	Kyrgyzstan	7.11.2002	16.1.2004	ICSID or UNCITRAL
24	Latvia	22.9.1999	14.4.2000	ICSID or UNCITRAL
25	Lithuania	20.9.1999	29.5.2003	ICSID or UNCITRAL
26	Montenegro	20.6.2014	Not in force	
27	Netherlands	26.9.1995	1.5.1997	ICSID
28	Poland	15.11.1994	27.7.1995	ICC International Court of Arbitration (Paris) or ICSID
29	Qatar	10.12.2012	27.6.2013	ICSID or UNCITRAL
30	Romania	14.8.1992	15.6.1997	ICSID or UNCITRAL
31	Russian Federation	17.3.1998	18.7.2001	Arbitration Institute of the SCC or UNCITRAL
32	Slovakia	7.4.2008	15.11.2009	ICSID or UNCITRAL
33	Slovenia	10.4.2003	1.6.2004	
34	Spain	11.5.2006	17.1.2007	UNCITRAL or ICSID
35	Switzerland	30.11.1995	29.11.1996	ICSID
36	Tajikistan	5.11.2002	20.10.2003	

No.	Country	Signature	In Force	Arbitration Option
37	Turkey	14.2.1994	16.5.1997	ICSID or UNCITRAL or ICC International Court of Arbitration (Paris)
38	Ukraine	29.8.1995	27.5.1996	ICSID or UNCITRAL
39	United Kingdom	19.3.1996	30.7.1998	ICSID
40	United States of America	21.4.1993	26.12.1994	ICSID or UNCITRAL
41	Uzbekistan	21.11.1995	17.1.1997	ICSID

[C] List of Investor-State Disputes (Concluded and Pending)[222]

No.	Parties and Year of Commencement	Arbitration Award	Treaty	Outcome
1	*Franck Charles Arif v. Republic of Moldova* (2011)	ICSID Case No. ARB/11/23, Award of 8 April 2013 (Prof Bernardo Cremades, Prof Bernard Hanotiau, Prof Rolf Knieper)	Moldova-France BIT	Decided in favor of investor
2	*Iurii Bogdanov, Agurdino-Invest Ltd. and Agurdino-Chimia JSC v. Republic of Moldova* (2004)	SCC, Award of 22 September 2005 (Giuditta Cordero Moss)	Moldova-Russia BIT	Decided in favor of investor
3	*Yury Bogdanov v. Republic of Moldova* (2009)	SCC Case No. V114/2009, Award of 30 March 2010 (Bo G.H. Nilsson)	Moldova-Russia BIT	Decided in favor of State
4	*Yuri Bogdanov and Yulia Bogdanova v. Republic of Moldova* (2012)	SCC Case No. V091/2012, Award of 16 April 2013 (Bengt Sjövall)	Moldova-Russia BIT	Decided in favor of investor
5	*Grand Torg SRL v. Moldova* (2013)	SCC (award is not public)	Moldova-Russia BIT	Decided in favor of State

---

222. Adopted from Investment Treaty Arbitration, http://www.italaw.com/browse/treaty (accessed 29 November 2016).

No.	Parties and Year of Commencement	Arbitration Award	Treaty	Outcome
6	TSIKinvest LLC v. Republic of Moldova (2014)	SCC Emergency Arbitration No. EA 2014/053, Award of 29 April 2014 (Prof Kaj Hober)	Moldova-Russia BIT	Decided in favor of investor
7	Energoalians SARL v. Republic of Moldova (2010)	UNCITRAL ad hoc, Award of 23 October 2013 (Mikhail Savranski, Viktor Volcinski, Dominic Pellew)	Moldova-Ukraine BIT	Decided in favor of investor
8	Link-Trading Joint Stock Company v. Department for Customs Control of the Republic of Moldova (1999)	UNCITRAL ad hoc, Award of 18 April 2002 (Ion Buruiana, Jeffrey Hertzfeld, Ivan Zykin)	Moldova-USA BIT	Decided in favor of State
9	State Enterprise "Energorynok" (Ukraine) v. The Republic of Moldova (2012)	SCC Case No. V175/2012, Award of 29 January 2015 (Nancy B. Turck, Prof Rolf Knieper, Joseph Tirado)	Energy Charter Treaty	Decided in favor of State
10	Kompozit LLC v. Republic of Moldova	SCC Emergency Arbitration No. EA 2016/095, Award of 14 June 2016 (Jose Rossel)	Moldova-Russia BIT	Decided in favor of investor
11	Evrobalt LLC v. Republic of Moldova	SCC Emergency Arbitration No. EA 2016/082, Award of 30 May 2016 (Georgios Petrochilos)	Moldova-Russia BIT	Decided in favor of State

§6.10 REFORM PROPOSALS

1.93 The Moldovan regulation of the commercial arbitration can be criticized for the establishment of the dualist regulation of domestic and international commercial arbitration.[223] The introduction of the two sets of procedural rules could have a chilling effect on the development of arbitration in the jurisdiction, which is relatively unfamiliar with that method of ADR.[224] More recent reports on this matter call for the consolidation of the legislation in order to create a more coherent framework for commercial arbitration carried out under Moldovan law.[225] The Government proclaimed the development of the commercial arbitration as one of the priority directions in its Strategy for reforming the justice system in 2011–2016.[226] The Government has pledged to strengthen the system of ADR by consolidating the national legislation on commercial arbitration and by strengthening the legal framework for the recognition and enforcement of foreign arbitral awards. It remains to be seen how and when these objectives will be realized. At the same time, the ICAC statistics indicate a significant increase in the caseload starting from 2012, especially in domestic arbitration cases.[227]

1.94 When it comes to the role of the judiciary in the commercial arbitration, the Republic of Moldova has mixed experiences in this field. As far as the actions for setting aside the arbitral awards are concerned, until recently the judicial competences have been concentrated in the District Economic Court. However, pursuant to the above-mentioned justice system reform, the most recent reorganization of courts has led to the abolishment of specialized courts and attributed their competences to the courts of general jurisdiction. When it comes to the recognition and enforcement of arbitral awards (both foreign and domestic), the judicial competences have already been decentralized. While the experience of the Moldovan courts with the enforcement of foreign awards remains limited, there have been several high impact cases, which

---

223. Moldovan legal scholars have argued that arbitration rules should be included in the CCP in order to elevate the significant of this ADR method and to remedy the current repetitions and inconsistencies between the legal provisions of the CCP and specialized arbitration laws. See Iurie Mihalache, *Recunoașterea arbitrajului ca formă a justiției private în materie civilă și comercială*, 7 Revista Națională de Drept 69–71 (2014).
224. See Alexandr Svetlicinii, *New Rules for Commercial Arbitration in the Republic of Moldova: A Step Forward?* 20 European Business Law Review, No. 5, 767–777 (2009).
225. See Zinaida Guțu, *Consolidarea cadrului legal privind arbitrajul în Republica Moldova*, 24 (Chișinău 2012), http://justice.gov.md/public/files/file/studii/studiu_2_arbitraj12_02.pdf (accessed 29 November 2016).
226. See Law No. 231 of 25 November 2011 approving the Strategy for reform of the justice sector for 2011–2016, published in the Official Gazette No. 1–6 on 6 January 2012; Parliament Decision No. 6 of 16 February 2012 approving the Plan of actions for the implementation of the Strategy for reforming the justice sector in 2011–2016, published in the Official Gazette No. 109–112 on 5 June 2012.
227. See Cristina Martin, *Arbitration in Moldova: per aspera ad astra* (12 June 2015), http://aci.md/arbitration-in-moldova-per-aspera-ad-astra/ (accessed 29 November 2016).

raised criticisms about the lower courts' incompetence in the matters of the recognition and enforcement.[228]

Bibliography

Legislation

Law No. 691 of 27 August 1991 on Declaration of Independence of the Republic of Moldova, published in the Official Gazette No. 11 on 27 August 1991.

Law No. 514 of 6 July 1995 on judicial organization, re-published in the Official Gazette No. 15-17 on 22 January 2013.

Law No. 789 of 26 March 1996 on the Supreme Court of Justice, re-published in the Official Gazette No. 15-17 on 22 January 2013.

Law No. 1335 of 1 October 1997 on franchising, published in the Official Gazette No. 82-83 on 11 December 1997.

Law No. 595 of 24 September 1999 on international treaties of the Republic of Moldova, published in the Official Gazette No. 24-26 on 2 March 2000.

Code No. 985 of 18 April 2002, published in the Official Gazette No. 128-129 on 13 September 2002.

Code No. 1107 of 6 June 2002, published in the Official Gazette No. 82-86 on 22 June 2002.

Law No. 1260 of 19 July 2002 on legal profession, re-published in the Official Gazette No. 159 on 4 September 2010.

Law No. 015 of 13 March 2003 on consumer protection, re-published in the Official Gazette No. 176-181 on 21 October 2011.

Code No. 154 of 28 March 2003, published in the Official Gazette No. 159-162 on 29 July 2003.

Code No. 225 of 30 May 2003 on civil procedure, re-published in the Official Gazette No. 130-134 on 21 June 2013.

Code No. 122 of 14 March 2003 of criminal procedure, re-published in the Official Gazette No. 248-251 on 5 November 2013.

Code No. 443 of 24 December 2004 on enforcement, re-published in the Official Gazette No. 214-220 on 5 November 2010.

Law No. 59 of 28 April 2005 on leasing, published in the Official Gazette No. 92-94 on 8 July 2005.

Law No. 198 of 26 July 2007 on legal aid guaranteed by state, published in the Official Gazette No. 157-160 on 5 October 2007.

Law No. 23 of 22 February 2008 on arbitration, published in the Official Gazette No. 88-89 on 20 May 2008.

Law No. 24 of 22 February 2008 on international commercial arbitration, published in the Official Gazette No. 88-89 on 20 May 2008.

---

228. *See* Alexandru Mardari, Victoria Sanduta & Livia Mitrofan, *Foreign Arbitral Awards Exequatur in the Republic of Moldova: Risks and Benefits* (9–12 June 2015), http://www.ejtn.eu/Documents/Themis%20Luxembourg/Written_paper_Republic_of_Moldova_1.pdf (accessed 29 November 2016).

Law No. 179 of 10 July 2008 on public-private partnerships, published in the Official Gazette No. 165-166 on 2 September 2008.
Law No. 231 of 25 November 2011 on approval of the Strategy for reform of justice sector for 2011-2016, published in the Official Gazette No. 1-6 on 6 January 2012.
Law No. 256 of 9 December 2011 on abusive clauses in consumer contracts, published in the Official Gazette No. 38-41 on 24 February 2012.
Law No. 137 of 3 July 2015 on mediation, published in the Official Gazette No. 224-233 on 21 August 2015.
Law No. 76 of 21 April 2016 on reorganization of courts, published in the Official Gazette No. 184-192 on 1 July 2016.
Parliament Decision No. 1331 of 26 September 1997 on accession of the Republic of Moldova to the European Convention on International Commercial Arbitration, published in the Official Gazette No. 67 on 16 October 1997.
Parliament Decision No. 87 of 10 July 1998 on accession of the Republic of Moldova to the Convention on Recognition and Enforcement of Foreign Arbitral Awards, published in the Official Gazette No. 71 on 30 July 1998.
Parliament Decision No. 6 of 16 February 2012 on approval of the Plan of actions for the implementation of the Strategy for reform of justice sector for 2011–2016, published in the Official Gazette No. 109–112 on 5 June 2012.
Government Decision No. 764 of 12 October 2012 on representation of the state in courts and before national and international arbitration tribunals, published in the Official Gazette No. 216–220 on 19 October 2012.
Plenum of the Supreme Court of Justice, Decision No. 3 of 9 June 2014 on application by courts of certain provisions of the European Convention of Human Rights and Fundamental Freedoms.
Plenum of the Supreme Court of Justice of the Republic of Moldova, Decision No. 2 of 30 March 2015 on application by the courts of the legal provisions related to certain issues in the judicial proceedings where parties have concluded an arbitration agreement.
Plenum of the Supreme Court of Justice of the Republic of Moldova, Decision No. 9 of 9 December 2013 on judicial practice of applying legislation concerning recognition and enforcement of foreign judgments and foreign arbitral awards.
Plenum of the Supreme Court of Justice of the Republic of Moldova, Decision No. 2 of 25 April 2016 on modification and completion of the Decision No. 9 of 9 December 2013 on judicial practice of applying legislation concerning recognition and enforcement of foreign judgments and foreign arbitral awards.
Chamber of Commerce and Industry, Statute No. 69 of 19 December 2008 of the International Commercial Arbitration Court attached to the Chamber of Commerce and Industry of the Republic of Moldova, published in the Official Gazette No. 19-21 on 3 February 2009.
Chamber of Commerce and Industry, ICAC Regulation on domestic arbitration procedure, adopted by the Decision of 19 December 2008, published in the Official Gazette No. 19-21 on 3 February 2009.

Chamber of Commerce and Industry, ICAC Regulation on international commercial arbitration procedure, adopted by the Decision of 19 December 2008, published in the Official Gazette No. 19-21 on 3 February 2009.

Chamber of Commerce and Industry, ICAC Regulation on mediation procedure, adopted by the Decision of 19 December 2008, published in the Official Gazette No. 19-21 on 3 February 2009.

Literature

Gheorge Avornic, *Importanța disciplinei Arbitrajul comercial internațional pentru formarea competențelor profesionale ale specialiștilor în drept în condițiile economiei de piață*, 7 Revista Națională de Drept 14–17 (2014).

Aurel Băieșu, *Rolul arbitrajului comercial internațional în înfăptuirea justiției*, 7 Revista Națională de Drept 2–7 (2014).

Oleg Bontea, *Arbitrajul – mijloc jurisdictional de soluționare pe cale pașnică a diferendelor internaționale*, 2 Revista Națională de Drept 62 (2008).

Dorin Cimil, *Criteriile de calificare a clauzelor abusive*, 1 Revista Institutului Național de Justiție 32–40 (2013).

Nicolae Clima, *Interacțiunea instanțelor de judecată cu Arbitrajul*, 7 Revista Națională de Drept 18–23 (2014).

Joel Dahlquist, *The First Known Investment Treaty Emergency Arbitration: TSIKinvest LLC v The Republic of Moldova, SCC Emergency Arbitration No EA 2014/053, 29 April 2014*, 17 Journal of World Investment & Trade 261–271 (2016).

Ion Druță & Ana Borș, Contestarea hotărîrilor arbitrale. Încuviințarea executării silite a hotărîrilor arbitrale in Mihai Poalelungi, Elena Belei & Diana Sârcu (eds.) Manualul judecătorului pentru cauze civile, 300–318 (Supreme Court of Justice, 3rd ed., 2013).

Lilia Gribincea, *Soluționarea de către arbitrajul comercial internațional a litigiilor ce apar din contractele comerciale internaționale*, 7 Revista Națională de Drept 13 (2002).

Lilia Gribincea, *Importanța Arbitrajului comercial internațional*, 9 Revista Națională de Drept 20 (2005).

Lilia Gribincea, *Arbitrajul ad-hoc*, 7 Revista Națională de Drept 72–74 (2014).

Lilia Gribincea, *Overview of International Commercial Arbitration of the Republic of Moldova*, 8(48) Revista Științifică a Universității de Stat din Moldova 151–156 (2016).

Zinaida Guțu, *Studiul I Evaluarea cadrului legal național în materie de arbitraj* (Chișinău 2012), http://www.justice.gov.md/public/files/file/reforma_sectorul_justitiei/pilon5/Studiul_evaluarea_cadrului_legal_national_in_materile_de_ar bitraj-_UNDP-2012.pdf (accessed November 29, 2016).

Zinaida Guțu, *Studiul II Consolidarea cadrului legal privind arbitrajul în Republica Moldova* (Chișinău 2012), http://justice.gov.md/public/files/file/studii/studiu_2_arbitraj12_02.pdf (accessed November 29, 2016).

Zinaida Guțu, *Studiul III Reglementarea și aplicarea mecanismelor de recunoaștere și executare a hotăr ârilor arbitrale străine în Republica Moldova* (Chișinău 2012), http://www.justice.gov.md/public/files/file/reforma_sectorul_justitiei/pilon5/ Studiul_regelementarera_si_aplicarea_mecanismului_de_recunoastere_si_execu tare_a_hotaririi_arbitrale_straine_in_RM-UNDP_Project-2012.pdf (accessed November 29, 2016).

Mariana Harjevschi & Svetlana Andrițchi, *UPDATE: Performing Legal Research: the Moldovan Experience* (April 2012), http://www.nyulawglobal.org/globalex/ Moldova1.htm (accessed November 29, 2016).

Robert Krč, *Overview of the PPP System in Moldova*, 10 Eur. Procurement & Pub. Private Partnership L. Rev. 292–297 (2015).

Diana Lazăr, *Cadrul de reglementări privind procedura recunoașterii și executării sentințelor arbitrale străine în sistemul Convenției de la New York din 1958*, 7 Revista Națională de Drept 79–92 (2014).

Alexandru Mardari, Victoria Sanduta & Livia Mitrofan, *Foreign Arbitral Awards Exequatur in the Republic of Moldova: Risks and Benefits* (2015), http://www.ejtn.eu/Documents/Themis%20Luxembourg/Written_paper_Republic_of_Mol dova_1.pdf (accessed November 29, 2016).

Cristina Martin, *Arbitration in Moldova: per aspera ad astra* (June 12, 2015), http://aci.md/arbitration-in-moldova-per-aspera-ad-astra/ (accessed November 29, 2016).

Anatolie Mereuta, *Analysis Of The Institution For Recognition And Enforcement Of Foreign Judgments In Domestic And Community Legal System, In The Context Of Association Of Moldova To The European Union*, 6(1) Contemporary Legal Institutions 192–206 (2014).

Iurie Mihalache, *Recunoașterea arbitrajului ca formă a justiției private în materie civilă și comercială*, 7 Revista Națională de Drept 69–71 (2014).

Tatiana Novac, *Arbitrul și judecătorul. Diferențieri statuare*, 7 Revista Națională de Drept 75–78 (2014).

Natalia Osoianu, *Custom as a Source of International Private Law of the Republic of Moldova*, 1-2 Studii Juridice Universitare 151–158 (2011).

Radu Panțîru, *Aspecte deficitare în realizarea justiției identificate de către Curtea Europeană a Drepturilor Omului în hotărârile împotriva Republicii Moldova* in Mihai Poalelungi, Elena Belei & Diana Sârcu (eds.) *Manualul judecătorului pentru cauze civile*, 77–97 (Supreme Court of Justice, 3rd ed., 2013).

Martins Paparinskis, *Franck Charles Arif v Republic of Moldova: Courts Behaving Nicely and What to Do About It*, ICSID Review 1–7 (2016).

Mihai Poalelungi, *Precedentul judiciar* in Mihai Poalelungi, Elena Belei & Diana Sârcu (eds.) *Manualul judecătorului pentru cauze civile*, 98-110 (Supreme Court of Justice, 3rd ed., 2013).

Mihai Poalelungi & Diana Sârcu, *Jurisprudența Curții Europene a Drepturilor Omului* in Mihai Poalelungi, Elena Belei & Diana Sârcu (eds.) *Manualul judecătorului pentru cauze civile*, 69–76 (Supreme Court of Justice, 3rd ed., 2013).

Dumitru Postovan, *Dezvoltarea arbitrajului în Republica Moldova*, 7 Revista Națională de Drept 8–13 (2014).

Dumitru Postovan, *"Dreptul discreționar"* în activitatea arbitrajului, 7 Revista Națională de Drept 54-59 (2014).
Michele Potesta, *Mr. Frank Charles Arif v. Republic of Moldova, ICSID Case No. ARB/n/23, Award, 8 April 2013 (Bernardo M. Cremades, Bernard Hanotiau, Rolf Knieper)* 15 Journal of World Investment & Trade 1013-1021 (2014).
Andrei Smochină, *Încălcarea principiilor fundamentale ale legislației Republicii Moldova sau a bunelor moravuri – temei de desființare a hotărîrii arbitrale*, 7 Revista Națională de Drept 50-53 (2014).
Alexandr Svetlicinii, *New Rules for Commercial Arbitration in the Republic of Moldova: A Step Forward?*, 20(5) European Business Law Review 767-777 (2009).
Alexandr Svetlicinii, *New Rules for Commercial Arbitration in the Republic of Moldova: A Step Forward?* 2 Revista moldovenească de drept internațional și relații internaționale 52-58 (2009).
Alexandr Svetlicinii, *Enforcement of Foreign Arbitral Awards in the Republic of Moldova: Evolution of the Pro-Arbitration Policy in the Case Law of the Supreme Court of Justice*, 24(3) Journal of International Arbitration 249-264 (2007).
Alexandr Svetlicinii, *Enforcement of Foreign Arbitral Awards and Foreign Judgments in the Republic of Moldova*, 10 Wuhan University International Law Review 194-213 (2009).
Alexandr Svetlicinii, *Arbitration of Investment Disputes: Experiences of the Republic of Moldova*, 11(1) Vindobona Journal of International Commercial Law and Arbitration 99-112 (2007).
Alexandr Svetlicinii, *Republic of Moldova as a Respondent State in the European Court of Human Rights*, 2(2) Eastern European Human Rights Law Journal 8-15 (2005).
Dumitru Visternicean & Mihai Buruiana, *Procedura de recunoaștere și executare a hotărârilor judiciare și arbitrale străine* in Mihai Poalelungi, Elena Belei & Diana Sârcu (eds.) *Manualul judecătorului pentru cauze civile*, 255-300 (Supreme Court of Justice, 3rd ed., 2013).

Investment Arbitration Awards

UNCITRAL ad hoc arbitration *Link-Trading Joint Stock Company v. Department for Customs Control of the Republic of Moldova*, Award of 18 April 2002 (Ion Buruiana, Jeffrey Hertzfeld, Ivan Zykin).
SCC Case *Iurii Bogdanov, Agurdino-Invest Ltd. and Agurdino-Chimia JSC v. Republic of Moldova*, Award of 22 September 2005 (Giuditta Cordero Moss).
SCC Case No. V114/2009 *Yury Bogdanov v. Republic of Moldova*, Award of 30 March 2010 (Bo G.H. Nilsson).
ICSID Case No. ARB/11/23 *Franck Charles Arif v. Republic of Moldova*, Award of 8 April 2013 (Prof Bernardo Cremades, Prof Bernard Hanotiau, Prof Rolf Knieper).
SCC Case No. V091/2012 *Yuri Bogdanov and Yulia Bogdanova v. Republic of Moldova*, Award of 16 April 2013 (Bengt Sjövall).
UNCITRAL ad hoc arbitration *Energoalians SARL v. Republic of Moldova*, Award of 23 October 2013 (Mikhail Savranski, Viktor Volcinski, Dominic Pellew).

SCC Emergency Arbitration No. EA 2014/053 *TSIKinvest LLC v. Republic of Moldova*, Award of 29 April 2014 (Prof Kaj Hober).

SCC Case No. V175/2012 *State Enterprise "Energorynok" (Ukraine) v. The Republic of Moldova*, Award of 29 January 2015 (Nancy B. Turck, Prof Rolf Knieper, Joseph Tirado).

SCC Emergency Arbitration No. EA 2016/082 *Evrobalt LLC v. Republic of Moldova*, Award of 30 May 2016 (Georgios Petrochilos).

SCC Emergency Arbitration No. EA 2016/095 *Kompozit LLC v. Republic of Moldova*, Award of 14 June 2016 (Jose Rossel).

CHAPTER 7
Russia

Alexey Kostin & Dmitry Davydenko

List of Abbreviations

AC Law 2002	Federal Law on Arbitration Courts in the Russian Federation of 24 July 2002 No. 102-FZ
BIT	Bilateral Investment Treaty
CCI	Russian Chamber of Commerce and Industry
CIS	Commonwealth of Independent States
CPC	Commercial Procedure Code
ECT	Energy Charter Treaty
FCC	Federal Commercial Court
ICA Law	Russian Law 'On International Commercial Arbitration'
ICAC	International Commercial Arbitration Court at the Chamber of Commerce and Industry of the Russian Federation
ICC	International Chamber of Commerce
ICSID Convention	Convention on the Settlement of Investment Disputes between States and Nationals of other States, 1965, Washington
LCIA	London Court of International Arbitration
MAC	Maritime Arbitration Commission
PCA	Permanent Court of Arbitration
RAA	Association for the Promotion of Arbitration
SCC	Stockholm Chamber of Commerce
UN	United Nations
UNCITRAL	United Nations Commission on International Trade Law

UNCITRAL Model Law	UNCITRAL Model Law on International Commercial Arbitration
USSR	Union of Soviet Socialist Republics

§7.01 GENERAL INTRODUCTION

[A] Historical Development of the Legal System

1.1. Russian legal system belongs to Romano-Germanic legal family.[1] The early written collection of Russian law *Russkaya Pravda*[2] dates back to XI century A.D. It constitutes the principal source of Russian law of ancient time and is in large part based on customs.

1.2. After ascent of the centralized Moscow State the so-called *Sudebniki* (restatements of law) were issued in 1497 of 1550. The most important legal text however appeared later, in 1649: *Sobornoye ulozhenie*, a complex code of feudal law. This text was largely influenced by Statute of Great Lithuanian Principality 1588[3] which in its turn found its source in Western legal tradition and, further, in Roman law.

1.3. In the epoch of Russian empire legislative texts proliferated and large-scale attempts to systemize them resulted in a Restatement of law of Russian empire (1830)[4] and *Sudebnyie ustavy* (Judicial statutes) of 1864.[5] In Soviet period the law continued to develop but under a strong influence of official ideology of socialism and predominance of State. Same was true, in particular, to civil law. For instance, Article 5 of Civil Code of 1964 provided that 'Civil rights shall be protected by law, with exception to cases where they are exercised in contradiction to destination of such rights in a socialist society in the period of formation of communism'.[6]

---

1. Isaev M.A., on the history of Russian law see in particular: *History of Russian state and law*; manual (MGIMO (University) MFA RF, M.: Statut, 2012) (Исаев М.А. История Российского государства и права: учебник / МГИМО (Университет) МИД России. М.: Статут, 2012. 840 с.).
2. In more detail see e.g.: Diakonov M.A., Kivlitskiy E.A., *Russkaya Pravda, monument of ancient Russian law* // *Encyclopedic dictionary of Brokhaus and Efron*, vol. 82, 4 suppl. (SPb, 1890–1907). *(Дьяконов М.А., Кивлицкий Е.А.Русская Правда, памятник древнерусского права* // Энциклопедический словарь Брокгауза и Ефрона: в 86 т. (82 т. и 4 доп.). – СПб., 1890–1907).
3. Vladimirskiy-Budanov M.F., *Relations between Lithuanian Statute and Ulozhenie of tsar Alexey Mikhailovich*, (Collection of state knowledge, Saint Petersburg, 1877) *(Владимирский-Буданов М. Ф. Отношения между Литовским Статутом и Уложением царя Алексея Михайловича* // Сборник государственных знаний. Т. IV. СПб . 1877).
4. Speranskiy M.M., *Review of historical data on the Restatement of law* (Odessa, 1889) *(Сперанский М. М. Обозрение исторических сведений о Своде законов.* – Одесса, 1889).
5. The Great reform: to 150-years anniversary of Judicial Statutes: in two volumes, *volume I: Statute of Civil Procedure. (E.A. Borisova, Yustitsinform, 2014)* (Великая реформа: К 150-летию Судебных Уставов: В 2 т. Т. I: Устав гражданского судопроизводства (под ред. Е.А. Борисовой). – 'Юстицинформ', 2014 г.).
6. Civil Code of Russian Soviet Federal Socialist Republic (RSFSR) (Гражданский кодекс РСФСР) (approved by Supreme Soviet of RSFSR on 11 June 1964), 24 Supreme Soviet Bulletin 407 (1964) ('Ведомости ВС РСФСР') .

1.4. Since the breakdown of Soviet Union, Russian legal system has been subject to rapid, complex and sometimes contradictory transformation. Various attempts have been made to modernize it and to adapt it to needs of market economy. Although considerable progress has been made in this regard, Russian legal system still actively changes.

[B] The Legal Profession

1.5. Federal law 'On advocates' activity and the bar in Russian Federation'[7] governs legal profession. Advocates are independent legal counsel. They may not enter into labour agreements, save for academic, teaching and other creative activity, and may not be in civil service. Currently there are more than 70,000 advocates in Russia and their number is constantly increasing.

1.6. A chamber of advocates exists in each constituent entity of Russian Federation. They are united by the Federal Chamber of Advocates.[8] Advocates are subject to Code of professional ethics and enjoy certain privileges in connection with their professional activity such as professional secrecy and witness immunity.

1.7. To become advocate it is necessary to pass a qualifying examination. All advocates must constantly improve their qualification. Failure to duly carry out professional activity may result in disciplinary sanctions such as exclusion from status of advocates. These measures aim to ensure maintaining high quality of legal services.

[C] Sources of Arbitration Law

1.8. Russia is a federal state. Domestic arbitration is regulated by Federal Law 'On Arbitration (arbitral proceedings) in the Russian Federation' of 29 December 2015 No.382-FZ ('Arbitration law') which entered into force on 1 September 2016. This law also contains general provisions on organizing permanent arbitral institutions. Before that date domestic arbitration was governed by Federal Law of Russian Federation 'On Arbitration Courts in the Russian Federation' of 24 July 2002 No. 102-FZ.

1.9. International commercial arbitration is subject to Law 'On International Commercial Arbitration' ('the ICA Law') dated 7 July 1993 (as amended) primarily based on the UNCITRAL Model Law on International Commercial Arbitration (UNCITRAL Model Law) version 2006.

---

7. Official internet-portal of legal information, Federal law of 31 May 2002 No. 63-FZ, http://www.pravo.gov.ru (accessed 30 January 2017).
8. Federal Chamber of Advocates, http://www.fparf.ru/ (accessed 30 January 2017).

[D] International Legal Framework, Supremacy of International Law

1.10. Russia is a co-founder of the United Nations (UN) and the Hague Conference on Private International Law.[9] In particular, Russia is the State successor of the Soviet Union[10] and as such is Party to numerous treaties entered into by the latter. In particular, Russia as the State-continuer of the Union of Soviet Socialist Republics (USSR) is a Party to the New York Convention on Recognition and Enforcement of Foreign Arbitral Awards 1956 ('New York Convention').[11]

1.11. Russia is a signatory to the European Convention on International Commercial Arbitration, 1961 ('Geneva Convention'), ratified by USSR in 1963. It is Party to over 60 Bilateral Investment Treaties (BITs) (see Appendix II). Russia has signed the Energy Charter Treaty (ECT) in 1994[12] and applied it on temporary basis until it decided not to become its Party in 2009.[13]

1.12. Russia is also Party to the Agreement on Settlement of Commercial Disputes (Kyiv, 1992) and the Convention on legal aid and legal relations in civil, family and criminal cases (Minsk, 1993) concluded by several former-USSR Member States.

1.13. Under Article 15(4) of the Russian Constitution 'If an international treaty or agreement of the Russian Federation fixes other rules than those envisaged by law, the rules of the international agreement shall be applied.'[14] As follows from current position of Russian legislator and the Constitutional Court, the principle of supremacy of international law does not apply where Russian Constitution is concerned.[15]

---

9. Embassy of the Russian Federation in the Kingdom of the Netherlands, *Russian participation in the Hague Conference on Private International Law*, http://www.rusembassy.nl/en/Russian_Federation_and_Hague_conference_on_private_international_law.php (accessed 30 January 2017).
10. Russia circulated a diplomatic note to such effect on 13 January 1992. See 2–3 Diplomatic bulletin 34 (1992) (Дипломатический вестник). See also William Elliott Butler, *The Law of Treaties in Russia and the Commonwealth of Independent States: Text and Commentary*, 15–18 (Cambridge University Press, 2002).
11. The Decree was published in the 'USSR Supreme Soviet Gazette' of 15 August 1960, No. 32 (1016), Art. 304. The Convention entered into force for the USSR on 22 November 1960. The text of the Convention was officially published in the 'USSR Supreme Soviet Gazette' of 23 November 1960, No. 46 (1030), Art. 421. The text was published in Russian only. There were no other official publications of the Convention in the USSR or in the Russian Federation. Since 24 December 1991, following the dissolution of the USSR, the Russian Federation continued the Soviet Union's membership of the UN and undertook all of its rights and obligations with respect to the Convention.
12. Russian Government Decree of 16 December 1994 No. 1390.
13. Russian Government Instruction of 30 July 2009 No. 1055-p.
14. Translation from website of the Constitution of the Russian Federation, http://www.constitution.ru/en/10003000-02.htm (accessed 30 January 2017).
15. Thus, Federal Constitutional law dated 14 December 2015 No. 7-ФКЗ 'On amending Federal constitutional law "On the Constitutional Court of the Russian Federation"' in Art. 3(1) empowers the Constitutional Court to 'resolve the issues on the possibility of execution of a judgment of intergovernmental body for protection of human rights and freedoms.' As follows from Art. 26(3) of such law, the Constitutional Court may decide that execution of such judgment is impossible if it would derogate from Russian Constitution.

[E] Available Dispute Resolution Mechanisms

1.14. Common dispute resolution mechanisms in Russia include litigation, arbitration, negotiation and mediation. Mediation is governed by a special federal law[16] and relevant provisions in other legislation. Negotiation is an informal procedure. Commercial ('Arbitrazh') Procedure Code governs litigation between businesses.[17] Civil Procedure Code provides regulation of litigation involving an individual (as a non-entrepreneur).[18]

1.15. In Soviet Russia, domestic commercial arbitration practically did not exist. On the contrary, due to the state monopoly on foreign trade international commercial arbitration constituted a predominant vehicle of settlement of disputes. However, since the dissolution of the Soviet Union the situation has changed significantly. Commercial arbitration has become increasingly popular as a method of commercial dispute resolution in Russia.

1.16. For the said historical reasons the number of cases settled through arbitration is still very small in comparison with cases brought before state courts (the disputes heard by arbitral tribunals currently amount to less than 1% of those heard by state courts). However, Russian companies involved in foreign trade on a regular basis often consciously choose international arbitration for resolution of their disputes.

[F] Judicial System

1.17. There are two principal systems of courts. The first is the system of *arbitrazh* (i.e., state commercial) courts.[19] They hear cases on commercial or other economic matters. Such courts form a united federal system. The second system is the courts of general jurisdiction. They are competent to hear, *inter alia*, both civil (non-commercial) and criminal cases, as well as some other matters. In terms of territory, as a general rule competence lies with the court that has jurisdiction over the territory in

---

16. Federal Law «On Alternative Dispute Resolution Procedure Involving a Mediator (Mediation Procedure)» [Федеральный закон 'Об альтернативной процедуре урегулирования споров с участием посредника (процедуре медиации)'] of 27 July 2010 No 193-FZ entered into force on 1 January 2011 (as amended). «Собрание законодательства РФ», 2 August 2010, No. 31, 4162.
17. Commercial Procedure Code of the Russian Federation (Арбитражный процессуальный кодекс Российской Федерации) adopted in 2002 (as amended). Collection of laws of Russian Federation (Собрание законодательства Российской Федерации), 29 July 2002, No. 30, 3012.
18. Civil Procedure Code of the Russian Federation (Гражданский процессуальный кодекс Российской Федерации) adopted in 2002. Collection of laws of Russian Federation (Собрание законодательства Российской Федерации), 18 November 2002 (as amended), No. 46, 4532.
19. The *arbitrazh* courts have nothing in common with arbitral (non-state) tribunals, whether domestic or international. So the Russian term '*arbitrazh*' (i.e. 'arbitration') as applied in modern Russian law has two meanings: the first refers to arbitral (non-state) tribunals while the second refers to the state commercial courts. This is a legacy of the Soviet era, caused by the historic peculiarities of domestic regulation.

which the debtor resides/is registered or, if the debtor's place of residence/registration is not in Russia or is unknown, where his assets are located.

[G] Arbitration Institutions

1.18. In Russia by virtue of law each arbitral institution operates as a unit of a non-profit organization. Under new law to establish and/or operate an arbitral institution it is necessary to obtain permission from the Russian Government. Such non-profit organization needs to qualify to certain requirements, in particular, compliance of its rules with federal statute, its reputation and capability to ensure high level of organization and financial support.[20]

1.19. However, two oldest arbitral institutions are exempted from such necessity. One of them is International Commercial Arbitration Court at the Chamber of Commerce and Industry of the Russian Federation (ICAC)[21] founded in 1932.[22]

1.20. Before 2017 ICAC administered only international commercial disputes. For instance, 314 claims were filed at ICAC by companies from various countries in 2014, 316 claims in 2015 and about 270 in 2016.[23] Now ICAC has four separate sets of institutional rules: for international commercial,[24] domestic, corporate and sport disputes, as well as rules for administering ad hoc arbitrations. The lists of ICAC's arbitrators include renowned Russian and foreign legal practitioners, scholars and professors of law. ICAC has principal office in Moscow and subdivisions in three major Russian cities: Ufa, Irkutsk and Rostov-on-Don.

1.21. Another such arbitral body is Maritime Arbitration Commission ('MAC')[25] founded in 1930. MAC administers civil law disputes arising out of merchant shipping, both Russian and foreign. MAC's competence includes, in particular, navigation of seagoing vessels, inland vessels on international rivers and disputes relating to the international shipping by inland vessels.

---

20. Article 44 of Arbitration Law.
21. The International Commercial Court, http://ICAC.tpprf.ru/en/ (accessed 30 January 2017).
22. *See* in detail about ICAC: *International commercial arbitration: experience of national regulation. eighty years of MAC at CCI USSR/CCI RF. 1930–2010: collection of selected documents and analytical materials* / In two volumes. Compiler and academic editor A.I. Muranov. 2012. – M. Статут (Moscow: Statut, 2012) (Международный коммерческий арбитраж: Опыт отечественного регулирования/саморегулирования. 80 лет МКАС при ТПП РФ: 1932–2012: Сборник избранных научных, нормативных, архивных, аналитических и иных материалов. В двух томах. Сост. и науч. ред. А.И. Муранов. – М. Статут 2012).
23. The International Commercial Arbitration Court, Statistics, http://mkas.tpprf.ru/ru/Stat/page.php (accessed 30 January 2017).
24. *See* CIS Arbitration Forum, Dmitry Davydenko, New rules of the ICAC at the Russian Chamber of Commerce: what has changed for international disputes? http://www.cisarbitration.com/2017/02/02/russian-icac-revises-rules-for-international-disputes-whats-new/ (accessed 9 March 2017).
25. The Maritime Arbitration Commission, http://mac.tpprf.ru/ (accessed 30 January 2017).

[H] Sovereign Immunity and International Arbitration

1.22. Russia has signed the UN Convention on Jurisdictional Immunities of States and Their Property of 2004 on 1 December 2006[26] but has not ratified it. However, in November 2015 Russia has adopted a federal law 'On jurisdictional immunities of a foreign state and property of the foreign state in the Russian Federation' (effective from 1 January 2016) which to a large extent mirrors its provisions. The law allows Russian courts to limit state immunity of a foreign state on basis of reciprocity, that is, if such state limits Russian state immunity, e.g. seizes Russian state assets upon claims of private persons (e.g., while enforcing arbitral awards against Russia).[27]

1.23. The law establishes the doctrine of restrictive (functional) immunity. It grants immunity from adjudication for acts performed in the exercise of sovereign power, rather than in course of commercial activity. Before such law entered into effect the provisions on jurisdictional immunity which a foreign state enjoys 'as a holder of power' were specified only in procedural codes.[28]

1.24. Under prevailing Russian legal doctrine, a state can take part in arbitral proceedings provided that it expressly waived its right to claim sovereign immunity, e.g. in arbitration agreement.[29] However, such waiver per se cannot be construed to authorize arbitral tribunal to impose interim measures against state assets. In addition, an arbitration clause does not constitute a waiver of immunity from execution and therefore to enforce an arbitral award against state assets a specific express waiver to such effect is required.[30] The waiver from state immunity must be effected by duly authorized persons.[31]

1.25. In practice Russia has concluded, mostly in 1990s, a number of large loan agreements, long-term concession and investment agreements which included express consent to have the disputes heard by arbitral tribunal without reference to sovereign immunity. Furthermore, some agreements expressly specified such waiver. This

---

26. Instruction of Government of Russian Federation of 27 October 2006 No. 1487-p.
27. *See* in more detail: *CIS Arbitration Forum, Anastasia Rogozina, New Rules on Jurisdictional Immunities of States in Russian Courts*, http://www.cisarbitration.com/2015/11/13/new-rules-on-jurisdictional-immunities-of-states-in-russian-courts/ (accessed 30 January 2017).
28. In particular, Art. 251 'Jurisdictional Immunity' of Commercial Procedure Code (in force until 1 January 2016).
29. 'Arbitration agreement may contain also other terms, for example, ... waiver by the state-party to the arbitration agreement from its immunity', Nikoliukin S.V., Arbitration agreements and competence of international commercial arbitration. Issues of theory and practice (Jurisprudence, 2009). Placed in ConsultantPlus legal reference database (Николюкин С.В., *Арбитражные соглашения и компетенция международного коммерческого арбитража. Проблемы теории и практики*, (Юриспруденция, 2009).
30. Federal law of 3 November 2015 No. 297-Ф 3 'On jurisdictional immunities of a foreign state and property of the foreign state in Russian Federation', Art. 5(4): *'Consent of a foreign state to exercising by a Russian Federation court of jurisdiction in respect of a specific dispute shall not touch upon immunity of the foreign state regarding security measures and(or) immunity of the foreign state regarding enforcement of the judgment'.*
31. *'An arbitration agreement concluded by persons which do not wield authorities to waive jurisdictional immunity, signed in violation of established order, shall not be considered as a legal ground for waiver from state immunity'* (Resolution of High Commercial Court Presidium of 12 December 2005 No. 9982/05 in case No. A40-47191/04-60-485).

practice has been reflected in Federal law 'On production sharing agreements'[32] which stipulates that an agreement with foreign persons may provide for waiver of jurisdictional immunity, of immunity from interim measures and from enforcement of arbitral award.[33]

§7.02 THE ARBITRATION AGREEMENT

[A] Introduction

1.26. Russian arbitration legislation contains a general definition of an arbitration agreement,[34] which is literally borrowed from the UNCITRAL Model Law on International Commercial Arbitration. From different theories underlying the nature of arbitration agreement the Russian doctrine favours sui generis approach which makes it possible to take into account specific combination of substantive and procedural elements thereof.[35] The derogation effect of an arbitration agreement in Russia is identical to the relevant provisions of Article II of the New York Convention and Article 8 of the UNCITRAL Model Law.

[B] Validity of the Arbitration Agreement

[1] General Provisions

1.27. The arbitration legislation does not directly determine requisites of the validity of an arbitration agreement. Rather, they come from the provisions of the New York Convention and domestic legislation concerning setting aside or enforcement of arbitration awards. These provisions are practically identical for domestic and international arbitration.

[2] Requisites of the Valid Arbitration Agreement

1.28. The law does not expressly specify the requisites of a valid arbitration agreement, but only provides that it shall be concluded in written form.[36] It follows from

---

32. Article 23. State immunity: 'Agreements concluded with foreign citizens and foreign legal persons may provide in accordance with legislation of Russian Federation for waiver from jurisdictional immunity, from immunity from interim measures and from enforcement of... arbitral award' (Federal law of 30 December 1995 No. 225-ФЗ (as of 19 July 2011) 'On Production Sharing Agreements').
33. Boguslavskiy M.M., *International private law: Manuel* (5th ed., Jurist, 2005). Placed in ConsultantPlus legal reference database) (Богуславский М.М. Международное частное право: Учебник. 5-е изд., перераб. и доп. М.: Юристъ, 2005. 606 с. Размещено в справочной правовой системе «КонсультантПлюс»).
34. Article 7 of Arbitration Law and Art. 7 of ICA Law.
35. *See* e.g. Chuprunov I.S., Admissibility of awarding damages resulting from violation of arbitration or prorogation agreements, 6 Civil law Bulletin (2011), reproduced in Russian law database 'ConsultantPlus' (Чупрунов И.С. Допустимость взыскания убытков из нарушения арбитражного или пророгационного соглашений. 'Вестник гражданского права', 2011, No. 6).
36. Article 7(2) of Arbitration Law and Art. 7(2) of ICA Law.

general provisions of Russian Civil Code applicable to any transactions that the parties need to enjoy full legal capacity defined in accordance with their personal statute.[37]

1.29. As any other transaction, an arbitration agreement may be found invalid if concluded resulting from fraud, duress or other 'error of the will' of a party.[38] Apart from that, the arbitration agreement shall not trespass the scope of arbitrability prescribed by applicable law.[39]

[C] Concluding the Arbitration Agreement

1.30. As noted above, the laws both on domestic and international arbitration provide that the arbitration agreement shall be made in writing. The laws specify the requirements of the written form of an arbitration agreement. Interestingly, the Arbitration Law reproduces the replica of Article 7 of the UNCITRAL Model Law of 1993 while the ICA law relies on the updated version of the Model Law of 2006. The ICA law introduces, *inter alia*, modern general formula of written form: the requirement of writing '... is deemed complied with, if an arbitration agreement is concluded in a form that allows the recording of information contained in it or the access to such information for subsequent use'.[40]

1.31. Both Laws specify the way of concluding an arbitration agreement envisaged in the UNCITRAL Model Law, i.e. via exchange of statements of claim and defence in which claimant alleges existence of an arbitration agreement and respondent does not deny it. This mode of conclusion of an arbitration agreement cannot be regarded purely by conduct since the claimant needs to refer to some writing to prove the existence of the arbitration agreement. As the current ICAC's practices show this latter way to conclude a written arbitration agreement is used where there is a serious ambiguity of the arbitration clause and, respectively, for the purpose to make clear the actual will of the parties with respect to arbitration.[41]

[D] The Doctrine of Separability

1.32. This approach in Russian doctrine more often is labelled as 'autonomy' of an arbitration agreement. For historic reasons this concept had primarily been developed within the framework of international commercial arbitration. By the time of adoption

---

37. Article 171 'Invalidity of a Transaction Made by a Citizen who has been Declared Lacking Dispositive Capacity' and Art. 173 'Invalidity of a Transaction by a Legal Person in Contradiction to Purposes of its Activity' of Russian Civil Code.
38. Article 179 'Invalidity of a Transaction Made under the Influence of Fraud, Duress, Threat, of an Ill-Intentioned Agreement of the Representative of One Party with Another Party or the Confluence of Harsh Circumstances' of Russian Civil Code.
39. With regard to arbitrable and non-arbitrable disputes please *see* 2.6.
40. Article 7(3) of ICA Law.
41. *See* for example the summary of ICAC case No. 1/2003. M.G. Rosenberg, *From the practice of ICAC*, Supplement to the journal Law and economics, 40 (2004) (М.Г. Розенберг. «Из практики МКАС. Приложение к ежемесячному журналу «Право и экономика» за 2004 Г., с. 40).

of the ICA Law in 1993, the arbitration practices of ICAC had taken a fairly obvious stand in favour of the separate nature of arbitration clause with regard to the principal contract. The leading 'precedent' from this standpoint is deemed to be the Foreign Trade Arbitration Commission (predecessor of ICAC) at the USSR Chamber of Commerce award[42] issued in 1984 with regard to the dispute between a Foreign trade combine 'Soyuznefteexport' and a Bermuda company 'Jock Oil Ltd'.[43]

1.33. Therefore, it was perfectly natural to incorporate the appropriate provision into ICAC Rules in 1987 and later to adopt the UNCITRAL Model Law formula on separability without any deviations in 1993. The same principle applies to domestic arbitration.

[E] Invalidity of the Arbitration Agreement

1.34. Invalidity of an arbitration agreement would lead either to inability to enforce it before an arbitral tribunal or a state court. Invalid arbitration agreement could also lead to setting aside of the arbitration award or bar its enforcement in the courts of law. Procedural legislation in Russia does not provide for a possibility to directly file a claim with the state courts in order to invalidate an arbitration agreement.

[F] Arbitrability

[1] Disputes Capable of Settlement by Arbitration

1.35. As a general rule only civil law disputes are arbitrable, unless otherwise provided by a federal law. There is only one federal law expressly prohibiting arbitration – the Law on bankruptcy.[44] Laws on arbitration in effect since 1 September 2016 contain express provisions as to the arbitrability of corporate disputes under certain conditions.[45]

---

42. Award published (in Russian) in the journal 'International Commercial Arbitration', 2007, No. 2. P. 135. *See also* A.A. Kostin, *Brief recollections of a long arbitration*. 2 International Commercial Arbitration 130, 134 (2007) (А.А. Костин. Краткие воспоминания о долгом арбитражном процессе. Международный коммерческий арбитраж . 2007. № 2. С. 130–134).
43. The English version of the award was published in the *Yearbook of commercial arbitration*, pp. 92–110 (Vol. XVIII, 1993). It is worth noting that this award had been taken into consideration during the drafting procedure of the Arbitration Act (in force since 1996) in England. *See*: V.V. Veeder, *From Florence to London via Moscow and New Delhi: how and why arbitral ideas migrate*, 1 Review of international commercial arbitration 51, 73 (2013), (В.В. Видер. Из Флоренции в Лондон через Москву и Нью-Дели: как и почему мигрируют арбитражные идеи // Вестник международного коммерческого арбитража № 1, М., 2013, с.с. 51–73).
44. Article 33(3) of the Federal law on insolvency (bankruptcy) of 26 October 2002 No. 127-ФЗ (as amended on 29 December 2015): '*A case on bankruptcy may not be submitted to arbitration*'.
45. Article 7(7) of Arbitration Law and Art. 7(8) of the ICA Law. *See also* Art. 225.1(2–5) of the Commercial Procedure Code.

[2] Special Provisions on Consumer and Labour Disputes

1.36. Russian legislation on arbitration does not contain any specific rules with regard to consumer disputes. Collective labour disputes may be resolved by arbitration under the Labour Code. If the parties to such dispute do not reach settlement of a collective labour dispute by direct negotiations and through a mediator, they must promptly discuss its resolution by labour arbitration.

1.37. Parties together with the respective governmental body may establish a temporary labour arbitration body. Apart from that, a trilateral commission on settlement of social and labour relations (consisting of representatives of employees, employer and the government body) may found a permanent arbitration body and approve its rules. It hears disputes submitted by agreement of the parties to a collective labour dispute.

1.38. Labour arbitration body shall resolve the dispute within three to five days from its formation. Arbitration is obligatory and its award is binding on the parties regardless of their agreement in cases where the law prohibits strike.[46] In other cases arbitration is optional and the award is non-binding unless the parties agreed otherwise.

1.39. For instance, in Moscow there is a Labour arbitration court for resolution of collective labour disputes founded in 2002. Usually it assists in resolving issues which the parties to collective labour agreements fail to agree upon, as well as disputes arising out of non-fulfilment of such agreements.[47]

[G] Effect of the Arbitration Agreement on Third Parties

1.40. Normally the arbitration agreement creates rights and obligations as between the parties only. Nevertheless, their substitution may take place either by operation of law or by mutual consent of the parties. One such was universal succession unless the prospective successor lacks specific features required to enforce the arbitration agreement. The parties may agree to make the substitution with the consent of third parties. Also, the arbitration agreement remains valid with the assignment of a claim or transfer of the debt or claims.[48]

[H] Termination of the Arbitration Agreement

1.41. The arbitration legislation does not establish specific rules for termination of arbitration agreements. It seems that the termination per se can be accomplished only by mutual agreement of the parties. In this respect the definition of 'termination' is more attributable to the situations where state courts or arbitral tribunals terminate the

---

46. Labour Code of the Russian Federation of 30 December 2001 No. 197-FZ (as of 30 December 2015). Art. 404.
47. At http://trudsud.ru/ (accessed 9 March 2017).
48. Article 7(10) of Arbitration Law and Art. 7(11) of ICA Law.

proceedings having found that the arbitration agreement is null and void, inoperative or incapable of being performed.

[I] Drafting Arbitration Clauses

1.42. Practical experience shows that the best way of drafting arbitration agreements is reliance on the existent models of arbitration clauses or submission agreements prepared and recommended by solid arbitration institutions tailored to their rules. In case of a prospective ad hoc arbitration, United Nations Commission on International Trade Law (UNCITRAL) Arbitration Rules 2010 equipped by Model Clause prove to be very helpful.

1.43. For instance, ICAC has developed the following arbitration clause which is recommended for the incorporation into international and domestic contracts: 'Any dispute, controversy or claim which may arise out of or in connection with the present contract (agreement), or the execution, breach, termination or invalidity thereof, shall be settled by the International Commercial Arbitration Court at the Chamber of Commerce and Industry of the Russian Federation in accordance with its applicable rules and regulations'.[49]

1.44. This recommendatory clause actually does not differ from similar clauses proposed by other reputable arbitration centres such as, for instance, the Court of International Arbitration at the International Chamber of Commerce (ICC), London Court of International Arbitration (LCIA) or the Stockholm Chamber of Commerce (SCC) Arbitration Institute. The desire of the parties to 'improve' the aforementioned clauses without a serious legal analysis may lead to an opposite result.

1.45. Under new Russian arbitration law certain issues need to be expressly specified in the parties' agreement rather than by reference to rules of an arbitral institution. In particular, the parties to an agreement providing for arbitration under the rules of a permanent arbitral institution may also stipulate that the arbitral award is final for them. To be legally valid, such agreement needs to be expressly specified.[50] Also, if the parties wish to exclude the possibility of challenging an arbitrator at a state court, they need to expressly specify this in their agreement.[51]

§7.03 APPLICABLE LAW

[A] Introduction

1.46. It is not very common in Russian arbitration practice for the parties to strongly dispute over the applicable law. However, such disputes do arise sometimes. For instance, where the choice-of-law clause in a contract of sale provides for the

---

49. The International Arbitration Court, Arbitration Agreement, http://mkas.tpprf.ru/en/lawstatus /arbitration_agreement/ (accessed on 30 January 2017).
50. Article 40 of Arbitration Law and Art. 34(1) of ICA Law.
51. Article 13(3) of Arbitration Law and Art. 13(3) of ICA Law.

applicable 'Russian legislation', parties often argue whether this includes only Russian domestic legislative texts, or the UN Convention on International Sale of Goods 1980 should apply as well. Legal doctrine is not uniform in this regard.[52] The issue of applicable law sometimes becomes controversial in various aspects. However, certain basic principles do exist and will be reviewed below.

[B] **The Law Governing the Arbitration (*Lex Arbitri*)**

1.47. If the place of arbitration is in the territory of the Russian Federation, then it is governed by the Arbitration Law. International commercial arbitration is subject to rules of the ICA Law. Matters which this Law does not cover (e.g., establishment and operation of permanent arbitration institutions in Russia) are regulated in accordance with the Arbitration Law.

[C] **Party Autonomy on Choice of Law Issues**

1.48. Under Russian conflict-of-laws rules the parties to transnational disputes (disputes involving a foreign factor)[53] enjoy considerable autonomy concerning the law applicable to their legal relations. For instance, the parties to a contract may select the law to govern their contractual rights and duties.[54] Selection of applicable law made by parties after the conclusion of a contract shall have retroactive effect and it shall be deemed valid, without prejudice to the rights of third persons and to validity of the contract, starting from the time of its conclusion.

1.49. It is now possible to choose the law applied to the agreements on foundation of a legal person and to the agreements concerning exercise of the rights of legal person's shareholder (Article 1214 of the Russian Civil Code). However, the option of selecting the law applicable to corporate agreements involving foreign persons remains seriously restricted: most corporate law issues are governed by mandatory rules of Russian law which cannot be derogated by choice of a foreign law.[55]

---

52. V.A. Kabatov, *Application of the Vienna Convention 1980 as a law of a Contracting State* // To ten years of its application by Russia / Compiler M.G. Rosenberg. 2nd edition (Moscow, Statute, 2002). P. 32 (Кабатов В.А. Применение Венской конвенции 1980 г. в качестве права государства – ее участника // Венская конвенция ООН о договорах международной купли-продажи товаров. К 10-летию ее применения Россией. / Сост. М.Г. Розенберг. 2-е изд. М.: Статут, 2002. С. 32).M.G. Rosenberg, *International treaty and foreign law in practice of International Commercial Arbitration Court* (Moscow, 1998) (Розенберг М.Г. Международный договор и иностранное право в практике Международного коммерческого арбитражного суда. Москва. 1998). Р. 28.
53. Article 1186 of Russian Civil Code.
54. Article 1210 'Selection of Law by the Parties to a Contract' of Russian Civil Code.
55. *See* D. Davydenko, K. Bulkina for Max Planck Institute for Comparative and International Private Law, *Overview of Recent Amendments to Russian Private International Law*, 7–8, http://www.mpipriv.de/files/pdf4/2014_09_01.pdf (accessed 26 January 2016).

[D] Restrictions on Party Autonomy

[1] General Observations

1.50. Party autonomy in selecting the law applicable to their relations is not absolutely unlimited: the legal relations must necessarily be connected to more than one state. Besides, rules on public policy and rules of direct application (mandatory rules) also establish limits on the parties' autonomy, as explained below.

[2] Close Connection Test

1.51. Where at the time of selection of applicable law that the contract is actually connected with only one country. The parties' selection of the law of another country shall not affect the imperative norms of the country with which the contract is actually connected.[56] In practice Russian courts frequently find Russian law applicable to contractual relations applying the 'close connection' test. For example, High Commercial Court concluded that since the transaction between a Cypriot company and an Irish citizen involved transfer of shares of a Russian company issued in Russia, the underlying relations are closely connected with Russia and therefore Russian substantive law is applicable.[57]

[3] National Public Policy

1.52. A norm of foreign law applicable in accordance with the Russian conflict-of-laws rules in exceptional cases shall not be applied when the consequences of its application would manifestly contradict the foundations of the legal order (public policy) of the Russian Federation, taking into account the nature of relations complicated with a foreign element. In such a case, if necessary, the respective norm of Russian law shall apply.[58]

[4] Mandatory Rules of Municipal Law

1.53. The choice of law does not affect the operation of those mandatory norms of the legislation of the Russian Federation that regulate the respective relations regardless of the applicable law (rules of direct application).[59] Such special status of legal rules may be indicated in the mandatory norms themselves or may follow from their special

---

56. Article 1210 of Russian Civil Code. Choice of Law by Parties to a Contract.
57. Resolution of the Presidium of High Commercial Court of 25 February 2014 No. 14467/13 in case No. A65-27211/2011.
58. On various contexts in which the notion 'public policy' appears in Russian legislation see: D. Davydenko, A. Khizunova, *Implications and function of the public policy exception in foreign and Russian law*, 2 Law, 31–38 (2013) (Давыденко Д.Л., Хизунова А.Н., Значение и функции оговорки о публичном порядке в иностранном и российском праве // Закон. 2013. № 2. C. 31–38).
59. Article 1192 'Rules of direct application' of Russian Civil Code.

significance, e.g. for ensuring the rights and interests protected by a statute of participants in civil commerce.

1.54. In the application of the law of any country the court may take into account the imperative norms of the law of another country having a close connection with the relation, if according to the law of that country such norms have the status of rules of direct application. In this case, the court must consider the purpose and nature of such norms as well as the consequences of their application or non-application.

1.55. The scope of mandatory rules of Russian municipal law includes human rights law, currency control and export control regulations, tax law. The arbitrators also need to consider potentially applicable mandatory rules of municipal law,[60] especially those of the state where the arbitral award will likely be enforced (unless this will result in rendering an unjust award).[61]

1.56. In particular, Russian courts found invalid a provision in a joint venture agreement in telecommunication industry relying on the concept of 'rule of direct application'. The courts applied a legal rule that organizations under foreign control may not establish control over business entities strategically important to Russian national defence and state security.[62] The joint venture agreement with foreign entities provided for English applicable law. However, Russian courts found that the contractual provision which implied that foreign persons would obtain shareholders' control over a Russian strategic entity is contrary to a Russian rule of direct application and therefore invalid.[63]

[5] International Public Policy

1.57. International (transnational) public policy comprises crucial legal principles acknowledged by majority of countries of the world and specified in international instruments. International public policy fulfils two key functions: bans the application of national law and, since recent times, tends to formulate its own binding legal rules which international arbitrators must always take into account.[64]

---

60. A.V. Asoskov, *Conflict-of-laws regulation of contractual obligations*, (Infotropic Media, 2012) (Асосков А.В. Коллизионное регулирование договорных обязательств. М.: Инфотропик Медиа, 2012. 640 с.) Placed in ConsultantPlus legal reference database.
61. A.N. Zhiltsov, *Mandatory rules in international commercial arbitration*, 2 International commercial arbitration, 36 (2004) (Жильцов А.Н. Императивные нормы в международном коммерческом арбитраже // Международный коммерческий арбитраж. 2004. № 2. С. 36).
62. Article 2(2) of Federal law of 29 April 2008 No. 57-ФЗ 'On the order of foreign investments into business entities having strategic importance to ensuring national defense and state security'.
63. Information letter of Presidium of High Commercial Court of Russian Federation of 9 July 2013 No. 158 'Review of case practice of hearing by commercial courts of cases involving foreign persons'. para. 16.
64. A.V. Asoskov, *Conflict-of-laws regulation of contractual obligations*, (Infotropic Media, 2012). (Асосков А.В. Коллизионное регулирование договорных обязательств. М.: Инфотропик Медиа, 2012. 640 с.) Placed in ConsultantPlus legal reference database.

[E] **No Explicit Choice of Law**

[1]   Introduction

1.58. International arbitrators in Russia, in contrast to state judges, have a wide discretion in choice of applicable law where the parties have not agreed on the applicable law. Using such discretion, the arbitrators sometimes tend to derogate from application of certain national choice-of-law rules which they believe to be contrary to international standards and to take into account individual interests of the parties and substantive factors.[65] Unlike state judges, international arbitrators may rely on foreign conflict-of-laws rules which they consider applicable.[66] However, in most cases international arbitrators in Russia do rely on Russian conflict-of-laws rules because the latter tend to proclaim the principle of close connection which is the most rational to apply.[67]

[2]   Relevant Conflict of Law Rules

1.59. Russian Civil Code provides detailed regulation for determining applicable law where the parties did not choose one. In the absence of an agreement of the parties on the applicable law, the law of the country where the party that conducts the characteristic performance was located (has the place of residence or the principal place of activity) at the time of the conclusion of the contract. Characteristic performance means a performance which has the decisive significance for the content of the contract. However, if it follows from the law, from the terms or nature of the contract, or from facts of the case that the contract is more closely connected with another country, the law of such country shall be applicable instead.[68]

[F]   **The Law Governing the Arbitration Agreement**

1.60. The parties' autonomy on choice of law implies that they may choose the law governing the arbitration agreement. That said, arbitration agreement is considered to be a separate independent contractual provision, and therefore choice of law applicable to a contract does not as such cover the arbitration agreement contained therein. Validity of arbitration agreement is determined by the law applicable to the place of

---

65. A.V. Asoskov, *Ibid.*
66. Article 28 of the ICA Law. *See also* Section §7.03[E][2] below.
67. *Commentary to part three of Civil Code of Russian Federation (article-by-article)*, Commentary to Art. 1211, (A.L. Makovsky, E.A. Sukhanov. M., Lawyer 2002) (Комментарий к части третьей Гражданского кодекса Российской Федерации' (постатейный) (под ред. А.Л. Маковского, Е.А. Суханова). М. 'Юристъ', 2002. Комментарий к статье 1211). Placed in ConsultantPlus legal reference database.
68. Article 1211(9) 'The Law Applicable to a Contract in the Absence of Agreement of the Parties on the Choice of Law' of Russian Civil Code.

arbitration (*lex loci arbitri*), unless the parties expressly agreed upon the law applicable to the arbitration agreement.[69]

1.61. The issue of the law governing the arbitration agreement may become important in two different contexts. First, the commercial court leaves a statement of claim without consideration if a party timely invokes an arbitration agreement, unless such agreement is invalid, has lost effect or cannot be executed.[70] The conclusion on the validity, effect and possibility to execute an arbitration agreement should be based on the law governing the arbitration agreement.

1.62. Second, when the state court decides on enforcement of an arbitral award, it also needs to determine the law applicable to the arbitration agreement. When enforcing domestic award the Russian state court shall apply 'the law to which the parties have subjected [the arbitration agreement] or, failing any indication thereon, ... the law of the country where the award was made'.[71] If arbitration agreement is not valid under such law, this constitutes a ground for refusal to recognize and enforce the award.

1.63. When enforcing Russian domestic award the Russian state court shall always apply Russian law to the arbitration agreement.[72] Arbitration agreement therefore must comply with the law applicable to arbitral proceedings, Russian civil law, Russian procedural law as well as with applicable international treaties.[73]

§7.04 THE ARBITRATORS

[A] Appointment of Arbitrators

[1] Appointment of Arbitrators under Municipal Law

1.64. The rules for appointment of arbitrators in domestic and international arbitration are similar and based on the provisions of the UNCITRAL Model law (Article 11). The parties are free to agree upon the procedure of selecting the arbitrators, e.g. refer to rules of an arbitral institution, with limits specified below. If either of the parties fails to comply with such procedure, or the parties or arbitrators cannot reach an agreement, or the arbitral institution fails to fulfil any of its functions according to the procedure,

---

69. Kostin A.A., *Issues of determining law applicable to arbitration agreement in practice of continental Europe states and English courts*, 1 Law (2014) (Костин А.А. Вопросы определения права, применимого к арбитражному соглашению, в практике стран континентальной Европы и английских судов // 'Закон', 2014, No. 1). Placed in ConsultantPlus legal reference database.
70. Article 148(1)(5) 'Grounds for Leaving a Statement of Claim without Consideration'.
71. Article 36(1)(1) of the ICA Law.
72. Article 239(2)(1) of Commercial Procedure Code 'Grounds for the Refusal to Issue a Writ of Execution for the Enforcement of an Arbitral tribunal Award': 'the commercial court may refuse to issue a writ of execution if the party to arbitral proceedings, against which the arbitral tribunal award was adopted, presents evidence, that the arbitration agreement is invalid on the grounds, stipulated in federal law'.
73. Kurochkin S.A., *International commercial arbitration and arbitral proceedings*, (Infotropic Media 2013) (Курочкин С.А. 'Международный коммерческий арбитраж и третейское разбирательство'. М. 'Инфотропик Медиа', 2013). Placed in ConsultantPlus legal reference database.

each party may request the competent state court to appoint the arbitrator or take other appropriate measures according to such procedure.

1.65. The parties are free to agree upon another procedure to avoid deadlock in appointment of the arbitrators. If the parties have chosen the administration of arbitral proceedings by a permanent arbitral institution, they may expressly exclude the possibility of deciding such issues by the state court. In such case arbitration is deemed to be terminated and the parties are free to file the claim on the merits of the dispute at a competent state court.[74]

1.66. Where the parties have not reached an agreement on the procedure of selecting the arbitrators, if the dispute is to be heard by three arbitrators, each party chooses one arbitrator, and the two arbitrators jointly select the third one. In case of deadlock each party may request the competent state court[75] to appoint the arbitrator. If the dispute is to be heard by a single arbitrator, if the parties fail to reach an agreement to select one, each party may request the competent state court to appoint the arbitrator.[76]

1.67. In all cases arbitrators must be 25 years old or older, and with full legal capacity.[77] The following persons may not serve as arbitrators: those persons who have been found guilty of a crime unless they were freed from punishment (e.g., because the court found that their person or the crime is no more dangerous due to a change or circumstances)[78] or their previous conviction has been extinguished due to elapse of time period specified by law;[79] those persons whose authorities as a judge, an advocate, a notary, an investigator, a prosecutor or other law enforcement officer have been terminated by due legal procedure for a wrongdoing incompatible with their professional activity; those persons whose status specified by law excludes his/her appointment as arbitrator.[80]

[2] Appointment under Institutional Rules

1.68. Under ICAC rules[81] arbitrators shall be chosen or appointed from persons possessing the requisite specialized knowledge in settling disputes within the jurisdiction of ICAC. The arbitrators shall be impartial and independent in fulfilling their

---

74. Article 11(4) of Arbitration Law.
75. An exception applies as to ICAC and MAC – the authority which appoints arbitrators in case of deadlock is not a state court but instead, the President of the Chamber of Commerce and Industry of Russian Federation (Art. 11 of the Regulation on ICAC and Art. 10 of the Regulation on MAC (Annex I and II to the ICA Law)).
76. Article 11(3) of Arbitration Law.
77. A court may limit or exclude one's legal capacity on certain grounds specified by law (*see* Arts 29 and 30 of the Civil Code).
78. Article 80(1) of the Criminal Code.
79. Article 86 of the Criminal Code.
80. Article 11(9–11) of Arbitration Law.
81. Rules in force since 27 January 2017 were approved by Order No. 6 of the Chamber of Commerce and Industry of the Russian Federation, 11 January 2017. The Regulation on Organizational Bases of ICAC ('ICAC Regulation') contains provisions to the same effect.

duties. None of them shall be a representative of either party to the dispute.[82] To serve an ICAC arbitrator it is not necessary to be on the list of arbitrators. Nevertheless, the chairperson of the arbitral tribunal shall be from such list unless the parties agree otherwise.[83]

1.69. Where an arbitral tribunal is to be composed of three arbitrators to arbitrate between multiple claimants and multiple respondents, the multiple claimants and the multiple respondents shall each choose one arbitrator. Where the claimants or respondents have not reached an agreement, the respective Appointment Committee of ICAC[84] shall appoint her/him. It may also appoint an arbitrator for the other party as well. Where a case is examined by a sole arbitrator, the Appointment Committee shall appoint him/her from the List of Arbitrators.[85]

1.70. It is possible to appoint a reserve arbitrator as well. In urgent cases the Appointment Committee may authorize ICAC Chairperson to decide on the appointment of an arbitrator.

1.71. Similar provisions can be found, e.g., in the Rules of the Association for the Promotion of Arbitration (the 'RAA'),[86] but, in contrast the appointing authority (RAA Arbitrator Nominating Committee)[87] shall communicate to each of the parties an identical list containing at least three names to number them in the order of its preference and/or delete some of them. The appointing authority shall appoint the sole arbitrator from among the names approved on the lists returned to it in accordance with the order of preference indicated by the parties. Otherwise it may exercise its discretion in appointing the sole arbitrator.[88] In the same way the presiding arbitrator is appointed where the arbitrators' number shall be three and the two arbitrators have not agreed on the choice of the presiding arbitrator.[89]

[B]   **Qualifications of Arbitrators**

1.72. *Domestic arbitration*

1.73. Under Russian law the parties are free to agree upon the qualifications of arbitrators with the following exception. Unless the parties agreed otherwise, the sole arbitrator or, if the tribunal consists of multiple arbitrators, the chairman of the arbitral

---

82. Paragraph 3(1) of ICAC Regulation.
83. Paragraph 16(1 and 7) of ICAC Rules on arbitration of international commercial disputes in force since 27 January 2017 ('ICAC Rules').
84. Under para. 7 of ICAC Regulation, ICAC establishes four separate Appointment Committees: on international, domestic, corporate and sport disputes.
85. Paragraph 16(9) of ICAC Rules.
86. The Association for the Promotion of Arbitration, founded in April 2013 in Moscow, in accordance with its Regulations for arbitral proceedings (the 'RAA Rules') administers disputes under the UNCITRAL Arbitration Rules. It has also developed Online Arbitration Rules (http://arbitrations.ru/upload/medialibrary/21a/arbitraj_block_01_20_fin.pdf).
87. Article 2.2 of RAA Rules.
88. Article 8 of RAA Rules.
89. Article 9 of RAA Rules.

tribunal shall have a university degree in jurisprudence confirmed either by appropriate diploma issued in Russia or by foreign documents recognized in Russia. Parties may agree that the chairman of a tribunal consisting of multiple arbitrators needs not to have such degree, but only if one of the other arbitrators has such degree.[90]

1.74. *International arbitration*

1.75. Under Russian law the parties are free to agree upon qualifications of arbitrators. The ICA Law additionally provides that the appointing authority must consider all parties' preferences in relation to the qualification of arbitrators.

[C] Powers and Duties of Arbitrators

1.76. *Interim measures*

1.77. Unless otherwise agreed by the parties, the arbitral tribunal may, at the request of a party, grant such interim measures which it finds appropriate: that is, order the other parties to perform some actions or to refrain from them. The arbitral tribunal may require the party requesting an interim measure to provide appropriate security in connection with the measure.[91]

1.78. The parties may also agree that before the composition of the tribunal, the permanent arbitral institution may order a party to take security measures which such institution believes appropriate.[92] Notably, before the commencement of arbitral proceedings the Chairperson of ICAC and MAC, respectively, may upon a party's request grant interim measures which may target both parties and third persons.[93]

1.79. *Determination of rules of procedure*

1.80. Failing the parties' agreement on the procedure to be followed by the arbitral tribunal in conducting the proceedings, the arbitral tribunal may, subject to the provisions of the arbitration law, conduct the arbitration in such manner as it considers appropriate. The power conferred upon the arbitral tribunal includes the power to determine the admissibility, relevance, materiality and weight of any evidence.[94]

1.81. *Appointment of an expert*

1.82. Unless otherwise agreed by the parties, the arbitral tribunal may appoint one or more experts to report on specific issues; may require a party to give the expert any relevant information or to produce, or to provide access to, any relevant documents,

---

90. Article 11(6, 7) of Arbitration Law.
91. Article 17(1) of Arbitration Law, Art. 17 of the ICA Law.
92. Article 17 of Arbitration Law.
93. Article 6 of the Regulation on ICAC and Art. 4 of the Regulation on MAC (Annex I and II to the ICA Law).
94. Article 19 of Arbitration Law, Art. 19 of the ICA Law.

goods or other property for his inspection.[95] The arbitral tribunal has a duty to consider the parties' opinion as to the expert and the issues to be clarified by him/her.[96]

1.83. Furthermore, arbitral tribunal can request disclosure of certain documents or attendance of witnesses. If a party fails to comply with such request, the tribunal can issue an award based on the available evidence. In addition, an arbitral tribunal can ask a state court for assistance in obtaining the necessary evidence.[97]

[D] Challenges and Replacement of Arbitrators

[1] *Challenges under Municipal Law*

1.84. *Grounds for challenge*

1.85. An arbitrator may be challenged only if circumstances exist that give rise to justifiable doubts as to his or her impartiality or independence, or if he or she does not possess qualifications agreed to by the parties. A party may challenge an arbitrator appointed by him, or in whose appointment he has participated, only for reasons of which he becomes aware after the appointment has been made.[98]

1.86. The parties are free to agree on a procedure for challenging an arbitrator. Failing such agreement, a party who intends to challenge an arbitrator shall, within fifteen days after becoming aware of the constitution of the arbitral tribunal or after becoming aware of any circumstance giving rise to justifiable doubts as to their impartiality or independence, send a written statement of the reasons for the challenge to the arbitral tribunal. Unless the challenged arbitrator withdraws from his office or the other party agrees to the challenge, the arbitral tribunal shall decide on the challenge. If a challenge under any procedure is not successful, the challenging party may request, within thirty days after having received notice of the decision rejecting the challenge, the competent state court[99] to decide on the challenge, which decision shall be subject to no appeal; while such a request is pending, the arbitral tribunal, including the challenged arbitrator, may continue the arbitral proceedings and make an award.[100]

[2] *Challenges under Institutional Rules*

1.87. Under ICAC Rules (paragraph 17) an arbitrator may be challenged by either of the parties having justifiable doubts as to his/her impartiality or independence or if the

---

95. Article 29(1) (1 and 2) of Arbitration Law, Art. 26 of the ICA Law.
96. Article 29(2) of Arbitration Law.
97. Article 30 of Arbitration Law, Art. 27 of the ICA Law.
98. Article 12 of Arbitration Law, Art. 12 of the ICA Law.
99. An exception applies as to ICAC and MAC – the authority which decide on the challenge of arbitrators in such case is not a state court but instead, the President of the Chamber of Commerce and Industry of Russian Federation (Art. 6 of the Law 'On international commercial arbitration', Art. 11 of the Regulation on ICAC and Art. 10 of the Regulation on MAC (Annex I and II to the Law 'On international commercial arbitration')).
100. Article 13 of Arbitration Law, Art. 13 of the ICA Law.

arbitrator lacks the qualifications stipulated by an agreement between the parties or applicable law. If the challenged arbitrator does not withdraw voluntarily or if the other party does not agree to the challenge, the decision on the release of the arbitrator from his/her appointment shall be made by ICAC Appointment Committee.

[E] Compensation of Arbitrators

1.88. If a permanent arbitral institution administers the arbitration, its rules govern the arbitrator's fee.[101] The Chamber of Commerce and Industry of Russian Federation establishes the rates of arbitrators' fees of ICAC and MAC.[102]

1.89. In ad hoc arbitration, the parties' agreement determines the arbitrator's fee, and where no such agreement exists, the arbitral tribunal decides on it considering the amount at issue, the complexity of the dispute, the time spent and any other relevant circumstances.[103]

§7.05 JURISDICTION OF THE ARBITRAL TRIBUNAL

[A] Introduction

1.90. Issuing an award on the merits of a case belongs to the exclusive authority of the arbitral tribunal examining a particular case. For that purpose, an arbitration clause of a contract shall be treated as an agreement independent of the other terms of the contract. A decision by the arbitral tribunal that the contract is null shall not automatically entail the invalidity of the arbitration clause.[104]

[B] The Arbitrators' Determination of Their Jurisdiction

1.91. Russian legislation recognizes the concept of *kompetenz-kompetenz*. An arbitral tribunal can decide on its jurisdiction, including any objections relating to the existence or validity of the arbitration agreement.[105] In addition, arbitral tribunal has the power to issue a separate ruling in relation to its competence. If a party denies that the arbitral tribunal has jurisdiction, it must make a statement during the arbitral proceedings. The arbitral tribunal must consider this statement and if the tribunal finds that it does not have jurisdiction, it may not consider the dispute on its merits.

---

101. Article 22(3) of Arbitration Law.
102. Article 2 of the Regulation on ICAC and Art. 1 of the Regulation on MAC (Annex I and II to the Law 'On international commercial arbitration')).
103. Article 22(4) of Arbitration Law.
104. This principle was first established in the award in *All-Union Foreign Trade Association 'Soyuznefteexport' v. Joc Oil Limited*, ICAC case No. 109/1980, 9 July 1984, van den Berg (ed) in Yearbook Commercial Arbitration. – Kluwer Law International, 1993. - Vol. XVIII. 1993. pp. 92–110.
105. Article 16(1) ICA Law.

[C] Court Review of Arbitrators' Jurisdiction

1.92. If the arbitral tribunal finds that it has jurisdiction, any dissenting party can apply to the competent state court with a request to decide on the jurisdiction of the arbitral tribunal. Rulings of the arbitral tribunal negating its jurisdiction are not appealable. If an arbitration agreement of the parties provides for administration of a dispute by a permanent arbitration institution, the parties may by their express agreement exclude this possibility. While the request is pending, the arbitral tribunal can proceed and issue an award.[106]

[D] Institutional Rules

1.93. The parties may refer to arbitration under ICAC respective rules their disputes subject to an agreement in writing between them. Disputes may also fall under its jurisdiction by virtue of international treaties.[107]

1.94. The issue of ICAC jurisdiction in a particular case shall be decided by an arbitral tribunal examining the case. The arbitral tribunal may take a separate decision on the jurisdiction issue before the case is examined on its merits, or deal with this issue in an award on the merits of the dispute.[108]

1.95. Same as under ICAC Rules, under RAA Rules the arbitral tribunal may rule on a jurisdiction plea either as a preliminary question or in an award on the merits; the arbitral tribunal may continue the arbitral proceedings and make an award, notwithstanding any pending challenge to its jurisdiction before a court.[109]

§7.06 THE PROCEDURE BEFORE THE ARBITRAL TRIBUNAL

[A] Introduction

1.96. The arbitral tribunal may conduct the arbitral procedure, as it considers appropriate, but shall always comply with the mandatory statutory rules and principles of arbitration,[110] the applicable arbitration rules and any rules mutually agreed upon by the parties.

[B] General Principles of Municipal Judicial Procedure

1.97. According to the Constitution of Russian Federation, the judicial power shall be exercised by means of constitutional, civil, administrative and criminal proceedings.[111]

---

106. Article 16(3) of Arbitration Law, Art. 16(3) ICA Law.
107. Paragraph 2 of ICAC Regulation.
108. Paragraph 25(2) of ICAC Rules.
109. Article 23 of RAA Rules.
110. *See* Section §7.06[C] below.
111. Article 118 of the Constitution of Russian Federation.

All people shall be equal before the law and court.[112] Judges shall be independent and submit only to the Constitution and the federal law. If after considering a case, the court of law decides that an act of the state or other body contradicts the law, it shall pass an appropriate decision according to the law.[113]

1.98. Examination of cases in all courts shall be open. Examinations in camera shall be allowed only in cases envisaged by the federal law. Judicial proceedings shall be held on the basis of adversarial proceedings and equality of the parties. In cases fixed by the federal law justice shall be administered by a court of jury.[114] The courts shall be financed only from the federal budget and the possibility of the complete and independent administration of justice shall be ensured in keeping with the requirements of federal law.[115] These principles of municipal judicial procedure are further elaborated in the federal constitutional law on judicial system[116] and in the procedural codes.[117]

1.99. The Russian courts pay considerable attention to the compliance of the procedural documents and evidence presented by the parties with the formal requirements established by the legislation. In fact, it is possible that a party whose legal position is clearly advantageous may lose the case simply because the form, details etc. of the evidence (documents) provided by such party do not meet the formal requirements, or some mandatory annexes are not enclosed with the presented documents.

1.100. A classic example of such approach is case where the three judges of the RF High Commercial Court upheld the judgments of inferior courts denying the recognition and enforcement of a foreign court judgment. The judges argued that the apostille affixed on the foreign judgment did not comply with the requirements of the Hague Convention Abolishing the Requirement of Legalization for Foreign Public Documents dated 5 October 1961, i.e., it was not in a square form with the size 9 to 9 centimetres but a rectangular form with the size 10 to 11 centimetres.[118] An analogous reasoning of the RF High Commercial Court regarding the incorrect form of the apostille may be found in another case.[119]

1.101. The court proceeding in Russia is characterized by a wide accessibility, partly due to its cheapness (low stamp duties and legal costs, including the lawyers' fees). Nowadays any person in Russia is officially entitled to represent the interests of a defendant or a claimant in court, even if he/she does not have the relevant education or experience. The exceptions to this rule are the Constitutional Court where only an

---

112. Article 19 of the Constitution of Russian Federation.
113. Article 120 of the Constitution of Russian Federation.
114. Article 123 of the Constitution of Russian Federation.
115. Article 124 of the Constitution of Russian Federation.
116. Federal Constitutional law of 31 December 1996 No. 1-FKZ 'On judicial system of Russian Federation'.
117. *See also* para. 1.5.
118. The Ruling of the High Commercial Court of the Russian Federation dated 20 July 2009 No. BAC-7426/09 regarding the case No. A40-7480/08-68-127.
119. Case No. A56-32532/2010.

advocate or a person with an academic degree in law may be representatives, as well as the criminal proceeding.

1.102. In principle, the parties may go through all court instances (the first, the appellate, two cassation and the supervisory instances) just in six – eight months, which confirms that the Russian court proceedings are rather expeditious.

1.103. The courts do not specialize on specific areas of law. The only exception is the Court for Intellectual Rights which serves as the court of the first and the cassation instance for consideration of the disputes concerning protection of the intellectual rights.[120]

1.104. In issuing their judgments the Russian courts always take into consideration the positions of superior courts, even where such a position was formed after the court rendered the judgment which does not comply with such position.

[C] General Principles of Arbitration Procedure

1.105. The Arbitration Law provides that arbitration shall be based on the principles of independence and impartiality of arbitrators, party autonomy, adversarial proceedings and equal treatment of the parties.[121]

1.106. *Independence and impartiality of arbitrators*

1.107. A potential arbitrator must disclose to the parties all circumstances that may give rise to reasonable doubts concerning the arbitrator's impartiality and independence. After being appointed the arbitrator must inform the parties about any relevant circumstances, if he failed to do that before.[122]

1.108. The Rules on Impartiality and Independence of Arbitrators (the Rules on Impartiality)[123] approved by President of the Russian Chamber of Commerce and Industry (CCI) in 2010 are designed to serve as guidance for state judges, arbitrators and bodies administering arbitrations and competent to decide on termination of the arbitrators' mandate. They represent a simplified version of the similar document issued by International Bar Association. The Rules on Impartiality specify the circumstances in which the arbitrator must withdraw from his office or at least notify the parties. Otherwise, he/she may be challenged by a party.

1.109. Parties may agree upon the details of arbitral procedure at their discretion (though subject to mandatory provisions of the arbitration law).[124] The parties shall be

---

120. The Court for Intellectual Rights, http://ipc.arbitr.ru/ (accessed on 30 January 2017).
121. Article 18 of the Arbitration Law.
122. *See also* Section '[D] Challenges and replacement of arbitrators' above.
123. International Commercial Arbitration Court, documents, http://mkas.tpprf.ru/en/documents/ (accessed 30 January 2017).
124. Article 19(1) of the Arbitration Law, Art. 19(1) of the ICA law.

treated with equality and each party shall be given a full opportunity of presenting his case.[125]

1.110. *Confidentiality*

1.111. Unless the parties agreed otherwise, arbitral proceedings are confidential and the hearing is closed to public. The arbitrators and the staff of permanent arbitral institutions shall refrain from disclosing information, which they become aware of during arbitration unless the parties have given them consent to do so.[126] Furthermore, arbitrators enjoy the immunity from being summoned at court as witnesses with regard to information they have become aware of in the course of arbitration.[127]

[D] Commencing the Arbitral Proceedings

[1] Municipal Law

1.112. Unless the parties agreed otherwise, the arbitral proceedings in respect of a particular dispute start when the respondent receives a copy of the statement of claim.[128] The Claimant bears the burden of proof of the date of such receipt (by hand or by mail). This date may be crucial to decide which arbitration rules as applicable: unless the parties agree otherwise, rules in effect as of the date of commencing the arbitral proceedings apply.[129]

[2] Institutional Rules

1.113. Under ICAC Rules arbitral proceedings shall commence with the filing of a statement of claim with ICAC. The filing date of the statement of claim shall be the date on which it is delivered to ICAC, or where the statement of claim is sent by mail it shall be the date of the postmark of the post office where it has been mailed. If it was sent by courier service, it shall be the date of waybill.[130]

1.114. Under RAA Rules arbitral proceedings shall be deemed to commence on the date on which the notice of arbitration is received by the respondent.[131] Unlike a statement of claim, notice of arbitration should specify only a brief description of the claim (and an indication of the amount involved, if any).[132]

---

125. Article 19(1) of the Arbitration Law, Art. 18 of the ICA law.
126. Article 21(1, 2) of the Arbitration Law.
127. Article 21(3) of the Arbitration Law, Art. 56(5.2) of the Commercial Procedure Code (effective since 1 September 2016).
128. Article 23 of the Arbitration Law, Art. 21 of the ICA law.
129. Article 45(2)(3) of the Arbitration Law.
130. Paragraph 2(2) of ICAC Rules.
131. Article 3(2) of RAA Rules.
132. Article 3(3) of RAA Rules.

[E] Conduct of Arbitration

[1] Written Submissions

1.115. All statements, documents or other information supplied to the arbitral tribunal by one party shall be communicated to the other party. Also any expert report or document of evidentiary value on which the arbitral tribunal may rely in making its decision shall be communicated to the parties.[133] Unless the parties agreed otherwise, it is in the discretion of the arbitral tribunal whether to allow the parties to present post-hearing briefs.

[2] Evidence (Admissibility, Documentary Evidence)

1.116. Each party must prove the circumstances to which it refers in its claim or defence. Therefore, the parties must disclose to each other and to the arbitrator(s) all of the documents that can serve as evidence. The arbitral tribunal may request disclosure of certain additional documents.[134] If a party fails to comply with the arbitrator's request, the tribunal can issue an award based on the available evidence. In addition, an arbitral tribunal in proceedings administered by a permanent arbitration institution, or a party with the approval of such arbitral tribunal can ask a state court for assistance in obtaining the necessary evidence.[135]

[3] Witness and Experts Testimony

1.117. Parties may refer to witness written testimony and expert reports to support their statements. The arbitral tribunal is free to decide on the admissibility and evidentiary weight of such testimony or report. Unless otherwise agreed by the parties, an arbitral tribunal may appoint one or more experts to report on specific issues, require a party to give the expert any relevant information, documents or other property for inspection. If a party so requests or the arbitral tribunal considers it necessary, the expert shall, after delivery of his report, participate in a hearing where the parties have the opportunity to put questions to him.[136]

[F] Hearings

1.118. Unless the parties agreed otherwise, the arbitral tribunal decides whether to hold oral hearings for the presentation of evidence or for oral argument, or whether the proceedings shall be conducted on the basis of written materials. The parties shall be given sufficient advance notice of any hearing and of any meeting of the arbitral

---

133. Article 27(3) of the Arbitration Law, Art. 24(3) of the ICA law.
134. Article 26 of the Arbitration Law.
135. Article 30 of the Arbitration Law, Art. 27 of the ICA law.
136. Article 29(3) of the Arbitration Law, Art. 26 of the ICA law.

tribunal for the purposes of inspection of goods, other property or documents.[137] If the parties agreed so, hearing may be conducted by videoconference communication.[138]

1.119. A record of the hearing of a case shall be drawn up unless the parties agree otherwise.[139] The arbitral tribunal may reopen the hearings at any time before the award is made.[140] In practice usually arbitral proceedings include at least one hearing which may last from two hours to two or three days depending on the complexity of the dispute.

§7.07 THE ARBITRAL AWARD

[A] Introduction

1.120. Typically the arbitral proceedings terminate with the rendering of a final award.[141] The arbitral tribunal endowed with appropriate jurisdiction can award any legitimate remedy requested by a party, including damages, costs, interest and declarations (e.g., declare a contract invalid). The type of remedy depends on the requesting party's preferences. An arbitral tribunal cannot award an injunction as a final remedy but, subject to this, remedies granted by arbitral tribunals do not differ significantly from the remedies awarded by state courts.

[B] Deliberation and Voting

1.121. Under Russian law, decision shall be issued by a sole arbitrator or by a majority vote. However, matters of procedure may be decided by a presiding arbitrator, if so authorized by the parties or all the other arbitrators.[142] When the arbitral tribunal finds that all the circumstances related to the dispute have been clarified in sufficient detail, it shall proceed to make an award. Usually arbitrators start deliberating after oral hearing. That said, the law and applicable rules normally do not oblige the arbitral tribunal to announce its award to the parties immediately after the hearing or at the same day: instead they can take time to deliberate on it.

1.122. When there is more than one arbitrator, an award shall be normally made by a majority vote of the arbitrators.[143] Under ICAC Rules if an award cannot be made by a majority vote (e.g., each arbitrator has a different opinion as to how to resolve the case), it shall be made by the presiding arbitrator. Any arbitrator disagreeing with the

---

137. Article 27(1, 2) of the Arbitration Law, Art. 24(1, 2) of the ICA law.
138. This is expressly specified in Art. 27(4) of the Arbitration Law.
139. Article 27(5) of the Arbitration Law.
140. Some institutional arbitration rules, e.g. para. 22(3) of MAC Rules, Art. 31(2) of RAA Rules provide for such effect.
141. The term 'award' in Russian practice normally means a decision on the merits.
142. Article 32 of the Arbitration Law, Art. 29 of the law on international commercial arbitration.
143. Paragraph 36(3) of ICAC Rules, Art. 33(1) of RAA Rules.

award made may express in writing his/her dissenting opinion, which shall be attached to the award.[144]

1.123. Under MAC Rules, unless the parties agreed otherwise, the case is usually heard by two arbitrators. They need to find consensus as to how the dispute must be resolved. Only where they fail to reach such agreement, they shall choose a third arbitrator as chairman of the tribunal.[145] Then the award should be made unanimously or by a majority vote. If this proves impossible, then it shall be made by the presiding arbitrator, whereas arbitrator disagreeing with the award may express in writing his/her dissenting opinion.[146]

[C] Different Kinds of Awards

1.124. *Separate awards*

1.125. Russian legislation does not expressly establish any specific rules for separate awards. However, in practice arbitrators do render such awards. ICAC Rules expressly provide in paragraph 38 that the arbitral tribunal may make separate awards on individual issues or a part of the claims. As explained in the commentary to the similar provision of previous ICAC Rules, the possibility of rendering a separate award implies awards on separate issues on the merits, rather than on procedural issues, therefore they sometimes are labelled as *partial awards*.[147]

1.126. In contrast, RAA Rules allow arbitrators to make separate awards 'on different issues at different times'.[148] A separate award shall be subject to the respective provisions of the Rules on content of arbitral awards.[149] A separate award should be distinguished from a separate decision on the jurisdiction issue the arbitral tribunal may take before the case is examined on its merits.[150]

1.127. *Interim awards*

1.128. Unless the parties agree otherwise, the arbitral tribunal may, at the request of a party, order the other party to take such interim measures of protection in respect of the subject matter of the dispute as it considers appropriate.[151] Usually such measures include orders to present evidence unavailable to the other party, or to keep such evidence untouched and unharmed; ensure the safety of the goods in dispute; measures to ensure subsequent enforcement of the award, e.g. seizure of respondent's

---

144. Paragraph 36(3) of ICAC Rules.
145. Paragraph 15(7) of the Maritime Arbitration Commission Rules.
146. Paragraph 33(3) of the Maritime Arbitration Commission Rules.
147. *Rules of the ICAC; academic and practical commentary*, 190-191 (A.S. Komarov, Infotropic Media 2012) (Регламент Международного коммерческого арбитражного суда при Торгово-промышленной палате Российской Федерации: науч.-практ. коммент. / Под общ. ред. А.С. Комарова. М.: Инфотропик Медиа, 2012. С. 190-191).
148. Article 34(1) of RAA Rules.
149. Paragraph 38(2) of ICAC Rules.
150. Paragraph 25(2) of ICAC Rules.
151. Paragraph 34 of ICAC Rules; also as follows from Art. 26 of RAA Rules.

assets, injunction to move them outside the jurisdiction.[152] It should be noted, however, that under Russian law interim awards remain unenforceable by state courts (*see* section §7.09[B][2] below).

1.129. *Consent awards*

1.130. If, in the course of the arbitral proceedings, the parties settle their dispute, the arbitral tribunal may, at the request of the parties, record such settlement in the form of an award on agreed terms ('consent award'). Such award shall be subject to the respective provisions of the Rules on content of arbitral awards.[153]

1.131. The settlement terms must comply with mandatory rules of applicable law. For instance, in ICAC case No. 44/2003 (award entered on 3 November 2003) the tribunal explained its obligation to first decide on its competence to hear the dispute and establish the applicable law, and then to check whether the settlement agreement is in line with such law.[154]

[D] Interest and Costs

1.132. *Interest*

1.133. Apart from the principal amount of debt, the claimant may claim interest as of a particular date. Where interest continues to accrue, the claimant shall indicate the amount accruing on the filing date of the claim.[155] The right to claim interest and the interest rate depend on the parties' agreement and applicable substantive law.[156]

1.134. Russian case law takes the position that where a party applies to state court to recover interest on the amount of arbitral award, such interest accrues only starting from the date when the court ruling on the award enforcement enters into force, rather than from the date of arbitral award.[157] The English High Court of Justice in case *Yukos*

---

152. Nikoliukin S.V., *Measures to secure a claim in international commercial arbitration*, six Commercial court of Moscow city Bulletin, (2009). Placed in ConsultantPlus legal reference database (Николюкин С.В. Меры по обеспечению иска в международном коммерческом арбитраже // 'Вестник Арбитражного суда города Москвы', 2009, № 6).
153. *See* in detail: Kryvoi Yaraslau, Davydenko Dmitry, *Consent Awards in International Arbitration: From Settlement to Enforcement*, 40 Brooklyn Journal of International Law 827–868 (7 November 2015), http://ssrn.com/abstract = 2580572 (accessed 29 January 2016).
154. Excerpt from the award reproduced in Russian language in the legal reference database ConsultantPlus.
155. Paragraph 4(1)(a) of ICAC Rules.
156. The applicable provision in Russian law is Art. 395 of the Civil Code 'Liability for Nonperformance of a Monetary Obligation'.
157. Resolution of Presidium of High Commercial Court of Russian Federation of 8 June 2010 No. 904/10 in case No. A40-33259/09-39-283, 10 Bulletin of High Commercial Court of Russian Federation (October 2010).

Capital SARL v. OJSC Rosneft Oil Company [2014] EWHC 2188 (Comm)[158] *also* invoked and relied upon this position.

1.135. *Costs*

1.136. As a general rule, the unsuccessful party (parties) bears the costs of the arbitration.[159] Such costs include, in particular, arbitration fee. Permanent arbitration courts establish their own fee schedules, which form the basis of the calculation of the fees by the arbitral tribunal. The fee may depend on the amount of the claim; the complexity of the dispute; time spent by the arbitrators; other relevant circumstances.[160]

1.137. The parties in an ad hoc arbitration can agree on the fees in their agreement. In the absence of agreement, the tribunal determines the fees on the basis of the above criteria.

1.138. Unless the parties have agreed otherwise, the arbitration fee shall be charged to the party against which the award is made. If a claim is granted in part, the arbitration fee shall be charged to the respondent in proportion to the amount of the granted claims.[161] The successful party may request the reasonable expenses incurred by him in the course of the arbitral proceedings, in particular, the expenses made to protect his interests through legal representatives, to be paid by the other party.[162]

1.139. However, the arbitral tribunal may, taking into account the circumstances of a particular case, order a different apportionment of the arbitration costs. In particular, under ICAC Rules, it may order one party to reimburse any additional expenses incurred by the other party through inappropriate or bad faith acts of such party (its representative), including acts causing unjustified delay in the arbitral proceedings.[163]

[E] Effects of the Award

[1] Execution

1.140. The parties by entering into arbitration agreement assume the duty to execute the arbitral award voluntarily[164] within the period of time fixed in the award. If the award does not specify such period, it shall be implemented immediately.[165] The

---

158. British and Irish Legal Information Institute, *Yukos Capital SARL v. OJSC Rosneft Oil Company [2014] EWHC 2188 (Comm) (03 July 2014)*, paras 43-49, http://www.bailii.org/ew/cases/EWHC/Comm/2014/2188.html (accessed 30 January 2017).
159. Article 22(5) of the Arbitration Law.
160. Article 22(4) of the Arbitration Law.
161. Article 22(5) of the Arbitration Law; para. 8 of the Schedule of arbitration fees and costs (appendix to ICAC Rules).
162. Article 22(6) of the Arbitration Law; para. 11 of the Schedule of arbitration fees and costs (appendix to ICAC Rules).
163. Paragraph 26(2) of ICAC Rules, para. 12 of the Schedule of arbitration fees and costs (appendix to ICAC Rules).
164. Article 22(6) of the Arbitration Law.
165. Paragraph 42(2) of ICAC Rules.

arbitral award cannot be reviewed on the merits. The arbitral tribunal and the parties have a duty to make the best efforts to ensure it is legally enforceable.[166]

[2] Res Judicata and Lis Pendens

1.141. An award becomes final and binding from the date thereof.[167] It constitutes res judicata for the parties, i.e. they become bound by its terms and may not file again the same claim on the matters covered by the award.[168] A claim submitted to a state court shall be rejected without consideration where an arbitral proceeding on the same claim is pending.[169]

[F] Correction and Interpretation of the Award

[1] Municipal Law

1.142. A party, with notice to the other party, may request the arbitral tribunal to correct in the award any errors in computation, any clerical or typographical errors or any errors of similar nature within thirty days of receipt of the award, unless another period of time has been agreed upon by the parties. The arbitral tribunal may also correct any such error of the type on its own initiative within thirty days of the date of the award.

1.143. Within the same period thirty days of receipt of the award, if so agreed by the parties, a party, with notice to the other party, may request the arbitral tribunal to give an interpretation of a specific point or part of the award. If the arbitral tribunal considers the request to correct/interpret the award to be justified, it shall make the correction or give the interpretation within thirty days of receipt of the request. The interpretation shall form part of the award.[170]

[2] Institutional Rules

1.144. Under ICAC Rules either party may, with notice to the other party, within a reasonable period of time after receiving the award, request the arbitral tribunal to

---

166. Article 38 of the Arbitration Law.
167. Paragraph 42(1) of ICAC Rules.
168. For example see Art. 150(1)(3) 'Grounds for the Termination of Proceedings' of the Commercial Procedure Code: 'The commercial court terminates proceedings, if it establishes that there exists an award of an arbitral tribunal rendered in the dispute between the same persons, on the same subject matter and on the same grounds, with the exception of cases, where the commercial court refuses to issue a writ of execution for the enforcement of the arbitral award'.
169. For example see Art. 148(1)(1) 'Grounds for Leaving a Statement of Claim without Consideration' of the Commercial Procedure Code: 'The commercial court leaves a statement of claim without consideration if, after its acceptance for judicial proceedings, it establishes that there is a case on a dispute between the same persons, on the same subject matter and on the same grounds under consideration of ... an arbitral tribunal'.
170. Article 37 of the Arbitration Law, Art. 33(1, 2) of the law on international commercial arbitration.

correct any computational, clerical or typographical errors, or other errors of similar nature. If the arbitral tribunal considers the request to be justified, it shall make relevant corrections within thirty days after receipt of the request.

1.145. The arbitral tribunal may also make such corrections on its own initiative within thirty days after the date of delivery of the award to the parties. If agreed between the parties, either of them may, by notice to the other party, within thirty days after receipt of the award, request the arbitral tribunal to give an interpretation of a particular point or part of the award.

1.146. If the arbitral tribunal considers the request to be justified, it shall give the required interpretation within thirty days after receipt of the request.[171] RAA Rules provide to the same effect, with exception that the interpretation shall be given in writing within forty-five days after the receipt of the request.[172]

§7.08 SETTING ASIDE THE AWARD

[A] Introduction

1.147. Unlike state court judgments, arbitral awards cannot be appealed but can be challenged in Russian state courts (either in the courts of general jurisdiction or commercial courts). Both international and domestic arbitral awards may be challenged by any of the parties or by any other person whose rights and duties are concerned by the arbitral award.[173] State courts while considering applications on setting the awards aside may not review the case on the merits.[174]

[B] Invalid Awards

1.148. To become valid an arbitral award needs to be signed by the sole arbitrator or, if the arbitral tribunal consists of more than one arbitrator, by all or the majority of

---

171. Paragraph 41 of ICAC Rules.
172. Articles 37 and 38 of RAA Rules.
173. Article 230(2) of the Commercial Procedure Code (as of 1 September 2016).
174. Strelov I.M., *Interaction between commercial and arbitration courts*, 4 Bulletin of High Commercial Court of Russian Federation 112 (2005): '*[Commercial Procedure Code] does not provide for possibility to appeal the arbitral award in a commercial court, whereas the rules on setting such awards aside establish the order which implies a formally legal control rather than review of the award on the merits. This constitutes a guarantee of "non-intervention" into activity of arbitration court and at the same time a guarantee of protection of the parties of arbitral proceedings from possible abuses*'. (Стрелов И.М., *Взаимодействие арбитражных и третейских судов*, Вестник BAC, No. 4, 112, (2005)). See also: '*The difference of challenging an arbitral award from traditional appeal consists of the following: while considering a case on application on setting aside an arbitral award the commercial court may not review it on the merits: it shall only establish circumstances which form ground for refusal to recognize the results of activity of the arbitral tribunal...*' – Practice of application of Commercial Procedure Code of Russian Federation (2nd edition revised and updated), (I.V. Reshetnikova, Yurait, 2012). Placed in ConsultantPlus legal reference database. (Практика применения Арбитражного процессуального кодекса Российской Федерации (2-еиздание, переработанное и дополненное) Отв. ред. И.В. Решетникова. "Юрайт", 2012. Размещено в СПС «КонсультантПлюс».

arbitrators (in the latter case it must specify the reason why other arbitrators' signatures are missing).[175]

1.149. An award must be dated and specify the place of arbitration, the arbitral tribunal and the order of its formation, the parties and their places of location, the competence of the arbitral tribunal, the parties claims/objections and motions, facts of the case, evidence and legal rules underlying the award, decision to sustain or reject the claim in full or in part; the expenses related to arbitration and their allocation between the parties. Where appropriate, the arbitral award should also specify the time and the order of its execution.[176]

[C] Challengeable Awards

[1] Grounds for Challenging the Award

1.150. The law establishes a limited list of grounds for challenging arbitral awards identical to those specified in the UNCITRAL Model Law.[177] This list is closed and cannot be expanded.[178] The state court *sua sponte* sets aside the award if it holds that the subject matter of the dispute is not arbitrable under the Russian law; the award is contrary to the Russian public policy. If the part of the award contrary to the Russian public policy is separable from the other part, then the court may set aside the former part of the award.[179]

[2] Waiver of Right to Challenge

1.151. Russian law expressly allows the parties to the arbitration agreement which provides for administering of the arbitration by a permanent arbitral institution to specify that arbitral award shall be final for them. A direct agreement of the parties is necessary (i.e., not by reference to rules of some arbitral institution). Such final arbitral award may not be challenged by such parties.[180] Therefore now the law confirms the approach previously taken by Russian state commercial courts that the parties can exclude the rights of challenge of an arbitral award by providing in their agreement on the finality of the award.[181]

---

175. Article 34(1) of the Arbitration Law, Art. 31(1) of the ICA law.
176. Article 34(2, 3) of the Arbitration Law (though this provision says that the parties may agree otherwise).
177. Article 233(3) of the Commercial Procedure Code (as of 1 September 2016).
178. Article 233(1) of the Commercial Procedure Code (as of 1 September 2016).*See also*: Yarkov V.V., *Challenging arbitral award*, The law, No. 1 (2008) (*Ярков В.В.* 'Оспаривание решения международного коммерческого арбитража' // 'Закон',   2008, No. 1): '*Purpose of challenging consists in providing to the interested party access to a limited judicial control over the arbitral award, because the Law establishes a closed list of grounds for its setting aside*'.
179. Article 233(4) of the Commercial Procedure Code (as of 1 September 2016).
180. Article 40 of the Arbitration Law, Art. 34(1) of the ICA law (as of 1 September 2016).
181. *See* e.g. resolution of Commercial court of Moscow circuit of 24 November 2015 in case No. A40-66296/15.

[D] Review of Jurisdictional Awards

1.152. An arbitral tribunal may decide on its jurisdiction as a preliminary issue or in the award on the merits. This allows the arbitral tribunal to evaluate the risk of 'delaying tactics' of arbitral proceedings (while challenging the jurisdiction award) and the peril of considerable monetary and temporary expenses for useless arbitration.[182] Russian arbitration practice does not usually name separate decisions on jurisdiction as 'awards' but rather as rulings. Either of the arbitrating parties may request the competent Russian state court to set aside the ruling on jurisdiction within a month from receipt of such ruling.[183]

§7.09 RECOGNITION AND ENFORCEMENT OF THE ARBITRAL AWARD

[A] Enforcement of Domestic Awards

[1] Enforcement Domestically

1.153. An arbitral award issued in Russia is enforceable in the local state courts. Both parties may attend the hearing and present their objections or comments. If an arbitral award is to be enforced by a commercial court, the procedure is regulated by Chapter 30 of the Commercial Procedure Code (CPC). The time limit for the request for recognition and enforcement of an arbitral award is three years from the date when the award becomes effective.

1.154. Arbitral awards of the so-called pocket Russian arbitral tribunals at business entities have often been non-enforceable or annulled as Russian state courts often perceive such tribunals as biased.[184] For example, Presidium of High Commercial Court in 2011 refused to enforce the award rendered by Court of Arbitration at the Investment and Construction company 'Sberbankinveststroy' in favour of Sberbank against a number of its debtors.[185]

[2] Enforcement Abroad

1.155. As noted above, Russia is a Party to the New York Convention. The Convention, signed by a representative of the USSR on 29 December 1958, gained the force of law in the USSR through its ratification by a Decree of the Presidium of the Supreme Soviet of the USSR (the highest legislative body according to the USSR Constitution, adopted

---

182. *Commentary to Federal law 'On arbitral tribunals in Russian Federation' (article-by-article)*, (A.L. Makovsky, E.A. Sukhanov, Statute, 2003). Placed in ConsultantPlus legal reference database (Комментарий к Федеральному закону 'О третейских судах в Российской Федерации' (постатейный) (отв. ред. А.Л. Маковский, Е.А. Суханов) ('Статут', 2003)).
183. Article 235(2) of the Commercial Procedure Code (as amended).
184. *See* A. Kalimanov, *Russia's Supreme Commercial Court Questions Impartiality of Party-Affiliated Arbitral Institutions*. 30 September 2013. http://www.cisarbitration.com/2013/09/30/russias-supreme-commercial-court-questions-impartiality-of-party-affiliated-arbitral-institutions/.
185. Resolution of Presidium of High Commercial Court of No. 17020/10 of 24 May 2011.

in 1936) dated 10 August 1960. Therefore, an arbitral award made in Russia can be recognized and enforced in other signatories to the New York Convention under the provisions of the Convention.[186]

1.156. Russia is also Party to many multilateral[187] and bilateral international treaties containing provisions on enforcement of arbitral awards, which are different from the New York Convention, for example, the Convention of 7 September 1940 concerning Turnover of Goods and Payments between the USSR and Sweden.

[B] Enforcement of Foreign Arbitral Awards

[1] Introduction to Recognition and Enforcement

1.157. Foreign arbitral awards are recognized and enforced in Russia by domestic courts under the mechanism established in the New York Convention. While acceding to the New York Convention the USSR in 1960 declared that it shall apply it to arbitral awards made in States that are not Parties to the Convention only subject to reciprocity.[188] This declaration is effective for the Russian Federation.

1.158. In accordance with Article 35 (1) of the ICA Law (based on the UNCITRAL Model Law) *'An arbitral award, irrespective of the country in which it was made, shall be recognized as binding and, upon application in writing to the competent court, shall be enforced...'*. Pursuant to Article VII of the Convention, any interested party may take advantage of this provision.

1.159. Russian laws essentially reproduce the provisions of the New York Convention. In interpreting the New York Convention and/or the implementing legislation the Russian courts have to comply with the general rules of interpretation and application of law rules provided by Russian regulations. These rules *inter alia* include: an obligation for the lower courts to follow superior judicial authorities' findings on points of law; regard for consistency in Russian court practice in interpreting and applying the law provisions.

---

186. *See* e.g. D.V. Marenkov, *Recognition and enforcement of the awards of ICAC at RF CCI, ICAC at Ukraine CCI and IAC at Belarusian CCI in Germany*, 2 International commercial arbitration bulletin 34, 62 (2011). (Маренков Д.В. Признание и исполнение решений МКАС при ТПП РФ, МКАС при ТПП Украины и МАС при БелТПП в Германии / Д.В. Маренков // Вестник международного коммерческого арбитража . – 2011. – № 2. – С. 34 – 62); Cour de Cassation, Chambre civile 1, du 30 Mars 2004, 01-14.311, Publié au bulletin.French courts even enforced a high-profile ICAC award annulled by Russian courts: Cour d'appel de Paris. Pôle 1 – Chambre 1. No. 12/15479. Novolipetski Mettalurguicheski Kombinat /Nikolay Maximov; Corte d'appello di Brescia, Sezione prima civile, No. 34/2015 of 9 March 2015, confirming the enforcement in Italy of ICAC award of 7 April 2013 in case No. 59/2013 (*AtomEnergosbyt JSC v. Angelo Ziglioli*).
187. For example Convention on resolution by arbitration of civil law disputes resulting from relations of economic and scientific and technical cooperation (Moscow, 26 May 1972).
188. Resolution of Presidium of Supreme Council of USSR of 10 August 1960 'On ratification of the Convention on Recognition and Enforcement of Foreign Arbitral Awards'. 32 Bulletin of Supreme Council of USSR, 304 (15 August 1960).

1.160. The Russian courts should also follow the provisions on interpretation established by Articles 31, 32 and 33 of the Vienna Convention on the Law of Treaties of 1969. As a matter of practice, the awards of well-known foreign arbitration courts are normally granted enforcement in Russia.[189]

[2] Separate, Partial and Interim Awards

1.161. Russian courts so far have consistently taken the position that only final arbitral awards are enforceable.[190] Therefore interim awards (e.g., awards on interim measures) are currently not enforceable in Russia. As regards separate and partial awards, Russian courts may grant their enforcement if the claimant shows that they are final under applicable arbitration rules.[191] However, Russian court held that an arbitral award on recovery of advance of arbitration fees is not enforceable separately from the award on the merits.[192]

[3] Grounds for Refusing Recognition and Enforcement

1.162. The grounds for recognition and enforcement of foreign awards are specified in the New York Convention. The party against whom enforcement is sought can submit its objections against the request for enforcement to a competent court orally or, preferably, in writing. However, a bilateral treaty of Russia may provide for a list of grounds which may be different from the New York Convention. For instance, the Agreement on Goods Turnover and Payments between the USSR and Sweden dated 7 September 1940, are more favourable to the debtor than the provisions of the Convention.[193] Provisions of a bilateral treaty prevail over the New York Convention pursuant to its Article VII.

---

189. *See* e.g. Ivan Philippov, *Notice of Arbitration to the Parent Company: Proper or Not?* 3 September 2014. http://www.cisarbitration.com/2014/09/03/notice-of-arbitration-to-the-parent-company-proper-or-not/ (accessed 31 July 2017).
190. For example Ruling of Supreme Court of Russian Federation of 4 February 2000 No. 5 Г00 4; Resolution of Presidium of High Commercial Court of Russian Federation of 5 October 2010 No. 6547/10.
191. Ruling of Supreme Court of Russian Federation of 11 January 2002 No. 5-Г01-168.
192. Resolution of Presidium of High Commercial Court of Russian Federation of 5 October 2010 in case No. 6547/10.
193. This treaty is still effective due to the Protocol between Russia and Sweden dated 29 September 1993. *See* in detail: A.I. Muranov, *One more view on issues of enforcement in Russia or arbitral awards rendered in Sweden; issues of application of almost forgotten bilateral treaty of 1940*, 2 International commercial arbitration bulletin 61, 102 (2010) (**Муранов А.И. Еще один взгляд на вопросы исполнения в России арбитражных решений, вынесенных в Швеции: проблемы применения почти что забытого двустороннего соглашения 1940 г. //Вестник международного коммерческого арбитража**. 2010. No. 2. C. 61 – 102), http://www.rospravo.ru/files/docs/echo_odin_vzglyad_na_voprosi_ispolneniya_v_Rossii_arbitraznih_resheniy.pdf (accessed 30 January 2017).

[a]   Lack of Capacity and Invalidity of Arbitration Agreement

1.163. This ground for refusal of awards enforcement is not often invoked in Russian courts. Sometimes defendants try to object to enforcement of arbitral award by referring to lack of authorities of a person who signed the arbitration agreement, e.g. failure to comply with due form of a power-of-attorney established by Russian Federation. However, such failure was not recognized as a good ground for refusal of the award enforcement in Russia.[194] Furthermore the defendant's argument on lack of capacity of the person to conclude the contract submitted to arbitration amounts to attempt to review the arbitral award on the merits which the law does not allow.[195]

[b]   Procedural Violations

1.164. It was very common for parties in Russian court to invoke various procedural violations of arbitral tribunals, mostly failure to duly notify the respondent on some steps in arbitral proceedings. However, state courts have gradually developed a balanced approach to deciding whether the procedural violation invoked by defendant constitutes a valid ground for refusal to enforce the award. In particular, the courts held that a party must take necessary measures to ensure the receipt of correspondence. Otherwise it shall bear the risks of failure to timely receive it.[196]

1.165. As the High Commercial Court held, the order of notification of the parties on the time and place of arbitral proceedings shall be governed by the parties' agreement, *lex arbitri* and of the enforcing state. The latter's role is to make sure that the arbitral tribunal met fundamental procedural guarantees of the parties' rights.[197]

[c]   Arbitral Award Not Binding

1.166. The Russian Supreme Court since late 1990s established a consistent position that the arbitral award to be enforceable in Russia must be final and binding on the parties.[198] The right of a party to challenge the award at a competent court shall not mean that the award is non-final.[199]

1.167. Interestingly, in 2001 the Supreme Court considered an award signed by all three members of arbitral tribunal two of whom made separate opinions, though on

---

194. Resolution of Federal Commercial Court of North-Western Circuit of 28 August 2003 No. A42-9072/02-C1.
195. Resolution of Federal Commercial Court of Moscow Circuit of 24 March 2004 No. A40/1836-04.
196. For example Ruling of Commercial Court of Sakhalin region of 14 July 2009 No. A59-2213/2009.
197. Ruling of High Commercial Court of Russian Federation of 25 July 2011 No. 6857/11.
198. Ruling of Supreme Court of Russian Federation of 11 January 2002 No. 5-Г01-168; Ruling of Supreme Court of Russian Federation of 4 February 2000 No. 5-Г00-4 (finding also that the court must find out when the arbitral award came into effect).
199. Ruling of Supreme Court of Russian Federation of 10 November 1997 No. 34-Г97-8.

different grounds. The court held that, the given such fact, the award was not rendered by majority of arbitrators and therefore non-binding and unenforceable.[200]

[d] Non-arbitrability

1.168. The courts check the arbitrability of the subject matter of the dispute (as well as compliance with public policy) on their own initiative.[201] As a general rule only civil law disputes (including corporate disputes under certain conditions) are arbitrable.[202]

[e] Public Policy

1.169. If a Russian court finds that the arbitral award violates Russian public policy, it may refuse to recognize and enforce it[203] or, in respective cases, set the award aside.[204] An international arbitral award violates Russian public policy if its enforcement would result in committing actions expressly forbidden by law or causing damage to sovereignty or security of the state. Other instances include cases where the enforcement would violate the principles of economic, political and legal systems, or infringe upon human rights; or contradict to basic principles of civil law, such as inviolability of property and freedom of the contract.[205]

1.170. For instance, a higher court considered an application of a Russian company to set aside on public policy ground ICAC award rendered in favour of an Irish company where the awarded damages exceeded the principal debt to 18%. The applicant alleged that the arbitral tribunal misinterpreted the contract, erroneously found it duly concluded and misapplied the Civil Code provisions on remedies for breach of contract. The court formulated the above public policy definition to find that such arguments clearly fall beyond its scope.[206]

1.171. Besides, the same court's ruling of 2005 includes state defence capacity interests in public policy. A Swiss company sought to enforce in Russia a German

---

200. Ruling of Supreme Court of Russian Federation of 9 November 2001 No. 5-Г01-142.
201. Karabelnikov B.R., *Enforcement and challenging international commercial arbitral awards. Commentary to the New York Convention 1958 and to Chapters 30 and 31 of Commercial Procedure Code 2002*, (Statute, 2008) (*Карабельников Б.Р. Исполнение и оспаривание решений международных коммерческих арбитражей. Комментарий к Нью-Йоркской конвенции 1958 г. и главам 30 и 31 АПК РФ 2002 г.* (3-е издание, переработанное и дополненное) // 'Статут', 2008): '... *the court is obliged at its own initiative (or upon request of the party objecting to enforcement of the foreign arbitral award) "check" the compliance of the award with the rules of this state on arbitrability and public policy*'.
202. Please *see* Section §7.02[F] above.
203. Article 244(1)(7) of the CPC and Art. 36(1)(2) of the Russian Federation law 'On International Commercial Arbitration'.
204. Article 34(2)(2) of the ICA Law.
205. Decision of judicial collegium of High Commercial Court of 6 December 2007 No. 13452/07. The High Commercial Court heard a case on the enforcement of an ICAC award compelling a Russian company to pay damages in the amount of USD 339,840 for the breach of a repair work contract in favour of a Ukrainian company. The High Commercial Court confirmed the lower court's conclusion that the award did not violate Russian public policy.
206. Moscow circuit FCC in the ruling of 3 April 2003 No. КГ-А40/1672.

arbitrator money award against a Russian company. The debtor was a former state-owned company privatized after the dissolution of the USSR. He argued that since the debt arose when the company was state-owned, the proper debtor was the Russian state as the USSR legal successor. On this ground he alleged that enforcing the award rendered against a wrong respondent was contrary to Russian public policy. However, the courts found that the enforcement nowise violates public policy which consists in '*fundamentals of legal order, universally accepted morality principles, as well as state defense interests*'.[207]

1.172. Russian courts came to understanding that the public policy exception may be applied only as *ultima ratio*, namely, where the arbitral award enforcement would violate the fundamental rules of the Russian law.[208] However, in some cases courts widely construe this notion, e.g. the Supreme Court found that awarding damages to a person for making unauthorized modifications with equipment owned by another person is contrary to Russian public policy.[209]

[4] Procedures for Recognition and Enforcement

1.173. A foreign arbitral award may be submitted for enforcement within three years of becoming legally binding.[210] Such request can be considered by a court of first instance where the debtor is registered/resides or, if the debtor's place of registration/residence is unknown, where his assets are located. The court notifies the applicant and the debtor of the place and the time of the hearing. In deciding a request, the court may not review the case on its merits. Enforcement of a foreign arbitral award within the courts of general jurisdiction and within commercial courts have similar procedures.

1.174. The Civil Procedure Code expressly provides a special procedure for recognizing arbitral awards which do not need to be compulsorily executed in Russia.[211] According to this procedure, there is no need for the award creditor to lodge a request for recognition with a competent court of general jurisdiction: the award is recognized without any further proceedings unless an interested party lodges objections with a competent court within one month of becoming aware of the award. Starting from September 2016 the same special procedure is applicable within the system of commercial courts.[212]

1.175. The procedures for an appeal against a decision refusing to enforce an award are generally similar for both the commercial courts and the courts of general

---

207. Moscow circuit FCC ruling of 29 September 2005 No. КГ-А40/9192-05.
208. This approach was specified in the Information letter of Presidium of High Commercial Court of Russian Federation of 22 December 2005 No. 96.
209. Ruling of the Supreme Court of Russian Federation No 305-ЭС14-2600 in case No. A40-87194/13-68-844 of 12 January 2015.
210. Article 246 (2) of Commercial Procedure Code.
211. Articles 413–416 of Civil Procedural Code.
212. Article 245.1 of Commercial Procedure Code.

jurisdiction: complaints are lodged in accordance with the applicable procedural rules and the competent courts consider such complaints.

§7.10 INVESTOR-STATE ARBITRATION

[A] General Overview of Law and Practice Related to Investor-State Arbitration

1.176. Russia pursues the policy of attracting foreign investments. Starting from 1989, Russia has concluded more than eighty-one investment protection treaties, sixty-four of which have become effective. Many international treaties of Russian Federation (including those concluded by the USSR as its legal predecessor) include arbitration clauses providing for arbitration of investor-state disputes. They may be divided into two groups.

1.177. First group includes the treaties which contain a 'narrow' investor-state arbitration clause, usually disputes concerning the amount of compensation or any other matter consequential upon an act of expropriation or a similar measure. For instance, this group includes BITs with Spain, United Kingdom (1989), Italy (1991). Such treaties do not endow the arbitral tribunal with competence to decide whether the expropriation did take place.

1.178. Second group includes treaties with a wide investor-state arbitration clause generally submitting to arbitration any disputes related to the investment. For instance, this group includes BITs with India (1994), with Sweden (1995), with Japan (1998). For instance, the Russian-China BIT (Beijing, 9 November 2006) provides in Article 9 that if an investment-related dispute between a Contracting Party and an investor of the other Contracting Party cannot be settled amicably through negotiations within six months from the date it has been raised by either party to the dispute, it shall be submitted to ICSID or to an ad hoc arbitration court in accordance with the UNCITRAL Arbitration Rules.

1.179. Russian domestic law on protection of foreign investments expressly establishes legal grounds for submitting disputes between a foreign investor and Russia to arbitration.[213] Under the ICA Law disputes arisen in connection with making foreign investments in Russia or Russian investments abroad may be submitted to international arbitration.[214]

1.180. Various arbitral tribunals have already heard a number of cases upon claims of foreign investors against Russia. One of the earliest cases *Compagnie Noga d'importation et D'exportation S.a. v. Russia* regarding termination of a

---

213. 'Article 10. ... A dispute of a foreign investor arisen in connection with exercising investment and business activity in the territory of Russian Federation shall be resolved in accordance with international treaties of Russian Federation and federal laws in state court or an international arbitral tribunal (arbitration court)' (Federal law of 9 July 1999 No. 160-ФЗ (in force as of 5 May 2014) 'On foreign investments in Russian Federation').
214. Article 1(3 and 4) of the ICA Law (as of 1 September 2016).

food-for-oil contract dates back to 1993. Frequently investors invoked breaches of fair and equitable treatment and (indirect) expropriation claims. Most of the claimants came from Europe: Italy, Germany, Belgium and Spain and UK and filed their claims under various BITs. Usually claimants applied at institutional arbitration, namely the SCC. Some ad hoc arbitrations under UNCITRAL Rules have also been instituted.[215]

1.181. However, the most important cases (in terms of the amount of claim) were heard under the Rules of Permanent Court of Arbitration (PCA) in Hague and related to Yukos Oil Company and its alleged expropriation by Russia in mid-2000s.[216] The claimants (incorporated in off-shore or tax haven jurisdictions – Isle of Men and Cyprus) filed their claims in 2007 and relied on the ECT provisions. As noted above in 1.4, Russia has signed the ECT in 1994 and applied it on temporary basis until it decided not to become its party in 2009.

1.182. Russia argued in particular that in fact the claimants did not qualify for the status of 'foreign investors': although they were companies instituted outside Russia, their beneficiaries were Russian nationals. The arbitrators rejected Russia's arguments and in mid-2015 awarded to the claimants the amount around USD 50 billion in damages. However, the District court of The Hague upon application of Russia set aside the awards (three interim awards and three final awards) in April 2016 on the ground that the arbitral tribunal had no jurisdiction against Russia.[217]

1.183. Most often the tribunals so far found no jurisdiction to hear a case against Russia,[218] or state courts subsequently annulled their awards.[219] However, there are cases in which the investor succeeded to obtain an award in his favour and to enforce it at least in part (*Mr Franz Sedelmayer v. the Russian Federation, SCC*).

---

215. For example Investment Policy, *Cesare Galdabini SpA v. Russia*, http://investmentpolicyhub.unctad.org/ISDS/Details/366 (accessed 30 January 2017).
216. *Hulley Enterprises Limited (Cyprus) v. The Russian Federation*, UNCITRAL, PCA Case No. AA 226 - *See* more at ITAlaw, http://www.italaw.com/cases/544#sthash.vWZhTxwg.dpuf (accessed 30 January 2017); *Yukos Universal Limited (Isle of Man) v. The Russian Federation*, UNCITRAL, PCA Case No. AA 227 - *See* more at ITAlaw, http://www.italaw.com/cases/1175#sthash.3Ix1oG1S.dpuf (accessed 30 January 2017); *Veteran Petroleum Limited (Cyprus) v. The Russian Federation*, UNCITRAL, PCA Case No. AA 228 - *See* more at ITAlaw, http://www.italaw.com/cases/1151#sthash.kLT7040Z.dpuf (accessed 30 January 2017).
217. *See* English text of the court judgment: De Rechtspraak, *Arbitration awards on multi-billion claims against Russia quashed*, http://uitspraken.rechtspraak.nl/inziendocument?id = ECLI%3ANL%3ARBDHA%3A2016%3A4230 (accessed 30 January 2017).
218. For example *Vladimir Berschader and Moïse Berschader v. the Russian Federation*, SCC Case No. 080/2004.
219. *Quasar de Valores SICAV S.A. et al v. the Russian Federation* (2012).

Chapter 7: Russia

APPENDIX 1. LIST OF INVESTMENT TREATIES RUSSIA HAS RATIFIED

1. Multilateral treaties

No.	Title of the treaty	Parties	Date of conclusion	Date of entry into force
1	Free Trade Agreement between the Eurasian Economic Union and its Member States, on One Part, and the Socialist Republic of Viet Nam, on the Other Part	Republic of Armenia; Republic of Belarus; Republic of Kazakhstan; Kyrgyz Republic; Russian Federation; Socialist Republic of Viet Nam	29/05/2015	05/10/2016
2	Treaty on the Eurasian Economic Union (Annex 16 'Protocol on Trade in Services, Establishment, Activity and Pursuit of Investments')	Republic of Belarus; Republic of Kazakhstan; Russian Federation	29/05/2014	01/01/2015
4	Agreement on Promotion and Reciprocal Protection of Investments in the Member States of the Eurasian Economic Community	Belarus; Kazakhstan; Kyrgyzstan; Tajikistan; Russian Federation	12/12/2008	11/01/2016
5	Agreement on Partnership and Cooperation Establishing a Partnership between the European Communities and Their Member States, on One Part, and Russia, on the Other Part	EU (European Union); Russian Federation	24/06/1994	01/12/1997
6	Convention on Protection of Investor's Rights	Armenia; Belarus; Moldova; Tajikistan; Kazakhstan; Kyrgyzstan; Russian Federation	28/03/1997	21/01/1999

2. Bilateral treaties on the promotion and reciprocal protection of investments

No.	Party (in alphabetical order)	Date of conclusion	Date of entry into force
1.	Albania	11/04/1995	29/05/1996
2.	Angola	26/06/2009	12/01/2011
3.	Argentina	25/06/1998	20/11/2000
4.	Armenia	15/09/2001	08/02/2006
5.	Austria	08/02/1990	01/09/1991
6.	BLEU (Belgium-Luxembourg Economic Union)	09/02/1989	18/08/1991
7.	Bulgaria	08/06/1993	18/12/2005
8.	Canada	20/11/1989	27/06/1991
9.	China	09/11/2006	01/05/2009
10.	Cuba	07/07/1993	08/07/1996
11.	Czech Republic	05/04/1994	06/06/1996
12.	Dem. People's Rep. Korea	28/11/1996	09/01/2006
13.	Denmark	04/11/1993	26/08/1996
14.	Egypt	23/09/1997	12/06/2000
15.	Finland	08/02/1989	15/08/1991
16.	France	04/07/1989	18/07/1991
17.	Germany	13/06/1989	05/08/1991
18.	Greece	30/06/1993	08/07/1996
19.	Hungary	06/03/1995	29/05/1996
20.	India	23/12/1994	05/08/1996
21.	Indonesia	06/09/2007	15/10/2009
22.	Italy	09/04/1996	07/07/1997
23.	Japan	13/11/1998	27/05/2000
24.	Jordan	13/02/2007	17/06/2009
25.	Kazakhstan	06/07/1998	11/02/2000
26.	Kuwait	21/11/1994	30/05/1996
27.	Lao People's Democratic Republic	06/12/1996	09/02/2006
28.	Lebanon	07/04/1997	11/03/2003
29.	Libya	17/04/2008	15/10/2010
30.	Lithuania	29/06/1999	24/05/2004
31.	Moldova, Republic of	17/03/1998	18/07/2001
32.	Mongolia	29/11/1995	26/02/2006
33.	Netherlands	05/10/1989	20/07/1991
34.	Nicaragua	26/01/2012	28/08/2013

Chapter 7: Russia

No.	Party (in alphabetical order)	Date of conclusion	Date of entry into force
35.	Norway	04/10/1995	21/05/1998
36.	Philippines	12/09/1997	29/10/1998
37.	Qatar	12/02/2007	04/06/2009
38.	Republic of Korea	14/12/1990	10/07/1991
39.	Romania	29/09/1993	20/07/1996
40.	Serbia	11/10/1995	19/07/1996
41.	Singapore	21/09/2010	16/06/2012
42.	Slovakia	30/11/1993	02/08/1996
43.	South Africa	23/11/1998	12/04/2000
44.	Spain	26/10/1990	28/11/1991
45.	Sweden	19/04/1995	07/07/1996
46.	Switzerland	01/12/1990	26/08/1991
47.	Syrian Arab Republic	27/01/2005	13/07/2007
48.	The former Yugoslav Republic of Macedonia	21/10/1997	09/07/1998
49.	Turkey	15/12/1997	17/05/2000
50.	Turkmenistan	25/03/2009	23/08/2010
51.	Ukraine	27/11/1998	27/01/2000
52.	United Arab Emirates	28/06/2010	19/08/2013
53.	United Kingdom	06/04/1989	03/07/1991
54.	Uzbekistan	15/04/2013	14/01/2014
55.	Venezuela	07/11/2008	26/11/2009
56.	Viet Nam	16/06/1994	03/07/1996
57.	Yemen	01/12/2002	17/06/2005

APPENDIX 2. LIST OF INVESTOR-STATE DISPUTES (CONCLUDED AND PENDING)

List of Russian Investment Arbitration Disputes

1. *Cesare Galdabini SpA v. the Russian Federation* (2011);[220]
2. *Compagnie Noga d'Importation et d'Exportation v. the Russian Federation* (SCC, 2001);
3. *Hulley Enterprises Limited (Cyprus) v. the Russian Federation*, Case No. AA 226 (PCA, 2014);
4. *Mr. Franz Sedelmayer v. the Russian Federation*, Case No. 106/1998 (SCC, 1998);

---

220. Lists given in alphabetical order.

5. *Quasar de Valores SICAV S.A. et al v. the Russian Federation*, Case No. 024/2007 (SCC, 2012);
6. *Renta 4 S.V.S.A, Ahorro Corporación Emergentes F.I., Ahorro Corporación Eurofondo F.I., Rovime Inversiones SICAV S.A., Quasar de Valores SICAV S.A., Orgor de Valores SICAV S.A., GBI 9000 SICAV S.A. v. The Russian Federation*, Case No. 24/2007 (SCC, 2012);
7. *Rosinvestco UK Ltd v. the Russian Federation*, Case No. V079/2005 (SCC, 2010);
8. *Russian Federation c/o Federal Customs Office of the Russian Federation v. I.M. Badprim SRL*, Case No. T 2454-14 (SCC, 2013);
9. *Sana Consulting & Management GmbH v. The Russian Federation* (UNCITRAL ad hoc arbitration, 2015);
10. *UK Bank v. Russian Federation* (SCC, 2000);
11. *Valle Esina S.p.A. v. The Russian Federation* (UNCITRAL ad hoc arbitration, 2014);
12. *Veteran Petroleum Limited (Cyprus) v. the Russian Federation*, Case No. AA 228 (PCA, 2014);
13. *Vladimir Berschader and Moïse Berschader v. the Russian Federation*, Case No. 080/2004 (SCC, 2006);
14. *Yukos Universal Limited (Isle of Man) v. the Russian Federation*, Case No. AA 227 (PCA, 2014).

Pending:

1. *Aeroport Belbek LLC and Mr Kolomoisky v. The Russian Federation*, Case No. 2015-07 (PCA);
2. *Artashes Rafikovich Amalyan v. Russian Federation* (UNCITRAL ad hoc arbitration);
3. *Everest Estate LLC and others v. The Russian Federation*, Case No. AA577 (PCA);
4. *Lugzor LLC and others v. The Russian Federation*, Case No. 2015-29 (PCA);
5. *Luxtona Limited v. The Russian Federation* (UNCITRAL ad hoc arbitration);
6. Naftogaz of Ukraine NJSC, State Joint Stock Company Chornomornaftogaz PJSC, *Ukrgasvydobuvannya PJSC and others v. The Russian Federation (PCA)*;
7. *Oschadbank JSC v. The Russian Federation* (PCA);
8. *Privatbank and Finance Company Finilion LLC v. The Russian Federation*, Case No. AA568 (PCA);
9. *Sergei Viktorovich Pugachev v. The Russian Federation* (UNCITRAL ad hoc arbitration);
10. *Stabil LLC and others v. The Russian Federation*, Case No. 2015-35 (PCA);
11. *Ukrnafta PJSC v. The Russian Federation*, Case No. 2015-34 (PCA);
12. *Yukos Capital S.A.R.L. v. the Russian Federation* (UNCITRAL ad hoc arbitration).

Chapter 7: Russia

Reform Proposals

The large-scale arbitration law reform has been implemented and resulted in adoption of the Arbitration Law (in effect from 1 September 2016) and amendment of various laws including the ICA Law. The main purpose of the reform has been to set quality standards for arbitration in Russia. This chapter takes into account such reform.

Bibliography

Asoskov A.V., *Conflict-of-Laws Regulation of Contractual Obligations*, (Infotropic Media, 2012). (Асосков А.В. Коллизионное регулирование договорных обязательств. М.: Инфотропик Медиа, 2012. 640 с.) Placed in ConsultantPlus legal reference database.

Boguslavskiy M.M., *International Private Law: Manuel* (5th ed., Jurist, 2005). Placed in ConsultantPlus legal reference database) (Богуславский М.М. Международное частное право: Учебник. 5-е изд., перераб. и доп. М.: Юристъ, 2005. 606 с. Размещено в справочной правовой системе «КонсультантПлюс»).

Chuprunov I.S., *Admissibility of Awarding Damages Resulting from Violation of Arbitration or Prorogation Agreements*, 6 Civil law Bulletin (2011), reproduced in Russian law database 'ConsultantPlus' (Чупрунов И.С. Допустимость взыскания убытков из нарушения арбитражного или пророгационного соглашений. 'Вестник гражданского права', 2011, No. 6. Размещено в справочной правовой системе «КонсультантПлюс»).

CIS Arbitration Forum, Anastasia Rogozina, New Rules on Jurisdictional Immunities of States in Russian Courts, http://www.cisarbitration.com/2015/11/13/new-rules-on-jurisdictional-immunities-of-states-in-russian-courts/ (accessed 30 October 2016).

CIS Arbitration Forum, Dmitry Davydenko, New Rules of the ICAC at the Russian Chamber of Commerce: What Has Changed for International Disputes? http://www.cisarbitration.com/2017/02/02/russian-icac-revises-rules-for-international-disputes-whats-new/ (accessed 9 March 2017).

Commentary to Federal Law 'On Arbitral Tribunals in Russian Federation' (article-by-article), (Makovsky A.L., Sukhanov E.A., Statute, 2003). Placed in ConsultantPlus legal reference database (Комментарий к Федеральному закону 'О третейских судах в Российской Федерации' (постатейный) (отв. ред. Маковский А.Л., Суханов Е.А.) ('Статут', 2003)).

Commentary to Part Three of Civil Code of Russian Federation (article-by-article), Commentary to Article 1211, (Makovsky A.L., Sukhanov E.A. M., Lawyer 2002) ('Комментарий к части третьей Гражданского кодекса Российской Федерации' (постатейный) (под ред. Маковского А.Л., Суханова Е.А.). М. 'Юристъ', 2002. Комментарий к статье 1211) Placed in ConsultantPlus legal reference database.

Davydenko D., Bulkina K. for Max Planck Institute for Comparative and International Private Law, *Overview of Recent Amendments to Russian Private International Law*, 7-8, http://www.mpipriv.de/files/pdf4/2014_09_01.pdf (accessed 26 January 2016).

Davydenko D.L., Khizunova A.N., *Implications and Function of the Public Policy Exception in Foreign and Russian Law*, 2 Law, 31-38 (2013) (Давыденко Д.Л., Хизунова А.Н., Значение и функции оговорки о публичном порядке в иностранном и российском праве // Закон. 2013. № 2. С. 31-38).

Diakonov M.A., Kivlitskiy E.A., *Russkaya Pravda, Monument of Ancient Russian Law // Encyclopedic dictionary of Brokhaus and Efron*, vol. 82, 4 suppl. (SPb, 1890-1907). (Дьяконов М.А., Кивлицкий Е.А. Русская Правда, памятник древнерусского права // Энциклопедический словарь Брокгауза и Ефрона: в 86 т. (82 т. и 4 доп.). - СПб., 1890-1907).

De Rechtspraak, *Arbitration Awards on Multi-Billion Claims Against Russia Quashed*, http://uitspraken.rechtspraak.nl/inziendocument?id=ECLI%3ANL%3ARBDHA%3A2016%3A4230 (accessed 30 October 2016).

Embassy of the Russian Federation in the Kingdom of the Netherlands, *Russian Participation in the Hague Conference on Private International Law*, http://www.rusembassy.nl/en/Russian_Federation_and_Hague_conference_on_private_international_law.php (accessed 30 October 2016).

International Commercial Arbitration: Experience of National Regulation. 80 years of MAC at CCI USSR/CCI RF. 1930-2010: Collection of Selected Documents and Analytical Materials / Chamber of Commerce and Industry of Russian Federation, Maritime Arbitration Commission at CCI RF, MGIMO(U) MFA RF, Department of private international and civil law; compiler and academic editor A.I. Muranov (Moscow: Infotropic Media, 2011. - 816 p.) (Международный коммерческий арбитраж: опыт отечественного регулирования. 80 лет МАК при ТПП СССР/ТПП РФ. 1930-2010 гг.: сб. избр. док. и аналит. материалов / Торгов.-пром. палата Российской Федерации, Морская арбитраж. комис. при ТПП РФ, МГИМО (У) МИД РФ, Каф. междунар. част. и гражд. права; сост. и науч. ред. А.И. Муранов. - М.: Инфотропик Медиа, 2011. - 816 с.).

International Commercial Arbitration: Experience of National Regulation. 80 years of MAC at CCI USSR/CCI RF. 1930-2010: collection of selected documents and analytical materials / In two volumes. Compiler and academic editor A.I. Muranov. 2012. - М.: Статут (Moscow: Statut, 2012) (Международный коммерческий арбитраж: Опыт отечественного регулирования/саморегулирования. 80 лет МКАС при ТПП РФ: 1932-2012: Сборник избранных научных, нормативных, архивных, аналитических и иных материалов. В двух томах. Сост. и науч. ред. А.И. Муранов. - М.: Статут, 2012).

Isaev M.A., *On the History of Russian Law See in Particular: History of Russian State and Law; Manual*, (MGIMO (University) MFA RF, M.: Statut, 2012). (Исаев М.А. История Российского государства и права: учебник / МГИМО (Университет) МИД России. М.: Статут, 2012. 840 с.)

Kabatov V.A., *Application of the Vienna Convention 1980 as a Law of a Contracting State //* To 10 years of its application by Russia / Compiler M.G. Rosenberg. 2nd edition (Moscow, Statute, 2002). P. 32 (Кабатов В.А. Применение Венской конвенции 1980 г. в качестве права государства – ее участника // Венская конвенция ООН о договорах международной купли-продажи товаров. К 10-летию ее применения Россией. / Сост. М.Г. Розенберг. 2-е изд. М.: Статут, 2002. С. 32).

Kalimanov A., *Russia's Supreme Commercial Court Questions Impartiality of Party-Affiliated Arbitral Institutions.* 30 September 2013. http://www.cisarbitration.com/2013/09/30/russias-supreme-commercial-court-questions-impartiality-of-party-affiliated-arbitral-institutions/ (accessed 30 October 2016).

Karabelnikov B.R., *Enforcement and Challenging International Commercial Arbitral Awards. Commentary to the New York Convention 1958 and to Chapters 30 and 31 of Commercial Procedure Code 2002,* (Statute, 2008) (Карабельников Б.Р. Исполнение и оспаривание решений международных коммерческих арбитражей. Комментарий к Нью-Йоркской конвенции 1958 г. и главам 30 и 31 АПК РФ 2002 г. (3-е издание, переработанное и дополненное) // 'Статут', 2008).

Kostin A.A., *Issues of Determining Law Applicable to Arbitration Agreement in Practice of Continental Europe States and English Courts*, 1 Law (2014) (Костин А.А. Вопросы определения права, применимого к арбитражному соглашению, в практике стран континентальной Европы и английских судов // 'Закон', 2014, No. 1). Placed in ConsultantPlus legal reference database.

Kryvoi Y., Davydenko D., *Consent Awards in International Arbitration: From Settlement to Enforcement,* 40 Brooklyn Journal of International Law 827–868 (7 November 2015), http://ssrn.com/abstract=2580572 (accessed 30 October 2016).

Kurochkin S.A., *International Commercial Arbitration and Arbitral Proceedings,* (Infotropic Media 2013) (Курочкин С.А. 'Международный коммерческий арбитраж и третейское разбирательство'. М. 'Инфотропик Медиа', 2013). Placed in ConsultantPlus legal reference database.

Lysov S.V., *Participation of Persons Non-signatories of the Arbitration Agreement in the Arbitral Proceedings,* 1 Review of international commercial arbitration 29, 42 (2015) (С.И. Лысов. Участие в арбитражном разбирательстве лиц, не являющихся подписантами арбитражного соглашения. Вестник международного коммерческого арбитража, № 1, 2015, Москва, с.с. 29 – 42).

Marenkov D.V., *Recognition and Enforcement of the Awards of ICAC at RF CCI, ICAC at Ukraine CCI and IAC at Belarusian CCI in Germany,* 2 International commercial arbitration bulletin 34, 62 (2011). (Маренков Д.В. Признание и исполнение решений МКАС при ТПП РФ, МКАС при ТПП Украины и МАС при БелТПП в Германии / Д.В. Маренков // Вестник международного коммерческого арбитража. – 2011. – № 2. – С. 34 – 62);

Muranov A.I., *One More View on Issues of Enforcement in Russia or Arbitral Awards Rendered in Sweden; Issues of Application of Almost Forgotten Bilateral Treaty of 1940,* 2 International commercial arbitration bulletin 61, 102 (2010) (Муранов А.И. Еще один взгляд на вопросы исполнения в России арбитражных решений, вынесенных в Швеции: проблемы применения почти что забытого двустороннего соглашения 1940 г. // Вестник международного коммерческого арбитража. 2010. No. 2. С. 61 - 102), http://www.rospravo.ru/files/docs/echo_odin_vzglyad_na_voprosi_ispo lneniya_v_Rossii_arbitraznih_resheniy.pdf (accessed 30 October 2016).

Nikoliukin S.V., *Arbitration Agreements and Competence of International Commercial Arbitration. Issues of Theory and Practice* (Jurisprudence, 2009) Placed in ConsultantPlus legal reference database (Николюкин С.В., *Арбитражные соглашения и компетенция международного коммерческого арбитража. Проблемы теории и практики,* (Юриспруденция, 2009) Размещено в справочной правовой системе «КонсультантПлюс»).

Nikoliukin S.V., *Measures to Secure a Claim in International Commercial Arbitration*, 6 Commercial court of Moscow city Bulletin, (2009). Placed in ConsultantPlus legal reference database (Николюкин С.В. Меры по обеспечению иска в международном коммерческом арбитраже // 'Вестник Арбитражного суда города Москвы', 2009, № 6).

Philippov Ivan, *Notice of Arbitration to the Parent Company: Proper or Not?* 3 September 2014. http://www.cisarbitration.com/2014/09/03/notice-of-arbitration-to-the-parent-company-proper-or-not/

Practice of Application of Commercial Procedure Code of Russian Federation (2nd edition revised and updated, I.V. Reshetnikova, Yurait, 2012. Placed in ConsultantPlus legal reference database). (Практика применения Арбитражного процессуального кодекса Российской Федерации (2-е издание, переработанное и дополненное) Отв. ред. И.В. Решетникова. 'Юрайт', 2012. Размещено в СПС «КонсультантПлюс».

Rosenberg M.G., *From the Practice of ICAC*, Supplement to the journal Law and economics, 40 (2004) (М.Г. Розенберг. «Из практики МКАС. Приложение к ежемесячному журналу «Право и экономика» за 2004 г., с. 40).

Rosenberg M.G., *International Treaty and Foreign Law in Practice of International Commercial Arbitration Court* (Moscow, 1998) (Розенберг М.Г. Международный договор и иностранное право в практике Международного коммерческого арбитражного суда. Москва. 1998). Р. 28.

Rules of the International Commercial Arbitration Court at the Chamber of Commerce and Industry of the Russian Federation: Academic and Practical Commentary, 190-191 (Komarov A.S., Infotropic Media 2012) (Регламент Международного коммерческого арбитражного суда при Торгово-промышленной палате Российской Федерации: науч.-практ. коммент. / Под общ. ред. Комарова А.С. М.: Инфотропик Медиа, 2012. С. 190 - 191).

Speranskiy M.M., *Review of Historical Data on the Restatement of Law* (Odessa, 1889) (*Сперанский М. М.* Обозрение исторических сведений о Своде законов. - Одесса, 1889).

Strelov I.M., *Interaction Between Commercial and Arbitration Courts,* 4 Bulletin of High Commercial Court of Russian Federation 112 (2005)

(Стрелов И.М., *Взаимодействие арбитражных и третейских судов*, Вестник ВАС, No. 4, 112, (2005)).

The Great reform: to 150-years anniversary of Judicial Statutes: in 2 volumes, volume I: Statute of Civil Procedure. (E.A. Borisova, Yustitsinform, 2014) (Великая реформа: К 150-летию Судебных Уставов: В 2 т. Т. I: Устав гражданского судопроизводства (под ред. Е.А. Борисовой). – 'Юстицинформ', 2014 г.)

Veeder V.V., *From Florence to London via Moscow and New Delhi: How and Why Arbitral Ideas Migrate*, 1 Review of international commercial arbitration 51, 73 (2013), (Подробнее см. В.В. Видер. Из Флоренции в Лондон через Москву и Нью-Дели: как и почему мигрируют арбитражные идеи // Вестник международного коммерческого арбитража № 1, М., 2013, с.с. 51–73).

Vladimirskiy-Budanov M.F., *Relations Between Lithuanian Statute and Ulozhenie of tsar Alexey Mikhailovich,* (Collection of state knowledge, Saint Petersburg, 1877) *(Владимирский-Буданов М.Ф. Отношения между Литовским Статутом и Уложением царя Алексея Михайловича //* Сборник государственных знаний. Т. IV. СПб. 1877).

William Elliott Butler, *The Law of Treaties in Russia and the Commonwealth of Independent States: Text and Commentary, 15-18* (Cambridge University Press, 2002).

Yarkov V.V., *Challenging Arbitral Award,* The law, No. 1 (2008) (*Ярков В.В.* 'Оспаривание решения международного коммерческого арбитража' // 'Закон', 2008, No. 1).

Yearbook of Commercial Arbitration, pp. 92–110 (Vol. XVIII, 1993).

Zhiltsov A.N., *Mandatory Rules in International Commercial Arbitration*, 2 International commercial arbitration, 36 (2004) (Жильцов А.Н. Императивные нормы в международном коммерческом арбитраже // Международный коммерческий арбитраж. 2004. № 2. С. 36).

Webliography

(accessed 31 July 2017)
CIS Arbitration Forum, http://www.cisarbitration.com/.
Arbitration Court, journal http://arbitrage.spb.ru/sud/SPISOKTS/spisokts.html.
Federal Chamber of Advocates, http://www.fparf.ru/.
Labour Arbitration Court, http://trudsud.ru/.
The Court for Intellectual Rights, http://ipc.arbitr.ru/.
The International Commercial Arbitration Court at the Russian Chamber of Commerce and Industry, http://mkas.tpprf.ru/en/.
The Maritime Arbitration Commission at the Russian Chamber of Commerce and Industry, http://mac.tpprf.ru/en/.

Association for the Promotion of Arbitration, http://arbitrations.ru/en/arbitration-association/.

The Constitution of the Russian Federation, http://www.constitution.ru/en/10003000-02.htm.

Legislation

Constitution of Russian Federation of 12 December 1993 adopted by nation-wide vote, as amended on 14 July 2014.

Civil Code of Russian Soviet Federal Socialist Republic approved by Supreme Soviet of RSFSR on 11 June 1964.

Civil Procedure Code of the Russian Federation of 14 November 2002, as amended on 15 September 2015, No. 46, 4532.

Criminal Code of the Russian Federation of 16 June 1996 No. 63-FZ.

Labour Code of the Russian Federation of 30 December 2001 No. 197-FZ.

Federal constitutional law of Russian Federation 'On judicial system of Russian Federation' of 31 December 1996 No. 1-FKZ.

Law of Russian Federation 'On International Commercial Arbitration' of 7 July 1993 No. 5338-1, as amended on 29 December 2015.

Federal Law 'On Arbitration (arbitral proceedings) in the Russian Federation' of 29 December 2015 No. 382-FZ ('Arbitration law').

Federal Law of Russian Federation 'On Alternative Dispute Resolution Procedure Involving a Mediator (Mediation Procedure)'of 27 July 2010 No. 193-FZ as amended on 23 July 2013.

Federal Law of Russian Federation 'On Arbitration Courts in the Russian Federation' of 24 July 2002 No. 102-FZ.

Federal law 'On advocates' activity and the bar in Russian Federation' of 31 May 2002 No. 63-FZ.

Federal law of Russian Federation 'On Foreign Investments in Russian Federation' of 09 July 1999 No. 160-FZ (as amended on 5 May 2014).

Federal law of Russian Federation 'On Insolvency (Bankruptcy)' of 26 October 2002 No. 127-ФЗ, as amended on 29 December 2015.

Federal law of Russian Federation 'On Jurisdictional Immunities of a Foreign State and Property of the Foreign State in Russian Federation' of 3 November 2015 No. 297-FZ.

Federal law of Russian Federation 'On Production Sharing Agreements' of 30 December 1995 No. 225-FZ, as amended on 19 July 2011).

Federal law of Russian Federation 'On the Order of Foreign Investments into Business Entities Having Strategic Importance to Ensuring National Defense and State Security' of 29 April 2008 No. 57-FZ.

Case law

British and Irish Legal Information Institute, *Yukos Capital SARL v. OJSC Rosneft Oil Company [2014] EWHC 2188 (Comm) (3 July 2014)*, Paragraphs 43–49, http://

www.bailii.org/ew/cases/EWHC/Comm/2014/2188.html (accessed 30 October 2016).

Corte d'appello di Brescia, Sezione prima civile, No. 34/2015 of 9 March 2015, confirming the enforcement in Italy of ICAC award of 7 April 2013 in case No. 59/2013 (*AtomEnergosbyt JSC v. Angelo Ziglioli*).

Cour d'appel de Paris. Pôle 1 – Chambre 1. No. 12/15479. Novolipetski Mettalurguicheski Kombinat / Nikolay Maximov.

Cour de Cassation, Chambre civile 1, du 30 Mars 2004, 01-14.311, Publié au bulletin.

Decision of Judicial Collegium of High Commercial Court of 6 December 2007 No. 13452/07.

Hulley Enterprises Limited (Cyprus) v. The Russian Federation, UNCITRAL, PCA Case No. AA 226 – *See* more at ITAlaw, http://www.italaw.com/cases/544#sthash.vWZhTxwg.dpuf (accessed 30 October 2016).

Information Letter of Presidium of High Commercial Court of Russian Federation of 22 December 2005 No. 96.

Information Letter of Presidium of High Commercial Court of Russian Federation of 9 July 2013 No. 158 'Review of case practice of hearing by commercial courts of cases involving foreign persons'. Paragraph 16.

Investment Policy, *Cesare Galdabini SpA v. Russia*, http://investmentpolicyhub.unctad.org/ISDS/Details/366 (accessed 30 October 2016).

ITAlaw, *Veteran Petroleum Limited (Cyprus) v. The Russian Federation*, UNCITRAL, PCA Case No. AA228, http://www.italaw.com/cases/1151 (accessed 30 October 2016).

Moscow Circuit FCC Ruling of 29 September 2005 No. КГ-А40/9192-05.

Quasar de Valores SICAV S.A. et al v. the Russian Federation (2012).

Resolution of Commercial Court of Moscow Circuit of 24 November 2015 in case No. A40-66296/15.

Resolution of Federal Commercial Court of Moscow Circuit of 19 December 2002 No. КГ-А40/8249-02.

Resolution of Federal Commercial Court of Moscow Circuit of 24 March 2004 No. A40/1836-04.

Resolution of Federal Commercial Court of North-Western Circuit of 28 August 2003 No. A42-9072/02-C1.

Resolution of High Commercial Court Presidium of 12 December 2005 No. 9982/05 in case No. A40-47191/04-60-485.

Resolution of Presidium of High Commercial Court of No. 17020/10 of 24 May 2011.

Resolution of Presidium of High Commercial Court of Russian Federation of 05 October 2010 in case No. 6547/10.

Resolution of Presidium of High Commercial Court of Russian Federation of 8 June 2010 No. 904/10 in case No. A40-33259/09-39-283, 10 Bulletin of High Commercial Court of Russian Federation (October, 2010).

Resolution of Presidium of High Commercial Court of Russian Federation of 5 October 2010 No. 6547/10.

Resolution of Presidium of Supreme Council of USSR of 10 August 1960 'On ratification of Convention on Recognition and Enforcement of Foreign Arbitral Awards'. 32 Bulletin of Supreme Council of USSR, 304 (15 August 1960).
Resolution of the Presidium of High Commercial Court of 25 February 2014 No. 14467/13 in case No. A65-27211/2011.
Ruling of Commercial Court of Sakhalin region of 14 July 2009 No. A59-2213/2009.
Ruling of High Commercial Court of 25 April 2011 in the case No. A56-32532/2010.
Ruling of High Commercial Court of Russian Federation of 25 July 2011 No. 6857/11.
Ruling of Supreme Court of Russian Federation of 4 February 2000 No. 5-Г00-4.
Ruling of Supreme Court of Russian Federation of 9 November 2001 No. 5-Г01-142.
Ruling of Supreme Court of Russian Federation of 10 November 1997 No. 34-Г97-8.
Ruling of Supreme Court of Russian Federation of 11 January .2002 No. 5-Г01-168.
Ruling of the High Commercial Court of the Russian Federation dated 20 July 2009 No. VAS-7426/09 in case No. A40-7480/08-68-127.
Ruling of the Supreme Court of Russian Federation dated 29 February 2016 in case No. 309-эС15-12928.
Ruling of the Supreme Court of Russian Federation No 305-эС14-2600 in case No. A40-87194/13-68-844 of 12 January 2015.
Veteran Petroleum Limited (Cyprus) v. The Russian Federation, UNCITRAL, PCA Case No. AA 228 – ITAlaw, http://www.italaw.com/cases/1151#sthash.kLT7040Z.dpuf (accessed 30 October 2016).
Vladimir Berschader and Moïse Berschader v. the Russian Federation, SCC Case No. 080/2004.
Yukos Universal Limited (Isle of Man) v. The Russian Federation, UNCITRAL, PCA Case No. AA 227 – ITAlaw, http://www.italaw.com/cases/1175#sthash.3Ix1oG1S.dpuf (accessed 30 October 2016).

Rules of international arbitration centres

International Commercial Arbitration Court Rules. Approved by Order No. 76 of the Chamber of Commerce and Industry of the Russian Federation on 18 October 2005 as amended by the Order No 28 of the Chamber of Commerce and Industry of the Russian Federation of 23 June 2010.
International Commercial Arbitration Court. Rules on arbitration of international commercial disputes. Approved by Order No. 6 of the Chamber of Commerce and Industry of the Russian Federation on 11 January 2017. In force since 27 January 2017.
Regulation on Organizational Bases of the International Commercial Arbitration Court at the Chamber of Commerce and Industry of the Russian Federation. Approved by Order No. 6 of the Chamber of Commerce and Industry of the Russian Federation on 11 January 2017. In force since 27 January 2017.
Maritime Arbitration Commission Rules. Approved by Order No. 93 of the Chamber of Commerce and Industry of the Russian Federation on 21 December 2006, as amended by the Order No 132 of the Chamber of Commerce and Industry of the Russian Federation of 27 December 2011.

Maritime Arbitration Commission Rules. Approved by Order No. 5 of the Chamber of Commerce and Industry of the Russian Federation on 11 January 2017. In force since 27 January 2017.

Arbitration Rules of the Association for the Promotion of Arbitration. Approved by the Decision of the Board of the Association for the Promotion of Arbitration on 21 April 2014.

The Chapter is current as of 31 July 2017.

CHAPTER 8
Tajikistan

Shirinbek Milikbekov & Zhanyl Abdrakhmanova

List of Abbreviations

CIS	Commonwealth of Independent States
Civil Code	Civil Code of Tajikistan, Part I No. 6 dated 30 June 1999, Part II No. 12 dated 12 December 1999, Part III No. 3 dated 1 March 2005
Civil Procedure Code	Civil Procedure Code of Tajikistan No. 1 dated 5 January 2008
Constitution of Tajikistan	Constitution of the Republic of Tajikistan dated 6 November 1994
Criminal Code	Criminal Code of Tajikistan No. 9 29 May 1998
Criminal Procedure Code	Criminal Procedure Code of Tajikistan No. 12 3 December 2009
Domestic Arbitration Law	Law of Tajikistan on Arbitration Courts No. 344 dated 5 January 2008
Economic Court Proceedings Code	Economic Court Proceedings Code of Tajikistan No. 1 dated 5 January 2008
International Arbitration Law	Law of Tajikistan on International Commercial Arbitration No. 1183 dated 18 March 2015
New York Convention	United Nations Convention on the Recognition and Enforcement of Foreign Arbitral Awards, 1958, New York

UNCITRAL	United Nations Commission on International Trade Law
UNCITRAL Model Law	UNCITRAL Model Law on International Commercial Arbitration 1985 (as amended in 2006)
USSR	Union of Soviet Socialist Republics

§8.01 GENERAL INTRODUCTION

[A] Historical Development of the Legal System

1.1. The legal system in Tajikistan is codified and is based on the continental and Soviet legal systems. It evolved as a part of the Soviet legal system during the Union of Soviet Socialist Republics (USSR) period. Tajikistan became independent in 1991 and started building its own legal system, which is still broadly based on the Soviet legal system in many respects. The current legal system of Tajikistan is similar to the legal systems of other former Soviet states containing Civil,[1] Civil Procedure,[2] Criminal,[3] Criminal Procedure,[4] Labour[5] and other Codes,[6] laws and secondary legislation adopted in their furtherance.

1.2. With its independence, Tajikistan inherited some of the international treaties signed by the USSR and has also signed a number of international treaties as an independent state. As a result, Tajikistan is now a party to most of the key international treaties in various areas recognised worldwide.[7]

1.3. Most recent legislation developments in Tajikistan demonstrate the country's willingness to improve the measures intended for foreign investment protection and the country's overall policy to establish a more investor-friendly environment.[8] These changes are related particularly to the establishment of neutral and impartial mechanisms for the protection of investors, such as international commercial arbitration.

---

1. Civil Code of Tajikistan, Part I No. 6 (30 June 1999), Part II No. 12 (12 December 1999), Part III No. 3 (1 March 2005), http://mmk.tj/ru/legislation/legislation-base/codecs/.
2. Civil Procedure Code of Tajikistan No. 1 (5 January 2008), http://mmk.tj/ru/legislation/legislation-base/codecs/.
3. Criminal Code of Tajikistan No. 9 (29 May 1998), http://mmk.tj/ru/legislation/legislation-base/codecs/.
4. Criminal Procedure Code of Tajikistan No. 12 (3 December 2009), http://mmk.tj/ru/legislation/legislation-base/codecs/.
5. Labour Code of Tajikistan No. 9 (15 May 1997), http://mmk.tj/ru/legislation/legislation-base/codecs/.
6. Codes of Tajikistan, http://mmk.tj/ru/legislation/legislation-base/codecs/.
7. International treaties of Tajikistan, http://mmk.tj/ru/international-legal-documents/multifeature/.
8. Laws of Tajikistan adopted for 2015, http://mmk.tj/ru/legislation/legislation-base/271/.

[B] The Legal Profession

1.4. Tajik legislation provides for a variety of legal professions, such as judges,[9] advocates,[10] notaries,[11] prosecutors,[12] etc.

1.5. Tajik laws do not restrict private legal practice to advocates only. Advocates (holding a licence) and qualified lawyers (holding a degree in law) are private practising lawyers in Tajikistan. This system is explained by the different regulatory frameworks applied to advocates and qualified lawyers, as well as different access to the legal practice and professional liability.

1.6. Criminal proceedings now require court representation of a party (defence) by advocates only.[13] Parties may be represented by advocates and qualified lawyers in all other (civil, administrative) cases. Moreover, the legal education of a court representative is not required at all in cases other than in criminal cases, and a party may be represented by any duly authorised representative, including its officers.

[C] Sources of Arbitration Law

1.7. There are two separate laws for international and domestic arbitration in Tajikistan. The Law on International Commercial Arbitration No. 1183 dated 18 March 2015 ('International Arbitration Law') governs international arbitration.[14] The UNCITRAL Model Law (as amended in 2006) served as a basis for the newly adopted International Arbitration Law. The International Arbitration Law applies to the establishment and work of institutional and ad hoc arbitration.[15] It is based on the principles of the equality of parties, freedom of the parties to appoint arbitrators, applicable law of the agreement, procedure of arbitration and language of the proceeding, contractual jurisdiction, and priority of internationally recognised principles of international law.[16]

1.8. The Law of Arbitration Courts No. 344 dated 5 January 2008 ('Domestic Arbitration Law') governs domestic arbitration matters.[17] Domestic Arbitration Law has a

---

9. Constitutional Law of Tajikistan on Courts No. 1084 (26 July 2014), http://mmk.tj/ru/legislation/legislation-base/.
10. Law of Tajikistan on Advocates and Advocacy No. 1182 (18 March 2015), http://mmk.tj/ru/legislation/legislation-base/.
11. Law of Tajikistan on Public Notaries No. 810 (16 April 2012), http://mmk.tj/ru/legislation/legislation-base/.
12. Constitutional Law of Tajikistan on Prosecution No. 107 (25 July 2005), http://mmk.tj/ru/legislation/legislation-base/.
13. Article 49(1) of the Criminal Procedure Code of Tajikistan.
14. Law of Tajikistan on International Commercial Arbitration No. 1183 (18 March 2015), http://mmk.tj/ru/legislation/legislation-base/.
15. Article 1(1) of the International Arbitration Law.
16. Article 4 of the International Arbitration Law.
17. Law of Tajikistan on Arbitration Courts No. 344 (5 January 2008), http://mmk.tj/ru/legislation/legislation-base/.

different scope of application. Article 1(3) of the Domestic Arbitration Law states that its provisions shall not apply to international arbitration. Article 4.1. of the Domestic Arbitration Law lists non-arbitrable disputes.

1.9. On 31 May 2012 the Lower Chamber of the Parliament passed Resolution No. 804 on the accession of the Republic of Tajikistan to the United Nation Convention on the Recognition and Enforcement of Foreign Arbitral Awards, which subsequently came into force in Tajikistan on 14 August 2012 and now constitutes an integral part of the Tajik national legal system, which prevails in the event of inconsistencies between its provisions and national laws.

1.10. Chapter 28 of the Tajik Economic Court Proceedings Code[18] and Chapter 44 of the Tajik Civil Procedure Code govern the recognition and enforcement of foreign arbitral awards.

[D]   International Legal Framework, Supremacy of International Law

1.11. Article 10 of the Tajik Constitution states that international legal acts recognised by Tajikistan constitute an integral part of the country's legal system and shall apply in cases of contradiction with domestic laws.[19] The same provision is repeated in the Law on International Treaties of the Republic of Tajikistan.[20]

1.12. As previously mentioned, Tajikistan is a party to the UN Convention on the Recognition and Enforcement of Foreign Arbitral Awards, 1958 (New York Convention) and various other international, regional and bilateral treaties.

[E]   Available Dispute Resolution Mechanisms

1.13. Disputes may be resolved through the state courts, domestic arbitration and international arbitration in Tajikistan.

1.14. There is currently no mediation in Tajikistan. The Draft Law on Mediation prepared by the Ministry of Justice, the President's Executive Office and the deputies of the lower Chamber of the Tajik parliament has been discussed, but has not yet been adopted.[21]

1.15. There are also several optional consent-based mechanisms available for dispute resolution in certain areas, such as conciliation commissions or quasi-arbitration for labour disputes that are used in practice.[22]

---

18. Economic Court Proceedings Code of Tajikistan No. 1 (5 January 2008), http://mmk.tj/ru/legislation/legislation-base/codecs/.
19. A. Taukhidi, Role and Place of Legislation in Formation and Development of the Private International Law: On the Example of the Republic of Tajikistan and the Islamic Republic of Iran, The Way of Science 2014, No. 2, p. 61.
20. Article 4(2) of the Law of Tajikistan on International Treaties of the Republic of Tajikistan No. 908 (11 December 1999), http://mmk.tj/ru/legislation/legislation-base/.
21. Asia Plus publication, http://news.tj/en/news/tajikistan/society/20140430/draft-mediation-law-discussed-dushanbe.
22. Chapters 15 and 16 of Labour Code of Tajikistan.

[F] Judicial System

1.16. The structure of the Tajik judicial system has been fairly stable during recent years. The Tajik court system involves the Constitutional Court having constitutional jurisdiction and general jurisdiction courts. Each branch of the courts of general jurisdiction has three instances (first, cassation and supervision). The Supreme Court and the Highest Economic Court head the courts of general jurisdiction, subject to their competence, and have special powers to issue binding opinions in cases of the contradictory application of the same rules by the general jurisdiction courts.[23]

[G] Arbitration Institutions

1.17. There are no international arbitration institutions established and functioning in Tajikistan. The only domestic arbitration institution established in Tajikistan is the Arbitration Court under the Republic of Tajikistan's Chamber of Commerce and Industry,[24] which is currently not active given that arbitration is still rather underdeveloped as an alternative dispute resolution mechanism in Tajikistan.

[H] Sovereign Immunity and International Arbitration

1.18. There is no specific law in Tajikistan governing its sovereign immunity. Meantime, the Soviet approach is taken by the country in regard to sovereign immunity. Thus, Tajikistan supports the absolute immunity doctrine i.e. immunity is not considered waived if the state is involved in commercial or economic relations. The waiver of immunity shall be expressly provided in the undertakings of the state. As an example may serve several provisions in the Law on Investment Agreement No. 344 dated 19 March 2013 referring to the possibility of providing for the waiver of sovereign immunity by Tajikistan in investment agreements.[25]

§8.02 ARBITRATION AGREEMENT

[A] Introduction

1.19. Tajikistan is currently in the very early stages of using arbitration as an alternative dispute resolution mechanism. Therefore, there is essentially no court practice established in this regard. Meantime, court practice, including that related to recognition and enforcement of foreign arbitral awards remains uncertain due to lack of public access to court decisions and publication of the same.

---

23. Constitutional Law of Tajikistan on Courts No. 1084 (26 July 2014).
24. Information about Arbitration Court under the Chamber of Commerce and Industry of Tajikistan, http://tpp.tj//dditem/AboutCourtofarbitration/.
25. Article 22 of the Law of Tajikistan on Investment Agreement No. 944 (19 March 2013), http://mmk.tj/ru/legislation/legislation-base/.

[B] Validity of the Arbitration Agreement

[1] Requirements of a Valid Arbitration Agreement

1.20. The validity of an arbitration agreement/clause depends on: (i) its form; (ii) its content; and (iii) the capacity of the parties to enter into the agreement. An arbitration agreement must be executed in writing.[26] Parties to an arbitration agreement shall be duly authorised to execute the agreement.

1.21. The Domestic Arbitration Law requires that the arbitration agreement contains the following in order to be valid: names of the parties, subject matter of the dispute, name of the arbitration court (if choosing the permanent one), number and names of the arbitrators, applicable rules, dispute trial period, penalties for non-performance of the obligations thereunder, location and time of execution. An arbitration agreement shall also specify the applicable arbitration rules in case of ad hoc arbitration.[27]

[C] Concluding the Arbitration Agreement

1.22. An arbitration agreement shall be executed in writing in form of: (i) a separate agreement; or (ii) an arbitration clause; or (iii) a reference in the arbitration agreement made to a written document containing an arbitration clause that makes this clause a part of the arbitration agreement.

1.23. An arbitration agreement is deemed to be executed in writing if it is made in a document signed by the parties or in an exchange of letters, telex, telegrams or other means of telecommunication that provide a record of the agreement, or in an exchange of statements of claim and defence in which the existence of an agreement is alleged by one party and is not denied by another.[28]

[D] The Doctrine of Separability

1.24. Article 21 of the International Arbitration Law provides that the arbitral tribunal may independently rule on its jurisdiction to hear the case, including on the existence and validity of the arbitration agreement. While doing so, the arbitrators are required to treat the arbitration clause independently from the conditions of the main agreement. Likewise, the invalidity of the latter shall not entail the invalidity of the arbitration clause.

1.25. Despite the statutory recognition of the arbitration clause separability, due to a lack of practice local courts' attitude towards this matter remains uncertain. It is therefore unclear how the Tajik courts would treat an arbitration clause in an agreement that does not bear the signatures of the parties, but has been exchanged in

---

26. Article 11 of the International Arbitration Law.
27. Article 6 of the Domestic Arbitration Law.
28. Article 11 of the International Arbitration Law.

other ways. As such, the question here is whether or not the courts would deem such an exchange as an adequate record of the agreement to arbitrate.

[E] Invalidity of the Arbitration Agreement

1.26. Arbitration agreements are subject to the general requirements of validity specified by the Tajik Civil Code. Grounds for invalidity may be classified as based on the type of defects the agreement may have. Invalid agreements are normally divided into agreements with a defect in form, subject, will and/or content.[29] Requirements pertaining to the formal validity of an arbitration agreement have already been discussed above.

1.27. Unfortunately, no statistics on the arbitration agreements found to be invalid is currently available in Tajikistan, but the state courts are not likely to be supportive of arbitration once it starts being used by contracting parties on a more regular basis for the resolution of disputes.

[F] Arbitrability

[1] Disputes Capable of Settlement by Arbitration

1.28. International Arbitration Law provides that the parties may submit for international commercial arbitration any cross-border disputes resulting from contractual and other civil law relationships arising during the course of foreign trade and other forms of international economic relations, and disputes if one of the commercial parties is located outside of Tajikistan.

1.29. Thus, pursuant to Article 1(2-3) of the International Arbitration Law the following disputes are capable of being resolved through arbitration under the agreement of the parties:

- disputes arising from contractual and other civil relations emerged in the course of cross-border and other international economic relations, provided one of the commercial parties is located outside Tajikistan;
- other disputes of economic nature submitted for international arbitration under the agreement of the parties if this submission does not contradict Tajik laws.

1.30. Restrictions on the arbitrability of certain disputes may only be envisaged by the law or international treaties of Tajikistan.

1.31. Disputes arising from civil and commercial relations may be referred to domestic arbitration in case if the parties involved in the dispute are local and in the extent allowed by the Domestic Arbitration Law.

---

29. Articles 192-204 of the Civil Code of Tajikistan.

[2] Disputes Not Capable of Settlement by Arbitration

1.32. Article 4(1) of the Domestic Arbitration Law provides that disputes arising from civil and commercial relations may be referred to arbitration, except for disputes:

(a) on the establishment of facts with legal importance;
(b) on the protection of honour, dignity and business reputation;
(c) on appeals on orders of the authorities dealing with administrative disputes;
(d) on bankruptcy;
(e) on the reimbursement of harm caused to the life and health of a person;
(f) disputes arising from the succession;
(g) disputes arising from making records on civil status acts;
(h) disputes regarding the procedure and terms of entering into and terminating a marriage;
(i) disputes regarding proprietary and personal non-proprietary relations arising in a family between spouses, parents and children or other family members;
(j) disputes arising in connection with the adoption, guardianship or patronage of children for raising;
(k) dispute on recognition of agreements as executed;
(l) housing disputes;
(m) disputes related to intellectual property;
(n) disputes that require a different procedure of consideration under Tajik law or the agreement of the parties.

1.33. Disputes related to privatisation of state property, seizure of property in state interest, disputes over immovable property located in Tajikistan, as well as corporate disputes arising from the constituent documents of a company are also considered non-arbitrable.[30] Although labour disputes are not specified as non-arbitrable by the Domestic Arbitration Law, these shall be tried by the state courts in accordance with the Tajik Labour Code and, consequently, are not subject to arbitration either.

[G] Effect of Arbitration Agreement on Third Parties (Party Substitution, Guarantee Agreements, Group of Companies Doctrine)

1.34. Tajik law is silent about the binding effect of an arbitration agreement on third parties. Moreover, and as noted above, there is no court practice in this regard at present.

---

30. Sh. Mengliev, Arbitratjnoe Rassmotrenie Vneshekonomicheskikh Sporov (Арбитражное рассмотрение внешэкономических споров), Dushanbe 'EJOD' 2009, p. 161.

1.35. Third parties may become bound under the arbitration agreement in the event of succession, or of the assignment or subrogation of an agreement containing an arbitration clause.

1.36. It is necessary to ensure that all the required formalities are met in the event of the succession, assignment or subrogation under an agreement containing an arbitration clause as the state courts will be rather formalistic when evaluating the effectiveness of the arbitration clause with regard to a third party.

[H] Termination of Arbitration Agreements

1.37. Tajik law does not contain any specific provisions regarding the termination of an arbitration agreement; therefore, such terminations shall be subject to the general agreement termination rules specified in the Tajik Civil Code.[31]

[I] Drafting Arbitration Clauses

1.38. The parties must carefully comply with all the applicable requirements set out in the Domestic and International Arbitration Laws when drafting arbitration agreements/clauses.[32]

1.39. It is also advisable to include the full scope of a dispute subject matter submitted to the arbitration along with the following wording in the arbitration clause for the avoidance of doubt as it is often left out by the parties: 'The arbitral award rendered under this Agreement is final and binding on the Parties.'

1.40. In the case of institutional arbitration, it is highly advisable not only to specify the name of the arbitral institution and its rules, but also to check the correct name of the arbitration institution in both languages in bilingual contracts. If the respective agreement is in two languages, which is often the case when Tajik parties are involved, it is highly recommended to check the correct name of the institution in both languages.

§8.03 APPLICABLE LAW

[A] Introduction

1.41. Article 43 of the International Arbitration Law states that the arbitral tribunal shall settle a dispute in accordance with the rules of law chosen by the parties as applicable to the substance of a dispute. Any reference made to the law or legal system of any state shall be interpreted as a reference to the material law of that state, but not to its conflict of law rules. If no law is chosen by the parties, the arbitral tribunal shall apply the law determined under the conflict of laws rules it considers applicable. In all

---

31. Chapters 25 and 28 of the Civil Code of Tajikistan.
32. Article 6 of the Domestic Arbitration Law and Art. 11 of International Arbitration Law.

cases, the arbitral tribunal shall make a decision in accordance with the terms of a contract and shall consider the trade customs applicable to the transaction.

[B] The Law Governing the Arbitration

1.42. Tajik law governs the following arbitration related issues: (i) the validity of arbitration agreements/clauses, (ii) arbitrability of the dispute subject matter, (iii) procedures for the enforcement of domestic arbitral awards and the recognition and enforcement of foreign arbitral awards.

[C] Party Autonomy on Choice of Law Issues

1.43. Tajik arbitration laws are silent about parties' autonomy in choosing law issues, therefore parties shall choose the law applicable to the substance of a dispute and the arbitration agreement subject to the general rules set out in the Tajik Civil Code.

[D] Restrictions on Party Autonomy

1.44. Article 1198 of the Tajik Civil Code states that the provisions contained in the section of the Civil Code on private international law do not limit the application of any mandatory rules governing the relations of the parties irrespective of the law chosen by them.

1.45. Article 1219(2) of the Civil Code states that in the event that no applicable law is chosen by the parties, the law of the country to which the contract is most closely connected shall apply. A contract is deemed to have the closest connection with the law of the country where a party responsible for the substantial performance of a contract resides or has the main place of its operations, unless the law or contract provides otherwise, and Article 1219(1) of the Civil Code contains a list of the parties responsible for substantial performance under different types of contracts (e.g., the seller in a purchase/sale contract and the creditor in a credit/loan contract).

1.46. Article 1197 of the Civil Code limits the application of foreign law in cases where its application contradicts the public policy of Tajikistan, whilst the refusal to apply foreign law may not be based merely on the difference between the legal, political or economic system of the respective state and the same systems of Tajikistan.

1.47. The notion of 'International public policy' is not recognised under Tajik law.

[E] No Explicit Choice of Law

[1] Introduction

1.48. As noted above, the law most closely connected with the legal relations shall apply to contractual obligations in the absence of the explicit choice of law.[33] The

---

33. Article 1219(2) of the Civil Code of Tajikistan.

general rule for tortious obligations is that the law of the state where a tortious act has taken place shall apply.[34]

[2] Relevant Conflict of Law Rules

1.49. Chapter 64 of the Civil Code covers conflict of law rules with regard to the legal status of individuals and legal entities, transactions, powers of attorneys, limitation period, intellectual property rights, rights in rem, contractual and tortious obligations, guardianship, IP and succession.

1.50. The principle of closest connection is clarified in Article 1219(2) of the Civil Code specifying the party responsible for substantial performance under different types of contracts (e.g., seller in a purchase/sale contract, creditor in a loan/credit agreement.)

[F] The Law Governing the Arbitration Agreement

1.51. Tajik law does not specify the law governing arbitration agreements, therefore parties may choose the law governing the arbitration agreement subject to the general rules set out in the Tajik Civil Code.

§8.04 THE ARBITRATORS

[A] Appointment of Arbitrators

1.52. The International Arbitration Law leaves the number, procedure of appointment and qualification of arbitrators at the discretion of the parties. Therefore, the parties may address these issues in the arbitration agreement. Parties to an arbitration agreement are free to elect either one or more arbitrators for a particular dispute. In the absence of an agreement between the parties on the number of arbitrators, each dispute must be resolved by three arbitrators. The failure by the parties to address them in the arbitration agreement gives the arbitral tribunal the right to resolve this issue independently.[35]

1.53. Parties are also free to decide upon the appointment procedure of arbitrators, subject to compliance with the provisions of the arbitration legislation. Article 16 of the International Arbitration Law stipulates that if the parties fail to agree upon the procedure for appointing arbitrators for arbitration consisting of three arbitrators, the claimant and the defendant shall appoint them in their respective statements of claims and defences. The third arbitrator shall be appointed by the arbitrators appointed in the statements of the parties. Failure to appoint the arbitrators leaves the resolution of this issue to the Chairman of the arbitral tribunal.

---

34. Article 1225 of the Civil Code of Tajikistan.
35. Article 16 of the International Arbitration Law.

1.54. The absence of an agreement on the appointment of a sole arbitrator leaves the resolution of this issue to the Chairman of the arbitral tribunal.

1.55. When dealing with the issue of the appointment of arbitrators, the Chairman of the tribunal is required to consider all the issues ensuring the appointment of a qualified, independent and impartial arbitrator. If an appointed arbitrator does not meet these requirements, a party may appeal against the appointment of this arbitrator.[36]

1.56. Decisions made by the arbitration tribunal regarding the appointment of the arbitrators may not be appealed.

[B] Qualification of Arbitrators

1.57. Requirements regarding the individuals nominated as arbitrators may be agreed upon by the parties or defined in the rules of the arbitration tribunal.

1.58. The International Arbitration Law defines an arbitrator as an individual who is at least 25 years old, has higher education, is independent from the parties, is not directly or indirectly interested in the outcome of a case and who has agreed to be an arbitrator.

1.59. A sole arbitrator shall have higher legal education and at least two years of legal experience. The Chairman of the arbitration tribunal shall have higher legal education in cases of collective dispute resolution.[37]

1.60. Article 15 of the International Arbitration Law specifies categories of individuals who may not be appointed by the parties as arbitrators. These include individuals who:

- are elected or appointed as judges in the competent courts of Tajikistan;
- have disabilities or limited capability as established by the courts;
- have a record of conviction that has not expired;
- are members of the parliament of Tajikistan;
- are public officials.

[C] Powers and Duties of Arbitrators

1.61. The main duty of arbitrators is to treat the parties equally and to ensure that each party is given the full opportunity to present its case.[38]

1.62. Arbitrators are also under an obligation to observe the agreement of the parties and the applicable procedural rules. The powers conferred upon the arbitral tribunal include the power to determine the admissibility, relevance, materiality and weight of any evidence presented by the parties.

---

36. Articles 17, 18 of the International Arbitration Law.
37. Article 15 of the International Arbitration Law.
38. Article 25 of the International Arbitration Law.

[D] Challenges and Replacement of Arbitrators

1.63. Parties may mutually agree upon the procedure for challenging an arbitrator. If the procedure for challenging an arbitrator is not agreed upon, the party interested in challenging shall file a written statement outlining the challenge with the tribunal based on valid grounds within fifteen days following the day on which the interested party learns about the appointment of the relevant arbitrator.[39]

1.64. If the arbitrator who has been challenged does not give notice of self-recusation or if the other party does not agree with the self-recusation, the matter shall be addressed by the other two arbitrators of the tribunal before case proceedings begin. If the arbitrators do not reach an agreement before the case proceedings begin, or if there is a challenge to two or more arbitrators or to the sole arbitrator, the challenge of the arbitrator(s) of a permanent arbitration tribunal or ad hoc arbitration tribunal shall be addressed by the Chairman of that tribunal.

1.65. Arbitration proceedings shall be postponed for the period required to resolve the matter of the challenge of the arbitrator(s). An order issued by the Chairman of the arbitration tribunal on the challenge of the arbitrator(s) may not be appealed. An arbitrator shall reject his/her powers and shall not perform his/her functions if the arbitrator proves to be incapable of performing them, or substantially delays case proceedings due to other reasons.[40]

1.66. The arbitrator's power may also be terminated based on the agreement of the parties. If no agreement is reached, either of the parties to a dispute tried by the permanent arbitration tribunal may refer to the Chairman of that tribunal and a party to a dispute tried by the ad hoc tribunal may refer to the tribunal with a request to terminate the arbitrator's authorities. A decision on this matter may not be appealed.

1.67. Other cases of terminating the arbitrator's authorities are defined by the arbitration rules. The powers of the arbitrators and the sole arbitrator shall also be terminated in the event of a challenge or self-recusation. If the arbitrator's authorities are terminated on the basis of a challenge or the party's request, another arbitrator shall be appointed under the procedure applied for the appointment of the replaced arbitrator.

[E] Compensation of Arbitrators

1.68. Article 23 of the International Arbitration Law defines the following types of arbitration costs:

- remuneration of arbitrator(s);
- costs incurred by arbitrators due to their participation in the arbitration proceedings including travel, accommodation and meal costs;
- amounts due to experts and translators;

---

39. Article 18 of the International Arbitration Law.
40. Article 19 of the International Arbitration Law.

- expenses incurred by the arbitrators in connection with the review and examination of written evidence and exhibits at their location;
- expenses incurred by witnesses;
- payment for the services of a representative of the party, in favour of which an arbitral award has been rendered;
- organisational and material costs of arbitration proceedings.

1.69. The amount of the arbitrator's remuneration shall be defined in line with a rating scale for the payment of the arbitrator's services envisaged by the arbitration rules. If no reference is made to the fixed arbitrator's remuneration, the tribunal may set the amount of the arbitrator's remuneration in each particular case subject to the amount of the claim, dispute complexity, etc.[41]

1.70. Costs connected with the resolution of a dispute by the arbitration shall be distributed by the arbitration pro rata to the satisfied and rejected claims unless the parties agree otherwise. The distribution of these costs shall be specified in an order or award of the arbitration tribunal.[42]

1.71. Payment for the services of a representative of the party in favour of which an arbitral award has been rendered, as well as other costs connected with the arbitration proceedings, may be laid on the other party if a claim for the reimbursement of incurred costs is brought during the arbitration proceedings and is satisfied.[43]

§8.05 JURISDICTION OF THE ARBITRATION TRIBUNAL

[A] Introduction

1.72. The International Arbitration Law respects the competence-competence principle and allows an arbitral tribunal to determine its own jurisdiction.

[B] The Arbitrators' Determination of Their Jurisdiction

1.73. Article 21 of the International Arbitration Law states that the arbitral tribunal may rule on its own jurisdiction, including any objections regarding the presence and validity of the arbitration agreement. If the tribunal rules that it has jurisdiction, any party may, within fifteen days after having received notice of that ruling, request that the Presidium of that arbitration tribunal makes a final decision on the competence. Arbitration proceedings shall be suspended while the competence matter is being considered.

1.74. A plea that the tribunal does not have jurisdiction shall be raised no later than the submission of the statement of defence and a plea that the tribunal is beyond the scope

---

41. Article 23(3) of the International Arbitration Law.
42. Article 24(1) of the International Arbitration Law.
43. Article 24(2) of the International Arbitration Law.

of its jurisdiction shall be raised as soon as the matter alleged to be beyond the scope of its jurisdiction is raised during the course of the arbitral proceedings.[44]

§8.06 THE PROCEDURE BEFORE THE ARBITRATION TRIBUNAL

[A] Introduction

1.75. The International Arbitration Law is based on the UNCITRAL Model Law approach and provides for a sufficient degree of flexibility for the tribunal and the parties in conducting the arbitration proceedings.

[B] General Principle of Non-interference

1.76. Article 5(3) of the International Arbitration Law prohibits any interference with the activity of a permanent arbitration court.

[C] General Principles of Arbitration Procedure

1.77. Article 26 of the International Arbitration Law states that 'subject to the provisions of this Law, the parties are free to agree on the procedure to be followed by the arbitral tribunal in conducting the proceedings'. The International Arbitration Law does not establish significant limits to the party's autonomy. Article 25 of the International Arbitration Law obliges the arbitral tribunal to treat the parties equally and to grant them a full opportunity to present their case.

1.78. Article 4 of the International Arbitration Law sets forth the following principles of the tribunal's activity:

- equality of the parties;
- free choice of arbitrators, applicable law, procedure and language for arbitration proceedings;
- contractual jurisdiction for all cases in question;
- priority of international law principles;
- independence of the arbitration tribunal and arbitrators;
- confidentiality of proceedings;
- promotion of the settlement of a dispute by executing a settlement agreement;
- rendering of final arbitral awards.

[D] Commencing the Arbitration Proceedings

1.79. Article 29 of the International Arbitration Law provides that the arbitration proceedings in respect of a particular dispute commence on the day on which a request

---

44. Article 21(2) of the International Arbitration Law.

for that dispute to be submitted for arbitration is received by the defendant, unless the parties agree otherwise. Proceedings at the permanent tribunal shall commence on the day set by the arbitration rules.

[E] Conduct of Arbitration

[1] Written Submissions

1.80. Subject to the provisions of the International Arbitration Law, the parties are free to agree upon the procedure to be followed by the arbitral tribunal in conducting the proceedings. The International Arbitration Law also provides for certain procedures to be followed in the absence of an agreement reached by the parties, for instance regarding the failure to submit a statement of defence or other documents. The level of party autonomy provided for by the International Arbitration Law is relatively high.[45]

[2] Post-Hearing Briefs

1.81. Post-hearing briefs are not envisaged by the International Arbitration Law. In light of lack of practice, it is rather impossible to draw a firm conclusion that post-hearing briefs may be allowed by the arbitral tribunal under the agreement of the parties.

[3] Evidence (Admissibility, Documentary Evidence)

1.82. Article 39 of the International Arbitration Law states that the parties have the right to provide evidence in order to prove the facts they rely upon to support their claims or defence.

[4] Witness and Expert Testimony

1.83. The International Arbitration Law contains certain rules regarding tribunal-appointed experts only.[46] The arbitrators may, at their own discretion, order examination by an expert. The International Arbitration Law does not contain special provisions regarding factual witness statements or party-appointed experts. There is also no practice established in this regard in Tajikistan at present.

[F] Hearings

1.84. Article 37 of the International Arbitration Law states that the arbitral tribunal shall decide whether to hold oral hearings for the presentation of evidence or oral arguments, or whether the proceedings shall be conducted on the basis of documents

---

45. Article 26 of the International Arbitration Law.
46. Article 40 of the International Arbitration Law.

and other materials. The arbitral tribunal shall hold such hearings at an appropriate stage of the proceedings, if they are requested by either of the parties.

1.85. The parties shall be given sufficient advance notice of any hearing and of any sitting of the arbitral tribunal for the purposes of the inspection of goods, other property or documents. If any party fails to appear at a hearing or fails to produce documentary evidence, the arbitral tribunal may continue the proceedings and render an award based on the available evidence.[47]

§8.07 THE ARBITRAL AWARD

[A] Introduction

1.86. The International Arbitration Law sets forth that the award must be in writing and signed by the sole arbitrator or arbitrators. The signatures of a majority of the arbitrators are sufficient for making a decision, provided that a reason why the signatures of the other arbitrators are missing is specified.

1.87. The award is final, shall enter into force immediately after it is rendered and may be appealed only in the cases provided by Article 51 of the International Arbitration Law.

1.88. It must state the reasons for rendering the award unless the parties have agreed otherwise. The arbitral award shall contain the date on which it is rendered and the location of the arbitration sitting. The award is deemed to be rendered at the location of the arbitration sitting.

1.89. The International Arbitration Law requires that after the award is made, a copy signed by the arbitrators must be delivered to each party.

[B] Deliberation and Voting

1.90. In arbitration proceedings with more than one arbitrator, any decision of the arbitral tribunal shall be made by a majority of all the arbitrators. Procedural matters may be decided upon by the chairing arbitrator, if he/she is authorised to do so by the parties or other arbitrators.[48]

[C] Different Kinds of Awards (Separate, Interim, Consent, Default, Etc.)

1.91. The International Arbitration Law does not provide for different kinds of awards. Special rules apply only to the awards on agreed terms.[49] Articles 47 and 49 of the International Arbitration Law are the only two articles in this Law referring to the term

---

47. Article 38(2) of the International Arbitration Law.
48. Article 45 of the International Arbitration Law.
49. Article 46 of the International Arbitration Law.

'final award' for the purposes of the termination of the arbitral proceedings in the event of Article 49. In other instances, the term 'award' is used.

[D] Interest and Costs

1.92. Interest is a matter of substantive Tajik law. Subject to contractual and applicable law provisions, interest on principal debt is normally awarded. Article 24 of the International Arbitration Law states that the costs connected with the resolution of a dispute by the arbitration shall be distributed by the arbitration pro rata to the satisfied and rejected claims, unless the parties agree otherwise. The distribution of such costs shall be specified in an order or an award by the arbitration tribunal.

[E] Effects of the Award

[1] *Execution*

1.93. Awards by tribunals operating in Tajikistan shall be enforced under the procedure set forth by the Tajik Economic Procedure Code discussed below.

1.94. Foreign arbitral awards shall be recognised and enforced in accordance with the Tajik Economic Procedure Law and international legal acts recognised by Tajikistan.

[2] *Res Judicata and Lis Pendens*

1.95. Article 149 of the Economic Procedure Code states that case court proceedings shall be terminated if there is an arbitral award rendered on a dispute between the same parties, regarding the same subject matter and on the same grounds, except for in the event that the economic court has refused to issue a writ of execution for the enforcement of an arbitral award.

1.96. Tajik Civil Procedure Code only contains a general rule regarding the termination of the proceedings in the event that there is an effective decision rendered on a dispute between the same parties, regarding the same subject matter and on the same grounds or a ruling on the termination of case proceedings due to the acceptance of the claimant's refusal from the claim or the approval of a settlement agreement between the parties.[50]

[F] Correction and Interpretation of the Award

1.97. Article 50 of the International Arbitration Law governs the modification, clarification or correction of an arbitral award. In accordance with this Article, any of the parties, having notified the other party, may request that the arbitral tribunal corrects any errors in computation in the award, any clerical or typographical errors or any

---

50. Article 225 of the Civil Procedure Code.

errors of a similar nature within thirty days following the receipt of the award, unless the parties agree otherwise. If the tribunal finds such a request justified, it shall correct the award or provide its interpretation within thirty days following the receipt of the request, unless the arbitration rules provide otherwise. Such a correction or interpretation becomes a part of the award. The arbitral tribunal may correct any such error upon its own initiative within the same period, having notified the parties of such a correction.

1.98. Any of the parties, having notified the other party, may request within thirty days following the receipt of the award that the arbitral tribunal makes an additional award on the claims brought during the course of the arbitral proceedings but omitted in the award, unless the arbitration rules provide otherwise. If the arbitral tribunal finds the request justified, it shall make the additional award within sixty days, unless the arbitration rules provide otherwise.

§8.08 SETTING ASIDE THE AWARD

[A] Introduction

1.99. Setting aside an award is the only way of challenging an award.[51]

1.100. A party seeking to set aside an arbitral award must file the respective application with the High Economic Court of Tajikistan within thirty days following the day on which the award is received and must provide proof supporting its application. Grounds for setting aside an award are contained in Article 51 of the International Arbitration Law and are discussed below.

1.101. An arbitral award may be set aside by the High Economic Court if the subject matter of a dispute is non-arbitrable under Tajik legislation or if it contradicts the public policy of Tajikistan. The grounds specified by the International Arbitration Law for setting aside an arbitral award mostly replicate the provisions of the New York Convention of 1958.[52]

1.102. The High Economic Court of Tajikistan may postpone the consideration of the application at the request of a party for up to one month. The delay is granted for the arbitral tribunal in order to be able to either resume hearings of the case or take other measures, which in the opinion of the arbitral tribunal will eliminate the grounds for the arbitral award to be set aside.

[B] Invalid Awards

1.103. The International Arbitration Law and the Domestic Arbitration Law do not distinguish types of awards for the purposes of the procedure for setting them aside, i.e.

---

51. Article 51(1) of the International Arbitration Law.
52. Article V of the New York Convention.

all awards rendered in Tajikistan could be equally challenged on the grounds provided in each of these laws as applicable.

1.104. Article 40 of the Domestic Arbitration Law states that an arbitral award may be appealed by a party to a case by filing a request for setting it aside with the competent court within three months following the receipt of the award unless the arbitration agreement states that the award is final.

[C] Challengeable Awards

[1] Grounds for Challenging an Award

1.105. An award rendered in an international arbitration seated in Tajikistan may be set aside by the Tajik court on the grounds specified in Article 51 of the International Arbitration Law.

1.106. An arbitral award may be set aside by the High Economic Court of Tajikistan within thirty days following the day on which the award is received only if a party seeking to set the award aside provides proof that:[53]

- a party had full or partial incapacity when executing the arbitration agreement or that the agreement is invalid under the law to which the parties have subjected it or under the law of the Republic of Tajikistan in the event of a failure to refer to such a law;
- a party was not properly notified of the appointment of an arbitrator or of the arbitral proceedings or could not present its case for any other valid reason;
- the award is issued on matters that are not specified by or do not fall within the terms of the arbitration agreement or contains matters that go beyond the scope of the arbitration agreement. Meanwhile, if the matters not covered by the arbitration agreement can be separated from those that do fall under its scope, only part of the award on the matters not covered by the agreement may be set aside;
- the structure of the arbitral tribunal or the arbitral proceedings was not in accordance with the agreement of the parties, unless such an agreement conflicts with the International Arbitration Law.

1.107. An arbitral award may be set aside by the High Economic Court if the subject matter of a dispute is non-arbitrable under Tajik legislation or if it contradicts the public policy of Tajikistan.

[2] Waiver of Right to Challenge

1.108. The International Arbitration, Domestic Arbitration Laws and both Procedural Codes of Tajikistan are silent about the possibility of waiving a right to challenge an

---

53. Article 51(2) of the International Arbitration Law.

award. Due to the absence of relevant court practice, it is not currently possible to comment on this matter.

[D] Review of Jurisdictional Awards

1.109. Article 22 of the International Arbitration Law states that the arbitral tribunal may rule on its own jurisdiction, including on any objections regarding the presence and validity of the arbitration agreement. If the tribunal rules that it has jurisdiction, any party may request, within fifteen days following receipt of a notice of that ruling, that the Presidium of that arbitration tribunal makes a final decision on the competence. Arbitration proceedings shall be suspended while the competence matter is being considered.

§8.09 RECOGNITION AND ENFORCEMENT OF THE ARBITRAL AWARD

[A] Enforcement of Domestic Awards

[1] Domestic Enforcement

1.110. There are two types of domestic awards rendered in Tajikistan: (i) awards rendered under the Domestic Arbitration Law, and (ii) awards rendered under the International Arbitration Law.

1.111. Article 52 of the International Arbitration Law states that an award rendered by the tribunal seated in Tajikistan shall be enforced in accordance with the Tajik economic procedural laws.

1.112. Chapter 27 of the Economic Procedure Code and Chapter 45 of the Civil Procedure Code govern the enforcement of awards rendered in Tajikistan. Chapter 28 of the Economic Procedure Code and Chapter 44 of the Civil Procedure Code govern the recognition and enforcement of foreign judgments and foreign arbitral awards (international commercial arbitration and arbitration tribunals).

1.113. The enforcement of arbitral awards rendered under the Domestic Arbitration Law is more or less straightforward compared to the enforcement of foreign arbitral awards in Tajikistan. It is also uncertain at this stage how arbitral awards rendered under the International Arbitration Law will be enforced in Tajikistan due to the lack of such practice.

[2] Enforcement Abroad

1.114. Tajik legislation does not deal with the enforcement of its domestic awards abroad. Such enforcement is subject to the applicable international treaty and national legislation of the country where the enforcement is sought.

[B] Enforcement of Foreign Arbitral Awards

[1] *Introduction to Recognition and Enforcement*

1.115. Foreign arbitral awards are recognised and enforced in Tajikistan only under international treaties duly recognised by Tajikistan. In the presence of international treaties foreign arbitral awards shall be enforced by the courts respectively.[54] Only a few foreign arbitral awards and judgments were recognised and enforced in the country until 2012 due to the scarce number of such treaties. These were mostly awards and judgments issued in the former Soviet countries, in particular, in Russia[55] and other countries with which Tajikistan has bilateral treaties such as China, Turkey, UAE, etc.

1.116. With Tajikistan's accession to the New York Convention of 1958 the number of cases of the recognition and enforcement of foreign arbitral awards is expected to grow. Due to the strictly confidential nature of arbitration, it is difficult to know how many cases of the recognition and enforcement of foreign arbitral awards have already been dealt with by Tajik courts during these three years. This information will probably become publicly available in the near future.

1.117. Upon its accession to the New York Convention, Tajikistan declared that it would apply the Convention only to arbitral awards made in the territories of other contracting states after the Convention entered into force for Tajikistan. It also declared that the Convention would not apply to disputes related to immovable property.[56]

1.118. Chapter 28 of the Economic Procedure Code governs the recognition and enforcement of foreign judgments and the power of recognition and enforcement of foreign arbitral awards (international commercial arbitration and arbitration tribunals) is vested on the state courts.

1.119. The Civil Procedure Code and Economic Procedure Codes grant jurisdiction over the enforcement of foreign arbitral awards to the state courts located in the place of the debtor's residence or location, or to the courts where the debtor's assets are located if the debtor's location is not known. A foreign arbitral award may be submitted for enforcement in Tajikistan within three years after it becomes effective. This period may be reinstated by the party seeking enforcement subject to the established procedure.

---

54. A. Taukhidi, Role and Place of Legislation in Formation and Development of the Private International Law: On the Example of the Republic of Tajikistan and the Islamic Republic of Iran, The Way of Science 2014, No. 2, p. 63.
55. Sh. Mengliev, Arbitratjnoe Rassmotrenie Vneshekonomicheskikh Sporov (Арбитражное рассмотрение внешэкономических споров), Dushanbe 'EJOD' 2009, p. 336.
56. Resolution of Parliament of Tajikistan No 804 on the Accession of the Republic of Tajikistan to the United Nation Convention on the Recognition and Enforcement of Foreign Arbitral Award dated 31 May 2012.

[2] Separate, Partial and Interim Awards

1.120. Tajik Civil Procedure and Economic Procedure Codes do not contain any special rules regarding the enforcement of separate, partial and interim awards.

[3] Grounds for Refusing Recognition and Enforcement

1.121. Grounds for refusal of recognition and enforcement of foreign arbitral award are provided in the international treaties and national legislation of Tajikistan. New York convention specifies in Article V the grounds for refusal of recognition and enforcement, which are duplicated in the International Arbitration Law. Such cases include the invalidity of arbitration agreement, lack of capacity, no fair hearing, excess of mandate, etc.

1.122. Economic procedure Code of Tajikistan deals with the issue of refusal of recognition and enforcement of foreign arbitral award in Article 223. Hence economic court may refuse to recognise and enforce a foreign arbitral award if it finds that:[57]

- the arbitral award has not entered into force in accordance with the law of the state where it is rendered;
- the party against whom the award is invoked has not been properly notified of the time and place of arbitration proceedings or has otherwise not been able to present its case;
- the case falls under the exclusive competence of Tajik courts under the legislation and international treaties duly recognised by Tajikistan;
- a final court decision has already been made by the Tajik court in respect of a dispute between the same parties, on the same subject matter and grounds;
- a case between the same parties on the same dispute, subject matter and grounds is being considered by a Tajik court, the latter initiated court proceedings before the initiation of the proceeding by a foreign court or the Tajik court was first to accept a claim on the same dispute between the same parties, on the same subject matter and grounds.
- the limitation period for the enforcement of a foreign arbitral award has lapsed and the economic court has not reinstated it;
- the enforcement of the award would contradict the public order of Tajikistan.

1.123. In addition to the grounds listed above, Article 54 of the International Arbitration Law reiterates mostly the provisions of the New York Convention in respect of the grounds of refusal of recognition and enforcement of an arbitral awards. Thus, recognition and enforcement may be refused:

---

57. Article 223 of the Economic Procedure Code of Tajikistan.

(i) a party against whom the arbitral award is invoked requests the refusal of its recognition and enforcement based on its application by providing the court with proof that:[58]
- either of the parties had a certain incapacity whilst executing the arbitration agreement;
- the arbitration agreement is invalid under the law to which the parties have subjected it or under the law of the country where the award is made in the event of the failure to define the applicable law;
- the party against whom the award is invoked has not been properly notified of the time and place of arbitration proceedings or has otherwise not been able to present its case;
- the award is made on a dispute that is not considered by or does not fall within the terms of the submission to arbitration, or it contains decisions on matters that go beyond the scope of the submission to arbitration, provided that, if a decision on the matters submitted to arbitration can be separated from those not submitted, the part of the award that contains decisions on matters submitted to arbitration may be recognised and enforced;
- the structure of the arbitral tribunal or the arbitral procedure was not in accordance with the agreement of the parties or was not in accordance with the law of the country where the arbitration had taken place in case of a failure to reach such an agreement;
- the award has not yet become binding on the parties, has been cancelled, or its enforcement has been suspended by the court of the country under whose law it has been rendered.

(ii) if the court establishes that the subject matter of a dispute is non-arbitrable under Tajik legislation or it contradicts the public policy of Tajikistan.

1.124. In determining the grounds for refusal of recognition and enforcement of foreign arbitral awards the economic courts of Tajikistan would mainly check the procedural issues without examining the substance of the award. The only substantive ground for refusal is considered contradiction of recognition and enforcement of foreign arbitral award with the public policy of Tajikistan. The current legislation of Tajikistan does not provide for the definition of public policy and thus, leaves this issue to the discretion of courts.

1.125. Article 1197 of the Tajik Civil Code provides that foreign law shall not be applied in case if its application would contradict order of Tajikistan. In this case the provisions of the national law shall be applicable. Meantime, this does not mean that foreign arbitral award based on the laws of Tajikistan would be recognised and enforced without the application of public policy test by courts. Article 194 of the Civil Code articulates that any agreement executed with the aim deliberately contradicting the principles of public order and moral is void.

---

58. Article 54 of the International Arbitration Law.

1.126. In the absence of the definition of public policy in the legislation courts may take a broad interpretation of the named concept in case of recognition and enforcement of foreign arbitral awards. Such interpretation may involve political, economic and security issues. Meantime, public policy is generally understood as the fundamental principles specified in the Constitution and other laws of Tajikistan, violations of which infringes on the foundations of the state.[59]

[4] Procedures for Recognition

1.127. The procedure for the recognition and enforcement of foreign arbitral awards is defined in Chapter 28 of the Economic Procedure Code of Tajikistan and Chapter 44 of the Civil Procedure Code. The issues pertaining to the recognition and enforcement of arbitral awards on economic disputes are considered by the respective economic courts at the location of the losing party based on the application of the party in favour of which the award is rendered.

1.128. A motion for the recognition and enforcement of a foreign arbitral award shall be accompanied by the following documents, which are prescribed by Article IV (1) of the New York Convention:

- duly authenticated award or duly certified copy thereof;
- original arbitration agreement or agreement containing an arbitral clause.

1.129. The motion shall be considered by one judge within one month following its submission, after which the parties to a case are notified of the time and place of a court sitting for consideration of the application.

1.130. When examining the motion in a court sitting, the economic court would determine whether grounds for the refusal to recognise and enforce a foreign arbitral award exist. In order to do so, the court would examine the arguments provided in support of the claims and defence, as well as the evidence provided by the parties without revisiting the merits of the case.

1.131. Having considered the motion for the enforcement and heard arguments of the parties, the judge renders a ruling either granting or denying the recognition and enforcement of the arbitral award. The ruling, upon its entry into force, serves as a ground for issuing a writ of execution, which triggers the execution procedure. Tajik Civil Procedure and Economic Procedure Codes allow appeals against the aforementioned ruling of a state court. Appealing on the ruling may substantially delay the award enforcement proceedings.

---

59. Sh. Mengliev, Arbitratjnoe Rassmotrenie Vneshekonomicheskikh Sporov (Арбитражное рассмотрение внешэкономических споров), Dushanbe 'EJOD' 2009, pp. 354–359.

§8.10 INVESTOR-STATE ARBITRATION

[A] General Overview of Law and Practice Related to Investor-State Arbitration

1.132. As a young state, Tajikistan is experiencing a great need for investments both local and foreign. The investment policy of the country is driven by this. A number of attempts have been made by the government to promote investment and improve the investment climate of the country. These were subsequently reflected in the Concept of State Policy for the Attraction and Protection of Investments of the Republic of Tajikistan approved under the Governmental Decree No. 755 dated 29 December 2012.[60] The concept highlights the development of investment regulatory framework in light of international development in this field as one of the major goals for the country to achieve.

1.133. The priority sectors considered to require investment include energy, infrastructure, mining, agriculture and tourism. Amongst these sectors, energy, mining and infrastructure are the ones that receive most foreign direct investment.

1.134. The Consultative Council on the Improvement of Investment Climate under the President[61] was established on the institutional level in 2007 in order to address the coordination of the state's investment policy. The authorised state body for investment is the State Committee on Investments and State Property Management. The powers of the investment committee include providing assistance to local and foreign investors in the extrajudicial resolution of disputes that may arise.[62]

1.135. The investment legal framework of Tajikistan consists of international treaties and national laws. Tajikistan entered into over forty bilateral investment treaties (BITs) and multilateral treaties with foreign states, including the Energy Charter Treaty. However, it did not sign the ICSID Convention.[63]

1.136. Tajikistan does not have a model for BITs. BITs executed since the country gained independence provide for the fair and equitable treatment of foreign investors, protection from expropriation, and the free transfer of funds. Most BITs concluded by Tajikistan allow for arbitration under the ICSID or United Nations Commission on International Trade Law (UNCITRAL) Rules. Domestic courts are also available for resolving investment disputes. However, since Tajikistan's accession to the New York Convention, arbitration is receiving more attention from investors.

---

60. Official web site of State Committee on Investments and State Property Management, http://www.gki.tj/files/zakon/121b94cff5d0f210540e59c0fba98884.pdf.
61. Official web site of Consultative Council under the President of Tajikistan, http://investmentcouncil.tj/en/.
62. Official web site of State Committee on Investments and State Property Management, http://gki.tj/ru/o_komitete/polozhenie/.
63. UNCTAD Investment Policy Review of Tajikistan, http://investmentpolicyhub.unctad.org/IPR/Index.

1.137. The repository of investment treaties and other international agreements of Tajikistan is the Ministry of Foreign Affairs. The country's international agreements are not publicly available and are provided upon request to interested persons.

1.138. Tajikistan's regulation of national investments comprises a number of scattered and unsystematised laws. The general regulation of investments is provided in the Law on Investments No. 1299 dated 15 March 2016 and the Law on Investment Agreements No. 944 dated 19 March 2013. Sector-specific regulations include the Law on Concessions No. 783 dated 26 December 2011, the Law on Production Sharing Contracts No. 238 dated 5 March 2007, and the Law on Subsoil No. 983 dated 20 July 1994. These laws mostly replicate the guarantees available to investors and assumed by the country under its international treaties.

1.139. An increasing trend for the use of investment agreements has been observed in Tajikistan since the adoption of the Law on Investment Agreements in 2013. The main reason for using this mechanism is rooted in tax and customs benefits, as well as in the international arbitration investors can enjoy thereunder. Six investment agreements have been concluded by the government following the adoption of the aforementioned law.[64]

[B] List of Investment Promotion Treaties Signed by Tajikistan

1.140. Tajikistan does not have a model investment promotion and protection treaty, but according to publicly available information it has entered into thirty-five BITs.[65]

[C] List of Investor-State Disputes (Concluded and Pending)

1.141. Only one investor-state dispute involving Tajikistan is publicly available as of 2016. Case No. V 064/2008 of the Stockholm Chamber of Commerce involving Tajikistan as a respondent was heard in 2000. The dispute concerned the breach of four exploration contracts executed by the state and a foreign investor due to the non-issuance of a licence to the claimant thereunder. The state lost the case.

1.142. Information on other concluded and pending investor-state disputes is not publicly available at present.

[D] Reform Proposals

1.143. The most recent development in this field is the adoption of the Law on International Commercial Arbitration in 2015.

---

64. Official web site of State Committee on Investments and State Property Management, http://gki.tj/ru//nvestitsii_v_rt/nformatsiya_i_statistika/reestr_soglashenii/.
65. *See* Appendix I with a list of Tajikistan's BITs.

1.144. There is currently no information available on the reforms in this field due to the extremely infrequent use of arbitration in the country. Meanwhile, reforms are expected to take place once demand for arbitration experiences significant growth in Tajikistan.

Chapter 8: Tajikistan

APPENDIX I LIST OF BITs SIGNED BY TAJIKISTAN

e#	Agreement Description	Date of signing/ entry into force
1	Agreement on the Promotion and Mutual Protection of Investments between the Government of the Republic of Tajikistan and the Government of the Chinese People's Republic	09.03.93/20.01.94
2	Agreement on the Promotion and Mutual Protection of Investments between the Republic of Tajikistan and the Czech Republic	11.02.94/06.12.95
3	Agreement on the Promotion and Mutual Protection of Investments between the Government of the Republic of Tajikistan and the Government of Slovak Republic	14.02.94/12.03.96
4	Agreement on the Promotion and Mutual Protection of Investments between the Government of the Republic of Tajikistan and the Government of the Republic of Korea	27.07.94/13.08.95
5	Agreement on the Promotion and Mutual Protection of Investments between the Government of the Republic of Tajikistan and the State of Kuwait	18.04.95/12.06.98
6	Agreement on the Promotion and Mutual Protection of Investments between the Government of the Republic of Tajikistan and the Government of the Islamic Republic of Iran	18.07.95/03.11.04
7	Agreement on the Promotion and Mutual Protection of Investments between the Government of the Republic of Tajikistan and the Government of the Republic of India	13.12.95/14.11.04
8	Agreement on the Promotion and Mutual Protection of Investments between the Republic of Tajikistan and the United Arab Emirates	17.12.95
9	Agreement on the Promotion and Mutual Protection of Investments between the Republic of Tajikistan and the Republic of Turkey	06.05.96/24.07.98
10	Agreement on the Promotion and Mutual Protection of Investments between the Government of the Republic of Tajikistan and the Government of the Republic of Belarus	05.09.98/25.08.99
11	Agreement on the Promotion and Mutual Protection of Investments between the Republic of Tajikistan and Socialist Republic of Vietnam	19.01.99

e#	Agreement Description	Date of signing/ entry into force
12	Agreement on the Promotion and Mutual Protection of Investments between the Government of the Republic of Tajikistan and the Government of the Russian Federation	17.04.99
13	Agreement on the Promotion and Mutual Protection of Investments between the Government of the Republic of Tajikistan and the Government of the Republic of Kazakhstan	16.12.33
14	Agreement on the Promotion and Mutual Protection of Investments between the Government of the Republic of Tajikistan and the Government of the Kyrgyz Republic	19.01.00
15	Agreement on the Promotion and Mutual Protection of Investments between the Government of the Republic of Tajikistan and the Cabinet of Ministers of Ukraine	06.07.01
16	Agreement on the Promotion and Mutual Protection of Investments between the Government of the Republic of Tajikistan and the Government of the Republic of Armenia	02.04.02
17	Agreement on the Promotion and Mutual Protection of Investments between the Government of the Republic of Tajikistan and the Government of the Kingdom of the Netherlands	24.07.02/01.04.04
18	Agreement on the Promotion and Mutual Protection of Investments between the Government of the Republic of Tajikistan and the Government of the Republic of Moldova	05.11.02/20.10.03
19	Agreement on the Promotion and Mutual Protection of Investments between the Government of the Republic of Tajikistan and the Government of the Republic of France	04.12.02/24.08.04
20	Agreement on the Promotion and Mutual Protection of Investments between the Republic of Tajikistan and the Federative Republic of Germany	27.03.03/25.05.06
21	Agreement on the Promotion and Mutual Protection of Investments between the Government of the Republic of Tajikistan and the Government of the Republic of Indonesia	28.10.03
22	Agreement on the Promotion and Mutual Protection of Investments between the Government of the Republic of Tajikistan and the Government of the Islamic Republic of Pakistan	13.05.04

Chapter 8: Tajikistan

e#	Agreement Description	Date of signing/ entry into force
23	Agreement on the Promotion and Mutual Protection of Investments between the Government of the Republic of Tajikistan and the Government of the Kingdom of Bahrain	09.08.05
24	Agreement on the Promotion and Mutual Protection of Investments between the Government of the Republic of Tajikistan and the Syrian Arab Republic	10.02.07
25	Agreement on the Promotion and Mutual Protection of Investments between the Government of the Republic of Tajikistan and the Government of the Republic of Azerbaijan	15.03.07/26.02.08
26	Agreement on the Promotion and Mutual Protection of Investments between the Government of the Republic of Tajikistan and the Government of the State of Qatar	06.05.07
27	Agreement on the Promotion and Mutual Protection of Investments between the Government of the Republic of Tajikistan and the Government of the Republic of Turkmenistan	04.10.07
28	Agreement on the Promotion and Mutual Protection of Investments between the Government of the Republic of Tajikistan and the Government of the People's Democratic Republic of Algeria	11.03.08
29	Agreement on the Promotion and Mutual Protection of Investments between the Republic of Tajikistan and the Economic Union of Belgium and Luxembourg	10.02.09
30	Agreement on the Promotion and Mutual Protection of Investments between the Government of the Republic of Tajikistan and the Government of the Republic of Lithuania	12.02.09/15.12.10
31	Agreement on the Promotion and Mutual Protection of Investments between the Government of the Republic of Tajikistan and Spain	26.10.90/28.11.91
32	Agreement on the Promotion and Mutual Protection of Investments between the Government of the Republic of Tajikistan and Swiss Federal Counsel	11.06.09/26.10.11
33	Agreement on the Promotion and Mutual Protection of Investments between the Republic of Tajikistan and the Republic of Austria	15.12.10/21.12.12
34	Agreement on the Promotion and Mutual Protection of Investments between the Government of the Republic of Tajikistan and the Government of the Islamic Republic of Afghanistan	26.03.14

e#	Agreement Description	Date of signing/ entry into force
35	Agreement on the Promotion and Mutual Protection of Investments between the Government of the Republic of Tajikistan and the Government of Mongolia	20.03.09/16.09.09

BIBLIOGRAPHY

A. Taukhidi, *Role and Place of Legislation in Formation and Development of the Private International Law: On the Example of the Republic of Tajikistan and the Islamic Republic of Iran*, The Way of Science No. 2, (2014) available at http://scienceway.ru/d/706321/d/the-way-of-science--2-(2)-april_1.pdf#page = 59.

A. Taukhidi, *The Comparative Analysis of a Number of Notions Similar in the Meaning to the Concept "Foreign Trade Transactions" (Taking into Account Legislation of the Republic of Tajikistan and the Islamic Republic of Iran)*, The Way of Science No. 2, (2014) http://scienceway.ru/d/706321/d/the-way-of-science--2-(2)-april_1.pdf#page = 59.

Sh. Mengliev, *Arbitratjnoe Rassmotrenie Vneshekonomicheskikh Sporov (Арбитражное рассмотрение внешэкономических споров* (2009).

Web Sources

Official website of the Arbitration Court under the Chamber of Commerce and Industry of the Republic of Tajikistan: http://tpp.tj//dditem/AboutCourtofarbitration/.

Official website of the National Centre for Legislation under the President of the Republic of Tajikistan: www.mmk.tj.

Official website of the State Committee on Investments and State Property Management: http://gki.tj/en/.

Official website of Consultative Council on the Improvement of Investment Climate under the President of the Republic of Tajikistan: http://investmentcouncil.tj/en/.

Legislation

United Nations Convention on the Recognition and Enforcement of Foreign Arbitral Awards, 1958, New York.

Constitution of the Republic of Tajikistan dated 6 November 1994, http://mmk.tj/ru/legislation/legislation-base/constitution/.

Civil Code of Tajikistan, Part I No. 6 (30 June 1999), Part II No. 12 (12 December 1999), Part III No. 3 (1 March 2005), http://mmk.tj/ru/legislation/legislation-base/codecs/.

Civil Procedure Code of Tajikistan No. 1 (5 January 2008), http://mmk.tj/ru/legislation/legislation-base/codecs/.

Criminal Code of Tajikistan No. 9 (29 May 1998), http://mmk.tj/ru/legislation/legislation-base/codecs/.

Criminal Procedure Code of Tajikistan No. 12 (3 December 2009), http://mmk.tj/ru/legislation/legislation-base/codecs/.

Economic Court Proceedings Code of Tajikistan No. 1 (5 January 2008), http://mmk.tj/ru/legislation/legislation-base/codecs/.

Labour Code of Tajikistan No. 9 (15 May 1997), http://mmk.tj/ru/legislation/legislation-base/codecs/.

Constitutional Law of Tajikistan on Courts No. 1084 (26 July 2014), http://mmk.tj/ru/legislation/legislation-base/.

Constitutional Law of Tajikistan on Prosecution No. 107 (25 July 2005), http://mmk.tj/ru/legislation/legislation-base/.

Law of Tajikistan on Advocates and Advocacy No. 1182 (18 March 2015) http://mmk.tj/ru/legislation/legislation-base/.

Law of Tajikistan on Public Notaries No. 810 (16 April 2012), http://mmk.tj/ru/legislation/legislation-base/.

Law of Tajikistan on International Commercial Arbitration No. 1183 (18 March 2015), http://mmk.tj/ru/legislation/legislation-base/.

Law of Tajikistan on Arbitration Courts No. 344 (5 January 2008), http://mmk.tj/ru/legislation/legislation-base/.

Law of Tajikistan on International Treaties of the Republic of Tajikistan No. 908 (11 December 1999), http://mmk.tj/ru/legislation/legislation-base/.

Law of the Republic of Tajikistan on Normative Legal Acts No. 506 (26 March 2009), http://mmk.tj/ru/legislation/legislation-base/.

CHAPTER 9
Turkmenistan

Rolf Knieper & Diora Ziyaeva

LIST OF ABBREVIATIONS

CPC	Civil Procedure Code (adopted in 2015, entered into force on July 1, 2016)
Directive	Directive on the Arbitral Tribunal, published as Annex 1 to the new Civil Procedure Code, effective July 1, 2016
ICSID Convention	Convention on the Settlement of Investment Disputes between States and Nationals of Other States
ICC	International Chamber of Commerce
International Arbitration Law	Law of Turkmenistan "On International Commercial Arbitration" of 2014
Law on International Treaties	Constitution of Turkmenistan and the Turkmenistan Law on International Treaties of Turkmenistan, No. 108-IV, dated May 10, 2010
MAC	Maritime Arbitration Commission
New York Convention	Convention on the Recognition and Enforcement of Foreign Arbitral Awards
SCC	Stockholm Chamber of Commerce
Soviet Union	Union of Soviet Socialist Republics
UNCITRAL Model Law	UNCITRAL Model Law on International Commercial Arbitration (1985), as amended in 2006
USSR	Union of Soviet Socialist Republics

§9.01 GENERAL INTRODUCTION

[A] Historical Development of the Legal System

1.1 Like that of its neighbors in Central Asia, the legal tradition of Turkmenistan has its oldest roots in the customs and practices of the nomadic peoples who have traditionally inhabited the land. In those traditions, elders called "aksakal" had societal authority to rule on disputes within their communities. Procedures, "merits" and enforcement were based on informal institutions, organization and social control, typically applying and sometimes elaborating on customary laws, called "adat."[1] Such customs were later partly accepted and somewhat legitimized under Soviet law. However, the Turkmen people and culture share a stronger affiliation to the mythic Oghuz Khan and his descendants than many of their other Central Asian neighboring nations. This sense of community has contributed to a historically strong cultural emphasis in Turkmenistan on kin groups and the adat, despite diverging lifestyles between nomadic pastoralists and sessile agrarian society.

1.2 Islamic law, too, has had an influence in shaping both institutions and substantive law in Turkmenistan. Yet despite the country's centuries of Islamic tradition, a series of interviews by Russian linguist A. Lomakin at the end of the nineteenth century indicated that the influence of Islam on Turkmen culture and behavior was far more limited than that of the pre-Islamic customary law, adat, especially when compared to the other peoples of Central Asia.[2] Lomakin in fact found that judges and spiritual leaders alike more commonly applied adat than shariah law.[3]

1.3 At the same time, the Turkmen legal system retains many vestiges, stemming from upwards of a hundred years under the influence of the Russian Empire and particularly the Union of Soviet Socialist Republics (USSR or Soviet Union).[4] Indeed, today, Turkmenistan is a civil law jurisdiction largely inheriting and building on the legal system and institutions from its former Soviet era.[5] Turkmenistan is a presidential republic. Its legislative branch is known as the Assembly or Mejlis. With respect to dispute settlement mechanisms owed to this period, State arbitration courts were created. They emerged in Soviet times as part of a procedure to implement and supervise the central plans. State arbitration courts were neither arbitral tribunals based on consensus of disputing parties nor part of the judiciary. Their role was less to ascertain enforceable claims but more to channel products and supplies between the State companies in accordance with the five-year plan. Some post-Soviet countries have abolished these arbitration courts altogether, some have maintained them

---

1. RAFIS ABAZOV, HISTORICAL DICTIONARY OF TURKMENISTAN (2003).
2. CAROLE BLACKWELL, TRADITION AND SOCIETY IN TURKMENISTAN: GENDER, ORAL CULTURE AND SONG 38 & n.13 (2001).
3. A. LOMAKIN, OBYCHNOE PRAVO TURKMEN: ADAT (Common Law of the Turkmen: Adat) (1993).
4. Oleg Stalbovskiy et al., *UPDATE: A Research Guide to the Turkmenistan Legal System*, NYU GLOBALEX (March 2014), http://www.nyulawglobal.org/globalex/Turkmenistan1.html.
5. U.S. Commercial Service, *Turkmenistan - Dispute Settlement*, EXPORT.GOV (August 15, 2016), https://www.export.gov/apex/article2?id = Turkmenistan-Dispute-Settlement.

transforming them into adjudicating courts, sometimes under the title of "economic courts" or by maintaining the denomination "arbitration court."

1.4 The current Constitution of Turkmenistan has its origins in the constitutions adopted on May 18, 1992 and September 26, 2008, which, in turn, differ significantly from its predecessors of 1927, 1937 and 1978. The Constitution was last amended by the Constitutional Law of Turkmenistan No. 448-V, dated September 14, 2016.

[B] The Legal Profession

1.5 The legal profession in Turkmenistan, collectively known as the Bar, is a self-regulating profession overseen by bar associations, with additional supervisory and grievance authority held by the Ministry of Justice and the courts of Turkmenistan.[6] The national Bar is composed of legal professionals enrolled in a regional level organization called a bar association. While membership is not mandatory for legal practice, even lawyers unaffiliated with any bar association have reporting obligations to the bar association presiding over the *welayat* or *welayat*-level city in which they practice.[7] Thus, one bar association may be formed in each *welayat* or city with the rights of a *welayat*.[8] In order to practice law in Turkmenistan, an individual must first become licensed as an advocate.[9] The base qualifications for licensing as an advocate are set out in the Law "On Advocacy and Legal Practice" of May 10, 2010, as amended.

1.6 In order to be a lawyer, a person has to meet the following criteria:

(1) In Turkmenistan, a citizen of Turkmenistan permanently residing in Turkmenistan, holding a law degree, possessing the status of a lawyer and engaging in the activities mentioned in Part Two of Article 1 of this Law may be a lawyer.
(2) The lawyer is an independent legal counsel.
(3) The lawyer may not hold public office or engage in other paid activities other than teaching, creative and research activities.
(4) A lawyer cannot be someone who has been dismissed from court by law enforcement authorities for committing a disciplinary offense, for one year from the date of dismissal, or a person convicted of a crime whose conviction has not been removed from the official records or expunged according to the procedure established by the law of Turkmenistan, or a person who has been declared incompetent or partially incapacitated, or a person who has been expelled from the bar association for actions incompatible with legal practice or whose license to provide legal assistance has been revoked.[10]

---

6. *See generally* Law of Turkmenistan "On Advocacy and Legal Practice," May 10, 2010.
7. Law of Turkmenistan "On Advocacy and Legal Practice," May 10, 2010, Art. 31.
8. Law of Turkmenistan "On Advocacy and Legal Practice," May 10, 2010, Art. 19(1).
9. Law of Turkmenistan "On Licensing Certain Activities," June 25, 2008, Art. 20(40).
10. Law of Turkmenistan "On Advocacy and Legal Practice," May 10, 2010, Art. 8.

1.7 Article 8(1) of the Law "On Advocacy and Legal Practice" conditions being a lawyer, in part, on possessing the "status of a lawyer." The requisite "status of a lawyer" is granted in one of two ways: by license and membership in a local bar association or by legal internship. For broad status as a lawyer, the person must both hold a license to practice and be a member of a *welayat* or *welayat*-level city bar association.[11] A license, in turn, requires the person to: (i) hold a law degree; and (ii) have continuous work experience in the legal profession for at least two years.[12] The other way to attain the status of a lawyer is by having completed an authorized six to twelve month internship at a law office.[13] In this case, the status only lasts for the period during which the person remains employed at the law office. In any case, experience collected during an internship also counts towards the "experience in the legal profession" requirement.[14]

1.8 The licensing authority for lawyers in Turkmenistan is the Ministry of Justice.[15] It grants and records the licenses issued to the candidates who meet the above requirements.

[C]   Sources of Arbitration Law

1.9 A number of sources form the body of arbitration law in force in Turkmenistan.

1.10 International commercial arbitration is governed by the Law of Turkmenistan "On International Commercial Arbitration" of 2014 ("International Arbitration Law") and other domestic laws.[16] The International Arbitration Law entered into force on January 1, 2016. The law limits the scope of "international commercial arbitration" to "[d]isputes resulting from contractual and other civil law relationships arising in the course of foreign trade and other forms of international economic relations, provided that the place of business of at least one of the parties is situated outside of Turkmenistan, and disputes arising between enterprises with foreign investment, international associations and organizations established in the territory of Turkmenistan; disputes between the participants of such entities; as well as disputes between such entities and other subjects of Turkmenistan law."[17] Thus the International Arbitration Law covers arbitral disputes between parties of which one is located outside Turkmenistan.

---

11. Law of Turkmenistan "On Advocacy and Legal Practice," May 10, 2010, Art. 9(1)(1), as amended by Law of Turkmenistan "On Amendments and Supplements to the Law of Turkmenistan 'On Advocacy and Legal Practice'" (No. 271-V), August 15, 2015, Art. 2.
12. Law of Turkmenistan "On Advocacy and Legal Practice," May 10, 2010, Art. 9(2).
13. Law of Turkmenistan "On Advocacy and Legal Practice," May 10, 2010, Art. 9(1)(2), as amended by Law of Turkmenistan "On Amendments and Supplements to the Law of Turkmenistan 'On Advocacy and Legal Practice'" (No. 271-V), August 15, 2015, Art. 2.
14. Law of Turkmenistan "On Advocacy and Legal Practice," May 10, 2010, Art. 12(4).
15. Law of Turkmenistan "On Advocacy and Legal Practice," May 10, 2010, Art. 9.
16. U.S. Commercial Service, *Turkmenistan - Dispute Settlement*, Export.Gov (August 15, 2016), https://www.export.gov/apex/article2?id=Turkmenistan-Dispute-Settlement.
17. Law of Turkmenistan "On International Commercial Arbitration," August 16, 2014, Art. 1(2).

1.11 Until recently, there was no equivalent law on domestic arbitration as that form of dispute resolution was not widely used or supported under the law of Turkmenistan. However, in the Directive on the Arbitral Tribunal, published as Annex 1 to the Civil Procedure Code (CPC) of 1963, as redrafted to be effective from July 1, 2016 (the "Directive"), Turkmen law formally established a procedure by which domestic parties can refer certain civil disputes to binding arbitration by a tribunal.

[D] International Legal Framework, Supremacy of International Law

1.12 Turkmenistan proclaimed its independence on October 27, 1991, in the course of the collapse of the USSR or Soviet Union. The Russian Federation declared that it was the "continuing State" of the former USSR. Turkmenistan, like certain other newly established states of the former USSR, was regarded as a successor state of the USSR. As a result, Turkmenistan acceded to a number of treaties concluded between the former USSR and third states.[18]

1.13 Many of the former Soviet states have rejected the traditional Soviet dualist approach to the implementation of international law in the domestic legal systems.[19] Some states proclaimed international law as part of the national law, and their constitutions provide a higher hierarchical status to international rules.[20] Others, like Turkmenistan, have made less specific references to international law in their constitutions.[21]

1.14 Specifically, the provisions governing the status of international treaties in the Turkmen legal system are found in the Constitution of Turkmenistan and the Turkmenistan Law on the International Treaties of Turkmenistan, No. 108-IV, dated May 10, 2010 ("Law on International Treaties"), which replaced the Turkmen "Law on the Procedure of Concluding, Implementing and Denouncing to International Treaties of Turkmenistan," dated June 15, 1995. In addition, Turkmenistan acceded as a party to the Vienna Convention on the Law of Treaties in 1996.[22] The latest amendments of the Constitution of Turkmenistan that further ensure compliance of national laws with international legal standards were introduced by the Constitutional Law of Turkmenistan No. 448-V dated September 14, 2016.[23]

---

18. For instance, on December 20, 1996 the Parliament of Turkmenistan (the *Mejlis*) acceded to the International Covenant on Civil and Political Rights and Optional Protocols which the USSR was a party to. For the Decision *see* Türkmenistanyň Mejlisiniň Maglumatlary, No. 4/1996 p. 56.
19. Gennady M Danilenko, Implementation of International Law in CIS Countries: Theory and Practice, 10 EUR. J. INT'L L. 51 (1999).
20. For instance, the Constitution of the Russian Federation, Constitution of the Republic of Moldova, the Constitution of Kazakhstan, etc.
21. For instance, the Constitution of the Republic of Uzbekistan and the Constitution of the Republic of Turkmenistan.
22. Süleyman Sırrı Terzioglu, International Treaties in the Legal System of Turkmenistan, IV(2) LAW & JUST. REV. 73 (2013).
23. "Turkmenistan Legal Capacity Building" https://www.dmiassociates.com/dmi/EN/turkmenistan-legal-capacity-building.

1.15 Article 9(2) of the recently amended Constitution of Turkmenistan states that Turkmenistan acknowledges "the primacy of generally recognized norms of international law." Moreover, the language used in Article 9(2) fails to clearly define what "generally recognized rules of international law" are. In our opinion, this phrase must be understood as a reference to customary law and the general principles of law mentioned in Articles 38(1) of the Statute of the International Court of Justice as sources of international law.[24] Though there is no provision in the Constitution that governs conflict of laws issues as between foreign laws and domestic laws, Article 4(2) of the Law on International Treaties may provide some useful insight into interpreting the provision on Article 9(2). Article 4(2) explains that where an international treaty establishes rules other than those established by the law of Turkmenistan, then the rules of the international treaty shall apply. Thus, Article 4(2) prioritizes international law over domestic law.

1.16 With regard to international law related to investment arbitration, Turkmenistan ratified the Convention on the Settlement of Investment Disputes between States and Nationals of Other States (the "ICSID Convention") in 1992, and it has remained in force since then. Section 9.10, *infra*, provides a more thorough examination of the investment law and treaties presently in force in Turkmenistan.

1.17 Notably, however, Turkmenistan has not ratified the Convention on the Recognition and Enforcement of Foreign Arbitral Awards (the "New York Convention"). This can have significant ramifications for arbitral disputes between Turkmen and non-Turkmen parties. Specifically, where such arbitrations have taken place outside Turkmenistan, the recognition and enforcement in Turkmenistan of any award rendered in such an arbitration would solely be governed by Turkmen arbitration law. Section 9.09[B], *infra*, examines the recognition and enforcement procedures under Turkmen law applicable to foreign arbitral awards.

1.18 If the arbitration is seated in Turkmenistan but its recognition and enforcement is sought abroad, any resulting award would be in the unusual position of being subject to the reciprocity declarations and reservations made by most Contracting Parties under Article I(3) of the New York Convention. Therefore, such awards would not be enforceable under the New York Convention in all but a few States.[25] Instead, the enforcement of any arbitral award originating out of Turkmenistan would be governed by each enforcing jurisdiction's domestic arbitration law.

1.19 Conversely to the New York Convention, Turkmenistan has ratified the Kiev Convention of 1992 on the Order of the Solution of Disputes Related to the Realization of Economic Activities. According to Article 3 of the Convention, it applies also to proceedings and awards of arbitral tribunals. Article 9 lists the reasons which allow the refusal of awards in other contracting States. They comprise the exception of res

---

24. Süleyman Sırrı Terzioglu, International Treaties in the Legal System of Turkmenistan, IV(2) LAW & JUST. REV. 73 (2013).
25. *See* New York Arbitration Convention, *Contracting States*, NEWYORKCONVENTION.ORG, http://www.newyorkconvention.org/countries (last accessed November 29, 2016).

judicata, incompetence of the arbitral tribunal, statute of limitation and lack of due process. Contrary to the New York Convention, a violation of public order does not give rise to a possible refusal of enforcement.

[E] Available Dispute Resolution Mechanisms

1.20 The judiciary is the most widely available dispute resolution mechanism in Turkmenistan, with a court in each province and district of Turkmenistan. Complementing the courts of general jurisdiction, however, the Turkmen judiciary also features a handful of less formal mechanisms for dispute resolution.

1.21 The State policy-driven arbitration courts of the former Soviet era have, with the exception of the Arbitration Court of the City of Ashgabat, become attached to the civil courts of general jurisdiction and nowadays serve to adjudicate disputes between corporations and other types of commercial disputes. Section 9.01[F], *infra*, revisits these courts and the functions of the general civil courts in greater detail.

1.22 Moreover, and as mentioned above, with the adoption and entrance into force of the International Arbitration Law, many transnational commercial disputes, as well as many types of civil disputes involving foreign investors, are now capable of being resolved by international commercial arbitration within Turkmenistan where the parties so agree.[26]

1.23 Finally, pursuant to the new CPC adopted in 2015, which entered into force on July 1, 2016, Turkmen law now provides a mechanism by which citizens can submit most kinds of civil disputes to binding ad hoc arbitration. Specifically, Annex 1 of the CPC (the Directive on the Arbitral Tribunal) permits citizens to submit any nonlabor, nonfamily dispute between them to arbitration, and to refer disputes that have arisen in accordance to a detailed arbitration agreement between the parties. Specifically, because the law has no default provisions, the parties must reach a consensus on and contract with their appointed arbitrator or arbitrators, and specify the procedure they are to follow in the arbitration proceedings. The formal and substantive requirements for arbitration agreements in domestic commercial arbitration are set out in greater detail in Section 9.02 below.

[F] Judicial System

1.24 The judicial system of Turkmenistan consists of three levels: the Supreme Court, the regional appeals courts at the appellate level, and local courts at the trial level. Additionally, the Turkmen judiciary provides for the Arbitration Court of the City of Ashgabat. The court has jurisdiction over disputes between corporations and other legal entities, including daughter companies, subsidiaries and branches of foreign

---

26. International Arbitration Law, Art. 1(2).

companies. However, appeals against the court's decisions are treated by the Turkmen Supreme Court, which thereby exercises a unifying function of judicial practice.

1.25 All appointments of judges are made by the President of Turkmenistan and appointment terms are for a period of five years.[27] Turkmen law recognizes the independence of the judiciary, as well as of each individual judge.[28]

[G] Arbitration Institutions

1.26 On February 28, 2015, the Law "On the Chamber of Commerce and Industry of Turkmenistan" of 1993 was updated to create a new body for international commercial arbitration, which would be regulated by the Chamber of Commerce and Industry of Turkmenistan.[29] Annex 1 to the International Arbitration Law already contains the provision that establishes this kind of court of international arbitration.[30] Under this provision, the court has the authority to hear *inter alia*: (1) disputes arising out of contractual and other civil law relationships resulting from the course of foreign trade so long as the business of at least one of the parties is outside of Turkmenistan, (2) disputes arising between entities with foreign investments, and (3) disputes between international associations and organizations established in Turkmenistan. Disputes arising out of civil law relationships, such as the purchase and sale of goods, works and services performed in the exchange of goods and/or services, joint businesses and other forms of industrial and business activities, can be referred to the International Commercial Arbitration Court. Thus, this forum was created to arbitrate civil disputes in foreign trade and international commerce between parties located in Turkmenistan and parties located outside Turkmenistan.[31] To date, however, no disputes have been administered in that forum. *See* Section 9.02[F], *infra*, for a discussion of subjective and objective arbitrability for international commercial arbitration in Turkmenistan.

---

27. Central Intelligence Agency, *Turkmenistan*, The World Factbook (November 22, 2016), https://www.cia.gov/library/publications/the-world-factbook/geos/tx.html.
28. Constitution of Turkmenistan of September 14, 2016, Arts. 6, 98.
29. U.S. Commercial Service, *Turkmenistan - Dispute Settlement*, Export.Gov (August 15, 2016), https://www.export.gov/apex/article2?id=Turkmenistan-Dispute-Settlement.
30. International Arbitration Law in Annex 2 also provides a mechanism for maritime-related arbitration through the Maritime Arbitration Commission ("MAC"). The MAC is then regulated by the Chamber of Commerce of Turkmenistan. The MAC was created solely for the purpose of addressing and resolving disputes arising out of contractual or other civil legal relations regarding, but not limited to, maritime shipping, marine insurance, maritime transport, accidents resulting from the collision of ships, as well as injury to the implementation of industrial fishing. The Maritime Arbitration Commission also resolves disputes that arise in connection with the sailing of seagoing vessels and inland waterway vessels on international rivers or bodies of water, like the Caspian Sea, which borders Turkmenistan on the west. Of particular note, the Chairman of the MAC has the authority to order the seizure of the vessel or cargo located in a port in Turkmenistan, at the request of the parties.
31. U.S. Commercial Service, *Turkmenistan - Dispute Settlement*, Export.Gov (August 15, 2016), https://www.export.gov/apex/article2?id=Turkmenistan-Dispute-Settlement.

[H] Sovereign Immunity and International Arbitration

1.27 Although Turkmenistan has not signed onto the United Nations Convention on Jurisdictional Immunities of States and Their Property, the new CPC recognizes the principle of sovereign immunity of States and their property under domestic law, and sets out the rules to be applied in that regard by Turkmen courts. Chapter 45 of the CPC follows the Convention's concept and codifies the principle of relative immunity. The immunity of foreign States is protected to the extent that it exercises sovereign authority and performs acts of public power, *puissance publique, acta iure imperii*. Diplomatic missions in the exercise of their functions and heads of State are equally protected. Conversely, States can no longer invoke their sovereign immunity before Turkmen courts or arbitral tribunals sitting in Turkmenistan if a claim against them concerns *acta iure gestionis*, commercial transactions, contracts of employment, tort and injuries, property rights, intellectual and industrial property, participation in companies or operation of a ship. They can equally not invoke their immunity if they have initiated the court or arbitral proceedings, have intervened by submissions relating to the merits, have brought a counterclaim or have agreed to commercial or investment arbitration (Articles 425–437 CPC). Securization of claims by interim measures and acts of enforcement are different matters. They necessitate an agreement by the concerned State and are restricted to types of property that are not used for purposes of sovereign power (Articles 438 and 439 CPC).

§9.02 THE ARBITRATION AGREEMENT

[A] Introduction

1.28 The International Arbitration Law of Turkmenistan is largely based on the UNCITRAL Model Law ("UNCITRAL Model Law"), as being confirmed by the UNCITRAL secretariat.[32] Therefore, many of its provisions regarding the arbitration agreement may not surprise a reader familiar with international arbitration. Conversely, the rather limited domestic arbitration statute presents both important and unusual regulations, as well as substantial omissions as compared to what is typically expected in domestic arbitration regulation.

[B] Validity of the Arbitration Agreement

[1] General Provisions

1.29 Article 7(1) of the International Arbitration Law provides a detailed definition of what makes an arbitration agreement valid for the purposes of international commercial arbitration. The law provides that:

---

32. UNCITRAL Model Law on International Commercial Arbitration (1985), as amended in 2006, http://www.uncitral.org/uncitral/en/uncitral_texts/arbitration/1985Model_arbitration_status.html.

> An "arbitration agreement" is an agreement by the parties to submit to arbitration all or certain disputes which have arisen or which may arise between them in respect of a defined legal relationship, whether contractual or not. An arbitration agreement may be in the form of an arbitration clause in a contract or in the form of a separate agreement.[33]

1.30 While the domestic arbitration statute does not have an express definition for what an arbitration agreement is, as detailed in Section 9.02[B][2] below, the Directive on the Arbitral Tribunal imposes significant form requirements on the arbitration agreement.

[2] Requisites of a Valid Arbitration Agreement

1.31 The International Arbitration Law follows the UNCITRAL Model Law approach that sets out both the definition and the form requirements of a valid arbitration agreement. Specifically, as to form, the International Arbitration Law states:

> The arbitration agreement shall be in writing. An agreement is in writing if it is contained in a document signed by the parties or in an exchange of letters, telex, telegrams or other means of telecommunication which provide a record of the agreement, or in an exchange of statements of claim and defense in which the existence of an agreement is alleged by one party and not denied by another. The reference in a contract to any document containing an arbitration clause constitutes an arbitration agreement provided that the contract is in writing and the reference is such as to make that clause part of the contract.[34]

1.32 Thus, the International Arbitration Law follows the UNCITRAL Model Law approach of requiring an agreement in writing but defining flexibly the form the writing can take.

1.33 On the other hand, domestic arbitration places a heavy burden on the formal requirements of an arbitration agreement. Thus, Article 5 of the Directive on the Arbitral Tribunal states:

> Article 5. The agreement on referring a dispute for consideration by an arbitration court shall contain:
> (1) the names of the parties and their places of residence;
> (2) the subject matter of the dispute;
> (3) the surnames, names and patronymics of the selected arbitrators;
> (4) the time period for resolving the dispute;
> (5) the place and time of the agreement.

1.34 Moreover, the Directive also indirectly imposes additional form requirements. This is because the Directive governing domestic arbitration does not contain any

---

33. International Arbitration Law, Art. 7(1).
34. International Arbitration Law, Art. 7(2).

default provisions.[35] Thus, the parties must, in the arbitration agreement, also provide provisions on procedure to be followed in the proceedings.[36]

[C] Concluding the Arbitration Agreement (Written, Oral, by Conduct)

1.35 For international arbitration, as indicated immediately above, the International Arbitration Law requires that the arbitration agreement "shall be in writing," meaning it is found in a document or a series of written exchanges of communication between the parties. However, an agreement to arbitrate will be considered concluded if, where parties are exchanging statements of claims and defenses, one party alleges an arbitration agreement exists and the other party does not deny it.[37]

1.36 Under the domestic ad hoc arbitration law, the arbitration agreement must be made in writing and, significantly, must be entered into after the dispute has arisen.[38] In other words, the new domestic ad hoc arbitration procedure is only accessible to parties by way of a written submission agreement.

[D] The Doctrine of Separability

1.37 With the new International Arbitration Law, Turkmen law now formally recognizes the concept of *kompetenz-kompetenz* (or competence-competence) and resultantly also the related doctrine of separability. Specifically, Article 16(1) of the International Arbitration Law provides that:

> The arbitral tribunal may rule on its own jurisdiction, including any objections with respect to the existence or validity of the arbitration agreement. For that purpose, an arbitration clause which forms part of a contract shall be treated as an agreement independent of the other terms of the contract. A decision by the arbitral tribunal that the contract is null and void shall not entail *ipso jure* the invalidity of the arbitration clause.

1.38 The second sentence, at least for the purpose of upholding the enforceability of arbitration agreements in otherwise unenforceable agreements, provides for the separation of arbitration clauses from the rest of the contract and ensures its validity in an otherwise unenforceable contract.

1.39 On the other hand, the Directive on the Arbitral Tribunal – the statute governing domestic arbitration – does not address questions of *kompetenz-kompetenz*. The related issue of separability is not addressed likely because the arbitration agreement in that case is, in fact, almost always a separate submission agreement rather than an arbitration clause within a broader contract. *See* Section 9.03[C] *supra*.

---

35. *See generally* Directive on the Arbitral Tribunal (CPC, Annex 1).
36. Directive on the Arbitral Tribunal (CPC, Annex 1), Art. 8 ("Cases shall be tried ... in accordance with the concluded agreement.").
37. International Arbitration Law, Art. 7(2).
38. Directive on the Arbitral Tribunal (CPC, Annex 1), Art. 1.

[E] Invalidity of the Arbitration Agreement

1.40 Since the International Arbitration Law recognizes the principle of separability of arbitration clauses, the tribunal's determination regarding the validity of the main contract has no bearing on the arbitration agreement's validity, and a separate determination of the arbitration clause's validity is necessary. In that regard, the provision of the International Arbitration Law regarding recognition and enforcement of awards suggests that the proper applicable law to assess the validity of the arbitration agreement is "the law to which the parties have subjected [the arbitration agreement] or, failing any indication thereon, ... the law of the country where the award was made."[39]

[F] Arbitrability

1.41 The laws of Turkmenistan diverge in their provisions on arbitrability with regard to domestic and international commercial arbitration. Each type of arbitration is subject to its own certain subjective arbitrability (or capacity) limitations. Moreover, domestic arbitration is subject to a greater number of objective arbitrability (or subject matter arbitrability) limitations. Insofar as capacity limitations are concerned, international arbitration is limited to disputes involving at least one party whose place of business is outside Turkmenistan, as well as disputes among enterprises with foreign investments in Turkmenistan, and their participants, as well as disputes between such enterprises and the other subjects of Turkmen law.[40]

[1] Disputes Capable of Settlement by Arbitration

1.42 The provisions governing each type of arbitration set out affirmative arbitrability rules. Thus, subject to the exclusions set out in Section 9.02[F][2] below, domestic arbitration is available to resolve any type of dispute between them.

1.43 For international commercial arbitration, in turn, the only disputes capable of settlement by arbitration are disputes resulting from contractual and other civil law relationships arising in the course of foreign trade and other forms of international economic relations. The International Arbitration Law also applies to disputes between foreign investors, international associations and organizations established in Turkmenistan, and their participants and members, as well as disputes between such entities and subjects of Turkmen law. On the other hand, domestic arbitration is only available to citizens of Turkmenistan.[41] This raises the question of whether arbitration is at all available for disputes between juridical persons of Turkmenistan who are not affiliated with a foreign investment.

---

39. International Arbitration Law, Art. 47(1)(1)(a); *see also id.*, Art. 45(2)(1)(a) (setting aside provision).
40. International Arbitration Law, Art. 1(2).
41. Directive on the Arbitral Tribunal (CPC, Annex 1), Art. 1.

[2] Disputes Not Capable of Settlement by Arbitration

1.44 The domestic arbitration law also sets limits on the types of disputes capable of settlement by arbitration. Specifically, the statute expressly carves out "disputes arising out of employment and family relationships" from the description of disputes referable to an arbitral tribunal for arbitration.[42] Thus, parties cannot submit family law or labor disputes to domestic arbitration.

[G] Termination of the Arbitration Agreement
[1] Termination with Respect to an Existing Dispute

1.45 An arbitration proceeding arising out of an international arbitration agreement is considered terminated when a final award or discontinuance order is issued.[43] The domestic arbitration Directive also contemplates a termination of existing arbitration proceedings on a temporal basis. Thus, Article 9 of the Directive provides:

> Citizens who have concluded an agreement referring a dispute for consideration by an arbitration court may not repudiate it before the expiration of the time period contemplated by the arbitration agreement, other than in the cases specified in Article 6 of this Statute.[44]

1.46 The time period contemplated by the arbitration agreement is one of the mandatory elements of the arbitration agreement that parties must set out in the arbitration agreement.[45] By its language, Article 9 effectively authorizes the termination of arbitration of an existing dispute by repudiation once the contracted period of time has lapsed.

§9.03 APPLICABLE LAW

[A] Introduction

1.47 Arbitration, especially international arbitration, presents a difficult landscape of applicable law to navigate, in which the law governing the arbitration, the substance of the dispute, and the arbitration agreement may be different. This section reviews how Turkmen law approaches some of the conflict of laws questions arising in the arbitration context.

[B] The Law Governing the Arbitration (*Lex Arbitri*)

1.48 The *lex arbitri*, or law governing the arbitration, provides the baseline procedural rules and limitations applicable to arbitration in Turkmenistan. For both domestic and

---

42. Directive on the Arbitral Tribunal (CPC, Annex 1), Art. 1.
43. International Arbitration Law, Art. 42(1)–(2).
44. Directive on the Arbitral Tribunal (CPC, Annex 1), Art. 9.
45. Directive on the Arbitral Tribunal (CPC, Annex 1), Art. 5(4).

international arbitrations seated in Turkmenistan, the *lex arbitri* is Turkmen law. For domestic arbitrations in Turkmenistan, the source of law is the CPC's Directive on the Arbitral Tribunal and the procedural rules created in accordance with the Directive. For international arbitrations seated in Turkmenistan, the source of the *lex arbitri* is the International Arbitration Law and, where applicable, the statute and rules on arbitration in the Chamber of Commerce and Industry.

[C] Party Autonomy on Choice of Law Issues

1.49 The International Arbitration Law sets out, in Article 38, a broad principle of party autonomy with regard to the parties' ability to designate the law governing their contractual relations:

(1) The arbitral tribunal shall decide the dispute in accordance with such rules of law as are chosen by the parties as applicable to the substance of the dispute. Any designation of the law or legal system of a given State shall be construed, unless otherwise expressed, as directly referring to the substantive law of that State and not to its conflict of laws rules.
(2) Failing any designation by the parties, the arbitral tribunal shall apply the law determined by the conflict of laws rules which it considers applicable.
(3) In all cases, the arbitral tribunal shall decide in accordance with the terms of the contract and shall take into account the usages of the trade applicable to the transaction.

1.50 Thus, subject to its competing duty to render an enforceable award, an international arbitration tribunal is bound by the parties' choice of substantive law and shall apply the same in resolving the dispute.

1.51 Conversely, the domestic arbitration provisions are silent on applicable law, save for waiving the requirement that tribunal procedures be governed by the CPC.[46] Whether or not parties may elect a different substantive law to govern their contractual dispute is an open question in light of the domestic character of these proceedings,

[D] Restrictions on Party Autonomy

[1] General Observations

1.52 On its face, the only restriction on party autonomy set out in Article 38 is that the designated law governing the dispute be that of a "State." Thus, the designation of an internationally recognized set of rules may not be sufficient. In that case, parties should incorporate those rules by reference but still designate a legal system as a lens to interpret and apply the incorporated rules.

---

46. Directive on the Arbitral Tribunal (CPC, Annex 1), Art. 10.

1.53 However, other provisions of the International Arbitration Law, largely duplicative of the UNCITRAL Model Law, infer certain additional familiar restrictions on party autonomy.

[2] Reasonable Connection Test

1.54 The text of Article 38 of the International Arbitration Law, quoted above in Section 9.03[C], does not appear to place any reasonable connection restriction or test on party autonomy in selecting applicable law.

[3] National Public Policy

1.55 The International Arbitration Law recognizes the fundamental public policy of principles of Turkmenistan as an affirmative constraint on party autonomy in international arbitration. Thus, it provides that any international arbitration award contrary to Turkmenistan's fundamental public policy is subject to be set aside (if made in Turkmenistan) and/or to nonrecognition and nonenforcement.[47]

[4] Mandatory Rules of Municipal Law

1.56 The International Arbitration Law affirmatively contemplates that Turkmen law may establish certain mandatory rules of law which may not be overcome by party autonomy when it envisions that certain arbitration agreements may be "null and void, inoperative or incapable of being performed" or would effectively refer to arbitration a dispute "not capable of settlement by arbitration under the law of Turkmenistan."[48] Indeed, the arbitration statutes themselves designate specific types of disputes that are not capable of settlement by arbitration. *See* Section 9.02[F][2] above. Moreover, the public policy restrictions set out in (Section 9.03[D][3]/9.03[D][5] above/below) may further compel application of mandatory rules of municipal law if failure to do so would constitute a violation of public policy. No concrete examples of such public policy rules can be quoted for the time being.

[E] No Explicit Choice of Law

[1] Introduction

1.57 The International Arbitration Law does not distinguish between express and implied choice of law by the parties. General principles of conclusion of contracts are applicable, as embedded in Book 1, Chapter 1, Section 1 of Article 75 of the Turkmen Civil Code. They accept the conclusion of contracts on implied terms.

---

47. International Arbitration Law, Arts. 45(2)(2)(b), 47(1)(2)(b).
48. International Arbitration Law, Arts. 8(1), 45(2)(2)(a), 47(1)(2)(a).

[2]   Relevant Conflict of Law Rules

1.58 Where the parties have not made any choice of law applicable to their contract, the International Arbitration Law provides that the tribunal first determine which country's conflict of laws rules it deems applicable and, on that basis, determine the law governing the contract:

> Failing any designation by the parties, the arbitral tribunal shall apply the law determined by the conflict of laws rules which it considers applicable.[49]

§9.04   THE ARBITRATORS

[A]   Appointment of Arbitrators

[1]   Appointment of Arbitrators under Municipal Law

1.59 Under the International Arbitration Law, the parties have autonomy to designate their own tribunal constitution mechanism. Failing that, the default rules provide that a tribunal shall consist of three arbitrators.[50] Each party appoints its own arbitrator and the parties, together, appoint the chairman. Where a party fails to designate its own arbitrator or the parties cannot agree on a chairman for the tribunal after thirty days, the Chairman of the Chamber of Commerce and Industry of Turkmenistan can, by request, make the necessary appointment.[51]

1.60 Under the domestic arbitration Directive, the parties' arbitration agreement itself must designate the persons who will serve as arbitrators.[52] The sole exception is that in the event of death, departure or serious illness of a party-appointed arbitrator, that party may appoint a new arbitrator.[53] If the same occurs with the sole arbitrator or chairman of the tribunal, then both parties' consent is necessary to appoint a replacement arbitrator.

[B]   Qualifications of Arbitrators

1.61 The International Arbitration Law broadly defines the qualifications an individual must have in order to serve as arbitrator. The law generally seeks not to unduly interfere with the arbitrator appointment. In fact, the only express requirement beyond appointment in accordance with the rules is that the individual be "capable."[54] Indeed, the International Arbitration Law specifically states that "[n]o person shall be precluded by reason of his nationality from acting as an arbitrator, unless otherwise agreed by the parties." However, once approached in connection with a possible appointment

---

49. International Arbitration Law, Art. 38(2).
50. International Arbitration Law, Art. 10(2).
51. International Arbitration Law, Arts. 11(3)(1), 6(1).
52. Directive on the Arbitral Tribunal (CPC, Annex 1), Art. 5(3).
53. Directive on the Arbitral Tribunal (CPC, Annex 1), Art. 7.
54. International Arbitration Law, Art. 2(1)(2).

as an arbitrator, the individual must disclose any circumstances likely to give rise to justifiable doubts as to his impartiality or independence.[55]

1.62 Conversely, the CPC sets out much stricter qualification and disqualification criteria for arbitrators in domestic ad hoc arbitration proceedings. Specifically, the Directive on the Arbitral Tribunal expressly excludes from service as arbitrator any individual who has not attained the age of majority, is under guardianship, is presently subject to a court order preventing them from holding a judicial or prosecutorial position or practicing law, or has an expunged or outstanding conviction.[56]

[C] **Powers and Duties of Arbitrators**

1.63 The International Arbitration Law gives arbitrators a broad range of powers in the performance of their role as arbitrators.

[D] **Challenges and Replacement of Arbitrators**

[1] Challenges under Municipal Law

[a] International Arbitration

1.64 In contrast to the International Arbitration Law's deferential approach to the standard for an arbitrator to qualify for appointment, the law provides a more rigorous standard for arbitrator challenges. Namely, under Article 12 of the International Arbitration Law, an arbitrator may be challenged "if circumstances exist that give rise to justifiable doubts as to his impartiality or independence, or if he does not possess qualifications agreed to by the parties."

1.65 Subject to an agreement between the parties on an alternate procedure, challenges to an arbitrator's appointment are made by communicating a written statement of the reasons for the challenge to the arbitral tribunal within fifteen days of that party becoming aware of the constitution of the arbitral tribunal or becoming aware of any circumstance giving rise to justifiable doubts as to the challenged arbitrator's impartiality, independence or party-agreed qualifications.[57] Note that a party challenging its own appointed arbitrator, however, may only do so for reasons of which it becomes aware after its appointment of that individual.[58]

[b] Domestic Arbitration

1.66 The domestic arbitration law also provides guidance on challenging arbitrators but is ultimately less flexible than its international counterpart. "Arbitrators may not be

---

55. International Arbitration Law, Art. 12(1).
56. Directive on the Arbitral Tribunal (CPC, Annex 1), Art. 4.
57. International Arbitration Law, Art. 13(3).
58. International Arbitration Law, Art. 2(2).

changed until consideration of the case is completed."[59] Moreover, there is no procedure for challenging arbitrators. Instead, "[a] party may repudiate an agreement if it proves that any of the arbitrators are interested in the outcome of the case and that it was unaware of this circumstance when entering into the agreement."[60] Thus, removal of an arbitrator by a showing of his or her unfitness generally results in dissolution of the tribunal rather than a replacement appointment process.

[E] Compensation of Arbitrators

1.67 The domestic arbitration statute expressly requires that arbitrators be paid a fee for their services: "Cases shall be tried in arbitral tribunals in exchange for a fee, on a contractual basis in accordance with the concluded [arbitration] agreement."[61]

§9.05 JURISDICTION OF THE ARBITRATION TRIBUNAL

[A] Introduction

1.68 The relatively new International Arbitration Law in Turkmenistan made significant headway in developing Turkmen law with regard to questions of jurisdiction of arbitral tribunals. The law introduced the concept of *kompetenz-kompetenz* and prescribed the timing and substance of judicial review of an arbitrator's or tribunal's determination of jurisdiction.

[B] The Arbitrators' Determination of Their Jurisdiction

1.69 As mentioned above, the International Arbitration Law of Turkmenistan recognizes arbitrators' ability to determine their own jurisdiction. Article 16(1) of the Law provides, in relevant part:

> The arbitral tribunal may rule on its own jurisdiction, including any objections with respect to the existence or validity of the arbitration agreement.

1.70 This power to rule on its own jurisdiction or competence ensures that the arbitrator or arbitrators can hear the parties' case right away without any prior court determination regarding the existence or validity of the arbitration agreement. Indeed, a challenge to the arbitrator or arbitrators' jurisdiction by a party is deemed waived, absent justification for the delay, if not made by the statement of defense.[62]

---

59. Directive on the Arbitral Tribunal (CPC, Annex 1), Art. 6.
60. *Id.*
61. Directive on the Arbitral Tribunal (CPC, Annex 1), Art. 8.
62. International Arbitration Law, Art. 16(2).

[C] Court Review of Arbitrators' Jurisdiction

1.71 Article 16(3) of the International Arbitration Law envisions a limited form of review of an arbitrator's or tribunal's determination on jurisdiction. Specifically, it provides:

> The arbitral tribunal may rule on a plea referred to in paragraph two of this article either as a preliminary question or in an award on the merits. If the arbitral tribunal rules as a preliminary question that it has jurisdiction, any party may request, within thirty days after having received notice of that ruling, the authority specified in article 6(1) of this Law to decide the matter, which decision shall be subject to no appeal; while such a request is pending, the arbitral tribunal may continue the arbitral proceedings and make an award.

1.72 Interestingly, the authority referenced in Article 6(1) of the International Arbitration Law is the Chamber of Commerce and Industry. Thus, the formal review of an arbitrator's or tribunal's determination on jurisdiction provided under the statute is not judicial but more akin to the internal review processes of the International Court of Arbitration in International Chamber of Commerce (ICC) Arbitration.[63]

1.73 However, the International Arbitration Law does envision another opportunity for preliminary judicial review of an arbitrator's jurisdiction:

> A court before which an action is brought in a matter which is the subject of an arbitration agreement shall, if a party so requests, not later than when submitting his first statement on the substance of the dispute, refer the parties to arbitration unless it finds that the agreement is null and void, inoperative or incapable of being performed.[64]

1.74 Thus, upon being presented with an action allegedly subject to an arbitration agreement and a party timely requesting referral of the matter to an arbitral tribunal, the court presiding over the matter must determine whether or not the arbitration agreement is null and void, inoperative or incapable of being performed. If the agreement does not suffer from those defects, the court must dismiss the case and refer the parties to arbitration. While this largely resembles the provisions of Article II of the New York Convention, an important distinguishing factor is that a Turkmen court is not authorized to engage in this analysis *sua sponte*; the statute requires that it be timely requested by a party.

1.75 The above does not prevent an arbitrator or tribunal from continuing proceedings until the court has ruled on the matter.[65]

---

63. *See* ICC Rules of Arbitration, Art. 6(3)-(4) (2012).
64. International Arbitration Law, Art. 8(1).
65. International Arbitration Law, Art. 8(2).

[D] Institutional Rules

1.76 Given the emphasis and responsibility that Article 16(3) of the International Arbitration Law places on the Chamber of Commerce and Industry in adjudicating issues of arbitrator jurisdiction, it is surprising that no published set of institutional rules is available yet from the Chamber. The absence of rules on this question potentially impairs predictability and party control of the jurisdiction review process.

§9.06 THE PROCEDURE BEFORE THE ARBITRATION TRIBUNAL

[A] General Principles of Arbitration Procedure

1.77 Under the International Arbitration Law, party autonomy is an overarching principle of arbitration procedures. Subject to the typical limitations of the UNCITRAL Model Law on party autonomy, the International Arbitration Law generally recognizes party autonomy as a general principle of arbitration procedure. *See* Section 9.03 above. Another principle embodied in the International Arbitration Law is the principle of equal treatment of the parties.

1.78 The domestic arbitration directive also emphasizes party autonomy and impartiality. Indeed, without parties specifying the procedure and timeframe by which to conduct the arbitration, the arbitration agreement is not effective for domestic arbitration.

[B] Commencing the Arbitral Proceedings

[1] Municipal Law

1.79 Under the International Arbitration Law, international arbitration proceedings are deemed to have commenced on the date on which the respondent party receives the claimant party's request for arbitration, unless the parties have agreed otherwise.[66]

[C] Conduct of Arbitration

1.80 The domestic arbitration law does not prescribe any particular guidelines on the conduct of the arbitration proceedings beyond stating that they need not comply with rules of procedure set out in the CPC of Turkmenistan.[67]

1.81 The International Arbitration Law permits the arbitral tribunal to appoint its own expert or experts on specific issues it deems require such expertise. Such expert shall deliver his or her oral or written report and thereafter participate in an oral hearing

---

66. International Arbitration Law, Art. 31.
67. Directive on the Arbitral Tribunal (CPC, Annex 1), Art. 10.

wherein he or she may be questioned by the parties and presented with the parties' expert testimony.[68]

[D] Hearings

1.82 In international arbitration, the arbitral tribunal has discretion as to whether to hold hearings for the presentation of evidence or for oral argument or whether to conduct the proceedings on the basis of submitted documents and other materials. However, if either party specifically wishes to hold a hearing and the parties have not expressly ruled it out, the tribunal shall organize hearings at an appropriate stage of proceedings.[69]

§9.07 THE ARBITRAL AWARD

[A] Introduction

[1] International Arbitration

1.83 Several formal requirements apply to awards arising out of international arbitrations. Specifically, the International Arbitration Law requires that awards:[70]

- be signed by a majority of the tribunal, and that an account be provided, detailing the reason for absence of any arbitrator's signature;
- other than consent awards, shall state the reasons upon which they are based, unless the parties agree otherwise; and
- state the date and place at which they are deemed to have been made.

[2] Domestic Arbitration

1.84 For domestic arbitration specifically, the relevant law sets out several formal requirements for an arbitral award. Specifically, Article 13 of the Directive provides:

1.85 The award shall be set out in writing and must state:

(1) the time and place the award was made and the composition of the arbitral tribunal;
(2) the arbitration agreement on the basis of which the court acted;
(3) the names of all participants in the dispute;
(4) the subject matter of the dispute;
(5) the reasons why the arbitral tribunal arrived at its findings; and
(6) the decision of the arbitral tribunal.

---

68. International Arbitration Law, Art. 36.
69. International Arbitration Law, Art. 34.
70. International Arbitration Law, Art. 41.

1.86 Furthermore, as discussed in Section 9.07[B] below, a domestic arbitration award must also include each arbitrator's signature.[71]

[B] Deliberation and Voting

1.87 The statute governing domestic arbitration procedure in Turkmenistan requires that awards be made by majority vote.[72] It also requires that the award state the reasons on which the arbitrators made their decision. However, the same statute further requires that *all* arbitrators sign the award.[73] Thus, even where a majority of the arbitrators vote in favor of the award, it may nevertheless be a defective document if the dissenting arbitrator refuses to sign the award.

[C] Different Kinds of Awards (Separate, Interim, Consent, Default, Etc.)

1.88 Both the domestic and international arbitration laws elaborate on awards resulting from certain circumstances and outcomes. However, the domestic arbitration Directive only addresses default awards.

[1] Interim Awards

1.89 Unless the parties decide otherwise, international arbitration tribunals are authorized by the International Arbitration Law to issue interim orders or awards,[74] as well as ex parte preliminary orders granting interim measures directing a party not to frustrate the purpose of the interim order requested. For interim awards related to the parties' circumstances, the requesting party must show (i) a likelihood of irreparable harm if the interim award is not issued, (ii) that such harm outweighs the burden the interim measure would impose on the other party and, (iii) without prejudice to a later determination by the tribunal to the contrary, a possibility that the requesting party will succeed on the merits of its claim.[75] The tribunal has greater discretion in determining whether an evidence preservation interim order is appropriate.[76]

1.90 Interim awards in international arbitration are enforceable in much the same way as final awards are. *See* Section 9.9[B][2] below.

[2] Consent Awards

1.91 With regard to consent awards, the International Arbitration Law deviates from the UNCITRAL Model Law in an important aspect. While Article 30 of the UNCITRAL

---

71. Directive on the Arbitral Tribunal (CPC, Annex 1), Art. 14.
72. Directive on the Arbitral Tribunal (CPC, Annex 1), Art. 12.
73. Directive on the Arbitral Tribunal (CPC, Annex 1), Art. 14 (emphasis added).
74. International Arbitration Law, Art. 17(1).
75. International Arbitration Law, Art. 18(1).
76. International Arbitration Law, Art. 18(2).

Model Law conditions the parties' right to memorialize their agreement in a consent award and the Tribunal's authority to issue the same on the parties' and Tribunal's willingness to do so, Article 40 of the International Arbitration Law requires that settlements be memorialized in an arbitral award. It provides:

(1) If, during arbitral proceedings, the parties settle the dispute, the arbitral tribunal shall terminate the proceedings and record the settlement in the form of an arbitral award on agreed terms.
(2) An award on agreed terms shall be made in accordance with the provisions of Article 41 of this Law and shall state that it is an award. Such an award has the same status and effect as any other award on the merits of the case.

1.92 The mandatory nature of the provision on consent awards can cause issues for the parties by forcing their post-arbitration agreement to meet the requirements of an enforceable arbitral award.

1.93 On the other hand, the domestic arbitration statute does not expressly recognize interim awards or consent awards. However, a party defaulting on arbitral proceedings[77] or the announcement of the award to and signing thereof by the parties[78] will nevertheless be deemed to have sufficient notice if otherwise compliant with Turkmen law.

[3] Default Awards

1.94 The International Arbitration Law expressly authorizes the Tribunal to continue proceedings and issue an award even where one of the parties fails to appear or produce demanded evidence without a showing of sufficient cause.[79]

1.95 A party's failure to appear in proceedings does not derail domestic arbitration proceedings either. Instead, although worded differently from the International Arbitration Law, the Directive on the Arbitral Tribunal specifically waives the requirement that the Tribunal hear both sides' pleadings prior to issuing an award where a party refuses to appear.[80]

[D] Interest and Costs

1.96 Turkmen arbitration law is silent on the questions of pre- and post-award interest for arbitral awards. However, the International Arbitration Law grants broad discretion

---

77. *See* Directive on the Arbitral Tribunal (CPC, Annex 1), Art. 10.
78. Directive on the Arbitral Tribunal (CPC, Annex 1), Art. 15.
79. International Arbitration Law, Art. 35(3).
80. Directive on the Arbitral Tribunal (CPC, Annex 1), Art. 10.

to the arbitral tribunal to set the amount of the costs of the proceeding[81] and apportion it as the tribunal may see fit.[82]

[E] Effects of the Award

[1] Res Judicata and Lis Pendens

1.97 Res judicata is a recognized principle of international arbitration under Turkmen law. In the International Arbitration Law, Article 46 mirrors the UNCITRAL Model Law's Article 35 in that it requires that an international arbitration award, "irrespective of the country in which it was made, shall be recognized as binding and, upon written application ... enforced subject to the provisions of ... Article 47 of this Law, and also in accordance with the procedural law of Turkmenistan and its international treaties."[83] Thus, subject to the criteria for nonrecognition of an international arbitration award, as discussed in Section 9.09[B] below, the parties are generally bound by the tribunal's determinations of issues and facts between them resolved within the award.

1.98 *Lis pendens* on the other hand is forgone in favor of the UNCITRAL Model Law's approach favoring greater autonomy for the arbitrator or arbitrators to commence proceedings despite the dispute pending in a different forum. Article 8 of the International Arbitration Law provides in relevant part:

> (2) Where an action ... has been brought [before a court], arbitral proceedings may nevertheless be commenced or continued, and an award may be made, while the issue is pending before the court.[84]

1.99 Thus, an arbitrator need not wait for dismissal of parallel court proceedings prior to assuming jurisdiction over a case.

[F] Correction and Interpretation of the Award

[1] Municipal Law

1.100 Article 44 of the International Arbitration Law permits parties to submit an arbitral award to the arbitral tribunal for correction or interpretation. Under the International Arbitration Law, any application for correction or interpretation must be submitted within thirty days by the petitioning party receiving the award in order to be considered by the Tribunal.[85]

---

81. International Arbitration Law, Art. 43(1).
82. International Arbitration Law, Art. 43(2).
83. International Arbitration Law, Art. 46(1).
84. International Arbitration Law, Art. 8(2).
85. International Arbitration Law, Art. 44(1).

§9.08 SETTING ASIDE THE AWARD

[A] Introduction

1.101 The International Arbitration Law permits judicial review of international commercial arbitration awards made in Turkmenistan.[86] An application to set aside the award, however, is the only court recourse available to the parties against an arbitral award.[87] Moreover, the only court with such competence is the Supreme Court of Turkmenistan.[88]

[B] Challengeable Awards

[1] Grounds for Challenging the Award

1.102 Article 45 of the International Arbitration Law specifies the grounds for which an arbitral award made in Turkmenistan may be set aside. The grounds for setting aside an award under this Article mirror those of Article 34 of the UNCITRAL Model Law and of Article V of the New York Convention. Thus, under the statute, the arbitral award may be set aside under the following four circumstances, which must be established by the petitioning party:[89]

- a party to the arbitration agreement was under some incapacity; or the arbitration agreement is not valid under the law to which the parties have subjected it or, failing any indication thereon, under the law of Turkmenistan;
- the petitioning party was not given proper notice of the appointment of an arbitrator or of the arbitral proceedings or was otherwise unable to present his case;
- the award deals with a dispute not contemplated by or not falling within the terms of the submission to arbitration, or contains decisions on matters beyond the scope of the submission to arbitration, provided that, if the decisions on matters submitted to arbitration can be separated from those not so submitted, only that part of the award which contains decisions on matters not submitted to arbitration may be set aside; or
- the composition of the arbitral tribunal or the arbitral procedure was not in accordance with the agreement of the parties, unless such agreement was in conflict with a provision of this Law from which the parties cannot derogate, or, failing such agreement, was not in accordance with this Law.

1.103 The statute also provides two further grounds by which the Supreme Court, presented with an application to set aside an award, may do so:[90]

---

86. International Arbitration Law, Art. 45.
87. International Arbitration Law, Art. 45(1).
88. International Arbitration Law, Art. 6(2).
89. International Arbitration Law, Art. 45(2)(1).
90. International Arbitration Law, Art. 45(2)(2).

- the subject-matter of the dispute is not capable of settlement by arbitration under the law of Turkmenistan; and
- the award is in conflict with the public policy of Turkmenistan.

1.104 Either of these grounds will be sufficient for the Supreme Court to set the award aside, and the statute does not require that either be expressly pleaded.

[2] Waiver of Right to Challenge

1.105 Petitions for setting aside an award must be made to the Supreme Court of Turkmenistan within three months of the later of the date on which the petitioning party received the award or the date of disposal of a request to the arbitral tribunal for correction or interpretation of the award in question.[91]

1.106 The same is not true for domestic arbitration in Turkmenistan, however. There, although the final award is required by law to be kept by the district or *etrap* court where the proceeding took place, the award itself is not executable.[92] If a party to the award does not comply with its terms voluntarily, the other party must petition the court where the award is kept for a writ of execution on the award.

[C] Review of Jurisdictional Awards

1.107 The International Arbitration Law limits parties' ability to challenge jurisdiction of the tribunal before a court after the fact. As described in Section 9.08[C][1] above, lack of jurisdiction is not a standalone ground for setting aside the award; instead, the party must challenge the award on one of the enumerated bases from Article 45 of the International Arbitration Law.

1.108 The statute does draw a distinction for preliminary decisions on jurisdiction – those are reviewable within thirty days by the Chamber of Commerce and Industry, as described in Section 9.05[C] above.

1.109 Domestic arbitration is silent on the arbitrators' powers to determine their own jurisdiction; it is equally silent on judicial review of such determinations.

§9.09 RECOGNITION AND ENFORCEMENT OF THE ARBITRAL AWARD

[A] Enforcement of Domestic Awards

[1] Enforcement Domestically

1.110 The Directive on the Arbitral Tribunal sets out an unusual enforcement mechanism for domestic arbitration awards. That is, "[a]n arbitral award that is not enforced

---

91. International Arbitration Law, Art. 45(3).
92. Directive on the Arbitral Tribunal (CPC, Annex 1), Arts. 16, 17.

voluntarily may be subject to compulsory enforcement on the basis of a writ of execution issued by an *etrap* or city court."[93] If the *etrap* or city court refuses to issue the writ of execution, the party seeking execution may file a special appeal to the same court within ten days.[94] Finally, "once the judge's determination on refusing to issue a writ of execution has entered into force, the dispute may be resolved in court by application of an interested party."[95]

[2] Enforcement Abroad

1.111 Since Turkmenistan is not party to the New York Convention, domestic awards in Turkmenistan would almost never qualify as New York Convention awards abroad since they are between resident citizens of Turkmenistan. Therefore, their enforcement abroad would generally be determined by the domestic recognition and enforcement laws in place in the enforcing jurisdiction vis-à-vis awards made in another jurisdiction.

[B] Enforcement of Foreign Arbitral Awards

[1] Introduction to Recognition and Enforcement

1.112 Unlike in petitions to set aside a non-domestic award (an international arbitral award made in Turkmenistan) described in Section 9.08 above, which can only be made in the Supreme Court, enforcement actions for foreign and non-domestic commercial arbitration awards can be brought in any of the five *welayat* (provincial) civil courts of Turkmenistan, as well as in the Commercial Court in the city of Ashgabat.[96]

1.113 With the adoption of the International Arbitration Law, Turkmenistan, despite not having signed the New York Convention, has become a relatively friendly jurisdiction for enforcement of foreign arbitral awards. The International Arbitration Law, in Article 46(1), provides that:

> An arbitral award, irrespective of the country in which it was made, shall be recognized as binding and, upon written application to a court of Turkmenistan shall be recognized and enforced subject to the provisions of paragraph two of this article and article 47 of this Law, and also in accordance with the procedural law of Turkmenistan and its international treaties.[97]

1.114 Article 46(2) provides the procedure applicable to international arbitration award enforcement actions. This procedure is described in Section 9.09[B][4] below. Article 47, in turn, provides the exclusive grounds for refusing recognition or

---

93. Directive on the Arbitral Tribunal (CPC, Annex 1), Art. 17.
94. *Id.*, Art. 18.
95. *Id.*, Art. 19.
96. International Arbitration Law, Art. 6(2).
97. International Arbitration Law, Art. 46(1).

enforcement of international arbitral awards, a topic explored in detail in Section 9.09[B][3] below.

1.115 Notably, the provisions of the International Arbitration Law apply only to "international commercial arbitration," with its subjective arbitrability scope discussed in Section 9.01[C] and Section 9.02[F][1] above. Thus, arbitral awards arising out of disputes related to foreign trade or international economic relations between two parties resident in Turkmenistan would not be recognized and enforced under this statute.[98] Conversely, no part of the statute precludes recognition and enforcement of a foreign arbitral award related to foreign trade or other international economic relations between two or more parties, none of which are domiciled in Turkmenistan.

[2] Separate, Partial and Interim Awards

1.116 The International Arbitration Law permits interim awards to be enforced in a mechanism similar to that applicable to final awards. Thus, Article 25(1) provides:

> An interim measure issued by an arbitral tribunal shall be recognized as binding and, unless otherwise provided by the arbitral tribunal, enforced upon application to the competent court, irrespective of the country in which it was issued, subject to the provisions of article 26 of this Law.

1.117 Article 26, in turn, enumerates the grounds for refusal to recognize or enforce interim awards. First, Article 26 mirrors the party-asserted and *sua sponte* grounds enumerated in Article 47. These are addressed in Section 9.09[B][3] below. Then, it also conditions interim award enforcement on requirements to provide security and limitations on the enforcing court's own powers.[99]

[3] Grounds for Refusing Recognition and Enforcement

1.118 Article 47 of the International Arbitration Law sets out the exclusive grounds for refusal of recognition or enforcement of an international arbitration award.[100] Article 47(1)(1) presents the grounds on which refusal to recognize or enforce may be based when asserted by the party resisting the award's recognition or enforcement. Article 47(1)(2) and 47(2), in turn, presents the grounds on which the enforcing court may *sua sponte* deny recognition or enforcement.

[a] Lack of Capacity and Invalidity of Arbitration Agreement

1.119 A Turkmen court can refuse recognition or enforcement if the party resisting recognition or enforcement of the arbitral award furnishes proof that:

---

98. International Arbitration Law, Art. 1(1)-(2).
99. International Arbitration Law, Art. 26(1)(1)-(2).
100. International Arbitration Law, Art. 47(1).

a party to the arbitration agreement referred to in Article 7 of this Law was under some incapacity; or the said agreement is not valid under the law to which the parties have subjected it or, failing any indication thereon, under the law of the country where the award was made... .[101]

[b] Procedural Violations

1.120 Likewise, a Turkmen court can also refuse recognition or enforcement if the party resisting recognition or enforcement of the arbitral award furnishes proof that:

> the party against whom the award is invoked was not given proper notice of the appointment of an arbitrator or of the arbitral proceedings or was otherwise unable to present his case.[102]

Or that:

> the composition of the arbitral tribunal or the arbitral procedure was not in accordance with the agreement of the parties or, failing such agreement, was not in accordance with the law of the country where the arbitration took place.[103]

[c] Excess of Mandate

1.121 Another ground by which a Turkmen court can refuse recognition or enforcement is if the party resisting recognition or enforcement of the arbitral award furnishes proof that:

> the award deals with a dispute not contemplated by or not falling within the terms of the submission to arbitration, or it contains decisions on matters beyond the scope of the submission to arbitration, provided that, if the decisions on matters submitted to arbitration can be separated from those not so submitted, that part of the award which contains decisions on matters submitted to arbitration may be recognized and enforced.[104]

[d] Arbitral Award Not Binding

1.122 A Turkmen court can also refuse recognition or enforcement if the party resisting recognition or enforcement of the arbitral award furnishes proof that:

> the award has not yet become binding on the parties or has been set aside or suspended by a court of the country in which, or under the law of which, that award was made.

---

101. International Arbitration Law, Art. 47(1)(1)(a).
102. International Arbitration Law, Art. 47(1)(1)(b).
103. International Arbitration Law, Art. 47(1)(1)(d).
104. International Arbitration Law, Art. 47(1)(1)(c).

[e] Non-arbitrability

1.123 Article 47(1)(2)(a) provides that recognition or enforcement may be refused if the court finds that "the subject-matter of the dispute is not capable of settlement by arbitration under the law of Turkmenistan." This provision parallels Article 36(1)(b)(i) of the UNCITRAL Model Law and Article V(2)(a) of the New York Convention. As in those texts, non-arbitrability, or objective arbitrability, under the International Arbitration Law is also determined with reference to the law of Turkmenistan.

[f] Public Policy

1.124 Article 47(1)(2)(b) provides that recognition or enforcement may be refused if the court finds that "the subject-matter of the dispute is not capable of settlement by arbitration under the law of Turkmenistan." This provision parallels Article 36(1)(b)(ii) of the UNCITRAL Model Law and Article V(2)(b) of the New York Convention. As in those texts, public policy under the International Arbitration Law is also determined with reference to the law of Turkmenistan.

[g] Sovereign Immunity

1.125 Notably, however, the International Arbitration Law adds an additional ground for refusal to recognize and enforce an international arbitral award to those listed in the UNCITRAL Model Law and Article V of the New York Convention. Article 47(2), namely, provides:

> Enforcement of an award may also be refused if its enforcement violates the principle of the sovereign immunity of Turkmenistan, provided that Turkmenistan has not explicitly waived such immunity.

1.126 Unlike the party-oriented language of Article 47(1)(1), the broad language of Article 47(2) indicates that it can be applied *sua sponte* by the court before which recognition or enforcement is sought.

[4] Procedures for Recognition

1.127 An international arbitration award for recognition and enforcement must be presented in original or certified copy to a court in the enforcing jurisdiction alongside the underlying arbitration agreement or a certified copy thereof. If either of these documents is in a foreign language, they must be translated into the official language of Turkmenistan.[105]

1.128 An enforcing court in Turkmenistan always has discretion to adjourn enforcement or order the enforcing party to offer security if the award whose enforcement is

---

105. International Arbitration Law, Art. 45(2).

sought is facing a petition for setting aside or suspension in a court of the country in which or under whose law the award was made.[106]

§9.10 INVESTOR-STATE ARBITRATION

[A] General Overview of Law and Practice Related to Investor-State Arbitration

1.129 Most contracts negotiated with the government provide for dispute resolution by arbitration.[107] There are three common types of commercial and investment arbitration disputes with the Government of Turkmenistan: (i) nonpayment of debts; (ii) nondelivery of goods; and (iii) contract renegotiations.[108] The Law of Turkmenistan "On Foreign Investment" of 2008 (the "Foreign Investment Law") prescribes three mechanisms for the resolution of disputes between foreign investors and the State: (i) negotiation; (ii) arbitration (or commercial) court proceedings; and (iii) if the parties so agree, before an arbitral tribunal.[109] As a result, investor-State arbitration is thus recognized as a valid means of resolving investment disputes. At the same time, because the statute does not designate any consent by Turkmenistan to arbitrate in any particular institution or under any particular rules, it leaves such forum and rules designation to the parties' agreement. Therefore, foreign investors would need to negotiate with the State in order to obtain Turkmenistan's consent to arbitration in its investment contract or in a subsequent arbitration agreement.[110]

1.130 In practice, Turkmenistan and its State-controlled entities have historically been quite liberal in agreeing to arbitration with different international institutions, including the ICC or the Stockholm Chamber of Commerce (SCC) when entering into commercial transactions. However, this seems to be a diminishing trend, especially in direct dealings with State authorities.

[B] List of Investment Treaties the Country Has Ratified

1.131 Turkmenistan has ratified and is a party to the following multilateral investment protection treaties:

- Energy Charter Treaty.
- ICSID Convention.

---

106. International Arbitration Law, Art. 47(3).
107. U.S. Commercial Service, *Turkmenistan - Dispute Settlement*, EXPORT.GOV (August 15, 2016), https://www.export.gov/apex/article2?id = Turkmenistan-Dispute-Settlement.
108. *See* e.g., Borzu Sabahi and Diora Ziyaeva, *Investor State Arbitration in Central Asia*, Transnational Dispute Management, 4 (2013).
109. Foreign Investment Law, Art. 29.
110. *See also* Law of Turkmenistan "On the Chamber of Commerce and Industry," February 28, 2015, Art. 16 (CCI arbitration is only available where agreed to by the parties); International Arbitration Law, Art. 47(2)(2) (an international arbitral award may also be refused if it violates the principle of Turkmenistan's sovereign immunity and Turkmenistan has not waived such immunity).

1.132 Turkmenistan has also signed bilateral investment protection treaties with the following counterparties. Unless indicated otherwise, the relevant treaty is ratified and in force:[111]

- Armenia (signed, not in force).
- Bahrain (signed, not in force).
- Belgium.
- China, People's Republic of.
- Egypt.
- France.
- Georgia.
- Germany.
- India.
- Indonesia (signed, not in force).
- Iran.
- Israel.
- Italy (signed, not in force).
- Luxembourg.
- Malaysia (signed, not in force).
- Pakistan (signed, not in force).
- Romania.
- Russia.
- Slovakia.
- Spain.
- Switzerland.
- Tajikistan (signed, not in force).
- Turkey.
- Ukraine (signed, not in force).
- United Arab Emirates.
- United Kingdom.
- Uzbekistan.

1.133 Most of the BITs refer investor-State disputes arising under them to investor-State arbitration under the ICSID Convention.

[C] List of Investor-State Disputes (Concluded and Pending)

1.134 There are two ICSID arbitrations presently pending against Turkmenistan, including one registered in August 2016 in relation to construction of a shopping and trade center.[112]

---

111. UNCTAD Division on Investment and Enterprise, *IIAs by Economy: Turkmenistan*, INVESTMENT POLICY HUB, http://investmentpolicyhub.unctad.org/IIA/CountryBits/215 (last accessed November 30, 2016).
112. *Görkem İnşaat Sanayi ve Ticaret Limited Şirketi v. Turkmenistan*, ICSID Case No. ARB/16/30.

1.135 On top of that, Turkmenistan was also involved in five concluded ICSID arbitration. Of the five concluded cases, Turkmenistan prevailed in two, lost in two and a fifth was discontinued. Turkmenistan's disputes' subject matter concerned the energy, telecommunications, construction and agro-industry sectors.

1.136 Turkmenistan also prevailed on jurisdiction in an UNCITRAL investment claim against it.[113] Another UNCITRAL investment claim against Turkmenistan was discontinued in August 2013 due to the claimant's inability to secure funding for the claim.[114]

§9.11 REFORM PROPOSALS

1.137 Though Turkmenistan's arbitration laws and institutions have evolved considerably from their pre-Soviet and Soviet roots, there are several reforms that Turkmenistan should consider in order to further develop its arbitration system. The following seven reforms would target those areas in need of development.

[A] Ratify the NY Convention

1.138 It is imperative that Turkmenistan ratify the New York Convention. Ratifying the convention would not only ensure the enforceability of arbitration awards, but it would also increase trade, increase foreign investments, improve interest rates and rates on return, and would allow Turkmen companies to enforce contracts in foreign countries. The New York Convention has been signed by 156 of the 193 U.N. member countries. It has a proven track record of working successfully for nearly sixty years and has been accepted in substantially different political and economic systems, including most of the countries that comprise the Commonwealth of Independent States. In order for international arbitration to be effective, arbitration awards must be enforceable across borders. If an arbitration award is unenforceable in the country in which the losing party has assets and income, the arbitration process will have been a waste of valuable resources, including time and money. Ratifying the New York Convention would ensure the enforceability of arbitration awards in Turkmenistan.

[B] Review the BITs as to the Consistency of Dispute Resolution Provision

1.139 Considering all of the business that takes place between Turkey and Turkmenistan, it is important that the dispute resolution provision of Article VII.2 in the Turkey-Turkmenistan BIT be understood consistently between the two nations.

---

113. *Erhas and others v. Turkmenistan (2013)*, UNCTAD INVESTMENT POLICY HUB (2013), http://investmentpolicyhub.unctad.org/ISDS/Details/517.
114. Luke Eric Peterson, *Central Asia round-up: updates on four UNCITRAL investment treaty arbitrations in the "Stans"*, IAREPORTER (March 11, 2014), http://www.iareporter.com/articles/central-asia-round-up-updates-on-four-uncitral-investment-treaty-arbitrations-in-the-stans/.

1.140 The Turkey-Turkmenistan BIT is rather unique in that the languages of the different versions of the dispute resolution clause of the BIT in Article VII.2 – English, Turkish and Russian – are not only inconsistent, but linguistically conflicting. The countries signed the BIT shortly after Turkmenistan proclaimed its independence. Hence, there has not been a period to carefully negotiate and review each provision of the treaty. Due to differences in the relevant languages in use, it remains unclear whether it is mandatory or optional for an investor to submit its dispute to the courts of the host State and receive the final award within one year from the date of submission of the case, before instituting arbitration proceedings in one of the fora in the manner permitted by Article VII.2. More than three ICSID Tribunals (e.g., *Kilic v. Turkmenistan*, *İçkale v. Turkmenistan*, *Sehil v. Turkmenistan*) to date have reviewed this issue of the interpretation of the dispute resolution provision. They have all arrived at conflicting points.

1.141 Conducting a formal review by Turkish and Turkmen officials, pursuant to Article VIII of the Turkey-Turkmenistan BIT, could assuage any doubts as to Article VII.2's interpretation and create a final and consistent interpretation of the dispute resolution clause.

[C] Set up an Independent Association for Lawyers to Regulate Admission to the Bar

1.142 Currently, lawyers have to regularly re-take the bar exam before the Ministry of Justice. A more efficient system would abrogate this requirement and do away with renewal requirements. Instead, Turkmenistan should create an independent professional association for lawyers to regulate the admissions to the Bar. This association would make final assessments of candidates so that lawyers would not be forced to go through the time-consuming process of retaking bar exams.

[D] Finalize and Open the New International Commercial Arbitration Court at the Turkmen Chamber of Commerce

1.143 The Decree attached to the Law on International Commercial Arbitration established an International Commercial Arbitration Court at the Turkmen Chamber of Commerce. This Court would have administrative functions in proceedings before arbitral tribunals sitting in Turkmenistan. Unfortunately, it appears that no cases have yet been administered by this Court. Turkmenistan should bring this new court into operation as decreed.

[E] Abolish the Arbitration Court of Ashgabat

1.144 The Arbitration Court of Ashgabat has survived from Soviet times and currently reviews all commercial matters. It does not fit into general structure of the judiciary and

Chapter 9: Turkmenistan §9.11[H]

should be fully integrated into it. Cases currently heard under this Court's jurisdiction should be reviewed by the courts of general jurisdiction.

[F] **Ratify the U.N. Convention on the Immunity of Property of States**

1.145 Turkmenistan should consider ratifying the U.N. convention on the immunity of property of States. Turkmenistan should not fear any sort of reprisal because the provisions of the Convention are already part of national Turkmen law. Ratifying the Convention would simply formally acknowledge Turkmenistan's acceptance and adherence to it, as expressed in the new CPC.

[G] **Align the National Arbitration of Annex 1 of the CPC to the UNCITRAL Model Law**

1.146 The current national arbitration system is still rudimentary. Aligning the current national arbitration law, codified in Annex 1 of the CPC, with the UNCITRAL Model Law, would create a more sophisticated and advanced system of arbitration.

[H] **Introduce a System of Tenure for Judges**

1.147 For the time being, judges are appointed for a limited period of five years, renewable. Experience in other countries shows that a system of tenure, life-long or until a retirement age, contribute to the independence of judges, a principle embedded in the Turkmen Constitution. It would be in line with this principle to accommodate the system of appointments and introduce a tenure, after a trainee period of three to five years.

APPENDIX I TURKMENISTAN BITs[115]

No.	Country	Signed	Ratified by Turkmenistan**	Entered into force for Turkmenistan***
1.	Armenia	19.03.1996		
2.	Bahrain	09.02.2011		
3.	Belgium/ Luxembourg	09.02.1989		18.08.1991
4.	China	21.11.1992		04.06.94
5.	Egypt	23.05.1995		28.02.1996
6.	France	28.04.1994		02.05.1996
7.	Georgia	20.03.1996		21.11.1996
8.	Germany	28.08.1997		19.02.2001
9.	India	20.09.1995		27.02.2006
10.	Indonesia	02.06.1994		
11.	Iran, Islamic Republic of	23.01.1996		29.04.2004
12.	Israel	24.05.1995		18.02.1997
13.	Italy	25.11.2009		
14.	Malaysia	30.05.1994		
15.	Pakistan	26.10.1994		
16.	Romania	16.11.1994		29.03.1996
17.	Russian Federation	25.03.2009		23.08.2010
18.	Slovakia	17.11.1994		10.03.1999
19.	Spain	26.10.1990		28.11.1991
20.	Switzerland	15.05.2008		02.04.2009
21.	Tajikistan	07.11.2007		
22.	Turkey	02.05.1992		13.03.1997
23.	Ukraine	29.01.1998		
24.	United Arab Emirates	09.06.1998		24.11.1999
25.	United Kingdom	09.02.1995		09.02.1995
26.	Uzbekistan	16.01.1996		02.08.1996

---

115. Texts of all Turkmenistan BITs are available at http://investmentpolicyhub.unctad.org/IIA/CountryBits/215.

APPENDIX II INVESTOR-STATE DISPUTES AGAINST TURKMENISTAN

List of concluded investment treaty arbitrations against Turkmenistan

1. *Garanti Koza LLP v Turkmenistan*, ICSID Case No. ARB/11/20, award dispatched on 19 December 2016;
2. *İçkale İnşaat Limited Şirketi v Turkmenistan*, ICSID Case No. ARB/10/24, award dispatched on 8 March 2016;
3. *Kılıç İnşaat İthalat İhracat Sanayi ve Ticaret Anonim Şirketi v Turkmenistan*, ICSID Case No. ARB/10/1, award dispatched on 2 July 2013;
4. *Erhas and others v Turkmenistan*, UNCITRAL;[116]
5. *Farouk Bozbey v Turkmenistan*, UNCITRAL;[117]
6. *Adem Dogan v Turkmenistan*, ICSID Case No. ARB/09/9, award dispatched 12 August 2014 (decision on annulment dispatched on 15 January 2016);[118]

List of pending investment treaty arbitrations against Turkmenistan

1. *Görkem Inşaat Sanayi ve Ticaret Limited Şirketi v Turkmenistan*, ICSID Case No. ARB/16/30.
2. *Muhammet Çap & Sehil Inşaat Endustri ve Ticaret Ltd. Sti. v Turkmenistan*, ICSID Case No. ARB/12/6.

Bibliography

RAFIS ABAZOV, HISTORICAL DICTIONARY OF TURKMENISTAN (2003).
CAROLE BLACKWELL, TRADITION AND SOCIETY IN TURKMENISTAN: GENDER, ORAL CULTURE AND SONG 38 & n.13 (2001).
GENNADY M DANILENKO, IMPLEMENTATION OF INTERNATIONAL LAW IN CIS COUNTRIES: THEORY AND PRACTICE, 10 EUR. J. INT'L L. 51 (1999).
A. LOMAKIN, OBYCHNOE PRAVO TURKMEN: ADAT [Common Law of the Turkmen: Adat] (1993).
Borzu Sabahi and Diora Ziyaeva, Investor State Arbitration in Central Asia, Transnational Dispute Management, 4 (2013).
Süleyman Sırrı Terzioglu, International Treaties in the Legal System of Turkmenistan, IV(2) LAW & JUST. REV. 73 (2013).

Webliography

Central Intelligence Agency, *Turkmenistan*, THE WORLD FACTBOOK (November 22, 2016), https://www.cia.gov/library/publications/the-world-factbook/geos/tx.html.

---

116. At https://www.iareporter.com/articles/an-uncitral-tribunal-declines-jurisdiction-over-a-joint-treaty-claim-brought-against-turkmenistan-by-a-series-of-unrelated-claimants/.
117. t http://www.italaw.com/cases/2465.
118. At http://www.italaw.com/cases/1454.

Erhas and others v. Turkmenistan (2013), UNCTAD INVESTMENT POLICY HUB (2013), http://investmentpolicyhub.unctad.org/ISDS/Details/517.

Luke Eric Peterson, Central Asia round-up: updates on four UNCITRAL investment treaty arbitrations in the "Stans," IAREPORTER (March 11, 2014), http://www.iareporter.com/articles/central-asia-round-up-updates-on-four-uncitral-investment-treaty-arbitrations-in-the-stans/.

New York Arbitration Convention, Contracting States, NEWYORKCONVENTION.ORG, http://www.newyorkconvention.org/countries (last accessed November 29, 2016).

Oleg Stalbovskiy et al., *UPDATE: A Research Guide to the Turkmenistan Legal System*, NYU GLOBALEX (March 2014), http://www.nyulawglobal.org/globalex/Turkmenistan1.html.

Turkmenistan Legal Capacity Building, https://www.dmiassociates.com/dmi/EN/turkmenistan-legal-capacity-building.

UNCTAD Division on Investment and Enterprise, *IIAs by Economy: Turkmenistan*, INVESTMENT POLICY HUB, http://investmentpolicyhub.unctad.org/IIA/CountryBits/215.

UNCITRAL Model Law on International Commercial Arbitration (1985), as amended in 2006, http://www.uncitral.org/uncitral/en/uncitral_texts/arbitration/1985Model_arbitration_status.html.

U.S. Commercial Service, *Turkmenistan – Dispute Settlement*, EXPORT.GOV (August 15, 2016), https://www.export.gov/apex/article2?id = Turkmenistan-Dispute-Settlement.

List of Laws and Statutes

Constitution of Turkmenistan of September 14, 2016.
Civil Code of Turkmenistan of 17 July 1998 (in force since March 1, 1999).
Civil Procedure Code of Turkmenistan of 18 August 2015 (in force since July 1, 2016).
Directive on the Arbitral Tribunal (Civil Procedure Code, Annex 1).
ICC Rules of Arbitration, Article 6(3)–(4) (2012).
Foreign Investment Law, Article 29.
Law of Turkmenistan "On Advocacy and Legal Practice," May 10, 2010.
Law of Turkmenistan "On the Chamber of Commerce and Industry," February 28, 2015.
Law of Turkmenistan "On International Commercial Arbitration," August 16, 2014.
Law of Turkmenistan "On Licensing Certain Activities," June 25, 2008.

CHAPTER 10
Ukraine

Olena Perepelynska

LIST OF ABBREVIATIONS

CIS	Commonwealth of Independent States
Civil Code	Civil Code of Ukraine No. 435-IV dated 16 January 2003
Civil Procedure Code	Civil Procedure Code of Ukraine No. 1618-IV dated 18 March 2004
Commercial Code	Commercial Code of Ukraine No. 436 dated 16 January 2003
Commercial Procedure Code	Commercial Procedure Code of Ukraine No. 1798-XII dated 6 November 1991
Constitution of Ukraine	Constitution of Ukraine No. 254K/96-BP dated 28 June 1996
Criminal Code	Criminal Code of Ukraine No. 2341-III dated 5 April 2001
Criminal Procedure Code	Criminal Procedure Code of Ukraine No. 4652-VI dated 13 April 2012
Domestic Arbitration Law	Law of Ukraine on Domestic Arbitration Courts No. 1701-IV dated 11 May 2004
Draft Law No. 4351	Draft Law No. 4351 on Amendments to Certain Laws of Ukraine concerning Judicial Control and Support of International Commercial Arbitration, registered in the Ukrainian Parliament on 31 March 2016
Geneva Convention	European Convention on International Commercial Arbitration, 1961, Geneva
ICAC	International Commercial Arbitration Court at the Ukrainian Chamber of Commerce and Industry
ICA Law	Law of Ukraine on International Commercial Arbitration No. 4002-XII dated 24 February 1994

ICAC Rules	Rules of the International Commercial Arbitration Court at the Ukrainian Chamber of Commerce and Industry, approved by the Decision of the Presidium of the Ukrainian Chamber of Commerce and Industry No. 18(1) of 17 April 2007, as amended by the Decision of the Presidium of the Ukrainian Chamber of Commerce and Industry No. 24(6) of 25 October 2012, No. 38(1) of 24 April 2014
ICSID Convention	Convention on the Settlement of Investment Disputes between States and Nationals of other States, 1965, Washington
Law on Advocate's Activity	Law of Ukraine on the Bar and Advocate's Activity No. 5076-VI dated 5 July 2012
MAC	Maritime Arbitration Committee at the Ukrainian Chamber of Commerce and Industry
New York Convention	United Nations Convention on the Recognition and Enforcement of Foreign Arbitral Awards, 1958, New York
PIL Law	Law of Ukraine on Private International Law No. 2709-IV dated 23 June 2005
SCU Resolution No. 12	Resolution of the Plenum of the Supreme Court of Ukraine on Practice of Consideration by the Courts of Motions for Recognition and Enforcement of Foreign Court Judgments and Arbitral Awards, and on Setting Aside the International Commercial Arbitration Awards Rendered within the Territory of Ukraine No. 12 dated 24 December 1999
UAA	Ukrainian Arbitration Association
UAA Draft Law	Proposals to improve arbitration legislation of Ukraine elaborated by the Working Group of the Ukrainian Arbitration Association in 2013-2015
UCCI	Ukrainian Chamber of Commerce and Industry
Ukrainian SSR	Ukrainian Soviet Socialist Republic
UNCITRAL	United Nations Commission on International Trade Law
UNCITRAL Model Law	UNCITRAL Model Law on International Commercial Arbitration 1985
USSR	Union of Soviet Socialist Republics

§10.01 GENERAL INTRODUCTION

[A] Historical Development of the Legal System

1.1. Ukraine is a civil law jurisdiction historically influenced by German law and Soviet law.[1] During the soviet period the legislation of Ukraine (then entitled the

---

1. There are many different views as to the role of the Roman law for the development of law in the Kievan Rus and in the Russian Empire (which during several centuries ruled over the major part of the modern Ukraine), as well as to qualification of the USSR law and its correlation with civil law – see Марченко М., *Сравнительное правоведение. Общая часть*, 459, 467 (Издательство «Зерцало», 2011).

Ukrainian Soviet Socialist Republic (Ukrainian SSR)) developed in line with the policies of the Union of Soviet Socialist Republics (USSR) and was quite similar to the legislation of other USSR Member States. The majority of international treaties for the USSR Member States were signed by the USSR itself, however, in a number of occasions the Ukrainian SSR was a separate signatory to international treaties.

1.2. In 1991 Ukraine became an independent state and started developing its own legislation. By virtue of the Law of Ukraine on Succession of Ukraine No. 1543-XII dated 12 September 1991[2] Ukraine confirmed its obligations under all the treaties signed by the Ukrainian SSR and conditionally confirmed its obligations under the treaties signed by the USSR. The legislation of the Ukrainian SSR continued to be in force insofar as it did not contradict the laws of Ukraine adopted after declaration of independence.

1.3. During the years of independence Ukraine has reformed its legislation and main codification acts. Most importantly, Ukrainian Parliament adopted the current Constitution of Ukraine[3] and 17 new Codes, including Civil Code,[4] Commercial Code,[5] Criminal Code,[6] Commercial Procedure Code,[7] Civil Procedure Code,[8] Code of Administrative Court Procedure[9] and new Criminal Procedure Code.[10]

1.4. New Civil Code of Ukraine has been developed according to the pandect system and taking into account recent reforms in several European states, the Principles of European Contract Law, the UNIDROIT documents, conventions of the Council of Europe and the Hague Conference on Private International Law as well as the Commonwealth of Independent States (CIS) Model Civil Code.[11]

1.5. In contrast, the Commercial Code of Ukraine elaborated by another working group inherited many archaic soviet law concepts and has been heavily criticized. In the

---

2. Law of Ukraine on Succession of Ukraine No. 1543-XII (12 September 1991), http://zakon5.rada.gov.ua/laws/show/1543-12.
3. Constitution of Ukraine No. 254к/96-ВР (28 June 1996), http://zakon3.rada.gov.ua/laws/show/254%D0%BA/96-%D0%B2%D1%80.
4. Civil Code of Ukraine No. 435-IV (16 January 2003), http://zakon4.rada.gov.ua/laws/show/435-15.
5. Commercial Code of Ukraine No. 436 (16 January 2003), http://zakon5.rada.gov.ua/laws/show/436-15.
6. Criminal Code of Ukraine No. 2341-III (5 April 2001), http://zakon3.rada.gov.ua/laws/show/2341-14.
7. Commercial Procedure Code of Ukraine No. 1798-XII (6 November 1991), http://zakon3.rada.gov.ua/laws/show/1798-12.
8. Civil Procedure Code of Ukraine No. 1618-IV (18 March 2004), http://zakon5.rada.gov.ua/laws/show/1618-15.
9. Code of Administrative Court Procedure of Ukraine No. 2747-IV (6 July 2005), http://zakon3.rada.gov.ua/laws/show/2747-15.
10. Criminal Procedure Code of Ukraine No. 4652-VI (13 April 2012), http://zakon3.rada.gov.ua/laws/show/4651-17.
11. *See Цивільне право України: Підручник: У 2-х кн.*, 23 (За ред. О.В. Дзери, Н.С. Кузнецової, Юрінком Інтер, 1999), as well as Довгерт А., *Вклад профессора Н. С. Кузнецовой в развитие цивилистической доктрины в Украине*, Гражданское общество и развитие гражданского права: Сборник статей к юбилею доктора юридических наук, профессора Наталии Семеновны Кузнецовой 40, 44 (Отв. ред. Р. А. Майданик и Е. В. Кохановская, ЧАО «Юридическая практика», 2014).

beginning of 2016 the Ministry of Justice of Ukraine and other regulatory authorities of Ukraine officially voiced for abolishing of the Commercial Code of Ukraine as it contains 'archaic norms repeating provisions of the specialised legislation'.[12] For that purpose in March 2016 the Ministry of Justice of Ukraine created a special working group to elaborate respective legislative proposals.[13]

[B]   The Legal Profession

1.6. Ukraine adopted special legislation governing different forms of legal profession, such as advocates,[14] notaries,[15] prosecutors,[16] investigators,[17] judges.[18]

1.7. Ukrainian legislation does not limit private legal practice to advocate's practice only. In fact, the private legal practice is carried out by advocates and 'lawyers-entrepreneurs'. This dual structure remains from early 1990s and is characterized by different regulatory frameworks applied to advocates and lawyers-entrepreneurs. The two groups are subject to different regulation of access to the practice of law and professional responsibility.[19]

1.8. Until recently Ukrainian legislation did not establish advocates' monopoly in parties' representations before the courts. In fact, only criminal procedure required representation (defence against the prosecution) by advocates only.[20] In civil litigation and administrative litigation a party could have been represented either by advocates or by 'other specialists in the field of law';[21] while in commercial litigation legal education of a representative was not required at all and a party could have been represented by any duly authorized representative or by a corporate body of a legal entity (e.g., director).[22]

---

12. The materials of press-conference: '*Abolishing of the Commercial Code: Opinion of the regulatory authorities and society*' is available at http://www.ukrinform.ua/rubric-pressconference/1944335-skasuvannya-gospodarskogo-kodeksu-dumka-regulyatoriv-zala-1.html.
13. *See* Order of the Ministry of Justice of Ukraine No. 82/7 dated 14 March 2016 on creation of the Working group for elaboration of concept of modernization of legal regulation of conditions for doing business in Ukraine, http://xn--80aagahqwyibe8an.com/minyust-ukrajini/nakaz-vid-14032016-pro-utvorennya-robochoji302634.html.
14. Law of Ukraine on the Bar and Advocate's Activity No. 5076-VI (5 July 2012), http://zakon3.rada.gov.ua/laws/show/5076-17.
15. Law of Ukraine on Notariate No. 3425-XII (2 September 1993), http://zakon3.rada.gov.ua/laws/show/3425-12.
16. Law of Ukraine on Public Prosecution No. 1697-VII (14 October 2014), http://zakon4.rada.gov.ua/laws/show/1697-18.
17. Criminal Procedure Code of Ukraine No. 4652-VI (13 April 2012), http://zakon3.rada.gov.ua/laws/show/4651-17.
18. Law of Ukraine on Judicial System and Status of Judges No. 1402-VIII (2 June 2016), http://zakon4.rada.gov.ua/laws/show/1402-19.
19. Kukharchuk V., Kulya M., *The Legal Profession in Ukraine* (2008), http://www.osce.org/odihr/36311?download = true.
20. Article 45 of the Criminal Procedure Code.
21. Article 12(1) of the Civil Procedure Code of Ukraine and Art. 16(2) of the Code of Administrative Court Procedure of Ukraine.
22. Article 28 of the Commercial Procedure Code of Ukraine.

1.9. However, the recently adopted amendments to the Constitution of Ukraine[23] provide that only an advocate shall represent a person before the court, and defend a person against prosecution. This rule will be implemented in several stages: since 1 January 2017 – for the proceedings before the Supreme Court of Ukraine and the cassation instance courts, since 1 January 2018 – for the proceedings before the appeal instance courts; since 1 January 2019 – for the proceedings before the first instance courts.[24] With regard to representation of the state and municipal bodies this rule shall apply starting from 1 January 2020.

1.10. Another block of reforms regarding advocate's activity is still pending.[25] As of now, the Law of Ukraine on the Bar and Advocate's Activity No. 5076-VI dated 5 July 2012 (Law on Advocate's Activity) provides rather complicated pathway to the status of an advocate. A person wishing to obtain such a status shall have higher legal education, command in Ukrainian language, two years of legal practice, shall pass the bar exam, pass six months of training or pupillage, make an advocate's oath and receive an advocate's certificate.

1.11. The law sets forth three forms of advocate's activity: individual practice, advocates' bureau or advocates' association.

1.12. All the advocates carrying out advocate's activity in Ukraine shall be included in the Unified Register of Advocates of Ukraine – http://erau.unba.org.ua.

1.13. Ukrainian advocates shall be members of the Ukrainian bar. Foreign advocates could be admitted to carry out advocate's activity in Ukraine if they apply to the respective qualification committee for inclusion in the Unified Register of Advocates of Ukraine and provided that they comply with the requirements of the Law on Advocate's Activity.

[C]   Sources of Arbitration Law

1.14. Ukraine has two separate laws and regimes for international and domestic arbitration. The international arbitration is governed by the Law of Ukraine on International Commercial Arbitration No. 4002-XII dated 24 February 1994 (ICA Law).[26] Domestic arbitration is governed by the Law of Ukraine on Domestic Arbitration Courts No. 1701-IV dated 11 May 2004[27] (Domestic Arbitration Law). These two

---

23. Respective amendments to the Constitution of Ukraine entered into force on 30 September 2016, http://zakon4.rada.gov.ua/laws/show/254%D0%BA/96-%D0%B2%D1%80.
24. Article 16-1(11) of Transitional provision of the Constitution of Ukraine.
25. *See* information at the website of the Council for Judicial Reform in Ukraine, http://jrc.org.ua/steps/step/advokatura_ta_bezoplatna_pravova_dopomoga.
26. Law of Ukraine on International Commercial Arbitration No. 4002-XII (24 February 1994), http://zakon4.rada.gov.ua/laws/show/4002-12; unofficial translation of the law into English, http://www.ucci.org.ua/en/legalbase/zua944002.html.
27. Law of Ukraine on Domestic Arbitration Courts No. 1701-IV (11 May 2004), http://zakon0.rada.gov.ua/laws/show/1701-15.

laws have different scope of application. According to Article 1(4) of the Domestic Arbitration Law its provisions shall not apply to international arbitration.

1.15. In terms of international arbitration Ukraine is a Model Law jurisdiction. Its ICA Law is almost a verbatim replica of the 1986 version of the UNCITRAL Model Law, with a few exceptions related to arbitrability rules, appointing authority, language of the award for enforcement purposes, annexes, etc.

1.16. The Domestic Arbitration Law is also based to certain extent on the UNCITRAL Model Law, but has additional provisions regarding creation and activity of the domestic arbitration courts.[28]

1.17. The function of judicial control over international arbitration is delegated to civil courts only and respective proceedings are governed by Chapter VII-1(1) (Setting aside of arbitral awards) and Chapter VIII (Enforcement of foreign court judgments) of the Civil Procedure Code.

1.18. For domestic arbitration these functions are split between commercial and civil courts depending on the status of the parties to the dispute and nature of the latter.[29] Respective proceedings are governed by Chapter VII-1 of the Civil Procedure Code and Chapter XIV-1 of the Commercial Procedure Code.[30]

1.19. In addition, both Procedural codes contain some arbitrability rules and the rules for enforcement of arbitration agreements by the courts (e.g., Articles 15(4), 17, 122, 130, 207, 235(5) of the Civil Procedure Code, Articles 2, 12(2), 80(5) of the Commercial Procedure Code).[31]

1.20. The Criminal Code of Ukraine contains provision regarding criminal liability of arbitrators for corruption and abuse of authority (Articles 18(4), 364, 365(2), 368(4)).

[D]   International Legal Framework, Supremacy of International Law

1.21. According to Article 9 of the Constitution of Ukraine:

> International treaties in force, consented by the Verkhovna Rada of Ukraine as binding, shall be an integral part of the national legislation of Ukraine.[32]

---

28. Жуков А., Перепелинская Е., *Статистика и проблемы третейского рассмотрения споров и взаимодействия третейских судов с государственными судами Украины*, 4(82) Журнал 'Третейский суд' 57, 58 (2012).
29. Жуков А., Перепелинская Е., *Третейские Суды Украины*, 32 ЭЖ ЮРИСТ, 4, 5 (2012). Закон и Бизнес, *Споры границ не знают*, http://zib.com.ua/ru/print/12878-15-16_noyabrya_v_kieve_sostoyalis_arbitrazhnie_dni.html.
30. Perepelynska O., *New Procedural Rules for Arbitration-Related Matters in Ukraine*, YIAG Newsletter (2011).
31. Перепелинская Е., *Арбитрабильность споров по законодательству Украины: проблемные вопросы*, Материалы II Международных арбитражных чтений памяти академика Побирченко И.Г. 37, 38 (2014).
32. *See* http://zakon4.rada.gov.ua/laws/show/254%D0%BA/96-%D0%B2%D1%80#Find.

1.22. The Law of Ukraine on International Treaties of Ukraine No. 1906-IV dated 29 June 2004 contains a similar provision in Article 19(1), but explains that the rules of the treaties operate as if they were the rules of the domestic legislation. It further clarifies in Article 19(2) that in case of a collision between a rule of the domestic legislation and a rule of the international treaty, to which Ukraine is a party and which has duly entered into force, the latter shall prevail. Similar rule is fixed in many laws and codes of Ukraine.

1.23. According to the Law of Ukraine on Compliance with Decisions and Application of Practice of the European Court of Human Rights No. 3477-IV dated 23 February 2006, the Ukrainian courts shall apply the Court's practice as a source of law.[33]

1.24. Ukraine is a party to all major international treaties in the field of international arbitration. It is one of the signatory to the United Nations Convention on the Recognition and Enforcement of Foreign Arbitral Awards, 1958 (New York Convention), and European Convention on International Commercial Arbitration, 1961 (Geneva Convention), ratified by the Ukrainian SSR in 1960 and in 1963 respectively. It acceded to the Convention on the Settlement of Investment Disputes between States and Nationals of other States, 1965 (ICSID Convention), in 2000, the Energy Charter Treaty in 1998, and singed over seventy bilateral investment treaties (BITs).

[E]   **Available Dispute Resolution Mechanisms**

1.25. Ukrainian legislation provides for resolution of disputes by the state courts, international arbitration and domestic arbitration.

1.26. Mediation is not regulated, but is used in practice. The Draft Law on Mediation has been registered and discussed within the Ukrainian Parliament,[34] but has not been adopted yet.

1.27. In addition, there are several optional consent-based mechanisms for dispute resolution in certain areas (e.g., conciliation commissions or quasi-arbitration for labour disputes).[35]

---

33. Article 17 of the Law of Ukraine on Compliance with Decisions and Application of Practice of European Court of Human Rights, http://zakon5.rada.gov.ua/laws/show/3477-15.
34. Information about and the text of the Draft Law on Mediation, http://w1.c1.rada.gov.ua/pls/zweb2/webproc4_1?pf3511=54558.
35. Article 7 of the Law of Ukraine on Procedure for Resolution of Collective Labour Disputes (Conflicts) No. 137/98-BP dated 3 March 1998, http://zakon4.rada.gov.ua/laws/show/137/98-%D0%B2%D1%80. A so-called labour arbitration is not based on arbitration legislation, and the final decision in such 'labour arbitration' is binding only if the parties so agree. The detailed procedure for this form of dispute resolution is set out by the Order of the National Service for Intermediary and Conciliation on Approval of the Regulation for Labour Arbitration No. 135 dated 18 November 2008.

[F] Judicial System

1.28. The judicial system of Ukraine has been reformed several times during the years of independence of the state, including in 2016.

1.29. According to the recent amendment[36] judicial system of Ukraine shall consist of the local courts, courts of appeal and the Supreme Court of Ukraine. In addition, special courts for IP and anti-corruption issues shall be created. Until implementation of these amendments, a current court system will remain in place. It has three branches of courts of general jurisdiction: civil & criminal, commercial and administrative courts, with three court instances (first, appeal and cassation) each, and the Supreme Court of Ukraine heading the whole system and having special powers to render binding opinions in case of contradictory application of the same rules by the cassation courts.[37]

[G] Arbitration Institutions

1.30. There are only two institutions administering international arbitrations in Ukraine – the International Commercial Arbitration Court at the Ukrainian Chamber of Commerce and Industry (ICAC)[38] and the Maritime Arbitration Committee at the Ukrainian Chamber of Commerce and Industry (MAC).[39] These institutions were created in 1991–1992[40] based on the Law of Ukraine on Foreign Economic Activity No. 959-XII dated 16 April 1991.[41] When the ICA Law was adopted the Regulations for both these institutions were included in the body of this law as annexes. The ICA Law does not contain any provision regarding creation of any new institutions in Ukraine.

1.31. In domestic arbitration the situation is different, and more than 500 domestic arbitration institutions have been registered in Ukraine since 2004 according to the procedure set forth by the Domestic Arbitration Law.[42] However, the majority of these courts are dormant. Since scope of the Domestic Arbitration Law does not include any matters related to international arbitration,[43] the procedure for registration of the domestic arbitration courts is not applicable to creation of institutions administering international arbitrations.

---

36. *See* amendments to the Constitution of Ukraine in force as of 30 September 2016 as well as Law of Ukraine on Judicial System and Status of Judges No. 1402-VIII (2 June 2016), http://zakon4.rada.gov.ua/laws/show/1402-19.
37. *See* previous (until 30 September 2016) edition of Articles 124–125 of the Constitution of Ukraine.
38. The official website of the ICAC is http://arb.ucci.org.ua/icac/en/icac.html.
39. The official website of the MAC is http://www.ucci.org.ua/arb/mac/en/mac.html.
40. The history of creation of the ICAC is available at its website: http://arb.ucci.org.ua/icac/ru/history.html.
41. Law of Ukraine on Foreign Economic Activity No. 959-XII (16 April 1991), http://zakon4.rada.gov.ua/laws/show/959-12.
42. Information on domestic arbitral institutions registered in Ukraine is available at the Unified Register of non-governmental institutions of the Ministry of Justice of Ukraine at http://rgf.informjust.ua/home/index.
43. Article 1(4) of the Domestic Arbitration Law.

[H] Sovereign Immunity and International Arbitration

1.32. Ukraine does not have special legislation governing the sovereign immunity of Ukraine, except for several provisions in the Law of Ukraine on Production-Sharing Contracts No. 1039-XIV dated 14 September 1999,[44] the Law of Ukraine on Public Private Partnership No. 2404-VI dated 1 July 2010[45] and the Budgetary Code of Ukraine No. 2456-VI dated 8 July 2010,[46] applicable to the waiver of immunity by Ukraine.

1.33. In 2015 a Draft Law on Jurisdictional Immunities and Responsibility of Foreign States was registered in the Ukrainian Parliament,[47] but has not been adopted yet.

§10.02 THE ARBITRATION AGREEMENT

[A] Introduction

1.34. In general, Ukraine is an arbitration-friendly jurisdiction. However, sometimes Ukrainian court practice with regard to arbitration agreements could still be rather formalistic.[48] Even in matters of interpretation of arbitration agreements Ukrainian courts are not always supportive to arbitration and respective court practice is not uniform. In practice, even a minor defect in arbitration agreement may cause problems in Ukrainian courts for the agreement itself and for an arbitral award rendered on its basis.[49]

1.35. The use of model arbitration clauses offered by the arbitral institutions does not always guarantee their enforceability in Ukraine as well[50] in view of unfortunate

---

44. Article 32 of the Law of Ukraine on Production-Sharing Contracts No. 1039-XIV (14 September 1999), http://zakon3.rada.gov.ua/laws/show/1039-14.
45. Article 19(3) of the Law of Ukraine on Public Private Partnership No. 2404-VI (1 July 2010), http://zakon4.rada.gov.ua/laws/show/2404-17, as amended on 26 May 2016.
46. Article 16(5) of the Budgetary Code of Ukraine No. 2456-VI (8 July 2010), http://zakon4.rada.gov.ua/laws/show/2456-17#Find.
47. Information about and the text of the Draft Law on Jurisdictional Immunities and Responsibility of Foreign States, http://w1.c1.rada.gov.ua/pls/zweb2/webproc4_1?pf3511 = 54404.
48. While *Kliuchkovskyi, Koriukalova and Uvarov* point out that the Ukrainian commercial courts '... tend to take a formal rather than a pragmatic approach and, despite parties' quite clear intention to arbitrate their dispute, refuse to enforce arbitration clauses where, for instance, the name of an arbitration institution is mentioned incorrectly', *Wietzorek* disagrees arguing 'that several agreements with incorrect or inaccurate references have also led Ukrainian commercial courts to discontinue the proceedings' – See Wietzorek M., *Ukrainian Courts on Agreements to Arbitrate in Switzerland*. 30 ASA Bulletin, Issue 3, Kluwer Law International, 552 (2012). Kliuchkovskyi, Koriukalova & Uvarov, *Ukraine*, in: The European & Middle Eastern Arbitration Review 2012, available at http://www.globalarbitrationreview.com/reviews/40/sections/141/chapters/1449/ukraine.
49. Perepelynska O., *Ukraine: How Minor Defects in Wording of Arbitration Clause May Result in a Big Problem*, CIS Arbitration Forum (2012), http://www.cisarbitration.com/2012/07/30/ukraine-how-minor-defects-in-wording-of-arbitration-clause-may-result-in-a-big-problem/.
50. Although *Pilkov* suggested that 'Ukrainian courts in the majority of cases would treat an arbitration agreement referring to the Swiss Rules as that one referring to an institutional arbitration, however without proper indication of and (sic!) arbitral institution' and *Kliuchkovskyi, Koriukalova & Uvarov* consider that 'the parties trying to evade arbitration sometimes challenge arbitration agreements where reference is made only to arbitration rules without

wording of the clarifications provided in this regard by the High Commercial Court of Ukraine in 2002.[51] However, as suggested by *Wietzorek* 'one should be very careful to make any generalization at this point in time, as the reported decisions also show that the practice of the Ukrainian commercial courts is not uniform with regard to some of the issues that typically arise in connection with Article II(3) NYC [New York Convention] and Article 8(1) uaLICA [ICA Law].'[52]

[B] Validity of the Arbitration Agreement

[1] General Provisions

1.36. Neither Ukrainian legislation nor international treaties of Ukraine provide for an exhaustive list of requisites of a valid arbitration agreement. Such a list could be identified based on a complex systematic analysis of international rules applicable to international arbitration.[53]

[2] Requisites of a Valid Arbitration Agreement

1.37. In Ukrainian law the general rules of validity of a transaction are set out in Article 203 of the Civil Code of Ukraine. However, these rules may not automatically apply to the validity of arbitration agreement in view of its mixed nature.

---

express designation of the arbitral institution', *Wietzorek* suggests that 'no recent Ukrainian judgment that accepted such argument could be retrieved'. *See*, Wietzorek M., *Ukrainian Courts on Agreements to Arbitrate in Switzerland*. 30 ASA Bulletin, Issue 3, Kluwer Law International, 559–560 (2012), Pilkov K., *Swiss Rules play a trick, of Why Ukrainian state court do not recognize 'arbitration in Geneva?'*, (2010), http://arbitration-blog.eu/swiss-rules-ukrainian-courts-recognize-arbitration-geneva, Kliuchkovskyi, Koriukalova & Uvarov, *Ukraine*, in: The European & Middle Eastern Arbitration Review 2012, available at http://www.globalarbitrationreview.com/reviews/40/sections/141/chapters/1449/ukraine.

51. Paragraphs 5 and 6 of the Clarifications of the Presidium of the High Commercial Court of Ukraine of 31 May 2002 No. 05-5/608 on Certain Practical Issues of Consideration of Cases Involving Foreign Commercial Entities and Organizations: *'that [arbitration] agreement must clearly indicate the body for the resolution of disputes chosen by the parties: the International Commercial Arbitration Court, the Maritime Arbitration Commission at the Ukrainian Chamber of Commerce and Industry or another court of the third person in Ukraine or abroad.... .an arbitration agreement cannot be performed if the parties have incorrectly stated the name of the court of the third person or have indicated an arbitration institution which does not exist.'* – http://zakon4.rada.gov.ua/laws/show/v_608600-02.As noted by *Wietzorek*: 'In this context, one should bear in mind that a Ukrainian commercial court might require evidence that a certain arbitration institution exists' – *See* Wietzorek M., *Ukrainian Courts on Agreements to Arbitrate in Switzerland*. 30 ASA Bulletin, Issue 3, Kluwer Law International (2012).
52. Wietzorek M., *Ukrainian Courts on Agreements to Arbitrate in Switzerland*. 30 ASA Bulletin, Issue 3, Kluwer Law International, 563 (2012).
53. Мальський М. *Арбітражна угода як умова розгляду спорів у міжнародному комерційному арбітражі*. Літопис (2013), http://www.ligazakon.ua/content/files/Arbitration_Agreement.pdf.

1.38. Validity of arbitration agreement depends on compliance with the requirement as to the: (i) form of arbitration agreement, (ii) capacity of the parties to arbitration agreement, (iii) content of arbitration agreement.[54]

1.39. Arbitration agreement shall be in writing.[55]

1.40. Parties to arbitration agreement shall have respective powers to enter into such an agreement. Unfortunately, the court practice does not give a definite confirmation that the scope of a power of attorneys rendered for entering into the main contract includes the power to enter into arbitration agreement as well. Thus, it is still advisable to stipulate that power separately.

1.41. Arbitration agreement shall contain the following conditions: (1) consent to refer the dispute to arbitration, (2) scope of legal relations, dispute out of which should be referred to arbitration, (3) type and name of arbitration: ad hoc arbitration or institutional arbitration competent to resolve the dispute.[56]

1.42. For domestic arbitration the Domestic Arbitration Law sets out the following rules as to the content of arbitration agreement: it shall contain information about names of the parties, their location, subject matter of the dispute, place and date of entering into the agreement.[57]

1.43. Ukrainian courts are inclined to conduct a full, rather than prima facie judicial review of the validity of arbitration agreements. One of the reasons for that, as explained by *Malskyy*[58] with reference to *Karabelnikov*, is the difference between the Russian and the English texts of Article II (3) of the New York Convention. The latter uses the term 'null and void', which should be translated as 'ничтожный'. Instead, the Russian version uses the term 'недействительный',[59] which comprises both void and voidable agreements. The same terms are used in the UNCITRAL Model Law. And following its Russian official text the ICA Law in Article 8 uses the term 'недійсний' instead of 'нікчемний'.

---

54. Мальський М. *Арбітражна угода як умова розгляду спорів у міжнародному комерційному арбітражі*. 90. Літопис (2013), http://www.ligazakon.ua/content/files/Arbitration_Agreement.pdf.
55. Article 7 of the ICA Law.
56. Мальський М. *Арбітражна угода як умова розгляду спорів у міжнародному комерційному арбітражі*. 90. Літопис (2013), http://www.ligazakon.ua/content/files/Arbitration_Agreement.pdf.
57. Article 12 (5) of the Domestic Arbitration Law.
58. Мальський М. *Арбітражна угода як умова розгляду спорів у міжнародному комерційному арбітражі*. 96. Літопис (2013), http://www.ligazakon.ua/content/files/Arbitration_Agreement.pdf.
59. Карабельников Б., *Исполнение и оспаривание решений международных коммерческих арбитражей: Комментарий к Нью-Йоркской конвенции 1958 г. и главам 30 и 31 АПК РФ 2002г*. 78. Статут (2008).

[C] Concluding the Arbitration Agreement (Written, Oral, by Conduct)

1.44. According to Article 7 of the ICA Law, the arbitration agreement must be in writing, either in the form of an arbitration clause in a contract or in the form of a separate agreement. An agreement is in writing if it is contained in a document signed by the parties or in an exchange of letters, telex, telegrams or other means of telecommunication which provide a record of the agreement, or in an exchange of statements of claim and defence in which the existence of an agreement is alleged by one party and not denied by another. The reference in a contract to a document containing an arbitration clause constitutes an arbitration agreement provided that the contract is in writing and the reference is such as to make that clause part of the contract.

[D] The Doctrine of Separability

1.45. According to Article 16(1) of the ICA Law, an arbitration clause, which forms part of a contract, shall be treated as an agreement independent of the other terms of the contract. A decision by the arbitral tribunal that the contract is null and void shall not entail *ipso jure* the invalidity of the arbitration clause.

[E] Invalidity of the Arbitration Agreement

1.46. In recent years the share of commercial court judgments on recognition of arbitration agreements invalid was insignificant and the courts usually dismissed respective claims.[60] However, this statistics concerns international arbitration only. In domestic arbitration the situation is different. There are many court cases with the only claim to recognize the arbitration clause invalid, used mostly as guerrilla tactics,[61] and despite critics from the arbitration community[62] respective court practice is not very supportive to arbitration.

1.47. In international arbitration, along with the well-grounded decisions on recognition of arbitration agreements invalid (e.g., courts recognized invalid arbitration agreement between Ukrainian companies with no foreign investment),[63] there were some questionable decisions (e.g., the court recognized invalid the arbitration agreement on settlement of disputes according to the rules of the German Arbitration

---

60. *See*, 'Ukraine. Arbitration-friendly jurisdiction: 2013–2014 statistical report' 20 (2014), http://c-n-l.eu/assets/files/ENFORCEMENT_OF_ARBITRATION_AWARDS_IN_UKRAINE_2013-2014%20(ENG).pdf.
61. Перепелинская Е., *Третейский лишний: процессуальные нюансы признания третейского соглашения недействительным*. Юридическая практика, № (2012).
62. Жуков А., Перепелинська О., *Стандартний підхід: українська судова практика з питань арбітражного (третейського) розгляду має розвиватися за найкращими світовими стандартами у цій сфері*. Судовий вісник № 11 (2014).
63. *See*, 'Ukraine. Arbitration-friendly jurisdiction: 2013–2014 statistical report' 20 (2014), http://c-n-l.eu/assets/files/ENFORCEMENT_OF_ARBITRATION_AWARDS_IN_UKRAINE_2013-2014%20(ENG).pdf.

Institution (DIS) as it found that the agreement did not contain the correct name of the arbitral institution).[64]

1.48. Although not in line with Ukrainian arbitration law and doctrine,[65] this case about the DIS Rules is an example of how the Ukrainian courts most often approach the validity of arbitration agreement. First, most probably they would apply *lex fori*, irrespective of whether the issue arose with respect to the enforcement of arbitration agreement, setting aside of the arbitral award or enforcement of the arbitral award. Second, the courts will consider validity from the perspective of the Civil Code of Ukraine provisions governing validity of transactions.[66]

[F] **Arbitrability**

[1] Disputes Capable of Settlement by Arbitration

1.49. According to the ICA Law, the parties may refer to the international commercial arbitration any cross-border disputes resulting from contractual and other civil law relationships arising in the course of foreign trade and other forms of international economic relations, and disputes involving Ukrainian enterprises with foreign investment, international associations and organizations established in the territory of Ukraine.

1.50. According to Article 1(2) of the ICA Law, the following may be referred to international commercial arbitration pursuant to an agreement of the parties:

- disputes resulting from contractual and other civil law relationships arising in the course of foreign trade and other forms of international economic relations, provided that the place of business of at least one of the parties is situated abroad; and
- disputes arising between enterprises with foreign investment, international associations and organizations established in the territory of Ukraine, disputes between the shareholders of such entities and disputes between such entities and other subjects of the law of Ukraine.

1.51. On 19 October 2016 the Law of Ukraine on Financial Restructuring[67] introduced temporary amendments to the scope of application of the ICA Law. These amendments

---

64. On 27 November 2013, the High Specialised Court on Civil and Criminal Matters upheld the court judgment of lower instances recognizing the arbitration clause referring to the DIS Arbitration Rules as invalid, http://www.reyestr.court.gov.ua/Review/35691495.
65. *See* Сліпачук Т., *Хто і як визначає право, що застосовується до арбітражної угоди, або... знову про головне*, 2 Юридичний журнал (2011), http://www.justinian.com.ua/article.php?id=3650 and Мальський М., *Визнання арбітражної угоди недійсною*. Держава і право (2010), http://dspace.nbuv.gov.ua/bitstream/handle/123456789/34352/62-Malskiy.pdf?sequence=1.
66. Articles 203, 215–236 of the Civil Code of Ukraine.
67. Law of Ukraine on Financial Restructuring No. 1414-VIII (14 June 2016), http://zakon4.rada.gov.ua/laws/show/1414-19.

shall apply during the period of effectiveness of the above-mentioned law (which is three years now – until 19 October 2019) and for this period they allow referring to international arbitration the disputes arising during financial restructuring covered by this law, even if a particular creditor is not a foreign entity or Ukrainian enterprise with foreign investment.

1.52. Exemptions from the ICA arbitrability rules may be established only by law or international treaty. In 2014–2016, several laws of Ukraine introduced positive 'exemptions' and allowed to refer to international arbitration certain categories of not cross-border disputes.

1.53. One of such positive 'exemptions' to the ICA Law arbitrability rules is provided by the Law of Ukraine on Creation of Special Economic Zone 'Crimea' and on Particularities of Carrying Out Commercial Activity within the Temporary Occupied Territory of Ukraine.[68] It sets forth special arbitrability rules for the period of temporary occupation of the territory of Crimea by the Russian Federation and allows referring to the ICAC or the MAC any disputes between the participants of commercial activity based in the Crimea and participants of commercial activity based in other part of the territory of Ukraine.

1.54. Another 'pro-arbitrability' exemption is provided in the Law of Ukraine on Privatization of the State-Owned Assets.[69] According to the amendments introduced to Article 27(10) of this law in 2016,[70] upon discretion of the privatization body any privatization agreement may provide for possibility to refer the disputes between the seller and the buyer of the privatization object arising out of or in connection with the privatization agreement to international arbitration. If the privatization agreement contains an arbitration clause, but the parties failed to agree on applicable institutional rules, respective disputes shall be finally resolved according to the Arbitration Rules of the Arbitration Institute of the Stockholm Chamber of Commerce.

1.55. In May 2016 arbitrability of disputes arising out of concession agreements and public private partnership agreements involving a foreign party or a Ukrainian enterprise with foreign investments was separately confirmed by amendments[71]

---

68. Law of Ukraine on Creation of Special Economic Zone 'Crimea' and on Particularities of Carrying Out Commercial Activity within the Temporary Occupied Territory of Ukraine No. 1636-VII (12 August 2014), http://zakon5.rada.gov.ua/laws/show/1636-18.
69. Law of Ukraine on Privatization of the State-Owned Assets No. 2163-XII (4 March 1992), http://zakon4.rada.gov.ua/laws/show/2163-12.
70. Law of Ukraine on Amending Certain Laws of Ukraine regarding Improvement of Privatization Procedure No. 1005-VIII (16 February 2016), http://zakon4.rada.gov.ua/laws/show/1005-19.
71. *See* Law of Ukraine on Amending Certain Laws of Ukraine to Eliminate Regulatory Barriers for Development of Public Private Partnership and Stimulating of Investments in Ukraine No. 817-VII (24 November 2015), http://zakon4.rada.gov.ua/laws/show/817-19, which entered into force on 24 May 2016.

introduced to the Law of Ukraine on Concessions[72] and the Law of Ukraine on Public Private Partnership.[73]

The Domestic Arbitration Law allows for referral to domestic arbitration of any domestic dispute arising from civil or commercial relations, except for certain cases envisaged by law.[74]

[2]   Disputes Not Capable of Settlement by Arbitration

1.56. Domestic Arbitration Law provides in Article 6 a rather long, but non-exhaustive,[75] list of non-arbitrable disputes, including:

(a) disputes regarding the invalidation of normative acts;
(b) disputes arising out of the conclusion, amendment, termination and performance of public procurement contracts;
(c) disputes related to state secrets;
(d) disputes arising from family relationships, except cases regarding marital agreements (contracts);
(e) bankruptcy disputes;
(f) disputes involving state or municipal authorities, their officials, state institutions or organizations;
(g) disputes related to immovable property, including land plots;
(h) cases about establishing facts of legal significance;
(i) labour disputes;
(j) disputes arising from corporate relations between a commercial company and its participant (founder or shareholder), including a participant that has withdrawn from the company, as well as between the participants (founders or shareholders) of commercial companies, in connection with the establishment, operation, management or winding up of the company;
(k) disputes involving a foreign party;
(l) disputes related to the protection of consumers' rights (including consumers of banking and credit union services);
(m) other disputes, which in accordance with the law are to be exclusively settled by the courts of general jurisdiction or by the Constitutional Ukraine Court of Ukraine (the latter ground applies, e.g., to petitions regarding the unconstitutionality of legal acts); and

---

72. See Art. 16(2) of the Law of Ukraine on Concessions No. 997-XIV (16 July 1999), http://zakon4.rada.gov.ua/laws/show/997-14.
73. Law of Ukraine on Public Private Partnership No. 2404-IV (1 July 2010), http://zakon4.rada.gov.ua/laws/show/2404-17.
74. Перепелинская Е., *Арбитрабильность споров по законодательству Украины: проблемные вопросы*, Материалы II Международных арбитражных чтений памяти академика Побирченко 32, 44 (2015), http://arbitration.kiev.ua/Uploads/kucher/Arb_Readings_2014_Arbitrability.pdf.
75. However, there is a Draft Law No. 3660 registered in the Ukrainian Parliament on 17 December 2015, which suggests to amend it and to make it exhaustive, http://w1.c1.rada.gov.ua/pls/zweb2/webproc4_1?pf3511 = 57458.

(n) disputes where the enforcement of the award to be issued by the domestic arbitration court requires certain action from the state or municipal authorities or their officials.

1.57. Other restrictions of arbitrability for domestic and/or international arbitration are set forth in Article 12 of the Commercial Procedure Code. In particular, it contains restrictions and prohibits disputes as described in items (a), (b) and (j) above from being submitted to arbitration.

1.58. After reforms made to the Commercial Procedure Code in February 2011 aimed at improving the legal framework for domestic arbitration-related cases, Article 12(2) of the Commercial Procedure Code was slightly amended. In particular, as regards international arbitrations, the new wording of Article 12 appears to restrict the non-arbitrability of the matters described above to domestic arbitration only, although initially (prior to the reform) it applied to international arbitration as well.[76]

1.59. For several years the scope of these restrictions and their correlation with the ICA Law arbitrability rules and other laws of Ukraine have been rather unclear, especially with regard to disputes related to public procurement contracts[77] and corporate governance.[78] The exact scope of the prohibition of referring to arbitration certain disputes arising out of corporate relations established in Article 12(2) of the Commercial Procedure Code was not clear, since Article 1(2) of the ICA Law was not amended and still allows the arbitrability of corporate disputes. At the same time, even according to that prohibition certain categories of disputes arising out of share purchase agreements remained arbitrable, e.g. disputes arising out of share turnover (except for disputes related to realization of the pre-emptive rights to acquire shares).[79]

1.60. Another restriction prohibiting referral to arbitration of cases on establishing certain facts of legal significance was introduced by new Civil Procedure Code of Ukraine in 2004. This exemption corresponds to the one introduced to Article 6 of the

---

76. Слипачук Т., *Арбитрабильность международных коммерческих споров в Украине*, 1 Вестник международного коммерческого арбитража 133, 142 (2010).
77. *See* the discussion regarding arbitrability of public procurement contracts and respective practice of recent years in Yaremko V., Karel O., Kluwer Arbitration Blog (2015), *Arbitrability of Corporate and Public Procurement Disputes in Ukraine*, http://kluwerarbitrationblog.com/2015/07/24/arbitrability-of-corporate-and-public-procurement-disputes-in-ukraine/. Перепелинская Е., *Все ясно: Ясность в вопросе арбитрабильности является важным фактором для иностранных инвесторов с точки зрения оценки ими рисков заключения договора*, 28-29 (864-865) Юридическая практика 18 (2014), Perepelynska O., Gontar O., *Arbitrability of Disputes Under Public Procurement Contracts In Ukraine: Recent Court Practice*, CIS Arbitration Forum (2014), http://www.cisarbitration.com/2014/08/25/arbitrability-of-disputes-under-public-procurement-contracts-in-ukraine-recent-court-practice/.
78. Wietzorek M., *Arbitrability of 'Corporate' Disputes in Ukraine – No News Is Good News?* CIS Arbitration Forum (2013), http://www.cisarbitration.com/2013/08/23/arbitrability-of-corporate-disputes-in-ukraine-no-news-is-good-news/.Perepelynska O., *Ukrainian Courts Review Arbitrability of Corporate Disputes*, CIS Arbitration Forum (2012), http://www.cisarbitration.com/2012/01/15/ukrainian-courts-review-arbitrability-of-corporate-disputes/.
79. However, the court practice in this regard is not uniform as well – *See* Савчук М., *Серый толк*, http://pravo.ua/article.php?id=100111532.

Domestic Arbitration Law during the reform of 2009. The wording of this restriction in the Civil Procedural Code as well as the content of its respective Section IV allows to conclude it does not apply to international arbitration.

1.61. Thus, as of today, Ukrainian legislation does not impose direct restrictions of the general arbitrability rules contained in the ICA Law, but the state court practice is still not uniform in this regard.[80] At the same time, certain matters are considered non-arbitrable in view of their nature. IP disputes, including validity of registered trademarks and/or patents and establishment of the IP owner, are not arbitrable.[81] Antitrust or competition issues can be considered arbitrable in relation to their effect on the civil law relationship of the parties.[82]

[3] Special Provisions on Consumer and Labour Disputes

1.62. As mentioned above, according to the Domestic Arbitration Law labour disputes are not arbitrable. Existing out of court forms for disputes resolution of labour disputes (conciliation commissions and quasi-arbitration) are not based on arbitration legislation.[83] The final decision in a so-called labour arbitration is binding only if the parties so agree.[84]

1.63. In contrast to rather clear arbitrability restrictions regarding the labour disputes, the restrictions imposed by the Domestic Arbitration Law on consumer disputes create many practical problems.

1.64. The wording of Article 6 of the Domestic Arbitration Law 'disputes related to the protection of consumers' rights (including consumers of banking and credit union services)' is understood in different manner by the arbitration community and the state courts.

---

80. *See* some examples of recent negative court practice in Кравчук. Г., *Арбитрабильность споров в контексте статьи 12 Хозяйственного процессуального кодекса Украины*, Материалы II Международных арбитражных чтений памяти академика Побирченко 15, 21 (2015), http://arb.ucci.org.ua/publ/rept2014reading.pdf.
81. *See* discussion regarding arbitrability of certain IP issues in Wietzorek M., *Decisions from Russia, Ukraine, and Kazakhstan related to Arbitration Proceedings Held in Switzerland.* 31 ASA Bulletin, Issue 3, Kluwer Law International, 590–591 (2013).
82. Perepelynska O., Taranyk D., *Arbitrability of Competition Law Issues in Ukraine*, Ukrainian Law Firms 2015. A Handbook for foreign clients (2015).
83. *See* the Law of Ukraine on Procedure for Resolution of Collective Labour Disputes (Conflicts) No. 137/98-BP dated 3 March 1998, http://zakon4.rada.gov.ua/laws/show/137/98-%D0%B2%D1%80. The detailed procedure for 'labour arbitration' is set out by the Order of the National Service for Intermediary and Conciliation on Approval of the Regulation for Labour Arbitration No. 135 dated 18 November 2008.
84. Article 12(5) of the Law of Ukraine on Procedure for Resolution of Collective Labour Disputes (Conflicts) No. 137/98-BP dated 3 March 1998, http://zakon4.rada.gov.ua/laws/show/137/98-%D0%B2%D1%80.

1.65. The literal interpretation of this clause as well as legislative history[85] of its adoption allows to conclude that the restriction applies to the narrow category of cases initiated by the consumers with regard to the breach of their consumer rights.[86]

1.66. The recent court practice and several binding opinions issued by the Supreme Court of Ukraine interpret this restriction as applicable to any dispute involving an individual, which is a client of a banking or credit institution, even if the proceedings are initiated by the banking or credit institution.[87]

1.67. In order to resolve these problems it is suggested[88] to amend the wording of respective provision of Article 6 of the Domestic Arbitration Law to prohibit referral to arbitration only disputes initiated by the consumers regarding protection of their rights provided by the Law of Ukraine on Protection of Consumers' Rights.

[G] Effect of Arbitration Agreement on Third Parties (Parties Substitution, Guarantee Agreements, Group of Companies Doctrine)

1.68. Ukrainian law is silent with regard to the effect of arbitration agreement on third parties.

1.69. The court practice in this regard is not uniform, but follows predominantly restrictive approach limiting the effect of the arbitration agreement to its parties only, except for the situation of the universal succession (e.g., merger of one of the parties).

1.70. As pointed out by *Slipachuk* 'third parties may also become bound through singular succession, such as through agency or an assignment or subrogation of an agreement containing an arbitration clause, but only where there exists a clear intention to assign the arbitration clause. Again it is necessary to ensure that all necessary formalities are met in the agreement as the state courts will be quite formalistic if they are asked to evaluate the effectiveness of the arbitration clause with regard to a third party'.[89]

---

85. Перепелинська О., *Споживачі в третейських судах. Чи вирішить законопроект № 6670-1 існуючі проблеми*, Юридична газета № 5 (2011).
86. The Arbitration Chamber of Ukraine launched public discussion regarding this problem, criticizing the opinions of the Supreme Court of Ukraine – *see* more at http://tpu.kiev.ua/komentar-treteyskoyi-palati-ukrayini-stosovno-pravovoyi-pozitsiyi-verhovnogo-sudu-ukrayini-vid-03-02-2016-roku-u-spravi-6-2630tss15-shhodo-zastosuvannya-p-14-st-6-zakonu-ukrayini-pro-treteyski-s/.
87. For example the Binding Opinion of the Supreme Court of Ukraine of 3 February 2016 in a case No. 6-2630 Цс15, Opinion of 02 September 2015 in a case No. 6-856 Цс15, Opinion of 11 November 2015 in a case No. 6-1716 Цс15, Opinion of 27 January 2016 in cases No. 6-2712 Ц 15 and No. 6-2892 Ц 15.
88. *See* Draft Law No. 3660 registered in the Ukrainian Parliament on 17 December 2015, http://w1.c1.rada.gov.ua/pls/zweb2/webproc4_1?pf3511=57458.
89. Slipachuk T., *Arbitration Guide – Ukraine*, IBA Arbitration Committee (2012).

[H] Termination of Arbitration Agreement

[1] *Termination with Respect to Existing Dispute*

1.71. The ICA Law[90] and the Domestic Arbitration Law[91] allow the parties to the pending arbitral proceedings to terminate the latter by their agreement. Although not stated explicitly, under the general procedural rules such termination, as any other termination of the proceedings, precludes the parties from initiating another set of arbitral proceedings regarding the same dispute. Put in other words, this would terminate the arbitration agreement with respect to existing dispute.

1.72. The Domestic Arbitration Law does not designate an appointing authority. Thus, the default rules for constitution of the arbitral tribunal in ad hoc arbitration may not operate to the full extent. In case of deadlock situations, the arbitration agreement with respect to existing dispute shall be terminated and the claimant may refer this dispute to the state court.[92]

1.73. Setting aside of an arbitral award by the Ukrainian state court does not automatically entail termination of the arbitration agreement with regard to the dispute resolved by the arbitral tribunal. According to the general rule set out in Article 51 of the Domestic Arbitration Law, setting aside of an arbitral award does not preclude the parties from initiating arbitration anew. The exceptions from this rule include the situations when the setting aside was based on invalidity of arbitration agreement, non-arbitrability of the subject matter of the dispute, or if the award dealt with a difference not contemplated or not falling within the terms of the submission of arbitration, or it contains decisions on matters beyond the scope of submission to arbitration.

[2] *Complete Termination*

1.74. Ukrainian law does not contain any specific rules regarding termination of arbitration agreement, thus in practice the courts, based on *lex fori*, apply general rules on termination of obligations set out in Chapter 50 of the Civil Code of Ukraine.

1.75. The ICA Law elaborated on the basis of the Russian version of the UNCITRAL Model Law, as well as the New York Convention (in its official Russian version most often used in Ukraine),[93] refer to the termination of the arbitration agreement in their respective Articles 8 and II(3), both using the same wording 'ceased to be in force'

---

90. Article 32(2) of the ICA Law.
91. Article 53(1) of the Domestic Arbitration Law.
92. For arbitrations with sole arbitration lack of parties' agreement to appoint a sole arbitrator, for arbitration with three arbitrators – default of the respondent to appoint his arbitrator or in disagreement of the two party-appointed arbitrators with regard to the presiding arbitrator – Art. 17(3)(1)–(2) of the Domestic Arbitration Law.
93. Russian version of the New York Convention is also published at the website of the Ukrainian Parliament: http://zakon2.rada.gov.ua/laws/show/995_070.

(*'утратило силу'*) in contrast to 'inoperative' used in the English version of both documents.

[I] Drafting Arbitration Clauses

1.76. In view of the risk of rather formalistic approach of the Ukrainian courts with regard to the wording of arbitration agreement,[94] the parties should be very careful when drafting their arbitration agreement.

1.77. If the parties agree on institutional arbitration it is advisable to specify in the agreement the name of the arbitral institution and not only its rules. If the respective agreement is in two languages, which is often the case when Ukrainian parties are involved, it is highly recommended to check the correct name of the institution in both languages and to provide that one of the languages will prevail in case of discrepancies.

1.78. In addition, taking into account recent court practice regarding the scope of the matters referred to arbitration by the parties, it would also appear important to state in the arbitration agreement the principal disputes that are subject to arbitration, i.e., arising out of or in connection with the contract, including its existence, validity, cancellation, termination or interpretation.[95]

§10.03 APPLICABLE LAW

[A] Introduction

1.79. Pursuant to Article 28 of the ICA Law, the arbitral tribunal shall decide the dispute in accordance with such rules of law as are chosen by the parties as applicable to the substance of the dispute. Otherwise the arbitral tribunal shall apply the law determined by the conflict of laws rules, which it considers applicable. The parties may authorize the arbitral tribunal to decide *ex aequo et bono* or as *amiable compositeur*. In all cases, the arbitral tribunal shall decide in accordance with the terms of the contract and shall take into account the usages of the trade applicable to the transaction.

[B] The Law Governing the Arbitration (*Lex Arbitri*)

1.80. According to the Ukrainian arbitration law and treaties *lex arbitri* shall govern the following issues for the purposes of arbitration proceedings and further enforcement of the arbitral award: (1) validity of arbitration agreement (for both form and

---

94. Марченко Р., Коптилин С., *Практика отмены арбитражных решений в Украине*, Юр газета (2012). *See also* the discussion in footnote 48.
95. Slipachuk T., Perepelynska O., Droug O., *Arbitration World – Ukrainian Chapter*. Arbitration World, 4th Edition, The European Lawyer, Thomson Reuters (2012).

substance), (2) arbitrability of the subject matter of the dispute and (3) rules of the arbitral procedure.[96]

[C] Party Autonomy on Choice of Law Issues

1.81. The ICA Law gives the parties freedom to determine the law applicable to the substance of the dispute[97] and the law applicable to the arbitration agreement.[98]

The parties may authorize the arbitral tribunal to decide *ex aequo et bono* or as *amiable compositeur*.[99]

1.82. In Ukrainian law the party autonomy principle is fixed in the Law of Ukraine on Private International Law No. 2709-IV dated 23 June 2005 (PIL Law).[100]

[D] Restrictions on Party Autonomy
[1] General Observations

1.83. One of the restrictions to the party autonomy principle is set out in Article 5(6) of the PIL Law, prohibiting choice of foreign law when the legal relations in question lack a so-called foreign element (i.e., factor connecting the relationship with a foreign jurisdiction via a party, a subject matter or a 'legal fact' in a way prescribed by Article 1(2) of the PIL Law).

1.84. Another important restriction is Article 10 of the PIL Law providing for invalidity of the choice of law if the latter aims at circumvention of the rules of the PIL Law.

1.85. Finally, Article 14 of the PIL Law sets forth that its provisions do not limit application of any mandatory rules governing the parties' relations irrespective of the law chosen by them.

[2] Reasonable Connection Test

1.86. The PIL Law sets out several instances when the law most closely connected with respective private legal relations shall apply.[101]

---

96. Сліпачук Т., *Хто і як визначає право, що застосовується до арбітражної угоди, або... знову про головне*, 2 Юридичний журнал (2011), http://www.justinian.com.ua/article.php?id=3 650.
97. Article 28(1) of the ICA Law.
98. Article 36(1)(1) of the ICA Law.
99. Article 28(3) of the ICA Law.
100. Articles 1(5), 5 of the Law of Ukraine on Private International Law No. 2709-IV (23 June 2005), http://zakon4.rada.gov.ua/laws/show/2709-15.
101. For example, if it is impossible to determine the applicable law based on the conflict of law rules (Art. 4), or such application is limited by public policy restrictions (Art. 12), or for certain mandatory rules (Art. 14(2) of the PIL Law).

1.87. For contractual relations the PIL Law fixes a presumption that the law most closely connected with the contract is the law of the country of residence or location of a party obliged to carry out characteristic performance.[102] Article 44 of the PIL Law contains an indicative list of parties obliged to carry out characteristic performance for different types of contracts (e.g., seller for the sale contract, lender for the loan agreement etc.).

[3] National Public Policy

1.88. The PIL Law provides for public policy restrictions limiting application of the foreign law provisions if 'such application leads to the results manifestly incompatible with foundations of the legal order (public order) of Ukraine'.[103]

1.89. Based on the case law and scholars' writings *Kysil* points out the following elements of the notion 'foundations of the legal order': '(a) the basic fundamental principles of the domestic law of Ukraine, including such mandatory rules of public, private and procedural law, that form the skeleton of existing legal order in Ukraine; (b) generally recognized principles of morality and justice, that are important for Ukrainian legal order and are dominant in the Ukrainian society; (c) the legitimate interests of Ukrainian legal entities and individuals, the state of Ukraine and the Ukrainian society, protection of which is the main task of the Ukrainian legal system; (d) the generally recognized principles and rules of international law constituting part of the Ukrainian legal system and especially the international legal standards of human rights'.[104]

[4] Mandatory Rules of Municipal Law

1.90. If the subject matter of the dispute is in any way connected with Ukraine or if one of the parties is incorporated or resides in Ukraine, then mandatory provisions of foreign currency, tax, customs and competition law, as well as certain provisions of the PIL Law may apply. Article 14 of the latter provides for application of the mandatory law of other jurisdictions (if it is closely connected with the respective legal relations) and sets forth conditions of its application in Ukraine. In all other cases, public policy restrictions of the seat shall apply.

[5] International Public Policy

1.91. Ukrainian law does not operate with 'international public policy' notion.

---

102. Article 32(3) of the PIL Law.
103. Article 12(1) of the PIL Law.
104. Довгерт А., Кисіль В., Штіка М., Серьогін О., Калакура В., Бірюков О., Галущенко Г., Криволапов Б., Капіца Ю., Виговський О., Забара І., Довжук О., Кармаза О., Черняк Ю., Ціраг Г., *Міжнародне приватне право. Науково-практичний коментар Закону*, Стаття 12, 97-98 (За ред. Довгерта А., ТОВ «Одіссей», 2008).

[E] No Explicit Choice of Law

[1] Introduction

1.92. In contractual obligations, in absence of the explicit choice of law, the law most closely connected with legal relations shall apply.[105]

1.93. In tortious obligations the general rule is that the law of the state where the tortious act took place shall apply.[106]

[2] Relevant Conflict of Law Rules

1.94. The PIL Law contains a set of conflict of law rules for different issues, such as legal status of individuals and legal entities, transactions, powers of attorneys, limitation period, intellectual property rights, rights in rem, contractual and tortious obligations, labour relations, family law, inheritance.

1.95. For contractual relations, the principle of closest connection is clarified in Article 44 of the PIL Law, indicating the party obliged to carry out characteristic performance for different types of contracts (e.g., seller for the sale contract, lender for the loan agreement, etc.).

[F] The Law Governing the Arbitration Agreement

1.96. According to the ICA Law,[107] the New York Convention,[108] the Geneva Convention[109] and prevailing doctrine, for the purposes of arbitration proceedings and further setting aside or enforcement of the arbitral award *lex arbitri* governs the substantive validity of arbitration agreement (if the parties have not agreed otherwise),[110] as well as formal validity of the arbitration agreement if the latter needs to be established by arbitrators.[111]

---

105. Article 44 of the PIL Law.
106. Articles 48, 49 of the PIL Law.
107. Articles 34(2)(a)(i) and 36(1)(a)(i) of the ICA Law.
108. Articles II(2), V(1)(2) of the New York Convention.
109. Article VI of the Geneva Convention.
110. Перепелинская Е., *Арбитрабильность споров по законодательству Украины: проблемные вопросы*, Материалы II Международных арбитражных чтений памяти академика Побирченко И.Г. 37, 38 (2014).
111. Сліпачук Т., *Хто і як визначає право, що застосовується до арбітражної угоди, або... знову про головне*, 2 Юридичний журнал (2011), http://www.justinian.com.ua/article.php?id=3650.

§10.04 THE ARBITRATORS

[A] Appointment of Arbitrators

[1] Appointment of Arbitrators under Municipal Law

1.97. The ICA Law does not impose any special restrictions on the parties' freedom to choose arbitrators. Under Article 10 of the ICA Law, the parties are also free to determine the number of arbitrators, failing which the number of arbitrators shall be three. According to Article 11(2) of the ICA Law, the parties are free to agree on a procedure of appointing the arbitrator or arbitrators, subject to compliance with the provisions of the ICA Law.

1.98. Pursuant to Article 11(3) of the ICA Law, in the absence of agreement by the parties:

- in an arbitration with three arbitrators, each party shall appoint one arbitrator, and the two arbitrators thus appointed shall appoint the third arbitrator; if a party fails to appoint the arbitrator within thirty days of receipt of a request to do so from the other party, or if the two arbitrators fail to agree on the third arbitrator within thirty days of their appointment, the appointment shall be made, upon request of a party, by the President of the Ukrainian Chamber of Commerce and Industry (UCCI);
- in an arbitration with a sole arbitrator, if the parties are unable to agree on the arbitrator, he or she shall be appointed, upon request of a party, by the President of the UCCI.

[2] Appointment under Institutional Rules

1.99. Article 5 of the current ICAC Rules[112] provides that arbitrators can be persons appointed by the parties in accordance with these Rules, or persons appointed by the President of the UCCI. In practice such appointment is limited to the pool of arbitrators included in a so-called the Recommendatory List of Arbitrators approved by the Presidium of the UCCI on the proposal of the ICAC Presidium.

1.100. Pursuant to Article 27 of the ICAC Rules, subject to the provisions of these Rules the parties are free to agree on a procedure of appointing the arbitrator or arbitrators. Failing such agreement, the default ICAC rules similar to those of Article 11 of the ICA Law shall apply. However, in an arbitration with three arbitrators the President of the UCCI shall make appointment within thirty days after receipt of a notice from the ICAC, or if the two arbitrators fail to agree on the third arbitrator within thirty days of their appointment.

---

112. ICAC is elaborating new version of its Rules, not yet disclosed to public.

1.101. For multiparty arbitration with three arbitrators the ICAC Rules provide that the multiple claimants and the multiple respondents shall each choose one arbitrator. Where the claimants or respondents have not reached an agreement within thirty days after receipt of a notice from the ICAC, an arbitrator shall be appointed by the President of the UCCI.

1.102. Article 29 of the ICAC Rules establishes the criteria the President of the UCCI shall consider in appointing an arbitrator, including qualifications required, securing the appointment of an independent and impartial arbitrator and, in the case of a sole arbitrator or a presiding arbitrator, – advisability of appointing an arbitrator of nationality other than those of the parties.

1.103. A decision by the President of the UCCI on appointment of arbitrators shall be subject to no appeal.

[B] Qualifications of Arbitrators

1.104. According to Articles 11(1) and 11(5) of the ICA Law, the parties may agree on qualifications required of an arbitrator and nationality considerations.

1.105. The Domestic Arbitration Law provides for much detailed regulation of the restrictions on choice of arbitrators. Pursuant to Article 18 of the Domestic Arbitration Law, the following persons may not act as arbitrators in domestic arbitration proceedings:

- minors and persons under guardianship;
- persons that do not meet the qualification requirements agreed by the parties or set forth in the rules of a domestic arbitration institution;
- persons with criminal record;
- persons that were declared legally incapable by court;
- judges of the general courts and judges of the Constitutional Court of Ukraine.

1.106. Furthermore, the Domestic Arbitration Law provides that in the event that case is heard by a sole arbitrator of the permanent arbitration court he or she shall have a law degree. In the event that case is heard by several arbitrators, the requirement to have a law degree extends only to the presiding arbitrator.

[C] Powers and Duties of Arbitrators

1.107. The main duty of arbitrators is to treat the parties equally and to ensure that each party is given a full opportunity to present its case.[113] The arbitrators must follow the parties' agreement and the applicable procedural rules. The powers conferred upon

---

113. Article 18 of the ICA Law.

the arbitral tribunal include the power to determine the admissibility, relevance, materiality and weight of any evidence.[114]

[D] Challenges and Replacement of Arbitrators

[1] Challenges under Municipal Law

1.108. The functions of making decision on challenge or termination of the mandate of an arbitrator are granted to the UCCI President (Articles 6(1), 13(3) and 14 of the ICA Law).

1.109. Pursuant to Article 13(1) of the ICA Law, the parties may agree between themselves on a procedure for challenging an arbitrator. At the same time, according to Article 13(3) of the ICA Law, if any such procedure agreed by the parties is not successful the challenging party may request, within thirty days after having received notice of the decision rejecting the challenge, the President of the UCCI to decide on the challenge, which decision shall be subject to no appeal.

1.110. In the event that the parties fail to reach agreement on a procedure for challenging an arbitrator, pursuant to Article 13(2) of the ICA Law, a party which intends to challenge an arbitrator shall, within fifteen days after becoming aware of the constitution of the arbitral tribunal or after becoming aware of any circumstance that gives rise to justifiable doubts as to arbitrator's impartiality or independence, send a written statement of the reasons for the challenge to the arbitral tribunal. Unless the challenged arbitrator withdraws from his or her office or the other party agrees to the challenge, the arbitral tribunal shall decide on the challenge. Failing that, the challenging party may resort to the procedure available under Article 13(3) of the ICA Law.

[2] Challenges under Institutional Rules

1.111. According to Article 12(1) of the ICA Law, persons approached in connection with their possible appointment as arbitrators must disclose any circumstances likely to give rise to justifiable doubts as to their impartiality or independence. Such obligation continues throughout the arbitral proceedings. There is no established practice as to what circumstances would be considered as giving rise to justifiable doubts as to the impartiality or independence of arbitrators.

1.112. Similar requirements in domestic arbitration are more specific. In particular, pursuant to Article 19 of the Domestic Arbitration Law, arbitrators may not take part in arbitration proceedings and, after appointment can be subject to challenge or required to resign if, *inter alia*: (i) they are interested either directly or indirectly in the outcome of the arbitration proceedings; (ii) they are relatives of one of the parties or other persons participating in the arbitration proceedings, or have any other special relations

---

114. Article 19 of the ICA Law.

with them; and (iii) they are resolving disputes which are either directly or indirectly related to the performance by such arbitrators of their public duties.

1.113. Pursuant to Article 13(1) of the ICA Law, the parties may agree on a procedure for challenging an arbitrator. According to Article 30 of the ICAC Rules, a party which intends to challenge an arbitrator must, within fifteen days of becoming aware of the constitution of the arbitral tribunal or of becoming aware of any circumstance that gives rise to justifiable doubts as to the arbitrator's impartiality or independence, send a written statement of the reasons for the challenge to the ICAC. Failure to meet this deadline amounts to a waiver of the right to challenge.

1.114. The ICAC Secretariat must give to the other party an opportunity to comment on the challenge. Unless the challenged arbitrator withdraws from office or the other party agrees to the challenge, the ICAC Presidium shall decide on the challenge. The challenged arbitrator can provide comments with respect to the challenge. The ICAC Presidium's decision to release from the appointment may not contain reasons.[115]

1.115. If a challenge is not successful, the challenging party may request, within thirty days after having received a notice of the decision rejecting the challenge, the President of the UCCI to decide on the challenge, which decision shall be subject to no appeal. While such a request is pending, the Arbitral Tribunal, including the challenged arbitrator, may continue the arbitral proceedings and make an award.[116]

[E] Compensation of Arbitrators

1.116. The ICAC Schedule on Arbitration Fees and Costs[117] operates with three types of fees & costs payable to the ICAC: registration fee, arbitration fee and additional costs of the arbitral proceedings.

1.117. The arbitration fee includes by definition the registration fee and is fixed as a lump sum depending on the amount in dispute. It covers arbitrators' fees and the ICAC administration fee, however the ICAC Schedule on Arbitration Fees and Costs does not provide the ratio between these types of fees. In other words, neither the parties nor the arbitrators are aware of the amount of the arbitrators' fee to be paid in a particular case at the time of his/her appointment. The ICAC arbitral awards do not contain such information either, which makes it rather difficult to analyse the respective practice of the institution.

1.118. The arbitrators' costs (travel expenses, accommodation, visa, etc.) shall be advanced by the parties as a part of the 'additional costs of the arbitral proceedings'. If the party fails either to deposit the required advance within the fixed period of time or to appoint any other arbitrator whose participation in the arbitral proceedings does not

---

115. Article 30(3) of the ICAC Rules.
116. Article 30(4) of the ICAC Rules.
117. The ICAC Schedule on Arbitration Fees and Costs http://arb.ucci.org.ua/icac/en/fees.html.

entail additional costs, the party shall be deemed to have waived its right to appoint an arbitrator, and the President of the UCCI shall appoint an arbitrator for such party.[118]

§10.05 JURISDICTION OF THE ARBITRATION TRIBUNAL

[A] Introduction

1.119. The ICA Law respects the competence-competence principle and allows an arbitral tribunal to determine its own jurisdiction.[119]

[B] The Arbitrators' Determination of Their Jurisdiction

1.120. Pursuant to Article 16 of the ICA Law, the arbitral tribunal may rule on its own jurisdiction, including any objections with respect to the existence or validity of the arbitration agreement. If the tribunal rules as a preliminary question that it has jurisdiction, any party may request within thirty days after having received notice of that ruling, the general court located at the seat of arbitration to decide the matter; such a decision shall not be subject to appeal. While such a request is pending, the arbitral tribunal may proceed with the arbitral proceedings and make an award.

[C] Court Review of Arbitrators' Jurisdiction

1.121. The functions of making decision on jurisdiction of the arbitral tribunal, when the latter rules on its own jurisdiction as a preliminary question, as well as decisions on setting aside of the final arbitral awards rendered in Ukraine are performed by local civil courts of Ukraine at the seat of arbitration.[120]

[D] Institutional Rules

1.122. Article 3 of the ICAC Rules sets forth the rules for pleas as to the ICAC jurisdiction. It generally follows the provisions of Article 16 of the ICA Law. At the same time, they specify that a plea that the ICAC does not have jurisdiction shall be raised not later than the submission of the Statement of Defence. A party is not precluded from raising such a plea by the fact that it has appointed, or participated in the appointment of, an arbitrator. A plea that the ICAC is exceeding the scope of its jurisdiction shall be raised as soon as the matter alleged to be beyond the scope of its jurisdiction is raised during the arbitral proceedings.

---

118. Section VII(3) of the ICAC Schedule on Arbitration Fees and Costs.
119. Article 16 of the ICA Law.
120. Articles 6(2), 16(3) and 34(2) of the ICA Law.

§10.06 THE PROCEDURE BEFORE THE ARBITRATION TRIBUNAL

[A] Introduction

1.123. The ICA Law follows the UNCITRAL Model Law approach and provides flexibility for the parties and the arbitral tribunal in conducting the proceedings.[121]

[B] General Principles of Municipal Judicial Procedure

1.124. Article 5 of the ICA Law limits the extent of court intervention as follows:

> In matters governed by the present Law, no court shall intervene except where so provided in the present Law.

1.125. An example of such non-interference is the ruling of the Shevchenkivskiy District Court of Kyiv of 3 June 2014,[122] in which the court refused to grant interim measures prohibiting arbitrators of the ICAC at the UCCI to decide on the competence of the arbitral tribunal and/or to make an arbitral award,[123] as well as the final ruling of this court in the same case of 29 July 2014[124] terminating the proceedings based on Article 5 of the ICA Law, as the claim relating to the appointment of arbitrator was beyond the scope of the court intervention allowed by the ICA Law.

[C] General Principles of Arbitration Procedure (Party Autonomy, Speed, Impartiality, Etc.)

1.126. Article 19(1) of the ICA Law sets out the following provisions on party autonomy 'subject to the provisions of this Law, the parties are free to agree on the procedure to be followed by the arbitral tribunal in conducting the proceedings'. The ICA Law contains a few rules of clearly mandatory nature[125] and thus not establishing significant limits to the party autonomy.[126] Article 18 of the ICA Law obliges the arbitral tribunal to treat the parties equally and to give them full opportunity to present the case.

---

121. Article 19 of the ICA Law.
122. Ruling of the Shevchenkivskiy District Court of Kyiv of 3 June 2014 (case No. 761/15766/14- Ц), http://www.reyestr.court.gov.ua/Review/39044483.
123. *See*, 'Ukraine. Arbitration-friendly jurisdiction: 2013–2014 statistical report' 11 (2014), http://c-n-l.eu/assets/files/ENFORCEMENT_OF_ARBITRATION_AWARDS_IN_UKRAINE_2013-2014%20(ENG).pdf.
124. Final ruling of the Shevchenkivskiy District Court of Kyiv of 29 July 2014 (case No. 761/15766/14- Ц), http://www.reyestr.court.gov.ua/Review/40120501.
125. Крупчан А., *Автономия воли сторон при определении арбитражной процедуры и ее пределы. Императивные нормы места арбитража*, Материалы ІІ Международных арбитражных чтений памяти академика Побирченко И.Г., 112–119 (2014), http://arb.ucci.org.ua/publ/rept2013reading.pdf.
126. Perepelynska O., *Party Autonomy vs. Mandatory Rules in International Arbitration*, Ukrainian Journal of Business Law 38, 39 (2012).

1.127. General principles of the ICAC arbitral proceedings are set forth in Article 9 of the ICAC Rules: 'The arbitral proceedings shall be conducted on an adversarial basis and on the principle of equality of the parties. The parties shall be treated with equality and each party shall be given a full opportunity of presenting his case ... The parties and their representatives shall make fair use of their procedural rights, refrain from abusing such rights, and observe the time limits designated for the exercise thereof.'

[D] Commencing the Arbitral Proceedings

[1] Municipal Law

1.128. Article 21 of the ICA Law sets out the default rule that the arbitral proceedings in respect of a particular dispute commence on the date on which a request for that dispute to be referred to arbitration is received by the respondent.

[2] Institutional Rules

1.129. According to Article 17 of the ICAC Rules, the proceedings in the case shall be initiated by the Resolution of the ICAC President upon duly filing of a Statement of Claim with the ICAC and payment of the registration fee by the Claimant. The filing date of the Statement of Claim shall be the date on which it is handed over to the ICAC, or where the Statement of Claim is sent by mail it shall be the date of the postmark of the post office where it has been mailed.

[E] Conduct of Arbitration

[1] Written Submissions

1.130. Subject to the provisions of the ICA Law, the parties are free to agree on the procedure to be followed by the arbitral tribunal in conducting the proceedings.[127] Both the ICA Law and the ICAC Rules provide for certain default procedures, in the absence of agreement, for example, regarding the non-submission of the statement of defence or other documents. The level of party autonomy provided for by the ICA Law is relatively high.

[2] Post-hearing Briefs

1.131. Such briefs are not envisaged in the ICA Law or the ICAC Rules. In the ICAC practice the date of the award is usually the date of the last hearing in the case.

---

127. Article 19(1) of the ICA Law.

[3] Evidence (Admissibility, Documentary Evidence)

1.132. The parties shall prove the facts they rely upon to support their claims or defence.[128] The ICA Law and the ICAC Rules do not contain special provisions regarding production of documents upon request of the other party. However, the arbitrators may require the parties to produce further evidence.[129] The IBA Rules on Evidence are usually not used. Under general practice, evidence is submitted together with written memorials, however additional written evidence could be submitted even at the hearing.[130]

[4] Witness and Experts Testimony

1.133. The ICA Law and the ICAC Rules set forth some rules regarding tribunal-appointed experts only.[131] The arbitrators may, at their discretion or at the request of either of the parties, order inspection by an expert and also call and hear witnesses.[132] In the latter case, the party requesting witnesses to be called will be responsible for the appearance of those witnesses before the tribunal.

1.134. Since neither the ICA Law nor the ICAC Rules contain special provisions regarding factual witness statements or party-appointed experts, there is no established practice with regard to these types of evidence.

[F] Hearings

1.135. According to Article 24 of the ICA Law if the parties have not agreed otherwise the arbitral tribunal shall decide whether to hold oral hearings for the presentation of evidence or for oral argument, or whether the proceedings shall be conducted on the basis of documents and other materials. However, unless the parties have agreed that no hearings shall be held, the arbitral tribunal shall hold such hearings at an appropriate stage of the proceedings, if so requested by a party.

1.136. The parties shall be given sufficient advance notice of any hearing and of any meeting of the arbitral tribunal for the purposes of inspection of goods, other property or documents. If any party which was duly notified fails to appear at a hearing or to produce documentary evidence, the arbitral tribunal may continue the proceedings and make the award on the evidence before it.[133]

---

128. Пильков К., *Международный коммерческий арбитраж: что нужно доказывать, кто должен доказывать?*, Аналитическое издание «Юрист и Закон» (2014), http://search.liga zakon.ua/l_doc2.nsf/link1/EA006233.html.
129. Article 42(1) of the ICAC Rules.
130. Слипачук Т., *Практические аспекты процесса доказывания в международном коммерческом арбитраже*, Право Украины (2010), http://www.sk.ua/sites/default/files/dok_v_mezhd_arb_pravo_ukrainy_2010_1.pdf.
131. Article 26 of the ICA Law, Art. 44 of the ICAC Rules.
132. Article 42(1) of the ICAC Rules.
133. Article 25 of the ICA Law.

§10.07 THE ARBITRAL AWARD

[A] Introduction

1.137. The ICA Law sets forth that the award must be in writing and signed by the arbitrators. It must state the reasons, the decision regarding satisfaction or rejection of the claim and the amount of the arbitration fee and costs and their apportioning. It must contain the date and the place of arbitration.

1.138. According to the ICAC Rules, the award must also contain the ICAC name, the full names of the arbitrators, names of the parties and their representatives, a reference to the subject matter and a brief description of the facts of the case. Any arbitrator disagreeing with the award made may express in writing his dissenting opinion, which shall be attached to the award.[134]

1.139. The ICA Law requires that after the award is made, a copy signed by the arbitrators shall be delivered to each party.

[B] Deliberation and Voting

1.140. In arbitral proceedings with more than one arbitrator, any decision of the arbitral tribunal shall be made, unless otherwise agreed by the parties, by a majority of all its members. However, questions of procedure may be decided by a presiding arbitrator, if so authorized by the parties or all members of the arbitral tribunal.[135]

[C] Different Kinds of Awards (Separate, Interim, Consent, Default, Etc.)

1.141. The ICA Law does not operate with different kinds of awards. Special rules apply only to the awards on agreed terms.[136] Article 32 of the ICA Law is the only article in the law referring to the term 'final award' for the purposes of termination of the arbitral proceedings. In other instance the term 'award' is used.

[D] Interest and Costs

1.142. Interest is a matter of substantive law in Ukraine. Subject to contractual and applicable law provisions interest on the principal debt is usually awarded. At the same time, in ICAC arbitrations interest as a rule can only be awarded in the form of a lump sum as part of the monetary claim covered by the arbitration fee.

1.143. The ICA Law does not regulate the issue of allocation of costs. For ICAC arbitrations the allocation of the arbitration fee is established by the schedule of arbitration fees and costs. In practice, at times the arbitral tribunals adopt different

---

134. Article 49(3)-(4) of the ICAC Rules.
135. Article 29 of the ICA Law.
136. Article 30 of the ICA Law.

approaches to the allocation of arbitration costs. In general, the arbitration fee shall be borne by the unsuccessful party, subject to any other rules, including agreement of the parties. The tribunal will be bound by any prior agreement of the parties as to costs. Where the claim is awarded partially, the arbitration fee shall be borne by the parties in relevant proportion. Parties are free to agree that the arbitration fee be allocated in a manner different to that provided in the schedule.

[E] Effects of the Award

[1] Execution

1.144. In view of applicable currency restrictions, it is currently not possible to voluntarily comply with an arbitral award if the amount in it is indicated in a foreign currency, since the payer must provide to its servicing bank an execution writ in addition to the arbitral award itself. The execution writ may be obtained only after a permission for enforcement of an arbitral award was given by a state court.

1.145. The local civil courts at the place of location/residence of the debtor or that of its assets are competent to consider motions for granting permissions to enforce foreign arbitral awards, as well as for arbitral awards rendered in international arbitrations seated in Ukraine.

[2] Res Judicata and Lis Pendens

1.146. Ukrainian procedural legislation regulates these issues only partially.

1.147. According to Article 122 of the Civil Procedural Code the judge shall refuse to commence proceedings if there is an arbitral award, rendered within the tribunal's jurisdiction, in a dispute between the same parties, regarding the same subject matter and on the same grounds, except for the situations, when the court has refused to grant leave for enforcement of the arbitral award or has set it aside, and consideration of the case in arbitration is impossible.

1.148. The Commercial Procedure Code does not contain similar explicit provision, setting forth only a general rule regarding termination of the proceedings if there is a decision rendered by a competent authority in a dispute between the same parties, regarding the same subject matter and on the same grounds.[137]

1.149. At the same time, Article 35 of the Commercial Procedure Code provides: 'the circumstances established in a court judgment in commercial, civil or administrative case, which has entered into force, except for those established by an arbitral award, need not be proven in the proceedings involving the same persons or person, these circumstances relate to.'

---

137. Article 80(2) of the Commercial Procedure Code.

[F] Correction and Interpretation of the Award

[1] Municipal Law

1.150. The provisions governing modification, clarification or correction of an arbitral award are set out in Article 33 of the ICA Law. This Article allows any of the parties, with notice to the other party, to request the arbitral tribunal to correct in the award any errors in computation, any clerical or typographical errors or any errors of similar nature within thirty days of receipt of the award, unless another period of time has been agreed upon by the parties. The arbitral tribunal may correct any such error on its own initiative within the same term.

1.151. Subject to the parties' agreement, any party, with notice to the other party, may request the arbitral tribunal to give an interpretation of a specific point or part of the award within thirty days of receipt of the award, unless another period of time has been agreed upon by the parties. If the arbitral tribunal considers the request to be justified, it shall make the correction or give the interpretation, which shall form part of the award.

1.152. Unless otherwise agreed by the parties, any of the parties, with notice to the other party, may request within thirty days of receipt of the award that the arbitral tribunal makes an additional award as to claims presented in the arbitral proceedings but omitted from the award. If the arbitral tribunal considers the request to be justified, it shall make the additional award.

[2] Institutional Rules

1.153. Articles 53 of the ICAC Rules repeats the rules of Article 33 of the ICA Law with the only deviation that the power to extend the period of time, within which the Arbitral Tribunal shall make a correction or interpretation, is conferred to the ICAC Presidium instead of Arbitral Tribunal indicated in the ICA Law.

§10.08 SETTING ASIDE THE AWARD

[A] Introduction

1.154. Following the Model Law approach setting aside the award is an exclusive recourse against the award.[138]

1.155. The statistics or recent years confirms rather supportive attitude of the Ukrainian courts with regards to the awards rendered according to the ICA Law in Ukraine.[139] The situation with awards rendered under the Domestic Arbitration Law is

---

138. Article 34 of the ICA Law.
139. Only 17% of the awards were challenged successfully in 2014, 83% of the requests for setting aside were dismissed, See 'Ukraine. Arbitration-friendly jurisdiction: 2013–2014 statistical

different, especially in view of controversial opinions of the Supreme Court of Ukraine given in 2015–2016 regarding arbitrability of consumer disputes in Ukraine.[140]

[B] Invalid Awards

1.156. There is no such concept in the Ukrainian law. The ICA Law and the Domestic Arbitration Law do not distinguish types of the awards for the purposes of setting aside procedure. So, all the awards rendered in Ukraine could be equally challenged on the grounds provided in each of these laws as applicable.

[C] Challengeable Awards

[1] Grounds for Challenging the Award

1.157. An award rendered in an international arbitration seated in Ukraine can be set aside by the Ukrainian courts, fully or partially, only on the grounds provided for in Article 34 of the ICA Law, mirroring the provisions of Article 34 of the Model Law.

1.158. According to the ICA Law, an arbitral award may be set aside by the local civil court in the seat of arbitration only if:

(1) the party making the application for setting aside furnishes proof that:
- a party to the arbitration agreement referred to in Article 7 of the ICA Law was under some incapacity, or that the said agreement is not valid under the law to which the parties have subjected it or, failing any indication thereon, under the law of Ukraine;
- it was not given proper notice of the appointment of an arbitrator or of the arbitral proceedings or was otherwise unable to present its case;
- the award was made regarding a dispute not contemplated by or not falling within the terms of the submission to arbitration, or contains decisions on matters beyond the scope of the submission to arbitration, provided that, if the decisions on matters submitted to arbitration can be separated from those not so submitted, only that part of the award which contains decisions on matters not submitted to arbitration may be set aside; or

---

report', available at http://c-n-l.eu/assets/files/ENFORCEMENT_OF_ARBITRATION_AWARDS_IN_UKRAINE_2013-2014%20(ENG).pdf.
140. Arbitration Chamber of Ukraine sent several official letter to the Supreme Court of Ukraine (on the most recent is available at http://tpu.kiev.ua/list-tpu-do-verhovnogo-sudu-ukrayini-pro-ne-rozglyad-verhovnim-sudom-vsih-dovodiv-storin-shhodo-pidvidomchosti-sporiv-treteyskim-sudam-ta-na-pidstavi-priynyatya-zayav-pro-pereglyad/) and launched public discussion regarding this problem, criticizing the opinions of the Supreme Court of Ukraine – *see* more at http://tpu.kiev.ua/komentar-treteyskoyi-palati-ukrayini-stosovno-pravovoyi-pozitsiyi-verhovnogo-sudu-ukrayini-vid-03-02-2016-roku-u-spravi-6-2630tss15-shhodo-zastosuvannya-p-14-st-6-zakonu-ukrayini-pro-treteyski-s/.

- the composition of the arbitral tribunal or the arbitral procedure was not in accordance with the agreement of the parties, unless such agreement was in conflict with a provision of the ICA Law from which Ukraine the parties cannot derogate, or, failing such agreement, was not in accordance with the ICA Law; or
(2) the court finds that:
- the subject matter of the dispute is not capable of settlement by arbitration under the law of Ukraine; or
- the award is in conflict with Ukrainian public policy.

[2] Waiver of Right to Challenge

1.159. The ICA Law, the Domestic Arbitration Law and both procedural codes are silent with regard to possibility to waive the right to challenge the award. The existing court practice does not confirm such possibility either.

[D] Review of Jurisdictional Awards

1.160. Pursuant to Article 16 of the ICA Law, the arbitral tribunal may rule on its own jurisdiction, including any objections with respect to the existence or validity of the arbitration agreement. If the tribunal rules as a preliminary question that it has jurisdiction, any party may request within thirty days after having received notice of that ruling, the civil court located at the seat of arbitration to decide the matter; such a decision shall not be subject to appeal. While such a request is pending, the arbitral tribunal may proceed with the arbitral proceedings and make an award.

§10.09 RECOGNITION AND ENFORCEMENT OF THE ARBITRAL AWARD

[A] Enforcement of Domestic Awards

[1] Enforcement Domestically

1.161. In view of the dualism of Ukrainian arbitration legislation there are two types of domestic awards: (i) rendered according to the Domestic Arbitration Law; and (ii) rendered according to the ICA Law. Their enforcement domestically is governed by different sets of rules.

1.162. Chapter XIV-I of the Commercial Procedure Code and Chapter VII-1 of the Civil Procedure Code apply to the former, while Chapter VIII of the Civil Procedure Code applies to the latter.

1.163. The enforcement of domestic arbitral awards type: (i) is faster and simpler, although it has some peculiarities when compared to the enforcement of type;

(ii) awards, the rules for enforcement of arbitral awards rendered under the ICA Law in arbitrations seated in Ukraine are the same as for foreign arbitral awards.[141]

[2] Enforcement Abroad

1.164. Ukrainian legislation does not contain specific rules regarding enforcement of its domestic awards abroad. Such enforcement is subject to applicable international treaty and national legislation in the place of enforcement.

[B] Enforcement of Foreign Arbitral Awards

[1] Introduction to Recognition and Enforcement

1.165. Recognition and enforcement of foreign arbitral awards is governed by Chapter VIII of the Civil Procedure Code and is delegated to the local civil courts.[142] In general the Ukrainian courts are supportive to the recognition and enforcement of foreign arbitral awards.[143]

1.166. The conditions and standards for such enforcement are set out in the ICA Law and applicable international treaties, including the New York Convention.[144] Some useful guidelines in this regard are provided for in the Resolution of the Plenum of the Supreme Court of Ukraine on Practice of Consideration by the Courts of Motions for Recognition and Enforcement of Foreign Court Judgments and Arbitral Awards, and on Setting Aside the International Commercial Arbitration Awards Rendered within the Territory of Ukraine (SCU Resolution No. 12).[145] In particular, it contains a definition of public policy in the context of enforcement of foreign arbitral awards.

1.167. The Civil Procedure Code grants jurisdiction over the enforcement of foreign arbitral awards to the civil courts located at the place of the debtor's residence or

---

141. *See* Section [B] below.
142. Мальський М., Анюхіна А., *Окремі питання визнання та виконання в Україні арбітражних рішень*, 4, 6 Правовий тиждень 13 (2013).
143. Local civil courts rarely refuse to grant the leave for enforcement of arbitral award (about 10% of the requests considered in 2013 and 18% in 2014) – *See* 'Ukraine. Arbitration-friendly jurisdiction: 2013–2014 statistical report', http://c n l.eu/assets/files/ENFORCEMENT_OF_ ARBITRATION AWARDS IN UKRAINE 2013-2014%20(ENG).pdf. Some case law in this regard is described in the following article: Perepelynska O., *Ukrainian Court Enforces Arbitral Awards Set Aside in the UK*, CIS Arbitration Forum (2012), http://www.cisarbitration.com/ 2012/09/17/ukrainian-court-enforces-arbitral-awards-set-aside-in-the-uk/ and Друг А., Перепелинская Е., *Украинско-английская взаимность в признании судебных решений* ЮрЛига (2012), http://jurliga.ligazakon.ua/news/2012/9/4/71405.htm.
144. Мальський М., Яремко В., *Нью-Йоркська конвенція чи Київська угода: хто кого?*, 33–34 Юридична газета 30 (2013), http://arzinger.ua/files/file/file_collection/en/Sc22013090415 220.pdf.
145. Resolution of the Plenum of the Supreme Court of Ukraine on Practice of Consideration by the Courts of Motions for Recognition and Enforcement of Foreign Court Judgments and Arbitral Awards, and on Setting Aside the International Commercial Arbitration Awards Rendered within the Territory of Ukraine No. 12 (24 December 1999), http://zakon2.rada.gov.ua/laws /show/v0012700-99.

location, or if the debtor does not have a place of residence or location in Ukraine, to the courts where the debtor's assets are located. A foreign arbitral award may be submitted for enforcement in Ukraine only within three years of it becoming effective, unless it provides for payment by instalments. An award providing for payment by instalments can be enforced any time within the general term for payment established in the award. However, the creditor can request only partial enforcement of such an award, namely the overdue payments for three years prior to filing application for enforcement.

[2] Separate, Partial and Interim Awards

1.168. Civil Procedure Code does not contain any special rules regarding enforcement of separate, partial and interim awards. In fact, the general rule of Article 390 of the Civil Procedure Code governing conditions of enforcement of decisions of 'foreign court' defines the latter rather broadly as including state courts, other competent authorities and arbitral tribunals.[146] However, the Chapter VIII of the Civil Procedure Code applicable to such enforcement does not set forth any qualification criteria as to the form and title of respective 'decision' of arbitral tribunals.

1.169. In 2011 Ukrainian courts enforced[147] the first partial award in the case *Sea Emerald S.A. (Panama) v. State-owned Enterprise 'Shipyard named after 61 Communars' (Ukraine)*,[148] while in 2016 after several rounds of consideration the same courts refused[149] to enforce the second partial award in the same case.

1.170. In 2015 Ukrainian courts in *JKX case* confirmed enforceability of Emergency Arbitrator Awards in Ukraine,[150] however, in the beginning of 2016 respective court judgments were quashed by the third instance court, and the case was returned to the Court of Appeal for a new consideration.[151] In a second round of consideration the

---

146. Blinov E., Boiarskyi I., *Enforcement in Ukraine of Foreign Court Orders Granting Provisional Measures in Support of Arbitration* (2013), http://arbitration-blog.com/international-arbitration/enforcement-in-ukraine-of-foreign-court-orders-granting-provisional-measures-in-support-of-arbitration/.
147. *See* Judgment of the High Specialised Court on Civil and Criminal Matters of 17 August 2011, http://www.reyestr.court.gov.ua/Review/17881099.
148. Wietzorek M., *The Enforcement of an LMAA Arbitral Award in Ukraine*, Reports From YIAG Members 37, 38 (2012).
149. *See* Ruling of the Court of Appeal of the Mykolaiv Region of 22 April 2016 (case No. 1423/15646/2012), http://www.reyestr.court.gov.ua/Review/57363710, Ruling of the High Specialised Court on Civil and Criminal Matters of 5 October 2016, http://www.reyestr.court.gov.ua/Review/62203095#.
150. Perepelynska O., Ivasechko V., *Enforceability of Emergency Arbitrator Awards in Ukraine*, CIS Arbitration Forum (2015), http://www.cisarbitration.com/2015/12/07/enforceability-of-emergency-arbitrator-awards-in-ukraine/.
151. *See* Ruling of the High Specialised Court on Civil and Criminal Matters of 24 February 2016 (case No. 6-30579ск15), http://www.reyestr.court.gov.ua/Review/56161176.

Court of Appeal allowed enforcement,[152] while the third instance court again disagreed.[153] The case is now considered by the Kiev City Court of Appeal for the third time.[154] Interestingly, all the court judgments in this case are rendered on the basis of the NYC.

1.171. Similarly, the courts of several instances[155] relied on NYC provisions in another case *Ostchem Holding Limited (Cyprus) v. Public Stock Company Odessa Port Plant (Ukraine)* with regard to enforcement of the SCC Emergency Arbitrator Award of 31 March 2016.[156] In this case Ostchem's application for enforcement was left without consideration (i.e., returned to the applicant without rendering the judgments on the merits) for formal reasons by the first instance court. Ostchem appealed against this ruling first to the Court of Appeal, and then to the third instance court, where the case is now pending.[157]

[3] Grounds for Refusing Recognition and Enforcement

[a] Lack of Capacity and Invalidity of Arbitration Agreement

1.172. This ground is not often invoked in practice, but it may have an interesting aspect related to the subjective arbitrability requirement set out in Article 1 of the ICA Law. The latter allows referring to international arbitration disputes between local Ukrainian entities, provided that at least one of them has over 10% of foreign investment in its authorized capital. In one of the reported cases the courts recognized invalid arbitration agreement between Ukrainian companies with no foreign investment.[158]

[b] Procedural Violations

1.173. In general, Ukrainian courts are rather cautious in accepting procedural violations objections, especially if breach of applicable arbitration rules is invoked. One of the recent and rather controversial examples is *JKX case*, where the courts rejected all

---

152. *See* Ruling of the Kiev City Court of Appeal of 17 May 2016, http://reyestr.court.gov.ua/Review/57985816.
153. *See* Ruling of the High Specialised Court on Civil and Criminal Matters of 2 November 2016 (case No. 757/5777/15-II), http://reyestr.court.gov.ua/Review/62524805.
154. *See* Ruling of the Kiev City Court of Appeal of 25 November 2016 (case No. 757/5777/15-II), http://reyestr.court.gov.ua/Review/63035783.
155. *See* Ruling of the Court of the City of Yuzhne of 25 July 2016 (No. 519/459/16-II), http://www.reyestr.court.gov.ua/Review/59411245; Ruling of the Court of Appeal of Odessa Region of 4 October 2016 (No. 519/459/16-II), http://www.reyestr.court.gov.ua/Review/61874533.
156. Emergency Award of Arbitration Institute of the Stockholm Chamber of Commerce of 31 March 2016, https://assets.documentcloud.org/documents/2790926/mr1020026.pdf.
157. *See* Ruling of the High Specialised Court on Civil and Criminal Matters of 27 October 2016 (case No. 519/459/16-II), http://www.reyestr.court.gov.ua/Review/62319526.
158. *See*, 'Ukraine. Arbitration-friendly jurisdiction: 2013–2014 statistical report' 20 (2014), http://c-n-l.eu/assets/files/ENFORCEMENT_OF_ARBITRATION_AWARDS_IN_UKRAINE_2013-2014%20(ENG).pdf.

such objections of the respondent – the State of Ukraine represented by the Ministry of Justice of Ukraine.[159]

[c] Excess of Mandate

1.174. Ukrainian courts quite rarely apply excess of mandate ground, and mostly in setting aside rather than enforcement context. One of such examples is *Argo* case considered by Ukrainian courts in 2009–2010.[160] In this case the courts set aside the ICAC award, having found that the arbitrator's interpretation of a defective arbitration agreement without the parties' request to do that amounted to the excess of mandate.[161]

[d] Arbitral Award Not Binding

1.175. Ukraine was one of the signatories of the New York Convention, and at the time of ratification and further succession it was not necessary to translate it officially into Ukrainian. So in practice during all these years Ukrainian arbitration practitioners relied on the official Russian version of the New York Convention in respective enforcement proceedings before the Ukrainian courts.

1.176. However, there is a crucial difference between the English and Russian language versions of Article V(1)(e) of the NYC. In particular, the English version requires the award to become 'binding' on the parties, while the Russian text contains the wording '*окончательный*' which means '*final*'.[162]

1.177. So far, the Ukrainian courts have not considered this difference and application of respective ground to refuse recognition of arbitral award has not been tested yet.

[e] Non-arbitrability

1.178. Non-arbitrability ground is often invoked by the parties if their disputes referred to arbitration relates to corporate or public procurement issues. For instance, this

---

159. Perepelynska O., Ivasechko V., *Enforceability of Emergency Arbitrator Awards in Ukraine*, CIS Arbitration Forum (2015), http://www.cisarbitration.com/2015/12/07/enforceability-of-emergency-arbitrator-awards-in-ukraine/. The High Specialised Court on Civil and Criminal Matters did not question these findings when quashed the ruling of the Court of appeal on 24 February 2016, but invoked some of them during the second round of case consideration when rendered its ruling of 2 November 2016.
160. At http://reyestr.court.gov.ua/Review/11754022.
161. Perepelynska O., *Ukraine: How Minor Defects in Wording of Arbitration Clause May Result in a Big Problem*, CIS Arbitration Forum (2012), http://www.cisarbitration.com/2012/07/30/ukraine-how-minor-defects-in-wording-of-arbitration-clause-may-result-in-a-big-problem/.
162. Perepelynska O., Ivasechko V., *Enforceability of Emergency Arbitrator Awards in Ukraine*, CIS Arbitration Forum (2015), http://www.cisarbitration.com/2015/12/07/enforceability-of-emergency-arbitrator-awards-in-ukraine/.

happened in Double W case on recognition of the VIAC award in Ukraine, and in several VAMED cases on setting aside ICAC awards.[163]

[f]   Public Policy

1.179. The SCU Resolution No. 12 defines public policy of Ukraine as 'the legal order of a state, the determinative principles and foundations, which constitute the basis of its policy (pertaining to its independence, integrity, autonomy and inviolability, its fundamental constitutional rights, freedoms, guarantees etc.)'. Ukrainian courts still rely on this definition while considering public policy objections against enforcement of the arbitral awards.[164]

1.180. One of the recent examples of refusal to enforce the award on this ground and on the 'threaten the interests of Ukraine' ground is judgment of the Kiev City Court of Appeal of 17 September 2015 in JKX case.[165] The Court found that the enforcement of the award shall entail the change of the tax rate applicable to the Claimants, while only the Tax Code of Ukraine may determine such issues. Granting courts the competence to alter tax rates in violation of the Tax Code of Ukraine would breach the fundamental and determinative principles of taxation established in Ukraine. Moreover, Ukraine would suffer significant losses, and they could cause economic deterioration of Ukraine.[166] However, on 24 February 2016 the High Specialized Court on Civil and Criminal Matters quashed[167] this decision and pointed out that the Court of Appeal failed to establish if the emergency arbitral award altered the tax system of Ukraine or substituted the provisions of the Tax Code of Ukraine. During the second round of case consideration, the Court of Appeal confirmed enforcement of the SCC Emergency Arbitrator Award,[168] but this ruling was also quashed by the third instance court on 2 November 2016,[169] and the case is pending before the Kiev City Court of Appeal for the third time.

---

163. *See* – Перепелинская Е., *Арбитрабильность споров по законодательству Украины: проблемные вопросы,* Материалы II Международных арбитражных чтений памяти академика Побирченко И. Г. 40, 44 (2014). For other examples of court practice – *See*: Marchukov D., *Refusing Recognition and Enforcement of Foreign Arbitral Awards in Ukraine (Procedural issues and application of non-arbitrability and public policy grounds)*, TDM 1 (2009), http://www.transnational-dispute-management.com/article.asp?key = 1368;   in Кравчук. Г., *Арбитрабильность споров в контексте статьи 12 Хозяйственного процессуального кодекса Украины,* Материалы II Международных арбитражных чтений памяти академика Побирченко 15, 21 (2015), http://arb.ucci.org.ua/publ/rept2014reading.pdf.
164. Алешин О., *Категория публичного порядка в международном частном праве,* Юридическая практика (2008), http://vkp.ua/ru/publications/articles/the_category_of_public_order_in_private_international_law/.
165. At http://www.reyestr.court.gov.ua/Review/51814205.
166. Perepelynska O., Ivasechko V., *Enforceability of Emergency Arbitrator Awards in Ukraine,* CIS Arbitration Forum (2015), http://www.cisarbitration.com/2015/12/07/enforceability-of-emergency-arbitrator-awards-in-ukraine/.
167. At http://www.reyestr.court.gov.ua/Review/56161176.
168. *See* Ruling of the Kiev City Court of Appeal of 17 May 2016 (case No. 757/5777/15-Ц), http://reyestr.court.gov.ua/Review/57985816.
169. *See* Ruling of the High Specialised Court on Civil and Criminal Matters of 2 November 2016 (case No. 757/5777/15-Ц), http://reyestr.court.gov.ua/Review/62524805.

[4] Procedures for Recognition

1.181. The court procedure for the motions for enforcement of foreign arbitral awards is set out in Article 395 of the Civil Procedure Code. If the motion for enforcement meets all the formal requirements established by the Civil Procedure Code and the ICA Law, the court sends it to the debtor and grants it one month for submitting its objections, if any. After that the judge schedules the hearing and informs the parties of its date.

1.182. At the hearing the judge determines whether any grounds to refuse enforcement exist. The grounds for refusal of enforcement in the ICA Law are the same as in the New York Convention. If the New York Convention is applicable, it prevails over the civil procedure code provisions, and in this case, there are no other grounds for refusal except those established by the Convention. The party applying for the recognition and enforcement of the foreign arbitral award may also request interim measures at any stage of the enforcement proceedings, which will be granted if the court establishes that failure to grant such interim relief may complicate or render the enforcement of the arbitral award impossible.

1.183. Having considered the motion for enforcement and heard the parties' arguments, the judge will render a ruling granting or denying the recognition and enforcement of the arbitral award. The ruling, after coming into force, serves as a basis for issuing a writ of execution, which triggers the execution procedure. Under the Civil Procedure Code, the above-mentioned rulings of local general courts can be appealed at the Appellate Court of the respective region and then, also to the High Specialized Court on Civil and Criminal Matters within a cassation proceeding. If so, the whole enforcement proceedings in all three instances could take around one year. The court fees are negligible and are not contingent on the amount of the award.

§10.10 INVESTOR-STATE ARBITRATION

[A] General Overview of Law and Practice Related to Investor-State Arbitration

1.184. Ukraine is a party to the ICSID Convention. It entered into and continues to conclude multilateral and BITs with foreign states. It does not have a model BIT. Its national legislation provides for national treatment and a number of guarantees for foreign investments. However, there is no integrated and coordinated system of investment legislation in Ukraine.

1.185. Ukraine is one of the most frequent respondents in the CIS region, with over fourteen concluded and over seven pending investment treaty cases. It usually defends itself with the help of the Ministry of Justice of Ukraine and external counsel (Ukrainian and international law firms), retained according to the special proceedings.

1.186. Investment arbitrations involving Ukraine have concerned different industries such as the petrochemical industry (*GEA Group Aktiengesellschaft v. Ukraine*), the sunflower oil industry (*Western NIS Enterprise Fund v. Ukraine*), the printing industry

(*Tokios Tokeles v. Ukraine*), radio broadcasting (*Joseph C Lemire v. Ukraine*), the poultry products industry (*Global Trading Resource Corp and Globex International Inc. v. Ukraine*), oil, gas & mining (*JSC Tatnafta v. Ukraine, JKX Oil&Gas PLC et al. v. Ukraine, Littop Enterprises Limited, Bridgemont Ventures Limited and Bordo Management Limited v. Ukraine, Emergofin B.V. and Velbay Holdings Ltd. v. Ukraine*) and maritime operations (*Inmaris Perestroika v. Ukraine and Laskaridis Shipping Co v. Ukraine*).

1.187. However, four investment arbitrations concerned the building industry, namely hotel development projects (*Alpha Projektholding GMBH v. Ukraine and Bosh International v. Ukraine*), construction of an office building (*Generation Ukraine Inc v. Ukraine*) and shipbuilding (*Laskaridis Shipping Co v. Ukraine*).

1.188. Ukraine has voluntarily paid respective amounts under the majority of the awards against it, however such payments were made only after completion of respective enforcement proceedings in Ukraine.[170]

[B] List of Investment Treaties the Country Has Ratified

1.189. Ukraine is party to the Energy Charter Treaty.

1.190. Ukraine does not have a model BIT, but has entered into seventy-two BITs.[171] In addition, Ukraine has signed, but not ratified, the CIS Treaty 'On cooperation in investment activity', thus the CIS Treaty is not in force for Ukraine.

[C] List of Investor-State Disputes (Concluded and Pending)

1.191. Ukraine has been involved in at least fourteen investment treaty arbitrations[172] and is currently involved in seven other pending proceedings:

---

170. *See* Ruling of the Pecherskyy District Court of the City of Kyiv of 23 June 2011 regarding enforcement of the ICSID award in *Alpha Projektholding GMBH v. Ukraine*, http://www.reyestr.court.gov.ua/Review/16679895; Ruling the Pecherskyy District Court of the City of Kyiv of 26 September 2012 regarding enforcement of the ICSID award in *Inmaris Perestroika v Ukraine*, http://www.reyestr.court.gov.ua/Review/26148630; Ruling of the High Specialised Court of Ukraine for Civil and Criminal Cases of 26 December 2012 regarding enforcement of the SCC award in *Remington Worldwide Limited v. Ukraine*, http://reyestr.court.gov.ua/Review/28571150.
171. *See* Appendix I with full list of Ukraine' BITs and their status.
172. *See* Slipachuk T., Perepelynska O., Makukha T. *Getting the Deal Through – Investment Treaty Arbitration (Ukraine section)*, Law Business Research Ltd (2015), as well as Slipachuk T., *Investment Treaty Arbitration. Ukraine: Overview of Investment Treaties*, Global Arbitration Review (2012), http://globalarbitrationreview.com/know-how/topics/66/jurisdictions/63/ukraine/%c2%a0.

1. *City-State N.V., Praktyka Asset Management Company LLC, Crystal-Invest LLC and Prodiz LLC v. Ukraine*, ICSID Case No. ARB/14/9.[173]
2. *Krederi Ltd. v. Ukraine*, ICSID Case No. ARB/14/17.[174]
3. *Gilward Investments B.V. v. Ukraine*, ICSID Case No. ARB/15/33.
4. *JKX Oil&Gas PLC et al. v. Ukraine*,[175] UNCITRAL (consolidated with ICSID and SCC arbitral proceedings launched by the same group of entities against Ukraine).[176]
5. *Ministry of Land and Property of the Republic of Tatarstan v. Ukraine*, ad hoc under UNCITRAL Arbitration Rules.[177]
6. *Littop Enterprises Limited, Bridgemont Ventures Limited and Bordo Management Limited v. Ukraine*, SCC V 2015/092.[178]
7. *Emergofin B.V. and Velbay Holdings Ltd. v. Ukraine*, ICSID Case No. ARB/16/35.[179]

1.192. In 2015–2016 a number of Ukrainian investors launched investment treaty arbitrations against the Russian Federation under the Ukraine-Russian BIT related to the Crimea.[180]

[D] Reform Proposals

1.193. On 31 March 2016, the Verkhovna Rada of Ukraine registered the Draft Law No. 4351 'On Amendments to certain laws of Ukraine concerning judicial control and support of international commercial arbitration' (Draft law No. 4351).[181]

---

173. Perepelynska O., Makukha T., *Arbitrations against Ukraine and Its State Bodies in Post-Revolution Period*, CIS Arbitration Forum (2015), http://www.cisarbitration.com/2015/05/13/arbitrations-against-ukraine-and-its-state-bodies-in-post-revolution-period/.
174. Perepelynska O., Makukha T., *Arbitrations against Ukraine and Its State Bodies in Post-Revolution Period*, CIS Arbitration Forum (2015), http://www.cisarbitration.com/2015/05/13/arbitrations-against-ukraine-and-its-state-bodies-in-post-revolution-period/.
175. Perepelynska O., Ivasechko V., *Enforceability of Emergency Arbitrator Awards in Ukraine*, CIS Arbitration Forum (2015), http://www.cisarbitration.com/2015/12/07/enforceability-of-emergency-arbitrator-awards-in-ukraine/.
176. Brief information about the consolidation was published at http://uk.reuters.com/article/idUKFWN10308820150724.
177. At http://www.centralbank.ie/regulation/securities-markets/prospectus/Pages/approved prospectus.aspx?DisplayID=31556.
178. At http://interfax.com.ua/news/economic/279495.html.
179. At https://icsid.worldbank.org/apps/icsidweb/cases/Pages/casedetail.aspx?CaseNo=ARB/16/35; http://globalarbitrationreview.com/article/1069924/rusal-files-icsid-claim-against-ukraine.
180. Dilevka S., *Arbitration Claims by Ukrainian Investors under the Russia-Ukraine BIT: between Crimea and a Hard Place?*, CIS Arbitration Forum (2016), http://www.cisarbitration.com/2016/02/17/arbitration-claims-by-ukrainian-investors-under-the-russia-ukraine-bit-between-crimea-and-a-hard-place/; Schwarz F., Khripkova K., *CEE Overview: International Arbitration in Central and Eastern Europe: An Overview and Key Developments*, ICLG Arbitration 2016 (2016), http://www.iclg.co.uk/practice-areas/international-arbitration/international-arbitration-2016/international-arbitration-in-central-and-eastern-europe-an-overview-and-key-developments.
181. At http://w1.c1.rada.gov.ua/pls/zweb2/webproc4_1?pf3511=58601.

1.194. In summary, Draft law No. 4351 contemplates two major groups of amendments, purporting to: (1) improving the efficiency of judicial control concerning (a) recognition and enforcement of international arbitration awards and (b) setting aside international arbitration awards and rulings; (2) fill existing gaps in matters of judicial support to international arbitration regarding provision of (a) court-ordered interim measures in support of international arbitration and (b) judicial assistance in taking of evidence for arbitral proceedings.

1.195. It will amend existing arbitrability rules contained in the procedural code of Ukraine and improve the court approach with regard to the enforcement of arbitration agreements.[182]

1.196. In addition, on 23 March 2017 the Draft Law No. 6232[183] amending three procedural codes of Ukraine was registered in the Ukrainian Parliament. It contains similar groups of amendments: judicial control over and support to domestic and international arbitration as well as new arbitrability rules. It also suggests amendments to certain provisions of the ICA Law.

1.197. Despite distinct approaches on a number of issues, the amendments proposed by both draft laws will, if adopted, allow many existing problems to be solved and to make Ukraine more arbitration-friendly jurisdiction. Those amendments are long-awaited, and the Ukrainian arbitration community hopes that they will be adopted soon by the Ukrainian Parliament.

---

182. *See* Perepelynska O., *Ukraine Reform its Arbitration-Related Procedural Legislation*, Ukrainian Journal of Business Law (2016).
183. At http://w1.c1.rada.gov.ua/pls/zweb2/webproc4_1?pf3511=61415.

APPENDIX I UKRAINE'S BITs*

No.	Country	Signed	Ratified by Ukraine*	Entered into force for Ukraine*
1.	Albania	25.10.2002	18.02.2004	18.02.2004
2.	Argentina	09.08.1995	11.04.1997	06.05.1997
3.	Armenia	07.10.1994	02.06.1995	07.03.1996
4.	Austria	08.11 1996	11.04.1997	01.12.1997
5.	Azerbaijan	24.03.1997	16.10.1997	09.12.1997
6.	Belarus	14.12.1995	06.12.1996	11.06.1997
7.	Belgium and Luxembourg	20.05.1996	26.02.1997	27.07.2001
8.	Bosnia & Herzegovina	13.03.2002	18.11.2003	22.01.2004
9.	Brunei	18.06.2004	04.04.2006	26.04.2006
10.	Bulgaria	08.12.1994	20.10.1995	10.12.1995
11.	Canada	24.10.1994	02.06.1995	24.07.1995
12.	Chile	30.10.1995	15.11.1996	26.07.1997
13.	China	31.10.1992		30.05.1993
14.	Democratic Republic of the Congo	11.10.2000	17.11.2010	17.11.2010
15.	Croatia	15.12.1997	10.02.2000	16.05.2001
16.	Cuba	20.05.1995	15.11.1996	04.12.1996
17.	Czech Republic	17.03.1994	20.10.1995	02.11.1995
18.	Denmark	23.10.1992		29.04.1994
19.	Egypt	22.12.1992		13.10.1993
20.	Equatorial Guinea	15.12.2005	19.09.2008	19.09.2008
21.	Estonia	15.02.1995	02.06.1995	05.07.1995
22.	Finland	07.10.2004	05.10.2005	07.12.2005
23.	France	03.05.1994	02.06.1995	26.01.1996
24.	Gambia	12.07.2001	19.01.2006	19.01.2006
25.	Georgia	09.01.1995	02.06.1995	18.12.1996

---

* Texts of all Ukraine's BITs in Ukrainian and other languages are available at http://arbitration.kiev.ua/en-US/Legislation/International-Treaties-of-Ukraine.aspx?ID = 167.
* The requirement to ratify intergovernmental treaties was first introduced by the Law of Ukraine on International Treaties of Ukraine No. 3767-XII (22 December 1993), http://zakon2.rada.gov.ua/laws/show/3767-12, and thus the intergovernmental treaties signed prior to the entry into force of this law were subject to other formal procedures.
* The data given regarding entry into force of treaties are taken from official Ukrainian sources. There are discrepancies regarding the date of entry into force between the official Ukrainian data and/or OECD and UNCTAD data in the treaties with Albania, Croatia, France, Georgia, Greece, Hungary, Jordan, Kazakhstan, Moldova, Singapore, Slovakia, Syria, Tajikistan and Turkmenistan. UNCTAD sources make no mention of the treaties with Kuwait, Libya, Panama and the United Arab Emirates.

Chapter 10: Ukraine

No.	Country	Signed	Ratified by Ukraine*	Entered into force for Ukraine*
26.	Germany	15.02.1993	11.10.1994	29.06.1996
27.	Greece	01.09.1994	15.11.1996	04.12.1996
28.	Hungary	11.10.1994	15.11.1996	20.12.1996
29.	India	01.12.2001	03.04.2003	12.08.2003
30.	Indonesia	11.04.1996	11.04.1997	06.08.1997
31.	Iran, Islamic Republic	22.05.1996	11.04.1997	05.07.2003
32.	Israel	24.11.2010	01.06.2011	20.11.2012
33.	Italy	02.05.1995	15.11.1996	12.09.1997
34.	Japan	05.02.2015	03.06.2015	26.11.2015
35.	Jordan	30.11.2005	15.03.2007	17.04.2007
36.	Kazakhstan	17.09.1994	02.06.1995	04.08.1995
37.	Korea, Republic	16.12.1996	16.10.1997	03.11.1997
38.	Kuwait	12.01.2002	06.02.2003	11.06.2003
39.	Kyrgyzstan (not in force)	23.02.1993		
40.	Latvia	24.07.1997	17.12.1997	30.12.1997
41.	Lebanon	25.03.1996	02.03.2000	26.05.2000
42.	Libya	23.01.2001	26.09.2002	23.04.2003
43.	Lithuania	08.02.1994	08.02.1995	27.02.1995
44.	Macedonia, TFYR	02.03.1998	10.02.2000	25.03.2000
45.	Moldova	29.08.1995	23.04.1996	20.05.1996
46.	Mongolia	05.11.1992		05.11.1992
47.	Morocco	24.12.2001	11.07.2002	28.04.2009
48.	Netherlands	14.07.1994	26.02.1997	01.06.1997
49.	Oman	14.01.2002	06.02.2003	06.02.2003
50.	Panama	04.11.2003	16.11.2005	13.06.2007
51.	Poland	12.01.1993		14.09.1993
52.	Portugal	25.10.2000	26.12.2002	18.07.2003
53.	Russia	27.11.1998	15.12.1999	27.01.2000
54.	San Marino	13.01.2006	19.09.2008	15.10.2008
55.	Saudi Arabia	09.04.2008	18.02.2009	18.02.2009
56.	Serbia	09.01.2001	05.07.2001	14.08.2001
57.	Singapore	18.09.2006	19.04.2007	17.07.2007
58.	Slovakia	26.02.2007	06.03.2008	20.08.2009
59.	Slovenia	30.03.1999	02.03.2000	01.06.2000

No.	Country	Signed	Ratified by Ukraine*	Entered into force for Ukraine*
60.	Spain	26.02.1998	10.02.2000	13.03.1997
61.	Sweden	15.08.1995	25.12.1996	01.03.1997
62.	Switzerland	20.04.1995	15.11.1996	21.01.1997
63.	Syria	21.04.2002	06.02.2003	16.03.2003
64.	Tajikistan	06.07.2001	22.05.2003	27.05.2003
65.	Turkey	27.11.1996	17.05.1997	21.05.1998
66.	Turkmenistan	29.01.1998	09.09.1999	28.09.1999
67.	United Arab Emirates	22.01.2003	18.09.2003	09.04.2004
68.	United Kingdom	10.02.1993		10.02.1993
69.	United States	04.03.1994	21.10.1994	16.11.1996
70.	Uzbekistan	20.02.1993		26.05.1994
71.	Vietnam	08.06.1994	21.10.1994	08.12.1994
72.	Yemen	19.02.2001	07.02.2002	07.02.2002

APPENDIX II INVESTOR-STATE DISPUTES AGAINST UKRAINE

List of concluded investment treaty arbitrations against Ukraine:

1. *Joseph C Lemire v. Ukraine* (ICSID Case No. ARB(AF)/98/1, award dispatched on 18 September 2000;
2. *Generation Ukraine Inc v. Ukraine*, ICSID Case No. ARB/00/9, award dispatched on 16 September 2003;
3. *Western NIS Enterprise Fund v. Ukraine*, ICSID Case No. ARB/04/2, order signed on 16 March 2006;
4. *Tokios Tokeles v. Ukraine*, ICSID Case No. ARB/02/18, award dispatched on 26 July 2007;
5. *AMTO LLC v. Ukraine*, SCC Case No. 080/2005; IIC 346 (2008), final award signed 26 March 2008;
6. *Alpha Projektholding GMBH v. Ukraine*, ICSID Case No. ARB/07/16, award dispatched on 8 November 2010;
7. *Global Trading Resource Corp and Globex International Inc. v. Ukraine*, ICSID Case No ARB/09/11, award dispatched on 1 December 2010;
8. *GEA Group Aktiengesellschaft v. Ukraine*, ICSID Case No. ARB/08/16, award dispatched on 31 March 2011;
9. *Remington Worldwide Limited v. Ukraine*, SCC, award dispatched 28 April 2011;[184]

---

184. Perepelynska O., '*Remington Worldwide Limited v Ukraine*' *Saga: The First ECT Arbitration Conducted in Russian*, CIS Arbitration Forum (2012), http://www.cisarbitration.com/2012/0 8/19/remington-worldwide-limited-v-ukraine-the-first-ect-arbitration-conducted-in-russian/.

Chapter 10: Ukraine

10. *Inmaris Perestroika Sailing Maritime Services GmbH and ors v. Ukraine*, ICSID Case No. ARB/08/8, award dispatched on 1 March 2012;[185]
11. *Laskaridis Shipping Co LTD, Lavinia Corporation, A K Laskaridis and P K Laskaridis v. Ukraine*, UNCITRAL;[186]
12. *Bosh International Inc and B&P Ltd Foreign Investments Enterprise v. Ukraine*, ICSID Case No. ARB/08/11, award dispatched on 25 October 2012;
13. *Joseph C Lemire v. Ukraine*, ICSID Case No. ARB/06/18; IIC 485 (2011), award dispatched on 28 March 2011; the ad hoc committee's decision on annulment issued on 8 July 2013;[187] and
14. *JSC "Tatnafta" v. Ukraine*, ad hoc under UNCITRAL Arbitration Rules, Award dated 29 July 2014.[188]

List of pending investment treaty arbitrations against Ukraine:

1. *City-State N.V., Praktyka Asset Management Company LLC, Crystal-Invest LLC and Prodiz LLC v. Ukraine*, ICSID Case No. ARB/14/9;[189]
2. *Krederi Ltd. v. Ukraine*, ICSID Case No. ARB/14/17;[190]
3. *Gilward Investments B.V. v. Ukraine*, ICSID Case No. ARB/15/33;
4. *JKX Oil&Gas PLC et al. v. Ukraine*,[191] UNCITRAL (consolidated with ICSID and SCC arbitral proceedings launched by the same group of entities against Ukraine);[192]

---

185. Perepelynska O., *ICSID Tribunal Found Unfair Treatment of a German Investor by Ukraine*, CIS Arbitration Forum (2013), http://www.cisarbitration.com/2013/05/20/icsid-tribunal-found-unfair-treatment-of-a-german-investor-by-ukraine/, as well as Perepelynska O., *ICSID Tribunal Orders Ukraine to Pay EUR 3 million to Inmaris Companies*, CIS Arbitration Forum (2012), http://www.cisarbitration.com/2012/03/26/icsid-tribunal-orders-ukraine-to-pay-eur-3-mln-to-inmaris-companies/.
186. Perepelynska O., *Arbitrations against Ukraine: Overview of 2012*, CIS Arbitration Forum (2013), http://www.cisarbitration.com/2013/02/20/arbitrations-against-ukraine-overview-of-2012/.
187. Perepelynska O., *Arbitrations against Ukraine: Overview of 2012*, CIS Arbitration Forum (2013), http://www.cisarbitration.com/2013/02/20/arbitrations-against-ukraine-overview-of-2012/.
188. Perepelynska O., Makukha T., *Arbitrations against Ukraine and Its State Bodies in Post-Revolution Period*, CIS Arbitration Forum (2015), http://www.cisarbitration.com/2015/05/13/arbitrations-against-ukraine-and-its-state-bodies-in-post-revolution-period/.
189. Perepelynska O., Makukha T., *Arbitrations against Ukraine and Its State Bodies in Post-Revolution Period*, CIS Arbitration Forum (2015), http://www.cisarbitration.com/2015/05/13/arbitrations-against-ukraine-and-its-state-bodies-in-post-revolution-period/.
190. Perepelynska O., Makukha T., *Arbitrations against Ukraine and Its State Bodies in Post-Revolution Period*, CIS Arbitration Forum (2015), http://www.cisarbitration.com/2015/05/13/arbitrations-against-ukraine-and-its-state-bodies-in-post-revolution-period/.
191. Perepelynska O., Ivasechko V., *Enforceability of Emergency Arbitrator Awards in Ukraine*, CIS Arbitration Forum (2015), http://www.cisarbitration.com/2015/12/07/enforceability-of-emergency-arbitrator-awards-in-ukraine/.
192. Brief information about the consolidation was published at http://uk.reuters.com/article/idUKFWN10308820150724.

5. *Ministry of Land and Property of the Republic of Tatarstan v. Ukraine*, ad hoc under UNCITRAL Arbitration Rules;[193]
6. *Littop Enterprises Limited, Bridgemont Ventures Limited and Bordo Management Limited v. Ukraine*, SCC V 2015/092;[194]
7. *Emergofin B.V. and Velbay Holdings Ltd. v. Ukraine*, ICSID Case No. ARB/16/35.[195]

Bibliography

Blinov E., Boiarskyi I., *Enforcement in Ukraine of Foreign Court Orders Granting Provisional Measures in Support of Arbitration* (2013), http://arbitration-blog.com/international-arbitration/enforcement-in-ukraine-of-foreign-court-orders-granting-provisional-measures-in-support-of-arbitration/.

BRIEF-JKX Oil & Gas says international arbitration tribunal issues interim award, Reuters (2015), http://uk.reuters.com/article/idUKFWN10308820150724.

Dilevka S., *Arbitration Claims by Ukrainian Investors under the Russia-Ukraine BIT: Between Crimea and a Hard Place?*, CIS Arbitration Forum (2016), http://www.cisarbitration.com/2016/02/17/arbitration-claims-by-ukrainian-investors-under-the-russia-ukraine-bit-between-crimea-and-a-hard-place/.

International Commercial Arbitration Court at the Ukrainian Chamber of Commerce and Industry, *The history of creation of the ICAC*, http://arb.ucci.org.ua/icac/ru/history.html.

Kliuchkovskyi, Koriukalova & Uvarov, Ukraine, in: The European & Middle Eastern Arbitration Review 2012, available at www.globalarbitrationreview.com/reviews/40/sections/141/chapters/1449/ukraine.

Kukharchuk V., Kulya M., *The Legal Profession in Ukraine* (2008), http://www.osce.org/odihr/36311?download=true (accessed 15 March 2016).

Marchukov D., *Refusing Recognition and Enforcement of Foreign Arbitral Awards in Ukraine (Procedural issues and application of non-arbitrability and public policy grounds)*, TDM 1 (2009), http://www.transnational-dispute-management.com/article.asp?key=1368 (accessed 11 March 2016).

Perepelynska O., *Arbitrations against Ukraine: Overview of 2012*, CIS Arbitration Forum (2013), http://www.cisarbitration.com/2013/02/20/arbitrations-against-ukraine-overview-of-2012/.

Perepelynska O., *ICSID Tribunal Found Unfair Treatment of a German Investor by Ukraine*, CIS Arbitration Forum (2013), http://www.cisarbitration.com/2013/05/20/icsid-tribunal-found-unfair-treatment-of-a-german-investor-by-ukraine/.

---

193. At http://www.centralbank.ie/regulation/securities-markets/prospectus/Pages/approvedprospectus.aspx?DisplayID=31556.
194. At http://interfax.com.ua/news/economic/279495.html.
195. At https://icsid.worldbank.org/apps/icsidweb/cases/Pages/casedetail.aspx?CaseNo=ARB/16/35; http://globalarbitrationreview.com/article/1069924/rusal-files-icsid-claim-against-ukraine.

Perepelynska O., Gontar O., *Arbitrability of Disputes Under Public Procurement Contracts In Ukraine: Recent Court Practice*, CIS Arbitration Forum (2014), http://www.cisarbitration.com/2014/08/25/arbitrability-of-disputes-under-public-procurement-contracts-in-ukraine-recent-court-practice/.

Perepelynska O., *ICSID Tribunal Orders Ukraine to Pay EUR 3 million to Inmaris Companies*, CIS Arbitration Forum (2012), http://www.cisarbitration.com/2012/03/26/icsid-tribunal-orders-ukraine-to-pay-eur-3-mln-to-inmaris-companies/.

Perepelynska O., Ivasechko V., *Enforceability of Emergency Arbitrator Awards in Ukraine*, CIS Arbitration Forum (2015), http://www.cisarbitration.com/2015/12/07/enforceability-of-emergency-arbitrator-awards-in-ukraine/.

Perepelynska O., Makukha T., *Arbitrations against Ukraine and Its State Bodies in Post-Revolution Period*, CIS Arbitration Forum (2015), http://www.cisarbitration.com/2015/05/13/arbitrations-against-ukraine-and-its-state-bodies-in-post-revolution-period/.

Perepelynska O., *New Procedural Rules for Arbitration-Related Matters in Ukraine*, YIAG Newsletter (2011).

Perepelynska O., *Party Autonomy vs. Mandatory Rules in International Arbitration*, Ukrainian Journal of Business Law 38, 39 (2012).

Perepelynska O., *'Remington Worldwide Limited v Ukraine' Saga: The First ECT Arbitration Conducted in Russian*, CIS Arbitration Forum (2012), http://www.cisarbitration.com/2012/08/19/remington-worldwide-limited-v-ukraine-the-first-ect-arbitration-conducted-in-russian/.

Perepelynska O., *Ukraine: How Minor Defects in Wording of Arbitration Clause May Result in a Big Problem*, CIS Arbitration Forum (2012), http://www.cisarbitration.com/2012/07/30/ukraine-how-minor-defects-in-wording-of-arbitration-clause-may-result-in-a-big-problem/.

Perepelynska O., *Ukraine Reform its Arbitration-Related Procedural Legislation*, Ukrainian Journal of Business Law (2016), http://www.integrites.com/en/publication/arbitration-related-procedural-legislatio.

Perepelynska O., *Ukrainian Court Enforces Arbitral Awards Set Aside in the UK*, CIS Arbitration Forum (2012), http://www.cisarbitration.com/2012/09/17/ukrainian-court-enforces-arbitral-awards-set-aside-in-the-uk/.

Perepelynska O., *Ukrainian Courts Review Arbitrability of Corporate Disputes*, CIS Arbitration Forum (2012), http://www.cisarbitration.com/2012/01/15/ukrainian-courts-review-arbitrability-of-corporate-disputes/.

Pilkov K., *Swiss Rules play a trick, of Why Ukrainian state court do not recognize 'arbitration in Geneva?'*, (2010), http://arbitration-blog.eu/swiss-rules-ukrainian-courts-recognize-arbitration-geneva.

Schwarz F., Khripkova K., *CEE Overview: International Arbitration in Central and Eastern Europe: An Overview and Key Developments*, ICLG Arbitration 2016,

(2016), http://www.iclg.co.uk/practice-areas/international-arbitration-/international-arbitration-2016/international-arbitration-in-central-and-eastern-europe-an-overview-and-key-developments.

Slipachuk T., *Arbitration Guide – Ukraine*, IBA Arbitration Committee (2012).

Slipachuk T., http://www.sk.ua, *What Law is Applicable to Arbitration Agreements: Who Is to Decide and How? Or Yet Again About the Things That Truly Matter...*, http://www.sk.ua/sites/default/files/article_slipachuk_intl_arbitration_yurzhurnal_eng_2_0.pdf.

Slipachuk T., *Investment treaty arbitration. Ukraine: Overview of investment treaties*, Global Arbitration Review (2012), http://globalarbitrationreview.com/know-how/topics/66/jurisdictions/63/ukraine/%c2%a0.

Slipachuk T., Perepelynska O., Droug O., *Arbitration World - Ukrainian Chapter*. Arbitration World, 4th Edition, The European Lawyer, Thomson Reuters (2012).

Slipachuk T., Perepelynska O., Makukha T. *Getting the Deal Through – Investment treaty arbitration (Ukraine section)*, Law Business Research Ltd (2015).

The materials of press-conference: '*Abolishing of the Commercial Code: Opinion of the regulatory authorities and society*' is available at http://www.ukrinform.ua/rubric-pressconference/1944335-skasuvannya-gospodarskogo-kodeksu-dumka-regulyatoriv-zala-1.html.

Ukraine. Arbitration-friendly jurisdiction: 2013-2014, Statistical report, http://c-n-l.eu/assets/files/ENFORCEMENT_OF_ARBITRATION_AWARDS_IN_UKRAINE_2013-2014%20(ENG).pdf.

Wietzorek M., *Arbitrability of 'Corporate' Disputes in Ukraine – No News is Good News?* CIS Arbitration Forum (2013), http://www.cisarbitration.com/2013/08/23/arbitrability-of-corporate-disputes-in-ukraine-no-news-is-good-news/.

Wietzorek M., *Decisions from Russia, Ukraine, and Kazakhstan related to Arbitration Proceedings Held in Switzerland*. 31 ASA Bulletin, Issue 3, Kluwer Law International, 583, 595 (2013).

Wietzorek M., *Decisions from Russia, Ukraine, and Kazakhstan related to Arbitration Proceedings Held in Switzerland*. 30 ASA Bulletin 548, 563 (3/2012).

Wietzorek M., *No Recognition and Enforcement in Germany of an Arbitral Award Set Aside in Ukraine*, YIAG, http://www.lcia.org/media/Download.aspx?MediaId=275.

Wietzorek M., *The Enforcement of an LMAA Arbitral Award in Ukraine*, Reports From YIAG Members 37, 38 (2012).

Wietzorek M., *Ukrainian Courts on Agreements to Arbitrate in Switzerland*. 30 ASA Bulletin, Issue 3, Kluwer Law International, (2012).

Yaremko V., Karel O., *Arbitrability of Corporate and Public Procurement Disputes in Ukraine*, Kluwer Arbitration Blog (2015), http://kluwerarbitrationblog.com/2015/07/24/arbitrability-of-corporate-and-public-procurement-disputes-in-ukraine/.

Алешин О., *Категория публичного порядка в международном частном праве*, Юридическая практика (2008), http://vkp.ua/ru/publications/articles/the_category_of_public_order_in_private_international_law/.

Довгерт А., Кисіль В., Щітка М., Серьогін О., Калакура В., Бірюков О., Галущенко Г., Криволапов Б., Капіца Ю., Виговський О., Забара І., Довжук О., Кармаза О., Черняк Ю., Цірат Г., *Міжнародне приватне право. Науково-практичний коментар Закону*, Стаття 12, 97-98 (За ред. Довгерта А., ТОВ «Одіссей», 2008).

Довгерт А., *Вклад профессора Н. С. Кузнецовой в развитие цивилистической доктрины в Украине*, Гражданское общество и развитие гражданского права: Сборник статей к юбилею доктора юридических наук, профессора Наталии Семеновны Кузнецовой 40, 44 (Отв. ред. Р. А. Майданик и Е. В. Кохановськая, ЧАО «Юридическая практика», 2014).

Друг А., Перепелинская Е., *Украинско-английская взаимность в признании судебных решений*, ЮрЛига (2012), http://jurliga.ligazakon.ua/news/2012/9/4/71405.htm.

Жуков А., Перепелинская Е., *Статистика и проблемы третейского рассмотрения споров и взаимодействия третейских судов с государственными судами Украины*, 4(82) Журнал 'Третейский суд' 57, 58 (2012).

Жуков А., Перепелинская Е. *Третейские Суды Украины*, 32 ЭЖ ЮРИСТ, 4, 5 (2012).

Жуков А., Перепелинська О., *Стандартний підхід: українська судова практика з питань арбітражного (третейського) розгляду має розвиватися за найкращими світовими стандартами у цій сфері*. Судовий вісник № 11 (2014).

Карабельников Б., *Исполнение и оспаривание решений международных коммерческих арбитражей: Комментарий к Нью-Йоркской конвенции 1958 г. и главам 30 и 31 АПК РФ 2002 г.* 78. Статут (2008).

Крупчан А.Д., *Автономии воли сторон при определении арбитражной процедуры и ее пределы. Императивные нормы места арбитража*, Материалы II Международных арбитражных чтений памяти академика Побирченко И. Г. 112-119 (2014), http://arb.ucci.org.ua/publ/rept2013reading.pdf.

Мальський М. *Арбітражна угода як умова розгляду спорів у міжнародному комерційному арбітражі.* Літопис (2013), http://www.ligazakon.ua/content/files/Arbitration_Agreement.pdf.

Мальський М., *Визнання арбітражної угоди недійсною.* Держава і право (2010), http://dspace.nbuv.gov.ua/bitstream/handle/123456789/34352/62-Malskiy.pdf?sequence=1.

Марченко М., *Сравнительное правоведение. Общая часть*, 459, 467 (Издательство «Зерцало», 2011).

Марченко Р., Коптилин С., *Практика отмены арбитражных решений в Украине*, Юр газета (2012), http://attorneys.ua/ru/publications/the-practice-of-setting-aside-arbitral-awards-in-ukraine/.

Пашковська Т., *Адвокатська монополія: юристи розділилися*, Юридична практика (2015), http://yur-gazeta.com/publications/events/advokatska-monopoliya-yuristi-rozdililisya.html.

Перепелинская Е., *Третейский лишний: процессуальные нюансы признания третейского соглашения недействительным*. Юридическая практика, № 1 (2012).

Перепелинская Е., *Арбитрабильность споров по законодательству Украины: проблемные вопросы*, Материалы II Международных арбитражных чтений памяти академика Побирченко, (2015), http://arbitration.kiev.ua/Uploads/kucher/Arb_Readings_2014_Arbitrability.pdf (2016).

Перепелинская Е., *Все ясно: Ясность в вопросе арбитрабильности является важным фактором для иностранных инвесторов с точки зрения оценки ими рисков заключения договора*, 28-29 (864-865) Юридическая практика 18, 18 (2014), http://arbitration.kiev.ua/Uploads/kucher/18_28-29.pdf.

Пильков К., *Международный коммерческий арбитраж: что нужно доказывать, кто должен доказывать?*, Аналитическое издание «Юрист и Закон» (2014), http://search.ligazakon.ua/l_doc2.nsf/link1/EA006233.html.

Савчук М., *Серый толк*, http://pravo.ua/article.php?id=100111532.

Слипачук Т., *Арбитрабильность международных коммерческих споров в Украине*, 1 Вестник международного коммерческого арбитража 133, 142 (2010), http://arbitration.kiev.ua/uploads/kucher/6_2010_Arbitrabilnost%20mezhdunarodnykh%20kommercheskikh%20sporov%20v%20Ukraine%20(Vestneyk%20MKA%20ianv-iiun).pdf.

Слипачук Т., *Практические аспекты процесса доказывания в международном коммерческом арбитраже*, Право Украины (2010), http://www.sk.ua/sites/default/files/dok_v_mezhd_arb_pravo_ukrainy_2010_1.pdf.

Цивільне право України: Підручник: У 2-х кн., 23 (За ред. О.В. Дзери, Н.С. Кузнєцової, Юрінком Інтер, 1999).

Web Source

Official website of the International Commercial Arbitration Court at the Ukrainian Chamber of Commerce and Industry, http://arb.ucci.org.ua/icac/en/icac.html.

Official website of the Maritime Arbitration Commission at the Ukrainian Chamber of Commerce and Industry, http://www.ucci.org.ua/arb/mac/en/mac.html.

Unified Register of non-governmental institutions of the Ministry of Justice of Ukraine, http://rgf.informjust.ua/home/index.

Website of the Ukrainian Arbitration Association, http://arbitration.kiev.ua/en-US/.

Legislation

Constitution of Ukraine No. 254к/96-ВР (28 June 1996), http://zakon3.rada.gov.ua/laws/show/254%D0%BA/96-%D0%B2%D1%80.

The Budgetary Code of Ukraine No. 2456-VI (8 July 2010), http://zakon4.rada.gov.ua/laws/show/2456-17#Find.

Civil Code of Ukraine No. 435-IV (16 January 2003), http://zakon4.rada.gov.ua/laws/show/435-15.

Commercial Code of Ukraine No. 436 (16 January 2003), http://zakon5.rada.gov.ua/laws/show/436-15.

Criminal Code of Ukraine No. 2341-III (5 April 2001), http://zakon3.rada.gov.ua/laws/show/2341-14.

Commercial Procedure Code of Ukraine No. 1798-XII (6 November 1991), http://zakon3.rada.gov.ua/laws/show/1798-12.

Civil Procedure Code of Ukraine No. 1618-IV (18 March 2004), http://zakon5.rada.gov.ua/laws/show/1618-15.

Code of Administrative Court Procedure of Ukraine No. 2747-IV (6 July 2005), http://zakon3.rada.gov.ua/laws/show/2747-15.

Criminal Procedure Code of Ukraine No. 4652-VI (13 April 2012), http://zakon3.rada.gov.ua/laws/show/4651-17.

Law of Ukraine on Amending Certain Laws of Ukraine regarding Improvement of Privatization Procedure No. 1005-VIII (16 February 2016), http://zakon4.rada.gov.ua/laws/show/1005-19.

Law of Ukraine on Amending Certain Laws of Ukraine to Eliminate Regulatory Barriers for Development of Public Private Partnership and Stimulating of Investments in Ukraine No. 817-VII (24 November 2015), http://zakon4.rada.gov.ua/laws/show/817-19, which entered into force on 24 May 2016.

Law of Ukraine on Compliance with Decisions and Application of Practice of European Court of Human Rights No. 3477-IV (23 February 2006), http://zakon5.rada.gov.ua/laws/show/3477-15.

Law of Ukraine on Concessions No. 997-XIV (16 July 1999), http://zakon4.rada.gov.ua/laws/show/997-14.

Law of Ukraine on Creation of Special Economic Zone 'Crimea' and on Particularities of Carrying out Commercial Activity within the Temporary Occupied Territory of Ukraine No. 1636-VII (12 August 2014), http://zakon5.rada.gov.ua/laws/show/1636-18.

Law of Ukraine on Domestic Arbitration Courts No. 1701-IV (11 May 2004), http://zakon0.rada.gov.ua/laws/show/1701-15.

Law of Ukraine on Financial Restructuring No. 1414-VIII (14 June 2016), http://zakon4.rada.gov.ua/laws/show/1414-19.

Law of Ukraine on Foreign Economic Activity, No. 959-XII (16 April 1991), http://zakon4.rada.gov.ua/laws/show/959-12.

Law of Ukraine on International Commercial Arbitration No. 4002-XII (24 February 1994), http://zakon4.rada.gov.ua/laws/show/4002-12, unofficial translation of the law into English http://www.ucci.org.ua/en/legalbase/zua944002.html.

Law of Ukraine on International Treaties of Ukraine No. 3767-XII (22 December 1993), http://zakon2.rada.gov.ua/laws/show/3767-12.

Law of Ukraine on Judicial System and Status of Judges No. 1402-VIII (2 June 2016), http://zakon4.rada.gov.ua/laws/show/1402-19.

Law of Ukraine on Notariate No. 3425-XII (2 September 1993), http://zakon3.rada.gov.ua/laws/show/3425-12.
Law of Ukraine on Private International Law No. 2709-IV (23 June 2005), http://zakon4.rada.gov.ua/laws/show/2709-15.
Law of Ukraine on Privatization of the State-Owned Assets No. 2163-XII (4 March 1992), http://zakon4.rada.gov.ua/laws/show/2163-12.
Law of Ukraine On Procedure for Resolution of Collective Labour Disputes (Conflicts) No. 137/98-BP dated 3 March 1998, http://zakon4.rada.gov.ua/laws/show/137/98-%D0%B2%D1%80.
Law of Ukraine on Production-Sharing Contracts No. 1039-XIV (14 September 1999), http://zakon3.rada.gov.ua/laws/show/1039-14.
Law of Ukraine on Public Private Partnership No. 2404-IV (1 July 2010), http://zakon4.rada.gov.ua/laws/show/2404-17.
Law of Ukraine on Public Prosecution No. 1697-VII (14 October 2014), http://zakon4.rada.gov.ua/laws/show/1697-18.
Law of Ukraine on Succession of Ukraine No. 1543-XII (12 September 1991), http://zakon5.rada.gov.ua/laws/show/1543-12.
Law of Ukraine on the Bar and Advocate's Activity No. 5076-VI (5 July 2012), http://zakon3.rada.gov.ua/laws/show/5076-17.
Information about and the text of the Draft Law on Introduction of Amendments to Certain Legislative Acts of Ukraine on the Matters of Judicial Control and Support of International Commercial Arbitration, http://w1.c1.rada.gov.ua/pls/zweb2/webproc4_1?pf3511=58601.
Information about and the text of the Draft Law on Mediation, http://w1.c1.rada.gov.ua/pls/zweb2/webproc4_1?pf3511=54558.
Information about and the text of the Draft Law on Jurisdictional Immunities and Responsibility of Foreign States, http://w1.c1.rada.gov.ua/pls/zweb2/webproc4_1?pf3511=54404.
Information about and the text of the Draft Law on Amending the Law of Ukraine on Domestic Arbitration Courts with the aim to Bring it in Line with International Arbitration Standards, http://w1.c1.rada.gov.ua/pls/zweb2/webproc4_1?pf3511=57458.
Information about and the text of the Draft Law on Amending Commercial Procedure Code, Civil Procedure Code and Code for Administrative court procedure as well as other laws of Ukraine, http://w1.c1.rada.gov.ua/pls/zweb2/webproc4_1?pf3511=61415.
Paragraphs 5 and 6 of the Clarifications of the Presidium of the High Commercial Court of Ukraine of 31 May 2002 No. 05-5/608 On Certain Practical Issues of Consideration of Cases Involving Foreign Commercial Entities and Organizations, http://zakon4.rada.gov.ua/laws/show/v_608600-02.
Resolution of the Plenum of the Supreme Court of Ukraine on Practice of Consideration by the Courts of Motions for Recognition and Enforcement of Foreign Court Judgments and Arbitral Awards, and on Setting Aside the International Commercial Arbitration Awards Rendered within the Territory of Ukraine No. 12 (24 December 1999), http://zakon2.rada.gov.ua/laws/show/v0012700-99.

CHAPTER 11
Uzbekistan

Foziljon Otakhonov & Alisher Umirdinov

List of Abbreviations

Arbitration Court of CCI	Arbitration Court of the Chamber of Commerce and Industry of Uzbekistan
Arbitration Law	The Law of the Republic of Uzbekistan 'On Arbitration Courts' No. 3PY-64 dated 16 October 2006
Administrative Responsibility Code	Administrative Responsibility Code of the Republic of Uzbekistan No. 2015-XII dated 22 September 1994
Civil Code	Civil Code of the Republic of Uzbekistan No. 163-I dated 21 December 1995
CLP	Centre for Legal Problems
Civil Procedural Code	Civil Procedural Code of the Republic of Uzbekistan No. 477-I dated 30 August 1997
Constitution of the Republic of Uzbekistan	Constitution of the Republic of Uzbekistan dated 8 December 1992
Criminal Code	Criminal Code of the Republic of Uzbekistan No. 2012-XII dated 22 September 1994
Criminal Procedural Code	Criminal Procedure Code of the Republic of Uzbekistan No. 2013-XII dated 22 September 1994
CCI	Chamber of Commerce and Industry of Uzbekistan
CIS	Commonwealth of Independent States
Economic Procedural Code	Economic Procedural Code of the Republic of Uzbekistan No. 478-I dated 30 August 1997
ECT	Energy Charter Treaty, 1991
GAFTA	Grain and Feed Trade Association

Hague Convention	Hague Convention on Civil Procedure, 1954, Hague
ICAC	International Commercial Arbitration Court (at the Chamber of Commerce and Industry of Uzbekistan)
ICA Draft Law	Draft of the Law 'On international commercial arbitration' produced by the Centre for Legal Problems
ICSID Convention	Convention on the Settlement of Investment Disputes between States and Nationals of other States, 1965, Washington
Kiev Agreement	CIS Agreement on the Procedure for Settling Disputes Arising Out of Business Activity 1992, Kiev
Law on Advocacy	Law of the Republic of Uzbekistan 'On Advocacy' No. 349-I dated 17 December 1996
Law on Guarantees for Protecting Legal Practice	Law of the Republic of Uzbekistan 'On Guarantees for Protecting Legal Practice and Social Security of Lawyers' No. 721-I dated 25 December 1998
Law on Courts	Article 61 of the Law of the Republic of Uzbekistan 'On Courts' No. 162-II dated 14 December 2000
Law On Execution of the Judicial Decisions	Law of the Republic of Uzbekistan 'On Execution of the Judicial Decisions and the Decisions of Other Organs' on the basis of the order of the competent court' No. 258-II dated 29 August 2001
Minsk Convention	Minsk Convention on Legal Assistance and Legal Relations in Civil, Family and Criminal Matters, 1993, Minsk
New York Convention	United Nations Convention on the Recognition and Enforcement of Foreign Arbitral Awards, 1958, New York
Presidential Decree on Measures on Further Reforming of the Bar	Presidential Decree on Measures on Further Reforming of the Bar in the Republic of Uzbekistan No. УП-3993 dated 1 May 2008
2012 Plenary Decision	Plenary Decision of the Higher Economic Court, On Some Issues of Application of Laws by the Economic Courts when Considering the Annulment of the Decision of the Arbitration Courts and the Issuance of a Writ of Execution to Enforce the Arbitral Award, No. 238, dated 15 June 2012
2013 Plenary Decision	Plenary Decision of the Higher Economic Court, On the Application of Laws to Some Issues of Recognition and Enforcement of Foreign Court Decision or Arbitral Award by Economic Courts No. 248 dated 24 May 2013
Programme of legal initiative for 2013	Programme for elaboration of drafts of Law and other legal acts for 2013 and submitting them to Legislative Chamber of Parliament of the Republic of Uzbekistan, Resolution of Cabinet Ministers of the Republic of Uzbekistan No. 81 dated 19 March 2013

CCI Regulation on Arbitration Court	Regulation on Arbitration Court at the Chamber of Commerce and Industry of Uzbekistan No. 43 dated 8 October 2007
CCI Regulation on Fees, Expenses and Costs	Regulation on Fees, Expenses and Costs of the Parties to the Arbitration Court at the Chamber of Commerce and Industry of Uzbekistan No. 43 dated 8 October 2007
UNCTAD	United Nation Conference on Trade and Development
UNCITRAL	United Nations Commission on International Trade Law
UNCITRAL Model Law	UNCITRAL Model Law on International Commercial Arbitration 1985
USSR	Union of Soviet Socialist Republics

§11.01 GENERAL INTRODUCTION

[A] Historical Development of the Legal System

1.1. Uzbekistan has a long history of legal systems starting from Khoresm, Bactria and Sugd in the eighth century BC. Many empires left traces of their legal traditions in the land once called Mavorounnahr – 'the land between two rivers' (the Amudarya and Syrdarya Rivers). Persian, Greco-Macedonian, Turkish, Islamic and finally Soviet law are only some of these. While during ancient times the people of Mavorounnahr used Avesto and Sugd writings, in the Middle Ages the Timurid and Shaybanid dynasties applied Islamic law and finally, after Russian conquest, the Uzbek khanates became subjects of the Russian Empire and then Soviet laws, respectively. The country announced its independence from the Soviet Union in August 1991, and after this period Uzbekistan independently developed its own peculiar legal system based on market relations.[1]

1.2. Article 53 of the Constitution of Uzbekistan clearly declares that the economy of the country is based on various forms of ownership and freedom of economic activity, along with the guarantee of the right to private property.[2] In order to facilitate economic activity and entrepreneurship, the Government of Uzbekistan initiated a series of judicial-legal reforms in the country. As a result of joint efforts of specialists and experts from various fields, Parliament has since adopted seventeen codes, including the Civil

---

1. *See* for a comprehensive analysis of Uzbek law, Bantekas I ed, The Law and Legal System of Uzbekistan, Juris Publishing (2005).
2. Конституция Республики Узбекистан (Constitution of the Republic of Uzbekistan), Газета «Народное слово» от 15.12.1992, № 247 (438), http://www.lex.uz/pages/getpage.aspx?lact_id=35869 (accessed 1 July 2017).

Code,[3] Civil Procedural Code,[4] Economic Procedural Code,[5] Administrative Responsibility Code,[6] –Criminal Code[7] and Criminal Procedure Code.[8]

1.3. Arbitration has also developed in line with the above legal traditions. Earlier documents show that under Islamic law, arbitral institutions existed as an alternative to *qadis* courts, despite the fact that arbitration closely resembled conciliation, due to the fact that Islamic teachings direct people towards reconciliation (sulh).[9] Arbitral institutions under Soviet law in the 1930s resolved disputes between entities conducting foreign economic activity.[10] Despite their independence from state courts, the state paid the salaries of arbitrators and state bodies controlled those institutions. Therefore, it is very hard to consider them commercial arbitration courts by modern standards.[11]

1.4. During the period of independence, that is, after 1991, with strong lobbying from the Chamber of Commerce and Industry of Uzbekistan (CCI), Parliament adopted the Law on Arbitration Courts (Arbitration Law), and it entered into force on 1 January 2007.[12] But this does not mean that Uzbekistan had not seen any type of arbitration during the previous period. For instance, GostavDon (current JSC 'Uzdonmahsulot'),[13] the state agency in charge of wheat production, had an arbitral institution under its

---

3. Гражданский Кодекс Республики Узбекистан (Civil Code of the Republic of Uzbekistan) Ведомости Олий Мажлиса Республики Узбекистан,1996, приложение к № 2, http://lex.uz/pages/getpage.aspx?lact_id = 111181 (accessed 1 July 2017).
4. Гражданский Процессуальный Кодекс Республики Узбекистан (Civil Procedural Code of the Republic of Uzbekistan) Ведомости Олий Мажлиса Республики Узбекистан,1997, № 9, http://lex.uz/pages/getpage.aspx?lact_id = 186098 (accessed 1 July 2017).
5. Хозяйственный Процессуальный Кодекс Республики Узбекистан (Economic Procedural Code of the Republic of Uzbekistan) Ведомости Олий Мажлиса Республики Узбекистан,1997, № 9, 234, http://lex.uz/pages/getpage.aspx?lact_id = 185981 (accessed 1 July 2017).
6. Кодекс Республики Узбекистан Об Административной Ответственности (Administrative Responsibility Code of the Republic of Uzbekistan) Ведомости Верховного Совета Республики Узбекистан, 1995, № 3, http://lex.uz/pages/getpage.aspx?lact_id = 97661 (accessed 1 July 2017).
7. Уголовный Кодекс Республики Узбекистан (Criminal Code of the Republic of Uzbekistan), Ведомости Верховного Совета Республики Узбекистан, 1995, № 1, http://lex.uz/pages/getpage.aspx?lact_id = 111457 (accessed 1 July 2017).
8. Уголовно-Процессуальный Кодекс Республики Узбекистан (Criminal Procedural Code of the Republic of Uzbekistan) Ведомости Верховного Совета Республики Узбекистан, 1995, № 2, http://lex.uz/pages/getpage.aspx?lact_id = 111463 (accessed 1 July 2017).
9. *See* Al-Ramahi A., Sulh: a crucial part of Islamic arbitration, LSE Law, Society and Economy Working Papers, No. 08-45, 1,15 (2008).
10. Rahimov A., Hakamlik Sudi: Tarix va Bugun, (Arbitration: History and Today) Oliy Hojalik Sudi Axborotnomasi, 43 (2014).
11. For a discussion of the Soviet arbitral system, *see* Butler W. ed, International Commercial Arbitration: Soviet Commercial and Maritime Arbitration, Oceana (1988).
12. Закон Республики Узбекистан 'О третейских судах' (The Law 'On Arbitration Courts'), № 3 РУ-64, Собрание законодательства Республики Узбекистан, 2006, № 42, 416, http://www.lex.uz/pages/GetAct.aspx?lact_id = 1072094&ONDATE = 15.05.2014 (accessed 1 July 2017).
13. For detailed information *see*, http://uzdon.uz/en/#en/content/about/history/ (accessed 1 July 2017).

umbrella which dealt with 156 cases between 1992 and 1993 that focused on local wheat producer entities; its decisions were enforced perfectly.[14]

1.5. Furthermore, the old Civil Procedural Code of Soviet Uzbekistan endorsed some elements of arbitration as understood today in a modern setting, which facilitated the early development of arbitration activity in Uzbekistan.[15] One such institution, the Centre for Legal Problems (CLP) in Tashkent City had already begun to set up arbitration centres in early 2002, which led to the opening of five such centres in Tashkent, Samarkand and Bukhara.[16] These centres decided more than sixty cases; nevertheless, a lack of legal foundations hampered their enforcement and plenty of misunderstandings resurfaced in practice.[17]

1.6. Since the adoption of the Arbitration Law, with the help of donor organisations, an Arbitration Development Centre was established in 2008, and in May 2009 the Association of Uzbekistan Arbitration Courts[18] began its work. The CCI established the Arbitration Courts Centre right after the adoption of the Arbitration Law.

[B] The Legal Profession

1.7. The main legislation governing the legal profession sector includes the Law on Advocacy,[19] the Law on Guarantees for Protecting Legal Practice and Social Security of Lawyer[20] and the Presidential Decree on Measures on Further Reforming of the Bar.[21]

---

14. Otakhonov F., Materials of Special Lecture on Implementation of Market-Oriented Legislation in Uzbekistan, Nagoya University Graduate School of Law, 4–6 February (2015).
15. *See* Civil Procedural Code of Soviet Uzbekistan, Regulation on Arbitration Courts, Third Appendix, 23 March 1963.
16. Kuchimov U., *Recognition and Enforcement of Arbitral Awards and the Practice of Uzbekistan Regarding Arbitral Awards* (2007). Available at http://papers.ssrn.com/sol3/papers.cfm?abstract_id=1886633 (accessed 1 July 2017).
17. For some of the examples of the cases decided by arbitration at the centre prior to the Arbitration Law *see* Комментарий к Закону Республики Узбекистан «О третейских судах» (Commentary to the Law on Arbitration Courts)// Авторы Ш.Асьянов, М.Куликова, А.Исаева, 2007. 202–203с, http://www.lprc.uz/treteyskiy.html (accessed 1 July 2017).
18. For the sake of clarity, the authors mean arbitral tribunals when use the term 'arbitration courts'. The reason for this is that the Arbitration Law of Uzbekistan named domestic arbitration in Uzbekistan after 'arbitration courts'. Therefore, the parties may bring their dispute to either ad hoc or permanent arbitration courts in the territory of Uzbekistan.
19. Закон Республики Узбекистан 'Об Адвокатуре' (Law of the Republic of Uzbekistan 'On Advocacy') № 349-I, Ведомости Олий Мажлиса Республики Узбекистан,1997, № 2, 48, http://www.lex.uz/pages/getpage.aspx?lact_id=58372 (accessed 1 July 2017).
20. Закон Республики Узбекистан 'О гарантиях адвокатской деятельности и социальной защите адвокатов' (Law on Guarantees for Protecting Legal Practice and Social Security of Lawyers) № 721-I, Ведомости Олий Мажлиса Республики Узбекистан,1999, № 1, 12, http://www.lex.uz/pages/GetAct.aspx?lact_id=1321 (accessed 1 July 2017).
21. Указ Президента Республики Узбекистан 'О мерах по дальнейшему реформированию института адвокатуры в Республике Узбекистан' (Presidential Decree on Measures on Further Reforming of the Bar in the Republic of Uzbekistan), from 1 May 2008, № УП-3993, http://lex.uz/Pages/GetAct.aspx?lact_id=1347567 (accessed 1 July 2017).

1.8. Uzbek citizens who hold a high law degree and have obtained a licence for legal practice can become an advocate and represent clients in courts.[22] In practice, however, upon getting the appropriate power of attorney from their companies, many in-house lawyers often act in court proceedings without a lawyer's licence. An advocate may work as a sole practitioner by establishing his own law office (bureau), setting up a law firm with other partners, joining a collegium of advocates on the basis of membership or practising in a legal consulting firm.[23] The above-mentioned four types of firms – bureau, law firm, collegium of advocates and legal consulting firm – are the organisational forms of legal practice in Uzbekistan.

1.9. Since the passage of the new law in 2008, the Chamber of Advocates carries out the coordination of legal practice, and its membership is compulsory for each advocate-practitioner. In 2010, a postgraduate training course was launched for new advocates over three years. All four types of organisational forms of legal practice must be registered in the regional Departments of the Ministry of Justice, which is in charge of licensing and registration issues.

1.10. Judges, public prosecutors and attorneys (called *advocates*) form distinct groups in the legal profession. Despite the fact that the Uzbek legal system originated in continental Europe, neither common examination nor joint training exists, with some exceptions,[24] for these three professions. Instead, as concerns formation and regulation of the activity of these three professions, Uzbekistan chose to establish different bodies.

1.11. The Tashkent State University of Law, Westminster International University in Tashkent, the University of World Economy and Diplomacy and the Academy of the Ministry of Internal Affairs are among the leading law schools in Uzbekistan.

[C] Sources of Arbitration Law

1.12. The Constitution stands as the main protector of private property and access to justice in the territory of Uzbekistan. Next to the Constitution, the Law on Courts, and the Law on Enforcement of Judicial Decisions and Decisions of Other Authorities stand as the main legal sources for the regulation of the judicial system in Uzbekistan. In addition to these and along with other relevant numerous by-laws, certain norms of the Civil Code, Civil Procedural Code, Economic Procedural Code and Tax Code are also highly relevant to arbitration procedure.[25]

---

22. *See* Art. 3 of the Law of the Republic of Uzbekistan 'On Advocacy'. № 349-I, Ведомости Олий Мажлиса Республики Узбекистан,1997, № 2, 48, http://www.lex.uz/pages/getpage.aspx?lact_id=58372 (accessed 1 July 2017).
23. *Ibid.*, Art. 4. Visit following web page for more information, http://www.ibanet.org/PPID/Constituent/Bar_Issues_Commission/ITILS_Uzbekistan.aspx (accessed 1 July 2017).
24. Although advocates and judges trained under the joint training system exist, this is not common for all three types of legal professions.
25. Both electronic versions Uzbek and Russian laws with latest updates are accessible by following the national database of www.lex.uz (accessed 1 July 2017).

1.13. As a primary source of arbitration in the territory of Uzbekistan, the Arbitration Law remains compatible with the UNCITRAL Model Law, though with important distinctions.[26] Indeed, it is not surprising that the United Nations Commission on International Trade Law (UNCITRAL) secretariat decided not to consider the Arbitration Law as being based on the UNCITRAL Model Law.[27] Unfortunately, the Arbitration Law failed to address foreign arbitration and arbitration between foreign parties. In other words, it deals exclusively with domestic disputes and more importantly, only Uzbek citizens can sit as an arbitrator. In order to overcome this hurdle, the project for a new law on international arbitration is being discussed in Parliament.[28]

[D] International Legal Framework, Supremacy of International Law

1.14. A wide network of international treaties and domestic law regulates arbitration proceedings in Uzbekistan. The country ratified a number of international treaties pertaining to arbitration, such as the 1954 Hague Convention on Civil Procedure,[29] the 1958 New York Convention on the Recognition and Enforcement of Foreign Arbitral Awards (New York Convention),[30] the 1965 Washington Convention on the Settlement of Investment Disputes (ICSID Convention),[31] the 1992 Commonwealth of Independent States (CIS) Agreement on Procedure for Settling Disputes Arising Out of Business Activity (Kiev Agreement)[32] and the 1993 Minsk Convention on Legal Assistance and Legal Relations in Civil, Family and Criminal Matters (Minsk Convention).[33]

---

26. The EBRD Report describes the Arbitration Law as a law of medium compliance with the Model Law. It has important differences from the Model Law such as assistance in taking evidence, appointment and challenge of arbitrators, applicable rules and interim measures. *See* Chapaev R., *International commercial arbitration assessment: report on the results of the assessment in the CIS* (Armenia, Azerbaijan, Georgia, Kazakhstan, Kyrgyz Republic, Moldova, Russia, Tajikistan, Turkmenistan, Ukraine, Uzbekistan) and Mongolia, EBRD, 65 (2007). http://www.ebrd.com/downloads/legal/judicial/arbitration.pdf (accessed 1 July 2017).
27. *See* http://www.uncitral.org/uncitral/en/uncitral_texts/arbitration/1985Model_arbitration_status.html (accessed 1 July 2017).
28. *See* Yuldashev N & Ruziev M., *Uzbekistan*, GLI – Litigation & Dispute Resolution, Fourth Edition, 327 (2015).
29. Hague Convention on Civil Procedure (1954) https://assets.hcch.net/docs/30f6092f-2a79-45f6-85a9-4f13c7c783c2.pdf (accessed 1 July 2017).
30. Convention on the Recognition and Enforcement of Foreign Arbitral Awards (1958). http://www.uncitral.org/pdf/english/texts/arbitration/NY-conv/New-York-Convention-E.pdf (accessed 1 July 2017).
31. Washington Convention on the Settlement of Investment Disputes (1965) https://icsid.worldbank.org/ICSID/StaticFiles/basicdoc_en-archive/ICSID_English.pdf (accessed 1 July 2017).
32. CIS Agreement on the Procedure for Settling Disputes Arising Out of Business Activity (Соглашение о порядке разрешения споров, связанных с осуществлением хозяйственной деятельности, 1992) http://zakon5.rada.gov.ua/laws/show/997_076 (accessed 1 July 2017).
33. Minsk Convention on Legal Assistance and Legal Relations in Civil, Family and Criminal Matters (1993) http://www.cisarbitration.com/2017/02/03/minsk-convention-on-legal-assistance-and-legal-relations-in-civil-family-and-criminal-matters/ (accessed 1 July 2017).

1.15. Uzbekistan also acceded to the Energy Charter Treaty (ECT) in 1994 and signed almost fifty Bilateral Investment Treaties (BITs).[34] Further, Uzbekistan is party to dozens of bilateral treaties on legal assistance in civil and commercial matters.[35]

1.16. International law enjoys priority over national law in case of conflict. The preamble of the Constitution recognises the priority of the generally accepted norms of international law over national law.[36] Similarly, the Arbitration Law specifically notes that if an international treaty – recognised by Uzbekistan – establishes provisions other than those found in the Arbitration Law, the regulations and norms of international treaties shall apply.[37]

[E] Available Dispute Resolution Mechanisms

1.17. There are state and alternative dispute resolution methods, which are commonly used as dispute settlement mechanisms in Uzbekistan. Alternative dispute resolutions – as part of the so-called non-governmental judicial system in Uzbekistan – consist of arbitration court proceedings and mediation. Because the Arbitration Law itself uses the term 'arbitration court' and as these institutions have a specific domestic character, the authors have decided to exclusively use the term 'arbitration court' throughout this chapter.

1.18. Since the establishment of the Law on Courts in 2001, the judicial system has undergone significant reform.[38] In particular, the courts have become more specialised and have been divided into criminal, civil and commercial matters. Furthermore, Uzbekistan has introduced the institution of Habeas Corpus to the courts, allowing them to expand their powers through granting the power to issue sanctions for arrest.[39] Here, one should acknowledge the important contribution and impact of international donor organisations to the development and democratisation of the judicial system of Uzbekistan.[40]

---

34. *See* The ECT And Related Documents: A Legal Framework For International Energy Cooperation (2004) http://www.ena.lt/pdfai/Treaty.pdf (accessed 1 July 2017).International Investment Agreements Navigator – Investment Policy Hub, http://investmentpolicyhub.unctad.org/IIA/CountryBits/226#iiaInnerMenu (accessed 1 July 2017).At http://investmentpolicyhub.unctad.org/IIA/CountryOtherIias/226#iiaInnerMenu (accessed 1 July 2017).
35. Visit following web page for more information, http://www.mfa.uz/en/cooperation/legalrelations/ (accessed 1 July 2017).
36. *See* Constitution of the Republic of Uzbekistan, Preamble, 1 Bulletin of the Supreme Council of the Republic of Uzbekistan (1993).
37. Arbitration Law, *supra* n. 12, at Art. 2(2).
38. Суд-хукук сохасини ислох этиш боскичлари (Stages of Judicial Reforms), Press Secretary of the Supreme Court of the Republic of Uzbekistan, https://www.gazeta.uz/uz/2016/02/23/sud/ (accessed 1 July 2017).
39. The Permanent Mission of the Republic of Uzbekistan to the United Nations, *On the Methods Needed to Improve the Judicial System* (2015), https://www.un.int/uzbekistan/news/way-improve-judicial-system (accessed 1 July 2017).
40. For related projects of European Bank of Reconstruction and Development, European Union and United Nations Development Program, *see* Legal Reform in Uzbekistan, http://www.ebrd.com/legal-reform/where-we-work/uzbekistan.html (accessed 1 July 2017); Support to Criminal Judicial Reforms in Uzbekistan, EU – Central Asia Rule of Law Platform, http://ruleoflaw.eu/

1.19. The arbitration courts have also become very active in the legal life of Uzbekistan. Furthermore, the draft of the Law on International Commercial Arbitration in Uzbekistan was submitted to Parliament[41] and is now under debate.[42]

1.20. Compared to the judicial system and arbitration courts, the mediation system, with limited success only in family disputes, is still in the early stages of its development. At the moment, the neighbourhood communities known as 'mahalla' have their own reconciliation committees and are applying procedures similar to mediation. Several well-respected people usually run the reconciliation committees which focus mainly on minor family and neighbourhood disputes. Unfortunately, as Karaketov rightly pointed out, the traditional mahalla system lacks legal foundations, something that has a hugely negative impact on the effective implementation of solutions proposed by committee members.[43] Moreover, due to the very heavy workload of the courts, especially in civil and economic matters, one can observe wide-ranging calls from various circles in the profession to introduce a mediation system to Uzbekistan in order to lessen the burden of the courts.[44]

1.21. There are no other systems of conciliation or other types of alternative dispute settlement mechanisms in Uzbekistan.

[F] Judicial System

1.22. The judicial system of Uzbekistan consists of courts of general jurisdiction, economic courts, military courts and the Constitutional Court.[45] Civil and criminal

---

projects-database/support-to-criminal-judicial-reforms-in-uzbekistan/ (accessed 1 July 2017); Rule of Law Partnership in Uzbekistan, UNDP Project, http://www.uz.undp.org/content/uzbekistan/en/home/operations/projects/democratic_governance/rule-of-law-partnership-in-uzbekistan-.html (accessed 1 July 2017).

41. For instance, for the draft of the Law 'On international commercial arbitration' produced by CLP, see Проект Закона Республики Узбекистан 'О международном коммерческом арбитраже' // Материалы Международных научно-практических конференций на тему 'Международный коммерческий арбитраж в контексте судебно-правовой реформы' (Materials of scientific-practical conference on 'International Commercial Arbitration in the Context of Judicial-Legal Reforms') 28 октября 2009 Г. –Т.: 'Chashma Print', 2010.– C.298–315.

42. See Программа по разработке и внесению в Законодательную палату Олий Мажлиса Республики Узбекистан проектов законов и других нормативно-правовых актов на 2013 год (Program for elaboration of drafts of Law and other legal acts for 2013 and submitting them to Legislative Chamber of Parliament of the Republic of Uzbekistan), Resolution of Cabinet Ministers of the Republic of Uzbekistan dated 19 March 2013, No. 81, http://www.lex.uz/pages/GetAct.aspx?lact_id=2144791 (accessed 1 July 2017).

43. See Karaketov M., Creating an Appropriate Model of Court-Connected Mediation for Uzbekistan, 258 Nagoya Journal of Law and Politics 207, 208 (2014).

44. Масадиков Ш.М., Сущность медиации и проблемы ее правового регулирования в Республике Узбекистан (The Essence of Mediation and Its Legal Regulation in Uzbekistan) //Автореферат дисс. на соис.ученой степени к.ю.н . – Г.: 2008. – Т.9; Отахонов Ф., Медиация – плюсы и минусы посредничества (Mediation: Its Plus and Minuses)// Материалы Международных научно-практических конференций на тему 'Международный коммерческий арбитраж в контексте судебно-правовой реформы' 28 октября 2009 Г. –Т.: 'Chashma Print, 2010.– C.253–259.

45. The Constitutional Court, in one case, also dealt with the interpretation of domestic investment law on jurisdictions of foreign arbitration. See for the analysis of foreign investment-related decisions, Bayzakova D., *Zarafshan-Newmont Case and International Investment Arbitration*

disputes belong to the jurisdiction of courts of general jurisdiction. While the upper level of courts is the Supreme Court that acts both as a Court of First Instance and as an appellate court, its lower level courts are divided into regional, city and district/inter-district courts for civil cases, and regional, city and district courts for criminal cases.

1.23. The economic courts have an exclusive jurisdiction on commercial disputes arising between legal entities, including foreign investors. Economic courts are divided into two levels: the Higher Economic Court which has the same functions as the Supreme Court and the regional (city) economic courts. According to Article 115(1) of the Economic Procedural Code, only the economic courts are granted the prerogative of issuing a writ of execution of arbitral awards.

1.24. As concerns qualification as a judge in Uzbekistan – except for Constitutional Court judges – candidates need a university law degree, with at least five years' practical experience as a lawyer before being eligible for appointment to the bench; they must also be at least 30 years of age.[46] Judges are selected for a five-year term, subject to re-appointment. The President of Uzbekistan nominates judges for higher courts, such as the Constitutional Court, Supreme Court and Higher Economic Court and this is then confirmed by parliament. Finally, we need to emphasize the fact that the newly-elected president of Uzbekistan, Shavkat Mirziyoyev has already started to push judicial reforms to address deficiencies of the system.

[G] Arbitral Institutions

1.25. Both permanent and ad hoc arbitration courts are permitted in Uzbekistan. Permanent arbitration courts may be established by any kind of legal entity, except governmental bodies. As of 2015, there are more than 200 permanent arbitration courts registered at the Ministry of Justice.[47] Each permanent arbitration court shall conduct arbitral proceedings in accordance with its own rules, determine the schedule of fees and keep the permanent list of arbitrators. Needless to say, the permanent arbitration courts handle the majority of arbitral disputes in Uzbekistan.

1.26. For the purpose of the development of arbitration courts, the Association of Arbitration Courts was established in May 2009, with fourteen regional branches. Another prominent and permanent arbitral institution in Uzbekistan is the Arbitration Court at the CCI. It has fourteen regional offices.[48] CCI also launched the International Commercial Arbitration Court (ICAC) under its own aegis in 2011.[49] Although the ICAC

---

against Uzbekistan: Interpretation of Consent by the Host State and Relevance of National Legislation, 9 J. World Investment & Trade 377 (2008).

46. Статья 61 Закона Республики Узбекистан 'О судах' (Art. 61 of the Law of the Republic of Uzbekistan 'On Courts') № 162-II, Ведомости Олий Мажлиса Республики Узбекистан, 2001, № 1–2, 10, http://www.lex.uz/pages/getpage.aspx?lact_id = 68521 (accessed 1 July 2017).
47. *See* for the list of registered permanent arbitration court in Uzbekistan, http://minjustuz.ru/uz/section.scm_sectionId = 24903&contentId = 24907.html (accessed 1 July 2017).
48. *See* Информация о третейских судах (Information about Arbitration Courts) http://chamber.uz/ru/page/4857 (accessed 1 July 2017).
49. *See* Международный коммерческий арбитражный суд (International commercial arbitration court) http://chamber.uz/ru/page/4838 (accessed 1 July 2017).

started its work with high enthusiasm and succeeded in attracting several multi-million dollar cases, the lack, and formal absence of a legal framework on international commercial arbitration made its activity almost dormant.

1.27. Overall, after the enactment of the Arbitration Law, due to its less time-consuming and less expansive character, the number of cases resolved by arbitration courts also increased drastically. According to statistics, arbitration courts under the Association and CCI handled 38,391 and 6,999 cases between 2010 and 2015, respectively.[50]

[H] Sovereign Immunity and International Arbitration

1.28. Uzbekistan still adheres to the doctrine of absolute immunity relating to claims of sovereign immunity. The country does not have separate legislation on foreign state sovereign immunity. Moreover, it has not yet signed up to the United Nations Convention on Jurisdictional Immunities of States and their Property. Despite such stance, developments reveal that Uzbekistan is going closer towards the restricted immunity doctrine. The country is very actively engaging in investment treaty making while, simultaneously, in May 2013, taking a pro-arbitration approach, with the Higher Economic Court announcing a resolution that is legally binding on the lower courts as concerns the enforcement of foreign arbitral awards.[51]

1.29. The issue of sovereign immunity gained attention when disputes arose between *Romak S.A.* and *Uzdon* on payment for a wheat supply contract. Gaining a favourable award under the Grain and Feed Trade Association (GAFTA) Arbitration in London, the claimant *Romak S.A.* pursued its execution against the specific bank account of Uzbekistan at HSBC in Paris. Although the claimant was initially successful in getting the bank account arrested by French officials, the Court of Cassation later rejected the claim by *Romak S.A.* and thereby confirmed that the state was not responsible for the acts of other independent legal entities operating on its territory.[52]

1.30. During consideration of the case, it seems that Uzbekistan relied on the principles of international law that provide immunity of the state from jurisdiction of foreign courts and asserted that under Uzbek civil law Uzdon had an independent legal personality from the State.[53] It should be noted that the claimant also failed to secure his claim in the Swiss Federal Supreme Court in 2013 under the same line of arguments. The Swiss court decided that foreign states should not be held liable for the debts of

---

50. Худайберганов А.С., Ҳакамлик судининг ҳал қилув қарорини ижроси этилиши (The Enforcement of Arbitration Court's Decision) http://chamber.uz/ru/page/4857 (accessed 1 July 2017).
51. *See* 2013 Plenary Decision.
52. *See* Arrêt n° 194 du 5 mars 2014 (12–22.406) – Cour de cassation – Première chambre civile – ECLI:FR:CCASS:2014:C100194 https://www.courdecassation.fr/jurisprudence_2/premiere_chambre_civile_568/194_5_28579.html.
53. *See* Ahmedov D & Rahmanova M., *French Court Supported Uzbekistan's Position Concerning Romak*, http://www.baltic-course.com/eng/markets_and_companies/?doc=94065 (accessed 1 July 2017).

state-owned companies registered in their territory with an independent legal personality.[54]

§11.02 THE ARBITRATION AGREEMENT

[A] Introduction

1.31. It should be noted that the UNCITRAL Model Law played a significant role during the drafting process of the Arbitration Law. The provision on the arbitration agreement is also not an exception in that regard, but with important distinctions. Uzbek law diverges from the UNCITRAL Model law significantly on the scope of the application of the law, court involvement, the clarity of interim measures, the choice of applicable law and recognition and enforcement of awards.[55]

1.32. The arbitration agreement should fulfil the same requirements as other types of contracts. Like in jurisdictions of other continental law countries, Uzbek courts also attach a great importance to all minor technical items in the arbitration agreement. Since arbitration court practice and the parties' involvement in arbitration disputes are still in the process of development, many misunderstandings have arisen in practice; we explore these later in the article.

[B] Validity of the Arbitration Agreement

[1] General Provisions

1.33. The Arbitration Law defines the arbitration agreement as the agreement of the parties to refer a dispute to resolution by an arbitration court.[56] A dispute can be referred to the arbitration court if there is a binding arbitration agreement between parties. The 2012 Plenary Decision of the Higher Economic Court emphasises that if the arbitration agreement contains a clause stating that *all disputes* which have arisen or which may arise between the parties are to be considered in an arbitration court, then the dispute over the invalidity of the arbitration agreement likewise belongs to the jurisdiction of the arbitration court.[57] Otherwise, the economic courts are the proper venue for the contestation of the invalidity of agreement.[58] The parties may conclude the arbitration agreement on the pending issue before the state courts until the competent state court has passed a judgment concerning the dispute.[59]

---

54. Ollivier N., *Attachment of State Assets – A Better Weapon Than Immunity: The Independent Legal Personality of the State-Owned Company*, International Litigation Letter Newspaper, 75, 78 (April 2013).
55. *See* Chapaev R., *supra* n. 26, 70 (2007).
56. Arbitration Law, *supra* n. 12, Art. 3.
57. *See* Art. 2(3) of 2012 Plenary Decision.
58. *Ibid.*, Art. 2(4).
59. Arbitration Law, *supra* n. 12, Art. 11(2).

[2] Requirements for a Valid Arbitration Agreement

1.34. The Arbitration Law requires arbitration agreements to be in writing only. In Article 12, it further provides that the arbitration agreement can be included as a clause in a contract or concluded as a separate agreement. The arbitration agreement is considered as concluded in writing if it is included in the document signed by the parties to the arbitration agreement, or is concluded by an exchange of letters or messages through the use of electronic or other means of communication that prove the conclusion of such an agreement.[60]

1.35. In practice, there is no reported case of the conclusion of an arbitration agreement via electronic methods. Furthermore, the arbitration agreement shall contain the provision that all or certain disputes which have arisen or can arise between the parties of the arbitration agreement are subject to consideration by arbitration, and also shall contain the name of the permanent arbitration court if the dispute is referred to resolution by the given arbitration court.[61] The CCI arbitration rules also state that if the defendant consents to the jurisdiction of the arbitration court in written form, it may also be considered as an arbitration agreement.[62]

[C] The Doctrine of Separability

1.36. The doctrine of separability also found its expression in the new law.[63] The arbitration court independently decides on the existence or absence of its competence to resolve a dispute referred to it for resolution, including cases where one of the parties to arbitral proceedings objects to the arbitration proceedings, motivating its objection by the absence or invalidity of the arbitration agreement. For this purpose, the arbitration agreement in the form of the contract clause should be considered to be separable from other treaty provisions.

1.37. The decision by the arbitration court that the contract containing the arbitration clause is void does not affect the validity of this arbitration clause. The Uzbek courts seem to respect this doctrine in their practices. In the *Toshkent paxtasanoat v. Pskent paxta tozalash zavodi & Spitamen-Siyavush-Invest* case, the claimant asked the economic court to find the logistics service agreement invalid.[64] During the process, it was revealed that there was an arbitral award in 2012 between the defendants according to the main logistics service contract. According to the separability doctrine – and behaving in a correct way – the economic court avoided addressing the invalidity of arbitral award.

---

60. *Ibid.*, Art. 12(2).
61. *Ibid.*, Art. 13(1).
62. Article 5(5) of Regulation of CCI Arbitration, No. 43, 8 October (2007).
63. Arbitration Law, *supra* n. 12, Art. 24(1).
64. Hamroqulov B., Hakamlik Sudlari Qarorlarini Bekor Qilish Bilan Bog'liq Ayrim Masalalar (Several Issues Related to Invalidity of Arbitral Awards), Oliy Xo'jalik Sudi Axborotnomasi, No. 2, 42–44 (2013).

[D] Invalidity of the Arbitration Agreement

1.38 The arbitration agreement is considered to be void under the following circumstances:

a) The agreement is not in a written form.[65]
b) The parties fail to register the written form of agreement as required in law.[66]
c) The parties fail to mention the name of the permanent arbitration court.[67]
d) One of the parties to the agreement is a state organ.[68]
e) The parties have agreed to submit disputes on administrative, family and labour relationships to arbitration.[69]

1.39. In addition to the above factors, an arbitration agreement can be found void and null if it contradicts the other norms of the Civil Code, Civil Procedural Code and Economic Procedural Code.[70]

[E] Arbitrability

1.40. The defined scope of arbitrability under the Arbitration Law is wide enough to encompass almost all disputes of a civil and commercial nature. Article 9 states that arbitration courts resolve disputes flowing from civil law disputes, including economic disputes arising between legal entities. This provision should be understood in conjunction with the second section of Article 9, which makes, specifically, administrative, family and labour relationships non-arbitrable in Uzbekistan.

1.41. Therefore, some problematic fields, which are considered as non-arbitrable in other jurisdictions, can be settled in arbitration courts in Uzbekistan. Those fields include intellectual property rights (patent, trademark and copyright),[71] issues of competition (unfair competition), consumer protection (product liability), corporate disputes and securities regulation (issuance of securities), although some governmental bodies have quasi-arbitral institutions to deal with specific legal disputes.[72]

---

65. Arbitration Law, *supra* n. 12, Art. 12(1).
66. *Ibid.*
67. *Ibid.*, Art. 13(1).
68. *Ibid.*, Art. 5(2).
69. *Ibid.*, Art. 9(2).
70. For instance, Art. 116 of the Civil Code of the Republic of Uzbekistan defines the invalidity of contracts which are contrary to the legal order and morality.
71. Клименко А.В., Гафарова С.Ф., Ҳакамлик мухокамаси буйича амалиётдаги юристлар ва низолашувчи тарафлар учун қулланма (Guide for Lawyers and Disputing Parties on Arbitration Court Procedure), Тошкент – 12-13 (2008).
72. For instance, the Agency of Intellectual Property established the Appeal Council for intellectual property disputes. *See*, http://ima.uz/en/disputes/pac.php (accessed 1 July 2017); the same function also can be found in the Uzbek Republican Commodity Exchange. *See* http://www.uzex.uz/ru/publications/2014/4/1/exchange-commissions/23 (accessed 1 July 2017).

1.42. However, the end of the second section of Article 9 also has somewhat unclear wording, reading '... and also other disputes provided by the law.' The very vague wording of the law opened the way for broad interpretation of the arbitrability concept of the Arbitration Law. For instance, in the *Gulnoz Hamedova* case, the claimant asked the arbitration court under the Khoresm Regional CCI to declare the invalidity of her entrepreneurship certificate issued by the local municipality.[73] Interestingly, the arbitration court found its jurisdiction on such administrative matters, decided the case in her favour and found her entrepreneurship certificate invalid. Subsequently, and not surprisingly, the local economic court overturned the decision of the arbitration court.

1.43. Against this backdrop, in its 2012 Plenary Decision, the Higher Economic Court clarified non-arbitrable disputes as follows. First of all, the parties may not contest decisions of governmental authorities, such as refusal to register, uncontested (without acceptance) orders on fines and budget funds at the arbitration court. Second, parties may not bring cases seeking invalidation (in whole or in part) of the acts of state bodies and bodies of self-government, which are illegal, violate the rights and legitimate interests of organisations and citizens.

1.44. In addition to them, the 2012 Plenary Decision also announced the application of administrative disposal and establishment of legal facts as non-arbitrable in Uzbek arbitration courts.[74] The peculiarities of the cases on the 'establishment of legal facts', such as the absence of parties to the dispute, and impossibility of concluding arbitration agreements which give arbitration courts the jurisdiction to resolve the case, put the former out of the scope of the Arbitration Law.[75]

[F] Effect of Arbitration Agreement on Third Parties

1.45. The Arbitration Law has not embraced any direct norm on this issue. It only mentions third parties' interests in one instance in Article 38. Accordingly, if the parties decide to amicably settle the issue during court proceedings, they may conclude an amicable settlement, but it should not violate the rights and legitimate interests of other parties.[76] In arbitral practice, such kind of consent awards used to pose a danger to third parties' lawful interest.

1.46. For instance, sometimes CEOs who are close to their retirement age abuse their position via entering into an agreement with the defendant party, something that infringes the rights of a third party, namely, the company's stock owners. In one of the cases in the Tashkent Region, a joint stock company and local limited liability company

---

73. Ibrohimov A., Hakamlik Sudlari:Tajriba va Amaliyot (Arbitration Courts: Experience and Practice), Huquq va Burch, No. 6, 2012, p. 16.
74. 2012 Plenary Decision, Art. 15(6).
75. Ўзбекистон Республикаси Олий Хўжалик Суди Пленумининг Қарори, Биринчи инстанция судида ишларни куришда Ўзбекистон Республикаси Хўжалик Процессуал Кодексининг Қулланилиши Тўгрисида, (Plenary Decision of Higher Economic Court, On Application of Economic Procedural Code in the Court of First Instance) No. 162, 11 (2007).
76. Arbitration Law, *supra* n. 12, Art. 38(4).

reached a consent award in arbitration and the CEO of the joint stock company agreed to transfer a large amount of money to the another party without the taking necessary approval of another 40% shareholder. According to Judge Isaev of the Tashkent Region Economic Court, the arbitration court made a procedural mistake by not confirming the protection of third parties' interests, but that also, nevertheless, the question arises as to whether the third party who was not a party to the consent award can contest the invalidity of consent award?[77]

1.47. Clarifying the situation on the demand of local economic courts, in its 2012 Plenary Decision, the Higher Economic Court noted that third parties may bring the dispute to the economic courts if in the particular case the arbitration court delivered an award affecting their interests without their participation in arbitral proceedings.[78] In Uzbekistan, plenary decisions usually explain the law on current topical issues. If so, the Higher Economic Court's explanation indicates a likely rise in claims by third parties to the state courts on arbitral awards.

[G] Termination of Arbitration Agreement

1.48. There are a number of grounds for the termination of an arbitration agreement under Uzbek law. First, in case of ad hoc arbitration, if the parties to the arbitration agreement fail to select the sole arbitrator within fifteen days, the dispute will be referred for resolution by the competent state court.[79] Thus, the arbitration agreement terminates. Second, the parties may terminate the arbitration agreement by mutual consent. Third, in case of nullity of the arbitration agreement, there is another ground for termination.[80] And fourth, liqudation of one of the parties or of a legal person may be another reason.

1.49. Furthermore, termination of the arbitration agreement may happen via the setting aside of arbitral awards. Such situations include when the arbitration court dealt with a non-arbitrable matter,[81] the award does not fall within the terms of the submission of arbitration[82] or the award contains decisions on matters beyond the scope of submission to arbitration.[83]

[H] Drafting Arbitration Clauses

1.50. As noted above, arbitration agreements should be in written form. Vigilant parties should determine the range of questions starting from arbitrable questions to the appointment of arbitrators. However, how to design arbitration agreements is no

---

77. Isaev H., Hakamlik Sudi Faoliyatining Ayrim Jihatlari (The Features of Arbitration Court's Activity), Oliy Hojalik Sudi Axborotnomasi, No. 12, 20–21, 2010.
78. 2012 Plenary Decision, Art. 5.
79. Arbitration Law, *supra* n. 12, Art. 15(3).
80. *See* Section 11.02[D] above.
81. *See* Gulnoza Hamedova case at Section 11.02[E].
82. *See* Art. 155.4(2) of Economic Procedural Code.
83. *Ibid.*

easy task – especially for an Uzbek entrepreneurial society that has relatively short experience in this field. Seeing this necessity, the CCI and international organisations have been actively engaged in the preparation of materials, including a model arbitration clause and an agreement for the reference of future potential parties to arbitration.[84]

1.51. One has to note also the pro-arbitration mindset of in-house lawyers: if they find arbitration a more convenient and efficient way than the courts, the number of arbitration agreements increase drastically. In fact, it is reported that a comparatively low arbitration fee and a faster procedure than state courts are the main factors for parties choosing arbitration courts.[85]

§11.03 APPLICABLE LAW

[A] The Law Governing the Arbitration (*Lex Arbitri*)

1.52. The arbitration court resolves disputes on the basis of Uzbek legislation.[86] This means that Uzbek procedural law regulates arbitral proceedings. The answer to how to define the exact procedural law lies in Article 25(4) of the Arbitration Law. Accordingly, the arbitration court may define its own procedure. In such situations, permanent arbitration courts apply their rules of procedure to the ongoing dispute. If they lack the necessary rules of procedure or in case of ad hoc arbitration, they may turn to relevant norms of the Civil Procedural Code or Economic Procedural Code according to the competence of the civil or economic courts on that particular issue.[87]

1.53. On the other hand, the parties may bring their case to the ICAC if they chose foreign law as a *lex arbitri* for their dispute.

[B] Party Autonomy on Choice of Law Issues

1.54. Party autonomy to choose the applicable law for their contract is very widely accepted in the field of arbitration. Not being an exception, Uzbekistan also adhered to this doctrine, with one important limitation: *the Arbitration Law limits the parties'*

---

84. *See* Arbitration Court of CCI, Regulations on Formation and Activity of Arbitration Courts in the Republic of Uzbekistan, Tashkent (2013).
85. Ermatova Sh., Ozbekiston Hakamlik Sudlari:Yangi Tizimdagi Qulayliklar (Arbitration Courts of Uzbekistan: Usability of New System), Oliy Xo'jalik Sudi Axborotnomasi, No. 11, 22–26 (2010).
86. Arbitration Law, *supra* n. 12, Art. 10.
87. As an example, Art. 35.2 of the Arbitration Law states that in the case of arbitration, parties or their representatives may participate; however, it fails to clarify the order of registration of the representative's authority. In such situations, the arbitration court may ask for guidance on the norms on representatives from the Economic Procedural Code (Arts 49–53) or Civil Procedural Code (Arts 50–55) *See* Комментарий к Закону Республики Узбекистан «О третейских судах» (Commentary to the Arbitration Law of Uzbekistan) // Авторы Ш.Асьянов, М.Куликова, А.Исаева, 30–31 (2007).

freedom on the choice of law within the bounds of Uzbek law.[88] Therefore, while deciding the case at hand, arbitrators should take the following legal norms into consideration: the Constitution, Laws, Presidential decrees, Resolutions of the Cabinet of Ministries, normative-legal acts of executive bodies, international agreements of Uzbekistan and other legal acts.

1.55. It seems that the Arbitration Law also applies to international arbitration in Uzbekistan as far as the parties' choice of law is the law of Uzbekistan and all arbitrators are citizens of Uzbekistan. On this point, Article 7 (Civil legislation and international treaties and agreements) of the Civil Code leaves some discretion to foreign parties. It states that if an international treaty or agreement establishes rules other than those stipulated by civil legislation, the rules of the international treaty and agreement shall apply.

[C] No Explicit Choice of Law

1.56. If the legislation of Uzbekistan does not directly regulate the conduct of the parties to the arbitration agreement or by the agreement of the parties to the arbitration, and there is no applicable customary rule in regard of this conduct, the arbitration court will apply legislative norms regulating similar conduct (analogy).[89]

1.57. If the use of analogy is impossible, the arbitration court shall determine the rights and duties of the parties to the arbitration agreement in accordance with the context of legislation and the principles of fairness, reasonableness and justice.[90]

[1] Introduction

Uzbekistan's conflict of laws has not yet codified into one single act. Rather, the Civil Code generally covers the matters related to private international law rules.

[2] Relevant Conflict of Law Rules

1.58. Article 1158 of the Civil Code regulates the determination of the law applicable to civil law relations complicated by a foreign element.[91] According to that norm, the law applicable to civil law relations with the participation of foreign citizens or foreign legal entities or complicated by another foreign element shall be determined on the

---

88. The head of the CCI commented that arbitration activities' 'compliance with the legislation of Uzbekistan allows, more specifically, to regulate the issues relating to dispute resolution and arbitration activity and to account for national peculiarities up to a maximum.' *See* for the short history of Arbitration Law and support of CCI, Interview – Topic Arbitration Courts in Uzbekistan Alisher Shaykov, Chairman of the Chamber of Commerce and Industry of Uzbekistan, http://www.silkpress.com/discovery-bc/archive/2007.9/10_12.php (accessed 1 July 2017).
89. Arbitration Law, *supra* n. 12, Art. 10(3).
90. *Ibid.*, Art. 10(3).
91. Civil Code, Art. 1158.

basis of either the Civil Code and other Uzbek laws, or international treaties and customs recognised, or on the basis of an agreement of the parties.

1.59. An agreement of the parties on an alternative law must be evidently expressed or directly followed from the conditions of a treaty and factual backgrounds considered in their body. If it is impossible to determine an applicable law according to above rules, the law which is closely connected with civil law relations complicated by a foreign element shall apply.

1.60. The above norm opens leeway for the parties to rely on foreign law in arbitral proceedings. For instance, if the dispute at the arbitration court in Uzbekistan concerns a sale and purchase agreement of real estate located in Kazakhstan between two Uzbek parties, then difficulties may potentially arise – something which requires the application of Kazakhstani law by the arbitration court in Uzbekistan. It is assumed that Article 1158 of the Civil Code of Uzbekistan permits the application of the substantive civil law of Kazakhstan in such situations.[92]

[D] The Law Governing the Arbitration Agreement

1.61. Article 10 explicitly states that arbitration courts in the territory of Uzbekistan resolve disputes on the basis of the legislation of Uzbekistan. This is why the problem of the governing law of arbitration agreements with an international legal character has not arisen in Uzbek arbitration courts. On the other hand, as a matter of fact, the CCI has established an ICAC in February 2011, and it is the institution which has the capacity to deal with arbitration agreements that have a transnational legal character.[93]

1.62. In a number of international arbitrations in the ICAC under the umbrella of CCI, one can notice the fact that both foreign and local parties selected the law of Uzbekistan as the applicable law to their arbitration agreement. In one dispute, two Belarusian claimants brought their case on the issue of payment of a delivered product and partially won their case. In another dispute, the ICAC failed to find jurisdiction due to lack of its jurisdiction. Furthermore, currently two international arbitrations against Chinese and Danish parties are currently pending at the ICAC.

1.63. However, the ICAC has been inactive due to the ambiguity of its legal nature and a lack of legal basis for the last several years. It is reported that currently arbitrators of the ICAC under the CCI are waiting for the adoption of a new law on international commercial arbitration by the Uzbek Parliament.

---

92. See Commentary to the Arbitration Law of Uzbekistan, *supra* n. 87, 29.
93. See Отахонов Ф., Организационно-правовые меры по развития международного коммерческого арбитража в Узбекистане (Organisational-legal Measures on Development of International Commercial Arbitration in Uzbekistan) website CIS Arbitration Forum: Russia- and CIS-related International Dispute Resolution, http://cisarbitration.com/2014/02/14/арбитраж-в-узбекистане/ (accessed 1 July 2017).

§11.04 THE ARBITRATORS

[A] Appointment of Arbitrators

[1] Appointment of Arbitrators under Municipal Law

1.64. Article 15 of the Arbitration Law lays down the appointment procedure of arbitrators for both permanent and ad hoc arbitration courts. Accordingly, in a permanent arbitration court, arbitrators are selected from the roster of arbitrators.

1.65. If a party fails to appoint the arbitrator(s) within fifteen days from the moment of receiving the request from the other party to the arbitration agreement, the parties to the arbitration agreement do not agree on the choice of the arbitrator (if a dispute is to be resolved by the sole arbitrator) or if two arbitrators fail to agree on the third arbitrator within 15 days from the moment of their election, then, upon the request of one party, the chairman of the permanent arbitration court shall appoint (an) arbitrator(s).[94]

1.66. In cases of ad hoc arbitration, if the above-mentioned three events occur, and the parties fail to agree on the appointment of the arbitrator(s), the arbitration agreement is then terminated.[95]

[2] Appointment under Institutional Rules

1.67. Institutional rules set more definite rules of appointment compared to municipal laws. For instance, according to Article 21 of the CCI Regulation, if the parties to the arbitration agreement have not agreed to submit the dispute to the sole arbitrator, then the arbitration court will function through a three-arbitrator panel. In that case, the secretary of the permanent arbitration court contacts the appointed arbitrators on the terms of their consent and gets their written consent to the appointment. Once the appointed arbitrator has signed the written consent, the president or vice-president of the permanent arbitration court issues orders on the composition of the arbitral tribunal.[96]

[B] Qualifications of Arbitrators

1.68. Pursuant to the Arbitration Law, only a citizen of Uzbekistan who is more than 25 years old can become an arbitrator.[97]

---

94. Arbitration Law, *supra* n. 12, Art. 15(2).
95. *Ibid.*, Art. 15(3).
96. Регламент Третейского суда при Торгово-промышленной палате Республики Узбекистан (Regulation on Arbitration Court at Chamber of Commerce and Industry of Uzbekistan), утверждено Протокол Исполнительного комитета Торгово-промышленной палаты Республики Узбекистан № 43 от 8 октября 2007 года, http://chamber.uz/ru/page/4857 (accessed 1 July 2017).
97. Arbitration Law, *supra* n. 12, Art. 14(1).

1.69. The educational background of potential candidates for the role of arbitrator merits attention. A sole arbitrator must have a higher education in law. In the case of a panel of arbitrators, at least the chairman of the panel must have a law degree.[98]

1.70. Parties to the arbitration agreement or the permanent arbitration court may establish other requirements for the qualification of the arbitrator.[99] For instance, Uzbek law does not require candidates to have work experience. It leaves that issue to the parties and rules of the permanent arbitration courts.

[C] Challenges and Replacement of Arbitrators

[1] Challenges under Municipal Law and Institutional Rules

1.71. Article 17 states that, if a procedure governing the challenge of an arbitrator is not defined by the rules of the permanent arbitration court or is not established by the parties to the arbitral proceedings, the written request on the challenge of the arbitrator should be submitted by the party to the arbitral proceedings to an arbitral panel.[100] If the challenged arbitrator does not withdraw himself or the other party in the arbitral proceedings does not agree with the challenge of the arbitrator, the issue of the challenge of the arbitrator is considered by other arbitrators that form the panel of the arbitration court.

1.72. In cases where the numbers of votes for and against the challenge are equal, the challenged arbitrator is considered to be withdrawn.[101]

1.73. In the *KAPITALBANK v. Kabir-Invest-Lider* case, the claimant filed a claim for recovery of the balance of a loan from the borrower through foreclosure of a mortgaged property.[102] While the claimant appointed his arbitrator on time, the defendant failed to do so and according to Article 15 of the Arbitration Law, the President of the Permanent Court under the CCI then appointed the claimant's arbitrator as a sole arbitrator. In turn, the representative of the respondent filed an application expressing the defendant's doubts about the impartiality of the sole arbitrator. The representative of the claimant objected to the removal of the respondent, stating that it was a way of delaying the process of the dispute. Eventually, the sole arbitrator dismissed the claims on the challenge of himself.

---

98. *Ibid.*, Art. 14(2).
99. *Ibid.*, Art. 14(3).
100. The Commentary on this norm mentions an important weakness of the Arbitration Law, which failed to articulate the exact period of request on challenge of the arbitrator to the panel. Although many permanent arbitration courts have their own sophisticated regulations, this is not the case for ad hoc arbitrations. See Commentary to the Arbitration Law of Uzbekistan, *supra* n. 87, 47.
101. *See* Arbitration Law, *supra* n. 12, Art. 17(5).
102. *KAPITALBANK v. Kabir-Invest-Lider*, Case № 2015/01-001, 11 March 2015. Arbitration Court at CCI.

[D] Compensation of Arbitrators

1.74. Pursuant to Article 21 of Arbitration Law, arbitrator fees are defined in accordance with the price of the claim, complexity of the dispute, time spent by the arbitrator on arbitral proceedings and other circumstances affecting the size of the fee.[103] In the permanent arbitration courts, the arbitrator fees are defined by the arbitration court in accordance with the scale of arbitrators' fees provided by the rules of the permanent arbitration court.[104] In cases of deferral of payment of compensation by the parties, the entity that formed the arbitration court may claim for the recovery of these costs from the corresponding party to the arbitral proceedings in a competent state court.[105]

1.75. In ad hoc arbitration courts, the arbitrator fees are defined in accordance with the agreement of the parties to the arbitral proceedings and the arbitration court, taking into account the provisions stipulated in the first part of this Article. Arbitrator fees are subject to taxation.[106]

§11.05 JURISDICTION OF THE ARBITRAL TRIBUNAL

[A] Arbitrators' Determination of Their Jurisdiction

1.76. Pursuant to Article 24 of the Arbitration Law, the arbitration court independently decides on the existence or absence of its competence to resolve a dispute referred to it for resolution, including cases when one of the parties to the arbitral proceedings objects to the arbitral proceedings, motivating its objection by the absence or invalidity of the arbitration agreement.[107]

1.77. The party to arbitral proceedings has the right to declare that the arbitration court acted ultra vires (in excess of its competence) in the following two instances. The first instance may happen if the issue of the arbitral proceedings fails to be a subject to arbitral proceedings in accordance with the arbitration agreement. In the second case, the party may protest if the issue of the arbitral proceedings fails to be subject to arbitral proceedings according to the law or the rules of the permanent arbitration court.[108]

---

103. *See* Arbitration Law, *supra* n. 12, Art. 21(1).
104. *See* for the details of compensation of arbitration the example of the CCI Regulation on Fees, Expenses and Costs. Accordingly, the lowest arbitration fee is set at 0.5% of the amount of the claim, but no less than two times the minimum wage. Arbitrators are paid from the arbitration fee according to the specific rules of the regulation in Art. 11(2). The Regulation in the Russian language is available at http://chamber.uz/en/page/4857 (accessed 1 July 2017).
105. 2012 Plenary Decision, Art. 5(1)(2).
106. Arbitration Law, *supra* n. 12, Art. 21; Мухамедбаев А., Гонорар и налоги третейского судьи (Fee and Taxes of Arbitrators), http://www.norma.uz/nashi_obzori/gonorar_i_nalogi_tretey skogo_sudi (accessed 1 July 2017).
107. Arbitration Law, *supra* n. 12, Art. 24(1).
108. *Ibid.*, Art. 24(3).

[B] Court Review of Arbitrators' Jurisdiction

1.78. The competent economic and civil courts may review the jurisdiction of the arbitration courts and annul arbitral awards if the dispute is not covered by the arbitration agreement, the arbitral award is rendered not in accordance with its conditions or the arbitral award went outside the scope of the arbitration agreement.[109]

1.79. A typical case here is where the parties to an arbitration agreement decide to submit 'disputes on performance of the contract' to arbitration; however, if the arbitration court focuses on the invalidity of the contract, then such an arbitral award would be annulled by the state court. This is because the parties only give the arbitration the power to check on the performance of the contract itself, not on invalidity issues.

1.80. In arbitral practice, arbitrators may exceed their power by going outside the scope of the arbitration agreement. As an example, in the *Praff Singer v. Latus Business* case (2009), a dispute arose from the transfer of plastic barriers which was not located in the area of a lease contract. In other words, the dispute erupted on the issue that had nothing to do with the lease contract. Because, the lease contract did not cover plastic barriers and left it outside the leasing area. However, the Tashkent city CCI arbitration court found its jurisdiction and decided the case. The award was subsequently set aside by the Tashkent city economic court.[110]

[C] Institutional Rules

1.81. Article 13 of the Regulation of Arbitration Court under the CCI establishes and clarifies the jurisdiction of the arbitration court. Accordingly, duly appointed arbitrators perform their functions according to the Regulation. Accordingly, the arbitration court issues rulings with respect to matters not related to the substance of the disputes, makes a decision after an examination of the facts of the dispute, and renders awards, clarifies the content of the award without altering its content, corrects typographical and arithmetical errors.[111]

§11.06 THE PROCEDURE BEFORE THE ARBITRAL TRIBUNAL

[A] Introduction

1.82. In the conduct of proceedings, the Arbitration Law again takes quite a different path than the UNCITRAL Model Law approach and imitates it more on domestic Civil

---

109. *See* Art. 155.4 of Economic Procedural Code. Art. 309.7 of Civil Procedural Code also generally follows the same provisions.
110. *See* Asqarov S., Hakamlik Bitimining Ahamiyati (Significance of Arbitration Agreement), Oliy Xo'jalik Sudi Axborotnomasi, No. 11, 43–45 (2011).
111. *See* Regulation on Arbitration Court at CCI, *supra* n. 96.

and Economic Procedural Codes norms. Subsequently, several important points, rules with respect to the appointment of experts were left blank in the Arbitration Law.

[B] General Principles of Municipal Judicial Procedure

1.83. The civil and economic courts deal with cases based on the following general principles of law: right to judicial protection,[112] implementation of justice only by a court and on the basis of the equality of citizens before the law and court,[113] independence of judges and their subordination only to the law,[114] competitiveness and equality of the parties[115] and the openness of judicial proceedings.[116]

[C] General Principles of Arbitral Procedure

1.84. Arbitration courts have to follow the following principles while carrying out their activities such as legality, independence, confidentiality of information of the arbitral proceedings and of arbitrators, competitiveness and equality of the parties of arbitral proceedings.[117]

1.85. Some authors have mentioned the absence of sanctions against breach of confidentiality principles either by parties or arbitration court members.[118] It is explained that arbitration court members may pay a penalty through the loss of their reputation in the arbitration industry. In addition to that, state courts are still considering the request of winning parties for the compulsory execution of arbitral awards, under the general and open procedure which should be reformed.[119]

[D] Commencing the Arbitral Proceedings

1.86. Before commencing arbitral proceedings, the parties have to define the rules of the arbitral procedure. Article 25 of the Arbitration Law says that if particular rules have not been agreed by the parties to the arbitral proceedings, and are not defined by the rules of the permanent arbitration court and the Arbitration Law, the arbitration court defines the rules of the arbitral proceedings.[120] The above rule is equally applicable when the parties have failed to define the place of arbitral proceedings.[121]

---

112. Civil Procedural Code, Art. 1.
113. *Ibid.*, Art. 6.
114. *Ibid.*, Art. 7.
115. *Ibid.*, Art. 8.
116. *Ibid.*, Art. 10.
117. Arbitration Law, *supra* n. 14, Art. 4.
118. Отахонов Ф., Правовые Вопросы Организации и Деятельности Третейских Судов (Legal Issues on Organizing and Activity of Arbitration Courts), http://chamber.uz/en/page/4857 (accessed 1 July 2017).
119. *Ibid.*, 6–7.
120. Arbitration Law, *supra* n. 12, Art. 25(4).
121. *Ibid.*, Art. 26(2).

Unless the parties to the arbitral proceedings have not agreed otherwise, arbitral proceedings are conducted in the state language, Uzbek.[122]

[E] Conduct of Arbitration

[1] Written Submissions

1.87. Under the Arbitration Law, the claimant commences the arbitral procedure by submitting the claim in written form with the attachment of necessary documents.[123] The claimant may also mention the name(s) of arbitrator(s) if the parties had already decided upon the composition of the arbitration in their arbitration agreement.

1.88. Arbitrator(s) should confirm whether the claimant also served the copy of the statement of claim to the respondent. The response to the statement of claim is presented to the claimant and to the arbitration court in accordance with the order and the time period provided by the rules of the arbitral proceedings.[124]

1.89. If the time limit for presenting a response to the statement of claim is not defined by the rules of the arbitral proceedings, the specified response is presented prior to the beginning of the arbitral session.[125] The parties to the arbitral proceedings have the right to change the claim requirements or objections to the claim during arbitral proceedings.[126] The Arbitration Law also permits the respondent to file a counterclaim for its consideration together with the initial claim.[127]

[2] Evidence

1.90. Each party to arbitral proceedings should prove the existence of the circumstances on which they substantiate their claims and objections to these claims.[128] The arbitration court may, if it considers the evidence presented to be insufficient, call upon the parties to produce additional evidence.[129] The Arbitration Law does not identify the

---

122. *Ibid.*, Art. 27(1).
123. *See* for the detail list of documents, *ibid.*, Art. 29.
124. *Ibid.*, Art. 30(2).
125. *Ibid.*, Art. 30(3).
126. *Ibid.*, Art. 30(4).
127. *Ibid.*, Art. 31.
128. In one arbitration case under the CCI rules, a foreign entity in Uzbekistan brought a case against a local company arguing that it had supplied low-quality goods. The defendant challenged the action, with reference to international standards, according to which for each laboratory sample for routine tests of the goods the claimant should take the laboratory sample of each product, including the name and designation of the material, place and date. However, the claimant could not submit such documents and thus failed to prove to the arbitration court his claims about the quality of goods. *See* Отахонов Ф., ВИНОВЕН? ДОКАЖИ! (Guilty?Prove!) http://www.norma.uz/nashi_obzori/ne_vinoven_dokaji (accessed 1 July 2017).
129. Arbitration Law, *supra* n. 12, Art. 33.

list of evidence, although the arbitrators can invite the parties to produce further evidence.[130]

1.91. It is important to note that under Uzbek law, the arbitration court is not entitled to request competent court assistance in taking evidence.[131] This may discourage potential parties to the dispute from bringing their cases to arbitration. In order to overcome this difficulty, Article 35 of the draft law on international commercial arbitration determines court assistance on evidence taking.[132]

[3]   Witness and Experts Testimony

1.92. Arbitration courts may also rely on expert opinion.[133] Arbitration expenses include the sum payable to experts and borne by witnesses.[134] But, in practice, parties hardly ever rely on witness and expert testimonies during arbitral proceedings.

[F]   Hearings

1.93. Notwithstanding the absence of mandatory requirements regarding the structure of hearings, the Arbitration Law guarantees the parties' equal opportunity to state their position and to protect their rights and interests during hearings. The arbitration court should properly notify parties of the time and place of the session of arbitration. Article 35 provides that unless the parties to the arbitral proceedings have not agreed otherwise, arbitral proceedings are carried out with the participation of the parties to arbitral proceedings or their representatives in a private meeting. The Arbitration Law permits arbitration courts to continue proceedings and to render decisions in the case of non-delivery of documents or absence of one party without a proper excuse.[135]

§11.07   THE ARBITRAL AWARD

[A]   Introduction

1.94. The Arbitration Law sets forth that the award shall be made in writing and shall be signed by the arbitrator(s) including the dissenting arbitrator. Furthermore, the Arbitration Law requires arbitrators to state the reasons upon which it is based in the award, its date and the place of arbitration as determined in accordance with Article 39.

---

130. *Ibid.*, Art. 33.
131. *See* 2013 Plenary Decision, Art. 16(8).
132. Проект Закона Республики Узбекистан 'О международном коммерческом арбитраже' (The draft of the Law 'On international commercial arbitration') Материалы Международных научно-практических конференций на тему 'Международный коммерческий арбитраж в контексте судебно-правовой реформы' 28 октября 2009 Г. –Т.: 'Chashma Print, 2010.- С.309–310.
133. Arbitration Law, *supra* n. 12, Art. 34(1).
134. *Ibid.*, Art. 20.
135. *Ibid.*, Art. 37.

[B] Deliberation and Voting

1.95. The arbitration court renders its decision by a majority of votes of all its members. If the arbitration court declares only the conclusion of the award, in such a case, a reasoned part of the award should be sent to the parties within no more than ten days.[136] Questions of procedure for deliberation and voting are not settled in the Arbitration Law sufficiently. Therefore, with the consent of parties, it is presumed that the presiding arbitrator or sole arbitrator may decide its order or may handle it according to particular institutional rules.

1.96. Regarding the form, the award shall be made in writing and shall be signed by all arbitrator(s) including the arbitrator with dissenting opinions. To be valid, an award must comprise a decision by the arbitration court specifying either satisfaction or refusal to satisfy each declared claim by parties. Moreover, the arbitration court has to show the amount of arbitration costs, allocation of that cost between parties and the time of enforcement in the final part of the award.[137]

[C] Different Kinds of Awards

1.97. The Arbitration Law provides for various types of awards. First of all, upon a party's request to the arbitration court, they may amicably settle the dispute during the proceedings and if that settlement does not infringe upon the rights of third parties, the arbitration court has to render the award stating the content of settlement in it.[138] The Higher Economic Court directs the lower courts which issue the writ of execution to approve the settlement agreement concluded by the parties during the execution process.[139]

1.98. Second, as set out in section 32(1) of the Arbitration Law, interim measures are permitted in order to preserve the enforcement of a pending arbitration outcome. Only state courts have the power to issue an interim order. In order to get an interim order, the party has to prove that the dispute has been submitted to the arbitration court. However, if the arbitration court eventually refuses to satisfy the claims, then the competent state court annuls the interim order.

1.99. Finally, the failure of an arbitration court to mention particular claims may force one of the parties to ask the arbitration court to issue an additional award within ten days of receiving the final award.[140]

---

136. *Ibid.*, Art. 38(2).
137. *Ibid.*, Art. 39(2).
138. *Ibid.*, Art. 38(4).
139. 2012 Plenary Decision, Art. 24(5).
140. Arbitration Law, *supra* n. 12, Art. 40(1).

[D] Interest and Costs

1.100. A question concerning costs and fees of arbitration arises in the fourth part of the Arbitration Law. It has no determination on interest, but one can find extensive rules on the fixing of costs and arbitration fees.[141] At the onset of proceedings, the arbitration court may demand a deposit in order to cover some part of the arbitration's expenses. Failure to pay the deposit amount within ten days of the claim means that the arbitration court will drop the case.[142]

1.101. Furthermore, the price of the claim, complexity of the dispute, time spent by arbitrators on arbitral proceedings and other circumstances affect the size of the arbitrators' remuneration.[143] The fee of the arbitrator is subject to taxation. Under Article 22, unless the parties come to an agreement on costs, the arbitration court shall determine the allocation of costs between parties in the award.[144]

1.102. Actually, in addition to the fast and confidential resolution of disputes by arbitration, one of the driving forces behind the drastic increase of alternative dispute resolution in Uzbekistan is the comparatively low level of arbitration fees. For instance, under the CCI Rules of Arbitration Fees parties have to pay 0.5% of the amount of the claim, but not lower than two times the lowest wage.[145] That price is almost ten times lower than the fees of the civil courts and two times lower than the economic courts of the country. Furthermore, the parties may receive a discount from the CCI depending on how many arbitrators are taking part in the process and whether parties are members of CCI.[146]

[E] Effects of the Award

[1] Execution

1.103. The award of the arbitration court shall be executed on a voluntary basis in accordance with the order and within the time limit that is established in this award. If the arbitration court fails to specify an execution date, then the award will be subject to immediate execution.[147] Should one party fail to honour the award, the winning party has to file an application for a writ of execution to the competent courts within six months after the end of the voluntary execution time period.[148]

---

141. For the costs of arbitration, see ibid., Art. 20.
142. Ibid., Art. 23.
143. Ibid., Art. 21(1).
144. Ibid., Art. 22.
145. See Art. 4, CCI Regulation on Fees, Expenses and Costs.
146. Ibid., Art. 8.
147. Arbitration Law, Art. 49(2).
148. Compulsory enforcement of the decision of the arbitration court is carried out in accordance with the Law 'On Execution of the Judicial Decisions and the Decisions of Other Organs' on the basis of the order of the competent court. See Закон Республики Узбекистан 'Об исполнении судебных актов и актов иных органов', № 258-II, Ведомости Олий Мажлиса Республики

1.104. The winning party must submit the following documents via a written request to the competent court:

a) Certified copy of the arbitral award.
b) Signed copy of the award by the chairman of the permanent arbitration court; the signature of the arbitrator in ad hoc arbitration should be certified by the notary.
c) Copy of the arbitration agreement.
d) The documents confirming payment of a state tax and also confirming the delivery of a copy of the statement to other participants in the arbitral proceedings.[149]

[2] Res Judicata and Lis Pendens

1.105. The Arbitration Law establishes the Res Judicata principle as one of the grounds for the termination of arbitral proceedings in Article 44. Accordingly, the economic court leaves a statement of claim without consideration in terms of whether there has been a final award which entered into force via an arbitration court.[150] Second, the *lis pendens* principle is established under Article 86 of Economic Procedural Code. The economic court refuses to consider a statement of claim if it establishes that there is an ongoing dispute between the same persons, on the same subject matter and on the same grounds under consideration by an arbitration court.[151]

[F] Correction and Interpretation of the Award

1.106. Under Articles 41 and 42, the arbitration court may make an exception to their '*functus officio*' in only in two instances: to correct typographical, arithmetical errors and to clarify any ambiguity in the award. On the first question, the Arbitration Law confers the arbitration court the power to correct its award, upon application of one of the parties to the dispute within ten days of receipt of the arbitral award. The arbitration court shall clarify the award without altering its content in the same amount of time. Interestingly enough, Uzbek law only permits the issuing of a ruling to clarify the award that will be part of the arbitral award, but not to deny the clarification of the award.[152]

1.107. Second, the arbitration court may, pursuant to an application of either party, correct typographical and arithmetical errors.[153] On this point, the question arises as to whether the arbitration court has the power correct on its own initiative. Furthermore,

---

Узбекистан, 2001, № 9-10, 169, http://www.lex.uz/pages/GetAct.aspx?lact_id = 13896 (accessed 1 July 2017).
149. *See* Art. 155.2(3) of Economic Procedural Code.
150. *Ibid.*, Art. 86.
151. *Ibid.*, Art. 117.
152. Arbitration Law, *supra* n. 12, Art. 41.
153. *Ibid.*, Art. 42.

many jurisdictions also use the word 'clerical' in line with 'typographical and arithmetical errors' or alone in order to confer a power to the arbitration court to correct, for example, a slip of the pen or something of that kind. How Uzbek arbitrators will handle such situations in the future is not yet clear. Finally, Uzbek legislators do not seem to have granted arbitration courts the power to re-examine disputes in view of newly discovered circumstances.

§11.08 SETTING ASIDE THE AWARD

[A] Introduction

1.108. Uzbek legislators have left some space for the judicial control of arbitral awards. The parties to the arbitral proceedings may ask for recourse to the competent court within thirty days after the receipt of the arbitral award. It should be noted that the award is not enforceable until the completion of the competent court's proceedings on this matter.[154] Notwithstanding such norms, the Arbitration Law clearly provides that the competent court has no power to investigate the circumstances established by the arbitration court, or to reconsider the arbitration court's decision on the substantive merits of the case.[155] Statistics show an astonishingly high rate of voluntary executions of arbitral awards by parties. For instance, if the arbitration courts in Uzbekistan rendered almost 6,000 awards during 2014, the parties filed only thirty-six cases to the economic courts to set aside the award, while twenty-one awards were annulled by the courts.[156]

[B] Challengeable Awards

[1] Grounds for Challenging the Award

1.109. The Arbitration Law enumerates several grounds for challenging the award. Accordingly, an arbitral award may be set aside by the court in the seat of arbitration only if:

(1) the party making the application to set aside furnishes proof that:
   a) The arbitration agreement is invalid under the law of Uzbekistan.
   b) The award deals with a dispute not contemplated by or not falling within the terms of the submission to arbitration, or contains decisions on matters beyond the scope of the submission to arbitration, provided that, if the decisions on matters submitted to arbitration can be separated from those not so submitted, only that part of the award which contains decisions on matters not submitted to arbitration may be set aside.

---

154. *Ibid.*, Art. 46.
155. *Ibid.*, Art. 47(1).
156. *See* the Archive of Higher Economic Court, http://oxs.uz/oliy-hzhalik-sudi-ahborotnomasi-aida.html (accessed 1 July 2017).

c) The arbitration court failed to observe the law of Uzbekistan during arbitral proceedings.
   d) The composition of the arbitration court or the arbitral procedure is not in accordance with the requirements of the Uzbek laws.
   e) The arbitration court failed to give an opportunity for one of the parties to present their case, or proper notice of the election (appointment) of arbitrators or of the time and place of the arbitral proceedings.
(2) the court finds that:
   a) The subject matter is not arbitrable under Uzbek law.[157]

1.110. Although the relevant norm on the grounds for challenging the award under the Arbitration Law often refers to other norms in the very Law and fails to copy the exact form from the UNCITRAL Model Law, in essence it would be not an exaggeration for one to argue that Uzbek law is quite compatible with the UNCITRAL Model Law. The only one noticeable difference is that, for unknown reasons, Uzbek lawmakers decided not to mention the public policy issue as one of the grounds for challenge by the court.

1.111. According to statistical data, between January and December of 2014 parties challenged thirty-nine cases in state courts out of which the competent state courts set aside thirteen awards mainly due to either awards having contained decisions on matters beyond the scope of the submission to arbitration or one of the parties not having given proper notice of arbitration proceedings.[158] It is important to note that the decisions delivered by arbitration courts under the CCI have never been set aside by state courts.

1.112. Judicial practice shows that sometimes state courts exceed their power and reconsider the arbitration court's decision on the substantive merits of the case. In the *Muborak gazni qayta ishlash zavodi v. Signal* case, the claimant challenged the arbitral award on the grounds of a) and d) above.[159] A Court of First Instance set aside the award because the defendant had failed to prove the fact that he had sent a request to the claimant to appoint the arbitrator(s). However, the court also reviewed the invalidity of the main agreement and touched upon the surcharge that the claimant paid to the defendant. Correcting the decision, a court of cassation upheld the judgment of the Court of First Instance on procedural irregularities. However, it annulled the relevant parts of latter's decision on the substantive part of arbitral award.[160]

---

157. Arbitration Law, *supra* n. 12, Art. 47.
158. Ўзбекистон Савдо-саноат палатаси, Хакамлик судининг хал қилув қарорини бекор қилиш тўғрисидаги аризалар бўйича маълумот, (Information on Cases of Setting Aside the Arbitral Awards) Ойлик статистик хисобот (2015).
159. Ibragimov A., Hakamlik Sudining Hal Qiluv Qarorini Bekor Qilish Bilan Bog'liq Ishlarni Xo'jalik Sudlarida Ko'rishning O'ziga Xos Xususiyatlari (The Features of Hearing the Cases regarding Termination of Arbitration Court's Awards in Economic Courts), Oliy Xo'jalik Sudi Axborotnomasi, No. 2, 17–19 (2013).
160. *Ibid.*

1.113. Furthermore, if the arbitral award is annulled, either in full or in part, due to the invalidity of the arbitral agreement, or because it is made in respect of a dispute not contemplated by or not falling within the terms of the arbitral agreement, or contains decisions on matters beyond the scope of the arbitral agreement, the relevant dispute shall not be subject to further examination by the arbitration court.[161]

§11.09 RECOGNITION AND ENFORCEMENT OF THE ARBITRAL AWARD

[A] Enforcement of Domestic Awards

[1] Enforcement Domestically

1.114. The parties are expected to voluntarily execute the arbitration court's decision in accordance with the order and within the time limit established in this decision. If the date of performance is not established in the decision of the arbitration court, it is subject to immediate execution.[162]

1.115. If the arbitration court's decision is not executed voluntarily within the time limit established by the decision of the arbitration court, it is subject to compulsory enforcement.[163] It is worth noting fact that in 2012 the Higher Economic Court adopted a plenary decision on several legal issues of enforcement of arbitration court decisions by economic courts.[164] Consequently, the Plenary Decision is expected to work for the further development of arbitration activity in Uzbekistan.

[2] Enforcement Abroad

1.116. A foreign legal entity or natural person stands as a plaintiff in the majority of cases and therefore, enforcement of domestic arbitral awards has not been problematic in Uzbekistan (at least the authors are not aware of such disputes in CCI arbitration courts). This is because Uzbekistan is a net capital importer country and this is thus not a surprising tendency. If such disputes arise, it will be decided according to the New York Convention and other international treaties that Uzbekistan has signed.

[B] Enforcement of Foreign Arbitral Awards

1.117. The authors' observations suggest that up until now, the majority of arbitral awards coming for recognition and enforcement to Uzbek courts originate from CIS

---

161. Arbitration Law, *supra* n. 12, Art. 48.
162. *Ibid.*, Art. 49.
163. It is fair to say that the compulsory enforcement mechanism is working quite effectively in Uzbekistan. Sometimes, courts grant a writ of execution even after passing the time limit for such claim. *See* Djuraev O., Hakamlik Sudining Hal Qiluv Qarorini Majburiy Ijro Etish Uchun Ijro Varaqasi Berish To'g'risidagi Ishlarni Xo'jalik Sudlarida Ko'rishning O'ziga Xos Xususiyatlari (The Features of Hearing the Cases regarding Issuing Writ of Compulsory Enforcement of Arbitral Awards in Economic Courts), Oliy Hojalik Sudi Axborotnomasi, No. 8, 26–29 (2012).
164. *See* 2012 Plenary Decision.

countries, such as the arbitral institutions of Russia and Ukraine. This may be due, first of all, to the strong economic ties with CIS countries rather than Western Europe, America and Asia. Second, courts in CIS countries give significant importance to the Minsk and Kiev Conventions, which facilitate smooth enforcement of dispute resolution in the region.[165] Finally, bilateral agreements on mutual legal assistance in trade, civil and family law matters with neighbouring countries significantly eases the enforcement of foreign arbitral awards.[166]

1.118. On the other hand, notwithstanding the fact that there are some awards, although rare, that came from Germany, France and the United Kingdom,[167] the absence of agreements on mutual legal assistance makes Uzbek courts hesitant to actively enforce arbitral awards from western European countries.

[1] Introduction to Recognition and Enforcement

1.119. According to the 2013 Plenary Decision, the Economic Courts handle the enforcement of foreign arbitral awards in Uzbekistan.[168]

1.120. Regarding recognition and enforcement of foreign awards, Uzbekistan has signed and ratified several international conventions, such as the New York Convention and Kiev Agreement. Uzbekistan also strongly relies on the principle of reciprocity through bilateral agreements on legal assistance.[169] For instance, to date Uzbekistan

---

165. The following example also vividly shows how inter-regional cooperation has the lion's share in enforcement of foreign court and arbitral decisions in Uzbek courts. From 1st January of 2008 until 31st December of that year, Uzbek courts received a total of 676 requests from the following foreign countries' courts and arbitrations on legal assistance and enforcement of decisions and awards: Russia-709, Ukraine-169, Belarus-11, Turkmenistan-8, Azarbaican-2, Armenia-1, Litva-1 and others. See Архив Министерства юстиции Республики Узбекистан за 2008 (Archive of Ministry of Justice for 2008); Сулейменова А.М., Халкаро Хусусий Хукукда Чет Эл Давлатлари Суд Карорларининг Ижро Этилиши (Enforcement of Foreign Court Decisions in International Private Law) Тошкент (2010).
166. Uzbekistan has concluded bilateral agreements on mutual legal assistance so far with Georgia, Russia, China, Turkey, Kazakhstan, Latvia, Azerbaijan, Ukraine and Turkmenistan. *Ibid.*
167. For example, in the *Aus-Trade GMBH v. Tashkent Tractor Factory* case (*Aus-Trade GMBH v. Tashkent Tractor Factory*, Case No. 10-1312/7922, 7 August 2013), the applicant asked the Tashkent city Economic Court to give a writ of execution in the amount of more than USD 15 million against the debt of the Tashkent Tractor Factory. The Court refused to grant a writ of execution because the arbitration in Frankfurt in Maine lacked the capacity to decide on the issue. The parties selected the law of Germany and arbitration in Frankfurt at the Maine arbitral institution; however, in a separate agreement they chose Uzbek law and Uzbek arbitration as proper law and arbitral institutions, respectively. Since the current dispute arose based on the latter agreement, the Uzbek court refused to recognise the award.
168. Article 1, 2013 Plenary Decision.
169. *See* Lee T., Ok V., Makhmudov M., *Key Things to Know: Arbitration in Uzbekistan*, Global Arbitration Review: The European, Middle Eastern and African Arbitration Review, Legal Max Law Firm (2013).

has signed such bilateral treaties with China, Turkey, Latvia, Lithuania, the Czech Republic, the Republic of Korea and Bulgaria.[170]

1.121. Though many have noted the difficulty in recognition and enforcement of foreign awards in Uzbekistan against state-owned enterprises,[171] a closer look at the issue may tell a different story. One brave move towards becoming a global arbitration-friendly jurisdiction was the Higher Economic Court's resolution regarding the recognition and enforcement of foreign arbitral awards in 2013 where it gave thorough explanations to the lower courts on how to recognise and enforce foreign arbitral awards consistently according to the New York Convention.[172] Taking into account the fact that state entities act as independent legal entities under their own capacity, the issue of sovereign immunity would not arise in domestic court proceedings.

[2] Grounds for Refusing Recognition and Enforcement

1.122. The 2013 Plenary Decision of the Higher Economic Court states that recognition and enforcement of the foreign arbitral award may be refused only based on Article 5 of the New York Convention.[173] It further states that the courts could refuse to recognise and enforce foreign arbitral awards only upon the submission of proven facts under the first section of Article 5 of that convention. However, courts may refuse to recognise and enforce arbitral awards under the second section of Article 5 upon submission of any evidence.[174]

1.123. Furthermore, Uzbek courts do not recognise and enforce procedural orders (appointment of expertise, hearing of parties, interrogation of witnesses, expert and other parties to hearing) of foreign arbitrations. If such an order is submitted, the courts should then refuse to accept it for consideration according to Article 117(1) of the Economic Procedural Code.[175] The time limit for accepting awards for recognition and enforcement is three years.[176]

1.124. Since the Uzbek courts have only started to summarise the trends of applications for recognition and enforcement of arbitral awards (2007), the authors have little data about real and long-term trends. For instance, between 2007 and 2011, the Uzbek courts handled fifty cases (including foreign court decisions and arbitral awards), out

---

170. For the complete list of international agreements on legal assistance and legal relations in civil, family and criminal matters, signed by Uzbekistan see http://www.mfa.uz/en/cooperation/legalrelations/ (accessed 1 July 2017).
171. See *Uzbekistan Mining Laws and Regulations Handbook*, International Business Publications, 159 (2013).
172. *See* the 2013 Plenary Decision.
173. *Ibid.*, Art. 14(2).
174. *Ibid.*
175. *Ibid.*, Art. 16(8).
176. *See* Civil Procedural Code, Art. 391 (Enforcement of Foreign Court Judgments and Arbitral Awards).

of which Uzbek courts gave a writ of execution in forty-four cases, refused five cases and finalised one case.[177]

1.125. A recent review of the judicial practice by the Higher Economic Court suggests that the Uzbek economic courts still do not possess a unified methodology for considering such cases.[178] First of all, local courts are sometimes guilty of procedural irregularities when they send applications directly for enforcement without taking appropriate steps for recognition.[179] Second, in the *Sigmafarm v. Farma-Service* case, the defendant failed to pay the due payment on time and the claimant got a favourable award from international commercial arbitration under the aegis of the Ukrainian Chamber of Commerce and Industry. When the Ukrainian party asked the Uzbek court to give a writ of execution, the Fergana Region Economic Court over-stepped its mandate by changing the amount of compensation.[180]

1.126. Also, under substantively similar facts, in the *Farmak v. Lahisam* case, the economic court of Tashkent City recognised the arbitral award and issued a writ of execution notwithstanding the fact that the parties had changed the contract, making the Kiev city economic court an appropriate place for dispute resolution.[181]

[a]   *Public Policy*

1.127. Pursuant to Article 14.2 of its Plenary Decision, the Higher Economic Court guides the lower courts not to recognise and enforce awards which are incompatible with the public policy of Uzbekistan according to Article V of the New York Convention.[182] However, the above provision is very general, lacking clear-cut scope of issues and there are no reported cases concerning the application of that doctrine.

1.128. On the other hand, in the famous *Romak v. Uzdon*, of 2 October 2000, Tashkent City Economic Court decided to return the application for recognition and enforcement of the GAFTA Award of the claimant on two grounds. The investment arbitration decision summarises the domestic flow of procedure as follows:

1.129. First, the application for recognition and enforcement of the GAFTA Award in Uzbekistan did not fulfil the requirements of Article IV of the New York Convention, which requires that the party applying for recognition and enforcement produce a translation of the original award and the underlying contract in an official language of the country in which enforcement of the award is sought – such language being Uzbek.

---

177. Oliy Xojalik Sudi, Chet davlat sudlari (xalqaro tijorat arbitrajlari) qarorlarini tan olish va ijroga qaratish tugrisidagi arizalarni korib chiqish hamda chet davlat sudlarining topshiriqlarini ijro etish bilan bogliq sud amaliyotini umumlashtirish natijalari haqida (Higher Economic Court, Summaries of Court Practices on Recognition and Enforcement of Decisions of Foreign Courts and the Issuance of a Writ of Execution to Enforce the Decisions of Foreign Courts) (2015).
178. *See* Lee T., Ok V., Makhmudov M., *supra* n. 169.
179. Summaries of Court Practices, *supra* n. 177, *FARMAK v. ADS Farm Group*, 460–461 (2011).
180. *Ibid.*, *Sigmafarm v. Farma-Service*, 461–462 (2008).
181. *Ibid.*, *Farmak v. Lahisam*, 459–460 (2010).
182. *See* the 2013 Plenary Decision.

1.130. Second, because Romak submitted no evidence to the Court that Uzdon had been duly notified of the appointment of the arbitrators, in accordance with the requirements of Article V(i)(b) of the New York Convention. Romak appealed the Economic Court's decision. On 24 November 2000, the Appellate Jurisdiction of the Tashkent City Economic Court confirmed the decision of the lower court.[183]

1.131. Interestingly enough, frustrated with the decision of the Uzbek court and without making any attempt to perfect and resubmit the application to the Higher Economic Court of Uzbekistan, the claimant hastily turned to the French courts and investment arbitration respectively which ended without a feasible solution.

[3]   Procedures for Recognition

1.132. The 2013 Plenary Decision of the Higher Economic Court requires an applicant to submit the following documents in order to be recognised and subsequently enforced:

a) Name of economic court.
b) Name of foreign arbitration, arbitration members, address.
c) Name of plaintiff, address or residence.
d) Name of defendent, address or residence.
e) Decision of arbitration.
f) Request of plaintiff.
g) Annex of other documents.[184]

1.133. Moreover, if the said arbitral award is not made in an official language of Uzbekistan, the applicant shall produce an Uzbek translation of the documents and shall notarise the translated award via a public notary.

§11.10   INVESTOR-STATE ARBITRATION

[A]   General Overview of the Law and Practice Related to Investor-State Arbitration.

1.134. Since its independence from the Soviet Union, Uzbekistan has always shown a welcome attitude towards foreign investment. The government offers different forms of capital investment opportunities to potential foreign investors: the creation of joint ventures, enterprises with 100% foreign investment and the purchase of a part or full

---

183. *See Romak v. Uzbekistan*, PCA Case No. AA280, Award, 26 November 2009, paras 65–66. http://www.italaw.com/sites/default/files/case-documents/ita0716.pdf (accessed 1 July 2017).
184. 2013 Plenary Decision, Art. 6(2).

package of shares of privatized enterprises.[185] Moreover, due to its double-landlocked geographical location, it presents potential investors with one of the most generous custom and tax privileges systems in the region.[186]

1.135. Although accurate data is unavailable, Uzbekistan is considered a net importer of foreign investment.[187] Being the most populous country, with the lowest labour cost potential in the Central Asian region, makes it a target of market-oriented and export investment. In addition, the country is also rich with natural resources such as gold, uranium, natural gas and other strategic minerals. Uzbekistan is also one of the five major producers of cotton in the world. Therefore, it is no surprise to see that in the last decade Uzbekistan has attracted the majority of its foreign direct investment in the natural resource sector. Coal, oil and gas are among the top foreign investment sectors, followed by chemicals, communications and transportation industries.[188]

1.136. Fierce international competition among developing countries to attract and retain foreign investment has also forced Uzbekistan to set up its own investment promotion agencies. An initiative from the President of Uzbekistan in 2007 established the 'UzInfoInvest' (Informational Support and Foreign Investments Promotion Agency) under the aegis of the Ministry of Foreign Economic Relations, Investments and Trade. The main purpose of the agency is to provide a 'one stop shop' for necessary information and other kinds of support to foreign investors. As an independent legal entity, the agency operates a website (www.uzinfoinvest.uz) where foreign investors can acquire useful information on the investment climate, legislation, and the investment potential of Uzbekistan.

1.137. Following legislative acts define rights and responsibilities of foreign investors in Uzbekistan:

- Law of the Republic of Uzbekistan 'On foreign investments' # 609-I, 30 April 1998.
- Law of the Republic of Uzbekistan 'On investment activities' # 719-I, 24 December 1998.
- Law of the Republic of Uzbekistan 'On guarantees and means of protection of foreign investors' rights' # 611-I, 30 April 1998.

---

185. *See*, Investment Policy of the Republic of Uzbekistan, http://www.uzinfoinvest.uz/eng/investment_guide/investment_policy_of_the_republic_of_uzbekistan/ (accessed 1 July 2017).
186. *See*, Privileges and Preferences for foreign direct investments, http://www.uzinfoinvest.uz/eng/investment_guide/privileges_and_preferences/ (accessed 1 July 2017).
187. *See*, UNCTAD, Country fact sheet: Uzbekistan, http://unctad.org/sections/dite_dir/docs/wir2016/wir16_fs_uz_en.pdf (accessed 1 July 2017).
188. *See* FDI Markets, 'FDI into Uzbekistan: January 2003 to June 2014', p. 7 http://www.fdireports.com/home/fdireports/static/docs/sample_country.pdf (accessed 1 July 2017).According to statistics provided by the Ministry of Foreign Economic Relations, Investment and Trade, the main part of foreign investments has been attracted into the following branches of industry in 2014: oil and gas (52.6%), power generation (10.4%), telecommunication and IT-technology (5.6%), construction and construction materials (4.7%), road construction (3.6%), drinking water supply and sewage (3.0%), textile (2.6%), agriculture and water management (1.9%). *See* 'Statistics investing activities', http://www.mfer.uz/en/investments/statistics/ (accessed 1 July 2017).

1.138. The above laws only set out the main principles of investment activity in Uzbekistan. There is also an array of by-laws on foreign investment activity which potential investors should be aware of. Furthermore, Uzbek legislation adopts different criteria for foreign investment when compared to the international standard. Accordingly, there are two types of foreign investment in Uzbekistan: enterprises with foreign participation and enterprises with foreign investment. The latter type of foreign investment may enjoy a wide range of tax and customs privileges *only* if that enterprise meets the following criteria:

- *foreign investor's share in the statutory capital is not less than 30%;*
- *the statutory capital not less than USD 150,000 equivalent;*
- *at least one of the foreign investors must be a legal entity.*

1.139. Significant foreign investments, which are more than USD 20 million, may also conclude investment agreements with the Government. The resolution of the Cabinet of Ministers #180, 2 August 2005 regulates the procedure of concluding an investment agreement between parties. In such a situation, the foreign investor may negotiate additional guarantees, tax and customs breaks, etc. The Ministry of Foreign Economic Relations, Investment and Trade represent the Government in investment agreements.[189] In the oil and gas sector, foreign investors may enter into contractual relationship with Uzbekneftgaz, a national holding company under the Law 'On Product Sharing Agreement' # 312- II, 7 December 2001.

1.140. Uzbekistan has concluded fifty BITs and five other instruments with investment chapters.[190] Out of fifty BITs, only three of them are not in force at the moment. Those BITs are with Bahrain (2009), Saudi Arabia (2011) and, notoriously, with the United States (1994).[191] All major investor home countries, such as Russia, South Korea, China, Singapore, United Kingdom and Netherlands singed a BIT with Uzbekistan. The absolute majority of BITs aim to protect foreign investments (except the Japan BIT), providing only post-establishment treatment.

1.141. Other instruments with investment chapters consist of the OIC Investment Agreement (1981),[192] the ECT (1994), EC (current EU)-Uzbekistan Cooperation Agreement (1996), the US-Central Asia TIFA (2004)[193] and the ECO Investment Agreement

---

189. See for the details of steps to conclude an investment agreement, UNDP, Investment Guide to Uzbekistan, 2009, p. 63, http://theiguides.org/guides/uzbekistan.pdf (accessed 1 July 2017).
190. See UNCTAD, International Investment Agreements Navigator, Investment Policy Hub, http://investmentpolicyhub.unctad.org/IIA/CountryBits/226#iiaInnerMenu (accessed 1 July 2017).
191. According to the Vandevelde, the BIT with the United States was ratified by Uzbekistan soon after its conclusion, and the Clinton Administration transmitted the BIT to the Senate in 1996. Nonetheless, it seems that due to the imposition of foreign exchange controls, contrary to the capital transfer provision of the BIT, the United States Senate has not consented to ratification of BIT with Uzbekistan. See Vandevelde K.J., *US International Investment Agreements*, Oxford, 2009, p. 64.
192. Agreement on Promotion, Protection and Guarantee of Investments amongst the Member States of the Organisation of the Islamic Conference.
193. Framework Agreement Between the Government of the United States of America, the Government of the Republic of Kazakhstan, The Government of the Kyrgyz Republic, the Government

(2005).[194] Apart from the Cooperation Agreement with the EU, all other agreements are multilateral investment treaties. It should be noted that the US-Central Asia TIFA and EC-Uzbekistan Cooperation Agreement focused on facilitation of cooperation and relations on investment and thus failed to embrace a strong dispute settlement mechanism.

1.142. Up until today, the Government of Uzbekistan has not publicly announced the model BIT and, therefore, it is no surprise to see that Uzbekistan has accepted the model of other contracting parties in most cases. One of the explanations as to why it has not yet developed its own model BIT may be that the majority of foreign investments are attracted under state contracts. This policy may divert Uzbekistan's attention towards sophistication of the content of the state contracts in particular fields of industry, rather than working on BITs.

1.143. Uzbekistan BITs tend to have similar, if not identical, definition of investment and investor. For instance, the BIT signed with Spain defines investment as:

> any kind of asset invested by investors of one Contracting Party in the territory of the other Contracting Party in accordance with the laws and regulations of the latter Contracting Party including, in particular, although not exclusively, the following:
>
> a) movable and immovable property and any other property rights such as mortgages, liens, pledges and similar rights;
> b) shares in, stocks and debentures of a company or any other form of participation in a company or business enterprise;
> c) claims to money or to any performance under contract having economic value and associated with an investment;
> d) intellectual and industrial property rights; technical processes, know-how and goodwill;
> e) rights to undertake economic and commercial activities conferred by law or by virtue of a contract, including concessions to search for, cultivate, extract or exploit natural resources.
>
> Not all, but some other BITs (such as those in China, Singapore and India BITs) require invested assets in accordance to domestic laws and regulations of the host state.

1.144. 'Investors' are defined under the BIT with Netherland in a wider form compared to other BITs of Uzbekistan:

> *(b) the term 'nationals' shall comprise with regard to either Contracting Party*
>   *i. natural persons having the nationality of that Contracting Party;*
>   *ii. legal persons constituted under the law of that Contracting Party;*
>   *iii. legal persons not constituted under the law of that Contracting Party but controlled, directly or indirectly, by natural persons as defined in (i) or by legal persons as defined in (ii) above.*

---

of the Republic of Tajikistan, the Government of Turkmenistan, and the Government of Uzbekistan concerning the Development of Trade and Investment Relations.

194. Agreement on Promotion and Protection of Investment among Member States of the Economic Cooperation Organisation.

1.145. Since Uzbekistan does not have a model BIT, the content of each BIT may differ. Therefore, the provisions of the relevant treaty must be carefully examined as to what types of protection are available. However, the following substantive protections are typically available in Uzbek BITs:

- *non-discriminatory treatment (national and most favoured nation treatments);*
- *fair and equitable treatment;*
- *full protection and security;*
- *expropriation;*
- *protection from civil disturbance or strife;*
- *guarantee of capital transfers.*

1.146. A number of BITs provide extra protection and some restrictions to the foreign investor. The BIT with Japan, for example, requires both parties to refrain from performance requirements and ensures transparency and publication of all laws and regulations relating to investments (the same in BIT with Austria). The China BIT provides the host country with discretion to deny treaty benefits to certain type of investors; the Singapore BIT allows contracting parties to apply prohibition or restrictions that are directed to protecting essential national interests, protection of public health or prevention of diseases.

1.147. On the other hand, Uzbekistan is one of the most active host states in the CIS in terms of investment arbitration.[195] Since 2006, investment cases against Uzbekistan have rapidly increased and they cover different sectors of the economy such as transportation (*Romak v. Uzbekistan*), mining (*Metal-Tech v. Uzbekistan*), textiles (*Spentex v. Uzbekistan*), gas distribution systems (*Federal Elektrik Yatirim v. Uzbekistan*), wholesale and retail trade (*Güneş Tekstil v. Uzbekistan*) and cement production (*Kim v. Uzbekistan*). It should be noted that some cases of investment arbitration against Uzbekistan are also the leading cases in global terms in relation to setting a precedent on definitions of investment[196] and corruption.[197]

1.148. Until now, international arbitral tribunals have rendered four awards against Uzbekistan. In the first award, *Romak v. Uzbekistan*, the Permanent Court of Arbitration dismissed the Claimant's arguments on jurisdictional grounds.[198] In particular, the tribunal determined that Romak's mere delivery of wheat to Uzbekistan could not be considered an 'investment' under the Swiss-Uzbekistan BIT.

---

195. *See* UNCTAD, Investment Dispute Settlement Navigator, Investment Policy Hub, http://investmentpolicyhub.unctad.org/ISDS/CountryCases/226?partyRole=2 (accessed 1 July 2017).
196. *See* Musurmanov I., *The Implications of Romak v. Uzbekistan for Defining the Concept of Investment*, 20 Austl. Int'l LJ 105 (2013).
197. *See* Umirdinov A., *Sharing Responsibilities on Corruption Allegations in Investor-State Arbitration: The Contribution of Metal-Tech v. Uzbekistan*, 264 Nagoya Journal of Law and Politics 43 (2015).
198. *See* Romak v. Uzbekistan, PCA Case No. AA280, Award, 26 November 2009, http://www.italaw.com/sites/default/files/case-documents/ita0716.pdf (accessed 1 July 2017).

1.149. In the *Metal-Tech Ltd v. Uzbekistan* award, the ICSID tribunal decided not to establish its jurisdiction over an investor claim because of corruption.[199] The dispute erupted after the termination of a raw materials supply contract and cancellation of an exclusive right to export of refined molybdenum oxide. Uzbekistan won a favourable decision at the jurisdictional stage by persuading the tribunal that the investment did not qualify as a 'legal investment'.[200] Similarly, in *Spentex v. Uzbekistan* the tribunal dismissed all claims of the investor due to corruption allegations, nonetheless majority of the tribunal urged the respondent to to donate an amount of USD 8 million to United Nations' Global Anti-Corruption Initiative.[201]

1.150. Finally, in the recent *Oxus Gold v. Uzbekistan* award, the investor pursued arbitral proceedings and a USD 400 million claim in relation to the loss of the Khandiza project and Amantaytau Goldfields mining projects located in Uzbekistan.[202] The UNCITRAL arbitration dismissed the claimant's argument against Uzbekistan almost entirely. It has found only that it breached the fair and equitable treatment provision in the UK-Uzbekistan BIT due to the host state's change of the taxation regime for the Amantaytau Goldfields joint venture; eventually, Oxus Gold was awarded USD 10.3 million in damages which led to suspension of trading of Oxus's shares in the London Stock Exchange in December 2015.[203]

1.151. Four Uzbek state entities have very recently filed an ICSID claim against neighbouring Kyrgyzstan in a dispute over the management and operation of a tourist resort.[204] It is not yet quite clear what made the Uzbek entities bring the case to ICSID.

1.152. The central repository of treaty preparatory materials is the Ministry of Foreign Affairs of Uzbekistan. Full text of BITs can be obtained from the Website of the National Electronic Data Base of Legislative Acts (www.lex.uz). Treaty ratifications by the Uzbek Parliament are publically recorded and promulgated in the government's official gazette Xalq So'zi (http://xs.uz/index.php/uzhzhatlar). In general, the Uzbek government is not required to make diplomatic correspondence publically available. The Ministry of Foreign Affairs keeps the archives of inter-governmental and inter-state documents.

---

199. *Metal-Tech Ltd. V. Republic of Uzbekistan* (ICSID Case No. ARB/10/3), Award, 4 October 2013.
200. For the full story of the case, see Alisher Umirdinov, *Metal-Tech v. Uzbekistan: No Jurisdiction Because of Corruption*, Case Comment, CIS Arbitration Forum, 16 December 2013.
201. Peterson, L. and Djanic V., *In an innovative award, arbitrators pressure Uzbekistan – under threat of adverse cost order – to donate to UN anti-corruption initiative; also propose future treaty-drafting changes that would penalize states for corruption*, International Arbitration Reporter, 22 June 2017.
202. *Oxus Gold plc v. Republic of Uzbekistan, the State Committee of Uzbekistan for Geology & Mineral Resources, and Navoi Mining & Metallurgical Kombinat*, UNCITRAL (1976), Final Award, 17 December 2015.
203. *See* Temporary Suspension of Trading on Aim, OXUS GOLD PLC, Regulatory Story, http://www.londonstockexchange.com/exchange/news/market-news/market-news-detail/other/12635167.html (accessed 1 July 2017).
204. *See* Lacey Yong, Uzbek State Entities take Kyrgyzstan to ICSID, Global Arbitration Review, 7 September 2016, http://globalarbitrationreview.com/article/1068445/uzbek-state-entities-take-kyrgyzstan-to-icsid. (accessed 1 July 2017).

1.153. Almost all of Uzbekistan's BITs and the ECT provide for arbitration in accordance with the ICSID Convention and an ad hoc tribunal constituted in accordance with the UNCITRAL rules. In practice, out of seven known investment treaty arbitrations involving Uzbekistan, five disputes relied on ICSID Convention and the remaining two cases were resolved under UNCITRAL Rules.

1.154. Uzbekistan consistently makes investment awards public. Until now, all three final awards, namely, *Romak v. Uzbekistan, Metal-Tech v. Uzbekistan and Oxus Gold v. Uzbekistan* are made public. The only exception is the jurisdictional decision concerning *Oxus Gold v. Uzbekistan*.

1.155. The Government does not usually employ a default mechanism for appointment of arbitral tribunals. The only arbitrator appointed two times is Professor Brigitte Stern (*Oxus Gold v. Uzbekistan* and *Spentex v. Uzbekistan*).

1.156. Uzbekistan usually defends itself through the Ministry of Justice and sometimes the ambassador of Uzbekistan in France is entrusted with defending Uzbekistan. Due to the increasing number of investor-state disputes and the associated workload in recent years, the Ministry has formed a special analytic group for international arbitration that closely works with counsels for each investment cases. This group is formally under the Department of International Legal Affairs of the Ministry and works with five experts. Except in the case *Romak v. Uzbekistan*, the international law firm White & Case is entrusted to defend Uzbekistan in all other cases.

[B] List of Investment Treaties the Country Has Ratified

No.	Partners	Signature	Entry into force
1.	Austria	2 June 2000	18 August 2001
2.	Azerbaijan	27 May 1996	2 November 1996
4.	Bangladesh	18 July 2000	24 January 2001
5.	Belgium-Luxembourg Economic Union	17 April 1998	6 February 2001
6.	Bulgaria	24 June 1998	31 March 1999
7.	China	19 April 2011	1 September 2011
8.	Czech Republic	15 January 1997	6 April 1998
9.	Egypt	16 December 1992	8 February 1994
10.	Finland	1 October 1992	22 October 1993
11.	France	27 October 1993	15 June 1996
12.	Georgia	4 September 1995	24 May 1999
13.	Germany	28 April 1993	23 May 1998
14.	Greece	1 April 1997	8 May 1998
15.	Hungary	28 October 2002	3 March 2003
16.	India	18 May 1999	28 July 2000

No.	Partners	Signature	Entry into force
17.	Indonesia	27 August 1996	27 April 1997
18.	Iran, Islamic Republic of	11 June 2000	11 July 2004
19.	Israel	4 July 1994	18 February 1997
20.	Italy	17 September 1997	14 October 1999
21.	Japan	15 August 2008	24 September 2009
22.	Kazakhstan	2 June 1997	8 September 1997
23.	Korea, Republic of	17 June 1992	20 November 1992
24.	Kuwait	19 January 2004	6 March 2006
25.	Kyrgyzstan	24 December 1996	6 February 1997
26.	Latvia	23 May 1996	29 January 1997
27.	Lithuania	18 February 2002	11 November 2002
27.	Malaysia	6 September 1997	20 January 2000
28.	Moldova, Republic of	21 November 1995	17 January 1997
29.	Netherlands	14 March 1996	1 July 1997
30.	Oman	30 March 2009	20 August 2009
31.	Pakistan	13 August 1992	15 February 2006
32.	Poland	11 January 1995	29 April 1995
33.	Portugal	11 September 2001	14 March 2010
34.	Romania	6 June 1996	30 May 1997
35.	Russian Federation	15 April 2013	14 January 2014
36.	Singapore	15 July 2003	23 November 2003
37.	Slovakia	6 March 2003	17 October 2003
38.	Slovenia	7 October 2003	18 May 2004
39.	Spain	28 January 2003	3 December 2003
40.	Sweden	29 May 2001	1 October 2001
41.	Switzerland	16 April 1993	5 November 1993
42.	Turkey	28 April 1992	18 May 1995
43.	Turkmenistan	16 January 1996	2 August 1996
44.	Ukraine	20 February 1993	6 June 1994
45.	United Arab Emirates	26 October 2007	22 April 2008
46.	United Kingdom	24 November 1993	24 November 1993
47.	Viet Nam	28 March 1996	6 March 1998

[C]   List of Investor-State Disputes (Concluded and Pending)

Case	Applicable IIA	Status/Forum
1. Federal Elektrik Yatirim v. Uzbekistan (2013)	Turkey-Uzbekistan BIT (1992)	Pending ICSID Case No. ARB/13/9

Case	Applicable IIA	Status/Forum
2. Güneş Tekstil v. Uzbekistan (2013)	Turkey-Uzbekistan BIT (1992)	Pending ICSID Case No. ARB/13/19
3. Kim v. Uzbekistan (2013)	Kazakhstan-Uzbekistan BIT (1997)	Pending ICSID Case No. ARB/13/6
4. Spentex v. Uzbekistan (2013)	Netherlands-Uzbekistan BIT (1996)	Decided in favour of State ICSID Case No. ARB/13/26
5. Oxus Gold v. Uzbekistan (2011)	United Kingdom-Uzbekistan BIT (1993)	Decided in favour of investor UNCITRAL
6. Metal-Tech v. Uzbekistan (2010)	Israel-Uzbekistan BIT (1994)	Decided in favour of State ICSID Case No. ARB/10/3
7. Romak v. Uzbekistan (2006)	Switzerland-Uzbekistan BIT (1993)	Decided in favour of State PCA Case No. AA280

§11.11 REFORM PROPOSALS

1.157. First of all, Uzbek scholars and judges are vociferously urging the parliament to adopt laws on international commercial arbitration[205] and mediation[206] respectively. The reasons behind these proposals are to lay the grounds for international commercial arbitration in a country which needs to attract new cases to the Arbitration Society of Uzbekistan, permitting foreign arbitrators to sit in arbitration panels and to react to the needs of business circles. As for mediation laws, the extraordinarily heavy workloads of the civil and economic courts is necessitating the accelerated adoption of the law.[207]

1.158. In addition to that, various authors have suggested the following proposals as the vital steps necessary for further development of alternative dispute resolution in Uzbekistan. One of the proposals includes revising certain provisions of the Arbitration Law so as to strengthen the requirements for the candidacy of arbitrators.[208] The reason behind this proposal has been the appointment of some local thieves-in-law as arbitrator and using their informal power to make the award enforced. In other words, the liberal requirements of the Arbitration Law for the candidate of arbitrators have led such kinds of people, although not many, to penetrate the Uzbek arbitration industry, and this should be resisted.

---

205. Ахметов Д., Международный Коммерческий Арбитраж в Разрешении Коммерческих Споров (International Commercial Arbitration in Commercial Dispute Resolution), Вестник Высшего Хозяственного Суда, No. 8, 88–89 (2014); see also Отахонов Ф., supra n. 93.
206. Berdiev Sh., Kelishmovchiliklar va Nizolar Echimi: Mediatsiya Institutini Taqazo Etmoqda (Dispute Resolution Needs Mediation Institute), Huquq va Burch, No. 5, 2014, 47–51; Rajabov O., Xo'jalik Nizolari: Ularni Hal Etishda Mediatsiyaning O'rni va Ahamiyati (Economic Disputes: the Role and Significance of Mediation for Resolution), Huquq va Burch, No. 1, 20–22 (2015).
207. Bobojonov M., Nizolarni Hal Etishning Muqobil Usullari (Methods of Alternative Dispute Resolution), Oliy Sud Axborotnomasi, No. 3, 18–20 (2015).
208. See Отахонов Ф., А кто будет «судить» самих судей? (Who will 'judge' the judges themselves?) http://www.norma.uz/nashi_obzori/a_kto_budet_sudit_samih_sudey (accessed 1 July 2017).

1.159. Furthermore, several authors have proposed clarifying the participation of third parties and the appointment of experts during arbitral proceedings,[209] lowering the payment for requests for competent court orders on compulsory execution and cancellation of arbitral awards[210] and granting the arbitration court the power to re-examine disputes in view of newly discovered circumstances.[211]

The chapter is current as of 1 July 2017.

---

209. Otakhonov F., *supra* n. 14.
210. *Ibid.*
211. Иноятова С., Некоторые Размышления о Проблемах Института Третейсокого Разбирательства (Discussions on Problems of Arbitration Proceeding's Institute), Вестник Вышего Хозяственного Суда, No. 4, 25 (2014); Hamroqulov B., *supra* n. 64, 42–43.

Appendices

Appendix 1. Map of the Commonwealth of Independent States
Appendix 2. Satistics of Cases Involving States of the CIS Region with Leading Arbitration Institutions
Appendix 3. The Most Important Domestic Enactments on International Arbitration in the CIS Region
Appendix 4. Ratification of Selected Arbitration Related Conventions by CIS States
Appendix 5. Agreement on the Settlement of Disputes Relating to the Exercising of Economic Activity 1992 (the Kiev Agreement)
Appendix 6. Convention on Legal Assistance in Civil, Family Relations and Criminal Matters 1993 (the Minsk Convention)
Appendix 7. Convention on Legal Assistance in Civil, Family Relations and Criminal Matters 2002 (the Kishinev Convention)
Appendix 8. Annex 16 to the 2014 Treaty on the Eurasian Economic Union Protocol on Trade in Services, Incorporation, Activities and Investments

Appendix 1
Map of the Commonwealth of Independent States

Map 1. The Commonwealth of Independent States (Member States and Associate States)

Appendix 1

Map 2. The Commonwealth of Independent States in the World

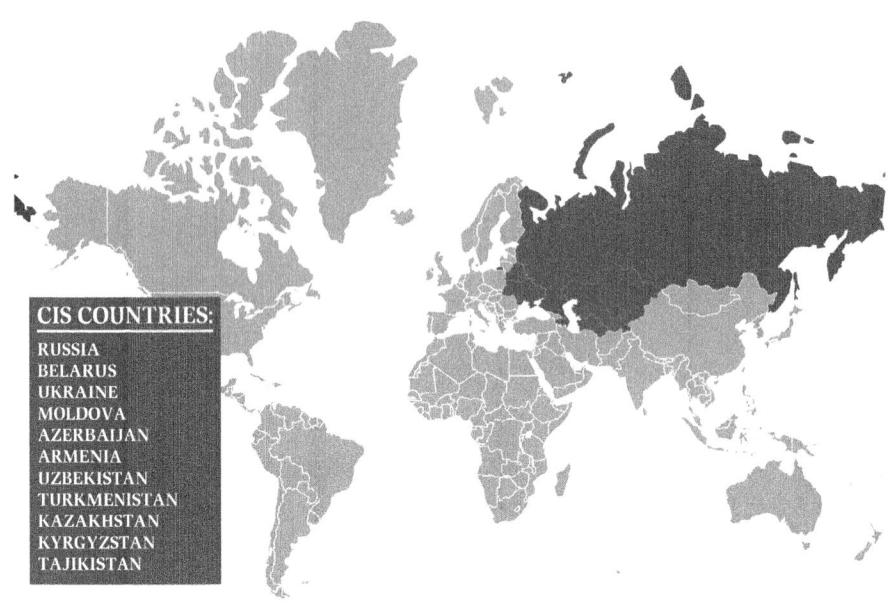

APPENDIX 2

Satistics of Cases Involving States of the CIS Region with Leading Arbitration Institutions

1. **The International Commercial Arbitration Court (ICAC) at the Russian Federation Chamber of Commerce and Industry**

	2010	2011	2012	2013	2014	2015	2016
Russia	281	238	222	299	315	242	292
Ukraine	16	37	45	32	39	18	26
Azerbaijan	4	4	3	1	1	3	3
Kazakhstan	3	15	11	15	28	14	17
Belarus		11	9	29	35	22	25
Turkmenistan			1				
Moldova		2	2	2	4	1	2
Kyrgyzstan				1	1	2	4
Uzbekistan	1	8	8	6	3	9	9
Tajikistan			2	2	2	1	1
Armenia			1			2	2
	305	315	304	387	428	314	381

Source: The International Commercial Arbitration Court at the Russian Federation Chamber of Commerce and Industry, available at http://mkas.tpprf.ru/ru/Stat/stat2012.php

Appendix 2

2. The International Court of Arbitration of the International Chamber of Commerce (ICC)

	2010[1]	2011[2]	2012[3]	2013[4]	2014[5]	2015[6]
Russia	13	25	23	13	27	26
Ukraine	9	13	9	9	5	3
Azerbaijan	2	2	1	6	3	
Kazakhstan	2	5	3	1	1	5
Belarus		1	1		3	
Turkmenistan	4					
Moldova		1			4	1
Uzbekistan	1	3	1			4
Tajikistan		1		1		
Armenia	2	1				
	33	51	38	30	43	39

[1] – 2010 Statistical Report, ICC International Court of Arbitration Bulletin - 22-1 (2011)
[2] – 2011 Statistical Report, ICC International Court of Arbitration Bulletin - 23-1 (2012)
[3] – 2012 Statistical Report, ICC International Court of Arbitration Bulletin - 24-1 (2013)
[4] – 2013 Statistical Report, ICC International Court of Arbitration Bulletin - 25-1 (2014)
[5] – 2014 Statistical Report, ICC Dispute Resolution Bulletin 2015 - Issue 1
[6] – 2015 Statistical Report, ICC Dispute Resolution Bulletin 2016 - Issue 1

3. The Arbitration Institute of the Stockholm Chamber of Commerce (SCC)

	2010	2011	2012	2013	2014	2015	2016
Russia	22	19	18	15	26	24	30
Ukraine	9	7	6	2	7	15	12
Azerbaijan						9	8
Kazakhstan	3	3	2	1	2	6	1
Belarus	2	2		1	1	2	1
Turkmenistan	0	0	0	0	0	1	0
Moldova	3	1	4	0	2	0	4
Kyrgyzstan	0	1					1
Uzbekistan	1	1	0	0	0	0	1
	40	34	30	19	37	57	58

* SCC Statistics, available at http://www.sccinstitute.com/statistics/ (accessed 18 May 2017)

Appendix 2

4. The London Court of International Arbitration (LCIA)*

	2010	2011	2012	2013	2014	2015
Russia	18	20	9	10	13	32
Ukraine		9				10
Kazakhstan			7			
	18	29	16	10	13	42

* LCIA Reports, available at http://www.lcia.org/LCIA/reports.aspx (accessed 18 May 2017)

5. State Respondents, the International Centre for Settlement of Investment Disputes (ICSID)

	2010	2011	2012	2013	2014	2015	2016
Ukraine					2	2	2
Kazakhstan	1	1		4		2	
Turkmenistan	2	2	1				
Moldova		1					
Kyrgyzstan				1			
	3	4	1	5	2	4	2

Source: The International Centre for Settlement of Investment Disputes, https://icsid.worldbank.org/en/ (accessed 18 May 2017)

6. State Respondents in Investor-State Disputes (ICSID, UNCITRAL, SCC)*

Year of initiation/State	2010	2011	2012	2013	2014	2015	2016
Ukraine					2	3	2
Kazakhstan	2	1		2		2	2
Turkmenistan	3	2	1	1			1
Moldova	1	1	2		1		1
Kyrgyzstan		1	2	4		1	1
Russia			1	1	2	7	3
	6	5	6	7	5	13	10

* Investment Public Policy Hub, UNCTAD, available at http://investmentpolicyhub.unctad.org/ISDS (accessed 18 May 2017)

APPENDIX 3
The Most Important Domestic Enactments on International Arbitration in the CIS Region

Country	LAW
Armenia	The Law of the Republic of Armenia "On Commercial Arbitration", of 22 January 2007 No. ZR-55
Azerbaijan	The Law of the Republic of Azerbaijan "On International Commercial Arbitration", of 18 November 1999
Belarus	The Law of the Republic of Belarus "On International Arbitration Court", of 29 May 2009 No. 698
Russia	Federal Law of the Russian Federation "On Arbitration in the Russian Federation", of 29 December 2015 No. 382-FZ
Ukraine	The Law of the Republic of Ukraine "On International Commercial Arbitration", of 24 February 1994 No. 4002-XII
Kazakhstan	The Law of the Republic of Kazakhstan "On Arbitration", of 8 April 2016 No. 488-V ZRK
Kyrgyzstan	The law "On arbitration courts in the Kyrgyz Republic", of 30 July 2002
Moldova	The Law of the Republic Of Moldova "On International Commercial Arbitration", of 22 February 2008 No. 24 XVI
Tajikistan	The Law of the Republic of Tajikistan "On international commercial arbitration", of 18 March 2015 No. 1183
Turkmenistan	The Law of Turkmenistan "On International Commercial Arbitration", of 16 August 2014 No. 101-V
Uzbekistan	The Law of the Republic of Uzbekistan "On Arbitration Courts", of 16 October 2006, No. 3PY-64

APPENDIX 4
Ratification of Selected Arbitration Related Conventions by CIS States

Appendix 4

Country	New York Convention *	Washington Convention***	Kiev Agreement***	Minsk Convention****	Energy Charter Treaty*****	Eurasian Economic Union******
Armenia	29 December 1997	16 September 1992	24 May 1994	22 November 1994	18 December 1997	4 December 2014
Azerbaijan	29 February 2000	18 September 1992	11 June 2003	11 July 1996	2 December 1997	-
Belarus	15 November 1960	10 July 1992	24 November 1992	10 June 1993		9 October 2014
Russia	24 August 1960	-	9 October 1992	11 November 1994	-	26 September 2014
Ukraine	10 October 1960	7 June 2000	19 December 1992	16 March 1995	6 February 1998	-
Kazakhstan	20 November 1995	21 September 2000	20 April 1994	20 April 1994	18 October 1995	1 October 2014
Kyrgyzstan	18 December 1996	Signed, not ratified	19 April 1994	19 January 1996	08 April 1997	20 May 2015
Moldova	18 September 1998	5 May 2011	Signed, not ratified	26 February 1996	10 June 1996	-
Tajikistan	14 August 2012	-	21 November 1994	21 November 1994	17 June 1997	-
Turkmenistan	-	26 September 1992	23 January 1998	21 January 1998	10 July 1997	-
Uzbekistan	7 February 1996	26 July 1995	6 May 1993	21 February 1994	22 December 1995	-

* Convention on the Recognition and Enforcement of Foreign Arbitral Awards (New York Convention), 1958, http://www.uncitral.org/uncitral/en/uncitral_texts/arbitration/NYConvention_status.html (accessed 27 February 2017).

** Convention on the Settlement of Investment Disputes between States and Nationals of Other States (Washington Convention), 1965, https://icsid.worldbank.org/en/Documents/resources/2006%20CRR_English-final.pdf (accessed 17 May 2017).

*** Agreement for the Settlement of Disputes Related to Commercial Activities (Kiev Agreement), 1992, http://cisarbitration.com/wp-content/uploads/2017/02/Kiev-Convention-on-Settling-Disputes-Related-to-Commercial-Activities-russian.pdf (accessed 18 May 2017).

**** The Convention on Legal Assistance and Legal Relations in Civil, Family and Criminal Matters (Minsk Convention), 1993, http://www.cis.minsk.by/page.php?id=614 (accessed 15 March 2017).

***** The 1994 Energy Charter Treaty, The treaty and related documents are available at http://www.energycharter.org/process/energy-charter-treaty-1994/energy-charter-treaty/ accessed 20 March 2017).

****** Treaty on the Eurasian Economic Union 2014, http://www.un.org/en/ga/sixth/70/docs/treaty_on_eeu.pdf (accessed 20 March 2017).

APPENDIX 5
Agreement on the Settlement of Disputes Relating to the Exercising of Economic Activity 1992 (the Kiev Agreement)

Adopted in Kiev on 20 March 1992

(unofficial translation)

Governments of the Member States of the Commonwealth of Independent States, Attaching great importance to the development of cooperation in the sphere of resolution of the disputes arising from economic activities between entities located in the different Member States of the Commonwealth of Independent States

Based on the need to ensure that all business entities have equal opportunities to protect their rights and legitimate interests,

Have agreed on the following:

Article 1

This Agreement governs the resolution of cases arising from the contractual and other civil law relations between economic entities, from their relations with state and other bodies, and also execution of decisions on the disputes.

Article 2

For the purposes of this agreement, economic entities are understood to mean enterprises, their associations, organizations of any organizational and legal forms, and also, citizens who have the status of an entrepreneur in accordance with legislation on the territory of Member States of the Commonwealth of Independent States, and their associations.

Article 3

Economic entities of each Member State of the Commonwealth of Independent States shall enjoy in the territory of another Member State of the Commonwealth of Independent States legal and judicial protection of their property rights and legitimate interests, on a par with economic entities of another state.

Economic entities of each Member State of the Commonwealth of Independent States has the right on the territory of other Member State of the Commonwealth of Independent States to file claims without hindrance to the courts, commercial (economic) courts, arbitration courts and other bodies, which have the competence to resolve the disputes mentioned in Article 1 of this Agreement (hereinafter - competent courts), may speak in the courts, initiate motions, make claims and perform other procedural actions.

Article 4

1. The competent court of a Member State of the Commonwealth of Independent States has the right to consider the disputes referred to in Article 1 of this Agreement, if on territory of this Member State of the Commonwealth of Independent States:

   A) the respondent had a permanent place of residence or a location for the day filing a claim.

   If there are several defendants in the territory of different Member States of the Commonwealth of Independent States, the dispute can be resolved at the territory of any of defendants subject to choice of the claimant;

   B) trade, industrial or other economic activities of the enterprise (branch) of the defendant are carried out;
   C) the obligation has been or should be fulfilled in full or in part from contract, which is the subject of a dispute;
   D) there was an action or other circumstance that served as the basis for claims for compensation for harm;
   E) has a permanent place of residence or location of the claimant for the defense of business reputation;
   E) there is a supplier-contractor, contractor or service provider (performing works) and the dispute concerns the conclusion, modification and termination of contracts.

2. The competent courts of Member States of the Commonwealth of Independent States also consider disputes in other cases, if there is written agreement of the parties to submit the dispute to this court.

   If there is such an agreement, the court of another Member State of the Commonwealth terminates the proceedings according to the defendant's application, if such a declaration is made before the decision on the merits is announced.

3. Claims of business entities on the right of ownership of real estate fall into exclusive jurisdiction of the court of the Member State in whose territory the property is located.
4. Cases of invalidation in whole or in part of acts of state and other bodies of non-regulatory character, as well as cases on recovery for damages caused to economic entities by such acts or arising due to improper performance by the said bodies of their responsibilities in relation to economic entities, are considered exclusively by the court of location of the said authority.

   The competence of courts specified in paragraphs 3 and 4 cannot be changed by an agreement of the parties.
5. The counterclaim and the claim for set-off, arising from the same legal relationship as the main claim, are subject to review in the court that considers the main claim.

Article 5

Competent Courts and other bodies of Member States of the Commonwealth of Independent States undertake to provide mutual legal assistance.

Mutual legal assistance includes the delivery and forwarding of documents and execution of procedural actions, in particular, examination, hearing of the parties, witnesses, experts and others.

When providing legal assistance, the competent courts and other bodies of the Member States of the Commonwealth of Independent States demolish each other directly.

When executing the instruction for rendering legal assistance, the competent courts and other bodies for which assistance is sought, apply the legislation of their State.

When applying for legal assistance and implementing decisions, the attached documents are set out in the language of the requesting state or in Russian.

Article 6

Documents issued or certified by the institution or specially authorized person within their competence in the prescribed form and sealed in the territory of one of the Member States of the Commonwealth of Independent States are accepted in the territory of other Member States of the Commonwealth of Independent States without any special certification.

Documents that are on the territory of one of the member states of the Commonwealth of Independent States are treated as official documents, have evidentiary force of official document on the territory of other CIS member states.

Article 7

The Member States of the Commonwealth of Independent States mutually recognize and enforce the decisions of the competent courts that came into force.

Appendix 5

Decisions rendered by the competent courts of one CIS Member State are subject to execution in the territory of other Member States of the Commonwealth of Independent States.

Decisions rendered by a competent court of one Member State of the Commonwealth of Independent States in respect of foreclosure on property of the defendant shall be enforceable in the territory of another Member State of the Commonwealth of Independent States by bodies designated by the court or certain legislation of this state.

Article 8

The enforcement of the decision is made at the request of the interested party.

The application shall be accompanied by:

duly certified copy of the decision, on compulsory execution of which a petition initiated;

official document proving that the decision has come into legal force, if it is cannot be seen from the text of the decision itself;

evidence of notification of another party about the process;

executive document.

Article 9

The enforcement of a decision may be refused at the request of the Party, against which it was initiated only if that Party submits to the competent court at the place where execution is requested, evidence that:

A) the court of the requested member state of the Commonwealth of Independent States has previously issued a legally binding decision in the case between the same parties, on the same subject and on the same basis;
B) there is a recognized decision of the competent court of a third Member State of the Commonwealth of Independent States or a non-member state of the Commonwealth, on the dispute between the same Parties, on the same subject and on the same basis;
C) the dispute is resolved by an incompetent court in accordance with this Agreement;
D) the other Party was not notified of the process;
E) the three-year period of limitation of compulsory enforcement of the decision has expired.

Article 10

The highest judicial bodies of the Member States of the Commonwealth of Independent States shall regulate disputes concerning the enforcement of the decision of the competent courts.

Article 11

Civil legislation of one Member State of the Commonwealth of Independent States shall be applied in the territory of another Member State of the Commonwealth of Independent States in accordance with the following rules:

A) civil legal capacity and legal capacity of legal entities and entrepreneurs is determined by the legislation of the Member State of the Commonwealth of Independent States, on whose territory a legal entity or an entrepreneur are registered;

B) to the relations arising from the owner's right the legislation where the property is located shall be applied. Ownership of transport to be registered in state registries is to be determined by the legislation of the state where the vehicle is registered;

C) the emergence and termination of the right of ownership or other proprietary right is determined by the laws of the state in whose territory the property was located at the time when the action or other circumstance which served as the basis for the emergence or termination of such a right took place.

The emergence and termination of the right of ownership or other proprietary right to that is the subject of the transaction is determined by the legislation of the place of fulfilment of the transaction, unless otherwise provided by the agreement of the Parties;

D) the form of the transaction is determined by the legislation of the place of its fulfilment. The form of transactions on buildings, other real estate and rights to it is determined according to the legislation where such property is located;

E) the form and term of validity of the power of attorney is determined by the legislation of the state on whose territory the power of attorney was issued;

F) the rights and obligations of the parties to the transaction are determined by the legislation of the place of its performance, unless otherwise provided by the agreement of the Parties;

G) the rights and obligations of the Parties for obligations arising from harm are determined by the legislation of the state where the action or other circumstance that served as the basis for the compensation of harm has raised.

This legislation does not apply if an action or other circumstance, which served as the basis for claims for compensation for harm, is not considered illegal under the laws of the place of consideration of the dispute;

H) the issues of limitation of actions are resolved according to the legislation of the state, regulating the corresponding relations.

Article 12

The highest judicial bodies and the Ministry of Justice of the Member States of the Commonwealth of Independent States present each other at the request of similar bodies of the other Party, information on the current or previous legislation and practice of its application in their States.

Appendix 5

Article 13

This Agreement is open for signature by the Member States of the Commonwealth of Independent States and is subject to ratification. It comes into force after its ratification by at least three Member States of the Commonwealth starting from the day of the deposit of the third instrument of ratification by the depositary State. For states ratifying the Agreement later, it shall enter into force on the day of deposit of their instruments of ratification.

APPENDIX 6

Convention on Legal Assistance in Civil, Family Relations and Criminal Matters 1993 (the Minsk Convention)

Minsk, 22 January 1993
as amended on 28 March 1997

(unofficial translation)

The member nations of the Commonwealth of Independent States participating in this Convention and hereinafter referred to as the "Contracting States",
Desirous of assuring their nationals and the other persons resident on their territories of the same degree of legal protection for their personal and proprietary rights in each of the Contracting States as is accorded to their own nationals; and
Considering it highly significant to develop cooperation between their judicial authorities in extending mutual legal assistance in civil, family, and criminal matters,
Hereby agree as follows:

Section I

General Provisions

Part I

Legal Protection

Article 1

Grant of Legal Protection

1. The nationals of each Contracting State and the other persons resident on its territory shall be entitled in all the other Contracting States to the same degree of legal protection for their personal and proprietary rights as is accorded to its own nationals.

Appendix 6

2. The nationals of each Contracting State and the other persons resident on its territory shall have the right of free and unimpeded recourse to the courts, public prosecutors' offices, police, and other institutions of the other Contracting States that have jurisdiction over civil, family, and criminal matters (hereinafter, the "judicial authorities"), and shall be entitled to apply thereto, submit petitions, file claims, and perform other procedural acts on the same conditions with its own nationals.
3. This Convention shall also be applicable to the legal entities organized under the laws of any of the Contracting States.

Article 2

Exemption From Duties and Reimbursement for Expenses

1. The nationals of each Contracting State and the other persons resident on its territory shall be exempted from any payment of, and from any reimbursement for, any judicial and notarial fees and expenses, and shall enjoy free legal assistance on the same conditions with its own nationals.
2. The privileges granted by Paragraph 1 of the present Article shall extend to all of the procedural acts performed in a particular matter, including, but not limited to, the enforcement of a judgment.

Article 3

Issue of Documents Evidencing Marital and Property Status

1. The privileges granted by Article 2 above shall be available on the basis of a document evidencing the marital and property status of the person initiating a petition. Such document shall be issued by a competent authority of the Contracting State where the petitioner is domiciled or resident.
2. If the petitioner is not domiciled or resident in any Contracting State, it may present a document issued by an appropriate diplomatic mission or consular office of that Contracting State of which it is a national.
3. The authority deciding on a petition for the above privileges may request additional data or necessary clarifications from the authority which has issued said document.

Part II

Legal Assistance

Article 4

Extension of Legal Assistance

1. The judicial authorities of the Contracting States shall extend legal assistance in civil, family, and criminal matters in accordance with the relevant provisions of the present Convention.

2. The judicial authorities of the Contracting States shall also grant legal assistance to other institutions in those matters specified in Paragraph 1 of the present Article.

Article 5
Liaison Procedure

When acting pursuant to this Convention, the competent judicial authorities of the Contracting States shall communicate with one another through their central, regional, and other agencies, unless a different liaison procedure is prescribed hereunder. The Contracting States shall determine lists of their central, regional, and other agencies duly empowered to maintain direct contacts by notice to the depositary.

Article 6
Scope of Legal Assistance

The Contracting States shall provide one another with legal assistance by performing such procedural and other acts as are stipulated by the legislation of the Contracting State requested to take such measures, including, but not limited to, the execution and sending of documents, the conduct of inspections and searches, the recovery and delivery of physical evidence, the performance of expert examinations, the interrogation of parties to the proceedings, third parties, suspects, indictees, victims, witnesses, and experts, efforts to track down certain individuals, criminal prosecution, the extradition of persons to be held criminally liable or face that punishment already fixed for them in appropriate sentences, the recognition and enforcement of judgments in civil matters, verdicts on civil claims, and executive endorsements, and the service of process.

Article 7
Contents and Form of Letters of Request for Legal Assistance

1. A letter of request for legal assistance shall:
   a) identify the authority whose assistance is sought;
   b) identify the authority seeking such assistance;
   c) specify the case regarding which the legal assistance is sought;
   d) indicate the first names, surnames, domiciles or residence addresses, nationalities, and occupations of the parties to the proceedings, witnesses, suspects, indictees, respondents, convicts, or victims, as well as, in criminal matters, their places and dates of birth and, if possible, the first names and surnames of their parents or, for legal entities, their names and registered and/or actual addresses;
   e) if those parties listed in paragraph d) above have any representatives, indicate the latter's first names, surnames, and addresses;
   f) describe the nature of the request and provide such other data as may be necessary for its satisfaction; and

g) in criminal matters, also describe and classify the misdeed in question and report the extent of the resulting damage, if any.
2. Such letter requesting the service of process shall also indicate the recipient's precise address and the heading of the document to be delivered.
3. A letter of request shall be signed and evidenced by an official seal of the authority seeking assistance.

Article 8

Performance Procedure

1. When acting upon a letter of request, the authority addressed shall apply the legislation of its own country. If petitioned by the authority seeking assistance, it may also apply the procedural rules of the Contracting State where the latter is based, unless such rules are inconsistent with the legislation of the Contracting State where such assistance is sought.
2. If the authority addressed is not competent to satisfy the request submitted, it shall pass it onto a competent authority and shall notify the authority requesting assistance accordingly.
3. If petitioned by the authority seeking assistance, the authority addressed shall notify the latter and the other parties concerned of the time and place of the request's fulfilment so that they should be able to attend its satisfaction in accordance with the legislation of the Contracting State where such assistance is sought.
4. Where the precise address of the person identified in a letter of request is unknown, the authority addressed shall take the measures necessary to ascertain such address in accordance with the legislation of the Contracting State where such authority is based.
5. After completing action on a letter of request, the authority addressed shall return the corresponding documents to the authority which applied for such assistance; where the legal assistance sought cannot be provided as requested, the authority addressed shall also report those circumstances that prevent such performance and shall return the corresponding documents to the authority seeking that assistance.

Article 9

Summons of Witnesses, Victims, Civil Claimants,

Civil Respondents, Their Representatives, and Experts

1. Regardless of their nationality, no witness, victim, civil claimant, civil respondent, their representative, or expert reporting to a judicial authority of the Contracting State seeking assistance on the basis of a summons served upon such person by an authority of the Contracting State addressed may be held

criminally or administratively liable, detained, or punished in the Contracting State seeking their assistance for any act committed before crossing the state border. Nor may any such person be held liable, detained, or punished in connection with their witness testimony or expert opinion offered in connection with the criminal matter in controversy.
2. Those persons specified in Paragraph 1 of the present Article shall forfeit the guarantee granted therein if they fail, despite being able to do so, to leave the Contracting State that sought assistance within 15 days from the date on which the interrogating judicial authority advised them of having no longer any need for their presence. Such period shall be exclusive of the time during which said persons are unable to leave the Contracting State that sought assistance other than through their own fault.
3. The Contracting State that sought assistance shall reimburse each witness, expert, victim, and the latter's lawful representatives for those expenses incurred for their travels and sojourn on its territory, as well as for the shortfall in their wages resulting from the days off from their regular work; an expert shall also be entitled to compensation for the examination performed. A summons shall specify the type of payment the persons summoned may have the right to receive; upon their request, the judicial authority of the Contracting State seeking assistance shall pay an advance to cover their corresponding expenses.
4. No summons for any of those persons specified in Paragraph 1 of the present Article and domiciled in any Contracting State to report to a judicial authority of another Contracting State shall contain any threat of coercion to follow in the event of their non-appearance.

Article 10
Letters Requesting Service of Process

1. That judicial authority addressed by a letter of request shall serve process in accordance with that procedure in effect in its Contracting State if the documents to be delivered have been executed in the latter's language or in Russian or are accompanied by duly certified translations into such languages. Otherwise, it shall pass such documents onto the recipient if the latter agrees to accept them voluntarily.
2. If the documents concerned cannot be delivered at the address indicated in a letter of request, the judicial authority addressed shall initiate the measures necessary to ascertain such address. Should it prove impossible for the judicial authority addressed to find out that address, it shall advise the judicial authority seeking assistance accordingly and return the documents due for service.

Article 11

Confirmation of Service of Process

The requested service of process shall be confirmed by an appropriate acknowledgement which shall be signed by the recipient and evidenced by the official seal of the judicial authority addressed, indicate the date of such service, and carry the signature of an officer of the serving judicial authority, or by another document issued by the latter and describing the manner, place, and time of the service performed.

Article 12

Powers of Diplomatic Missions and Consular Offices

1. The Contracting States may serve process on their own nationals through their diplomatic missions or consular offices.
2. Upon requests from their competent authorities, the Contracting States may interrogate their own nationals through their diplomatic missions or consular offices.
3. In those matters described in Paragraphs 1 and 2 of the present Article, it shall not be permitted to have recourse to any coercion or any threat thereof.

Article 13

Validity of Documents

1. Those documents which have been executed or certified on the territory of one of the Contracting States by an authority or duly authorized person within their terms of reference and according to the form required in that Contracting State and evidenced by an official seal shall be subject to acceptance in the other Contracting States without the need for any special further certification.
2. Those documents which are accepted as official in any Contracting State shall enjoy the evidentiary force of official documents also in the other Contracting States.

Article 14

Sending of Civil-Status and Other Documents

1. The Contracting States shall satisfy requests for civil registration certificates to be sent without being translated and free of charge to one another directly through their civil registry offices subject to appropriate document transfer notices to the corresponding individuals.
2. Each Contracting State addressed shall satisfy requests for documents evidencing training standards, job seniority, and other documents concerning the personal or proprietary rights and interests of its nationals or other persons domiciled on its territory to be sent – without having such documents

translated and free of charge – to another Contracting State requesting such assistance.

Article 15

Legal Information

The central judicial authorities of the Contracting States shall provide one another upon request with information about the internal legislation in effect or which was in effect on their territories and about the practices of its application by the judicial authorities.

Article 16

Ascertainment of Addresses and Other Data

1. The Contracting States shall assist one another - upon request and in accordance with their respective legislation - in ascertaining the addresses of persons domiciled on their territories, if necessary for the exercise by their nationals of their rights. In such matters, the Contracting State seeking assistance shall supply that data at its disposal which may help establish the address of the person identified in its request.
2. The judicial authorities of a Contracting State shall assist those of another Contracting State in identifying the employers and ascertaining the income levels of persons domiciled in the Contracting State addressed and facing property claims made by the judicial authorities of the Contracting State seeking assistance in civil, family, or criminal matters.

Article 17

Language

The judicial authorities of the Contracting States shall use the latter's state languages or the Russian language in their liaising hereunder. Should any documents be executed in the Contracting States' state languages, these shall be accompanied by duly certified translations into Russian.

Article 18

Expenses for Legal Assistance

No Contracting State addressed shall seek reimbursement for any of the expenses incurred for the legal assistance rendered. The Contracting States shall themselves bear any and all of the expenses for the extension of legal assistance on their territories.

Article 19

Refusal of Legal Assistance

A request for legal assistance may be turned down, in full or in part, if the grant of such assistance may be detrimental to the sovereignty or security, or is inconsistent with the

Appendix 6

legislation, of the Contracting State addressed. In such case, the Contracting State seeking legal assistance shall be promptly advised of the reasons why its corresponding request has been denied.

Section II

Legal Relations in Civil and Family Matters

Part I

Competence

Article 20

General Provisions

1. Unless stipulated otherwise in Parts II–V of the present Section, claims against persons resident in a Contracting State, regardless of their nationality, shall be filed with a court of such Contracting State, while those against a legal entity shall be filed with a court of that Contracting State where such legal entity's governing body, representative office, or branch is located.

    Where proceedings involve several respondents resident or based on the territories of different Contracting States, the case shall be heard in that jurisdiction where any respondent of the claimant's own choice is resident or based.
2. Courts on the territory of a Contracting State shall also be competent where it is in the latter that:
    a) the respondent's enterprise or branch maintains trade, industrial operations, or other business; or
    b) the contractual obligation which is the subject of the dispute was performed or has to be performed in whole or in part; or
    c) the claimant in proceedings instituted to uphold the latter's honour, dignity, and business reputation is domiciled or resident.
3. The only courts competent to hear cases initiated over title and other rights in rem to real property shall be those of the place where the property in dispute is located.

Such claims against a carrier as arise out of or in connection with a contract for the transportation of freight, passengers, or luggage shall be filed at the place where the administration of the carrier duly confronted with an appropriate grievance is located.

Article 21

Contractual Jurisdiction

1. Courts of the Contracting States may hear also other cases where the parties have agreed in writing to submit the corresponding disputes to such courts.

    However, the exclusive competence stemming from Paragraph 3 of Article 20 and other provisions of Parts II–V of the present Section, and from

the internal legislation of the Contracting State concerned, may not be altered by agreement of the parties.
2. If there is an agreement to refer a dispute to another court, the court hearing such dispute shall dismiss the proceedings in the case upon the respondent's request.

Article 22
Interrelated Proceedings

1. Where proceedings have been instituted in a matter involving the same parties, regarding the same subject matter, and over the same cause of action in courts of two Contracting States as are competent to hear such disputes hereunder, the court that initiated its proceedings at the later date shall dismiss the case.
2. Such counter-claims and requests for offsets as emanate from the same legal relationship as the principal action shall be subject to the court dealing with the principal action.

Article 22-1
Requests for Public Prosecutors' Involvement in Civil Proceedings

A public prosecutor in a Contracting State may apply to a public prosecutor in another Contracting State for the institution of proceedings to protect the rights and lawful interests of nationals of the Contracting State seeking such assistance, or for the opportunity to participate in the trial of such matters, or for a cassation appeal, private protest, or supervisory protest to be lodged against judicial resolutions handed down in such matters.

Part II
Personal Status
Article 23
Legal Capacity

1. The legal capacity of a natural person shall be subject to the legislation of the Contracting State of which he is a national.
2. The legal capacity of a stateless person shall be subject to the law of the country where he is domiciled.
3. The legal capacity of a legal entity shall be subject to the legislation of the State under whose laws such legal entity has been established.

Article 24

Pronunciation of Persons to Be of Limited Legal Capacity or Legally Incapable.

Reinstatement of Legal Capacity

1. A court of that Contracting State of which the respondent is a national shall have jurisdiction in proceedings initiated to pronounce such person to be of limited legal capacity or legally incapable, with the exception of cases provided by Paragraphs 2 and 3 of the present Article.
2. Where a court of a Contracting State learns of any reasons why a person resident on the latter's territory, but being a national of another Contracting State should be pronounced to be of partial legal capacity or legally incapable, such court shall give an appropriate notice to a court of the Contracting State of which such person is a national.
3. Where that court of a Contracting State which has been notified of a reason why a person should be pronounced to be of partial legal capacity or legally incapable fails to initiate appropriate proceedings or to come back with its own opinion on the matter within the following three months, the case for the pronunciation of such person to be of limited legal capacity or legally incapable shall be taken up by a court of that Contracting State where the person concerned is resident. The judgment pronouncing a person to be of partial legal capacity or legally incapable shall be sent to a competent court of the Contracting State of which such person is a national.
4. The provisions of Paragraphs 1–3 of the present Article shall also be applicable to the reinstatement of legal capacity.

Article 25

Pronunciation of Persons to Be Missing or Deceased.

Establishment of Facts of Death

1. The judicial authorities competent in proceedings initiated for a person to be pronounced missing or deceased or for a fact of death to be established shall be those of the Contracting State of which the person concerned was a national when last known to be alive or, in the case of other persons, those of the Contracting State where they were last known to be resident.
2. The judicial authorities of each Contracting State may pronounce a national of another Contracting State or any other person who was resident on its territory to be missing or deceased or establish the fact of their death on the basis of a petition filed by those persons concerned and resident on its territory whose rights and interests are based on the legislation of such Contracting State.
3. When conducting proceedings initiated for the pronunciation of a person to be missing or deceased or for the establishment of a fact of death, the judicial authorities of the Contracting States shall apply the latter's own legislation.

Part III
Family Matters
Article 26
Conclusion of Marriages

Marriage terms for each of the future spouses shall be subject to the legislation of the Contracting State of which they are a national or, for stateless persons, the legislation of the Contracting State where they are domiciled. Furthermore, any obstacles to a marriage shall be subject to the legislation of the Contracting State where it is concluded.

Article 27
Relations Between Spouses

1. Personal and property relations between spouses shall be subject to the legislation of the Contracting State where the spouses jointly reside.
2. If one of the spouses is resident in one Contracting State, while another is resident in another Contracting State, but both spouses share the same nationality, their personal and property relations shall be subject to the legislation of that Contracting State of which they are nationals.
3. If one of the spouses is a national of one Contracting State and the other is a national of another Contracting State and should one of the spouses be resident in one Contracting State and the other be resident in another Contracting State, their personal and property relations shall be subject to the legislation of the Contracting State where they last had their joint residence.
4. If those persons specified in Paragraph 3 of the present Article did not have any joint residence in any of the Contracting States, the governing legislation shall be that of the Contracting State whose authority is hearing their case.
5. Those relations of spouses which concern their real property shall be subject to the legislation of the Contracting State where such real property is located.
6. The authorities competent in proceedings over spouses' personal and property relations shall be those of the Contracting State whose legislation is applicable by virtue of Paragraphs 1 – 3, 5 of the present Article.

Article 28
Dissolution of Marriages

1. Divorce cases shall be subject to the legislation of the Contracting State of which the spouses were nationals at the time when they filed an application for the dissolution of their marriage.
2. If one of the spouses is a national of one Contracting State, while the other is a national of another Contracting State, the governing legislation shall be that of the Contracting State whose authority is hearing the divorce case.

Article 29
Competence of Contracting States' Authorities

1. The judicial authorities competent in divorce proceedings in cases provided for in Paragraph 1 of Article 28 shall be those of the Contracting State of which the spouses were nationals at the time when they filed an application for the dissolution of their marriage. If both spouses were resident in another Contracting State at the time when they filed such application, the judicial authorities of the latter Contracting State shall likewise be competent.
2. The judicial authorities competent in divorce proceedings in those cases provided for by Paragraph 2 of Article 28 shall be those of the Contracting State where both spouses are resident. If one of the spouses is resident in one Contracting State, while the other is resident in another Contracting State, the judicial authorities of both Contracting States where the spouses are resident shall be competent to conduct proceedings for the dissolution of their marriage.

Article 30
Annulment of Marriages

1. Proceedings initiated to have a marriage annulled shall be subject to the same legislation of the corresponding Contracting State which was applicable pursuant to Article 26 to the conclusion of the marriage.
2. The competence of judicial authorities in proceedings to have a marriage annulled shall be determined in accordance with Article 27.

Article 31
Establishment and Challenging of Paternity or Maternity

Paternity and maternity shall be established and challenged according to the legislation of the Contracting State of which the child is a national by birth.

Article 32
Relations Between Parents and Children

1. The rights and obligations of parents and children, including the parental obligations to maintain children, shall be subject to the legislation of the Contracting State where they are jointly domiciled or, in the absence of such joint domicile, the mutual rights and obligations of the parents and their child shall be subject to the legislation of the Contracting State of which the child is a national.

    Should a claimant so request, maintenance obligations shall be subject to the legislation of the Contracting State where the child is domiciled.

2. The maintenance obligations of adult children in favour of their parents and the maintenance obligations of other family members shall be subject to the legislation of the Contracting State where they shared a joint residence. If they had no such joint residence, such obligations shall be subject to the legislation of the Contracting State of which the claimant is a national.
3. The courts competent in proceedings concerning relations between parents and children shall be those of the Contracting State whose legislation is applicable by virtue of Paragraphs 1 and 2 of the present Article.
4. The enforcement of court judgments rendered in proceedings concerning the upbringing of children shall proceed in the manner prescribed by the legislation of the Contracting State where the child is resident.
5. The Contracting States shall assist one another in tracking down a respondent in proceedings for the recovery of alimony where there is reason to believe that the respondent is to be found in another Contracting State and a court has ordered a search for the respondent.

Article 33

Tutorship and Guardianship

1. Tutorship and guardianship shall be appointed or terminated according to the legislation of the Contracting State of which the ward covered by such tutorship or guardianship is a national.
2. Relations between a tutor or guardian and their ward shall be subject to the legislation of that Contracting State whose judicial authority has appointed the tutor or guardian.
3. The obligation to act as a tutor or guardian shall be imposed according to the legislation of the Contracting State of which the person to act in that capacity is a national.
4. The tutor or guardian of a person who is a national of one Contracting State shall be a national of another Contracting State if resident in the Contracting State where such tutorship or guardianship is to be exercised.

Article 34

Competence of Contracting States' Judicial Authorities in Matters of Tutorship and Guardianship

The judicial authorities competent in proceedings for the appointment or termination of tutorship or guardianship shall be those of the Contracting State of which the ward covered by such tutorship or guardianship is a national, unless otherwise established hereunder.

Article 35

Procedure for Taking Measures by Way of Tutorship and Guardianship

1. Where necessary to take measures towards tutorship or guardianship in the interest of a national of one Contracting State who is domiciled or resident or whose property is located in another Contracting State, a judicial authority of the latter Contracting State shall promptly notify that judicial authority competent under Article 34 above accordingly.
2. In cases brooking no delay, a judicial authority of another Contracting State may itself initiate the necessary temporary measures under the latter's own legislation. In such case, it shall promptly notify that judicial authority competent under Article 34 above accordingly. Such measures shall continue in effect until that judicial authority specified in Article 34 above resolves otherwise.

Article 36

Procedure for Transfer of Tutorship or Guardianship

1. That judicial authority competent under Article 34 above may transfer tutorship or guardianship to a judicial authority of another Contracting State where the ward covered by such tutorship or guardianship is domiciled or resident or where such person's property is located. The tutorship or guardianship concerned shall then be deemed transferred with effect as from the moment when the judicial authority addressed accepts such tutorship or guardianship and notifies the requesting judicial authority accordingly.
2. That judicial authority accepting tutorship or guardianship pursuant to Paragraph 1 of the present Article shall exercise the same in the manner prescribed by the legislation of its own Contracting State.

Article 37

Adoptions

1. An adoption shall take effect or be rendered ineffective under the legislation of that Contracting State of which the foster parent was a national when filing an application for such adoption to become valid or be terminated.
2. The adoption of a child who is a national of another Contracting State shall take effect or be rendered ineffective subject to consent from such child's lawful representative and a competent government agency, as well as from the child himself if required under the legislation of the Contracting State of which the child is a national.
3. If a child is adopted by spouses one of whom is a national of one Contracting State and the other is a national of another Contracting State, the adoption shall take effect or be rendered ineffective on those terms as established by the legislation of both Contracting States.

4. The judicial authority competent in proceedings for an adoption to take effect or be rendered ineffective shall be that of the Contracting State of which the foster parent was a national when filing an application for such adoption to become valid or be terminated or, in the case specified in Paragraph 3 of the present Article, that of the Contracting State where the spouses have or had their last joint domicile or residence.

Part IV

Property Relations

Article 38

Ownership Rights

1. Ownership rights in real property shall be subject to the legislation of the Contracting State where it is located. The question of which property falls under the category of real property shall be determined according to the legislation of the Contracting State where it is located.
2. Ownership rights in vehicles liable to be recorded in state registers shall be subject to the legislation of the Contracting State where the judicial authority that has registered the corresponding vehicle is located.
3. Ownership rights or other rights in rem in property shall arise and be terminated under the legislation of the Contracting State where such property was located when that act or another circumstance which has resulted in such rights arising or being terminated took place.
4. Ownership rights or other rights in rem in any property constituting the subject matter of a transaction shall be subject to the legislation of the Contracting State where such transaction was executed, unless the parties agree otherwise.

Article 39

Form of Transaction

1. The form of a transaction shall be subject to the legislation of the Contracting State where it is executed.
2. The form of a transaction involving real property and related rights shall be subject to the legislation of the Contracting State where such real property is located.

Article 40

Power of Attorney

The form and validity period of a power of attorney shall be subject to the legislation of the Contracting State where such power of attorney is issued.

Article 41

Rights and Obligations of Parties to Transaction

The rights and obligations of the parties to a transaction shall be subject to the legislation of the Contracting State where such transaction is executed, unless the parties agree otherwise.

Article 42

Compensation for Damage

1. Any obligations to provide compensation for damage, other than those which arise out of or in connection with contracts or other legitimate acts, shall be subject to the legislation of the Contracting State where that act or another circumstance which has resulted in the claims of such damages took place.
2. If the tortfeasor and the victim are nationals of the same Contracting State, the legislation of this Contracting State shall be applied.
3. The court competent to deal with such matters as are specified in Paragraphs 1 and 2 of the present Article shall be that of the Contracting State where that act or other circumstance which has constituted grounds for the claims of damages took place. The aggrieved party may also have recourse to a court in the Contracting State where the respondent is resident.

Article 43

Statute of Limitations

Any period-of-limitation matters shall be subject to the legislation that is applicable to the respective legal relationship.

Part V

Succession

Article 44

Principal of Equality

The nationals of each of the Contracting States may inherit property or rights in the other Contracting States by law or testament on the same terms and to the same extent as its own nationals.

Article 45

Succession Rights

1. Other than in that case which is provided for in Paragraph 2 of the present Article, succession rights in property shall be subject to the legislation of that Contracting State where the testator was last domiciled.
2. Succession rights in real property shall be subject to the legislation of that Contracting State where such real property is located.

Appendix 6

Article 46
Procedure for Decedent's Estate to Pass Onto the State

If the State is a successor under the legislation of a Contracting State which is applicable to a succession, the movable estate shall pass onto the Contracting State of which the testator was a national at the time of his demise, while the real estate shall pass onto that Contracting State where such property is located.

Article 47
Testament

A person's ability to draw up and revoke a testament, as well as the form of the testament and that of the act revoking the same, shall be subject to the legislation of that Contracting State where the testator was resident when executing the document. However, neither a testament nor an act revoking the same may be invalidated by reason of failure to observe the prescribed form if its form complies with the relevant requirements in effect in the Contracting State where the document was executed.

Article 48
Competence in Succession Matters

1. The judicial authorities competent in succession proceedings over movable estate shall be those of the Contracting State where the testator was resident at the time of his demise.
2. The judicial authorities competent in succession proceedings over real estate shall be those of the Contracting State where such property is located.
3. The provisions of Paragraphs 1 and 2 of the present Article shall also be applicable to disputes arising out of succession proceedings.

Article 49
Competence of Diplomatic Missions and Consular Offices in Succession Matters

The diplomatic missions or consular offices of each of the Contracting States may represent its nationals, if these are absent or have failed to appoint their representatives, in succession matters, including disputes, without a power of attorney (but shall not be entitled to renounce succession rights).

Article 50
Measures to Protect Estate

1. The judicial authorities of the Contracting States shall take the measures necessary under their legislation to protect that estate left on their territories by any nationals of the other Contracting States or to manage such estate.

2. The diplomatic mission or consular office of the Contracting State of which the successor is a national shall be promptly notified of those measures taken pursuant to Paragraph 1 of the present Article. Such mission or office may take part in the implementation of such measures.
3. Those measures taken in accordance with Paragraph 1 of the present Article may be modified, called off, or suspended upon an appropriate petition lodged by a judicial authority competent to conduct succession proceedings, or by a diplomatic mission or consular office.

Section III

Recognition and Enforcement of Judgments

Article 51

Recognition and Enforcement of Judgments

On the terms and conditions herein contained, each of the Contracting States shall recognize and enforce the following judgments rendered in the other Contracting States:

a) judgments rendered by judicial authorities in civil and family cases, including amicable settlements approved by courts in such cases and notarial acts in respect of monetary obligations ("judgments"); and
b) judgments rendered by courts in criminal cases and ordering damages to be paid.

Article 52

Recognition of Unenforceable Judgments

1. Those judgments which have been rendered by any judicial authorities in any Contracting State and become res judicata which, by their nature, do not require enforcement shall be recognized in the other Contracting States without the need for any special further proceedings unless:
    a) a judicial authority in the Contracting State addressed has already rendered a judgment in the case and such judgment has the effect of res judicata; or
    b) in accordance with this Convention or, in those cases left uncovered hereunder, with the legislation of the Contracting State where the judgment is to be recognized, the matter falls within the exclusive competence of the judicial authorities of such Contracting State.
2. The provisions of Paragraph 1 of the present Article shall be also applicable to judgments concerning tutorship and guardianship, as well as divorces, and rendered by such judicial authorities as are competent to decide such matters under the legislation of the Contracting State where the corresponding judgments have been rendered.

Article 53

Petitions for Enforcement of Judgments

1. A petition for the enforcement of a judgment shall be filed with a competent court in the Contracting State where such judgment is to be executed. Such petition may also be lodged with the court of first instance that has rendered the judgment. Such court shall then resend the petition to that court competent to decide on the same.
2. Such petition shall be accompanied by:
    a) judgment or its certified copy, as well as an official document evidencing that the judgment has the effect of res judicata and is enforceable or that it is to be enforced before becoming res judicata, unless this follows from the judgment itself;
    b) document to confirm that the party who did not take part in the proceedings and against whom the judgment has been rendered was duly served timely summons to the court or, if procedurally incapable, was duly represented;
    c) document confirming a partial enforcement of the judgment by the time it was sent; and
    d) document attesting to the parties' agreement in matters subject to contractual jurisdiction.
3. A petition for the enforcement of a judgment, and accompanying documents shall be submitted together with their certified translations into the language of the Contracting State addressed or into Russian.

Article 54

Procedure for Recognition and Enforcement of Judgments

1. Such petitions for the recognition and enforcement of judgments as are provided for in Article 51 shall be considered by appropriate courts of the Contracting State where such enforcement is sought.
2. A court considering a petition for the recognition and enforcement of a judgment shall limit itself to determining that the relevant terms of this Convention have been observed. Subject to their observance, the court shall rule to proceed with the enforcement sought.
3. The enforcement procedure shall be subject to the legislation of the Contracting State where such enforcement is sought.

Article 55

Refusal of Recognition and Enforcement of Judgments

The recognition of a judgment pursuant to Article 52 and the declaration of enforceability may be refused if:

a) the judgment does not have the effect of res judicata or is not enforceable under the legislation of the Contracting State of origin, unless such judgment is enforceable before becoming res judicata; or
b) the respondent did not take part in the proceedings as a result of either the respondent itself or its duly authorized representative not having been duly served timely summons to the court; or
c) a judgment has already been rendered and has the effect of res judicata, or a judgment rendered by a court in a third state has already been recognized, in the Contracting State addressed in a case involving the same parties, regarding the same subject matter, and based on the same cause of action, or a judicial authority in that Contracting State has already instituted proceedings in such case; or
d) pursuant to this Convention or, in those cases not addressed hereunder, to the legislation of the Contracting State addressed, a judicial authority of that Contracting State has exclusive jurisdiction over the matter concerned; or
e) there is no documented evidence to confirm that the parties have agreed on contractual jurisdiction in respect of the matter in question; or
f) the period of limitation applicable to enforcement according to the legislation of the Contracting State addressed has expired.

Section IV

Legal Assistance and Legal Relations in Criminal Matters

Part I

Extradition

Article 56

Obligation of Extradition

1. The Contracting States hereby agree on the terms and conditions herein contained to extradite certain persons found on their territories to one another upon request for such persons to be held criminally liable or face the punishment already fixed for them in appropriate sentences.
2. Extradition procedures shall be invoked to hold a person criminally liable for such acts as are punishable - by imprisonment of at least one year or by stricter penalties – according to the legislation of both that Contracting State seeking such extradition and the Contracting State addressed.
3. Extradition procedures shall be invoked to administer the punishment already fixed for such acts as are punishable according to the legislation of both that Contracting State seeking such extradition and the Contracting State addressed where the person concerned has been sentenced to imprisonment of at least six months or to a stricter penalty.

Article 57
Refusal of Extradition

1. No extradition shall take place if:
   a) the person sought is a national of the Contracting State addressed;
   b) at the time when the extradition request was received, no criminal prosecution was possible according to the legislation of the Contracting State addressed or the sentence may not be executed due to the expiry of the period of limitation or for any other legal reason; or
   c) a sentence has already been passed in the Contracting State addressed to convict the person sought for the same crime or a resolution has already been issued and became res judicata in such Contracting State to dismiss the proceedings in the case; or
   d) the criminal prosecution is sought on private charges (upon the victim's request) according to the legislation of the Contracting State requesting such extradition or of the Contracting State addressed.
2. An extradition request may be refused if the crime for which the person in question is sought has been committed in the Contracting State addressed.
3. Should its extradition request be refused, the requesting Contracting State shall be advised of the reason for such refusal.

Article 58
Extradition Request

1. An extradition request shall indicate or contain the following:
   a) names of the requesting judicial authority and the judicial authority addressed;
   b) description of the facts of the corresponding act and the text of the requesting Contracting State's law qualifying such act as a crime, with an indication of the punishment due for such crime under the law;
   c) first name, middle name, surname, year of birth, nationality, and domicile or residence address of the person to be extradited, as well as, if possible, a description of such person's appearance, his photograph, fingerprints, and other personal data; and
   d) information about the extent of the damage caused by the crime.
2. An extradition request for criminal prosecution purposes shall be accompanied by a certified copy of the resolution ordering that the person concerned be taken into custody.
3. An extradition request for the purposes of enforcing a sentence shall be accompanied by a certified copy of such sentence bearing a note to confirm that it has come into force and by the text of that provision in the criminal law whereby such person has been convicted. If the convict has already served a part of the sentence, this shall also be reported.

4. Extradition requests and accompanying documents shall be executed in accordance with the requirements set out in Article 17.

Article 59
Additional Data

1. If an extradition request does not contain all of the required information, the Contracting State addressed may request additional data to be made available over a period of up to one month. Such period may be further extended by up to one month on the basis of an appropriate petition from the requesting Contracting State.
2. Should the requesting Contracting State fail to provide the additional data requested on time, the Contracting State addressed shall release the person taken into custody.

Article 60
Search for Person and Taking Into Custody

Immediately upon receiving an extradition request, the Contracting State addressed shall take the measures necessary to track down the person sought and take him into custody, except in cases where such extradition may not take place.

Article 61
Taking Into Custody or Detention Prior to Receipt of Extradition Request

1. On the basis of a special petition to such effect, the person sought may be taken into custody even before the receipt of an extradition request in his respect. Such petition shall refer to the resolution ordering that the person concerned be taken into custody or to the sentence having the effect of res judicata, and shall promise that the extradition request is forthcoming. Such petition requesting that a person be taken into custody before the receipt of an extradition request may be submitted by mail, telex, or fax.
2. The person concerned may also be detained without that petition provided for in Paragraph 1 of the present Article if there are statutory grounds for suspecting such person of having committed such crime in another Contracting State as will entail his extradition.
3. The other Contracting State shall be immediately advised of any such person having been taken into custody or detained before the receipt of an extradition request in his respect.

Appendix 6

Article 61-1

Search for Person Prior to Receipt of Extradition Request

1. Upon being petitioned to do so, the Contracting States shall search for certain persons prior to receiving a request for their extradition where there is reason to believe that such persons may be found in the Contracting State thus petitioned.
2. Such search petitions shall be executed in accordance with the requirements of Article 7 above, and shall contain the fullest possible description of the person sought along with any other data making it possible to establish his whereabouts, as well as a request to take such person into custody along with a promise that an extradition request in his respect is forthcoming.
3. A search petition shall be accompanied by a certified copy of a resolution issued by a competent judicial authority and ordering that the person concerned be taken into custody or by a sentence having the effect of res judicata, information about the time still to be served thereby, and the wanted person's photograph and fingerprints, if any.
4. The Contracting State petitioning a search shall be immediately advised of the taking of the corresponding person into custody or of the other results of the search.

Article 61-2

Calculation of Time Spent in Custody

The time spent in custody by a person taken into custody by virtue of Articles 60, 61, and 61-1 shall be counted, should such person be extradited, towards the total period spent in custody in accordance with the legislation of the Contracting State to which the person has been extradited.

Article 62

Release of Person Detained or Taken Into Custody

1. That person taken into custody in accordance with Paragraph 1 of Articles 61 and 61-1 shall be released upon the receipt of the requesting Contracting State's notice requiring such person to be set free or if the Contracting State addressed fails to receive an extradition request complete with all accompanying documents required by Article 58 hereof within 40 days from the day on which the person concerned was taken into custody.
2. That person detained in accordance with Paragraph 2 of Article 61 shall be released unless a petition for such person to be taken into custody pursuant to Paragraph 1 of Article 61 is received within the statutory detention period.

Article 63
Deferral of Extradition

If a person requested to be extradited has been held criminally liable or convicted of other crime committed in the Contracting State addressed, the extradition of such person may be deferred pending the completion of such criminal prosecution, enforcement of the sentence, or release from punishment.

Article 64
Temporary Extradition

1. Where the deferral of extradition as provided for in Article 63 may entail the expiry of the period of limitation applicable to criminal prosecution or interfere with the investigation of the crime, the person requested to be extradited may be extradited temporarily.
2. The person that was extradited temporarily shall be returned upon the completion of the act making part of the criminal proceedings for which such person has been extradited, but at all times within three months from the extradition date. Where substantiated, such period, however, may be extended.

Article 65
Collision of Extradition Requests

Where extradition requests are received from several countries, the Contracting State addressed shall decide which request to grant at its own discretion.

Article 66
Restrictions on Criminal Prosecution of Extradited Persons

1. A person extradited may not – other than with the consent of the Contracting State addressed - be held criminally liable or punished for any crime committed before the extradition, unless such crime constitutes the reason for such extradition.
2. Nor may such person be extradited to any third country other than with the consent of the Contracting State addressed.
3. No such consent from the Contracting State addressed shall be necessary where the person extradited failed to leave the requesting Contracting State, or voluntarily returned thereto, within one month of the completion of the criminal proceedings or, if such person has been convicted, one month of the completion of the sentence or of the release from punishment. Such period shall not include the time during which the person extradited was unable to leave the requesting Contracting State other than through his own fault.

Article 67

Handover of Extradited Person

The Contracting State addressed shall notify the requesting Contracting State of the place and time when the extradition is to take place. If the requesting Contracting State fails to accept the person subject to extradition within 15 days of the extradition date thus scheduled, such person shall be released from custody.

Article 67-1

Repeat Detention or Taking Into Custody

A person's release by virtue of Paragraph 2 of Article 59, Paragraphs 1 and 2 of Article 62, and Article 67 shall not prevent such person from being detained and taken into custody again for the purpose of extradition if an appropriate extradition request has subsequently been received.

Article 68

Repeat Extradition

Should a person extradited evade from criminal prosecution or from the service of sentence and if it returns to the Contracting State addressed, such person shall be extradited on the basis of a new request, but without the need for those documents listed in Articles 58 and 59 to be provided.

Article 69

Notice Reporting Results of Criminal Proceedings

The Contracting States shall keep one another informed on the results of criminal proceedings against those persons extradited thereto. Copies of final judgments shall likewise be sent upon request.

Article 70

Transit Transportation

1. If petitioned by another Contracting State, a Contracting State shall authorize the transit transportation through its territory of those persons extradited to such other Contracting State or handed over thereto temporarily by a third country.
2. Petitions for such authorization shall be considered in accordance with the same procedure as extradition requests.
3. The Contracting State addressed shall authorize the transit transportation sought to be carried out in the manner such Contracting State itself finds the most appropriate.

Article 71

Expenses for Extradition and Transit Transportation

Those expenses incurred for extradition or temporary handover procedures shall be borne by that Contracting State where such expenses were suffered, while transit transportation costs shall be borne by the Contracting State that has requested such transportation.

Part II

Criminal Prosecution

Article 72

Obligation of Criminal Prosecution

1. If requested by another Contracting State, each Contracting State shall be obliged in accordance with its own legislation to carry out the criminal prosecution of its own nationals suspected of having committed a crime in the requesting Contracting State.
2. Should that crime which has prompted the initiation of criminal proceedings entail civil-law claims from its victims, such claims shall be considered as part of the proceedings provided that the claimants have filed applications for damages.

Article 73

Criminal Prosecution Request

1. A criminal prosecution request shall indicate or contain the following:
   a) name of the requesting judicial authority;
   b) description of the act that has prompted the criminal prosecution request;
   c) time and place of such act, which shall be indicated as exactly as possible;
   d) the text of that legislative provision of the requesting Contracting State qualifying the act as a crime, as well as the texts of other legislative provisions of material relevance to the proceedings;
   e) first name, surname, and nationality of the suspect, and other personal information regarding the same;
   f) applications filed by victims for the institution of the criminal proceedings concerned and for damages; and
   g) indication of the extent of the damage caused by the crime.

   Such request shall be accompanied by the briefs prepared and evidence gathered in the course of the relevant criminal proceedings that the requesting Contracting State has at its disposal.
2. Where the requesting Contracting State sends a file covering ongoing criminal proceedings, the Contracting State addressed shall continue the investigation of such matter in accordance with its own legislation. Each of the documents

attached to the file shall be evidenced by an official stamp of the competent judicial authority of the requesting Contracting State.
3. A criminal prosecution request and accompanying documents shall be executed in accordance with the requirements of Article 18.
4. If an indictee was at the time when a criminal prosecution request was sent in custody in the requesting Contracting State, the indictee shall be taken to the Contracting State addressed.

Article 74
Notice of Results of Criminal Prosecution

The Contracting State addressed shall notify the requesting Contracting State of the final judgment. The requesting Contracting State shall also be sent a copy of the final judgment upon request.

Article 75
Consequences of Issue of Judgment

Where a Contracting State has been sent a criminal prosecution request by virtue of Article 72 after the sentence became res judicata or after a judicial authority in the Contracting State addressed issued another final judgment, no judicial authority in the requesting Contracting State may institute related criminal proceedings and that criminal case already opened shall be dismissed.

Article 76
Mitigating or Aggravating Circumstances

During the investigation of crimes and the hearing of criminal cases by the courts, each Contracting State shall take account of those mitigating and aggravating circumstances which are provided for by the legislation of the Contracting States, regardless of the Contracting State where such circumstances have occurred.

Article 76-1
Acknowledgement of Verdicts

When deciding whether a person should be pronounced an especially dangerous repeat offender, has committed crimes repeatedly, or breached the terms of a suspended sentence, postponement of a sentence, or parole, the judicial authorities of the Contracting States may acknowledge and act with due regard for those verdicts passed by the courts or tribunals of the former Soviet Union and its constituent republics, or the Contracting States' courts.

Appendix 6

Article 77

Procedure for Dealing With Cases Falling Under the Jurisdiction of Courts in Two or More Contracting States

Where a person or a group of persons are indicted on several counts falling within the jurisdiction of courts in two or more of the Contracting States, the court competent to deal with such cases shall be one in the Contracting State where the preliminary investigation has been completed. Such proceedings shall conform to the judicial procedures in effect in such Contracting State.

Part III

Special Provisions on Legal Assistance and Legal Relations in Criminal Matters

Article 78

Transfer of Exhibits

1. The Contracting States shall provide one another upon request with:
    a) such items as were used during a crime entailing the extradition of the criminal in accordance with this Convention, including instruments of the crime, property obtained as a result of the crime or as a reward for the crime, or assets exchanged for such property; and
    b) items which may have the significance of evidence in a criminal case; they shall also be transferred where the criminal cannot be extradited as a result of the latter's demise or escape, or for other reasons.
2. Should the Contracting State addressed need those items listed in Article 78.1 above as evidence in a criminal case, their transfer may be delayed until the completion of the criminal proceedings in question.
3. Third-party rights in the items transferred shall remain valid. Following the completion of proceedings in a case, such items shall be returned, free of charge, to the Contracting State which has made them available.

Article 78-1

Temporary Transfer of Person Held in Custody or Serving Time

1. Should it be necessary to interrogate a person held in custody or serving time in another Contracting State as a witness or a victim, or to perform any other investigative action with the participation of such person, the Contracting State addressed may transfer such person, regardless of its nationality and upon a substantiated request from the General Procurator (Prosecutor) of the requesting Contracting State, to the latter temporarily, provided that the person concerned is held in custody and returned when due.
2. A request for such temporary transfer of a person described in Paragraph 1 of the present Article shall be executed in accordance with the requirements of

Article 7, and shall indicate the time for which such person is required to be present in the requesting Contracting State.
3. No person described in Paragraph 1 of the present Article shall be subject to such temporary transfer:
   a) other than upon his own consent; or
   b) if required to be present during the preliminary investigation or hearing in the Contracting State addressed; or
   c) if the transfer may entail a breach of the time during which such person is required to remain in custody or in prison to serve the sentence.
4. Those persons described in Paragraph 1 of the present Article shall be entitled to those guarantees granted by Paragraph 1 of Article 9.

Article 79

Notices of Convictions and Criminal Records

1. Each Contracting State shall annually provide the other Contracting States with reports on res judicata convictions rendered by its courts against the nationals of the respective Contracting States together with the convicts' fingerprints.
2. Each Contracting State shall provide the other Contracting States, upon request and free of charge, with the criminal records of persons previously convicted by its courts if such persons are held criminally liable in the requesting Contracting State.

Article 80

Special Liaison Procedures

Contacts regarding extradition and criminal prosecution issues shall be maintained by the General Procurators (Prosecutors) of the Contracting States.

Contacts regarding the performance of procedural or other acts requiring authorization from a public prosecutor or a court shall be maintained by public prosecutors' offices in accordance with the procedures prescribed by the General Procurators (Prosecutors) of the Contracting States.

Section V

Final Provisions

Article 81

Implementation Issues

Any issues arising out of or in connection with the implementation of this Convention shall be resolved by the competent authorities of the Contracting States by mutual agreement.

Appendix 6

Article 82
Convention's Relationship with Other International Agreements

This Convention shall not affect the provisions of other international agreements to which the Contracting States are parties.

Article 83
Coming Into Force

1. This Convention shall be subject to ratification by its signatory nations. The instruments of ratification shall be surrendered for custody to the Government of the Belarus Republic, which shall act as the depositary of this Convention.
2. This Convention shall come into force on the 30th day after the day on which the third instrument of ratification is surrendered to the depositary. For each Contracting State which surrenders its instrument of ratification to the depositary after this Convention has already entered into force, this Convention shall take effect on the 30th day after the day on which its instrument of ratification was surrendered to the depositary.

Article 84
Term

1. This Convention shall be valid for five years after its effective date. Upon the expiry of that period, this Convention shall be automatically extended, each time for another five-year term.
2. Any Contracting State may withdraw from this Convention by written notice to the depositary 12 months prior to the expiry of the five-year term then in effect.

Article 85
Retroactive Force

This Convention shall also apply to those legal relations which have arisen before its effective date.

Article 86
Accession Procedure

After this Convention comes into force, other nations may accede hereto – subject to the consent of all of the Contracting States – by providing the depositary with appropriate accession documents. Each accession shall be deemed effective upon the expiry of 30 days after the day on which the depositary received the last notice of consent to such accession.

Article 87

Depositary's Obligations

The depositary shall promptly notify all of the signatories of this Convention and those nations having acceded hereto of the date on which each instrument of ratification or accession document is surrendered for custody, the Convention's effective date, and the depositary's receipt of other notices.

Done in the city of Minsk on 22 January 1993 in a single original copy in Russian. The original shall be on file in the Archives of the Government of the Belarus Republic, which shall send a certified copy of the Convention to each nation that is a party to this Convention.

APPENDIX 7
Convention on Legal Assistance in Civil, Family Relations and Criminal Matters 2002 (the Kishinev Convention)

Adopted in Kishinev on 7 October 2002

(unofficial translation)

Member states of the Commonwealth of Independent States, participating in the present Convention and hereafter referred to as the "Contracting States",
 Being guided by the desire to provide to citizens of the Contracting Parties and persons residing in their territories legal protection of their personal and property rights similar to those of the native inhabitants of all Contacting States,
 Attaching great importance to the development of cooperation in the sphere of granting legal assistance in civil, family, and criminal matters,
Hereby agree as follows:

Part I

General Provisions

Section I

Legal Protection

Article 1

Granting legal protection

1. Citizens of each Contracting State and other persons residing in their territories have the right to use the same legal protection of their personal and property rights as native citizens of Contracting Parties.
2. Citizens of each Contracting State and other persons residing in their territories have the right to free and unimpeded recourse to the courts, public prosecutors' offices, police, security agencies, and other institutions of the other

Contracting States whose competence covers civil, family, and criminal matters (hereafter, the "judicial authorities"), and shall be entitled to apply thereto, hand petitions, file claims, and perform other procedural acts on the same conditions as native citizens.
3. The term "civil matters" used in this Convention also includes matters relating to resolution of economic disputes.
4. This Convention shall also be applicable to legal entities.

Article 2

Exemption from Payment of Duties and Reimbursement for Expenses

1. Citizens of each Contracting State and persons residing in their territories are exempted from any payment of, and any reimbursement for, any judicial and notarial fees and expenses, and have the right to free legal aid on the same conditions as native citizens.
2. The privileges granted by Paragraph 1 of the present Article shall extend to all of the procedural acts performed in civil, family and criminal matters, including the enforcement of a decision or judgment.

Article 3

Presenting documents on Marital and Property Status

1. The privileges granted by Article 2 of this Convention shall be available on the basis of a document evidencing the family and property status of the person handing the petition. These documents shall be issued by a competent authority of the Contracting State where the petitioner is domiciled or resident.
2. If the petitioner is not domiciled or resident in any Contracting State they may present a document issued by an appropriate diplomatic mission or consular office of that Contracting State of which it is a national.
3. The authority deciding on a petition for the above privileges may request some additional information or clarifications from the authority which has issued the document.

Section II

Legal Aid

Article 4

Extension of Legal Aid

1. The judicial authorities of the Contracting States shall extend legal aid in civil, family, and criminal matters in accordance with the relevant provisions of the present Convention.

2. The judicial authorities of the Contracting States shall also grant legal assistance to other institutions in those matters specified in Paragraph 1 of the present Article.
3. Legal assistance is provided on the basis of instructions and other requests provided for by this Convention, sent by judicial institutions of the Contracting State to the judicial institutions of the requested Contracting State.

Article 5
Liaison Procedure

1. When providing legal assistance, the competent judicial authorities of the Contracting States shall communicate with one another through their central, regional, and other agencies, unless a different liaison procedure is presupposed hereunder. The Contracting States shall prepare lists of their central, regional, and other agencies duly empowered to maintain direct contacts by notice to the depositary at the time of the deposit of the instruments of ratification or accession.

   On the changes to the list of central, regional and other bodies, the Contracting Parties must/shall notify the depositary.
2. Relations concerning the execution of instructions for conducting procedural actions and investigations requiring the sanction of the prosecutor (court) are exercised through the prosecutor's office.

Article 6
Types of Legal Aid

The Contracting States shall provide one another with legal assistance by performing such procedural and other acts as are stipulated by the legislation of the Contracting State and are required to take such measures, including, but not limited to, the execution and sending of documents, the conduct of inspections and searches, the recovery and delivery of physical evidence, the performance of expert examinations, the interrogation of parties to the proceedings, third parties, suspects, indictees, victims, witnesses, civil plaintiffs, civil defendants, their representatives, legal representatives of the accused, experts, identification, through the use of video communication, video recording and other technical means, tracing individuals, carrying out criminal investigations, prosecuting persons, extraditing them for criminal liability or executing a sentence, search and seizure of money and property obtained by criminal means, as well as profits obtained by criminal means, search for property and funds of civil defendants for the execution on civil cases, commercial and other economic disputes, recognition and execution of executive orders, judgments in civil cases and sentences.

The Contracting Parties may provide mutual legal assistance in other forms and types, based on specific circumstances, the interests of justice and society as a whole and in accordance with the domestic legislation of the Contracting Parties.

Appendix 7

Article 7

Contents and Form of Letters of Request for Legal Assistance

1. A letter of request for legal assistance shall:
    a) identify the authority of the Contracting State whose assistance is sought;
    b) identify the authority of the Contracting State seeking such assistance;
    c) specify the case regarding which the legal aid is requested;
    d) provide information on the natural person: the first names, surnames, patronymics, domiciles or residence addresses, nationalities, and occupations; for juridical persons: name, legal address or location, bank details and fiscal codes;
    e) if those parties listed in paragraph d) above have any representatives, indicate the latter's first names, surnames, and addresses;
    f) ensure the confidentiality of instructions and information received during its execution;
    g) describe the nature of the request and provide such other information as may be necessary for its satisfaction; and
2. Such letter requesting the service of process shall also indicate the recipient's precise address and the name of the document to be delivered.
3. A letter of request shall be signed and evidenced by an official seal of the authority seeking assistance. The request must also include contact numbers and other contact details.
4. A letter of request for legal assistance in accordance with the requirements of paragraphs 1 to 3 of this article shall be forwarded to the judicial authority of the requested Contracting State by the head of the judicial institution of the requesting Contracting State, subject to the provisions of Article 5 of this Convention.
5. In cases that are urgent, a request for legal assistance issued in accordance with the rules of this article may be sent by facsimile or by any other means of communication. At the same time, the original order must be sent by mail or courier.

Article 8

Performance Procedure for a Request for Legal Assistance

1. When acting upon a letter of request, the authority addressed applies laws of its country. If petitioned by the authority seeking assistance, it may also apply the procedural rules of the Contracting State where the latter is based, unless such rules are inconsistent with the legislation of the Contracting State where such assistance is sought. In this case, the requesting Contracting State shall submit the text of the procedural law.
2. If the authority addressed is incompetent to satisfy the request submitted, it must pass it onto a competent authority within 5 days and notify the authority requesting assistance about this.

3. If petitioned by the authority seeking assistance, the authority addressed shall notify the latter and the other parties concerned of the time and place of the request's fulfilment so that they should be able to attend its satisfaction in accordance with the legislation of the Contracting State where such assistance is sought;, and where this does not contradict the legislation of the requesting Contracting State, it shall take part in the implementation of the procedural actions and investigative activities.
4. Where the precise address of the person identified in a letter of request is unknown, the authority addressed shall take the necessary measures to ascertain such address in accordance with the legislation of the Contracting State where such authority is based.
5. After complying with a letter of request, the authority addressed shall return the corresponding documents to the authority which applied for such assistance, unless otherwise provided by this Convention. Where the legal assistance sought cannot be provided as requested, the authority addressed shall also report those reasons that prevent its performance and shall return the corresponding documents to the authority seeking that assistance.

Article 9
Summons of Witnesses, Victims, Civil Claimants, Civil Respondents, Their Representatives, Experts, and Other Parties

1. Regardless of their nationality, no witness, victim, civil claimant, civil respondent, their representative, or expert reporting to a judicial authority of the Contracting State seeking assistance on the basis of a summons served upon such person by an authority of the Contracting State addressed may be held criminally or administratively liable, detained, or punished in the Contracting State seeking their assistance for any act committed before crossing that state's border. Nor may such person be held liable, detained, or punished in connection with their witness testimony or expert opinion offered in connection with the criminal matter in dispute.
The issue of their criminal liability is to be decided in accordance with the provisions of Section IV of this Convention.
2. The summoned persons shall forfeit the guarantee granted therein if they fail, despite being able to do so, to leave the Contracting State that sought assistance within 15 days from the date on which the inquiring judicial authority decides their presence is no longer needed. Such period shall be exclusive of the time during which said persons are unable to leave the Contracting State that sought assistance other than through their own fault.
3. The requesting Contracting State shall reimburse the person referred to in paragraph 1 of this article for expenses related to travel, and accommodation in its territory and unpaid wages for days of absence from work; experts also have the right to remuneration for the conduct of examinations. The call should indicate which payments the summoned persons are eligible to receive;

at their request, the judicial authority of the requesting Contracting State may pay an advance to cover the relevant costs.
4. No summons for any of those persons specified in Paragraph 1 of the present Article and domiciled in any Contracting State reporting to a judicial authority of another Contracting State shall contain any threat of coercion to follow in the event of their non-appearance.

Article 10

Organization of Expert Examinations

1. The judicial authority of the Contracting Parties shall provide mutual legal assistance in organizing and conducting expert examinations in civil, family and criminal cases in specialized expert, research and other competent institutions of the Contracting Parties.
2. While organizing and conducting such examinations, the judicial authorities of the Contracting Parties are subject to domestic law. The expert opinions given in the requested Contracting State in accordance with the legislation of that Contracting State shall have the same validity in the requesting Contracting State and shall be accepted by the judicial institutions of that Contracting State without any special certification.
3. The costs of organizing and conducting expert examinations in such cases shall be borne by the requesting Contracting State, unless otherwise agreed by the Contracting Parties.

Article 11

Summons of witnesses, victims, civil plaintiffs, civil defendants, their representatives and experts

1. The judicial authority addressed by a letter of request shall act in accordance with that procedure in effect in its state if the documents to be delivered have been executed in the latter's language or in Russian or are accompanied by duly certified translations into such languages. Otherwise, it shall pass such documents onto the recipient if the latter agrees to accept them voluntarily.
2. If the documents concerned cannot be delivered at the address indicated in a letter of request, the judicial authority addressed shall take any measures necessary to ascertain such address. Should it prove impossible for the judicial authority addressed to identify that address, it shall advise the judicial authority seeking assistance accordingly and return the documents due for service.
3. The requested service of process shall be confirmed by an appropriate acknowledgement which shall be signed by the recipient and evidenced by the official seal of the judicial authority addressed, indicate the date of such service, and carry the signature of an officer of the serving judicial authority, or by another document issued by the latter and describing the manner, place,

and time of the service performed. If the addressee refused to receive documents or from signing the confirmation, the judicial authority of the requested Contracting State shall notify the judicial institution of the requesting Contracting State.

Article 12
Validity of Documents

1. Those documents which have been executed or certified on the territory of one of the Contracting States by an authority or duly authorized person within their terms of reference and according to the form required by that Contracting State and confirmed by an official seal shall be subject to acceptance in the other Contracting States without the need for any special further certification.
2. Those documents which are accepted as official in any Contracting State shall enjoy the same evidentiary validity as official documents in the other Contracting States.

Article 13
Sending of Civil-Status and Other Documents

1. The Contracting States shall satisfy requests for civil status certificates to be sent without being translated and free of charge to one another directly through their civil registry offices subject to appropriate document transfer notices to the corresponding individuals.
2. Each Contracting State addressed shall satisfy requests for documents evidencing training standards, job seniority, and other documents concerning the personal or proprietary rights and interests of its citizens or other persons domiciled on its territory to be sent – without having such documents translated and free of charge – to another Contracting State requesting such assistance.

Article 14
Powers of Diplomatic Missions and Consular Offices

Diplomatic missions and consular offices of the Contracting Parties have the right to transfer judicial and non-judicial documents or to execute letters of request for the taking of evidence for the vessels of the represented Contracting State in accordance with existing international agreements or, in the absence of such agreements, in any other order not inconsistent with the legislation of the Contracting State, on the territory of which they are located.

Article 15

Legal Information

The central judicial authorities of the Contracting States shall provide one another upon request with information about the internal legislation operating or operated on their territories and on practical application of these laws by the judicial authorities.

Article 16

Ascertainment of Addresses and Other Data

1. The judicial authorities of the Contracting States shall assist one another - upon request and in accordance with their respective legislation - in ascertaining the addresses of persons domiciled on their territories, if necessary for the exercise by their nationals of their rights. In such matters, the Contracting State seeking assistance shall supply that data at its disposal which may help establish the address of the person identified in its request.
2. The judicial authorities of a Contracting State shall assist those of another Contracting State in identifying the employers and ascertaining the income levels of persons domiciled in the Contracting State addressed and facing property claims made by the judicial authorities of the Contracting State seeking assistance in civil, family, or criminal matters.

Article 17

Language

The judicial authorities of the Contracting States shall use the latter's state languages or the Russian language in their liaising hereunder. Should any documents be executed in the Contracting States' state languages, these shall be accompanied by duly certified translations into Russian.

Article 18

Expenses for Legal Assistance

1. Expenses related to the provision of legal assistance shall be borne by that Contracting State in whose territory they arise, unless otherwise provided by this Convention.
2. The requesting Contracting State shall bear the costs of the transfer and transportation of items of historical and cultural value, as well as large material cost.

Article 19

Appeal against actions of officials. Compensation for damage caused

1. Citizens and legal entities of each of the Contracting Parties, as well as other persons on its territory, have the right to appeal against the actions of officials of the judicial institutions of other Contracting Parties that they have carried out in the implementation of the provisions of this Convention in the manner provided by the legislation of the Contracting State at the place of commission such actions, unless otherwise specified by the Convention.
2. If the wrongful acts of officials of the judicial institutions of the Contracting Parties committed in the performance of this Convention to persons referred to in paragraph 1 of this article are harmed, they are entitled to demand compensation in accordance with the legislation of the Contracting State, officials of the institutions of justice of which such harm caused.

Article 20

Confidentiality of Information in the Provision of Legal Assistance

1. The judicial authority of the requested Contracting State, at the request of the judicial institution of the requesting Contracting State, shall take all necessary measures to ensure confidentiality of the fact of receipt and contents of the instruction for rendering legal assistance and data obtained as a result of its execution.
2. The judicial institutions of the requesting and requested Contracting Parties, if necessary, agree on the terms and conditions for preserving the confidentiality of the information obtained as a result of the execution of the instruction.

Article 21

Refusal of Legal Assistance

A request for legal assistance may be turned down, in full or in part, if the grant of such assistance may be detrimental to the sovereignty or security, or is inconsistent with the legislation, of the Contracting State addressed. In such case, the Contracting State seeking legal assistance shall be promptly advised of the reasons why its corresponding request has been denied.

Appendix 7

Part II
Legal Relations in Civil and Family Matters

Section I
Competence

Article 22
General Provisions

1. Unless stipulated otherwise in Parts II–V of the present Section, claims against persons resident in a Contracting State, regardless of their nationality, shall be filed with a court of such Contracting State, while those against a legal entity shall be filed with a court of that Contracting State where such legal entity's governing body, representative office, or branch is located.
   Where proceedings concern several defendants, residing on the territories of different Contacting States, the case is considered in any involved country on the choice of the claimant.
2. Courts on the territory of a Contracting State shall also be competent where it is in the latter that:
   a) the respondent's enterprise or branch maintains trade, industrial operations, or other business; or
   b) the contractual obligation which is the subject of the dispute was performed or has to be performed in whole or in part; or
   c) the claimant in proceedings instituted to uphold the latter's honour, dignity, and business reputation is domiciled or resident.
3. The only courts competent to hear cases initiated over title and other rights in rem to real property shall be those of the place where the property in dispute is located.
   Such claims against a carrier as arise out of or in connection with a contract for the transportation of freight, passengers, or luggage shall be filed at the place where the administration of the carrier duly confronted with an appropriate grievance is located.

Article 23
Contractual Jurisdiction

1. Courts of the Contracting States may hear also other cases where the parties have agreed in writing to submit the corresponding disputes to such courts.
   However, the exclusive competence stemming from Paragraph 3 of Article 20 and other provisions of Parts II–V of the present Section, and from the internal legislation of the Contracting State concerned, may not be altered by agreement of the parties.

2. If there is an agreement to refer a dispute to another court, the court hearing such dispute shall dismiss the proceedings in the case upon the respondent's request.

Article 24
Interrelated Proceedings

1. Where proceedings have been instituted in a matter involving the same parties, regarding the same subject matter, and over the same cause of action in courts of two Contracting States as are competent to hear such disputes hereunder, the court that initiated its proceedings at the later date shall dismiss the case.
2. Such counter-claims and requests for offsets as emanate from the same legal relationship as the principal action shall be subject to the court dealing with the principal action.

Article 25
Requests for Public Prosecutors' Involvement in Civil Proceedings

A public prosecutor in a Contracting State may apply to a public prosecutor in another Contracting State for the institution of proceedings to protect the rights and lawful interests of nationals of the Contracting State seeking such assistance, or for the opportunity to participate in the trial of such matters, or for a cassation appeal, private protest, or supervisory protest to be lodged against judicial resolutions handed down in such matters.

Section II
Personal Status

Article 26
Legal Capacity

1. The legal capacity of a natural person shall be subject to the legislation of the Contracting State of which he is a national.
2. The legal capacity of a stateless person shall be subject to the law of the country where he is domiciled.
3. The legal capacity of a legal entity shall be subject to the legislation of the State under whose laws such legal entity has been established.

Article 27
Pronunciation of Persons to Be of Limited Legal Capacity or Legally Incapable.
Reinstatement of Legal Capacity

1. A court of that Contracting State of which the respondent is a national shall have jurisdiction in proceedings initiated to pronounce such person to be of limited legal capacity or legally incapable, with the exception of cases provided by Paragraphs 2 and 3 of the present Article.
2. Where a court of a Contracting State learns of any reasons why a person resident on the latter's territory, but being a national of another Contracting State should be pronounced to be of partial legal capacity or legally incapable, such court shall give an appropriate notice to a court of the Contracting State of which such person is a national.
3. Where that court of a Contracting State which has been notified of a reason why a person should be pronounced to be of partial legal capacity or legally incapable fails to initiate appropriate proceedings or to come back with its own opinion on the matter within the following three months, the case for the pronunciation of such person to be of limited legal capacity or legally incapable shall be taken up by a court of that Contracting State where the person concerned is resident. The judgment pronouncing a person to be of partial legal capacity or legally incapable shall be sent to a competent court of the Contracting State of which such person is a national.
4. The provisions of Paragraphs 1–3 of the present Article shall also be applicable to the reinstatement of legal capacity.

Article 28
Pronunciation of Persons to Be Missing or Deceased.
Establishment of Facts of Death

1. The judicial authorities competent in proceedings initiated for a person to be pronounced missing or deceased or for a fact of death to be established shall be those of the Contracting State of which the person concerned was a national when last known to be alive or, in the case of other persons, those of the Contracting State where they were last known to be resident.
2. The judicial authorities of each Contracting State may pronounce a national of another Contracting State or any other person who was resident on its territory to be missing or deceased or establish the fact of their death on the basis of a petition filed by those persons concerned and resident on its territory whose rights and interests are based on the legislation of such Contracting State.
3. When conducting proceedings initiated for the pronunciation of a person to be missing or deceased or for the establishment of a fact of death, the judicial authorities of the Contracting States shall apply the latter's own legislation.

Appendix 7

Section III
Family Matters
Article 29
Conclusion of Marriages

Marriage terms for each of the future spouses shall be subject to the legislation of the Contracting State of which they are a national or, for stateless persons, the legislation of the Contracting State where they are domiciled. Furthermore, any obstacles to a marriage shall be subject to the legislation of the Contracting State where it is concluded.

Article 30
Relations Between Spouses

1. Personal and property relations between spouses shall be subject to the legislation of the Contracting State where the spouses jointly reside.
2. If one of the spouses is resident in one Contracting State, while another is resident in another Contracting State, but both spouses share the same nationality, their personal and property relations shall be subject to the legislation of that Contracting State of which they are nationals.
3. If one of the spouses is a national of one Contracting State and the other is a national of another Contracting State and should one of the spouses be resident in one Contracting State and the other be resident in another Contracting State, their personal and property relations shall be subject to the legislation of the Contracting State where they last had their joint residence.
4. If those persons specified in Paragraph 3 of the present Article did not have any joint residence in any of the Contracting States, the governing legislation shall be that of the Contracting State whose authority is hearing their case.
5. Those relations of spouses which concern their real property shall be subject to the legislation of the Contracting State where such real property is located.
6. The authorities competent in proceedings over spouses' personal and property relations shall be those of the Contracting State whose legislation is applicable by virtue of Paragraphs 1 – 3, 5 of the present Article.

Article 31
Dissolution of Marriages

1. Divorce cases shall be subject to the legislation of the Contracting State of which the spouses were nationals at the time when they filed an application for the dissolution of their marriage.
2. If one of the spouses is a national of one Contracting State, while the other is a national of another Contracting State, the governing legislation shall be that of the Contracting State whose authority is hearing the divorce case.

Article 32
Competence of Contracting States' Authorities

1. The judicial authorities competent in divorce proceedings in cases provided for in Paragraph 1 of Article 31 shall be those of the Contracting State of which the spouses were nationals at the time when they filed an application for the dissolution of their marriage. If both spouses were resident in another Contracting State at the time when they filed such application, the judicial authorities of the latter Contracting State shall likewise be competent.
2. The judicial authorities competent in divorce proceedings in those cases provided for by Paragraph 2 of Article 31 shall be those of the Contracting State where both spouses are resident. If one of the spouses is resident in one Contracting State, while the other is resident in another Contracting State, the judicial authorities of both Contracting States where the spouses are resident shall be competent to conduct proceedings for the dissolution of their marriage.

Article 33
Annulment of Marriages

1. Proceedings initiated to have a marriage annulled shall be subject to the same legislation of the corresponding Contracting State which was applicable pursuant to Article 26 to the conclusion of the marriage.
2. The competence of judicial authorities in proceedings to have a marriage annulled shall be determined in accordance with Article 32.

Article 34
Establishment and Challenging of Paternity or Maternity

Paternity and maternity shall be established and challenged according to the legislation of the Contracting State of which the child is a national. If it is impossible to determine citizenship - under the legislation of the Contracting State of which the child is a national after birth.

Article 35
Relations Between Parents and Children

1. The rights and obligations of parents and children, including the parental obligations to maintain children, shall be subject to the legislation of the Contracting State where they are jointly domiciled or, in the absence of such joint domicile, the mutual rights and obligations of the parents and their child shall be subject to the legislation of the Contracting State of which the child is a national.

    Should a claimant so request, maintenance obligations shall be subject to the legislation of the Contracting State where the child is domiciled.

2. The maintenance obligations of adult children in favour of their parents and the maintenance obligations of other family members shall be subject to the legislation of the Contracting State where they shared a joint residence. If they had no such joint residence, such obligations shall be subject to the legislation of the Contracting State of which the claimant is a national.
3. The courts competent in proceedings concerning relations between parents and children shall be those of the Contracting State whose legislation is applicable by virtue of Paragraphs 1 and 2 of the present Article.
4. The enforcement of court judgments rendered in proceedings concerning the upbringing of children shall proceed in the manner prescribed by the legislation of the Contracting State where the child is resident.
5. The Contracting States shall assist one another in tracking down a respondent in proceedings for the recovery of alimony where there is reason to believe that the respondent is to be found in another Contracting State and a court has ordered a search for the respondent.

Article 36
Tutorship and Guardianship

1. Tutorship and guardianship shall be appointed or terminated according to the legislation of the Contracting State of which the ward covered by such tutorship or guardianship is a national.
2. Relations between a tutor or guardian and their ward shall be subject to the legislation of that Contracting State whose judicial authority has appointed the tutor or guardian.
3. The obligation to act as a tutor or guardian shall be imposed according to the legislation of the Contracting State of which the person to act in that capacity is a national.
4. The tutor or guardian of a person who is a national of one Contracting State shall be a national of another Contracting State if resident in the Contracting State where such tutorship or guardianship is to be exercised.

Article 37
Competence of Contracting States' Judicial Authorities in Matters of Tutorship and Guardianship

The judicial authorities competent in proceedings for the appointment or termination of tutorship or guardianship shall be those of the Contracting State of which the ward covered by such tutorship or guardianship is a national, unless otherwise established hereunder.

Article 38
Procedure for Taking Measures by Way of Tutorship and Guardianship

1. Where necessary to take measures towards tutorship or guardianship in the interest of a national of one Contracting State who is domiciled or resident or whose property is located in another Contracting State, a judicial authority of the latter Contracting State shall promptly notify that judicial authority competent under Article 34 above accordingly.
2. In cases brooking no delay, a judicial authority of another Contracting State may itself initiate the necessary temporary measures under the latter's own legislation. In such case, it shall promptly notify that judicial authority competent under Article 34 above accordingly. Such measures shall continue in effect until that judicial authority specified in Article 34 above resolves otherwise.

Article 39
Procedure for Transfer of Tutorship or Guardianship

1. That judicial authority competent under Article 37 above may transfer tutorship or guardianship to a judicial authority of another Contracting State where the ward covered by such tutorship or guardianship is domiciled or resident or where such person's property is located. The tutorship or guardianship concerned shall then be deemed transferred with effect as from the moment when the judicial authority addressed accepts such tutorship or guardianship and notifies the requesting judicial authority accordingly.
2. That judicial authority accepting tutorship or guardianship pursuant to Paragraph 1 of the present Article shall exercise the same in the manner prescribed by the legislation of its own Contracting State.

Article 40
Adoptions

1. An adoption shall take effect or be rendered ineffective under the legislation of that Contracting State of which the foster parent was a national when filing an application for such adoption to become valid or be terminated, if otherwise is not provided by the domestic law of the Contracting State of which the child is national.
2. The adoption of a child who is a national of another Contracting State shall take effect or be rendered ineffective subject to consent from such child's lawful representative and a competent government agency, as well as from the child himself if required under the legislation of the Contracting State of which the child is a national.
3. If a child is adopted by spouses one of whom is a national of one Contracting State and the other is a national of another Contracting State, the adoption

shall take effect or be rendered ineffective on those terms as established by the legislation of both Contracting States, subject to the provisions of paragraphs 1 and 2 of this article.
4. The judicial authority competent in proceedings for an adoption to take effect or be rendered ineffective shall be that of the Contracting State of which the foster parent was a national when filing an application for such adoption to become valid or be terminated or, in the case specified in Paragraph 3 of the present Article, that of the Contracting State where the spouses have or had their last joint domicile or residence.

Section IV
Property Relations
Article 41
Ownership Rights

1. Ownership rights in real property shall be subject to the legislation of the Contracting State where it is located. The question of which property falls under the category of real property shall be determined according to the legislation of the Contracting State where it is located.
2. Ownership rights in vehicles liable to be recorded in state registers shall be subject to the legislation of the Contracting State where the judicial authority that has registered the corresponding vehicle is located.
3. Ownership rights or other rights in rem in property shall arise and be terminated under the legislation of the Contracting State where such property was located when that act or another circumstance which has resulted in such rights arising or being terminated took place.
4. Ownership rights or other rights in rem in any property constituting the subject matter of a transaction shall be subject to the legislation of the Contracting State where such transaction was executed, unless the parties agree otherwise.

Article 42
Form of Transaction

1. The form of a transaction shall be subject to the legislation of the Contracting State where it is executed.
2. The form of a transaction involving real property and related rights shall be subject to the legislation of the Contracting State where such real property is located.

Article 43
Power of Attorney

The form and validity period of a power of attorney shall be subject to the legislation of the Contracting State where such power of attorney is issued. Such power of attorney with a notarized translation into the language of the Contracting State in the territory of which it will be used, either in the Russian language is accepted on the territory of other Contracting Parties without any special license.

Article 44
Rights and Obligations of Parties to Transaction

The rights and obligations of the parties to a transaction shall be subject to the legislation of the Contracting State where such transaction is executed, unless the parties agree otherwise.

Article 45
Compensation for Damage

1. Any obligations to provide compensation for damage, other than those which arise out of or in connection with contracts or other legitimate acts, shall be subject to the legislation of the Contracting State where that act or another circumstance which has resulted in the claims of such damages took place.
2. If the tortfeasor and the victim are nationals of the same Contracting State, the legislation of this Contracting State shall be applied.
3. The court competent to deal with such matters as are specified in Paragraphs 1 and 2 of the present Article shall be that of the Contracting State where that act or other circumstance which has constituted grounds for the claims of damages took place. The aggrieved party may also have recourse to a court in the Contracting State where the respondent is resident.

Article 46
Statute of Limitations

Any period-of-limitation matters shall be subject to the legislation that is applicable to the respective legal relationship.

Section V
Succession

Article 47
Principal of Equality

Citizens of each of the Contracting States may inherit property or rights in the other Contracting States by law or testament on the same terms and to the same extent as its own nationals.

Article 48
Succession Rights

1. Other than in that case which is provided for in Paragraph 2 of the present Article, succession rights in property shall be subject to the legislation of that Contracting State where the testator was last domiciled.
2. Succession rights in real property shall be subject to the legislation of that Contracting State where such real property is located.

Article 49
Procedure for Decedent's Estate to Pass Onto the State

If the State is a successor under the legislation of a Contracting State which is applicable to a succession, the movable estate shall pass onto the Contracting State of which the testator was a national at the time of his demise, while the real estate shall pass onto that Contracting State where such property is located.

Article 50
Testament

A person's ability to draw up and revoke a testament, as well as the form of the testament and that of the act revoking the same, shall be subject to the legislation of that Contracting State where the testator was resident when executing the document. However, neither a testament nor an act revoking the same may be invalidated by reason of failure to observe the prescribed form if its form complies with the relevant requirements in effect in the Contracting State where the document was executed.

Article 51
Competence in Succession Matters

1. The judicial authorities competent in succession proceedings over movable estate shall be those of the Contracting State where the testator was resident at the time of his demise.
2. The judicial authorities competent in succession proceedings over real estate shall be those of the Contracting State where such property is located.
3. The provisions of Paragraphs 1 and 2 of the present Article shall also be applicable to disputes arising out of succession proceedings.

Article 52
Competence of Diplomatic Missions and Consular Offices in Succession Matters

The diplomatic missions or consular offices of each of the Contracting States may represent its nationals, if these are absent or have failed to appoint their representatives, in succession matters, including disputes, without a power of attorney (but shall not be entitled to renounce succession rights).

Article 53
Measures to Protect Estate

1. The judicial authorities of the Contracting States shall take the measures necessary under their legislation to protect that estate left on their territories by any nationals of the other Contracting States or to manage such estate.
2. The diplomatic mission or consular office of the Contracting State of which the successor is a national shall be promptly notified of those measures taken pursuant to Paragraph 1 of the present Article. Such mission or office may take part in the implementation of such measures.
3. Those measures taken in accordance with Paragraph 1 of the present Article may be modified, called off, or suspended upon an appropriate petition lodged by a judicial authority competent to conduct succession proceedings, or by a diplomatic mission or consular office.

Part III
Recognition and Enforcement of Judgments

Article 54
Recognition and Enforcement of Judgments

On the terms and conditions herein contained, each of the Contracting States shall recognize and enforce the following judgments rendered in the other Contracting States:

a) judgments rendered by judicial authorities in civil and family cases, including amicable settlements approved by courts in such cases and notarial acts in respect of monetary obligations ("judgments");
b) sentences (decisions) of courts on criminal cases of the damages, fines and confiscation; and
c) court decisions on seizure of property, including money in bank accounts, in order to ensure the claim.

2. Recognition and enforcement of decisions referred to in paragraph 1 of this Article shall be made in accordance with the law of the requested Contracting State.

Article 55
Recognition of Unenforceable Judgments

1. Those judgments which have been rendered by any judicial authorities in any Contracting State and become res judicata which, by their nature, do not

require enforcement shall be recognized in the other Contracting States without the need for any special further proceedings unless:
   a) a judicial authority in the Contracting State addressed has already rendered a judgment in the case and such judgment has the effect of res judicata; or
   b) in accordance with this Convention or, in those cases left uncovered hereunder, with the legislation of the Contracting State where the judgment is to be recognized, the matter falls within the exclusive competence of the judicial authorities of such Contracting State.
2. The provisions of Paragraph 1 of the present Article shall be also applicable to judgments concerning tutorship and guardianship, as well as divorces, and rendered by such judicial authorities as are competent to decide such matters under the legislation of the Contracting State where the corresponding judgments have been rendered.

Article 56
Petitions for Enforcement of Judgments

1. A petition for the enforcement of a judgment shall be filed with a competent court in the Contracting State where such judgment is to be executed. Such petition may also be lodged with the court of first instance that has rendered the judgment. Such court shall then resend the petition to that court competent to decide on the same.
2. Such petition shall be accompanied by:
   a) judgment or its certified copy, as well as an official document evidencing that the judgment has the effect of res judicata and is enforceable or that it is to be enforced before becoming res judicata, unless this follows from the judgment itself;
   b) document to confirm that the party who did not take part in the proceedings and against whom the judgment has been rendered was duly served timely summons to the court or, if procedurally incapable, was duly represented;
   c) document confirming a partial enforcement of the judgment by the time it was sent; and
   d) document attesting to the parties' agreement in matters subject to contractual jurisdiction.
3. A petition for the enforcement of a judgment, and accompanying documents shall be submitted together with their certified translations into the language of the Contracting State addressed or into Russian.

Article 57

Procedure for Recognition and Enforcement of Judgments

1. Such petitions for the recognition and enforcement of judgments as are provided for in Article 54 shall be considered by appropriate courts of the Contracting State where such enforcement is sought.
2. A court considering a petition for the recognition and enforcement of a judgment shall limit itself to determining that the relevant terms of this Convention have been observed. Subject to their observance, the court shall rule to proceed with the enforcement sought.
3. The enforcement procedure shall be subject to the legislation of the Contracting State where such enforcement is sought.

Article 58

Enforcement of court decisions on recovery of fines, forfeiture of illegally obtained property

1. Decisions of the court of the requesting Contracting State to the recovery of fines, confiscation, or to apply to the income and property of subjects of the state in a criminal case or confiscation of illegally performed the requested Contracting State on the grounds and in the manner prescribed in Articles 8, 54, 56, 57, 59 of this Convention.
2. The amounts of the fines collected are transmitted to the requesting Contracting State.
3. Only the requesting Contracting State shall be entitled to revise the decision on confiscation. The procedure of confiscation is determined by the law of the requested Contracting State.

The requested Contracting State bound by the findings relating to the establishment of the facts in so far as they are stated in a conviction or other judicial decision, decree requesting Contracting State, or to the extent to which the judgment or other judicial decision is based on these findings.

Confiscated property or its equivalent property may be transferred in whole or in part of the Contracting State in which decreed the confiscation.

In each case, the requesting and requested Contracting Parties agree on the division of property received by the Contracting State in the execution of the confiscation order in accordance with this Convention.

Article 59

Refusal of Recognition and Enforcement of Judgments

The recognition of a judgment pursuant to Article 52 and the declaration of enforceability may be refused if:

a) the judgement is rendered with violations of the provisions of this Convention; or
b) in accordance with the law of the Contracting State in whose territory the award is invoked did not enter into force and are not enforceable, except in cases where the decision is enforceable before the entry into force; or
c) the respondent did not take part in the proceedings as a result of either the respondent itself or its duly authorized representative not having been duly served timely summons to the court; or
d) a judgment has already been rendered and has the effect of res judicata, or a judgment rendered by a court in a third state has already been recognized, in the Contracting State addressed in a case involving the same parties, regarding the same subject matter, and based on the same cause of action, or a judicial authority in that Contracting State has already instituted proceedings in such case; or
e) pursuant to this Convention or, in those cases not addressed hereunder, to the legislation of the Contracting State addressed, a judicial authority of that Contracting State has exclusive jurisdiction over the matter concerned; or
f) there is no documented evidence to confirm that the parties have agreed on contractual jurisdiction in respect of the matter in question; or
g) the period of limitation applicable to enforcement according to the legislation of the Contracting State addressed has expired; or
h) recognition and execution of the decision is contrary to the public policy of the requested Contracting State.

Part IV

Legal Assistance and Legal Relations in Criminal Matters

Section I

ORDER OF RENDERING LEGAL ASSISTANCE IN CRIMINAL MATTERS

Article 60

Content and form of instruction for legal assistance in a criminal case

1. Instruction for legal assistance in a criminal case shall be made in accordance with the requirements of Article 7 of this Convention.
2. The instruction must also be specify:
    a) description and qualification of the crime, the extent of loss data, if it was caused by a criminal act;
    b) a detailed list of procedural actions, investigative or search operations to be carried out within the framework of the criminal case, as well as other information necessary for the execution of the order;
    c) a list of questions to be find out during the interrogation;
    d) the full text of the rules of law, on the grounds of which that a criminal case is being investigated.

3. Duly certified, and where necessary, authorized in accordance with legislation of the requesting Contracting State shall decisions on the procedural actions, investigative or search operations shall be attached to the instruction on legal assistance in a criminal case.

Article 61

Execution of orders for legal assistance in a criminal case

1. The competent judicial authorities of the Contracting Parties shall ensure the implementation of orders for legal assistance in criminal matters in accordance with the requirements of Article 8 of the Convention.
2. The provisions of the judicial authorities of the requesting Contracting State referred to in paragraph 3 of Article 60 of this Convention, are the basis for the production of specified therein procedural and other actions. Additional legalization of the order is not required, if it is not contrary to the domestic law of the requested Contracting State.
3. For the most complete and accurate execution of orders judicial authority of the requested Contracting State may request from the judicial authorities of the requesting Contracting State for more information.

    During the execution judicial institutions of the requesting and requested Contracting Parties may exchange information on the progress of investigation, investigations or search operations, provide one another for more information, and to coordinate issues on additional investigation, investigative or search operations.
4. After the execution of the order the judicial authority of the requested Contracting State sends the received materials to the Department of Justice of the requesting Contracting State or the initiator instructions with the notification on the execution of the order by judicial authorities order the requesting Contracting State.

Article 62

Requests execution dates for legal assistance in criminal matters

1. Orders for legal assistance in criminal matters are executed within the period prescribed by the legislation of the Contracting State.
2. If necessary, the period of execution of the order for legal assistance in coordination of the competent institutions of justice of the Contracting Parties may be extended.

Article 63

Establishment and operation of joint investigative team

1. For the purpose of rapid and thorough investigation of the crimes committed by one or more persons in the territories of two or more Contracting Parties or affecting them, may set up joint investigation group.
2. The proposal to set up a joint investigation group shall be in accordance with the procedure under Article 60 of this Convention.
3. The requested Contracting State shall, within 15 days after receipt of the proposal to establish a joint investigation group shall notify the requesting Contracting State of the decision, and in the case of consent it provides at the same time a list of the officials included in that group.
4. The members of the joint investigation group directly interact with each other, agree on the basic direction of the investigation, investigative actions, investigative or search operations, exchange the received information. Coordination of their activities is exercised by the initiator of the creation of a joint investigation group or one of its members.
5. Investigative actions, investigative or search operations carried out by members of joint investigation group of the Contracting State in whose territory they are held. Participation of members of the joint investigation group of one Contracting State in the conduct of investigative actions, investigative and search operations on the territory of the other Contracting State pursuant to the procedure provided for in Article 8 of the Convention.

Article 64

Execution of orders on certain conditions

1. Department of Justice of the requested Party may postpone the execution of orders or execute it partially, if its immediate execution prevent investigation or proceeding which is produced in the territory of the Contracting State.
2. Before addressing the issue of postponement of execution of the order or partial performance of his judicial authority of the Contracting State shall consider the possibility of execution of the order on certain conditions. If the judicial authority of the requesting Contracting State agrees to such conditions, it shall notify in writing the judicial authority of the requested Contracting State and meet its conditions.

Article 65

The legal value of evidence obtained as a result of execution of the order

Evidence obtained in the requested Contracting State as result of execution of instructions in accordance with its legislation, have the same probative value in the requesting Contracting State.

Appendix 7

Section II

Extradition

Article 66

Obligation of Extradition

1. The Contracting States hereby agree on the terms and conditions herein contained to extradite certain persons found on their territories to one another upon request for such persons to be held criminally liable or face the punishment already fixed for them in appropriate sentences.
2. Extradition procedures shall be invoked to hold a person criminally liable for such acts as are punishable – by imprisonment of at least one year or by stricter penalties – according to the legislation of both that Contracting State seeking such extradition and the Contracting State addressed.
3. Extradition procedures shall be invoked to administer the punishment already fixed for such acts as are punishable according to the legislation of both that Contracting State seeking such extradition and the Contracting State addressed where the person concerned has been sentenced to imprisonment of at least six months or to a stricter penalty.
4. When deciding whether an act for issuance of the request, is considered to be criminal under the domestic law of the requested and requesting contracting parties, the differences in the description of the individual features of a crime and the terminology used are irrelevant.

Article 67

Extradition Request

1. An extradition request shall indicate or contain the following:
   a) names of the requesting judicial authority and the judicial authority addressed;
   b) description of the facts of the corresponding act and the text of the requesting Contracting State's law qualifying such act as a crime, with an indication of the punishment due for such crime under the law;
   c) first name, middle name, surname, year of birth, nationality, and domicile or residence address of the person to be extradited, as well as, if possible, a description of such person's appearance, his photograph, fingerprints, and other personal data; and
   d) information about the extent of the damage caused by the crime.
2. An extradition request for criminal prosecution purposes shall be accompanied by a certified copy of the resolution ordering that the person concerned be taken into custody.
3. An extradition request for the purposes of enforcing a sentence shall be accompanied by a certified copy of such sentence bearing a note to confirm

that it has come into force and by the text of that provision in the criminal law whereby such person has been convicted. If the convict has already served a part of the sentence, this shall also be reported.
4. Extradition requests and accompanying documents shall be executed in accordance with the requirements set out in paragraph 3 Article 7 and Article 17.

Article 68

Search for Person and Taking Into Custody

Immediately upon receiving an extradition request, the Contracting State addressed shall take the measures necessary to track down the person sought and take him into custody, except in cases where such extradition may not take place.

Article 69

Search for Person Prior to Receipt of Extradition Request

1. Upon being petitioned to do so, the Contracting States shall search for certain persons prior to receiving a request for their extradition where there is reason to believe that such persons may be found in the Contracting State thus petitioned.
2. Such search petitions shall be executed in accordance with the requirements of Article 7 above, and shall contain the fullest possible description of the person sought along with any other data making it possible to establish his whereabouts, as well as a request to take such person into custody along with a promise that an extradition request in his respect is forthcoming.
3. A search petition shall be accompanied by a certified copy of a resolution issued by a competent judicial authority and ordering that the person concerned be taken into custody or by a sentence having the effect of res judicata, information about the time still to be served thereby, and the wanted person's photograph and fingerprints, if any.
4. The Contracting State petitioning a search shall be immediately advised of the taking of the corresponding person into custody or of the other results of the search.

Article 70

Taking Into Custody or Detention Prior to Receipt of Extradition Request

1. On the basis of a special petition to such effect, the person sought may be taken into custody even before the receipt of an extradition request in his respect. Such petition shall refer to the resolution ordering that the person concerned be taken into custody or to the sentence having the effect of res judicata, and shall promise that the extradition request is forthcoming. Such petition

requesting that a person be taken into custody before the receipt of an extradition request may be submitted by mail, telex, or fax.
2. The person whose extradition is sought may be arrested before receipt of a request for extradition and an ad it into an international (intergovernmental) wanted. The basis of his detention in such cases is the entered into force decision of the competent judicial authorities of the requesting Contracting State of taking into custody as a preventive measure or a sentence.
3. The person concerned may also be detained without that petition provided for in Paragraph 1 of the present Article if there are statutory grounds for suspecting such person of having committed such crime in another Contracting State as will entail his extradition.

Article 71
Terms of the extradition request

1. The request for extradition shall be considered within 30 days after its receipt by the competent judicial authority of the Contracting State, unless otherwise stipulated by the legislation of that Contracting State. A judicial authority of the requesting Contracting State shall be notified on the results of consideration of the request for the extradition.
2. If the request for extradition does not contain all the necessary data, the judicial authority of the requested Contracting State may request additional information, which set a deadline of 30 days. This period may be extended up to 30 days at the request of judicial authorities of the requesting Contracting State.

Article 72
Custodial Expenses

1. The grounds for placing a person taken into custody (detained) in respect of which the issue of extradition is addressed in detention facilities is a decision on detention order issued by a competent judicial authorities of the requesting Party, or the decision of the competent judicial authorities of the requested Contracting State if it is provided in its law.
2. Expenses of the person taken into custody (detained), are carried out in accordance with the law of the requested Contracting State.

Article 73
Extension of the detention of a person to be extradited

Where the circumstances prevent the extradition of a person in time frames under this Convention, the competent judicial authority of the requesting Contracting State, in charge of the criminal proceedings, resolves in accordance with the domestic law the issue of the extension of the term of detention of the extradited person and sends to the Department of Justice of the Contracting Parties a duly certified copy of such decision.

Article 74

Calculation of the period of detention

Time of apprehension and detention of the extradited person in the territory of the Contracting State, as well as the time of a transfer of the requesting Contracting State shall be counted in the total period of his detention.

Article 75

Release of a person taken into custody

A person taken into custody in the territory of the Contracting State in accordance with this Convention shall immediately be released if:

a) there is a notification of the competent judicial authority of the requesting Contracting State to release that person;
b) a request for extradition and the accompanying documents provided for in Article 67 of this Convention shall be submitted within 40 days after the arrest and detention of the person sought;
c) the additional information to the request for the extradition requested by the requested Contracting State in accordance with paragraph 2 of Article 71 of this Convention, is not filed within the prescribed period of this article;
d) period of detention subject to extradition specified in the decision on the detention expired, and the requesting Party has not submitted a copy of the decision on the extension of this period.

Article 76

Ensuring the right of defence

1. Person taken into custody (arrested) in accordance with the provisions of this Convention shall have the right to protection in the territory of each of the Contracting Parties in accordance with their legislation.
2. Complaints of persons held in custody, their lawyers or legal representatives on the use of remand in custody, the extension of the period of detention shall be filed to the court, or other competent judicial authority of the requesting Contracting State.

Court, other competent judicial authority of the requested Contracting State at the place of detention (arrest) of the person is limited to verifying compliance with the provisions of this Convention when dealing with complaints of these persons.

Article 77
Deferral of Extradition

1. If a person requested to be extradited has been held criminally liable or convicted of other crime committed in the Contracting State addressed, the extradition of such person may be deferred pending the completion of such criminal prosecution, enforcement of the sentence, or release from punishment.
2. The requesting Party shall be notified on the postponement of the extradition.

Article 78
Temporary Extradition

1. Where the deferral of extradition as provided for in Article 77 may entail the expiry of the period of limitation applicable to criminal prosecution or interfere with the investigation of the crime, the person requested to be extradited may be extradited temporarily.
2. The person that was extradited temporarily shall be returned upon the completion of the act making part of the criminal proceedings for which such person has been extradited, but at all times within 90 days from the extradition date. Where substantiated, such period, however, may be extended by the competent judicial authorities of the requested Contracting State at the request of the competent judicial authorities of the requesting Contracting State.

Article 79
Collision of Extradition Requests

Where extradition requests are received from several countries, the Contracting State addressed shall decide which request to grant at its own discretion.

Article 80
Restrictions on Criminal Prosecution of Extradited Persons

1. A person extradited may not – other than with the consent of the Contracting State addressed - be held criminally liable or punished for any crime committed before the extradition, unless such crime constitutes the reason for such extradition.
2. Nor may such person be extradited to any third country other than with the consent of the Contracting State addressed.
3. The consent of the Contracting Parties referred to in paragraphs 1 and 2 of this Article shall not be required if the extradited person before the expiration of 30 days after the end of criminal proceedings, and in the event of a conviction - before the expiration of 30 days after completion of sentence or release does not leave the territory against him the requesting Contracting State or if he

returns there voluntarily. This period does not include the time during which the extradited person could not leave the territory of the requesting Contracting State for reasons beyond him.

Article 81

Non-application of the death penalty

For the purposes of this Convention and without prejudice to the legislation of the requesting and requested Contracting Parties the death penalty shall not apply by the requesting Party against a person, extradited in accordance with the provisions of this Convention, if this penalty does not apply the requested Contracting State.

Article 82

Handover of Extradited Person

1. In the case of satisfaction of the request for the extradition the requested Contracting State shall notify the requesting Contracting State of the place and time of the transmission of the extradited person and deliver it to the transfer place.
2. If the requesting Party does not accept the person to be extradited within 15 days after the agreed date of transfer, the person must be released from custody. In justified cases, the transmission period of the extradited person may be extended to 15 days at the request of the competent judicial authorities of the requesting Contracting State.

Article 83

Re-arrest in connection with the extradition

1. Release of the person in accordance with paragraph "a" of article 75, paragraph 2 of Article 82 of this Convention shall not prejudice re-arresting him for purposes of extradition in the case of the issuance of a new request.
2. A person released in accordance with paragraph "b", "c" and "d" of Article 75 of this Convention, may be re-taken into custody for the purpose of extradition in cases where an extradition request, additional information to the request for extradition or the decision the extension of the detention period will be received after the deadline.

Article 84

Repeat extradition

1. If an extradited person evades prosecution or serving a sentence for an offense in respect of which it was issued, and will return to the territory of the Contracting State, the new extradition request is to be issued without providing the materials referred to in Article 67 of this Convention.
2. Re-extradition shall be carried out on a common basis in accordance with this Convention where the person commits a new crime on the territory of the requesting Contracting State or the sanction against him has changed.

Article 85

Notice Reporting Results of Criminal Proceedings

The Contracting States shall keep one another informed on the results of criminal proceedings against those persons extradited thereto. Copies of final judgments shall likewise be sent upon request.

Article 86

Transit Transportation

1. If petitioned by another Contracting State, a Contracting State shall authorize the transit transportation through its territory of those persons extradited to such other Contracting State or handed over thereto temporarily by a third country. The permit for transit transportation is not required if it is carried out by air without intermediate stops in the territory of the Contracting State of transit.
2. Petitions for such authorization shall be considered in accordance with the same procedure as extradition requests.
3. The Contracting State addressed shall authorize the transit transportation sought to be carried out in the manner such Contracting State itself finds the most appropriate.

Article 87

Expenses for Extradition and Transit Transportation

Those expenses incurred for extradition or temporary handover procedures shall be borne by that Contracting State where such expenses were suffered, while transit transportation costs shall be borne by the Contracting State that has requested such transportation.

Appendix 7

Article 88

The procedure for the relations on extradition

Actions on the issues extradition are exercised by Attorney Generals (prosecutors) of the Contracting Parties, unless otherwise specified in their domestic laws.

Article 89
Refusal of Extradition

1. No extradition shall take place if:
   a) the person sought is a national of the Contracting State addressed;
   b) at the time when the extradition request was received, no criminal prosecution was possible according to the legislation of the Contracting State addressed or the sentence may not be executed due to the expiry of the period of limitation or for any other legal reason; or
   c) a sentence has already been passed in the Contracting State addressed to convict the person sought for the same crime or a resolution has already been issued and became res judicata in such Contracting State to dismiss the proceedings in the case; or
   d) the criminal prosecution is sought on private charges (upon the victim's request) according to the legislation of the Contracting State requesting such extradition or of the Contracting State addressed.
   e) extradition is likely to intervene the sovereignty, security of the requested Contracting Parties;
   f) there are reasonable grounds to believe that the extradition request is related to the persecution of a person on grounds of race, sex, religion, ethnicity or political opinion;
   g) the offense for which extradition is sought, is related to the military offences under the law of the Contracting State;
   h) the person whose extradition is requested has been previously extradited by the requested Contracting State to a third State and the consent of the State received on the issue;
   i) the person whose extradition is requested, granted asylum in the territory of the Contracting State;
   j) there are other grounds stipulated in international treaties which the requesting and requested Contracting Parties are parties to.
2. Extradition may be refused if the offense for which extradition is requested was committed in the territory of the requested Contracting State.
3. In case of refusal the requesting Party shall be informed of the grounds for refusal within 10 days after the decision on this.

Article 90

Prosecution non-extradited

In case of refusal to extradite the requested person a competent judicial authority of the requested Contracting State on the basis of an application and materials of the competent judicial authorities of the requesting Contracting State, in accordance with the law of the Contracting Parties decides the issue of criminal prosecution of the person whose extradition was denied.

Section III
Criminal Prosecution

Article 91
Obligation of Criminal Prosecution

1. If requested by another Contracting State, each Contracting State shall be obliged in accordance with its own legislation to carry out the criminal prosecution of its own nationals suspected of having committed a crime in the requesting Contracting State.

    Criminal prosecution is carried out by the Contracting Parties in respect of stateless persons and foreign nationals, within their territories, in the case of refusal to extradite them.

2. Should that crime which has prompted the initiation of criminal proceedings entail civil-law claims from its victims, such claims shall be considered as part of the proceedings provided that the claimants have filed applications for damages, or such claims can also be considered within civil proceedings.

3. The criminal prosecution in the requested Contracting State can be provided if a committed act is considered to be a criminal in that Contracting State.

    When convicting the punishment for a crime should not be more severe than the punishment provided for by the legislation of the requesting Contracting State.

Article 92
Criminal Prosecution Request

1. A criminal prosecution request shall indicate or contain the following:
    a) name of the requesting judicial authority of the Contracting State;
    b) description of the act that has prompted the criminal prosecution request;
    c) time and place of such act, which shall be indicated as exactly as possible;
    d) the text of that legislative provision of the requesting Contracting State qualifying the act as a crime, as well as the texts of other legislative provisions of material relevance to the proceedings;
    e) first name, surname, and nationality of the suspect, and other personal information regarding the same;

f) applications filed by victims for the institution of the criminal proceedings concerned and for damages; and
g) indication of the extent of the damage caused by the crime.

Such request shall be accompanied by the briefs prepared and evidence gathered in the course of the relevant criminal proceedings that the requesting Contracting State has at its disposal and which in accordance with its domestic law, have the same evidentiary value as in the requested Contracting State.
2. Where the requesting Contracting State sends a file covering ongoing criminal proceedings, the Contracting State addressed shall continue the investigation of such matter in accordance with its own legislation. Prior to the delivery of the request on prosecution, requesting Party shall decide on the extension of the investigation, detention of the accused and the resumption of the proceedings.
3. A criminal prosecution request and accompanying documents shall be executed in accordance with the requirements of Articles 7 and 17 of this Convention.
4. If an indictee was at the time when a criminal prosecution request was sent in custody in the requesting Contracting State, the indictee shall be taken to the Contracting State addressed.

Article 93

Detention of its own citizens prior obtaining request on prosecution

1. Each Contracting State shall, at the request of the other Contracting State may take custody of their own citizens to obtain instructions on the implementation of the criminal prosecution against them for committing grave and especially grave crimes. The petition shall contain a reference to a detention order and an indication that the order on prosecution will be presented later.

    The petition and the ruling on detention prior obtaining the order on prosecution can be transmitted using the technical means of communication with simultaneous originals by mail or by courier.
2. The requesting party in charge of the criminal case shall be immediately notified (by fax, by telephone, telegraph, etc.) on taking into custody a person who is a citizen of the requested Contracting State, and in accordance with Article 91 of this Convention, should be questioned on the direction of the respective materials for the prosecution of that person.
3. For the prosecution of such person, the law of the requested Contracting State shall apply.
4. A person arrested pursuant to paragraph 1 of this Article shall be released if the order on prosecution with all the attached documents provided for in Article 92 of this Convention, will not be received by the requested Contracting State within 40 days from the date of arresting that person.

    The requested Contracting State shall decide whether to prosecute that person on the basis of domestic law.

Article 94

The procedure for the liaison of criminal prosecution

Criminal prosecution liaison is exercised by Attorney General (prosecutors) of the Contracting Parties, unless otherwise specified in their domestic laws.

Article 95

Transfer of jurisdiction

1. Since the adoption of the criminal case to the production of the requested Contracting State, the requested Contracting State may not involve a suspect, an accused person responsible for the act in respect of which raised the question of criminal prosecution.
2. The right of prosecution proceeds to the requesting Contracting State, if the requested Contracting State does not take steps to comply with its request or refuse to perform it.
3. In the cases described in paragraph 2 of this article, the requested Contracting State shall return the materials referred to it by the prosecution and evidence.

Article 96

The procedure for the transfer of criminal cases pending before the courts

1. Criminal cases against the accused who refuse to appear before court hearings and is hiding from the court, when establishing their place of residence and the citizenship in the requested Contracting State or in the case of refusal to issue, after the lifting of the suspension of the proceedings, refer for prosecution in competent judicial authority of the Contracting State in the manner provided in Article 92 of this Convention.
2. In a further investigation, the end of the investigation and the proceedings, the law of the Contracting State and the Article 90 of this Convention shall apply.

Article 97

Notice of Results of Criminal Prosecution

The Contracting State addressed shall notify the requesting Contracting State of the final judgment. The requesting Contracting State shall also be sent a copy of the final judgment upon request.

Article 98

Consequences of Issue of Judgment

Where a Contracting State has been sent a criminal prosecution request by virtue of Article 91 after the sentence became res judicata or after a judicial authority in the Contracting State addressed issued another final judgment, no judicial authority in the requesting Contracting State may institute related criminal proceedings and that criminal case already opened shall be dismissed.

Article 99
Mitigating or Aggravating Circumstances

1. During the investigation of crimes and the hearing of criminal cases by the courts, each Contracting State shall take account of those mitigating and aggravating circumstances which are provided for by the legislation of the Contracting States, regardless of the Contracting State where such circumstances have occurred.
2. When deciding on the recognition of a person by an especially dangerous recidivist, or the presence in his actions different types of recurrence, on establishment of the facts of the crime and re violation of duties related to probation, suspending sentence or parole, the judicial authorities of the Contracting Parties may recognize and consider the sentences imposed by the courts (tribunals) of the former Soviet Union and its former constituent republics of the Union, as well as the courts of each Contracting State.

Article 100
Merger of criminal cases

1. If a person or group of persons commit offense in the territory of two or more Contracting Parties, the criminal cases at the request of the relevant competent authorities of the Contracting Parties of Justice can be merged into one.
2. Merger of cases shall be done in compliance with the requirements of Articles 91 and 92 of this Convention.

Article 101
Procedure for Dealing With Cases Falling Under the Jurisdiction of Courts in Two or More Contracting States

Where a person or a group of persons are indicted on several counts falling within the jurisdiction of courts in two or more of the Contracting States, the court competent to deal with such cases shall be one in the Contracting State where the preliminary investigation has been completed. Such proceedings shall conform to the judicial procedures in effect in such Contracting State.

Article 102
Refusal to criminal prosecution

1. The criminal prosecution shall be refused if:
    a) at the time of receipt of the order to prosecute statute of limitations for bringing a person to criminal liability has expired;

b) the prosecution against the same person in the territory of the Contracting State for the same crime was terminated, or the sentence has come into force, or it has be refused to initiate criminal proceedings against him;
c) there is an act of amnesty, which eliminates the possibility of punishment for the offense;
d) the person at the time of commission of a socially dangerous act, according to the law of the requested Contracting State has not reached the age of criminal responsibility.
2. The criminal prosecution may be refused on any other grounds stipulated by the legislation of the Contracting State.
3. In the event of a failure in the implementation of prosecution the requesting Contracting State shall be notified in writing of the grounds for refusal within 10 days after such decision.

Section IV

Special Provisions on Legal Assistance and

Legal Relations in Criminal Matters

Article 103

Transfer of Exhibits

1. The Contracting States shall provide one another upon request with:
   a) such items as were used during a crime entailing the extradition of the criminal in accordance with this Convention, including instruments of the crime, property obtained as a result of the crime or as a reward for the crime, or assets exchanged for such property; and
   b) items which may have the significance of evidence in a criminal case; they shall also be transferred where the criminal cannot be extradited as a result of the latter's demise or escape, or for other reasons.
2. Should the Contracting State addressed need those items listed in paragraph 1 of this Article as evidence in a criminal case, their transfer may be delayed until the completion of the criminal proceedings in question.
3. Third-party rights in the items transferred shall remain valid. Following the completion of proceedings in a case, such items shall be returned, free of charge, to the Contracting State which has made them available.

Article 104

Legal assistance in the investigation, arrest and confiscation of property maintenance

1. The Contracting Parties in accordance with its laws and the provisions of this Convention shall provide each other with legal assistance in the search for, arrest and seizure of property, money and valuables obtained by criminal

means, as well as belonging to the accused (defendant convicted) of proceeds of crime, damages to victims of crime (civil claimant), execution of court judgments for the recovery of fines and confiscation.
2. To this purpose, the competent judicial authorities of the Contracting Parties on the basis of orders for legal assistance in criminal matters in accordance with domestic law, carry out all the necessary investigations, investigative and operational-search measures aimed to detect the property, money and valuables obtained by criminal means, as well as belonging of the accused (defendant convicted) of proceeds of crime.

   When such property, money, values and profits are established, the competent judicial authorities of the Contracting Parties shall take measures to ensure their safety in the form of attachment to prevent any transactions with them and their removal.
3. The competent judicial authorities of the Contracting Parties, in establishing its jurisdiction over property, money and values obtained by criminal means, transmit them to the competent judicial authorities of the requesting Contracting State with a view to inclusion in the criminal case as evidence, and subsequent return to their rightful owners, repayment caused by crimes damage.
4. The competent judicial authorities of the requested Contracting State, seize the money, valuables and property of the accused (defendant convicted), the proceeds of criminal activities and ensure their safety in view of the subsequent appeal to the repayment of the damage caused by the crime and the confiscation on the basis of an enforceable judgment the court of the requesting Contracting State, subject to the rules provided for in Article 58 of this Convention.
5. The competent judicial authorities of the requested Party may delay the handing over of judicial authorities of the requesting Contracting State of the property, money and valuables obtained by criminal means, as well as belonging to the accused (defendant convicted) of proceeds from criminal activities, if required by him in connection with pending criminal proceedings or the resolution of disputes about the rights of other (third) parties.

Article 105

Use of video

The competent judicial authorities of the Contracting Parties while providing legal assistance shall be entitled by mutual agreement to use video tool. The regulation of the use of the video is subject to domestic legislation of the Contracting Parties.

Article 106

Temporary Transfer of the person in custody or the confined person

1. If necessary, the questioning as a witness or injured person in custody or serving a sentence of imprisonment in the territory of the other Contracting State, as well as carrying out other investigative actions with his participation, that person, whatever his nationality, upon reasonable request of the requesting Contracting State may be transferred to it at the time of the decision of the central body of the judicial authorities of the requested Contracting State subject to condition of his detention and returning on time.
2. The request for the temporary transfer of the person referred to in paragraph 1 of this Article shall be made in accordance with the provisions of Article 7 of this Convention and shall also contain an indication of the time during which the presence of that person in the requesting Contracting State is required.
3. Temporary transfer of the person referred to in paragraph 1 of this Article shall not be made if:
   a) his consent to the transfer is not received;
   b) his presence is necessary at the preliminary investigation or proceedings in the territory of the Contracting State;
   c) such transfer may result in violation of the terms of the person in custody or serving their sentences of imprisonment.
4. The person referred to in paragraph 1 of this Article, subject to the safeguards provided for in paragraph 1 of Article 9 of this Convention.

Article 107

Notices of Convictions and Criminal Records

1. Each Contracting State shall annually provide the other Contracting States with reports on res judicata convictions rendered by its courts against citizens of the respective Contracting States together with the convicts' fingerprints.
2. Each Contracting State shall provide the other Contracting States, upon request and free of charge, with the criminal records of persons previously convicted by its courts if such persons are held criminally liable in the requesting Contracting State.

Article 108

Controlled delivery

The Contracting Parties shall in accordance with domestic law take measures to ensure the use of method of controlled deliveries on the basis of mutual agreement of the competent judicial authorities investigating criminal cases in order to identify persons involved in the commission of a crime, obtain evidence and to ensure prosecution.

Section V

Recognition and Enforcement of Sentences

Article 109

Recognition and enforcement of judgments

1. Each of the Contracting Parties under the terms of this Convention, recognizes and executes sentences, decrees of the courts of other Contracting Parties, in the case of extradition of a person convicted by a court of one Contracting State and not confined punishment for criminal prosecution on the territory of the other Contracting State, as well as the failure of one Contracting State to extradite a person for the execution of a sentence imposed by a court of another Contracting State.
2. Recognition and enforcement of judgments is carried out on the basis of legislation of the Contracting State in the territory of which such sentences will be recognized and enforced.

Article 110

An application for recognition and enforcement of the sentence

1. An application for recognition and enforcement of the sentence by the competent judicial authorities of the requesting Contracting State shall be transferred to the competent judicial authority of the requested Contracting State.
2. The application shall be accompanied by:
    a) a duly certified copy of an enforceable judgment and available decisions of higher instances, the official document proving that the sentence has come into force and its enforcement;
    b) the identity and nationality of the person in respect of whom the application for recognition and enforcement of the sentence is filed;
    c) The text of the articles of the law, on the basis of which the person has been convicted;
    d) information on the unserved part of the main and additional sentence, the amount of damages.
3. If necessary, the competent judicial authority of the requested Contracting State may request additional documents and information.
4. Documents attached to the application are supplied by a certified translation into the language of the requested Contracting State or in the Russian language.
5. The competent judicial authority of the requested Contracting State shall send petitions for recognition and enforcement of the judgment to the competent court of its Contracting State.

Article 111

The procedure for recognition and enforcement of a sentence

1. An application for recognition and enforcement of the sentence is considered by the competent court of the Contracting State in accordance with its domestic law.
2. The competent court of the Contracting Parties shall decide on the recognition and enforcement of the judgment prior the actual transfer of the extradited person to its territory.
3. The competent court of the Contracting State on the basis of the decision of the sentence of the court of the requesting Contracting State shall determine, in accordance with the domestic law of the same punishment as designated by the verdict.
4. If under the law of the requested Party the sentence is less for the act is less severe than issued by the verdict, the court shall determine the maximum penalty provided for a similar offense law of the requested Contracting State.
5. Part of the punishment, confined on the territory of the requesting Contracting State, shall be included in the sentence in accordance with the law of the Contracting Parties dealing with application for recognition of a sentence. At the same the issue of order execution shall be solved.
6. The penalty applies in the case, if it is provided by the laws of the requesting and requested Contracting Parties.

Article 112

Refusal of recognition and enforcement of the sentence

Recognition and enforcement of the judgment may be refused if:

a) The sentence cannot be executed due to expiration of limitation period or for other legitimate reasons, as well as the sentence, judgment are rendered in the absence of the defendant;
b) person either confined punishment in the territory of the Contracting State for the act committed or has been acquitted or the, or criminal case was dismissed in accordance with the law, and if the person is released from punishment by the competent judicial authorities of the requested Contracting State;
c) the law of the requested Contracting State does not provide punishment similar to the punishment in the territory of the requesting Contracting State;
d) there are reasonable grounds to believe that the conviction is related to the prosecution of a person on grounds of race, sex, religion, ethnicity or political opinion.

Article 113

The order of addition of punishments in the execution of sentences

Addition of penalties when executing sentences is carried out by the rules established by the legislation of the Contracting State in whose territory sentences will be executed.

Article 114

Application of mercy and amnesty

The mercy and amnesty of the person against whom the decision on the recognition and enforcement of the sentence is issued, shall be carried out both by the requesting and the requested Contracting Parties in accordance with their domestic law.

Article 115

The procedure for review of sentence

Revision the judgment transferred for the execution of the sentenced person may be carried out only by a competent court of the Contracting State in whose territory the sentence was decreed.

Article 116

Execution of changed and annulled sentences

1. If during the execution of the sentence it will be changed by a competent court of the Contracting State in the territory of which a sentence was decreed, a copy of the decision shall be immediately sent to the Contracting State enforcing sentences to decide the issue of the execution of such a decision in accordance with the requirements of this Convention.
2. If during the execution of the sentence it will be annulled, a copy of the decision shall be immediately sent for execution to the competent authority of the Contracting Parties for enforcement.
3. If in the course of execution of sentence has been annulled and a new investigation or judicial review have been ordered, a copy of this decision, materials of the criminal case and instructions on prosecution in accordance with Article 92 of this Convention shall be sent to the competent judicial authorities of the Contracting Parties to enforce sentences.

Appendix 7

Part VI

Final Provisions

Article 117

Implementation Issues

Any issues arising out of or in connection with the implementation of this Convention shall be resolved by the competent authorities of the Contracting States by mutual agreement.

Article 118

Convention's Relationship with Other International Agreements

1. In relations between the Contracting Parties which are also Parties to one or more of the Council of Europe conventions in the criminal sphere, the provisions that affect the subject of the present Convention shall apply only to those of its provisions that complement these Council of Europe Convention or facilitate application of the principles contained therein.
2. In relations between the Contracting Parties - participants of the above-mentioned Council of Europe conventions and the Contracting Parties which are not parties to such conventions, the provisions of this Convention shall apply.
3. The provisions of this Convention shall not affect the rights and obligations of the Contracting Parties arising from other international treaties to which they are parties or may become parties.
4. At the request of one of the Contracting Parties its the central institutions of justice shall hold consultations on the relationship of this Convention and other international agreements involving, if necessary, representatives of other governmental authorities of the Contracting Parties.

Article 119

Amendments

With the consent of the Contracting Parties the provisions of this Convention may be amended and supplemented by relevant protocols that are an integral part thereof and shall enter into force in accordance with the procedure provided for in Article 120 of the Convention.

Article 120

Coming Into Force

1. This Convention shall be subject to ratification by its signatory nations. The instruments of ratification shall be surrendered for custody to the Executive Committee of the Commonwealth of Independent States, which shall act as the depositary of this Convention.

2. This Convention shall come into force on the 30th day after the day on which the third instrument of ratification is surrendered to the depositary. For each Contracting State which surrenders its instrument of ratification to the depositary after this Convention has already entered into force, this Convention shall take effect on the 30th day after the day on which its instrument of ratification was surrendered to the depositary.
3. The Convention on Legal Assistance and Legal Relations in Civil, Family and Criminal Cases of 22 January 1993 and the Protocol thereto of 28 March 1997 ceases to apply between the Parties to this Convention.
4. The Convention and the Protocol indicated in paragraph 3 of this Article continue to apply in the relations between the state - party to this Convention and States that are party to which this Convention is not yet in force.

Article 121

Term

1. This Convention shall be valid for five years after its effective date. Upon the expiry of that period, this Convention shall be automatically extended, each time for another five-year term.
2. Any Contracting State may withdraw from this Convention by written notice to the depositary 12 months prior to the expiry of the five-year term then in effect.

Article 122

Retroactive Force

This Convention shall also apply to those legal relations which have arisen before its effective date.

Article 123

Accession Procedure

After this Convention comes into force, other nations may accede hereto – subject to the consent of all of the Contracting States – by providing the depositary with appropriate accession documents. Each accession shall be deemed effective upon the expiry of 30 days after the day on which the depositary received the last notice of consent to such accession.

Article 124

Depositary's Functions

The depositary shall promptly notify all of the signatories of this Convention and those nations having acceded hereto of the date on which each instrument of ratification or accession document is surrendered for custody, the Convention's effective date, and the depositary's receipt of other notices.

Appendix 7

Done in the city of Kishinev on 7 October 2002 in a single original copy in Russian. The original shall be on file in the Executive Committee of the Commonwealth of Independent States, which shall send a certified copy of the Convention to each state that is a party to this Convention.

For the Republic of Azerbaijan
G. ALIEV
For the Republic of Armenia
R. KOCHARYAN
For the Republic of Belarus
A. LUKASHENKO
For Georgia
E. SHEVARNADZE
For the Republic of Kazakhstan
N. NAZARBAYEV
For the Kyrgyz Republic
A. AKAYEV
For the Republic of Moldova
V. VORONIN
For the Russian Federation
V. PUTIN
For the Republic of Tajikistan
E. RAKHMONOV
For Ukraine
L. KUCHMA

The Convention was signed by the Republic of Azerbaijan with the reservation:

"1. Implementation on the basis of a request of search operations in the framework of this Convention to the extent possible, which allows the existing national legislation of the Azerbaijan Republic only by its competent authorities.
2. Within the framework of this Convention only instruments and means used in committing a crime, as well as property obtained by criminal means can be confiscated on the basis of a court decision.
3. Articles 63 and 108 of the Convention have no legal effect for the Republic of Azerbaijan."

The Convention was signed by Ukraine with reservations:

"1. Ukraine undertakes obligations to provide legal assistance to the extent provided for by Article 6 of the Convention, except for the recognition and enforcement of executive inscriptions.
2. Ukraine undertakes obligations to accept and carry out the decisions made on the territories of the states – parties to the Convention under sub-paragraph "a" of paragraph 1 of Article 54 of the Convention, except for notarial acts in respect of financial obligations."

Translated from Russian into English by Anna Lanshakova.

APPENDIX 8

Annex 16 to the 2014 Treaty on the Eurasian Economic Union Protocol on Trade in Services, Incorporation, Activities and Investments

(unofficial translation)

I. General Provisions

1. This Protocol has been developed in accordance with Articles 65-69 of the Treaty on the Eurasian Economic Union (hereinafter "the Treaty") and determines the legal basis for regulating trade in services, incorporation, activities and investments in the Member States.
2. The provisions of this Protocol shall apply to any and all measures taken by the Member States with regard to the supply and receipt of services, as well as incorporation, activities and investments.

    Specific features of legal relations arising in connection with the trade in telecommunication services shall be in accordance with Annex 1 to this Protocol.

    "Horizontal" restrictions maintained by the Member States in respect of all sectors and activities shall be determined in accordance with Annex 2 to this Protocol.

    Individual national lists of restrictions, exceptions, additional requirements and conditions (hereinafter "the national lists"), provided for by paragraphs 15-17, 23, 26, 28, 31, 33 and 35 of this Protocol, shall be approved by the Supreme Council.
3. The provisions of this Protocol shall apply to created, acquired, controlled juridical persons of the Member States, opened branches, representative offices, registered individual entrepreneurs still existing on the effective date of the Treaty, as well as to created, acquired, controlled juridical persons of the

Appendix 8

Member States, opened branches, representative offices, registered individual entrepreneurs after the effective date of the Treaty.

Notwithstanding the provisions of paragraphs 15-17, 21, 24, 27, 30 and 32 of this Protocol, the Member States shall reserve the right to adopt and enforce any measures with regard to new services, that is, those that did not exist on the effective date of the Treaty.

In the case of adoption or enforcement of a measure that affects a new service and is incompatible with the provisions of the above paragraphs, the respective Member State shall inform all other Member States and the Commission of such a measure no later than 1 month from the date of its adoption or enforcement, whichever comes first. Corresponding changes in the national list of that Member State shall be approved by decision of the Supreme Council.

4. As regards the cases of supply of services specified in the second and third indents of sub-paragraph 22 of paragraph 6 of this Protocol, the provisions of this Protocol shall not apply to the rights of air transportation and services directly related to the rights of transportation, except for the repairs and maintenance of aircraft, supply and marketing of air transportation services and services of computer booking systems.
5. The Member States shall not use mitigation of any requirements provided by their legislation for the protection of human life and health, the environment, and national security, as well as labour standards, as a mechanism to attract persons of other Member States and third states to incorporate on the territories of Member States.

II. Terms and Definitions

6. The terms used in this Protocol shall have the following meanings:
    1) "recipient state" means a Member State on the territory of which the investments are made by investors from other Member States;
    2) "activities" means business and other activities (including trade in services and manufacture of goods) conducted by juridical persons, branches, representative offices or individual entrepreneurs listed in indents two to six of sub-paragraph 24 of this paragraph;
    3) "investment activities" means possession, use and/or disposal of investments;
    4) "income" means funds generated as a result of investment, in particular, dividends, interest and royalties, fees and other remunerations;
    5) "legislation of a Member State" means legislation and other regulatory legal acts of a Member State;
    6) "applicant" means a person of a Member State having applied for a permit to the competent authority of that or another Member State;
    7) "investments" means tangible and intangible assets invested by an investor of a Member State into subjects of entrepreneurial activity on the

territory of another Member State in accordance with the legislation of the latter, including:

funds (cash), securities and other property;

rights to engage in entrepreneurial activities granted under the legislation of the Member States or under a contract, including, in particular, the right to exploration, development, production and exploitation of natural resources;

property rights and other rights having monetary value;

8) "investor of a Member State" means any person of a Member State making investments on the territory of another Member State in accordance with the legislation of the latter;

9) "competent authority" means any authority or organisation exercising control, authorisation or other regulatory functions with respect to matters covered by this Protocol under the powers delegated by the Member State, in particular, administrative authorities, courts, professional and other associations;

10) "person of a Member State" means any natural person or juridical person of a Member State;

11) "measure of a Member State" means the legislation of a Member State, as well as any decision, action or omission of an authority or official of that Member State adopted or applied at any level of state or local authorities or organisations in the exercise of the powers delegated thereto by such authorities.

In the case of adoption (publication) by the authority of a Member State of an official non-binding document, this recommendation may be deemed a measure of the Member State applied for the purposes of this Protocol if it is proven that, in practice, the recommendation is observed by a predominant portion of its subjects (state, regional and/or municipal authorities, non-governmental authorities, as well as persons of the Member State, persons of other Member States, and persons of any third state);

12) "service recipient" means any person of a Member State a service is supplied to or intending to use a service;

13) "service supplier" means any person of a Member State supplying a service;

14) "representative office" means a separate division of a juridical person located outside of its location that represents and protects the interests of the juridical person;

15) "permit" means confirmation by a competent authority, as provided for by the legislation of a Member State and based on an applicant's request, of the rights of the applicant to engage in certain activities or perform certain actions, including by its introduction into the registry and issuance of an official document (license, approval, conclusion, diploma, certificate of attendance, certificates, etc.). A permit may be granted on the basis of competitive selection;

16) "authorisation procedures" means a set of procedures implemented by competent authorities in accordance with the legislation of a Member State relating to the issuance and re-issuance of permits and duplicates thereof, termination, suspension, resumption or extension and withdrawal (cancellation) of permits, refusal to grant permits, as well as review of all respective claims;
17) "authorisation requirements" means a set of standards and/or requirements (including licensing and qualification requirements) to the applicant, permit holder and/or a service supplied or activity undertaken under the relevant legislation of a Member State, aimed at ensuring the fulfilment of regulation objectives determined by the legislation of the Member State.
With regard to permits for activities, authorisation requirements may be aimed at, among other things, ensuring the competence and ability of the applicant to carry out trade in services and other activities in accordance with the legislation of the Member State;
18) "treatment" means a set of measures of the Member States;
19) "service sector":
for the purposes of Annex 2 to this Protocol and of the lists approved by the Supreme Council, one, several or all sub-sectors of a certain service;
in other cases – an entire service sector, including all sub-sectors;
20) "territory of a Member State" means the territory of a Member State, as well as its exclusive economic area and the continental shelf, in respect of which it exercises sovereign rights and jurisdiction in accordance with the international law and its legislation;
21) "economic feasibility test" means determining grounds for issuing permits based on the economic feasibility or market demand, assessment of the potential or existing business or economic impact of respective activities or assessment of compliance of the activities with economic planning objectives set by the competent authority. This term shall not include any conditions associated with non-economic planning and based on the grounds of public interest, such as social policy, implementation of socio-economic development programs approved by local authorities within their competence, or protection of the urban environment, including implementation of urban development plans;
22) "trade in services" means supply of services, including manufacture, distribution, marketing, sale and delivery of services, conducted in the following ways:
from the territory of one Member State to the territory of any other Member State;
on the territory of one Member State by a person of this Member State to a service recipient of another Member State;

by a service supplier of one Member State through its incorporation on the territory of another Member State;

by a service supplier of one Member State through the presence of natural persons of that Member State on the territory of another Member State;

23) "third state" means a state that is not a Member State;
24) "incorporation":

creation and/or acquisition of a juridical person (participation in the capital of a created or incorporated juridical person) with any organisational legal form and form of ownership provided for by the legislation of the Member State on the territory of which such juridical person is created or incorporated;

acquisition of control over a juridical person of a Member State through obtaining of an opportunity to, either directly or via third persons, determine decisions to be adopted by such juridical person, including through the management of votes granted by voting shares (stakes) and participation in the board of directors (supervisory board) and other management authorities of such juridical person;

opening of a branch;

opening of a representative office;

registration as an individual entrepreneur.

Incorporation shall be carried out, among other things, for the purposes of trade in services and/or manufacture of goods;

25) "natural person of a Member State" means a national of a Member State in accordance with the legislation of the Member State;
26) "branch" means a separate division of a juridical person incorporated outside of its location and performing all of its functions, or part thereof, including the function of a representation;
27) "juridical person of a Member State" means an organisation with any organisational legal form, created or incorporated on the territory of a Member State in accordance with the legislation of that Member State.

7. For the purposes of this Protocol, the service sectors shall be identified and classified based on the Central Products Classification approved by the United Nations Statistical Commission.

III. Payments and Transfers

8. Except for the cases provided for in paragraphs 11-14 of this Protocol, each Member State shall cancel all effective and shall not introduce new restrictions on transfers and payments in connection with trade in services, incorporation, activities and investments, in particular with regard to:
   1) income;
   2) funds transferred in repayment of loans and credits recognised by the Member States as investments;

3) funds received by an investor in connection with a partial or complete liquidation of a profit organisation or sale of investments;
4) funds received by an investor in recovery of damages in accordance with paragraph 77 of this Protocol and compensations referred to in paragraphs 79-81 of this Protocol;
5) salaries and other remuneration received by investors and nationals of other Member States allowed to perform investment-related activities on the territory of the recipient state.

9. Nothing in this section shall affect the rights and obligations of any Member State arising out of its membership in the International Monetary Fund, including the rights and obligations regarding any currency transactions control measures, provided that such measures of the Member States comply with the Articles of Agreement of the International Monetary Fund of July 22, 1944, and/or provided that the Member State does not impose restrictions on transfers and payments that are incompatible with its obligations under this Protocol regarding such transactions, except as specified in paragraphs 11-14 of this Protocol or in case of restrictions imposed on request from the International Monetary Fund.

10. Transfers under paragraph 8 of this Protocol may be made in any freely convertible currency. Funds shall be converted without undue delay, at the exchange rate applicable on the territory of the Member State on the date of the transfer of funds and payments.

IV. Restrictions on Payments and Transfers

11. In the case of deterioration of the balance of payments, a significant reduction in foreign exchange reserves, sharp fluctuations of the national currency exchange rate or a threat thereof, a Member State may impose restrictions on transfers and payments provided for in paragraph 8 of this Protocol.

12. The restrictions referred to in paragraph 11 of this Protocol:
    1) shall not create discrimination between the Member States;
    2) shall comply with the Articles of Agreement of the International Monetary Fund of July 22, 1944;
    3) shall not cause excessive damage to the commercial, economic and financial interests of any other Member State;
    4) shall not be more burdensome than required to overcome the circumstances referred to in paragraph 11 of this Protocol;
    5) shall be temporary and be phased out with the disappearance of the circumstances referred to in paragraph 11 of this Protocol.

13. When determining the sphere of the restrictions specified in paragraph 11 of this Protocol, the Member States may give priority to the supply of those goods or services that are more critical to their economic or development

programs. However, such restrictions shall not be imposed or maintained for the protection of a certain economic sector.
14. Any restrictions imposed or maintained by the Member States in accordance with paragraph 11 of this Protocol or any changes thereto shall be immediately communicated to all other Member States.

V. State Participation

15. The treatment accorded by each Member State to persons of another Member State on its territory with regard to participation in privatisation shall be no less favourable than that accorded to persons of its Member State, subject to the restrictions, exceptions and additional requirements and conditions specified in the national lists or Annex 2 to this Protocol.
16. If any juridical persons operating on the territory of a Member State have participation of that Member State in their capital or are controlled by the Member State, the Member State shall ensure that these persons:
    1) operate for commercial considerations and participate in relations governed by this Protocol:

    on the basis of the principle of equality with the other participants of these relations;

    on the basis of the principle of non-discrimination of other participants of these relations according to their nationality, place of registration (incorporation), organisational legal form or form of ownership;
    2) are not granted any rights, privileges or obligations solely because of the participation of the Member State in their capital or control of that Member State over these persons.

    These requirements shall not apply when the activities of such juridical persons are aimed at solving problems of the social policy of the Member State, as well as to all restrictions and conditions specified in the national lists or Annex 2 to this Protocol.
17. The provisions of paragraph 16 of this Protocol shall also apply to juridical persons having formal or de facto exclusive rights or special privileges, except for juridical persons with rights and/or privileges included, pursuant to sub-paragraphs 2 and 6 of paragraph 30 of this Protocol, in the national lists or Annex 2 to this Protocol, and juridical persons the activities of which are governed by Section XIX of the Treaty.
18. Each Member State shall ensure that all state or local authorities of that Member State at any level are independent of and unaccountable to any person engaged in business activities in the economic sector regulated within the competence of the respective authority, without prejudice to the provisions of Article 69 of the Treaty.

Measures of that Member State, including decisions of the above authority and rules and procedures determined and applied thereby, shall be unbiased and objective in relation to all persons engaged in economic activities.

19. In accordance with the obligations arising from Section XIX of the Treaty and notwithstanding the provisions of paragraph 30 of this Protocol, each Member State may retain in its territory any juridical persons that are the subjects of natural monopolies. A Member State retaining such juridical persons on its territory shall ensure that these juridical persons act in a manner consistent with the obligations of the Member State arising from Section XIX of the Treaty.
20. Should the juridical persons of a Member State referred to in paragraph 19 of this Protocol compete directly or via controlled juridical persons outside the sphere of their monopoly rights with juridical persons of other Member States, the first Member State shall ensure that such juridical persons do not abuse their monopoly position acting on the territory of the first Member State in a manner inconsistent with the obligations of the first Member State arising out of this Protocol.

VI. Trade in Services, Incorporation and Activities

1. National Treatment for Trade in Services, Incorporation and Activities

21. The treatment accorded by each Member State in respect of services, service suppliers and service recipients of another Member State regarding all measures affecting trade in services shall be no less favourable than that accorded under the same (similar) circumstances to its own same (similar) services, service suppliers and service recipients.
22. Each Member State may perform the obligations referred to in paragraph 21 of this Protocol through the provision of formally similar or formally different treatment to services, suppliers and recipients of services of any other Member State as compared to the treatment accorded by that Member State to its own same (similar) services, or suppliers or recipients of services.
Formally similar or formally different treatment shall be considered less favourable if it modifies the terms of competition in favour of services, service suppliers and/or service recipients of that Member State as compared to the same (similar) services, service suppliers and/or recipients of any other Member State.
23. Notwithstanding the provisions of paragraph 21 of this Protocol, each Member State may impose certain restrictions and conditions specified in the national lists or Annex 2 to this Protocol in respect of services, service suppliers and service recipients of another Member State.
24. The treatment accorded by each Member State to persons of any other Member State in respect of incorporation and activities shall be no less favourable than that accorded under the same (similar) circumstances to its own persons on its territory.
25. Each Member State may perform the obligations referred to in paragraph 24 of this Protocol through the provision of formally similar or formally different

treatment to persons of any other Member State as compared to the treatment accorded by that Member State to its own persons. The treatment shall be deemed less favourable if it modifies the terms of competition in favour of persons of that Member State as compared to persons of any other Member State.
26. Notwithstanding the provisions of paragraph 24 of this Protocol, each Member State may impose certain restrictions and conditions specified in the national lists or Annex 2 to this Protocol in respect of incorporation or activities of persons of another Member State.

2. Most Favoured Nation Treatment for Trade in Services, Incorporation and Activities

27. The treatment accorded by each Member State, under the same (similar) circumstances, with regard to services, service suppliers and recipients of any other Member State, shall be no less favourable than that accorded to the same (similar) services, service suppliers and recipients of third states.
28. Notwithstanding the provisions of paragraph 27 of this Protocol, each Member State may impose certain exceptions specified in the national list or Annex 2 to this Protocol in respect of services, service suppliers and service recipients of any other Member State.
29. The treatment accorded by each Member State, under the same (similar) circumstances, to persons of any other Member State and persons incorporated thereby in respect of their incorporation and activities in its territory shall be no less favourable than that accorded to persons of third states and persons incorporated thereby.

3. Quantitative and Investment Measures

30. The Member States shall not introduce or apply to persons of any Member State any restrictions with respect to trade in services, incorporation and activities regarding:
    1) the number of service suppliers in the form of quota, economic feasibility tests or any other quantitative form;
    2) the number of juridical persons, branches or representative offices created, acquired and/or controlled and individual entrepreneurs registered;
    3) transactions of any service supplier in the form of quota, economic feasibility tests or any other quantitative form;
    4) transactions of juridical persons, branches or representative offices created, acquired and/or controlled and individual entrepreneurs registered, conducted in the course of their activities in the form of quotas, economic feasibility tests or any other quantitative form;

5) forms of incorporation, including the organisational legal form of a juridical person;
6) acquired shares in the authorised capital of a juridical person or the degree of control over a juridical person;
7) limitations of the total number of natural persons that may be employed in a particular service sector or the number of natural persons that may be employed by a service supplier and are required and directly relevant to the supply of certain services in the form of numerical quotas or economic feasibility tests.
31. In respect of service suppliers and recipients of any Member State, each Member State may impose and apply the restrictions specified in paragraph 30 of this Protocol, if such restrictions are specified in the national list or Annex 2 to this Protocol.
32. No Member State shall be entitled to introduce or apply the following additional requirements to persons of the Member States and persons incorporated thereby as conditions for their incorporation and/or activities:
    1) on exportation of all manufactured goods or services or any part thereof;
    2) on importation of goods or services;
    3) on the purchase or use of goods or services originating from a Member State;
    4) any requirements restricting the sale of goods or supply of services on the territory of that Member State, the import of goods into the territory of that Member State or export of goods from its territory that are based on the volume of goods manufactured (service supplied) or on the use of local goods or services or restrict access to foreign exchange payable in connection with transactions referred to in this sub-paragraph;
    5) on the transfer of technology, know-how and other information of commercial value, except in the case of their transfer pursuant to a court order or an order issued by a authority in the field of protection of competition, subject to the rules of the competition policy determined by other international treaties of the Member States.
33. Each Member State may introduce and apply to persons of other Member States any additional requirements referred to in paragraph 32 of this Protocol, if such restrictions are provided for by the national list or Annex 2 to this Protocol.
34. The requirements specified in paragraph 32 of this Protocol shall not be grounds for obtaining any preferences by persons of any Member State in connection with their incorporation or activities.

4. Migration of Natural Persons

35. Except for the restrictions and requirements specified in the national list or Annex 2 to this Protocol, subject to the provisions in Section XXVI of the Treaty, no Member State shall apply or impose in its territory any restrictions

on employment of workers for activities of juridical persons, branches or representative offices created, acquired and/or controlled and individual entrepreneurs registered.
36. The provisions of paragraph 35 of this Protocol shall not apply with respect to the requirements for education, experience, qualifications, and professional qualities, if their application does entail actual discrimination against workers on the ground of their national origin.
37. Subject to the provisions of Section XXVI of the Treaty, no Member State shall apply or impose restrictions on natural persons involved in trade in services in the procedure specified in the fifth indent of subparagraph 22 of paragraph 6 of this Protocol and present on the territory of that Member State.

5. Establishment of a Common Market of Services

38. For the purposes of this section, the common market of services shall refer to such a state of the market of services of a particular sector when each Member State grants to persons of any other Member State the right to:
   1) supply and receive services under the conditions specified in paragraphs 21, 24, 27, 29, 30 and 32 of this Protocol, without any restrictions, exceptions and additional requirements, except for the conditions and restrictions provided for in Annex 2 to this Protocol;
   2) supply services without additional incorporation of a juridical person;
   3) supply services on the basis of permit for the supply of services obtained by the service supplier on the territory of its Member State;
   4) recognize professional qualifications of the staff of the service supplier.
39. The rules of the common market of services shall apply to the Member States on a reciprocal basis.
40. The common market of services within the Union shall operate in the service sectors approved by the Supreme Council on the basis of proposals agreed by the Member States and the Commission.
41. The Member States shall seek to spread, on a reciprocal basis, the rules of the common market of services onto the maximum number of service sectors, including through gradual elimination of exceptions and restrictions provided for by national lists.
42. The procedure and the stages of establishment of the common market of services shall be determined for individual sectors in liberalisation plans developed on the basis of proposals agreed by the Member States and the Commission to be approved by the Supreme Council (hereinafter "the liberalisation plans").
43. Liberalisation plans may provide for certain Member States extended deadlines for the liberalisation of individual service sectors, which shall not prevent other Member States from establishment of the common market in these sectors on the basis of reciprocity.

Appendix 8

44. The provisions of subsections 1-4 of this section shall apply to sectors not regulated by the rules of the common market of services.

6. Relations with Third States on Trade in Services, Incorporation, Activities and Investments

45. Nothing in this Protocol shall preclude the Member States from concluding with third states international treaties on economic integration in compliance with the requirements of paragraph 46 of this Protocol.

    Each Member State having concluded such a treaty on economic integration shall make concessions in respect of the Member States under the same (similar) conditions as granted under the international treaty.

    Concessions in this paragraph refer to cancellation by the Member State of one or more restrictions provided for by its national list.

46. For the purposes of this Protocol, international treaties on economic integration between a Member State and a third state shall refer to all international treaties meeting the following criteria:
    1) covering a significant number of service sectors and under no circumstances knowingly a priori preclude any mode of supply of services or aspects of incorporation and activities;
    2) focusing on the elimination of existing and prohibition of new discriminatory measures;
    3) aimed at liberalising the trade in services, incorporation and activities.

    These international treaties shall be intended to facilitate trade in services and the conditions of incorporation and activities applied between parties thereto. Such treaty shall not create for any third state an increase in the overall number of barriers to trade in services in certain sectors or subsectors as compared to the situation existing prior to the conclusion of such treaty.

47. A Member State having concluded with a third state an international treaty on economic integration shall be obliged to inform other Member States thereof within 1 month from its signing date.

48. The Member States shall be free to determine their foreign trade policy in relation to trade in services, incorporation, activities and investments with third states.

7. Additional Rights of Service Recipients

49. Subject to the provisions of Section XV of the Treaty, each Member State shall not impose any requirements or special conditions for a service recipient restricting its rights to obtain, use or pay for the services rendered (provided) by a service supplier of another Member State, including with regard to the

selection of a service supplier or mandatory permits to be obtained from competent authorities.
50. Subject to the provisions of Section XV of the Treaty, each Member State shall ensure non-application with respect to service recipients of any discriminatory requirements or special conditions on the grounds of their nationality, place of residence or place of incorporation or activities.
51. Each Member State shall oblige:
    1) service suppliers to provide the necessary information to service recipients in accordance with the Treaty and the legislation of the Member State;
    2) competent authorities to take measures to protect the rights and legitimate interests of service recipients.
52. Nothing in this Protocol shall affect the right of a Member State to take any measures required for the implementation of its social policies, including for ensuring pension and social support of its population.
    All issues regarding consumer access to services covered by Sections XIX, XX and XXI of the Treaty and the treatment accorded to consumers of such services shall be governed by the provisions of these Sections, respectively.

8. Mutual Recognition of Permits and Professional Qualifications

53. Recognition of permits for the supply of services in sectors for which the liberalisation plans are implemented shall be recognised after the taking measures referred to in paragraphs 54 and/or 55 of this Protocol.
54. On the basis of mutual consultations (including on the interdepartmental level), the Member States may decide on the mutual recognition of permits for the supply of services in specific sectors upon achievement of substantial equivalence of regulation in these sectors.
55. Liberalisation plans shall ensure:
    1) gradual convergence of mechanisms ensuring admission to activities (including authorisation requirements and procedures) through the harmonisation of legislation of the Member States, setting sector-specific completion dates of such harmonisation;
    2) the establishment of administrative cooperation mechanisms in accordance with Article 68 of the Treaty;
    3) recognition of professional qualifications of employees of service suppliers.
56. When professional examinations are required prior to admission to the implementation of professional services, each Member State shall ensure a non-discriminatory procedure for passing such professional examinations.

9. Internal Regulation in Trade in Services, Incorporation and/or Activities

57. Each Member State shall ensure that all measures of that Member State affecting trade in services, incorporation and activities are applied in a reasonable, objective and impartial manner.
58. Each Member State shall maintain and create as soon as practicable all judicial, arbitration or administrative authorities or procedures that shall, on request of persons of other Member States the interests of which have been affected, promptly review respective issues and adopt reasonable measures to alter administrative decisions affecting trade in services, incorporation and activities. In cases where such procedures are not independent of the authority entrusted with the respective administrative decision, the Member State shall ensure that the procedures guarantee an objective and impartial review.
59. The provisions of paragraph 58 of this Protocol shall not require a Member State to establish authorities or procedures referred to in paragraph 58 of this Protocol when it is inconsistent with its constitutional procedure or the nature of its judicial system.
60. Should it be required to obtain a permit for trade in services, incorporation and/or activities, the competent authorities of the Member State shall, within a reasonable period of time after the submission of the respective application deemed executed in accordance with the legislation of the Member State and applicable regulation provisions, inform the applicant of the review of the application and the results obtained thereupon.

    The above application shall not be deemed duly arranged until all documents and/or information have been received as specified in the legislation of the Member State.

    In any case, the applicant shall be given the opportunity to make technical corrections in the application.

    At the request of the applicant, competent authorities of the Member State shall provide information about the progress of application processing without undue delay.
61. In order to ensure that authorisation requirements and procedures do not constitute unnecessary barriers to trade in services, incorporation and activities, the Commission shall, in agreement with the Member States, develop respective rules to be approved by the Supreme Council. These rules shall be intended to ensure that such authorisation requirements and procedures, among other things:
    1) are based on objective and overt criteria such as competence and the ability to conduct trade in services and activities;
    2) are not more burdensome than required to ensure the security of ongoing activities, as well as the safety and quality of services supplied;
    3) do not restrict trade in services, incorporation and/or activities.

Appendix 8

62. The Member States shall not apply any authorisation requirements and procedures that invalidate or reduce benefits and:
    1) do not meet the criteria specified in paragraph 61 of this Protocol;
    2) have not been determined by the legislation of the Member State and applied by the Member State as on the signing date of the Treaty.
63. When confirming fulfilment by a Member State of the obligations referred to in paragraph 62 of this Protocol, international standards of international organisations open for membership to all the Member States shall be taken into account.
64. If a Member State applies authorisation requirements and procedures in relation to trade in services, incorporation and/or activities, it shall ensure that:
    1) the names of competent authorities issuing authorisations have been published or otherwise communicated to the general public;
    2) all authorisation requirements and procedures have been determined in the legislation of the Member State and any act determining or applying any authorisation procedures and requirements has been published prior to its effective date (entry into force);
    3) competent authorities have decided to issue or refuse to issue a permit within a reasonable period of time specified in the legislation of the Member State and generally equal to up to 30 working days from the date of receipt (arrival) of the application deemed arranged in accordance with the legislation of the Member State. This period shall be determined based on the minimum time required to obtain and process all documents and/or information necessary for the implementation of the authorisation procedure;
    4) any fees charged in connection with the submission and consideration of the application, except for the fees charged for the right to engage in activities, did not constitute a restriction on trade in services, incorporation or activities and were based on the expenses of the competent authority incurred with regard to the consideration of the application and issuance of the permit;
    5) upon expiration of the period referred to in sub-paragraph 3 of this paragraph and at the request of the applicant, the competent authority of the Member State informed the applicant in accordance with paragraph 60 of this Protocol of the status of its application, indicating whether the application was deemed duly executed.
    In any case, the applicant shall be granted the rights provided for in paragraphs 57, 58, 60, 62 and 64 of this Protocol;
    6) upon written request of an applicant whose application was rejected, the competent authority that rejected the application informed the applicant in writing of the reasons for this rejection. This provision shall not be construed to require the competent authority to disclose information if it prevents due enforcement of the law or is otherwise contrary to the public interest or critical security interests of the Member State;

7) in case of rejection of an application by the competent authority due to its improper execution, the applicant was able to reapply;
8) permits issued for the supply of services were effective on the entire territory of the Member State specified in such permits.

VII. Investments

1. General Provisions

65. The provisions of this section shall apply to all investments made by investors of the Member States on the territory of another Member State starting from December 16, 1991.
66. Incorporation within the meaning of sub-paragraph 24 of paragraph 2 of this Protocol shall constitute a form of investment. All provisions of this Protocol, except for the provisions of paragraphs 69-74 of this Protocol, shall apply to such investments.
67. Changes in investment methods, as well as in forms of investment or reinvestment, shall not affect their qualification as investments provided that such changes do not contradict the legislation of the recipient state.

2. Legal Treatment and Protection of Investments

68. Each Member State shall ensure on its territory fair and equitable treatment to investments and investment-related activities conducted by investors of other Member States.
69. The treatment specified in paragraph 68 of this Protocol shall not be less favourable than the treatment accorded by the Member State in respect of investments and investment-related activities conducted by its domestic (national) investors.
70. The treatment accorded by each Member State, under the same (similar) circumstances, to investors of any other Member State, their investments and investment-related activities shall be no less favourable than the treatment accorded to investors of any third state, their investments and activities related to such investments.
71. The treatments provided for in paragraphs 69 and 70 of this Protocol shall be accorded by the Member States as selected by the investor, depending on the most favourable treatment.
72. Each Member State shall create favourable conditions for investment in its territory to investors of other Member States and shall enable such investments in accordance with its legislation.
73. Each Member State shall, in accordance with its legislation, reserve the right to restrict the activities of investors of other Member States, as well as to apply and introduce other exceptions to the national treatment referred to in paragraph 69 of this Protocol.

74. The provisions of paragraph 70 of this Protocol shall not be construed as obliging a Member State to extend to investments and related activities of investors of other Member States the benefits of any treatment, preferences or privileges that are available or may be made available in the future to that Member State under international treaties on the avoidance of double taxation or other agreements on taxation, as well as the treaties referred to in paragraph 46 of this Protocol.
75. Each recipient state shall guarantee the following to investors of other Member States, upon completion by the latter of their obligations under all tax-related and other legislation of the recipient state:
   1) the right to use and dispose of the income generated as a result of investments for any purpose not prohibited by the legislation of the recipient state;
   2) the right to use and dispose of the income generated as a result of investments for any purpose not prohibited by the legislation of the recipient state;
   3) the right to freely transfer investment-related funds (cash) and payments referred to in paragraph 8 of this Protocol to any country, at the discretion of the investor.
76. Each Member State shall guarantee and ensure on its territory, in accordance with its legislation, the protection of investments of investors of other Member States.

3. Indemnity and Guarantees of Investors

77. Investors shall be entitled to indemnification for damages caused to their investments as a result of civil unrest, hostilities, revolutions, insurrection, state of emergency or other similar circumstances on the territory of a Member State.
78. These investors shall be accorded treatment no less favourable than that accorded by the recipient state to its domestic investors or to investors of third states in respect of measures taken by the Member State in relation to compensation for such damage, depending on the most favourable treatment for the investor.

4. Guarantees of Rights of Investors in Expropriation

79. Investments of investors of a Member State made on the territory of another Member State shall not be subject to direct or indirect expropriation, nationalisation and other measures with consequences equivalent to those of expropriation or nationalisation (hereinafter "expropriation"), except in cases where such measures are taken for the public benefit in the procedure

Appendix 8

determined by the legislation of the recipient state, are not discriminatory and involve prompt and adequate compensation.

80. The compensation referred to in paragraph 79 of this Protocol shall correspond to the market value of investments expropriated from investors on the date immediately preceding the date of their actual expropriation or the date when it becomes known about the upcoming expropriation.

81. The compensation referred to in paragraph 79 of this Protocol shall be paid without delay, within the period provided for by the legislation of the recipient state, but not later than within 3 months from the date of expropriation and shall be freely transferable abroad from the territory of the recipient state in a freely convertible currency.

In case of a delayed payment of compensation, interest shall be accrued in the period from the date of expropriation till the date of actual payment of the compensation, to be calculated at the domestic interbank market rate for actually provided loans in US dollars for up to 6 months, but not below the rate of LIBOR, or in the procedure determined by agreement between the investor and the Member State.

5. Transfer of Rights of Investor

82. A Member State or its authorised authority having completed payments to an investor of their state based on the guarantees of protection against non-commercial risks in connection with an investment of such investor on the territory of a recipient state may exercise the rights of such investor under subrogation to the same extent as the investor.

83. The rights referred to in paragraph 82 of this Protocol shall be exercised in accordance with the legislation of the recipient state, but without prejudice to the provisions of paragraphs 21, 24, 27, 29, 30 and 32 of this Protocol.

6. Procedure for Settlement of Investment Disputes

84. All disputes between a recipient state and an investor of another Member State arising from or in connection with an investment of that investor on the territory of the recipient state, including disputes regarding the size, terms or order of payment of the amounts received as compensation of damages pursuant to paragraph 77 of this Protocol and the compensation provided for in paragraphs 79-81 of this Protocol, or the order of payment and transfer of funds provided for in paragraph 8 of this Protocol, shall be, where possible, resolved through negotiations.

85. If a dispute may not be resolved through negotiations within 6 months from the date of a written notification of any of the parties to the dispute on negotiations, it may be referred to the following, at investor's option:

Appendix 8

1) a court of the recipient state duly competent to consider relevant disputes;
2) international commercial arbitration court at the Chamber of Commerce of any state as may be agreed by the parties to the dispute;
3) ad hoc arbitration court, which, unless the parties to the dispute agree otherwise, shall be established and act in accordance with the Rules of Arbitration of the United Nations Commission on International Trade Law (UNCITRAL);
4) the International Centre for Settlement of Investment Disputes established pursuant to the Convention on the Settlement of Investment Disputes between States and Nationals of Other States of March 18, 1965, in order to resolve the dispute under the provisions of the Convention (provided that it has entered into force for both Member States that are parties to the dispute) or under the Additional Facility Rules of the International Centre for Settlement of Investment Disputes (if the Convention has not entered into force for one or both the Member States that are parties to the dispute).

86. An investor having referred a dispute for settlement to a national court or one of the arbitration courts specified in sub-paragraphs 1 and 2 of paragraph 85 of this Protocol shall not have the right to redirect the dispute to any other court or arbitration.

The choice made by an investor with respect to a court or arbitration referred to in paragraph 85 of this Protocol shall be final.

87. Any arbitration decision on a dispute considered pursuant to paragraph 85 of this Protocol shall be final and binding on the parties to the dispute. Each Member State shall ensure enforcement of such decisions in accordance with its legislation.

Index

A

Applicable law
  Choice choice of law
    explicit, 109, 139–140, 183–184, 270, 320–321, 359–360, 405, 456
    implicit, 270, 359
    reasonable connection test, 138, 182, 359, 403
  conflict of laws rules, 61, 110, 184, 270, 321, 357, 405, 456
  ex aequo et bono, 402–403
  lex arbitri, 62–63, 66, 81, 110, 137, 140, 181, 267, 292, 357, 402, 405, 455
    seat of arbitration, 15, 18–19, 358, 410, 417–418, 468
  party autonomy, 110–111, 137–138, 182, 267, 320, 358, 403, 455–456
  restrictions on party autonomy
    international public policy, 139, 183, 241, 269, 320, 404
    mandatory rules, 24, 109, 139, 183, 268–269, 284, 359, 403–404
    national public policy, 25, 63, 112, 138, 182–183, 268, 359, 404

Arbitrability
  bankruptcy, 60, 81, 134, 178, 264, 318, 397
  consumer disputes, 107, 223–224, 265, 399, 417
  corporate disputes, 12, 23–25, 60, 106, 134, 264, 318, 398, 452
  labour disputes, 23, 98, 107, 265, 314, 318, 389, 397, 399
  public procurement contracts, 397

Arbitral award
  correction, 76, 149–150, 195, 232–233, 234, 286–287, 328–329, 368, 416, 467–468
  deliberation and voting, 73, 148, 193, 232, 282–283, 327, 366, 414, 465
  effects of the award
    execution, 5, 27, 44, 75, 148–149, 194, 233, 285–286, 328, 368, 415, 466–467
    final and binding, 31, 32, 38, 57, 200, 201, 225, 286, 292, 319
    lis pendens, 75, 149, 194–195, 233–234, 286, 328, 368, 415, 467
    res judicata, 75, 149, 194–195, 233–234, 286, 328, 368, 415, 467
  grounds for challenging, 76, 150, 196, 235, 288, 330, 369, 417, 468
  interpretation, 76, 149–150, 195, 234, 286–287, 328–329, 368, 416, 467–468
  recognition and enforcement
    domestic, 78–79, 151–152, 198, 236–237, 289, 331, 370–371, 418–419, 470–471

Index

foreign, 44, 79–82, 153, 198, 237, 289–290, 331, 371, 419, 470
setting aside
excess of mandate, 154–155, 199, 240, 373, 422
lack of capacity, 154, 199, 238–239, 292, 372–373, 421
New York Convention, 154, 198, 200, 290
8, 54, 58, 77–78, 80, 93, 114, 154, 198, 200, 216, 238, 242, 258, 290–291, 329, 332, 369, 371, 374, 377, 392, 401, 405, 419, 422, 424, 445, 470, 472
nNon-arbitrability, 60–61, 136, 155, 200, 240–241, 293, 374, 398, 422–423
public policy, 155–156, 200, 241, 293–294, 374, 423, 473–474
types of awards
interim, 80, 148, 154, 193, 199, 232–233, 238, 291, 327–328, 333, 366, 372, 414, 420–421
jurisdictional, 151, 197, 236, 289, 331, 370, 418
partial, 154, 199, 238, 291, 333, 372, 420–421
separate, 148, 154, 193, 199, 232–233, 238, 291, 327–328, 333, 366, 372, 414, 420–421
Arbitral institutions
Arbitration Institute of the Stockholm Chamber of Commerce (SCC), 3, 14, 38–39, 243, 490
Foreign Trade Arbitration Commission (FTAC), 4–6
International Centre for Settlement of Investment Disputes (ICSID), 29, 31, 34, 36, 38–39, 42, 85, 95, 117, 202, 206, 237, 244–246, 491
International Commercial Arbitration Court (ICAC) at the Russian Federation Chamber of Commerce and Industry, 13–14, 390, 409, 489
International Court of Arbitration, International Chamber of Commerce (ICC), 14–15, 243, 363, 490
London Court of International Arbitration (LCIA), 14–15, 266, 491
Maritime Arbitration Commission (MAC), 4–6, 260, 352
Permanent Court of Arbitration (PCA), 33, 40, 41, 296
Arbitration agreement
arbitrability, 60–61, 105–107, 133–135, 178–179, 222–224, 264–265, 317–318, 356–357, 395–400, 452–453
complete termination, 136, 180, 401–402
consent, 30, 57, 131, 133, 176, 179, 199, 202
drafting clauses, 61–62, 109, 136–137, 181, 224–225, 266, 319, 402, 454–455
formal validity, 61, 184, 317, 405
separability, 59, 104–105, 133, 177, 222, 263–264, 316–317, 355, 394, 451
substantive validity, 184, 405
termination, 61, 108, 136, 180–181, 265, 319, 357, 401, 454
third parties
group of companies doctrine, 61, 108, 135, 179–180, 318–319, 400
guarantee agreements, 135, 179–180, 318–319, 400
parties substitution, 135, 179, 265, 318, 400
Arbitrators, Arbitral tribunal
appointment, 23, 64, 140–141, 184–185, 220, 225–226, 239, 271–273, 321–322, 360, 406–407, 411, 454, 458

Index

challenges, 66, 142–143, 186–187, 226–227, 275–276, 323, 361–362, 408, 459
compensation, 67, 85, 143, 187–188, 227, 276, 323, 362, 409–410, 460, 503
jurisdiction of the tribunal, 67, 143, 188, 227, 324, 362, 410, 460
impartiality, 5, 18, 19, 56, 66, 71, 112–113, 142, 145, 186, 187, 189, 226, 229, 275, 279–280, 361, 364, 408, 409, 411, 459
independence, 18, 19, 66, 71, 142, 187, 226, 275, 279–280, 361, 408, 409
powers and duties, 65–66, 142, 186, 226, 274–275, 322, 361, 407–408
qualifications, 20, 23, 64–65, 141–142, 185–186, 213, 226, 273–274, 360–361, 407, 458–459

B

Bilateral Investment Treaty (BIT), 28, 36–38, 40–42, 82, 84, 85, 120, 121, 159, 201, 243, 244, 246, 247, 295, 377, 378, 424–426, 476–479, 481, 482
model BIT, 36–38, 84, 159, 424, 425, 477

C

Commonwealth of Independent States (CIS)
arbitration institutions, 56, 99, 129–130, 174, 218–219, 260, 315, 352, 390
Crimea, 18, 30, 41, 396, 426
Economic Court, 6, 34
Eurasian Economic Union (*see* Eurasian Economic Union (EEU))

history, 52–53, 90–91, 126, 170, 212–213, 256–257, 312, 346–347, 384–386, 441–443
judicial system, 55–56, 97–98, 129, 173–174, 218, 259–260, 315, 351–352, 390, 447–448
legal profession, 53, 91–92, 126–127, 141, 170–171, 213–214, 257, 313, 347–348, 386–387, 443–444
Conciliation, 55, 96, 135, 219, 314, 389, 399, 442, 447
Corruption, 3, 7, 16, 82, 271, 388, 390, 478–479
bribery, 16
Costs
allocation, 194, 414–415, 465, 466
determination of, 74, 148, 233
lawyers' fees, 43, 74, 278
security for costs, 16

D

Damages, 26, 34, 35, 40, 43, 74, 116, 159, 219, 226, 262, 282, 293, 294, 296, 479, 501, 508, 520, 522, 525, 530, 545, 554, 556, 562, 570, 571, 575, 577, 588, 599, 600

E

Energy Charter Treaty (ECT), 28, 30–33, 40, 44, 48, 49, 55, 95, 173, 202, 216, 247, 258, 296, 336, 375, 389, 425, 446, 476, 480, 496, 497
Eurasian Economic Union (EEU), 3, 6, 30, 35–36, 48, 52, 82, 297, 496, 583–601
Experts, 9, 10, 43, 71–72, 74, 147, 187, 191, 192, 231, 233, 274–275, 281, 323, 326, 364, 365, 413, 441, 462, 464, 472, 480, 483, 501, 507–509, 539, 541–543

605

Index

F

Foreign direct investment (FDI), 6, 29, 30, 82, 115, 156, 157, 336, 475

I

ICSID Convention. *See* Washington Convention
Investor-State arbitration
  absolute immunity, 45, 46, 315, 449
  BIT (*see* Bilateral Investment Treaty (BIT))
    cooling-off period, 37, 243
    expropriation, 17, 28, 32, 39, 40, 158, 295–296, 336, 478
    fair and equitable treatment, 37, 39, 82, 84, 158, 296, 336, 478
    MFN principle (*see* Most-favoured nation (MFN)), 32, 40–41, 82, 158
    national treatment, 32, 37, 82, 84, 424
    umbrella clause, 37, 158
  ECT (*see* Energy Charter Treaty (ECT))
  FDI (*see* Foreign direct investment (FDI))
  history, 28–29, 55, 314–315, 388–389
  ICSID, 29–32, 34, 36–39, 42–44, 85, 115, 117, 118, 158–160, 201, 202, 242–246, 295, 336, 375–377, 424, 426, 479, 480
  investment climate, 30, 43, 82, 83, 117, 336, 475
  investment treaty, 38–42, 85, 201, 202, 207, 243, 381, 425, 430
  201, 243
  investor, 16, 28–36, 39–41, 44, 46, 55, 83, 85, 92, 95, 116, 130, 157, 243, 296, 336, 375, 475
  model BIT, 36–38, 84, 159, 424, 425, 477
  restrictive immunity, 45, 46

State immunity, 3, 40, 44–46, 56–57, 130–131, 174, 261

J

Jurisdiction
  competence-competence, 67, 188, 227, 324, 355, 410
  Court review, 68, 144, 188, 228, 277, 363, 410, 461

L

Legal profession, 53, 91–92, 126–127, 141, 170–171, 213–214, 257, 313, 347–348, 386–387, 443–444

M

Mediation, 55, 96, 97, 119, 129, 135, 173, 193, 217–220, 225, 259, 314, 389, 446, 447, 482
Most-favoured nation (MFN), 32, 37, 40, 41, 82, 84, 478, 591

N

New York Convention, 5, 8–10, 20, 27, 31, 42, 44, 48, 52, 54, 58, 60, 77–80, 93, 95, 101, 105, 114, 115, 129, 140, 148–151, 153, 154, 173, 198, 200, 216, 237, 238, 242, 258, 262, 289–291, 314, 329, 332, 333, 335, 336, 350, 351, 363, 369, 371, 374, 377, 389, 392, 393, 401, 405, 419, 422, 424, 445, 470–474, 496
National courts, 4, 5, 7, 11, 16, 25, 26, 31, 42, 43, 44, 54, 59, 61, 79, 81, 97–98, 112, 128–129, 131–132, 135, 144, 145, 151, 153, 160, 171, 173, 176, 183, 195, 198, 200, 215, 218, 228, 233, 236, 240, 259, 269, 271,

Index

277–278, 287, 291, 294, 315, 330, 351, 363, 370, 387, 390, 394, 400, 410, 461

P

Procedure
  Conduct of arbitration
    evidence
      admissibility, 71, 147, 192, 231, 281, 326, 413
      IBA Rules, 71, 413
      experts, 71–72, 147, 192, 231, 281, 326, 413, 464
      hearing, 72, 147, 192–193, 231, 281–282, 326–327, 413, 464
      post-hearing briefs, 70, 146–147, 191, 230–231, 326, 412
      witness, 71–72, 147, 192, 231, 281, 326, 413, 464
      written submission, 70, 146, 191, 230, 281, 326, 412, 463
    guerrilla tactics, 21–22, 394
    interim measures, 74, 220, 243, 411, 424
Provisional measures, 22, 142, 420
Public policy, 4, 19, 22, 24–26, 28, 60, 61, 63, 69, 76, 77, 79–81, 112, 115, 118, 138, 139, 155, 156, 182–183, 197, 200, 241, 268, 269, 288, 293–294, 320, 329, 330, 334, 335, 359, 370, 374, 404, 418, 419, 423, 469, 473–474, 491, 559
  international public policy (*see* international public policy)
  national public policy (*see* national public policy)

R

Regional treaties
  Agreement on the Settlement of Disputes Relating to the Exercising of Economic Activity 1992 (the Kiev Agreement), 9–10, 445, 496, 499
  Agreement on Promotion and Reciprocal Protection of Investments in the Member States of the Eurasian Economic Community (the EAEC Convention), 34–35
  Convention on Legal Assistance in Civil, Family Relations and Criminal Matters (the Kishinev Convention), 10–11, 48, 537
  Convention on Legal Assistance and Legal Relations in Civil, Family, and Criminal Matters (the Minsk Convention), 9–10, 48, 96, 445, 496, 505

S

Sanctions, 18–19, 30, 257, 446, 462, 539, 568
Sources of Arbitration Law
  international law generally, 8, 53, 92, 127, 214, 257, 313, 348, 387, 313
  international treaties, 8, 54–55, 95–96, 128, 215–216, 258, 313, 314, 349, 388–389, 445
    provisional application, 8, 44
    ratification, 11, 48, 220, 495
    signed, 10, 29, 120–121
  municipal law, 139, 140, 142, 146, 149, 183, 184, 187, 190, 195, 225, 226, 229, 234, 268, 271, 275, 280, 286, 359, 360, 361, 364, 368, 404, 406, 408, 412, 416, 458–459
  national law, 11, 61, 95, 102, 126, 269, 314, 446

Index

principles, 9, 12, 69, 112, 145, 189, 229, 277, 279, 325, 364, 411, 462, 456

regional treaties, *See Regional treaties*

Soviet law, 5, 8, 20, 346, 384, 385, 441, 442

State immunity, 3, 40, 44–46, 56–57, 130–131, 174, 220, 261–262, 315, 353, 374, 391, 449, 472

absolute immunity, 45, 46, 315, 449

diplomatic immunity, 40, 57

principle of reciprocity, 27, 46, 261, 290, 350, 471

restrictive immunity, 45–46, 175, 261

immunity from interim measures, 46, 262

waiver, 40, 46, 57, 130–131, 261–262, 315, 391

U

UNCITRAL Model law, 11, 20, 52, 54, 55, 58, 90, 93, 101, 105, 111, 125–127, 145, 160, 170, 172, 189, 191, 202, 214, 229–232, 256, 257, 262–264, 271, 288, 290, 312, 313, 325, 345, 353, 354, 359, 364, 366, 368, 369, 374, 379, 384, 388, 393, 401, 411, 441, 445, 450, 461, 469

W

Washington Convention, 3, 29, 31, 39, 42, 43, 115, 129, 158, 160, 173, 201, 237, 336, 350, 375, 389, 424, 445, 480

Additional facility rules, 29, 31, 32, 34, 36, 38, 39, 601